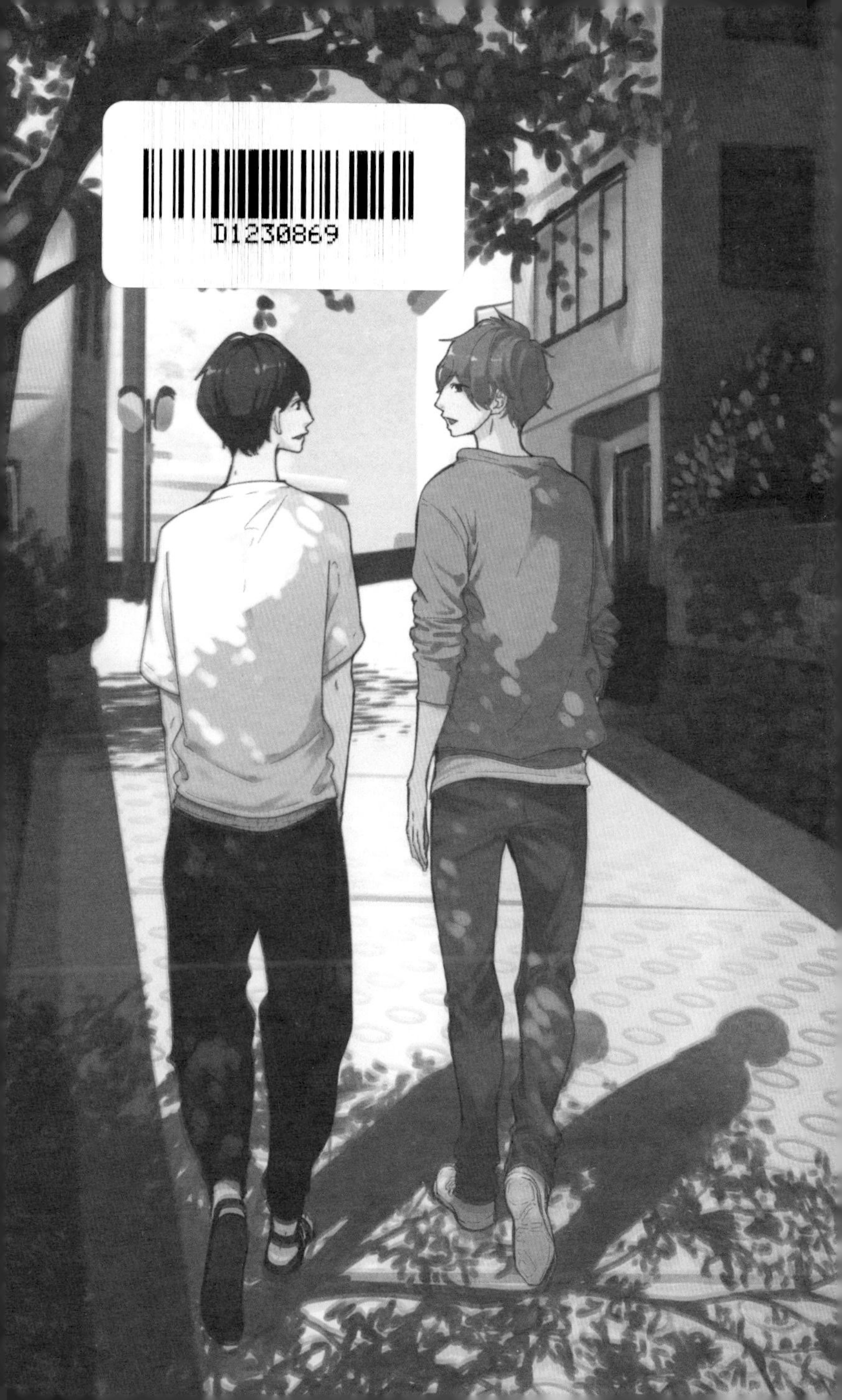

KOIMONOGATARI

LOVE STORIES

KOIMONOGATARI: LOVE STORIES

Tohru Tagura

CHARACTER

YAMATO YOSHINAGA

IS IN THE CLOSET. HE HAS A CRUSH ON KYOUSUKE.

YUIJI HASEGAWA

WAS IN YAMATO'S CLASS BUT NEVER HAD DIRECT CONTACT WITH HIM UNTIL ACCIDENTALLY STUMBLING INTO THE KNOWLEDGE THAT YAMATO IS GAY.

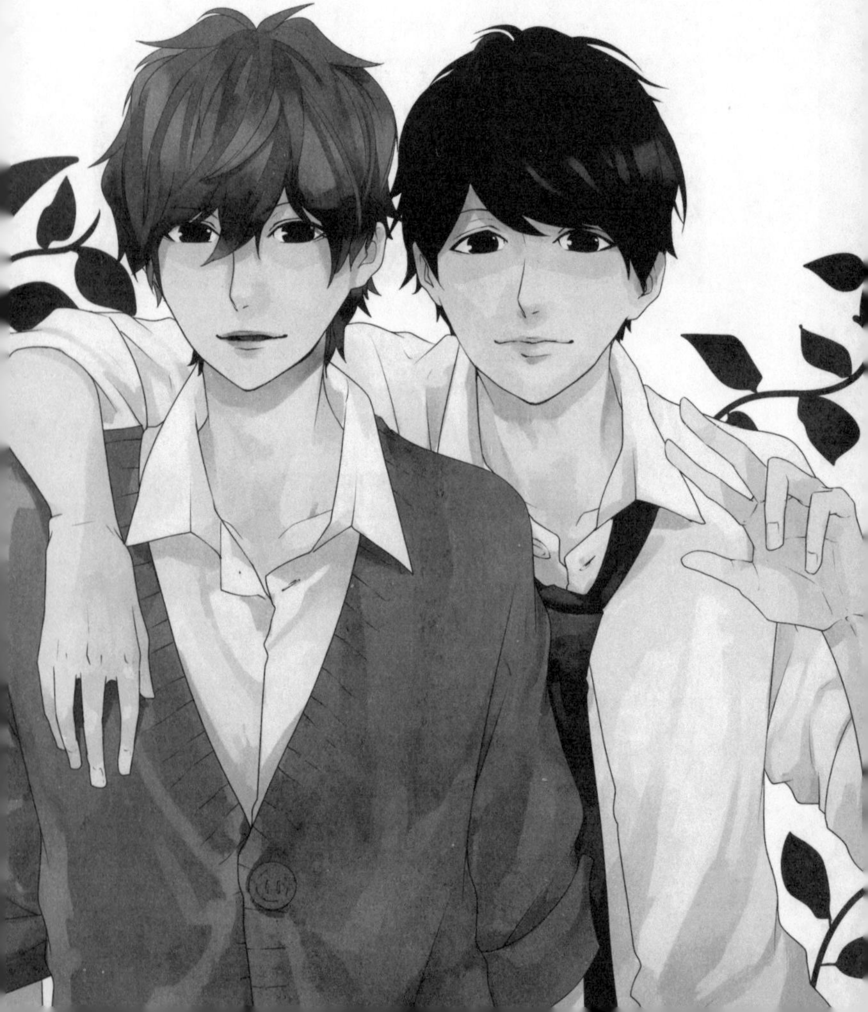

KYOUSUKE HONGOU
YUIJI'S FRIEND.

KAZUTAKA SEKI
YAMATO'S FRIEND.

NATSUMI SHIBATA
YAMATO'S CONFIDANT.

MAYU NEMOTO
YUIJI'S GIRLFRIEND.

AKITO SAKURA
A GAY STUDENT YAMATO MET IN CRAM SCHOOL. HE GOES TO A DIFFERENT HIGH SCHOOL.

AKIYAMA
SAKURA'S CLASSMATE. USED TO ATTEND THE SAME JUNIOR HIGH AS YUIJI.

STORY

DESPITE BEING IN THE SAME CLASS AS YAMATO, YUIJI NEVER HAD CONTACT WITH HIM BEFORE ACCIDENTALLY OVERHEARD THAT YAMATO IS GAY. WHEN HE FINDS OUT THAT YAMATO HAS A CRUSH HIS FRIEND KYOUSUKE, YUIJI CAN'T HELP BUT THINK THAT YAMATO'S LOVE WILL NEVER BE RECIPROCA AFTER ATTENDING A STUDY GROUP TOGETHER, YUIJI REALIZES THAT YAMATO'S A PRETTY GOOD GUY, A HE MAKES IT HIS MISSION TO HELP THE COMPLICATED AND BUMBLING YAMATO FIND HAPPINESS. DUR SUMMER CRAM SCHOOL, YUIJI'S JUNIOR HIGH FRIEND, AKIYAMA, INTRODUCES YAMATO TO HIS CLASSM SAKURA. IN PRIVATE, SAKURA CONFESSES TO YAMATO THAT HE'S ACTUALLY ALSO GAY.

CONTENTS

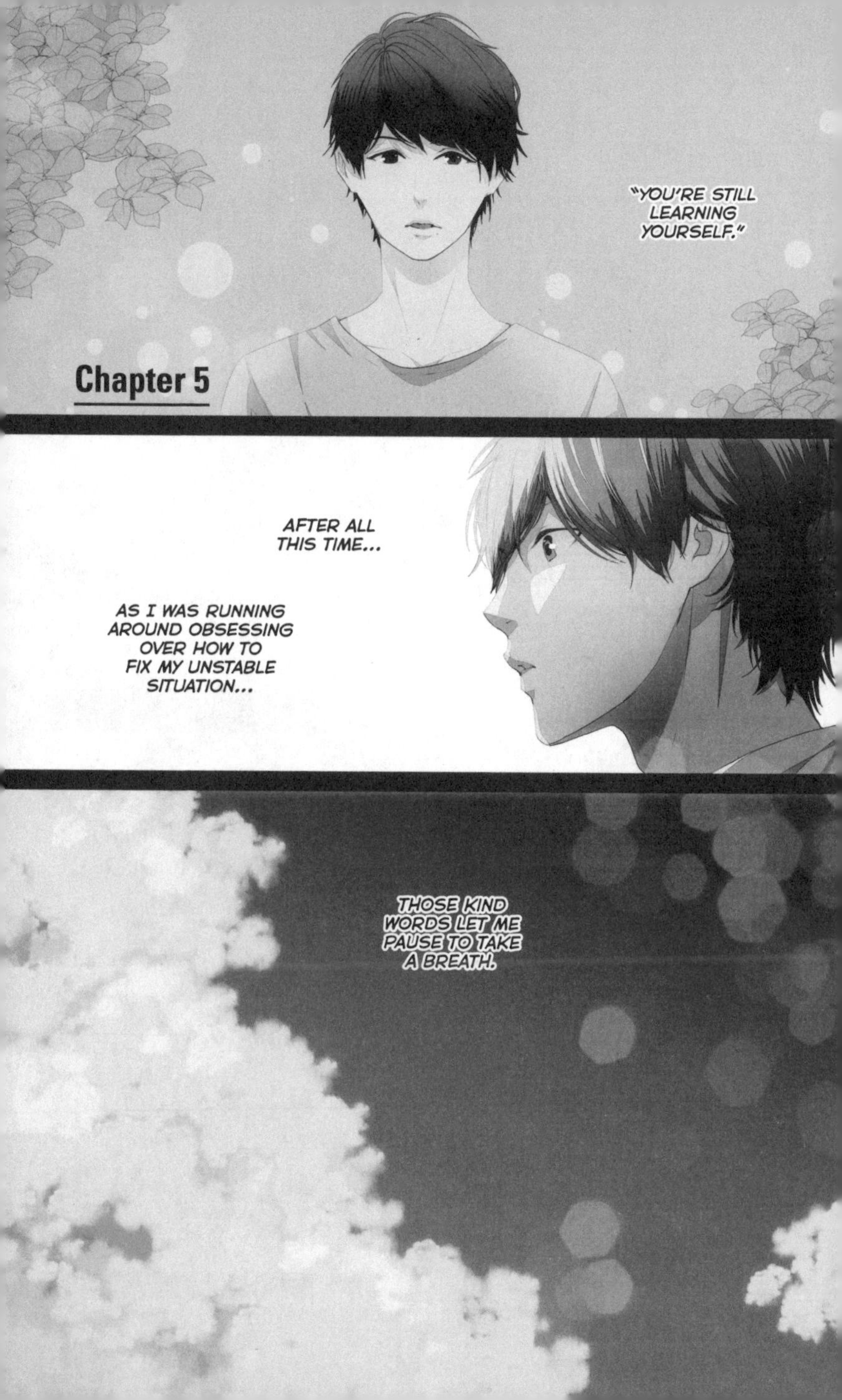
Chapter 5
"YOU'RE STILL LEARNING YOURSELF."
AFTER ALL THIS TIME...
AS I WAS RUNNING AROUND OBSESSING OVER HOW TO FIX MY UNSTABLE SITUATION...
THOSE KIND WORDS LET ME PAUSE TO TAKE A BREATH.

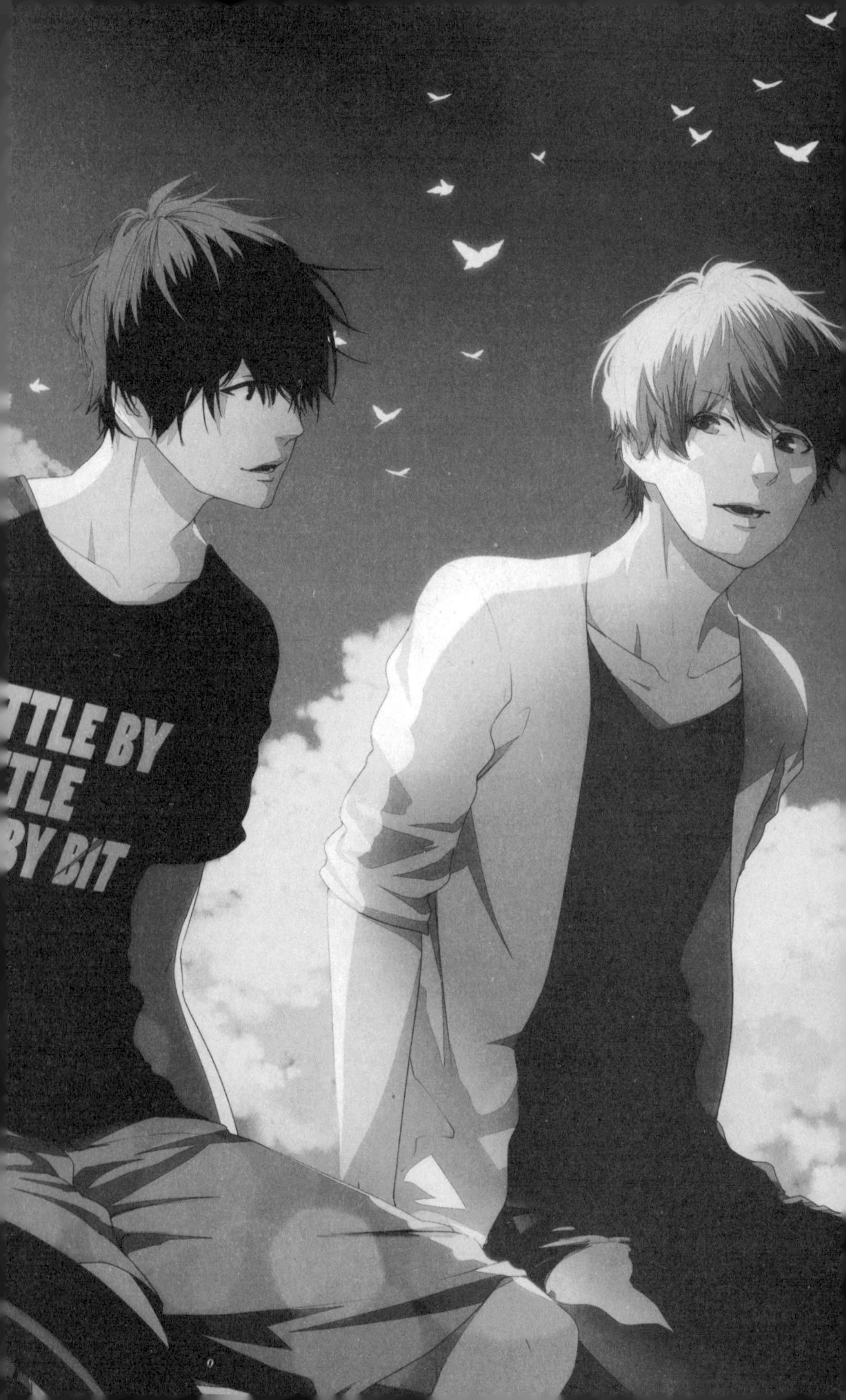
TTLE BY
TLE
BY BIT

Chapter 5

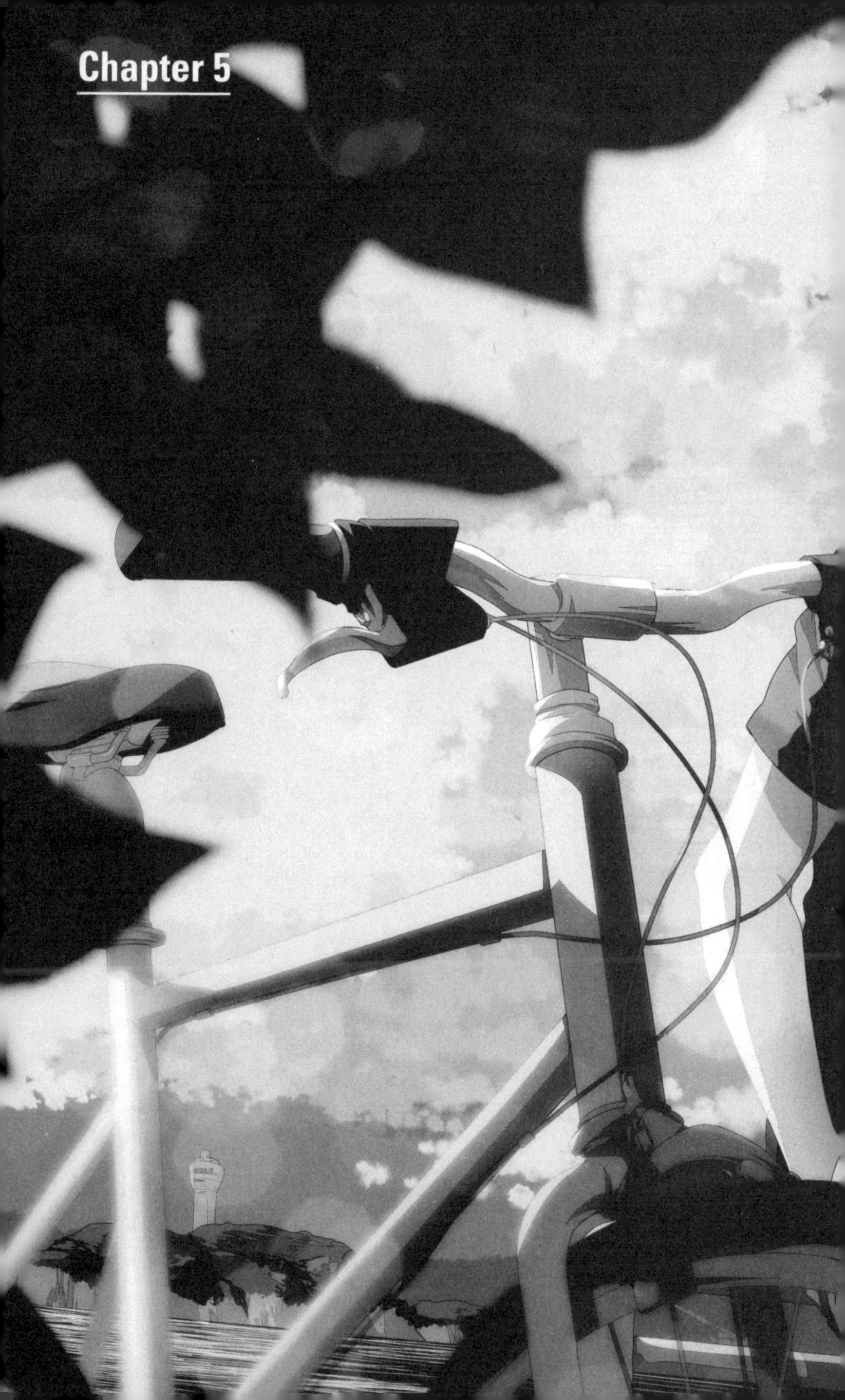

KOIMONOGATARI:
LOVE STORIES

2

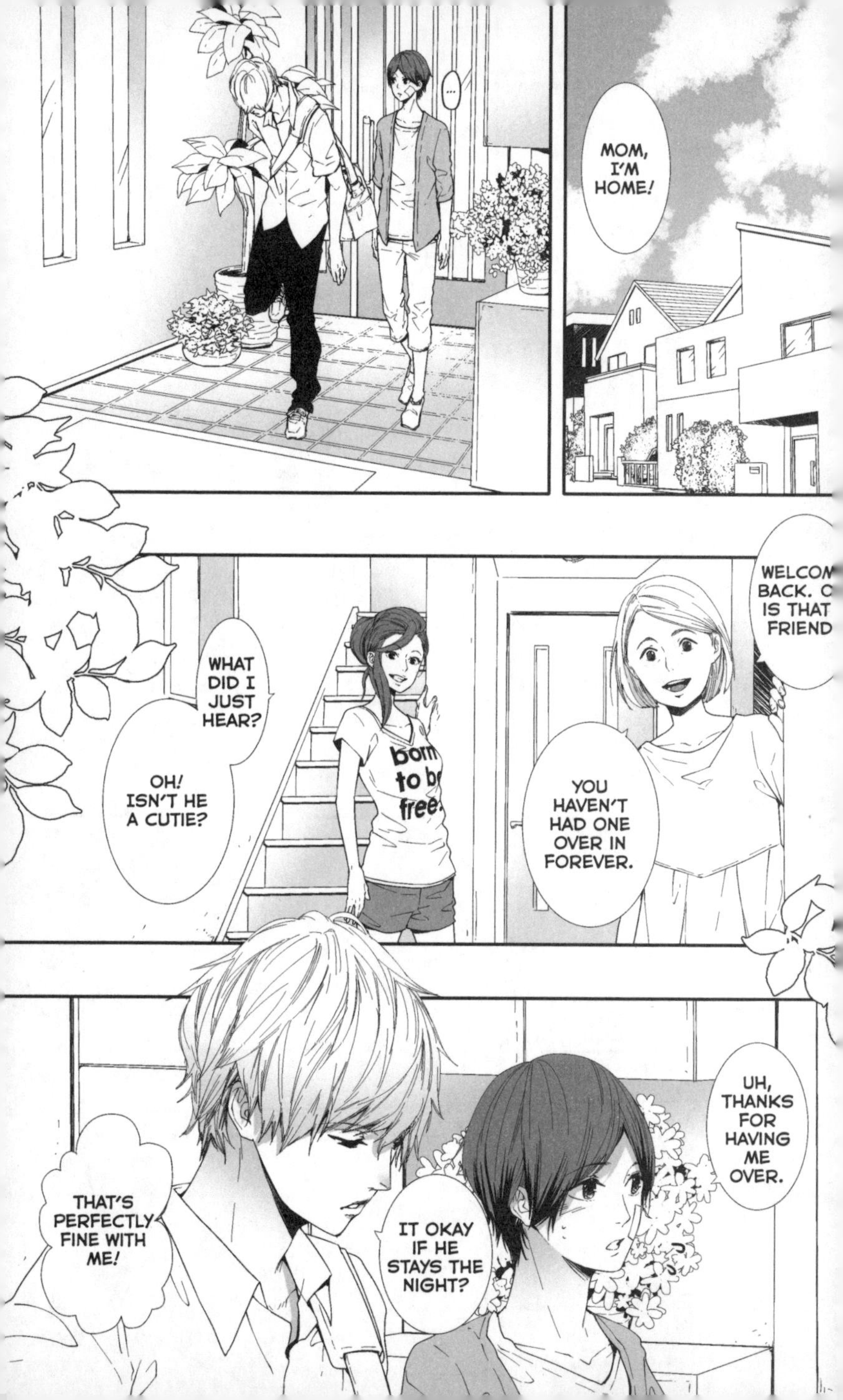
MOM, I'M HOME!
...
WELCOM BACK. O IS THAT FRIEND
YOU HAVEN'T HAD ONE OVER IN FOREVER.
WHAT DID I JUST HEAR?
OH! ISN'T HE A CUTIE?
born to be free.
UH, THANKS FOR HAVING ME OVER.
IT OKAY IF HE STAYS THE NIGHT?
THAT'S PERFECTLY FINE WITH ME!

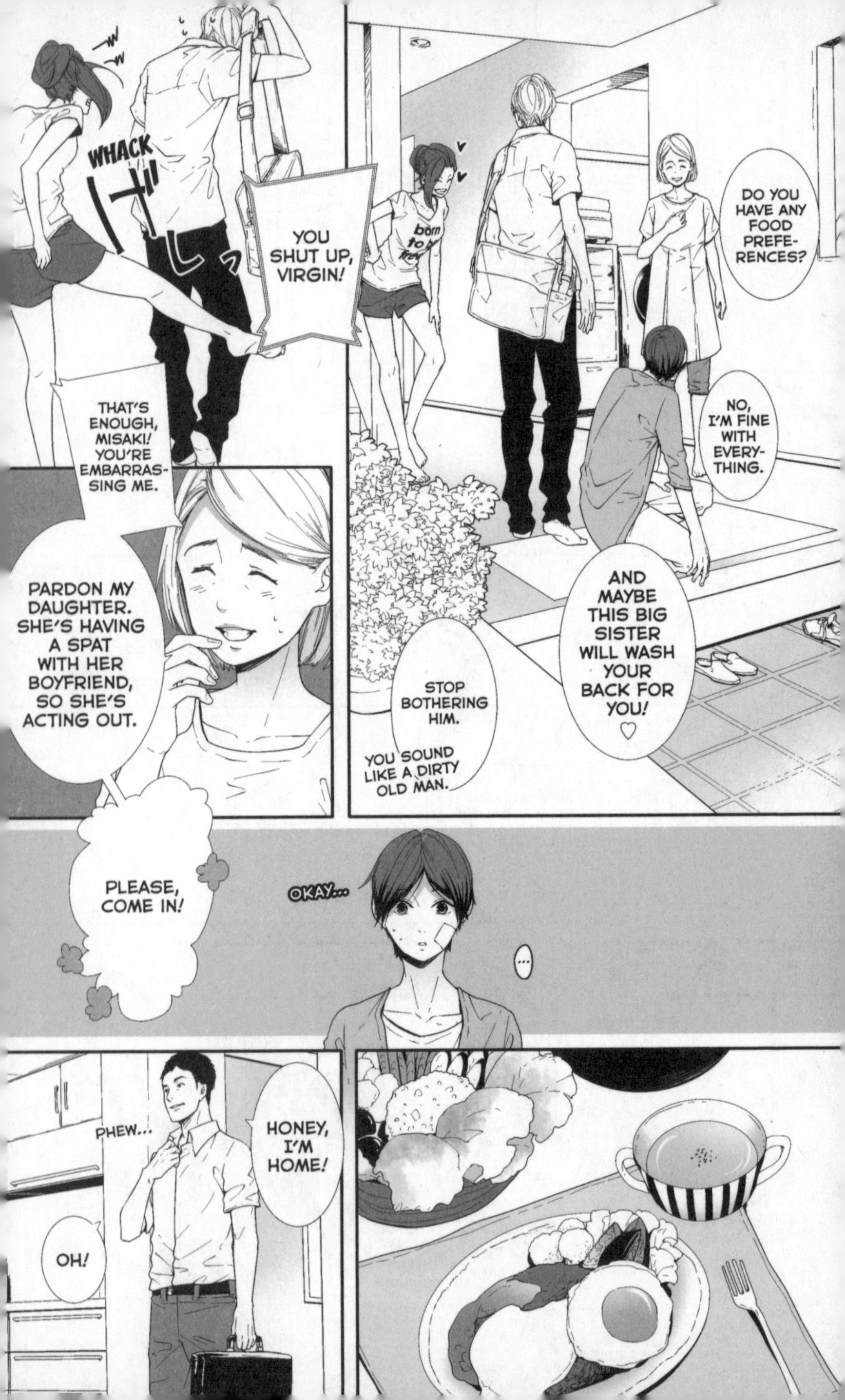
DO YOU HAVE ANY FOOD PREFE-RENCES?
NO, I'M FINE WITH EVERY-THING.
AND MAYBE THIS BIG SISTER WILL WASH YOUR BACK FOR YOU! ♡
STOP BOTHERING HIM.
YOU SOUND LIKE A DIRTY OLD MAN.
WHACK
YOU SHUT UP, VIRGIN!
THAT'S ENOUGH, MISAKI! YOU'RE EMBARRAS-SING ME.
PARDON MY DAUGHTER. SHE'S HAVING A SPAT WITH HER BOYFRIEND, SO SHE'S ACTING OUT.
...
OKAY...
PLEASE, COME IN!
HONEY, I'M HOME!
PHEW...
OH!

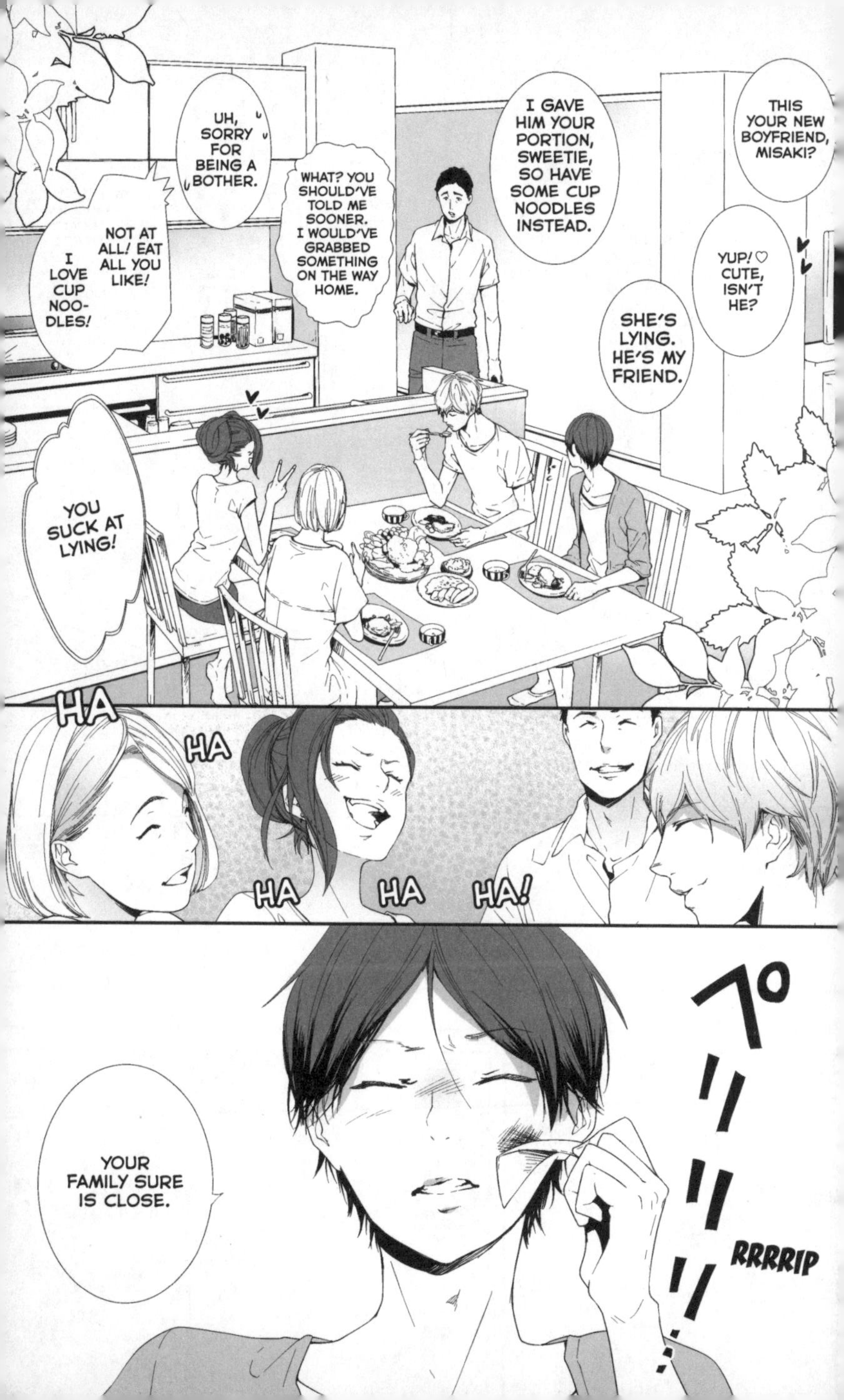
THIS YOUR NEW BOYFRIEND, MISAKI?
YUP! ♡ CUTE, ISN'T HE?
SHE'S LYING. HE'S MY FRIEND.
I GAVE HIM YOUR PORTION, SWEETIE, SO HAVE SOME CUP NOODLES INSTEAD.
WHAT? YOU SHOULD'VE TOLD ME SOONER. I WOULD'VE GRABBED SOMETHING ON THE WAY HOME.
UH, SORRY FOR BEING A BOTHER.
NOT AT ALL! EAT ALL YOU LIKE!
I LOVE CUP NOO-DLES!
YOU SUCK AT LYING!
HA
HA
HA
HA
HA!
ペリリリ
RRRRIP
YOUR FAMILY SURE IS CLOSE.

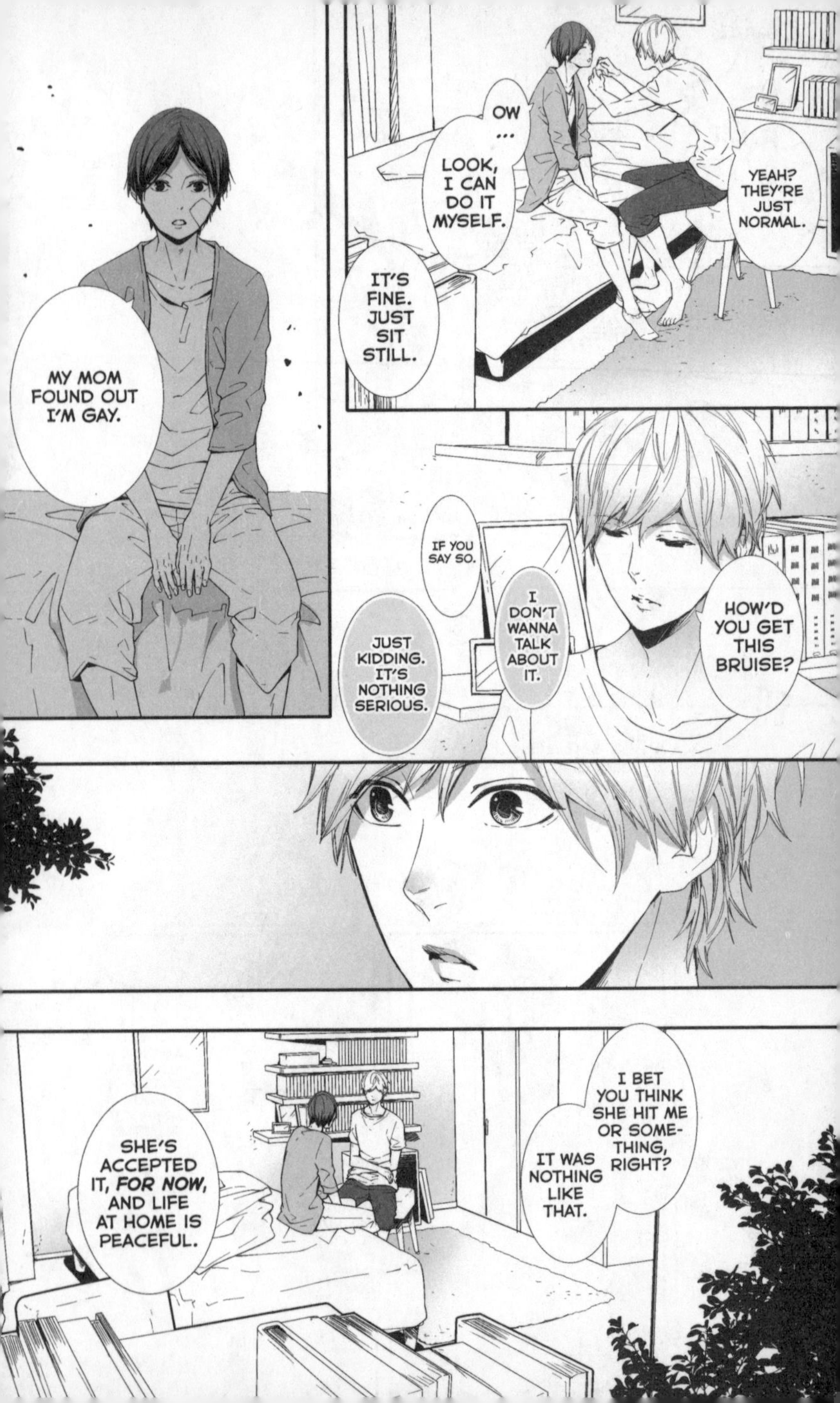
YEAH? THEY'RE JUST NORMAL.
OW ...
LOOK, I CAN DO IT MYSELF.
IT'S FINE. JUST SIT STILL.
HOW'D YOU GET THIS BRUISE?
I DON'T WANNA TALK ABOUT IT.
IF YOU SAY SO.
JUST KIDDING. IT'S NOTHING SERIOUS.
MY MOM FOUND OUT I'M GAY.
I BET YOU THINK SHE HIT ME OR SOME-THING, RIGHT?
IT WAS NOTHING LIKE THAT.
SHE'S ACCEPTED IT, *FOR NOW*, AND LIFE AT HOME IS PEACEFUL.

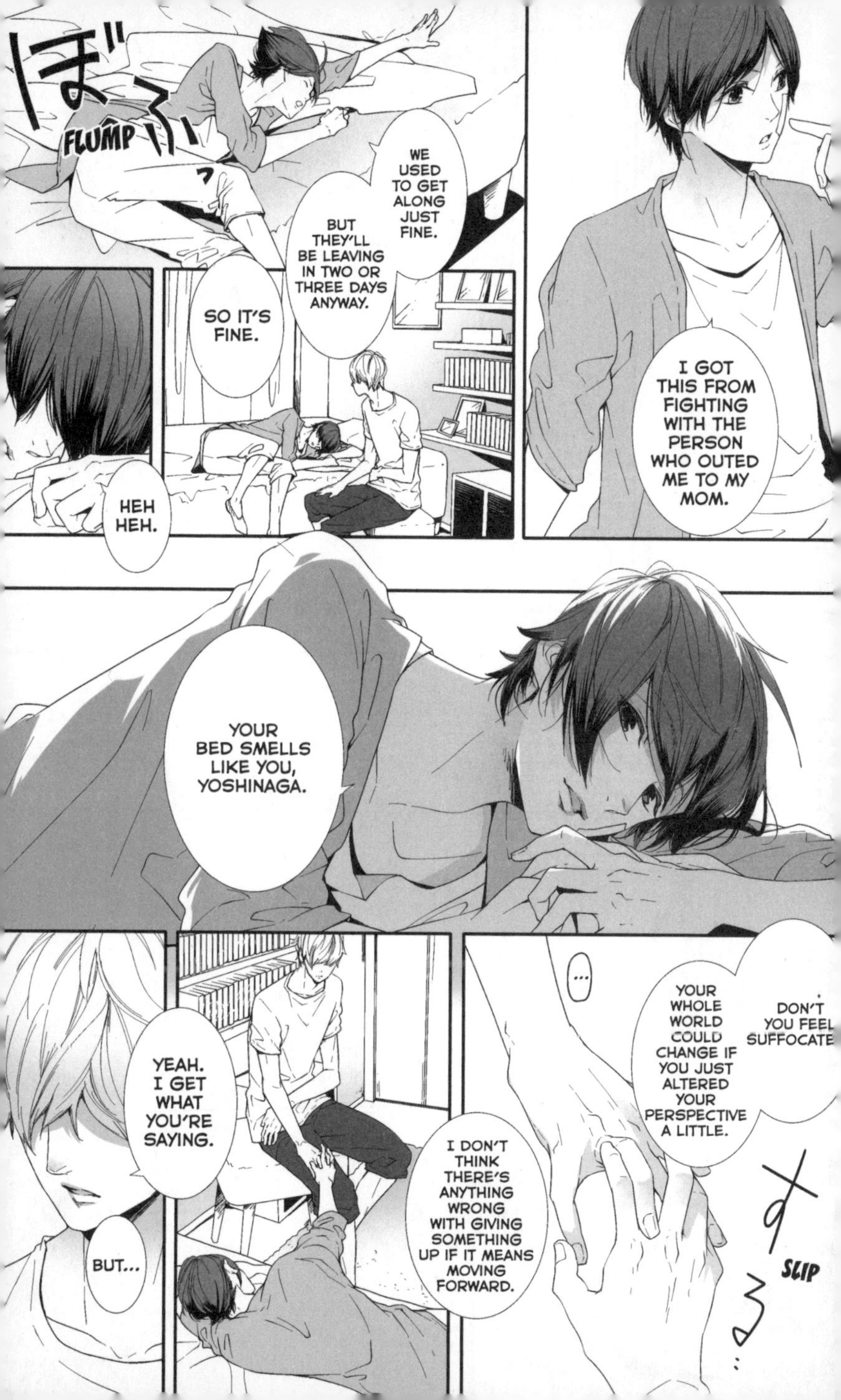
I GOT THIS FROM FIGHTING WITH THE PERSON WHO OUTED ME TO MY MOM.
ぼふ
FLUMP
WE USED TO GET ALONG JUST FINE.
BUT THEY'LL BE LEAVING IN TWO OR THREE DAYS ANYWAY.
SO IT'S FINE.
HEH HEH.
YOUR BED SMELLS LIKE YOU, YOSHINAGA.
...
DON'T YOU FEEL SUFFOCATE
YOUR WHOLE WORLD COULD CHANGE IF YOU JUST ALTERED YOUR PERSPECTIVE A LITTLE.
する…
SLIP
I DON'T THINK THERE'S ANYTHING WRONG WITH GIVING SOMETHING UP IF IT MEANS MOVING FORWARD.
YEAH. I GET WHAT YOU'RE SAYING.
BUT...

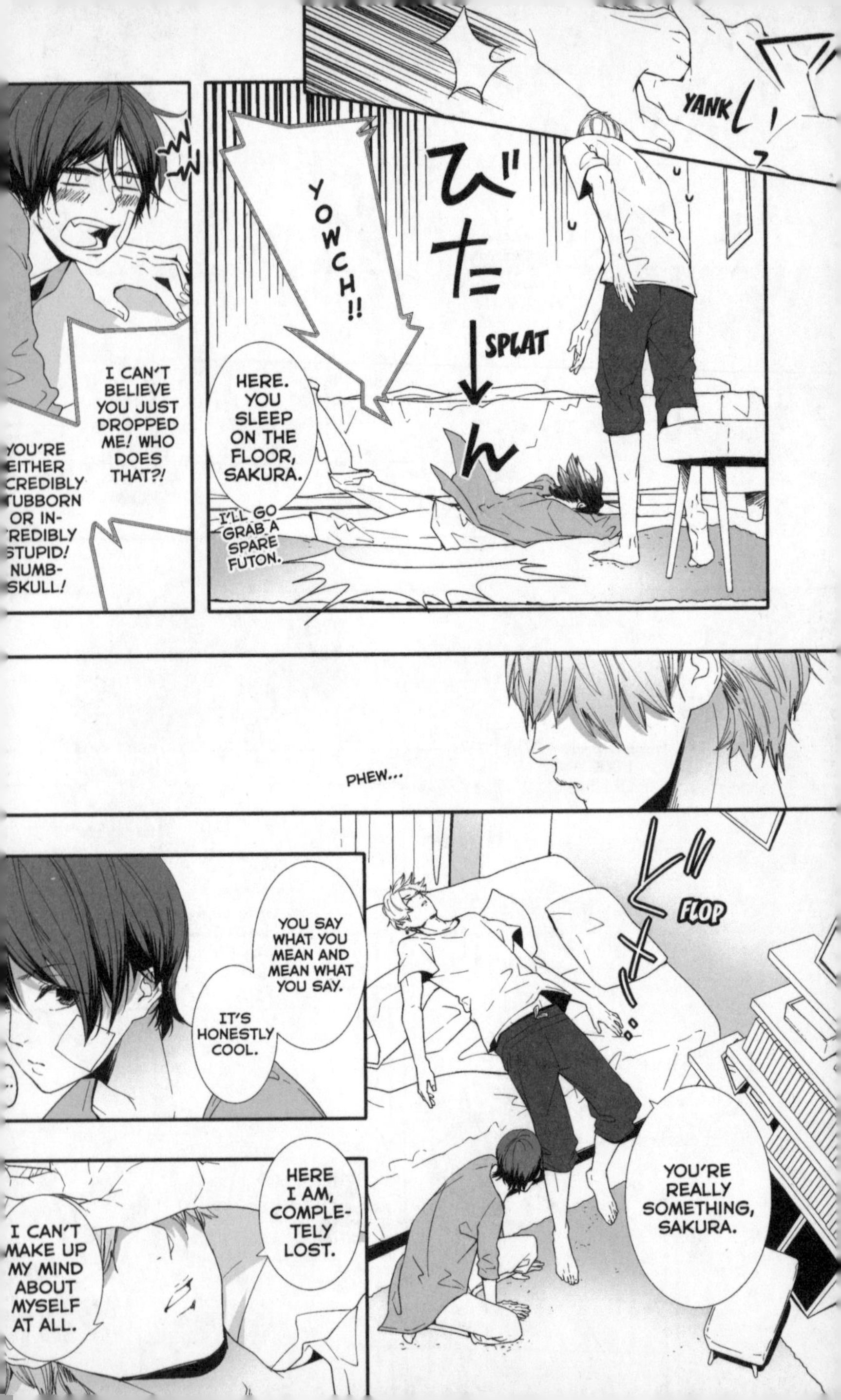
YANK
びたーん
SPLAT
YOWCH!!
HERE. YOU SLEEP ON THE FLOOR, SAKURA.
I'LL GO GRAB A SPARE FUTON.
I CAN'T BELIEVE YOU JUST DROPPED ME! WHO DOES THAT?!
YOU'RE EITHER CREDIBLY TUBBORN OR IN- REDIBLY STUPID! NUMB- SKULL!
PHEW...
FLOP
YOU'RE REALLY SOMETHING, SAKURA.
YOU SAY WHAT YOU MEAN AND MEAN WHAT YOU SAY.
IT'S HONESTLY COOL.
HERE I AM, COMPLETE- LY LOST.
I CAN'T MAKE UP MY MIND ABOUT MYSELF AT ALL.

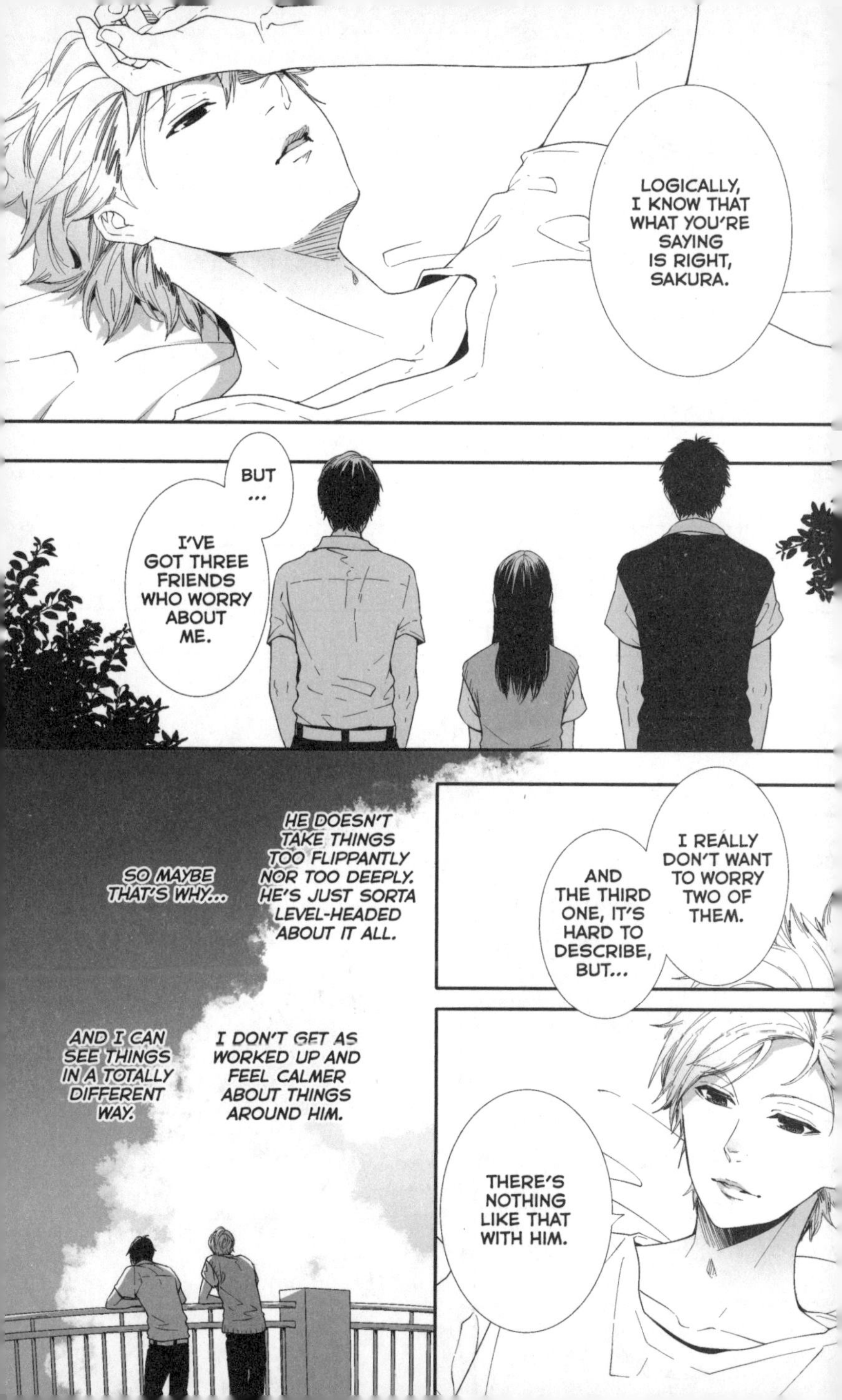
LOGICALLY, I KNOW THAT WHAT YOU'RE SAYING IS RIGHT, SAKURA.
BUT ...
I'VE GOT THREE FRIENDS WHO WORRY ABOUT ME.
I REALLY DON'T WANT TO WORRY TWO OF THEM.
AND THE THIRD ONE, IT'S HARD TO DESCRIBE, BUT...
THERE'S NOTHING LIKE THAT WITH HIM.
HE DOESN'T TAKE THINGS TOO FLIPPANTLY NOR TOO DEEPLY. HE'S JUST SORTA LEVEL-HEADED ABOUT IT ALL.
SO MAYBE THAT'S WHY...
I DON'T GET AS WORKED UP AND FEEL CALMER ABOUT THINGS AROUND HIM.
AND I CAN SEE THINGS IN A TOTALLY DIFFERENT WAY.

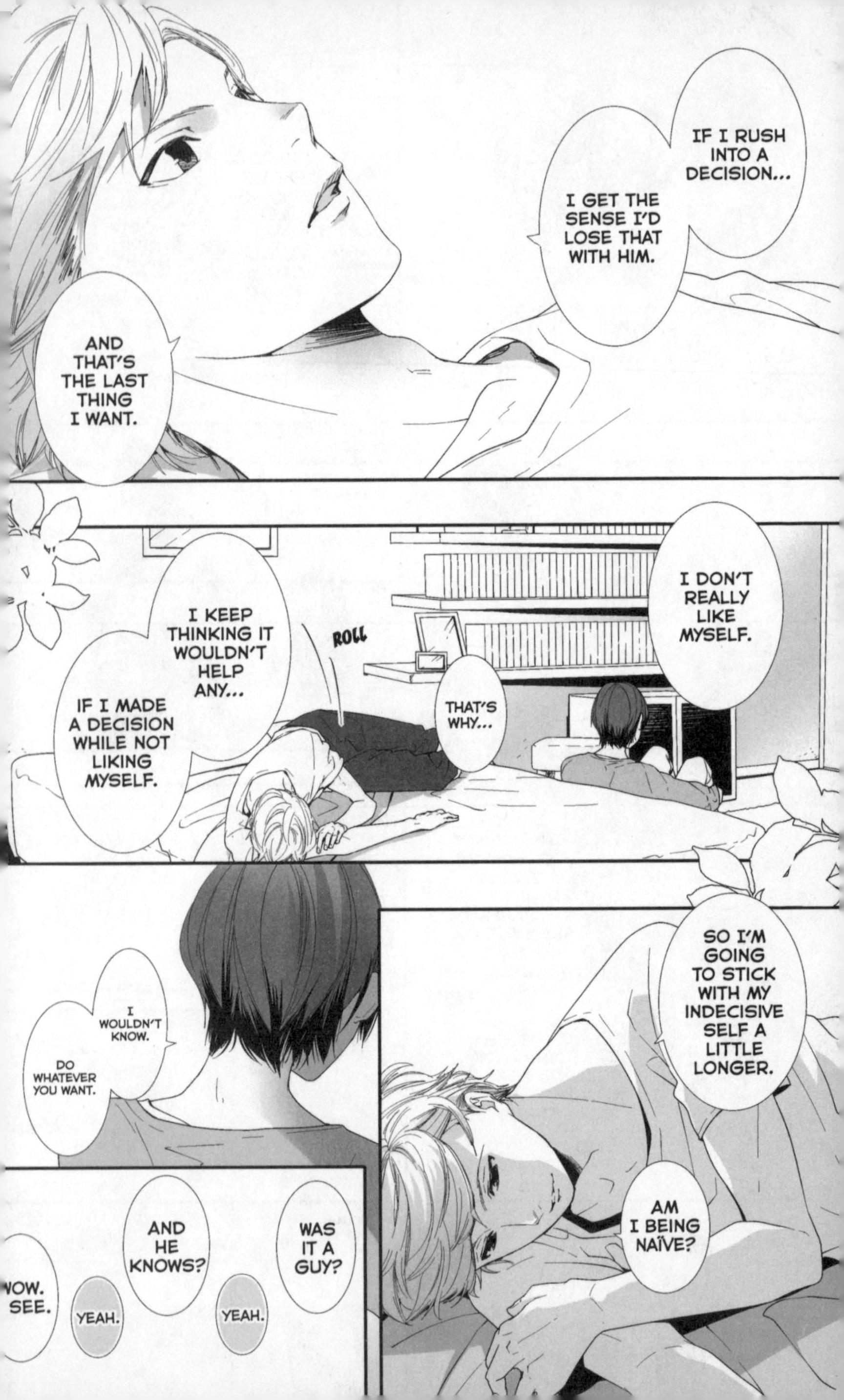
IF I RUSH INTO A DECISION...
I GET THE SENSE I'D LOSE THAT WITH HIM.
AND THAT'S THE LAST THING I WANT.
I DON'T REALLY LIKE MYSELF.
THAT'S WHY...
ROLL
I KEEP THINKING IT WOULDN'T HELP ANY...
IF I MADE A DECISION WHILE NOT LIKING MYSELF.
SO I'M GOING TO STICK WITH MY INDECISIVE SELF A LITTLE LONGER.
AM I BEING NAÏVE?
I WOULDN'T KNOW.
DO WHATEVER YOU WANT.
WAS IT A GUY?
YEAH.
AND HE KNOWS?
YEAH.
OW. SEE.

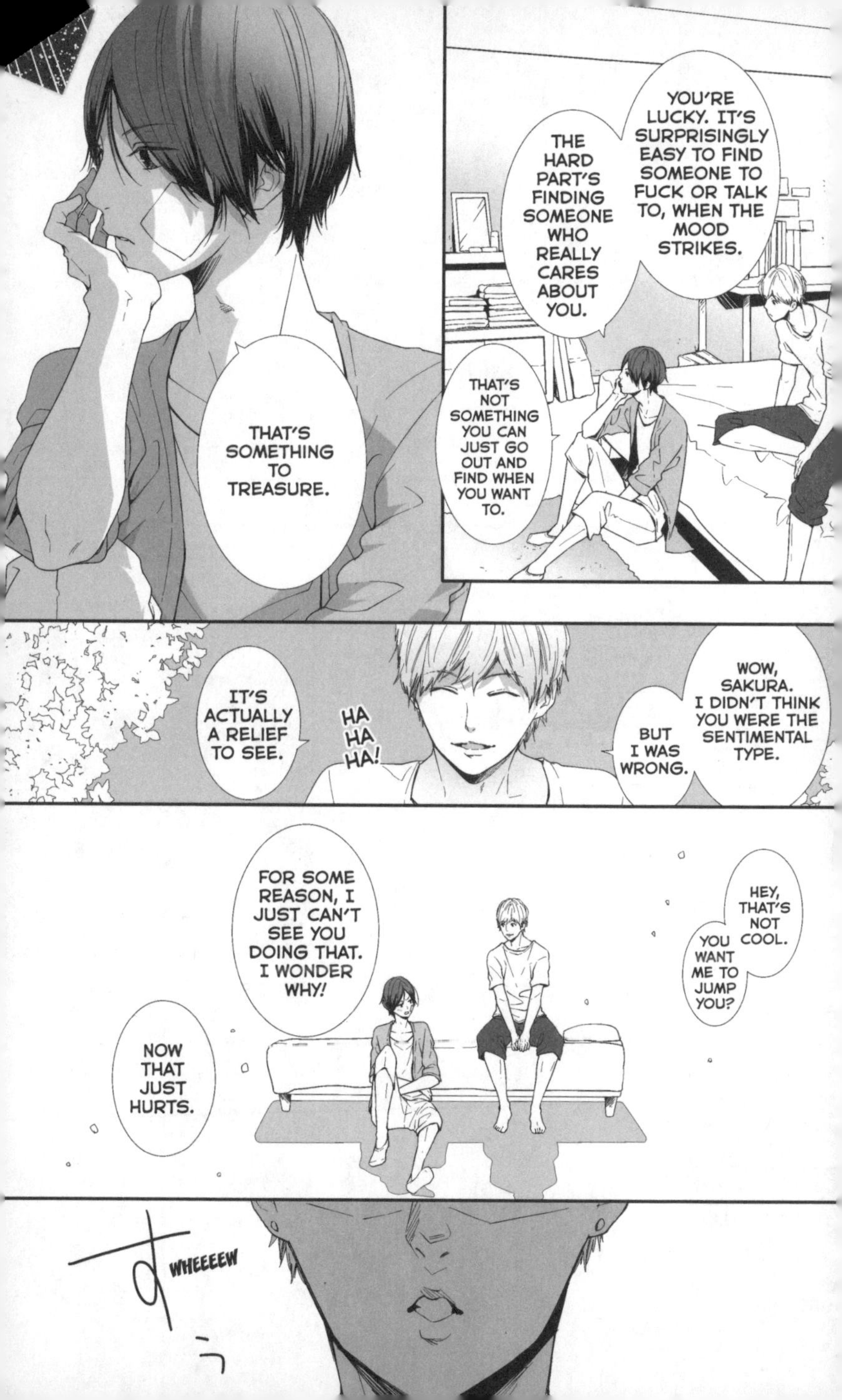
YOU'RE LUCKY. IT'S SURPRISINGLY EASY TO FIND SOMEONE TO FUCK OR TALK TO, WHEN THE MOOD STRIKES.
THE HARD PART'S FINDING SOMEONE WHO REALLY CARES ABOUT YOU.
THAT'S NOT SOMETHING YOU CAN JUST GO OUT AND FIND WHEN YOU WANT TO.
THAT'S SOMETHING TO TREASURE.
WOW, SAKURA. I DIDN'T THINK YOU WERE THE SENTIMENTAL TYPE.
BUT I WAS WRONG.
HA HA HA!
IT'S ACTUALLY A RELIEF TO SEE.
HEY, THAT'S NOT COOL.
YOU WANT ME TO JUMP YOU?
FOR SOME REASON, I JUST CAN'T SEE YOU DOING THAT. I WONDER WHY!
NOW THAT JUST HURTS.
WHEEEEW

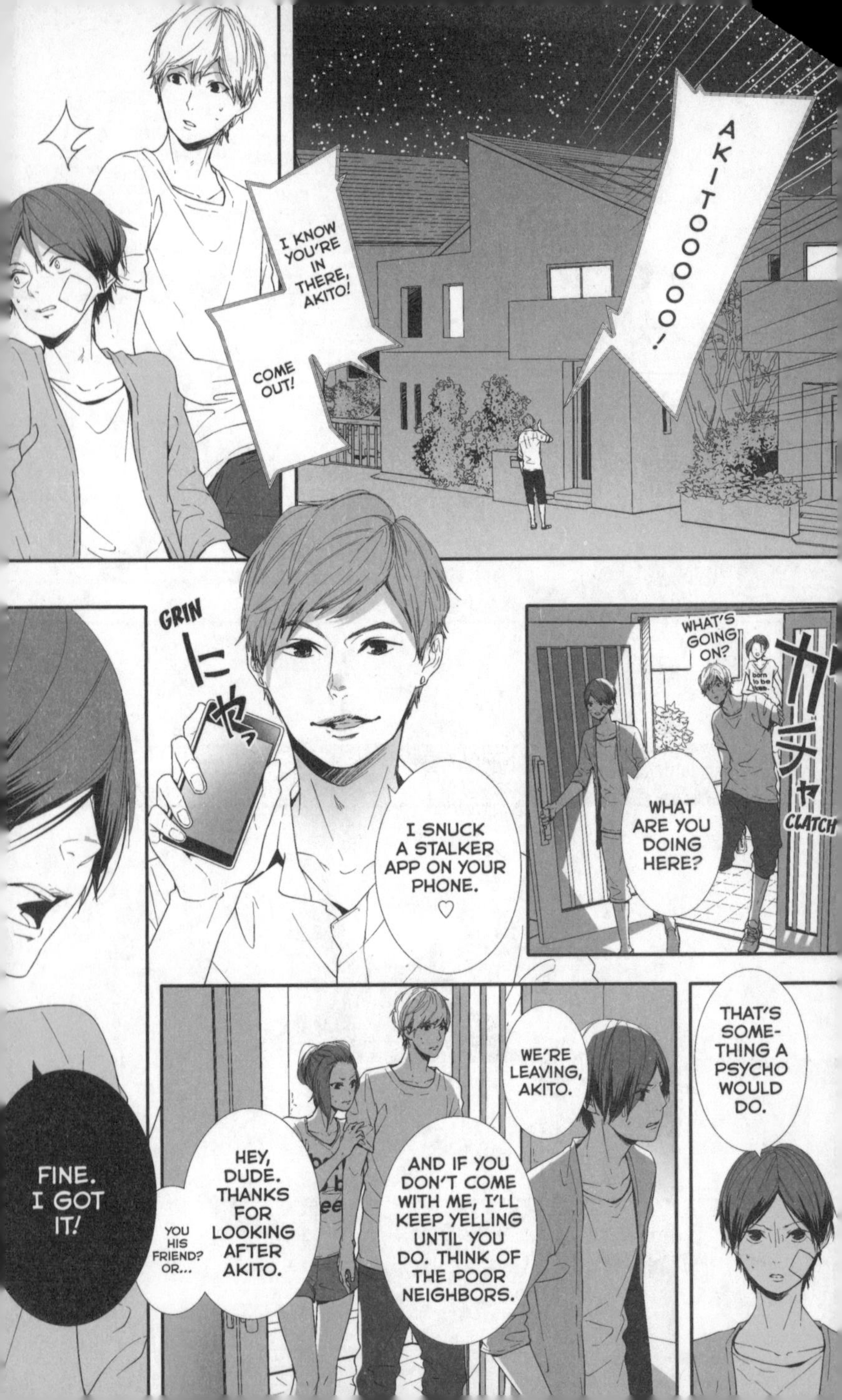
AKITOOOOOO!
I KNOW YOU'RE IN THERE, AKITO!
COME OUT!
WHAT'S GOING ON?
ガチャ
CLATCH
WHAT ARE YOU DOING HERE?
GRIN
にやっ
I SNUCK A STALKER APP ON YOUR PHONE. ♡
THAT'S SOMETHING A PSYCHO WOULD DO.
WE'RE LEAVING, AKITO.
AND IF YOU DON'T COME WITH ME, I'LL KEEP YELLING UNTIL YOU DO. THINK OF THE POOR NEIGHBORS.
HEY, DUDE. THANKS FOR LOOKING AFTER AKITO.
YOU HIS FRIEND? OR...
FINE. I GOT IT!

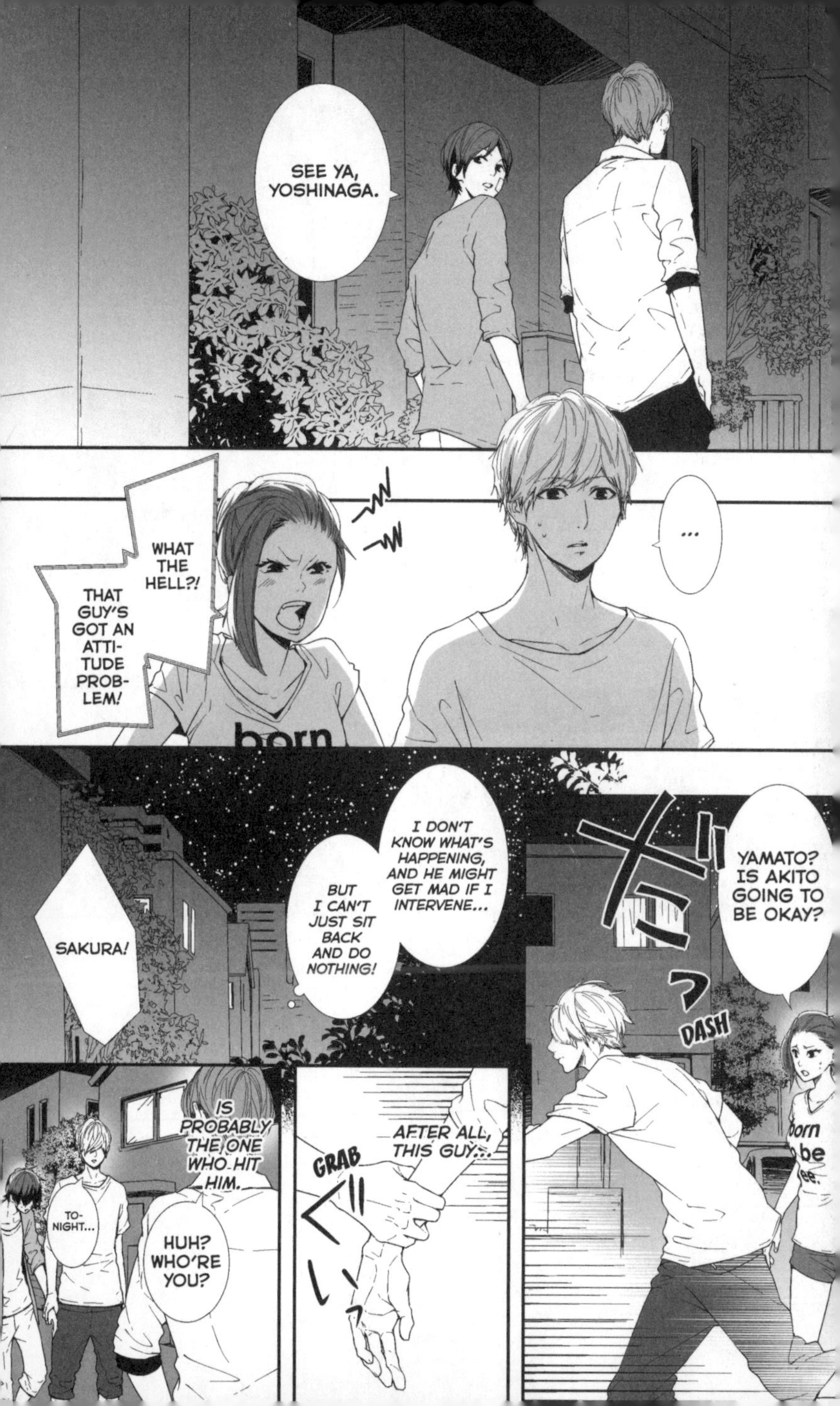
SEE YA, YOSHINAGA.
...
WHAT THE HELL?!
THAT GUY'S GOT AN ATTI-TUDE PROB-LEM!
YAMATO? IS AKITO GOING TO BE OKAY?
DASH
I DON'T KNOW WHAT'S HAPPENING, AND HE MIGHT GET MAD IF I INTERVENE...
BUT I CAN'T JUST SIT BACK AND DO NOTHING!
SAKURA!
AFTER ALL, THIS GUY...
GRAB
IS PROBABLY THE ONE WHO HIT HIM.
HUH? WHO'RE YOU?
TO-NIGHT...

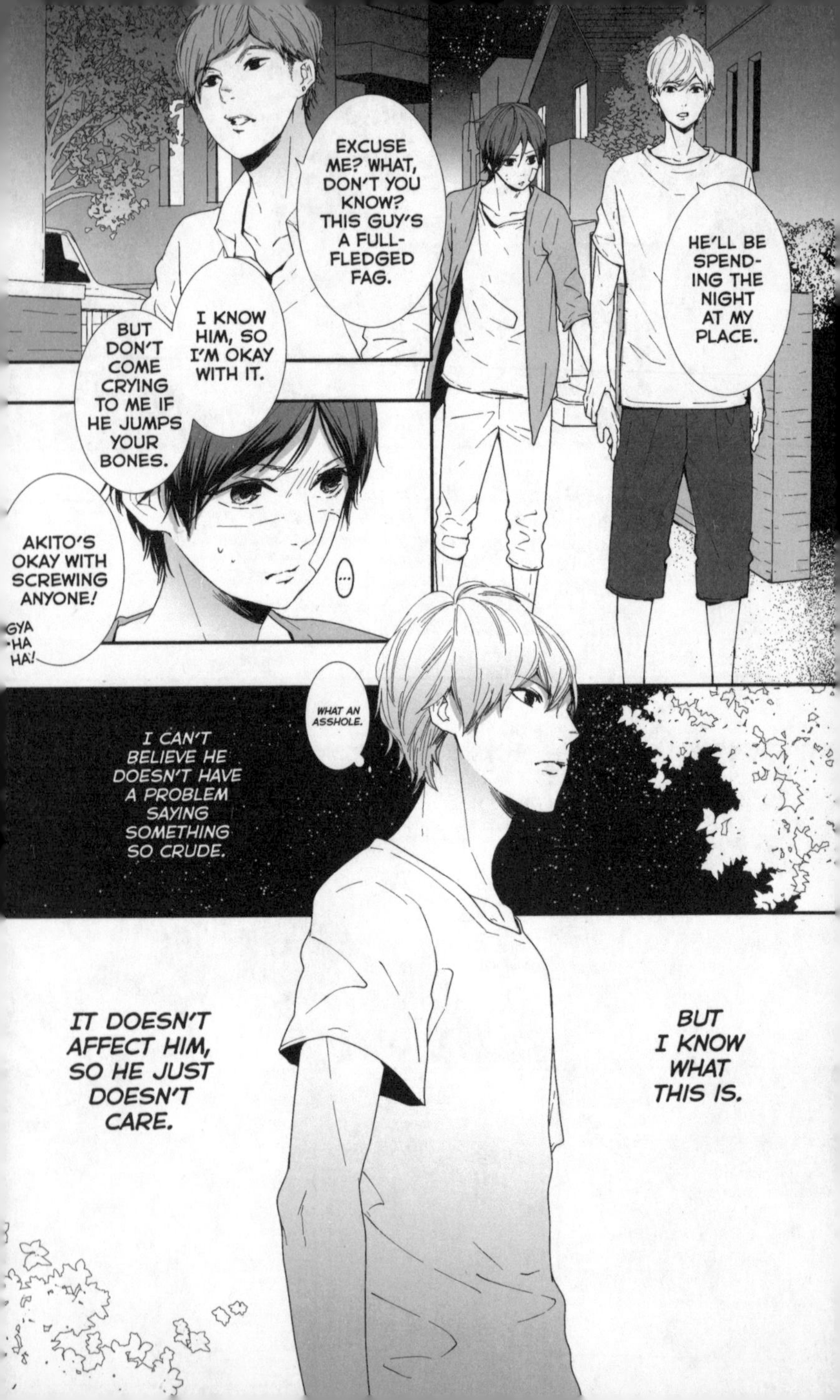
HE'LL BE SPENDING THE NIGHT AT MY PLACE.
EXCUSE ME? WHAT, DON'T YOU KNOW? THIS GUY'S A FULL-FLEDGED FAG.
I KNOW HIM, SO I'M OKAY WITH IT.
BUT DON'T COME CRYING TO ME IF HE JUMPS YOUR BONES.
...
AKITO'S OKAY WITH SCREWING ANYONE!
GYA-HA HA!
WHAT AN ASSHOLE.
I CAN'T BELIEVE HE DOESN'T HAVE A PROBLEM SAYING SOMETHING SO CRUDE.
IT DOESN'T AFFECT HIM, SO HE JUST DOESN'T CARE.
BUT I KNOW WHAT THIS IS.

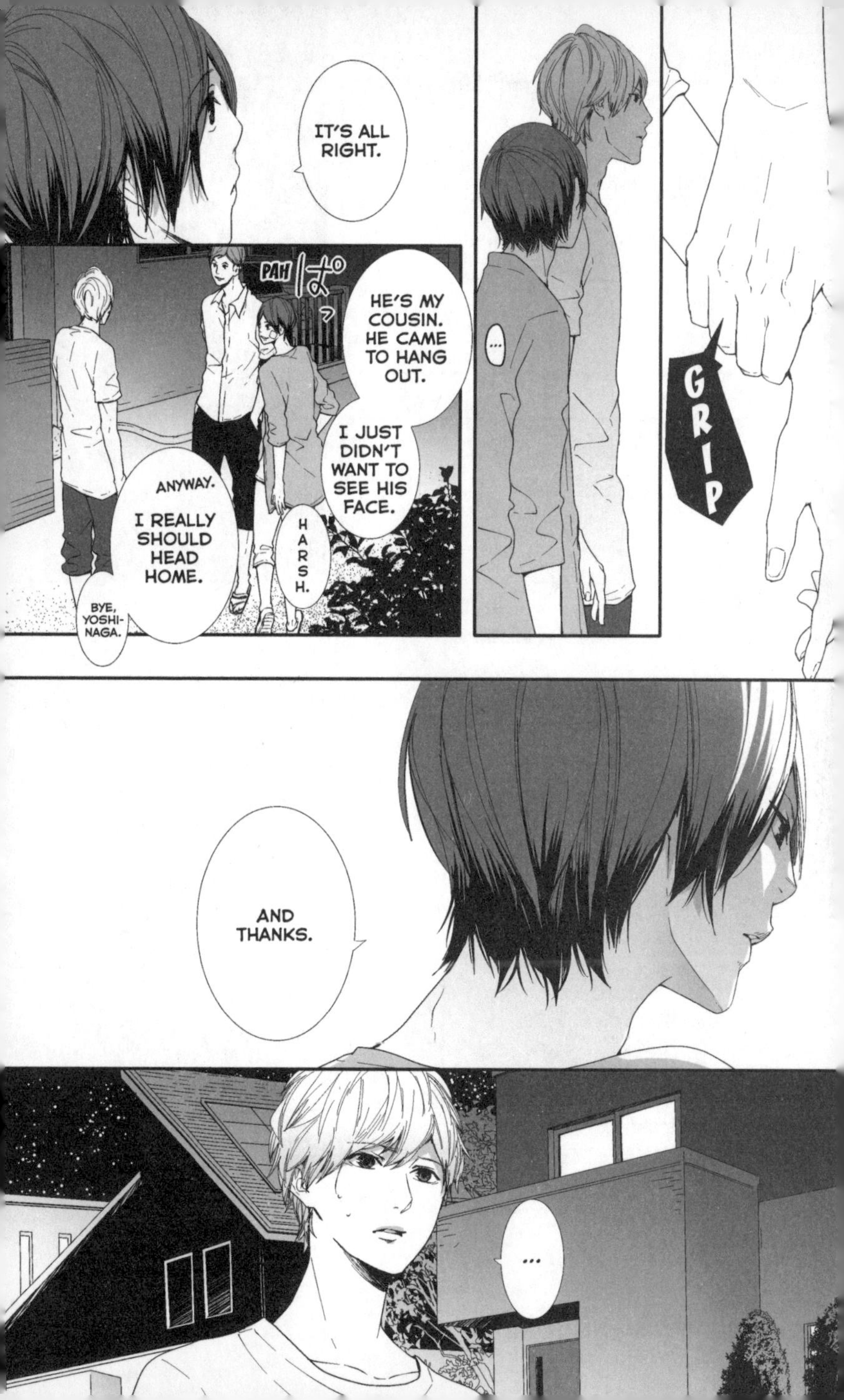
GRIP
...
IT'S ALL RIGHT.
PAH ぱっ
HE'S MY COUSIN. HE CAME TO HANG OUT.
I JUST DIDN'T WANT TO SEE HIS FACE.
HARSH.
ANYWAY.
I REALLY SHOULD HEAD HOME.
BYE, YOSHI-NAGA.
AND THANKS.
...

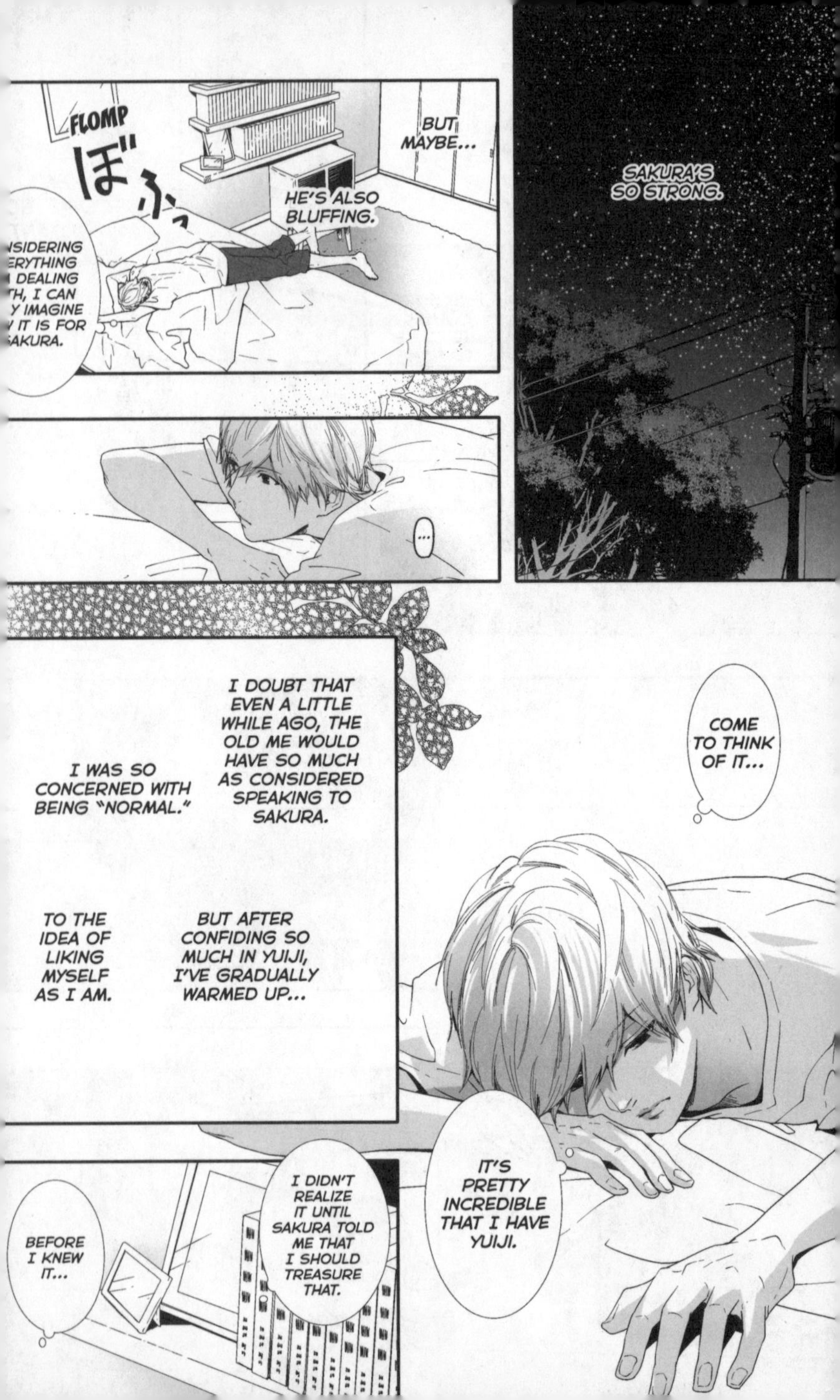
SAKURA'S SO STRONG.
BUT MAYBE...
HE'S ALSO BLUFFING.
FLOMP
ぼふっ
NSIDERING ERYTHING DEALING TH, I CAN Y IMAGINE IT IS FOR SAKURA.
...
COME TO THINK OF IT...
IT'S PRETTY INCREDIBLE THAT I HAVE YUIJI.
I DOUBT THAT EVEN A LITTLE WHILE AGO, THE OLD ME WOULD HAVE SO MUCH AS CONSIDERED SPEAKING TO SAKURA.
I WAS SO CONCERNED WITH BEING "NORMAL."
BUT AFTER CONFIDING SO MUCH IN YUIJI, I'VE GRADUALLY WARMED UP...
TO THE IDEA OF LIKING MYSELF AS I AM.
I DIDN'T REALIZE IT UNTIL SAKURA TOLD ME THAT I SHOULD TREASURE THAT.
BEFORE I KNEW IT...

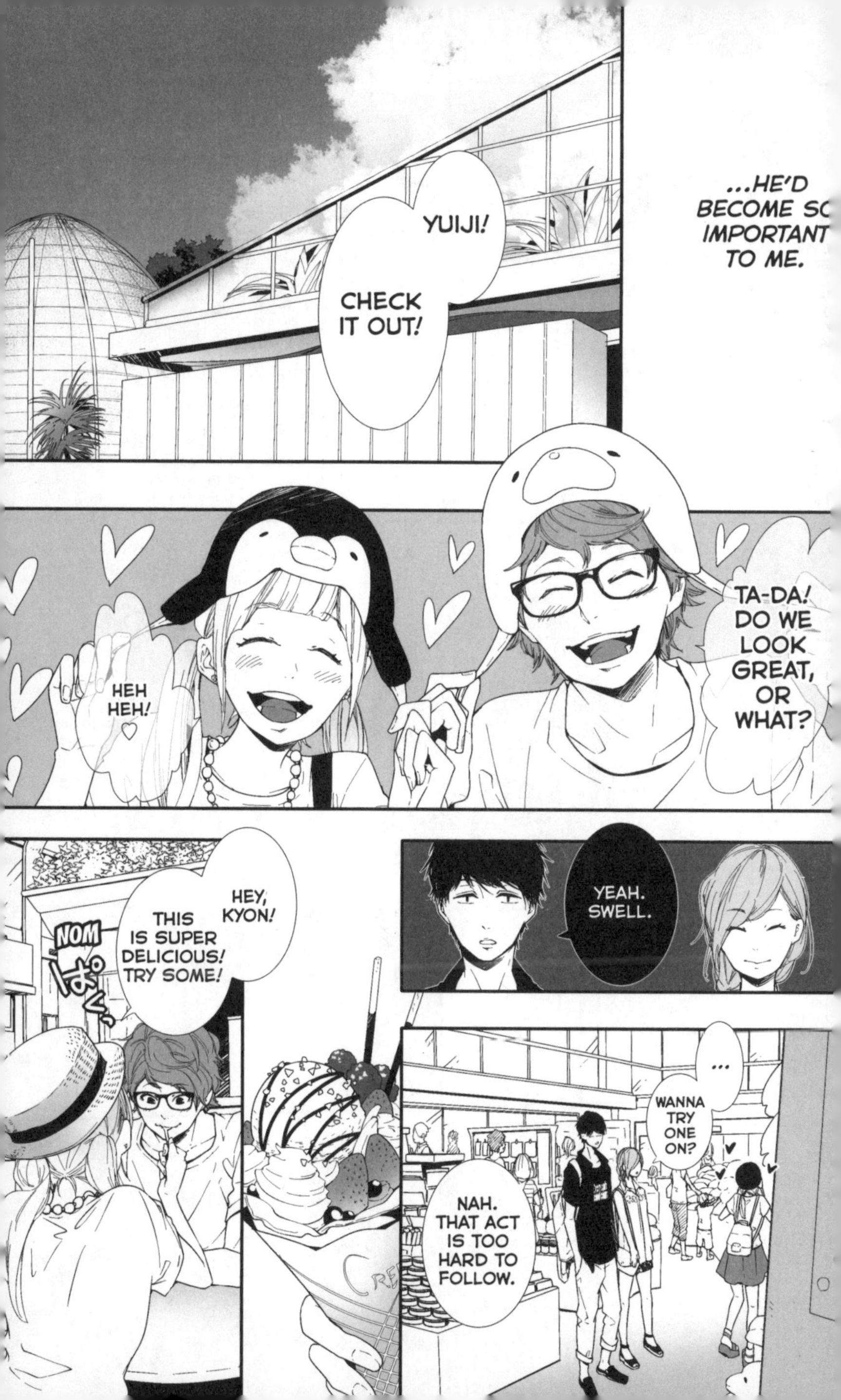

...HE'D BECOME SO IMPORTANT TO ME.
YUIJI!
CHECK IT OUT!
TA-DA! DO WE LOOK GREAT, OR WHAT?
HEH HEH! ♡
YEAH. SWELL.
...
WANNA TRY ONE ON?
NAH. THAT ACT IS TOO HARD TO FOLLOW.
HEY, KYON!
THIS IS SUPER DELICIOUS! TRY SOME!
NOM
ぱく

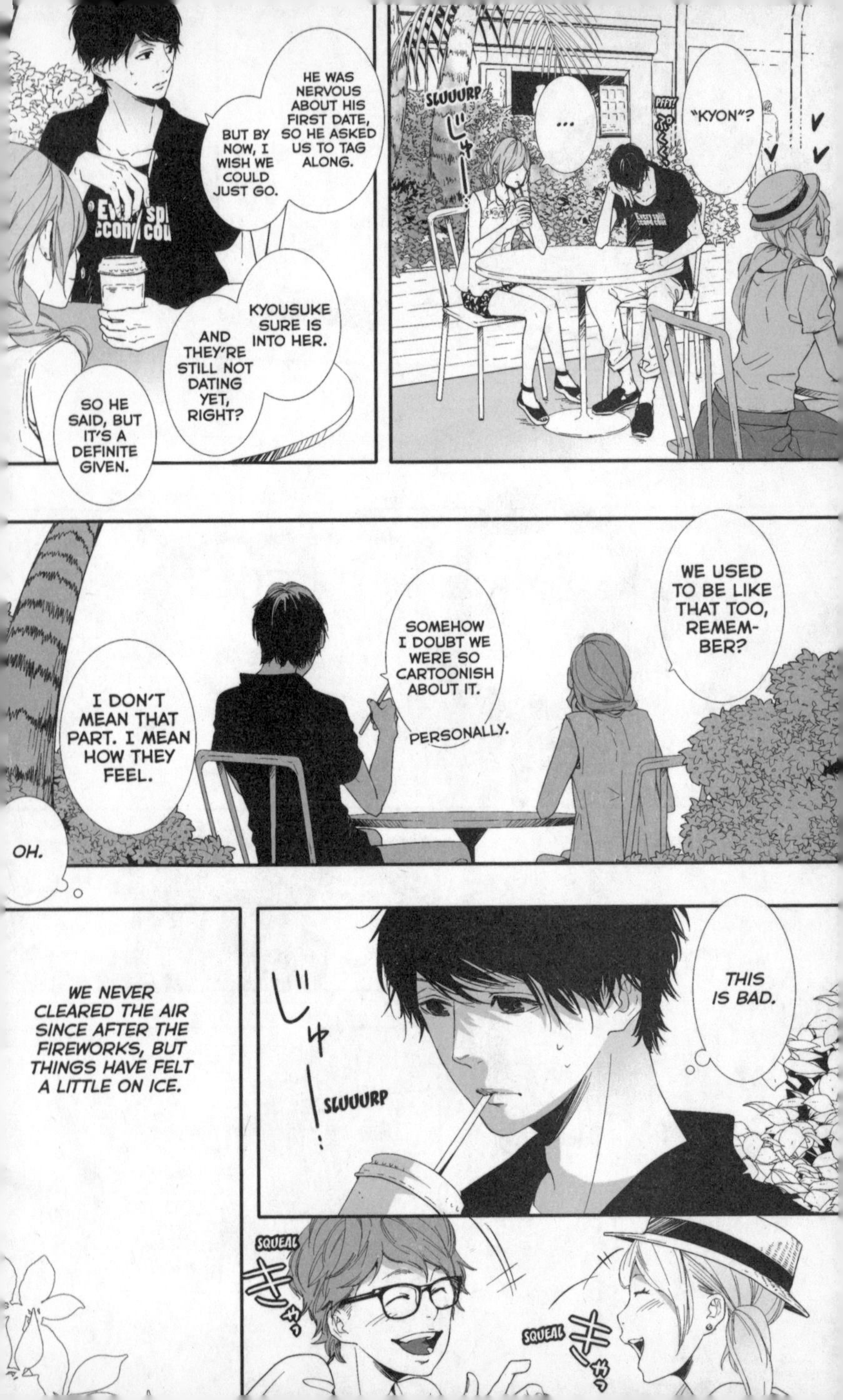
"KYON"?
...
PFFT!
SLUUURP
HE WAS NERVOUS ABOUT HIS FIRST DATE, SO HE ASKED US TO TAG ALONG.
BUT BY NOW, I WISH WE COULD JUST GO.
KYOUSUKE SURE IS INTO HER.
AND THEY'RE STILL NOT DATING YET, RIGHT?
SO HE SAID, BUT IT'S A DEFINITE GIVEN.
WE USED TO BE LIKE THAT TOO, REMEMBER?
SOMEHOW I DOUBT WE WERE SO CARTOONISH ABOUT IT.
PERSONALLY.
I DON'T MEAN THAT PART. I MEAN HOW THEY FEEL.
OH.
THIS IS BAD.
SLUUURP
WE NEVER CLEARED THE AIR SINCE AFTER THE FIREWORKS, BUT THINGS HAVE FELT A LITTLE ON ICE.
SQUEAL
SQUEAL

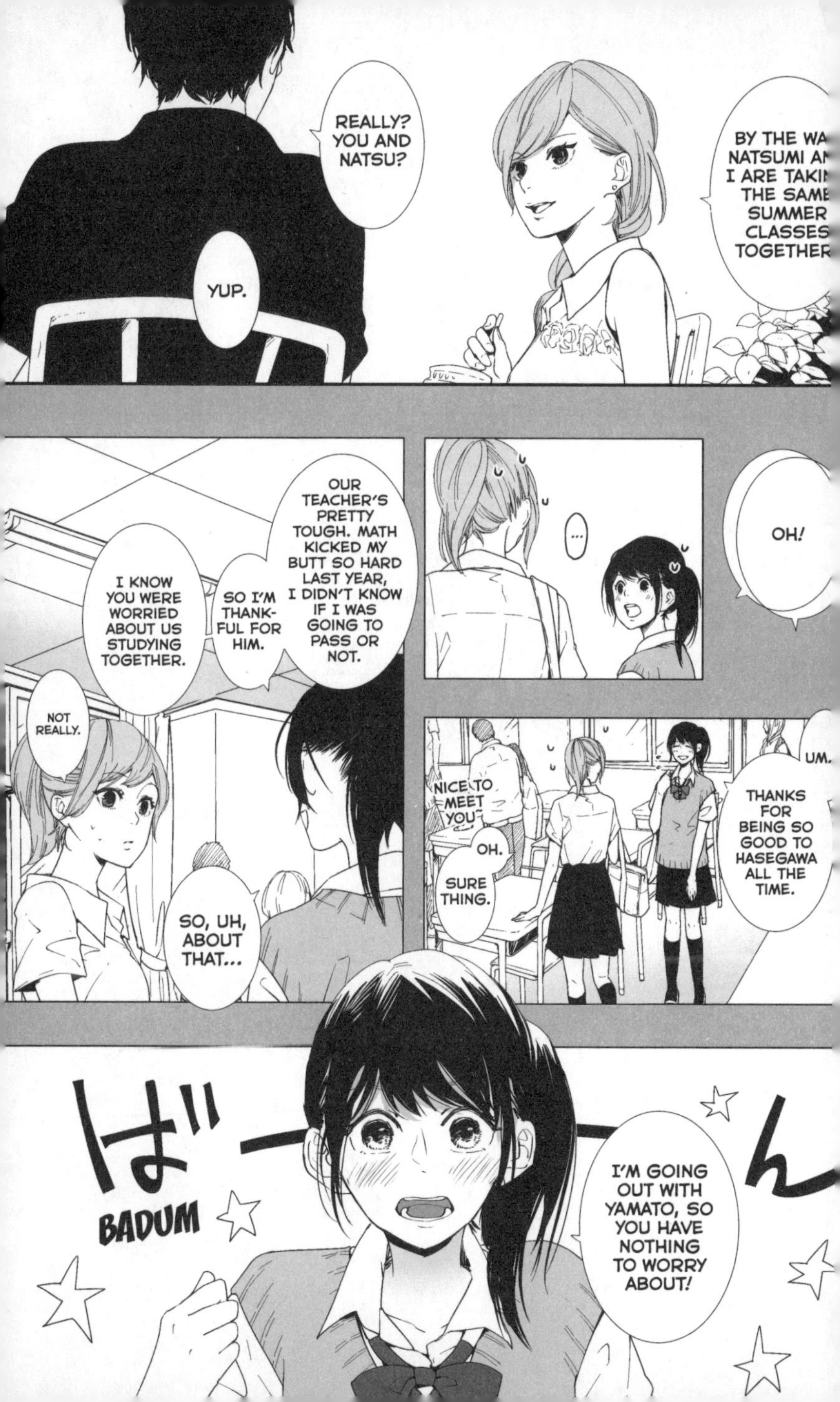
BY THE WA NATSUMI AN I ARE TAKIN THE SAME SUMMER CLASSES TOGETHER
REALLY? YOU AND NATSU?
YUP.
OH!
...
UM.
THANKS FOR BEING SO GOOD TO HASEGAWA ALL THE TIME.
NICE TO MEET YOU~
OH.
SURE THING.
OUR TEACHER'S PRETTY TOUGH. MATH KICKED MY BUTT SO HARD LAST YEAR, I DIDN'T KNOW IF I WAS GOING TO PASS OR NOT.
SO I'M THANK-FUL FOR HIM.
I KNOW YOU WERE WORRIED ABOUT US STUDYING TOGETHER.
NOT REALLY.
SO, UH, ABOUT THAT...
ばーん
BADUM
I'M GOING OUT WITH YAMATO, SO YOU HAVE NOTHING TO WORRY ABOUT!

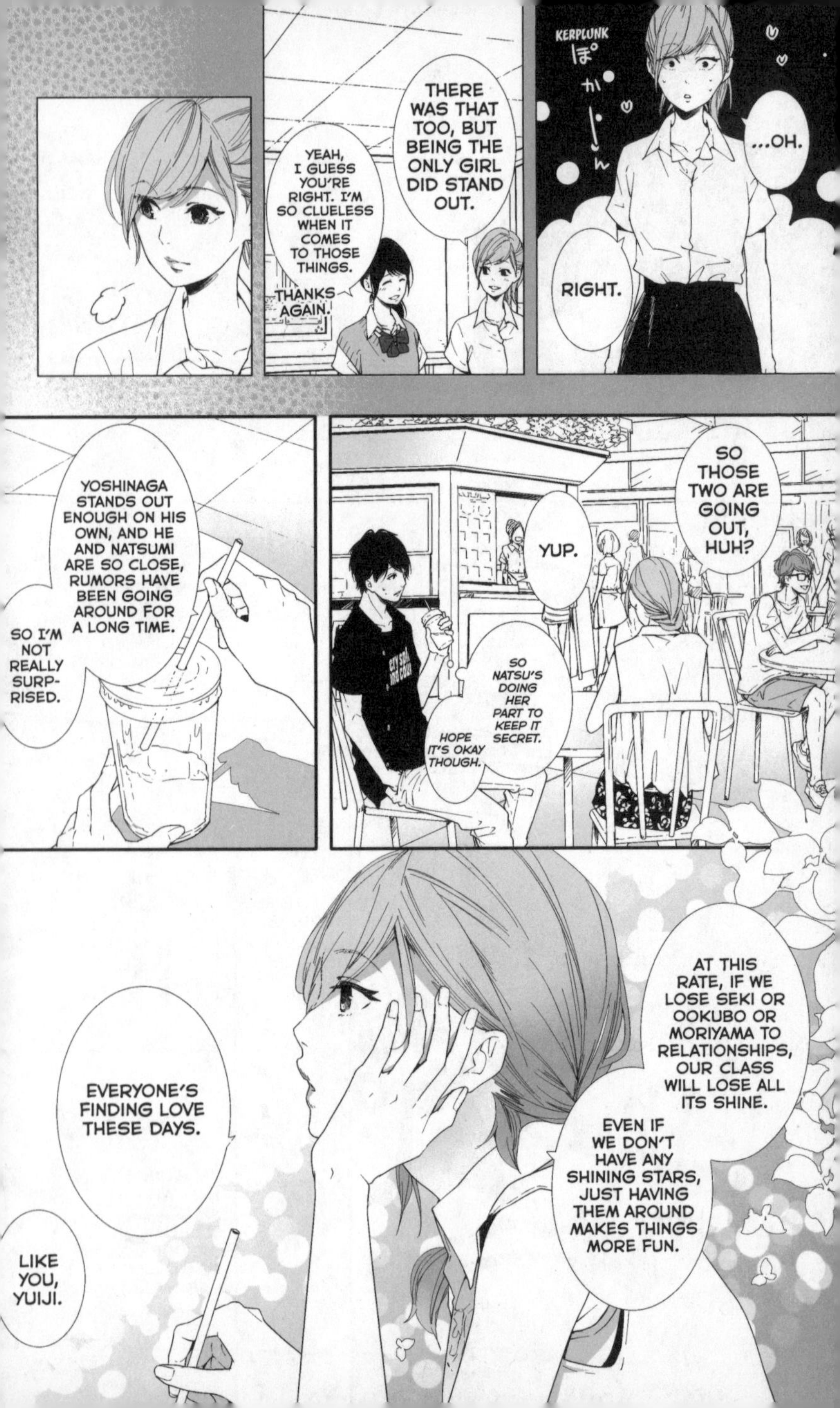
KERPLUNK
ぽかーん
...OH.
RIGHT.
THERE WAS THAT TOO, BUT BEING THE ONLY GIRL DID STAND OUT.
YEAH, I GUESS YOU'RE RIGHT. I'M SO CLUELESS WHEN IT COMES TO THOSE THINGS.
THANKS AGAIN.
SO THOSE TWO ARE GOING OUT, HUH?
YUP.
SO NATSU'S DOING HER PART TO KEEP IT SECRET.
HOPE IT'S OKAY THOUGH.
YOSHINAGA STANDS OUT ENOUGH ON HIS OWN, AND HE AND NATSUMI ARE SO CLOSE, RUMORS HAVE BEEN GOING AROUND FOR A LONG TIME.
SO I'M NOT REALLY SURPRISED.
AT THIS RATE, IF WE LOSE SEKI OR OOKUBO OR MORIYAMA TO RELATIONSHIPS, OUR CLASS WILL LOSE ALL ITS SHINE.
EVEN IF WE DON'T HAVE ANY SHINING STARS, JUST HAVING THEM AROUND MAKES THINGS MORE FUN.
EVERYONE'S FINDING LOVE THESE DAYS.
LIKE YOU, YUIJI.

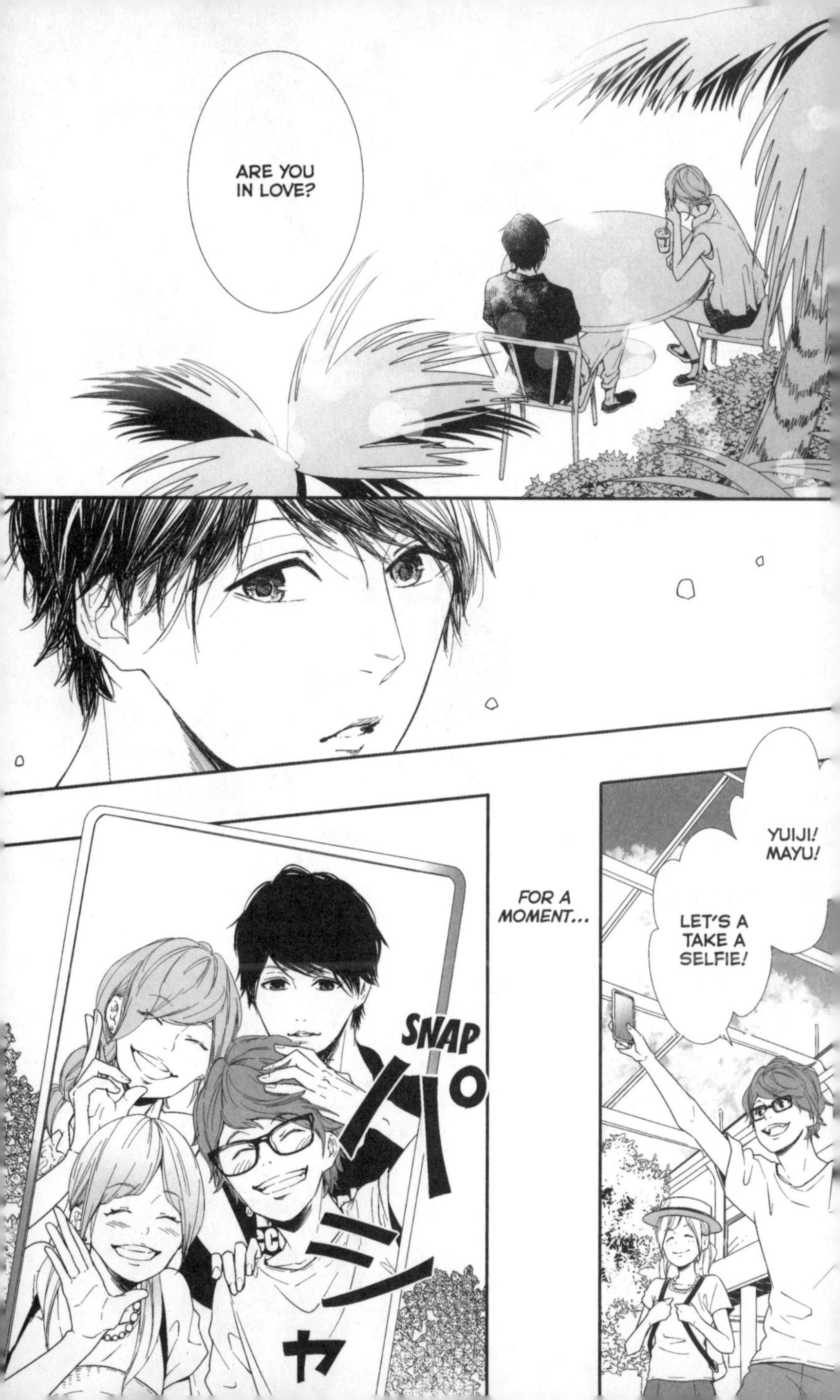
ARE YOU IN LOVE?
YUIJI! MAYU!
LET'S A TAKE A SELFIE!
FOR A MOMENT...
SNAP

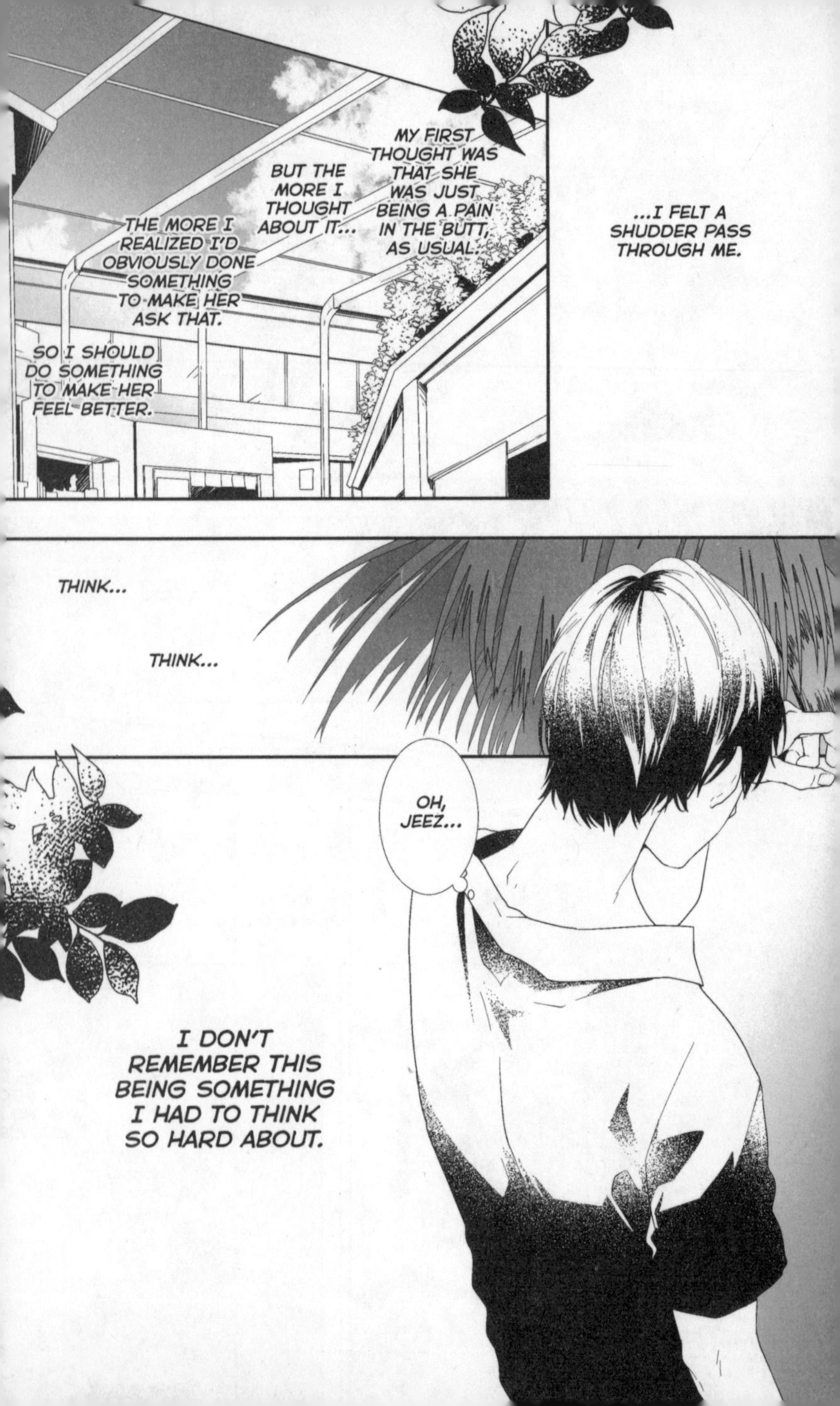
...I FELT A SHUDDER PASS THROUGH ME.
MY FIRST THOUGHT WAS THAT SHE WAS JUST BEING A PAIN IN THE BUTT, AS USUAL.
BUT THE MORE I THOUGHT ABOUT IT...
THE MORE I REALIZED I'D OBVIOUSLY DONE SOMETHING TO MAKE HER ASK THAT.
SO I SHOULD DO SOMETHING TO MAKE HER FEEL BETTER.
THINK...
THINK...
OH, JEEZ...
I DON'T REMEMBER THIS BEING SOMETHING I HAD TO THINK SO HARD ABOUT.

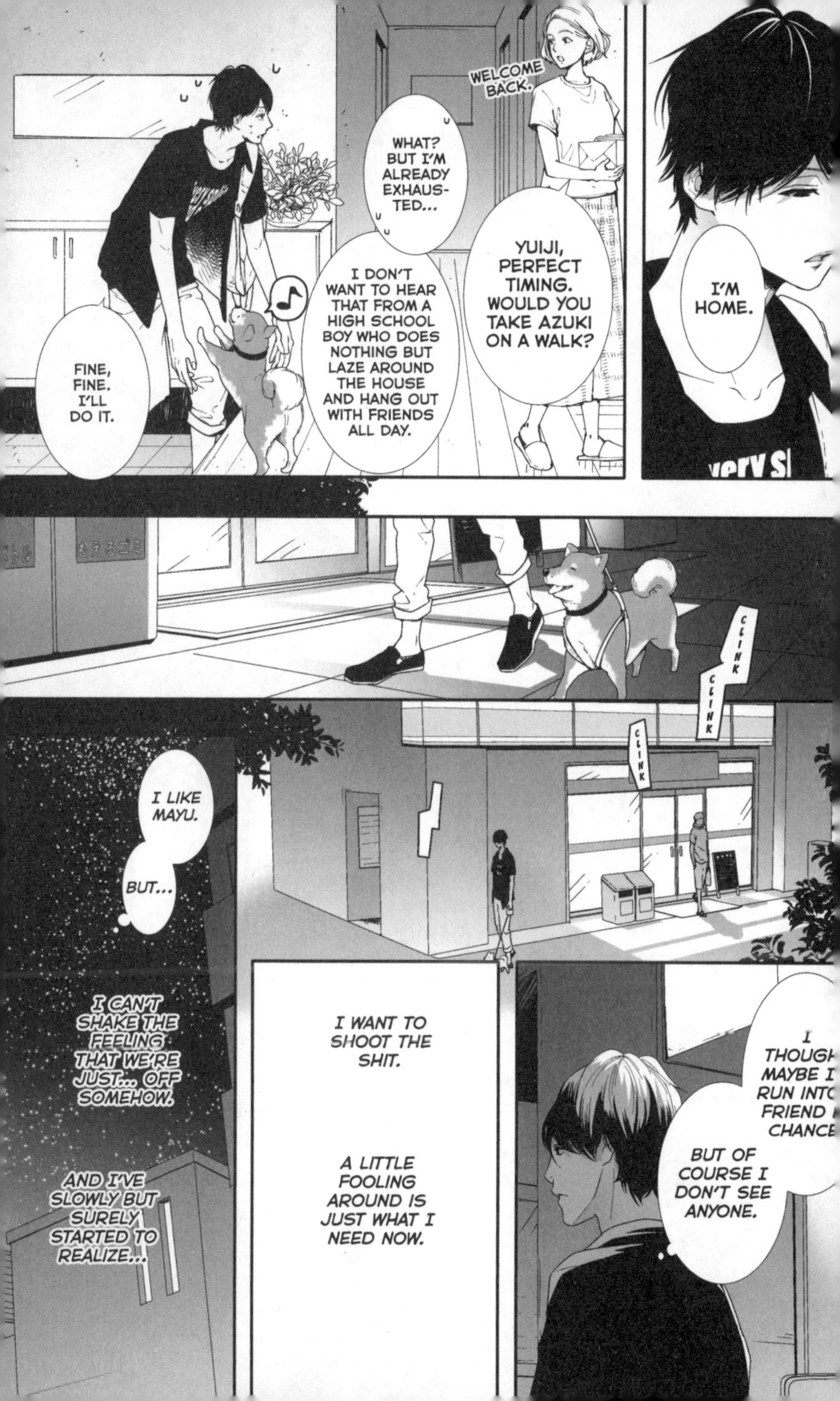
I'M HOME.
WELCOME BACK.
YUIJI, PERFECT TIMING. WOULD YOU TAKE AZUKI ON A WALK?
WHAT? BUT I'M ALREADY EXHAUS-TED...
I DON'T WANT TO HEAR THAT FROM A HIGH SCHOOL BOY WHO DOES NOTHING BUT LAZE AROUND THE HOUSE AND HANG OUT WITH FRIENDS ALL DAY.
FINE, FINE. I'LL DO IT.
もえるゴミ
CLINK
CLINK
CLINK
I THOUGH MAYBE I RUN INTO FRIEND CHANCE
BUT OF COURSE I DON'T SEE ANYONE.
I WANT TO SHOOT THE SHIT.
A LITTLE FOOLING AROUND IS JUST WHAT I NEED NOW.
I LIKE MAYU.
BUT...
I CAN'T SHAKE THE FEELING THAT WE'RE JUST... OFF SOMEHOW.
AND I'VE SLOWLY BUT SURELY STARTED TO REALIZE...

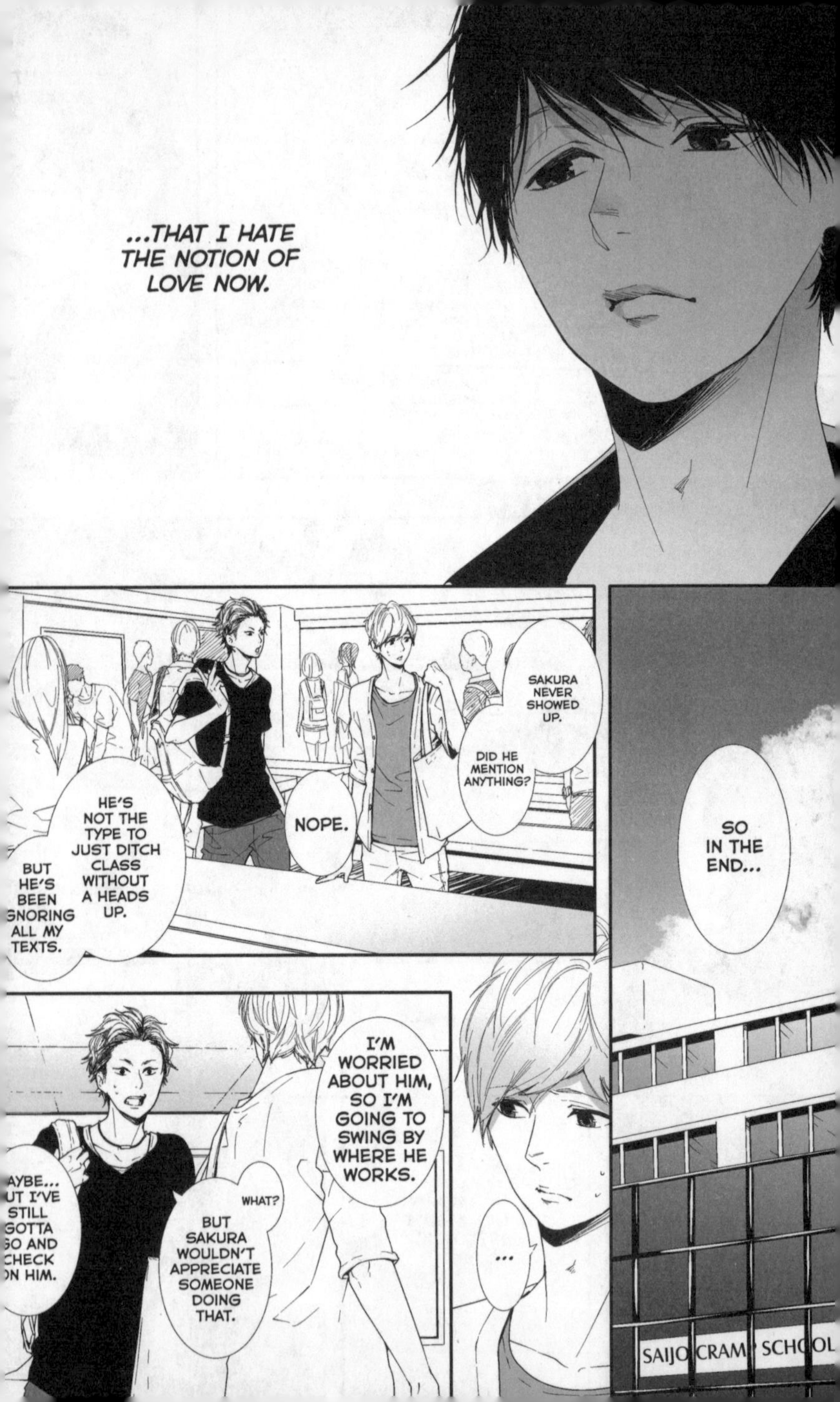
...THAT I HATE THE NOTION OF LOVE NOW.
SO IN THE END...
SAKURA NEVER SHOWED UP.
DID HE MENTION ANYTHING?
NOPE.
HE'S NOT THE TYPE TO JUST DITCH CLASS WITHOUT A HEADS UP.
BUT HE'S BEEN GNORING ALL MY TEXTS.
SAIJO CRAM SCHOOL
I'M WORRIED ABOUT HIM, SO I'M GOING TO SWING BY WHERE HE WORKS.
...
WHAT?
BUT SAKURA WOULDN'T APPRECIATE SOMEONE DOING THAT.
AYBE... UT I'VE STILL GOTTA GO AND CHECK ON HIM.

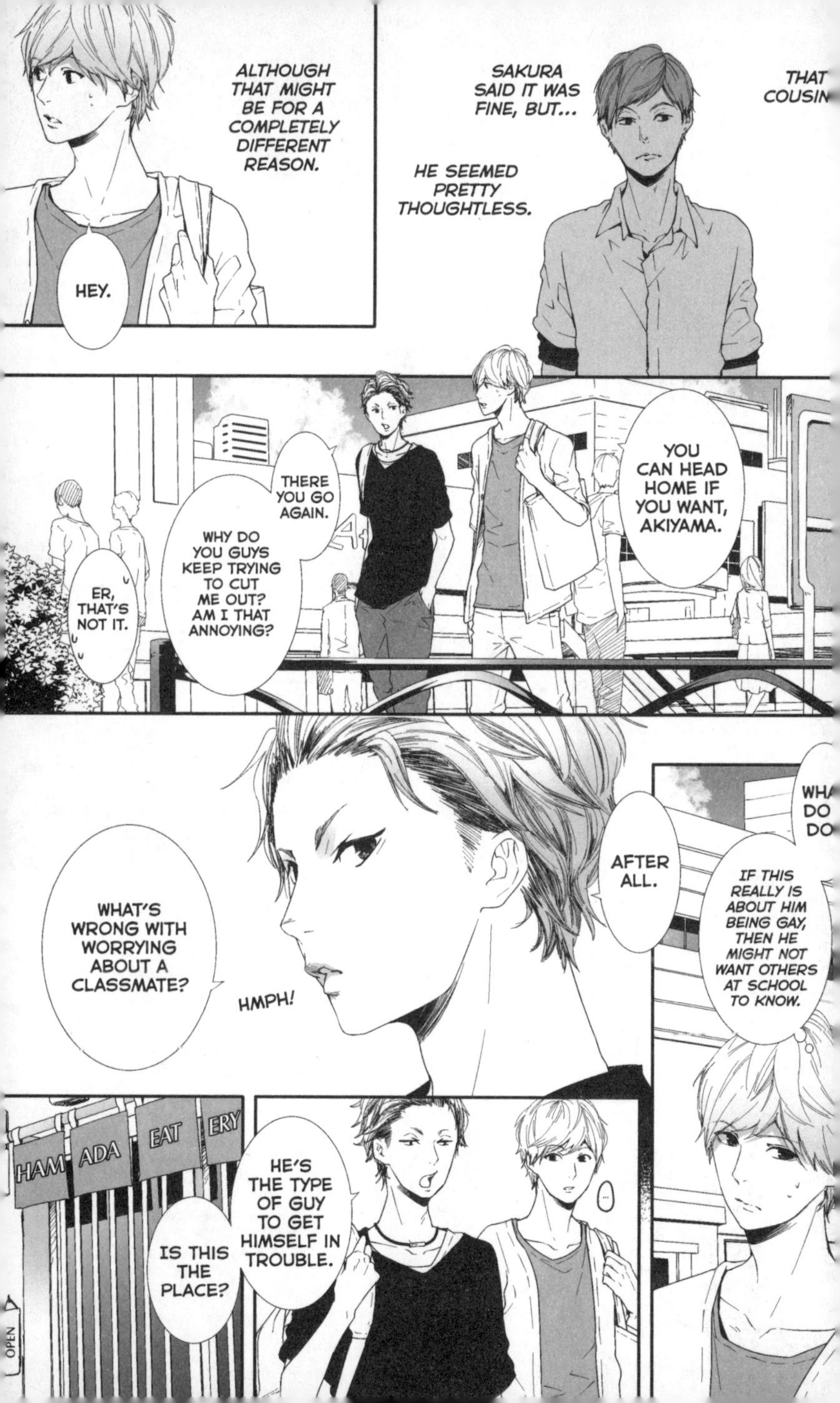

THAT COUSIN
SAKURA SAID IT WAS FINE, BUT...
HE SEEMED PRETTY THOUGHTLESS.
ALTHOUGH THAT MIGHT BE FOR A COMPLETELY DIFFERENT REASON.
HEY.
YOU CAN HEAD HOME IF YOU WANT, AKIYAMA.
THERE YOU GO AGAIN.
WHY DO YOU GUYS KEEP TRYING TO CUT ME OUT? AM I THAT ANNOYING?
ER, THAT'S NOT IT.
WHA DO DO
IF THIS REALLY IS ABOUT HIM BEING GAY, THEN HE MIGHT NOT WANT OTHERS AT SCHOOL TO KNOW.
AFTER ALL.
WHAT'S WRONG WITH WORRYING ABOUT A CLASSMATE?
HMPH!
...
HE'S THE TYPE OF GUY TO GET HIMSELF IN TROUBLE.
IS THIS THE PLACE?
HAM ADA EAT ERY
OPEN

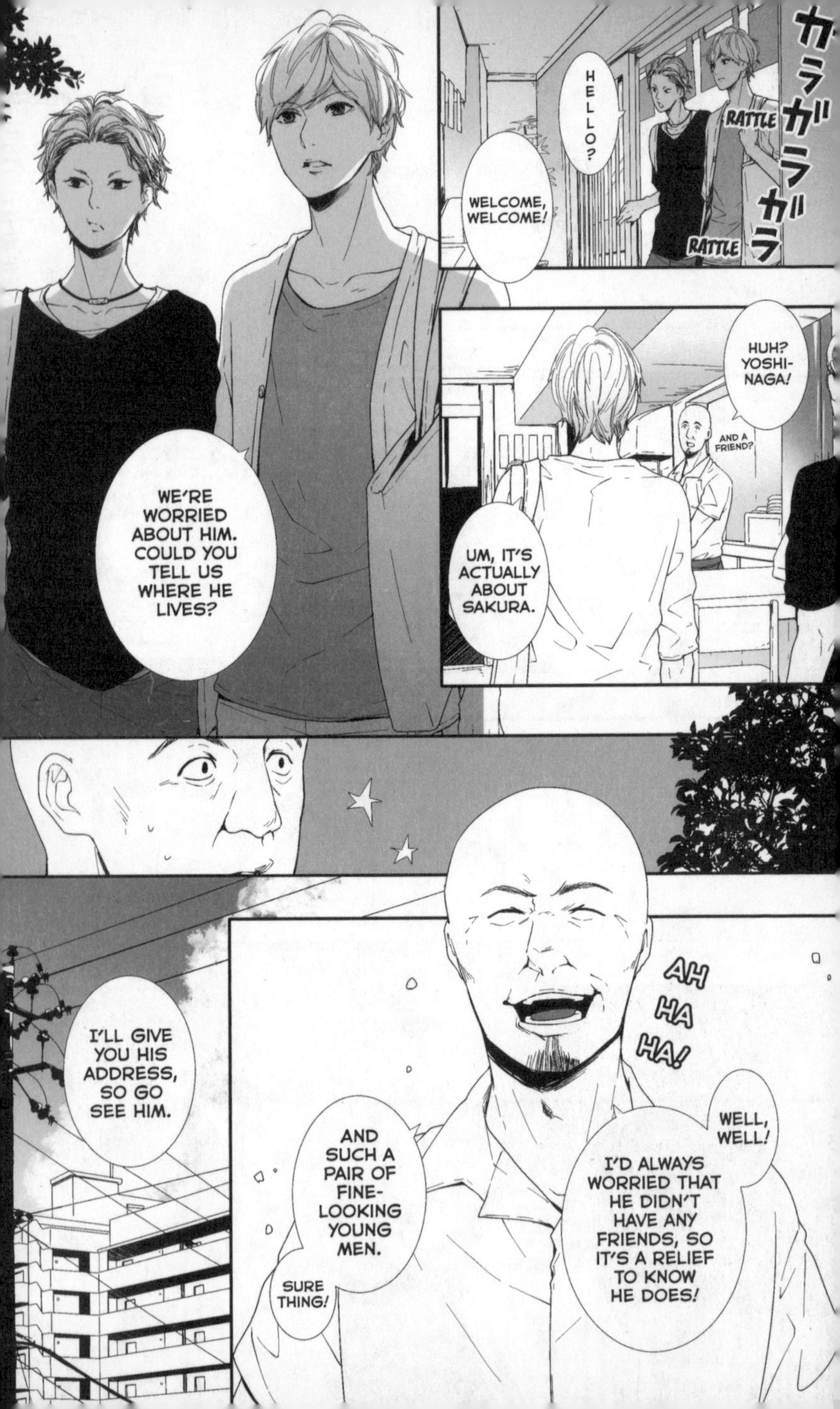
カラガラガラ
RATTLE
RATTLE
HELLO?
WELCOME, WELCOME!
HUH? YOSHINAGA!
AND A FRIEND?
UM, IT'S ACTUALLY ABOUT SAKURA.
WE'RE WORRIED ABOUT HIM. COULD YOU TELL US WHERE HE LIVES?
AH HA HA!
WELL, WELL!
I'D ALWAYS WORRIED THAT HE DIDN'T HAVE ANY FRIENDS, SO IT'S A RELIEF TO KNOW HE DOES!
AND SUCH A PAIR OF FINE-LOOKING YOUNG MEN.
SURE THING!
I'LL GIVE YOU HIS ADDRESS, SO GO SEE HIM.

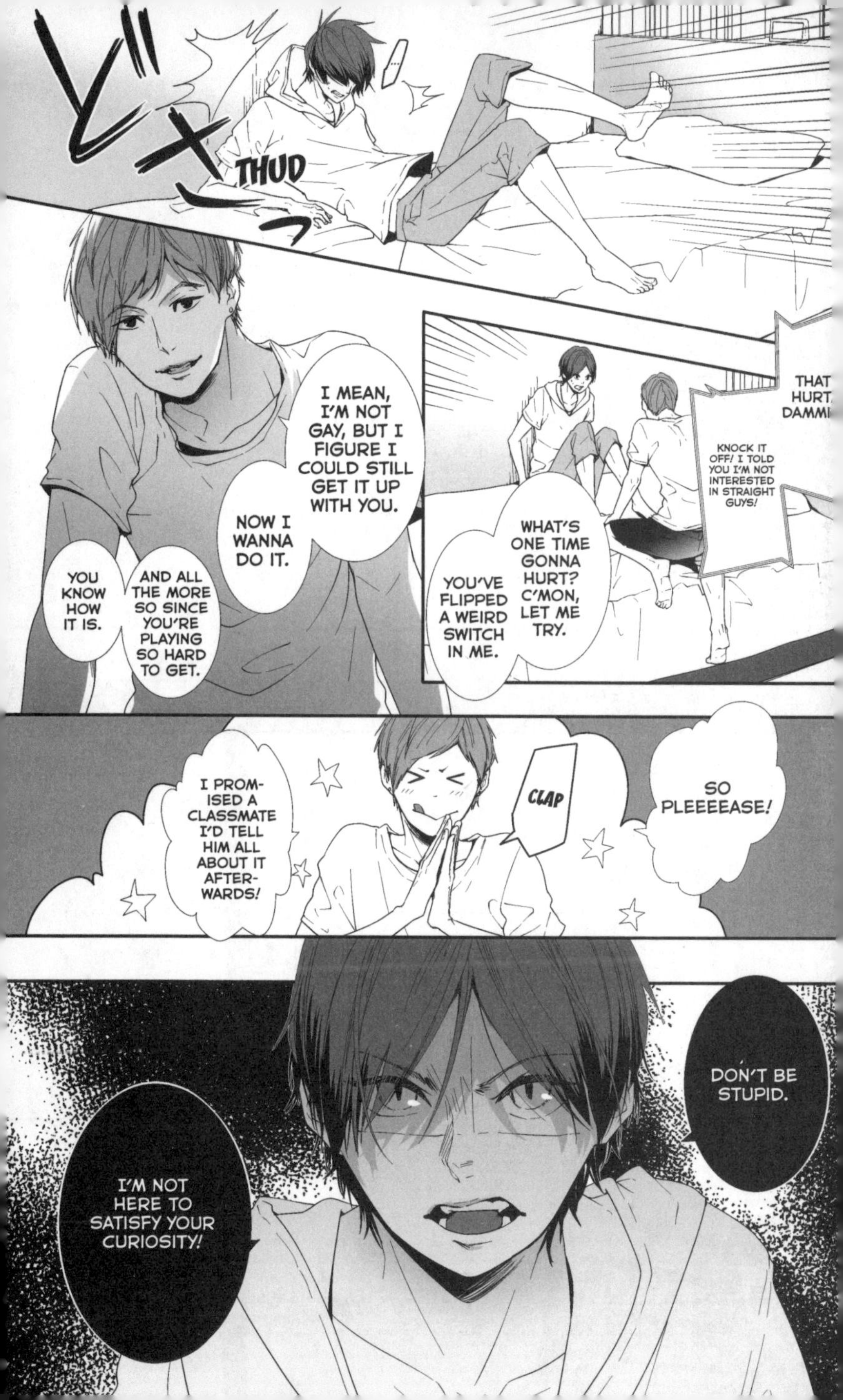
…!
THUD
THAT HURT, DAMMI
KNOCK IT OFF! I TOLD YOU I'M NOT INTERESTED IN STRAIGHT GUYS!
WHAT'S ONE TIME GONNA HURT? C'MON, LET ME TRY.
YOU'VE FLIPPED A WEIRD SWITCH IN ME.
I MEAN, I'M NOT GAY, BUT I FIGURE I COULD STILL GET IT UP WITH YOU.
NOW I WANNA DO IT.
AND ALL THE MORE SO SINCE YOU'RE PLAYING SO HARD TO GET.
YOU KNOW HOW IT IS.
SO PLEEEEASE!
CLAP
I PROMISED A CLASSMATE I'D TELL HIM ALL ABOUT IT AFTERWARDS!
DON'T BE STUPID.
I'M NOT HERE TO SATISFY YOUR CURIOSITY!

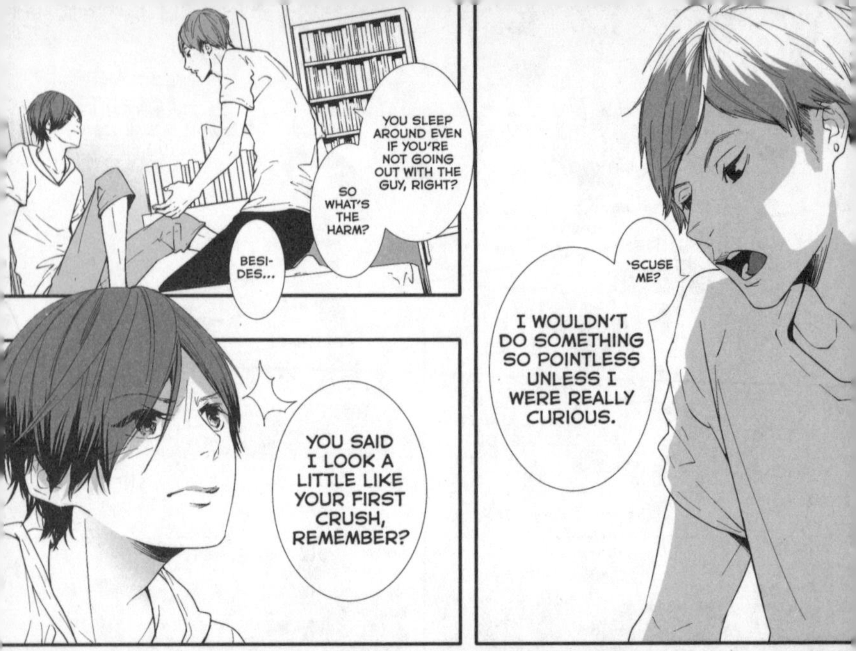
'SCUSE ME?
I WOULDN'T DO SOMETHING SO POINTLESS UNLESS I WERE REALLY CURIOUS.
YOU SLEEP AROUND EVEN IF YOU'RE NOT GOING OUT WITH THE GUY, RIGHT?
SO WHAT'S THE HARM?
BESI-DES...
YOU SAID I LOOK A LITTLE LIKE YOUR FIRST CRUSH, REMEMBER?

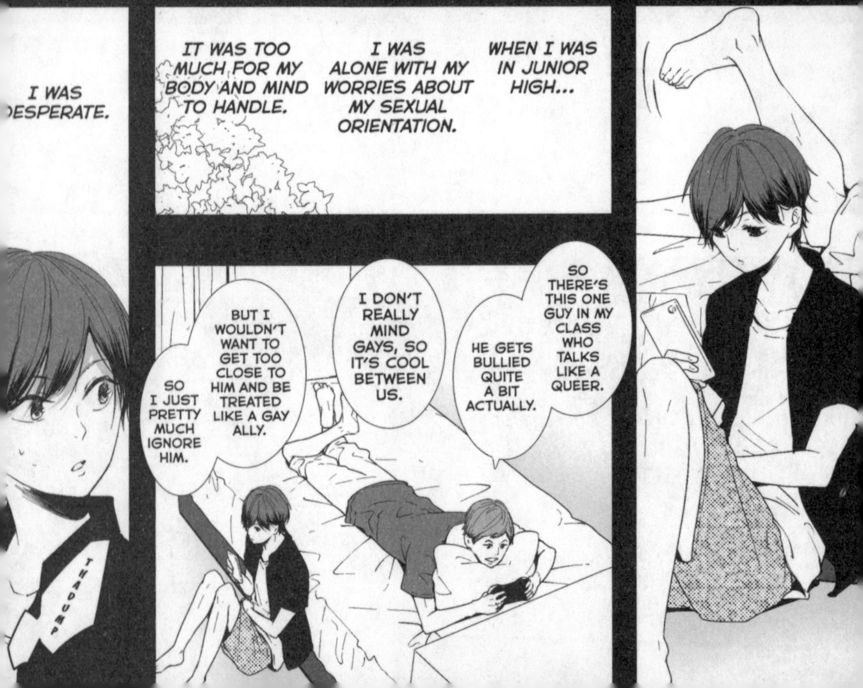
WHEN I WAS IN JUNIOR HIGH...
I WAS ALONE WITH MY WORRIES ABOUT MY SEXUAL ORIENTATION.
IT WAS TOO MUCH FOR MY BODY AND MIND TO HANDLE.
SO THERE'S THIS ONE GUY IN MY CLASS WHO TALKS LIKE A QUEER.
HE GETS BULLIED QUITE A BIT ACTUALLY.
I DON'T REALLY MIND GAYS, SO IT'S COOL BETWEEN US.
BUT I WOULDN'T WANT TO GET TOO CLOSE TO HIM AND BE TREATED LIKE A GAY ALLY.
SO I JUST PRETTY MUCH IGNORE HIM.
I WAS DESPERATE.
THADUMP

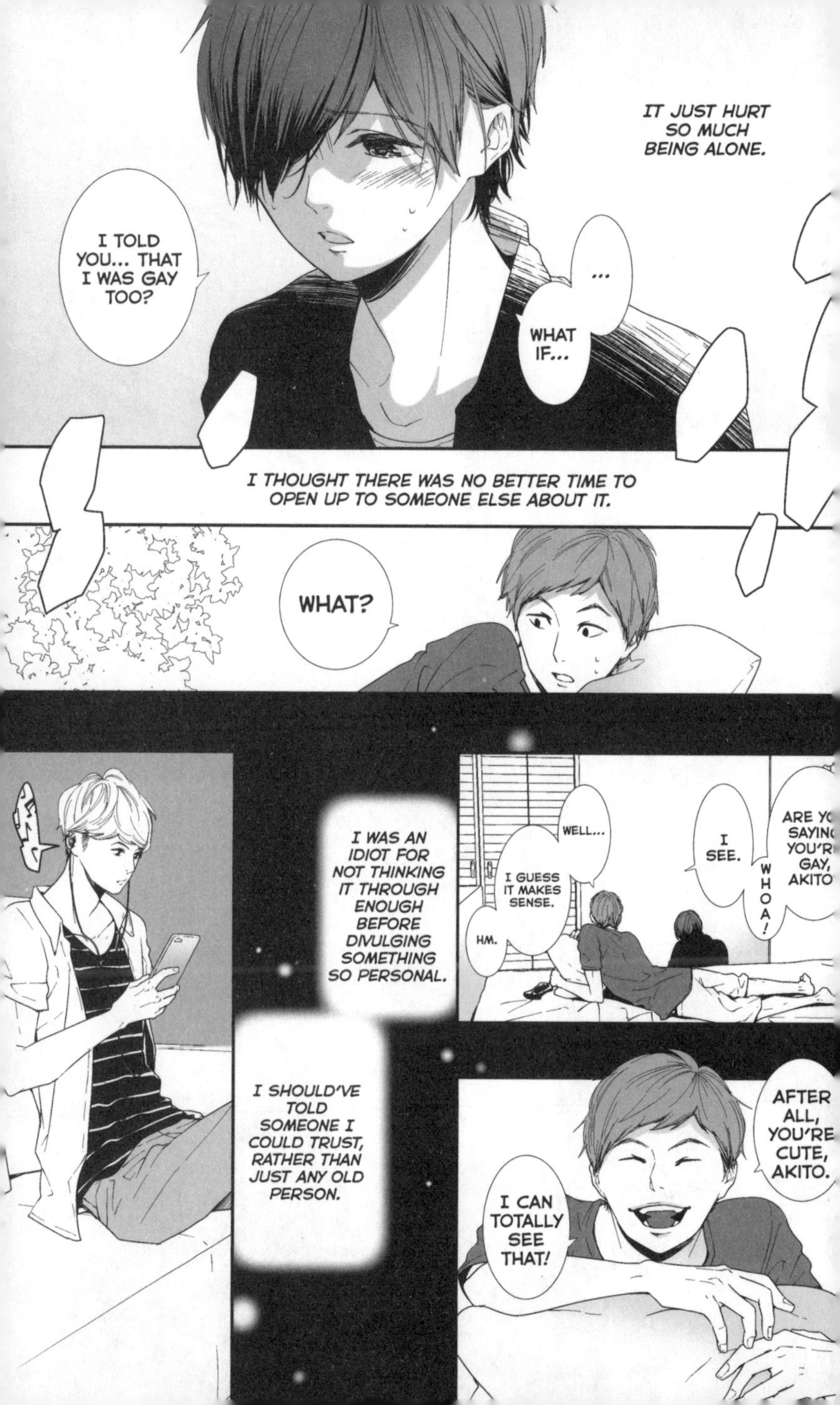
IT JUST HURT SO MUCH BEING ALONE.
...
WHAT IF...
I TOLD YOU... THAT I WAS GAY TOO?
I THOUGHT THERE WAS NO BETTER TIME TO OPEN UP TO SOMEONE ELSE ABOUT IT.
WHAT?
ARE YO SAYIN YOU'R GAY, AKITO
WHOA!
I SEE.
WELL...
I GUESS IT MAKES SENSE.
HM.
I WAS AN IDIOT FOR NOT THINKING IT THROUGH ENOUGH BEFORE DIVULGING SOMETHING SO PERSONAL.
AFTER ALL, YOU'RE CUTE, AKITO.
I CAN TOTALLY SEE THAT!
I SHOULD'VE TOLD SOMEONE I COULD TRUST, RATHER THAN JUST ANY OLD PERSON.

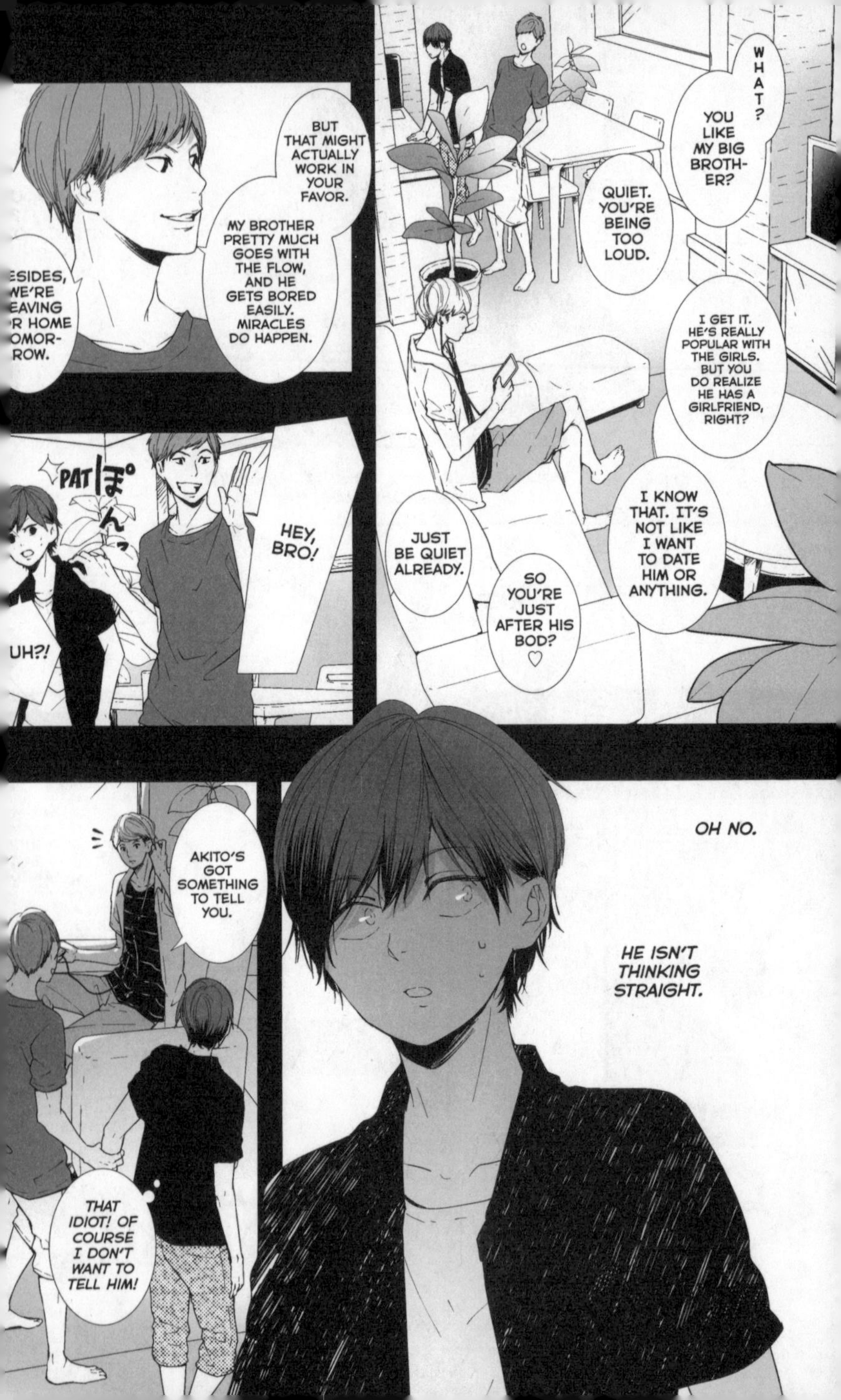
WHAT? YOU LIKE MY BIG BROTHER?
QUIET. YOU'RE BEING TOO LOUD.
I GET IT. HE'S REALLY POPULAR WITH THE GIRLS. BUT YOU DO REALIZE HE HAS A GIRLFRIEND, RIGHT?
I KNOW THAT. IT'S NOT LIKE I WANT TO DATE HIM OR ANYTHING.
SO YOU'RE JUST AFTER HIS BOD? ♡
JUST BE QUIET ALREADY.
BUT THAT MIGHT ACTUALLY WORK IN YOUR FAVOR.
MY BROTHER PRETTY MUCH GOES WITH THE FLOW, AND HE GETS BORED EASILY. MIRACLES DO HAPPEN.
ESIDES, WE'RE EAVING R HOME OMOR-ROW.
HEY, BRO!
PAT ぽんっ
UH?!
OH NO.
HE ISN'T THINKING STRAIGHT.
AKITO'S GOT SOMETHING TO TELL YOU.
THAT IDIOT! OF COURSE I DON'T WANT TO TELL HIM!

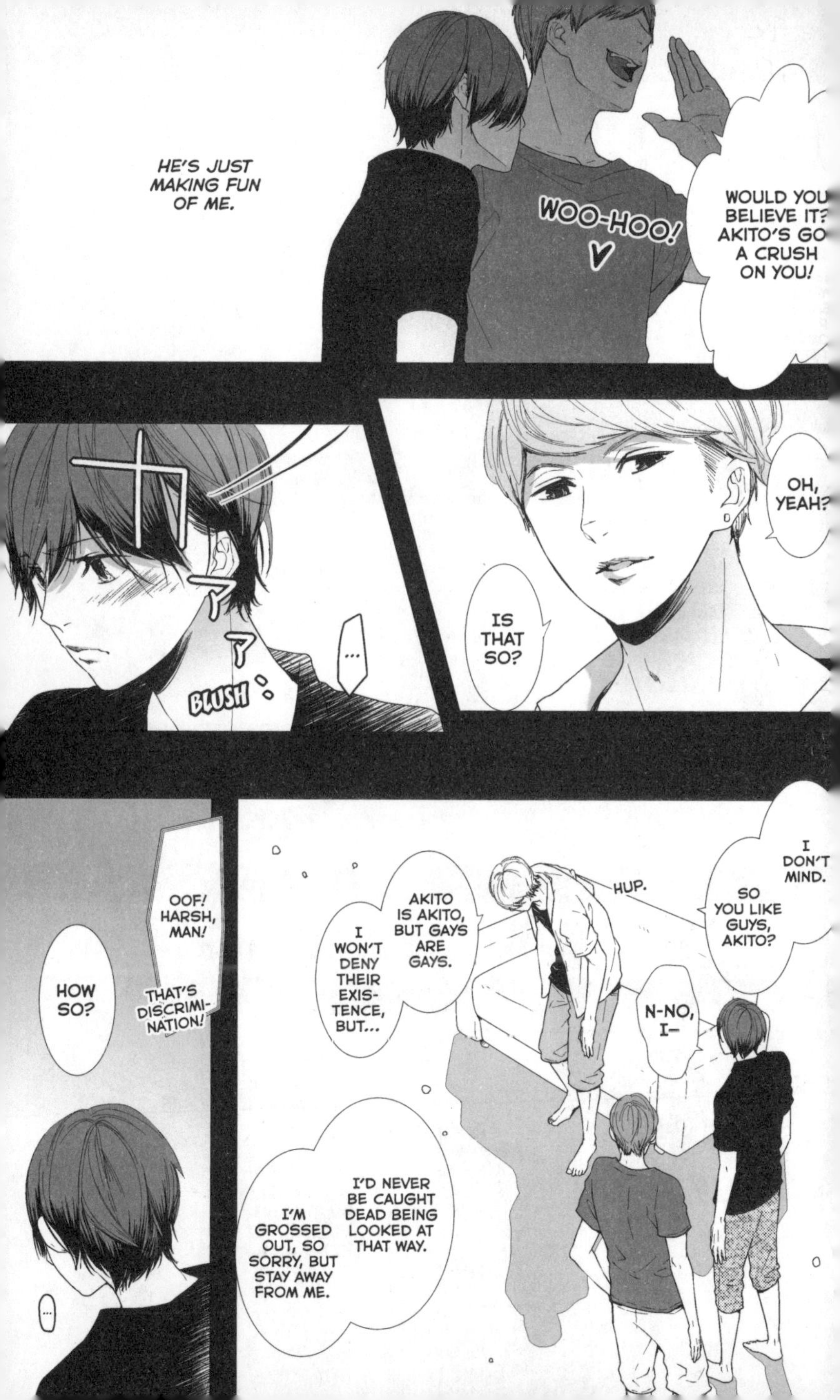

WOULD YOU BELIEVE IT? AKITO'S GO A CRUSH ON YOU!
WOO-HOO! ♥
HE'S JUST MAKING FUN OF ME.
OH, YEAH?
IS THAT SO?
...
BLUSH
I DON'T MIND.
SO YOU LIKE GUYS, AKITO?
HUP.
N-NO, I–
AKITO IS AKITO, BUT GAYS ARE GAYS.
I WON'T DENY THEIR EXISTENCE, BUT...
I'D NEVER BE CAUGHT DEAD BEING LOOKED AT THAT WAY.
I'M GROSSED OUT, SO SORRY, BUT STAY AWAY FROM ME.
OOF! HARSH, MAN!
THAT'S DISCRIMINATION!
HOW SO?
...

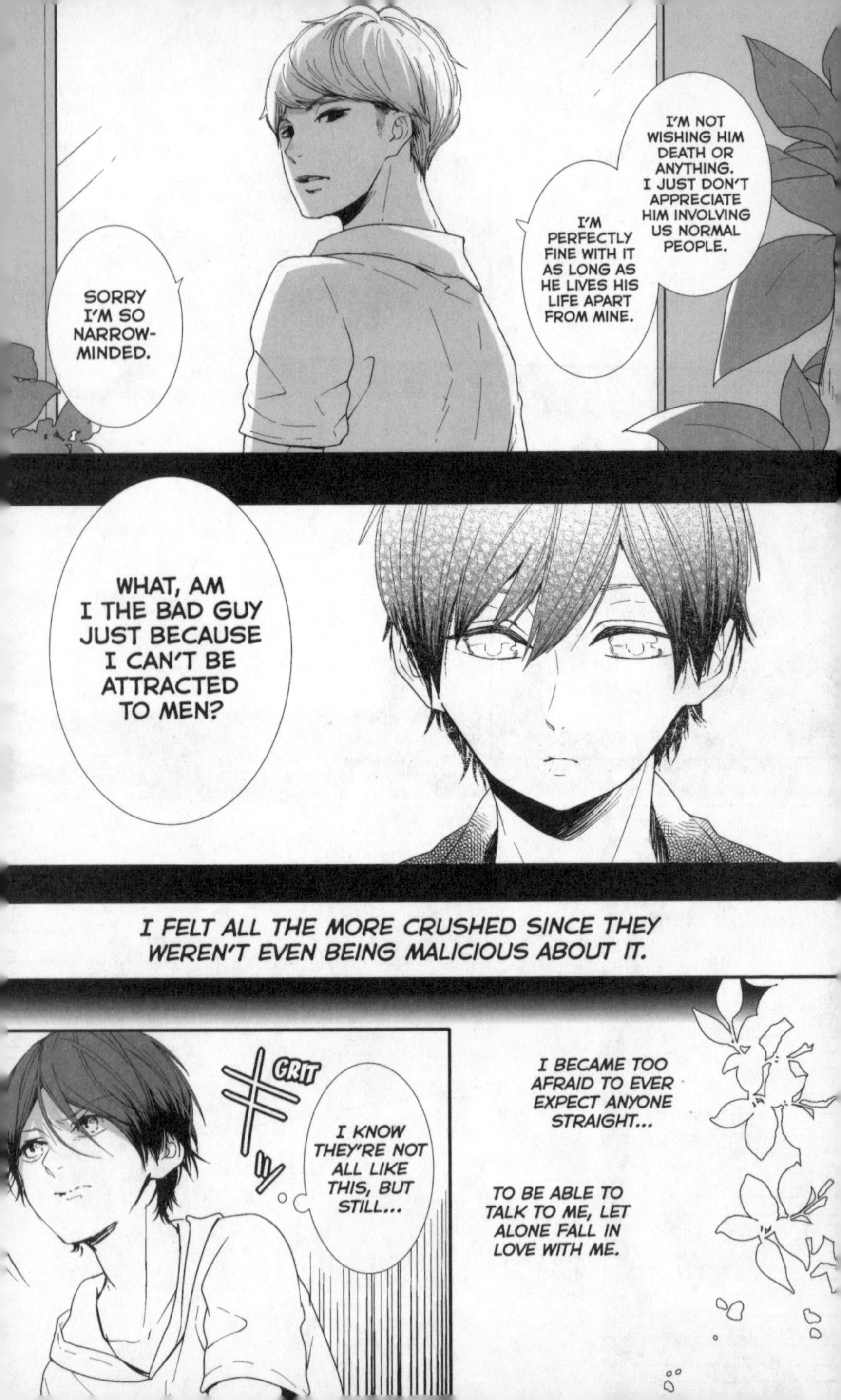
I'M NOT WISHING HIM DEATH OR ANYTHING. I JUST DON'T APPRECIATE HIM INVOLVING US NORMAL PEOPLE.
I'M PERFECTLY FINE WITH IT AS LONG AS HE LIVES HIS LIFE APART FROM MINE.
SORRY I'M SO NARROW-MINDED.
WHAT, AM I THE BAD GUY JUST BECAUSE I CAN'T BE ATTRACTED TO MEN?
I FELT ALL THE MORE CRUSHED SINCE THEY WEREN'T EVEN BEING MALICIOUS ABOUT IT.
I BECAME TOO AFRAID TO EVER EXPECT ANYONE STRAIGHT...
TO BE ABLE TO TALK TO ME, LET ALONE FALL IN LOVE WITH ME.
GRIT
I KNOW THEY'RE NOT ALL LIKE THIS, BUT STILL...

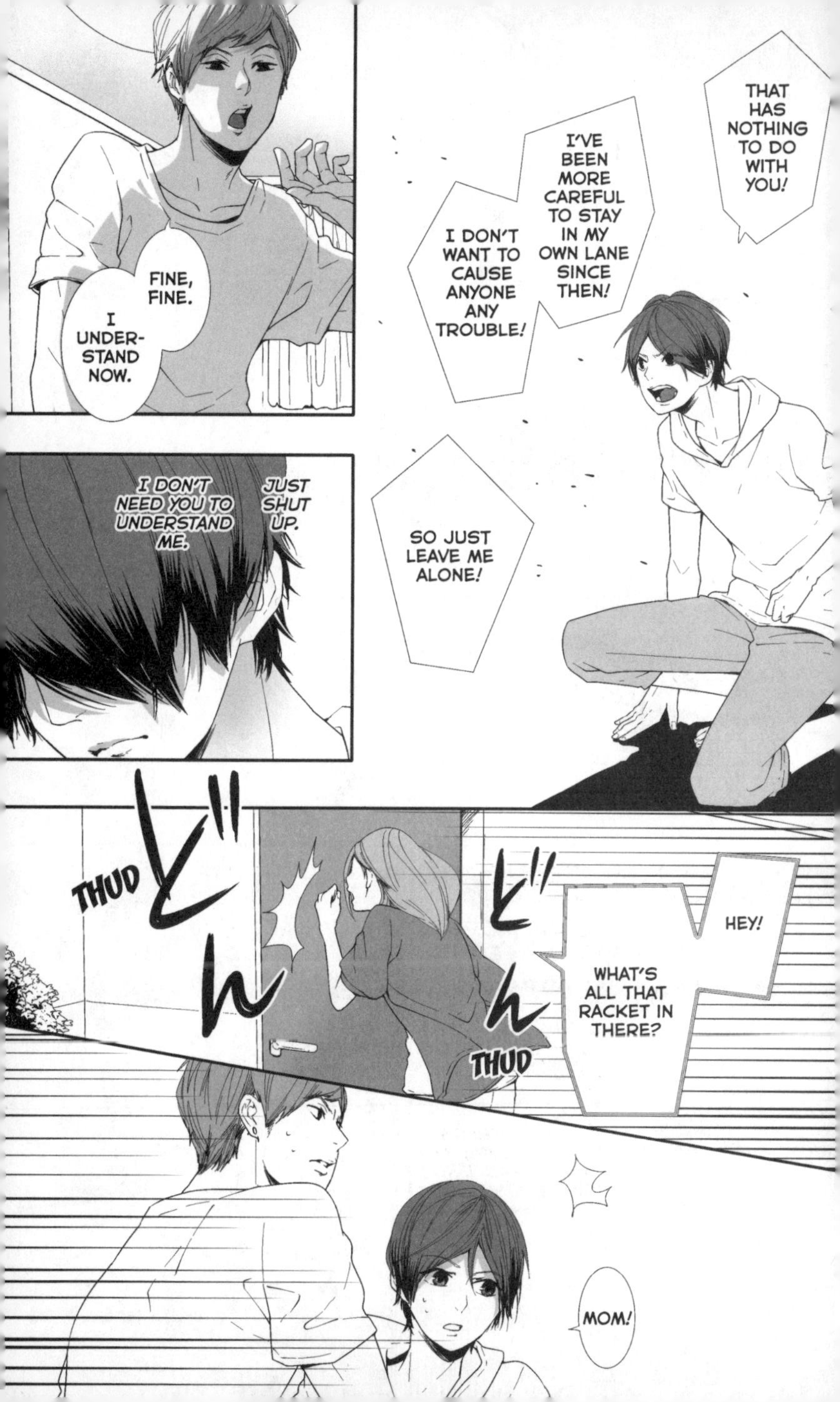

THAT HAS NOTHING TO DO WITH YOU!
I'VE BEEN MORE CAREFUL TO STAY IN MY OWN LANE SINCE THEN!
I DON'T WANT TO CAUSE ANYONE ANY TROUBLE!
SO JUST LEAVE ME ALONE!
FINE, FINE.
I UNDER-STAND NOW.
JUST SHUT UP.
I DON'T NEED YOU TO UNDERSTAND ME.
HEY!
WHAT'S ALL THAT RACKET IN THERE?
どん
THUD
どん
THUD
MOM!

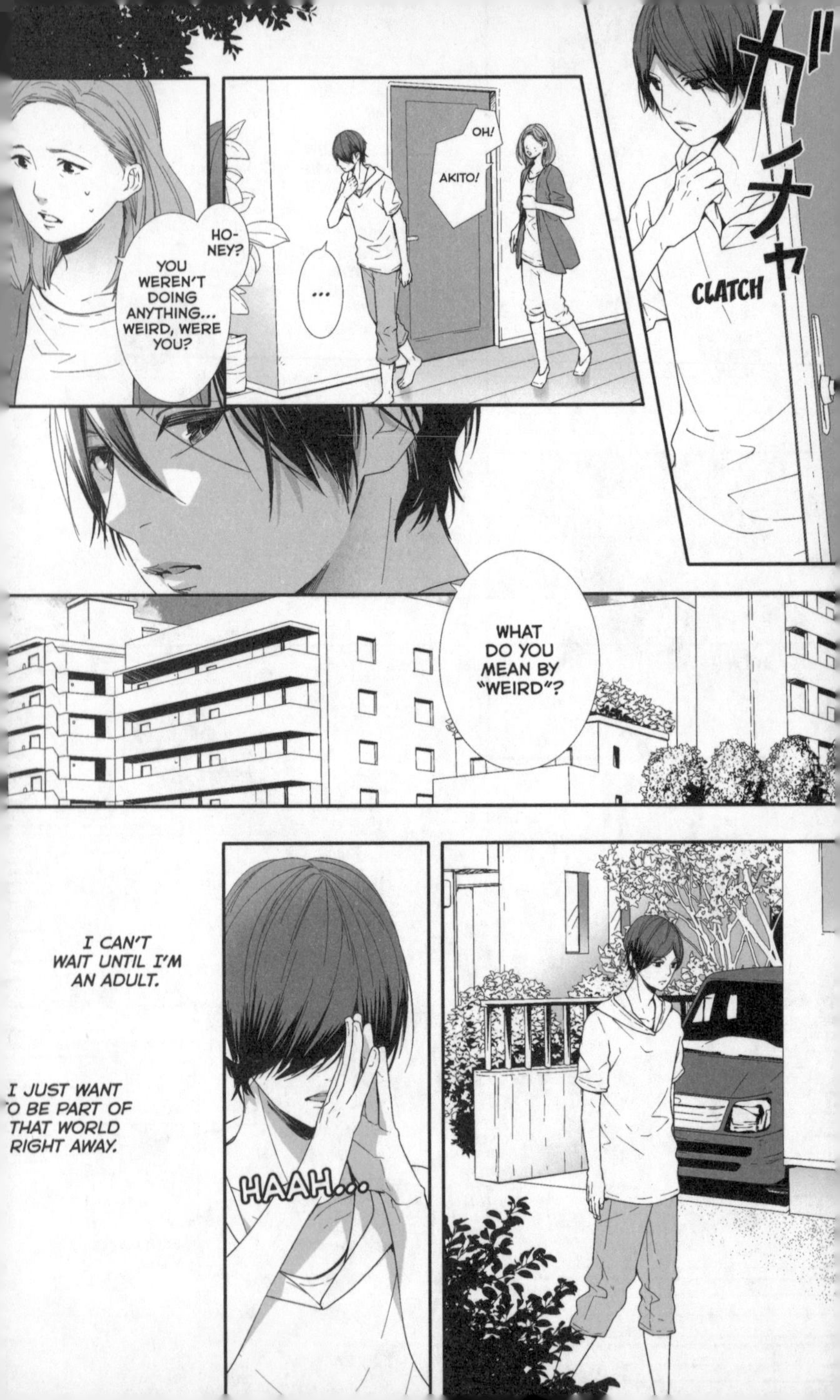
ガチャ
CLATCH
OH!
AKITO!
...
HO-NEY?
YOU WEREN'T DOING ANYTHING... WEIRD, WERE YOU?
WHAT DO YOU MEAN BY "WEIRD"?
HAAH...
I CAN'T WAIT UNTIL I'M AN ADULT.
I JUST WANT 'O BE PART OF THAT WORLD RIGHT AWAY.

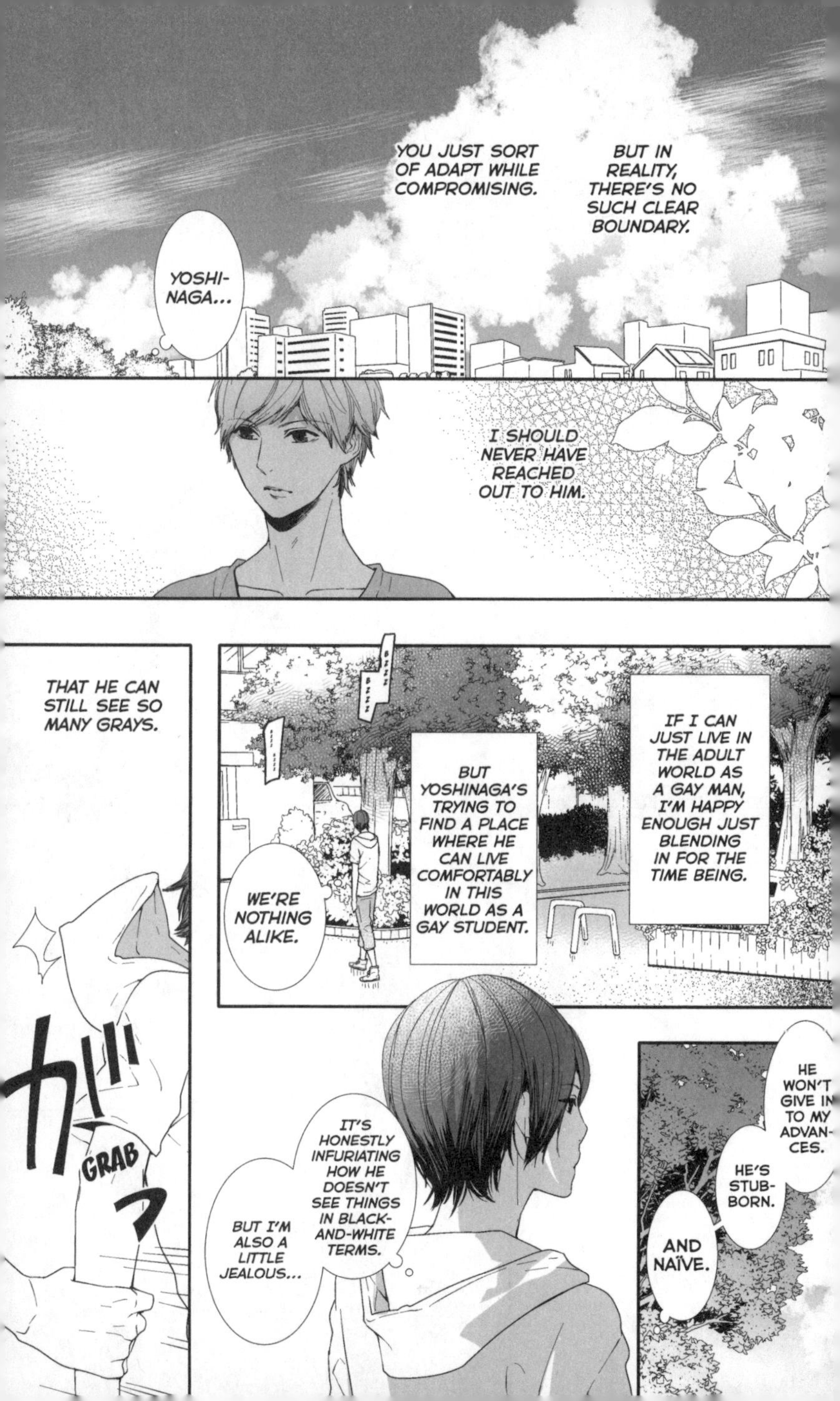
BUT IN REALITY, THERE'S NO SUCH CLEAR BOUNDARY.
YOU JUST SORT OF ADAPT WHILE COMPROMISING.
YOSHI-NAGA...
I SHOULD NEVER HAVE REACHED OUT TO HIM.
IF I CAN JUST LIVE IN THE ADULT WORLD AS A GAY MAN, I'M HAPPY ENOUGH JUST BLENDING IN FOR THE TIME BEING.
BUT YOSHINAGA'S TRYING TO FIND A PLACE WHERE HE CAN LIVE COMFORTABLY IN THIS WORLD AS A GAY STUDENT.
BZZZ
WE'RE NOTHING ALIKE.
HE WON'T GIVE IN TO MY ADVAN-CES.
HE'S STUB-BORN.
AND NAÏVE.
IT'S HONESTLY INFURIATING HOW HE DOESN'T SEE THINGS IN BLACK-AND-WHITE TERMS.
BUT I'M ALSO A LITTLE JEALOUS...
THAT HE CAN STILL SEE SO MANY GRAYS.
GRAB

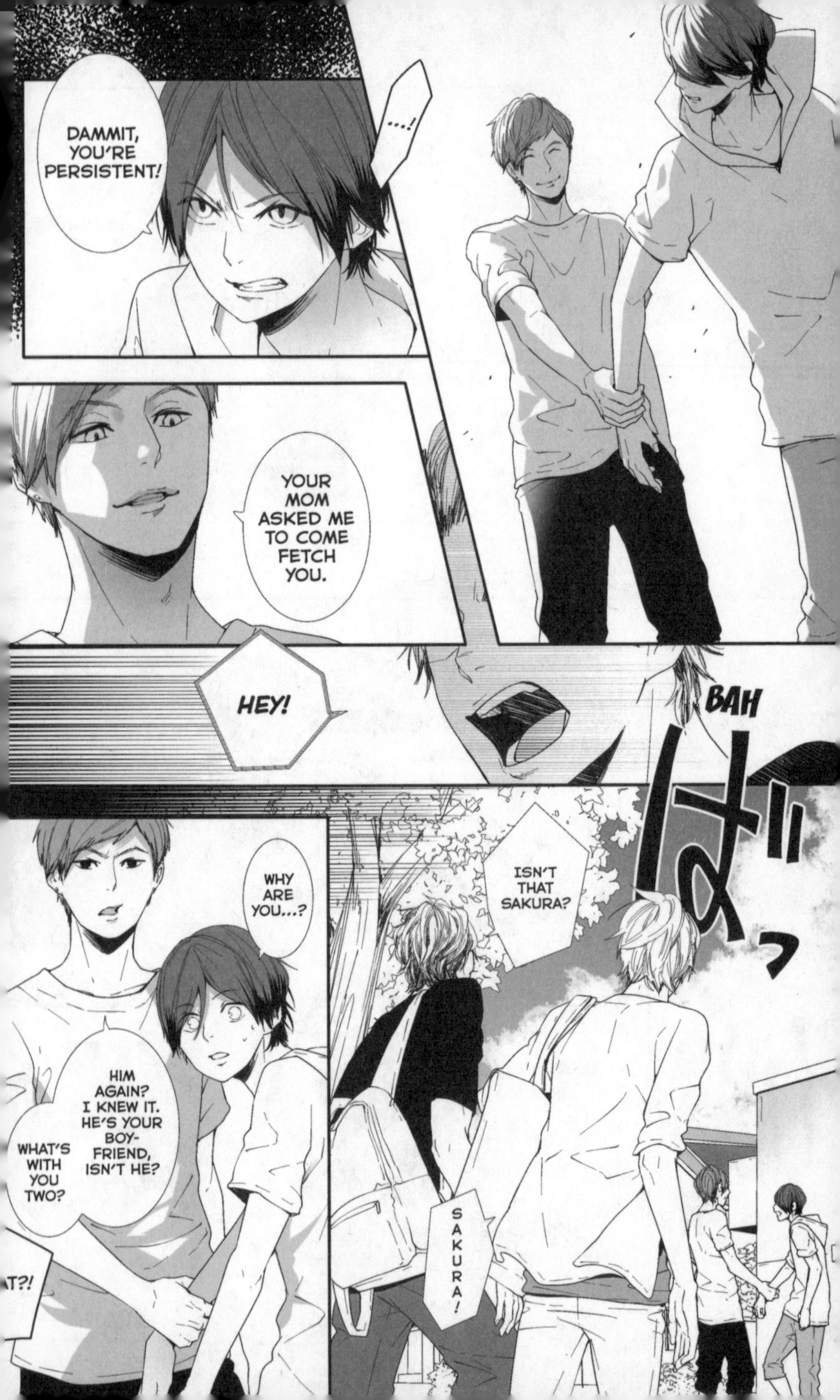
...!
DAMMIT, YOU'RE PERSISTENT!
YOUR MOM ASKED ME TO COME FETCH YOU.
HEY!
BAH
ISN'T THAT SAKURA?
SAKURA!
WHY ARE YOU...?
HIM AGAIN? I KNEW IT. HE'S YOUR BOY-FRIEND, ISN'T HE?
WHAT'S WITH YOU TWO?

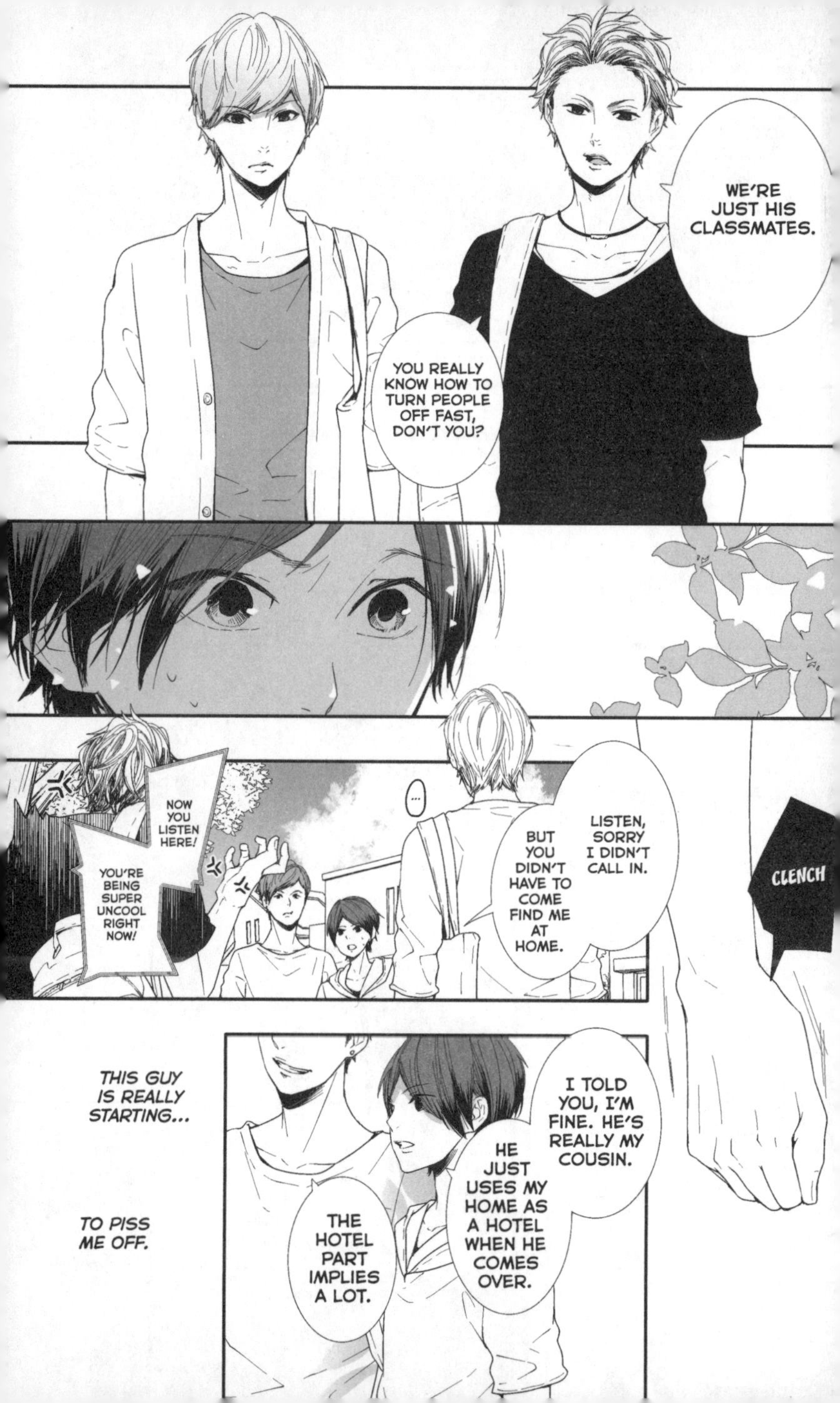
WE'RE JUST HIS CLASSMATES.
YOU REALLY KNOW HOW TO TURN PEOPLE OFF FAST, DON'T YOU?
CLENCH
LISTEN, SORRY I DIDN'T CALL IN.
BUT YOU DIDN'T HAVE TO COME FIND ME AT HOME.
...
NOW YOU LISTEN HERE!
YOU'RE BEING SUPER UNCOOL RIGHT NOW!
I TOLD YOU, I'M FINE. HE'S REALLY MY COUSIN.
HE JUST USES MY HOME AS A HOTEL WHEN HE COMES OVER.
THE HOTEL PART IMPLIES A LOT.
THIS GUY IS REALLY STARTING...
TO PISS ME OFF.

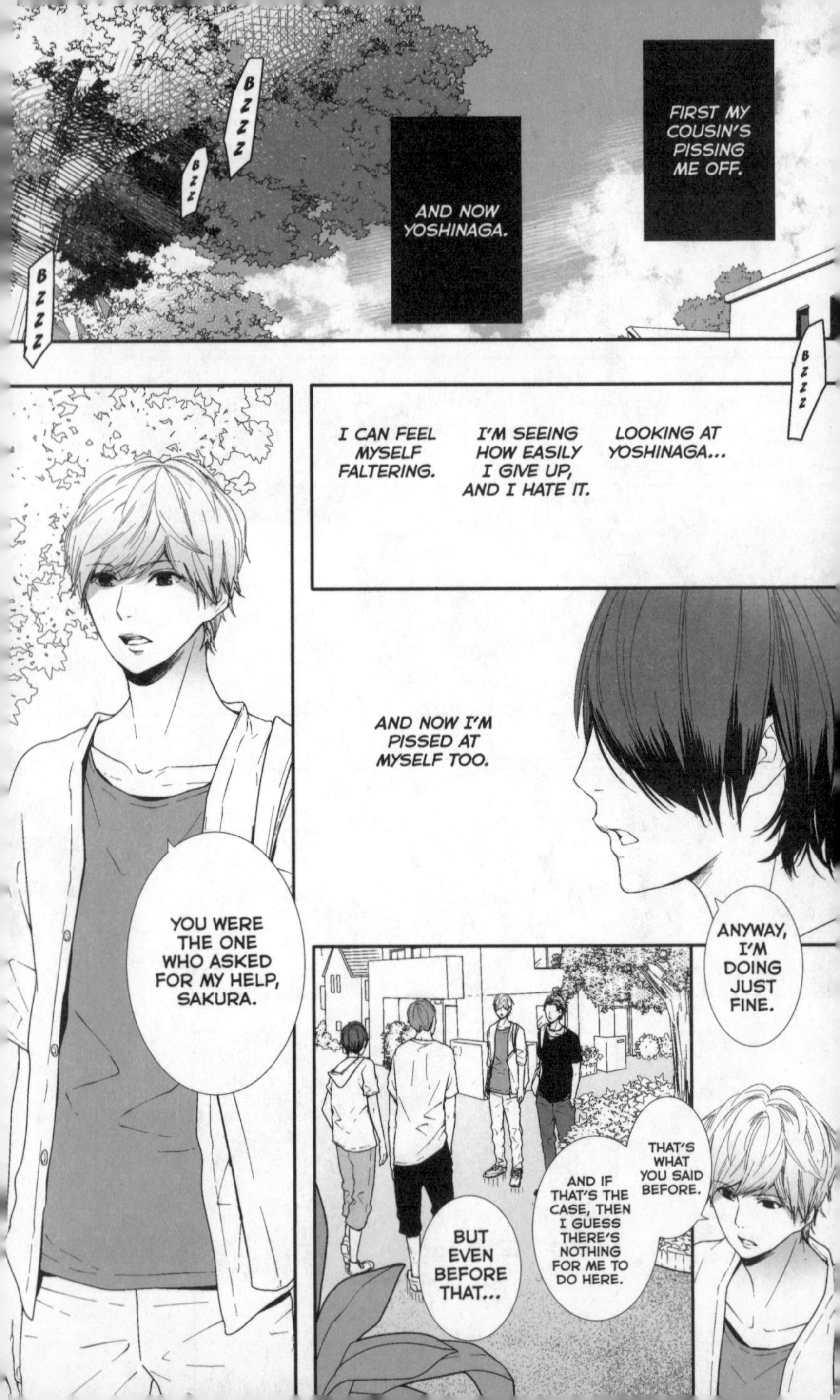
B Z Z Z
FIRST MY COUSIN'S PISSING ME OFF.
AND NOW YOSHINAGA.
B Z Z
B Z Z Z
B Z Z Z
LOOKING AT YOSHINAGA...
I'M SEEING HOW EASILY I GIVE UP, AND I HATE IT.
I CAN FEEL MYSELF FALTERING.
AND NOW I'M PISSED AT MYSELF TOO.
ANYWAY, I'M DOING JUST FINE.
THAT'S WHAT YOU SAID BEFORE.
AND IF THAT'S THE CASE, THEN I GUESS THERE'S NOTHING FOR ME TO DO HERE.
BUT EVEN BEFORE THAT...
YOU WERE THE ONE WHO ASKED FOR MY HELP, SAKURA.

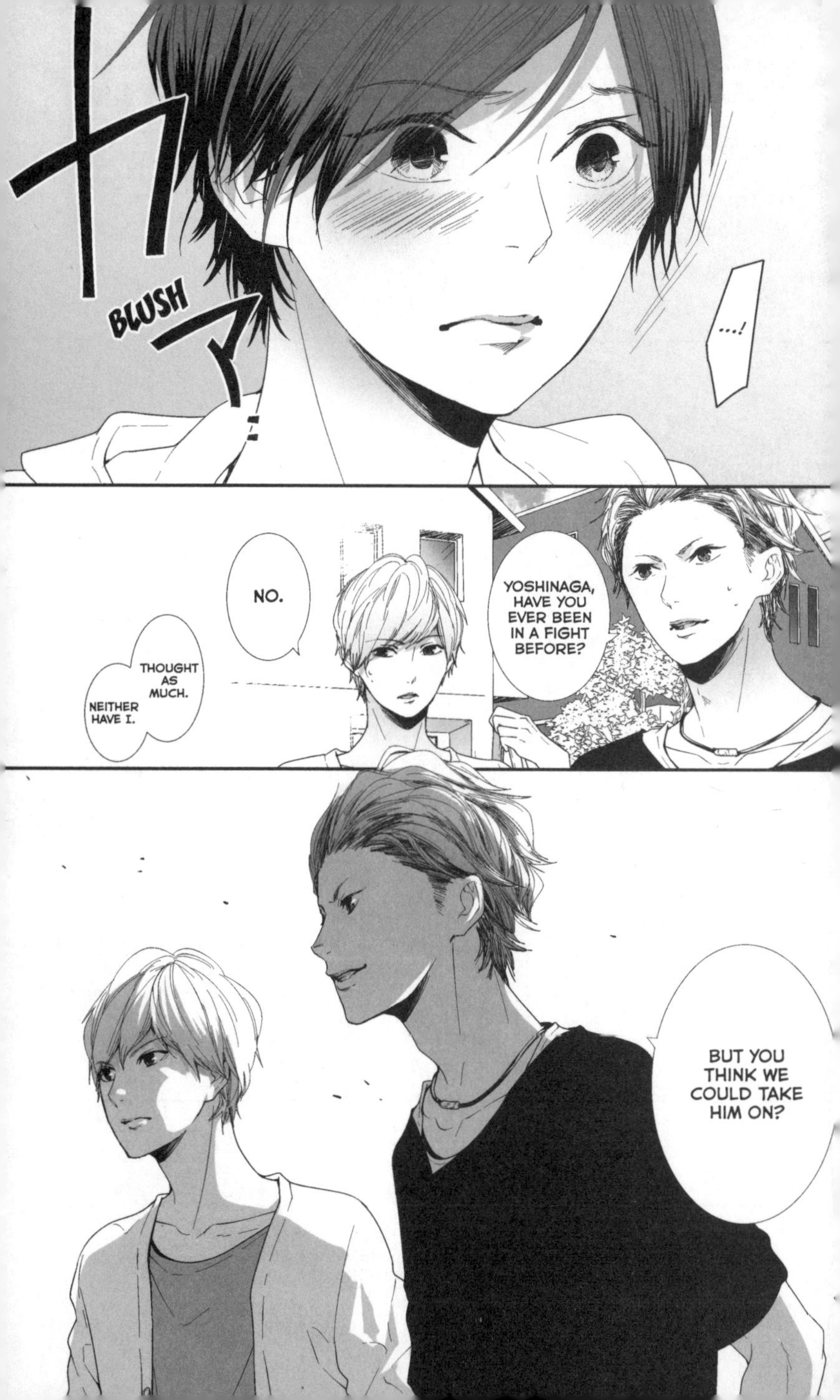
...!
BLUSH
YOSHINAGA, HAVE YOU EVER BEEN IN A FIGHT BEFORE?
NO.
THOUGHT AS MUCH.
NEITHER HAVE I.
BUT YOU THINK WE COULD TAKE HIM ON?

KOIMONOGATARI

LOVE STORIES

Character Intros (4)

Misaki Yoshinaga
Yamato's older
sister. She's in college.

Akiyama
Sakura's
classmate.
He went to the
same junior
high as Yuiji.

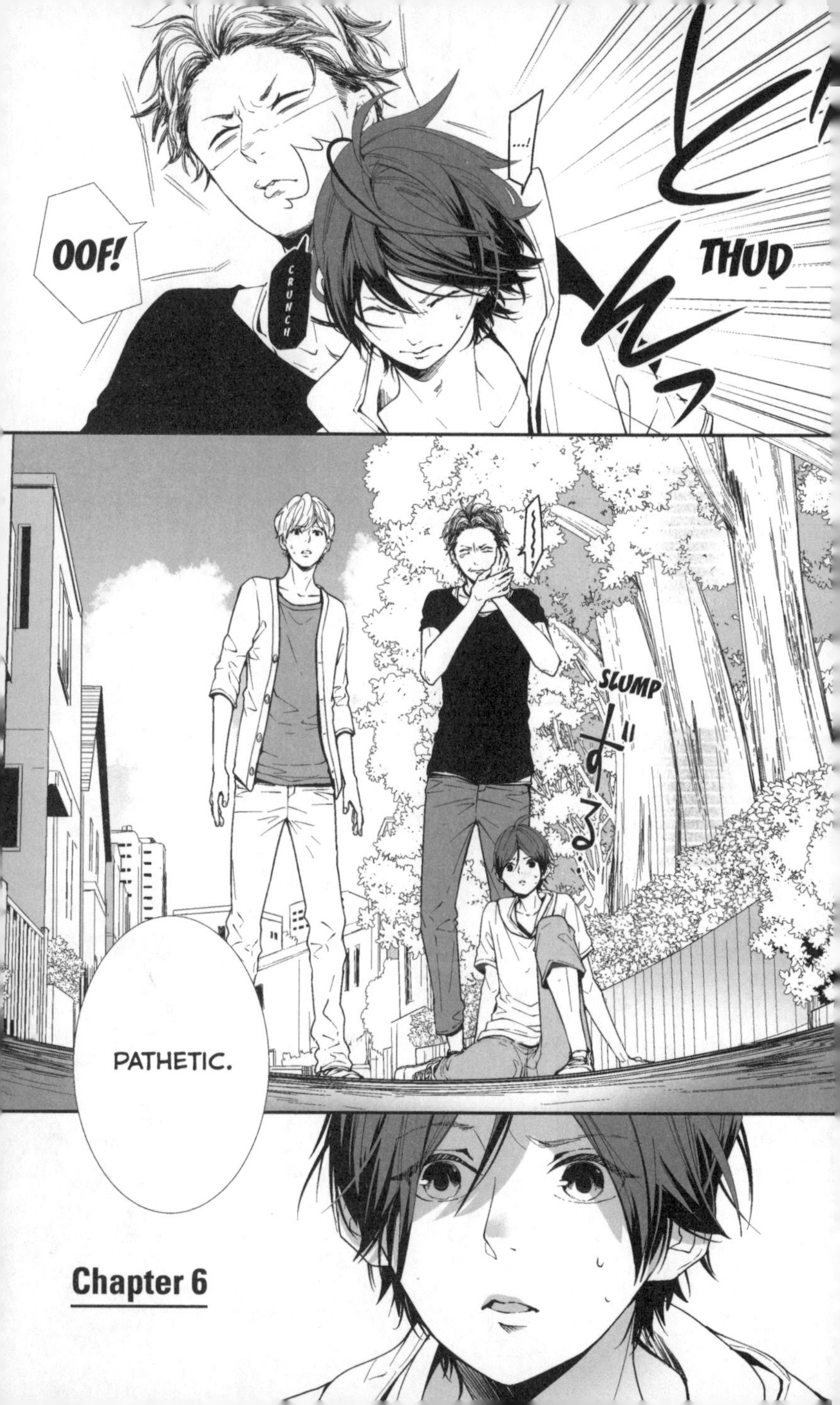

...!
THUD
CRUNCH
OOF!
...!
SLUMP
PATHETIC.
Chapter 6

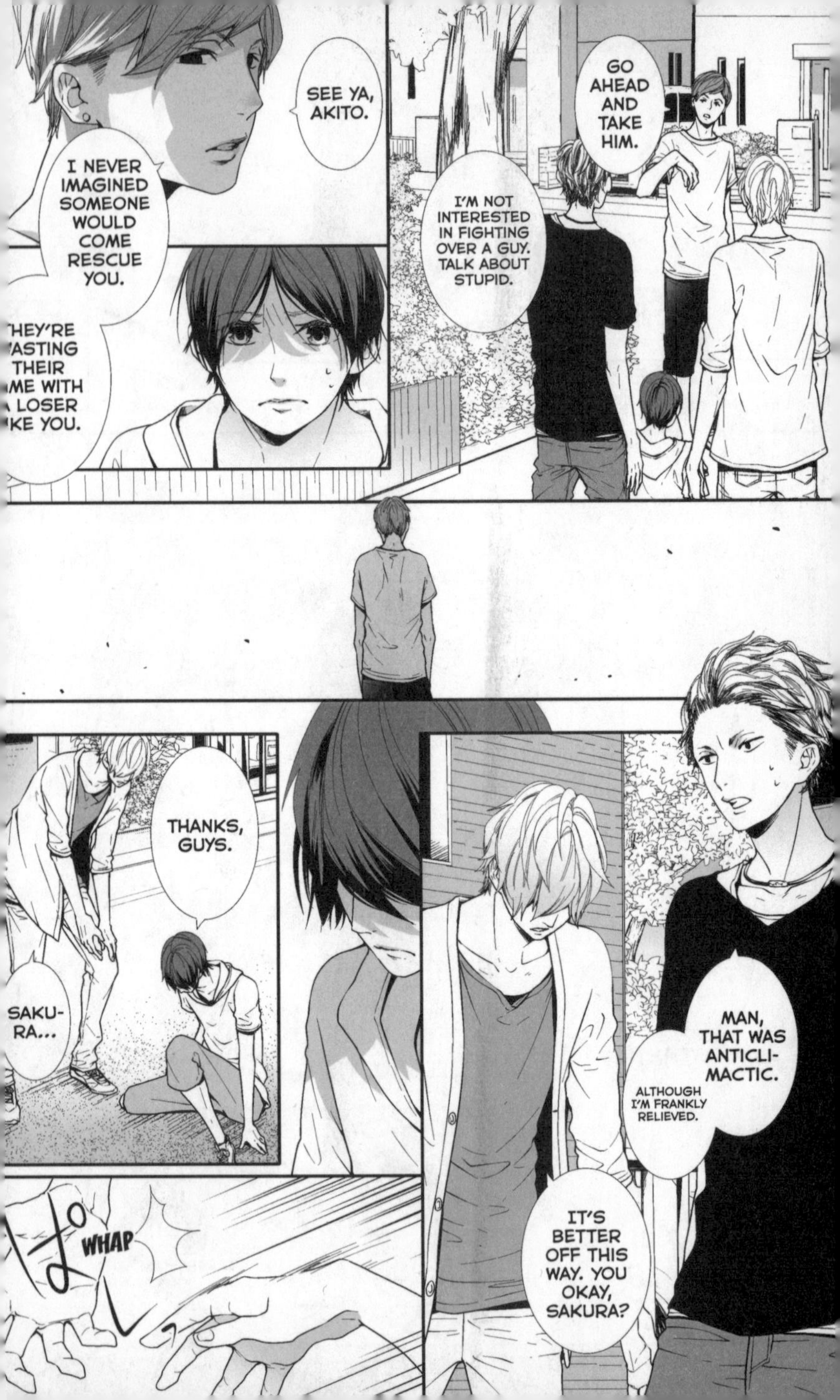
GO AHEAD AND TAKE HIM.
I'M NOT INTERESTED IN FIGHTING OVER A GUY. TALK ABOUT STUPID.
SEE YA, AKITO.
I NEVER IMAGINED SOMEONE WOULD COME RESCUE YOU.
HEY'RE ASTING THEIR ME WITH LOSER KE YOU.
MAN, THAT WAS ANTICLI-MACTIC.
ALTHOUGH I'M FRANKLY RELIEVED.
IT'S BETTER OFF THIS WAY. YOU OKAY, SAKURA?
THANKS, GUYS.
SAKU-RA...
WHAP

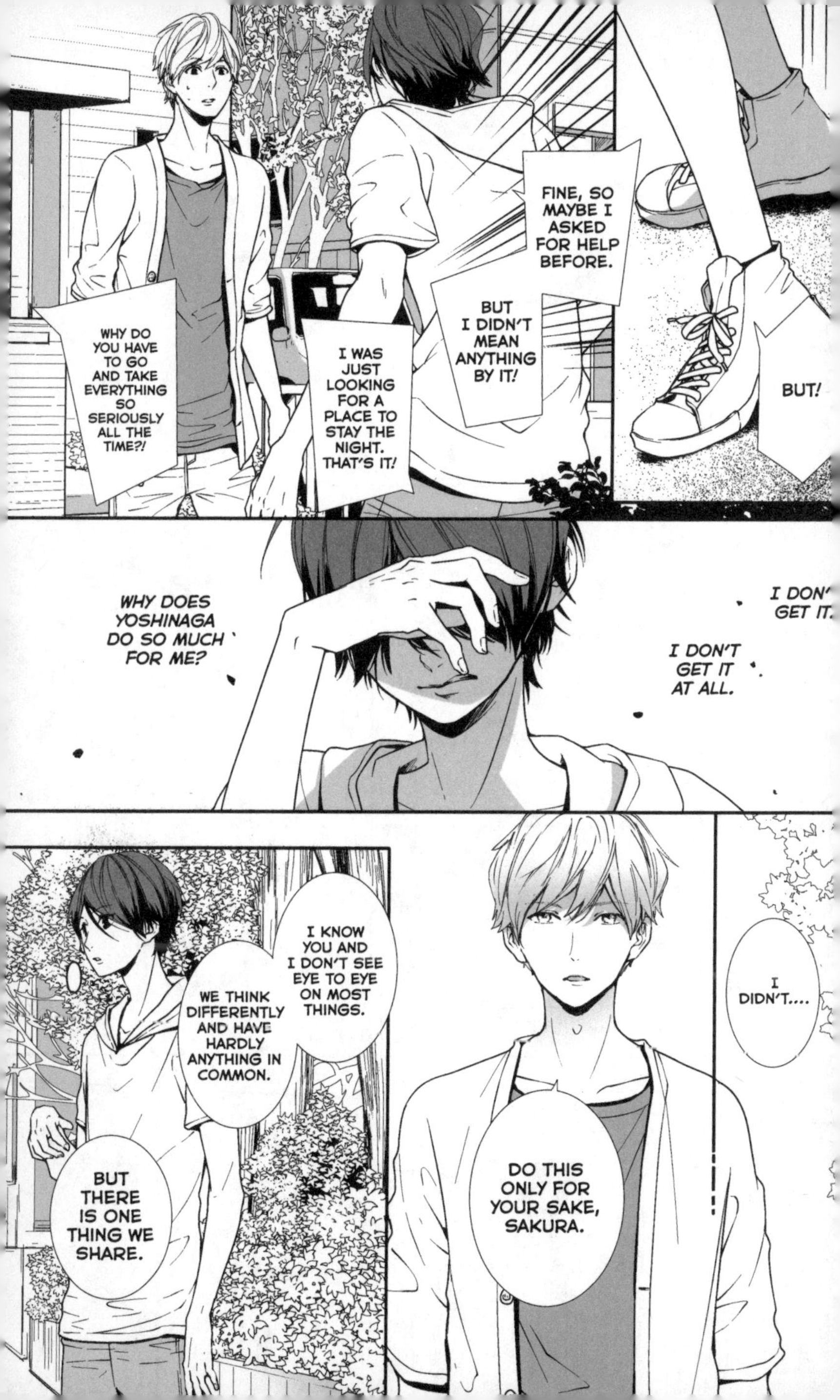
BUT!
FINE, SO MAYBE I ASKED FOR HELP BEFORE.
BUT I DIDN'T MEAN ANYTHING BY IT!
I WAS JUST LOOKING FOR A PLACE TO STAY THE NIGHT. THAT'S IT!
WHY DO YOU HAVE TO GO AND TAKE EVERYTHING SO SERIOUSLY ALL THE TIME?!
I DON' GET IT.
I DON'T GET IT AT ALL.
WHY DOES YOSHINAGA DO SO MUCH FOR ME?
I DIDN'T....
DO THIS ONLY FOR YOUR SAKE, SAKURA.
I KNOW YOU AND I DON'T SEE EYE TO EYE ON MOST THINGS.
WE THINK DIFFERENTLY AND HAVE HARDLY ANYTHING IN COMMON.
BUT THERE IS ONE THING WE SHARE.

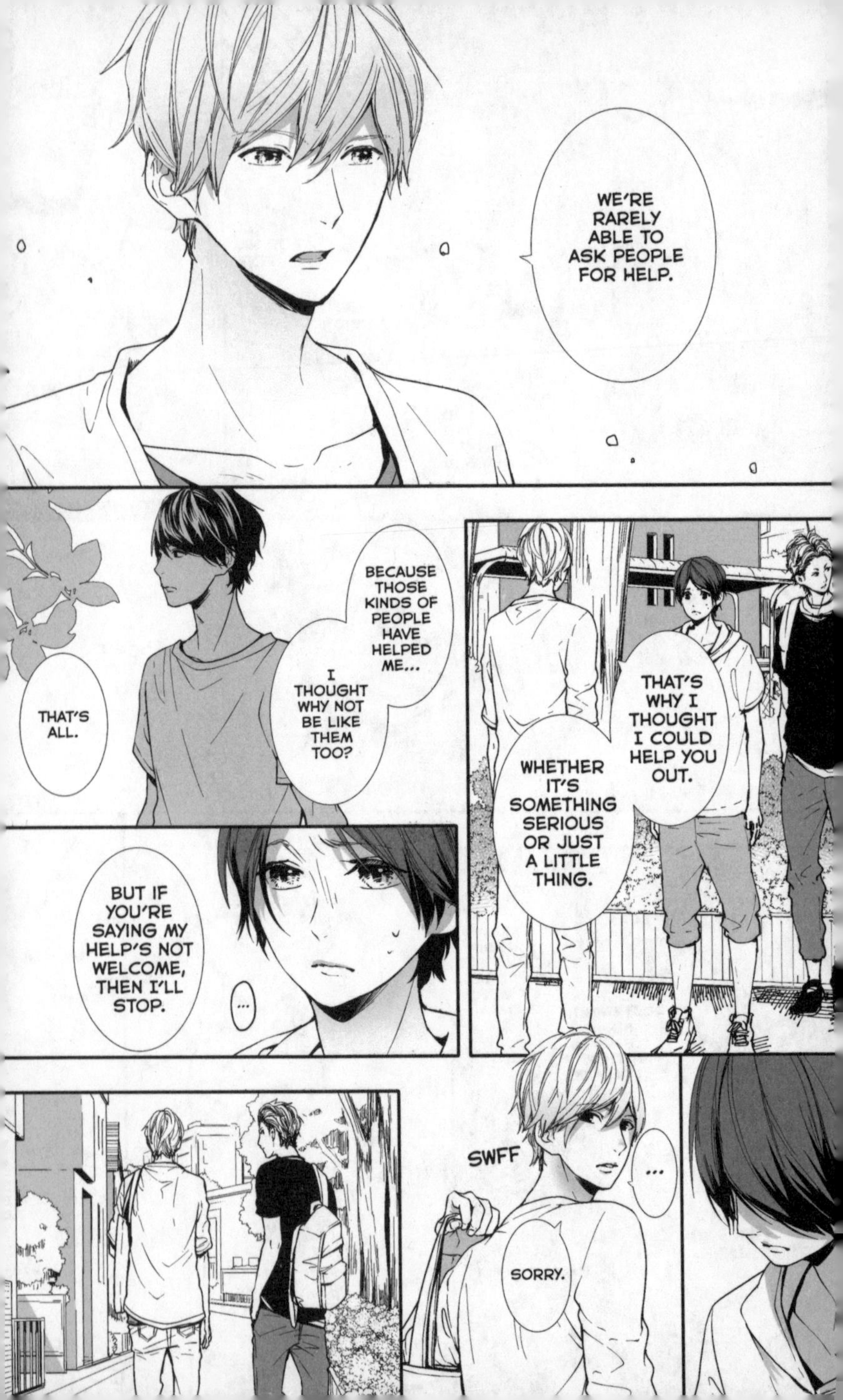
WE'RE RARELY ABLE TO ASK PEOPLE FOR HELP.
THAT'S WHY I THOUGHT I COULD HELP YOU OUT.
WHETHER IT'S SOMETHING SERIOUS OR JUST A LITTLE THING.
BECAUSE THOSE KINDS OF PEOPLE HAVE HELPED ME...
I THOUGHT WHY NOT BE LIKE THEM TOO?
THAT'S ALL.
BUT IF YOU'RE SAYING MY HELP'S NOT WELCOME, THEN I'LL STOP.
...
...
SWFF
SORRY.

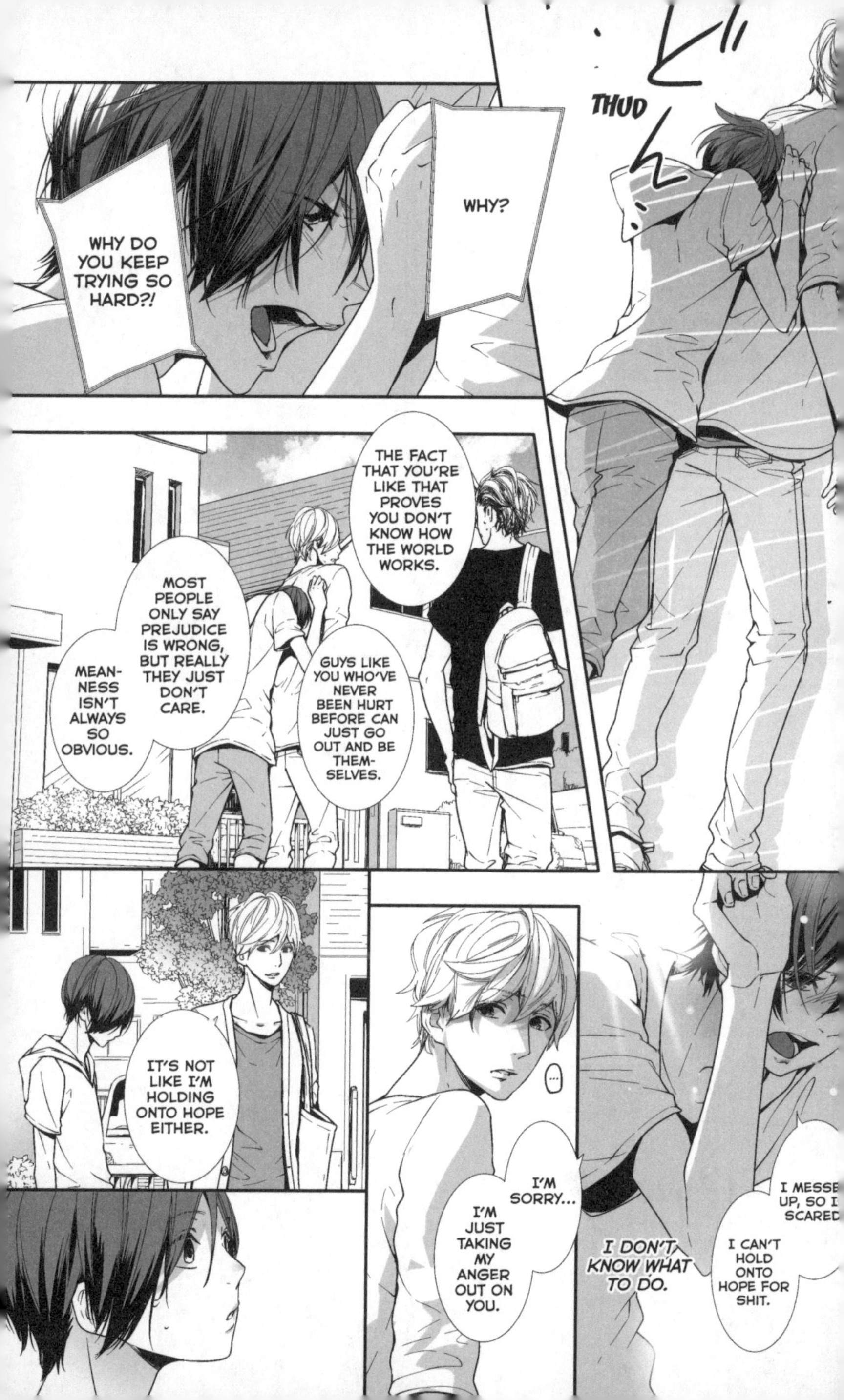

どん
THUD
WHY?
WHY DO YOU KEEP TRYING SO HARD?!
THE FACT THAT YOU'RE LIKE THAT PROVES YOU DON'T KNOW HOW THE WORLD WORKS.
GUYS LIKE YOU WHO'VE NEVER BEEN HURT BEFORE CAN JUST GO OUT AND BE THEM-SELVES.
MOST PEOPLE ONLY SAY PREJUDICE IS WRONG, BUT REALLY THEY JUST DON'T CARE.
MEAN-NESS ISN'T ALWAYS SO OBVIOUS.
I MESSE UP, SO I SCARED
I CAN'T HOLD ONTO HOPE FOR SHIT.
I DON'T KNOW WHAT TO DO.
...
I'M SORRY...
I'M JUST TAKING MY ANGER OUT ON YOU.
IT'S NOT LIKE I'M HOLDING ONTO HOPE EITHER.

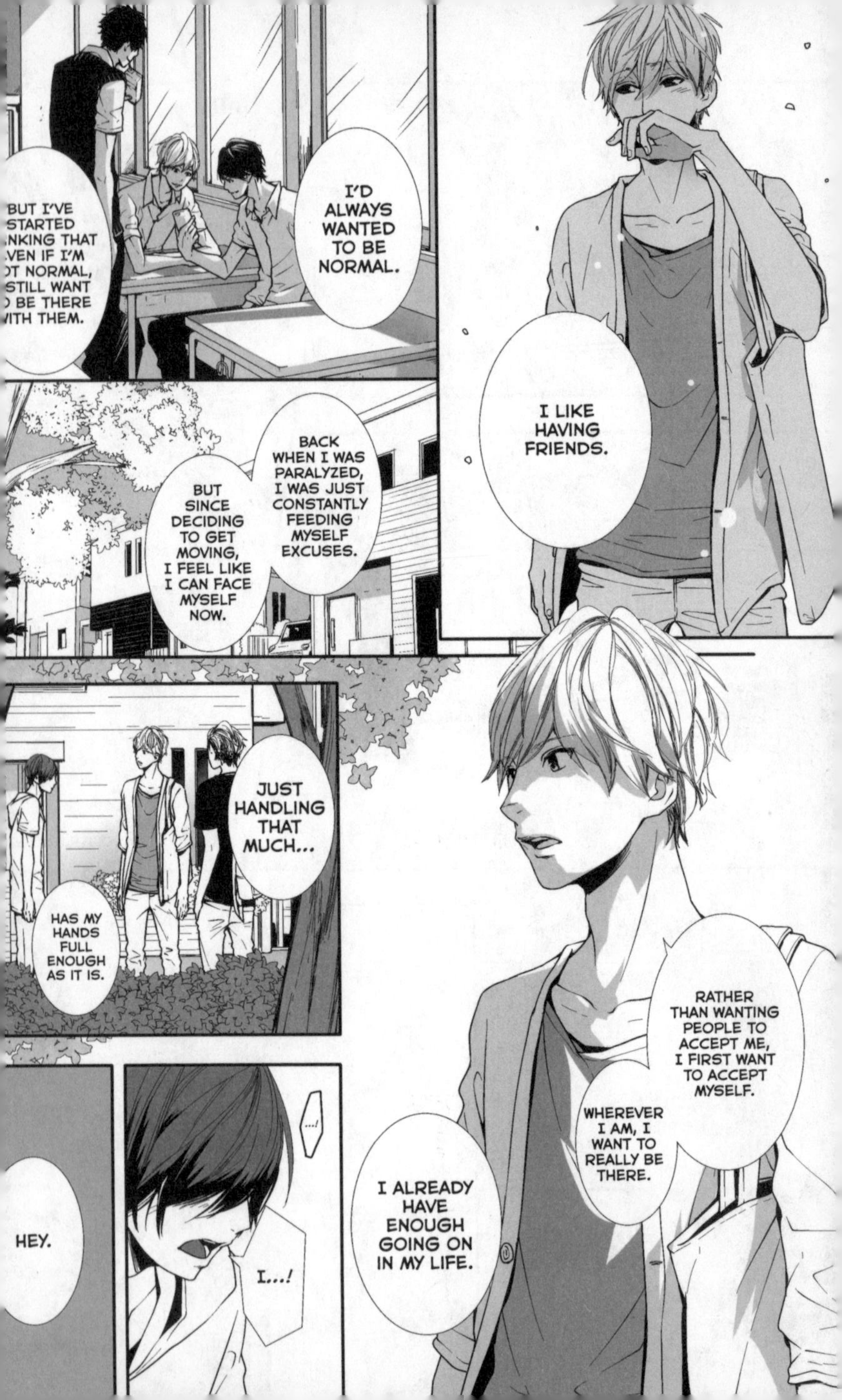
I LIKE HAVING FRIENDS.
I'D ALWAYS WANTED TO BE NORMAL.
BUT I'VE STARTED NKING THAT VEN IF I'M OT NORMAL, STILL WANT O BE THERE WITH THEM.
BACK WHEN I WAS PARALYZED, I WAS JUST CONSTANTLY FEEDING MYSELF EXCUSES.
BUT SINCE DECIDING TO GET MOVING, I FEEL LIKE I CAN FACE MYSELF NOW.
RATHER THAN WANTING PEOPLE TO ACCEPT ME, I FIRST WANT TO ACCEPT MYSELF.
WHEREVER I AM, I WANT TO REALLY BE THERE.
I ALREADY HAVE ENOUGH GOING ON IN MY LIFE.
JUST HANDLING THAT MUCH...
HAS MY HANDS FULL ENOUGH AS IT IS.
...!
I...!
HEY.

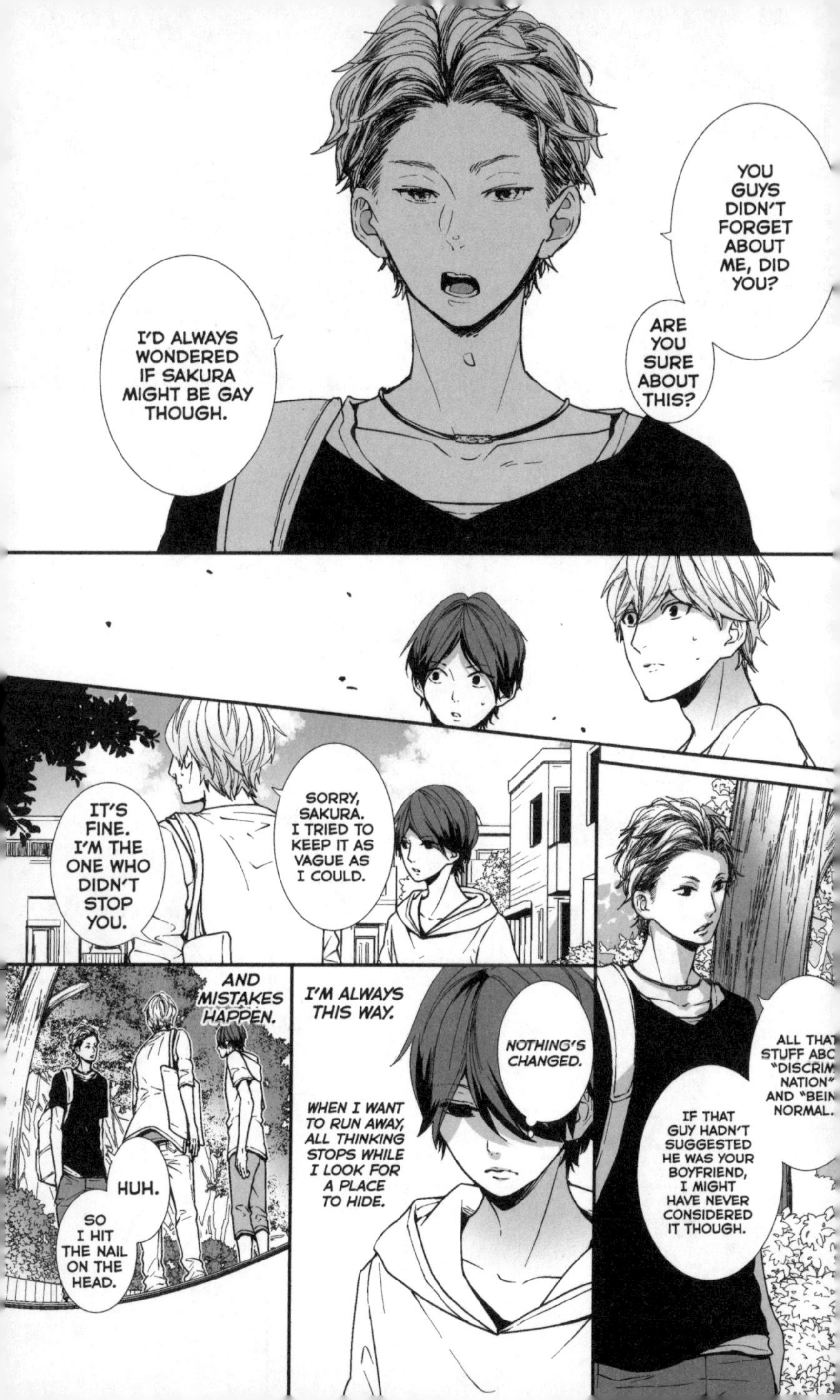
YOU GUYS DIDN'T FORGET ABOUT ME, DID YOU?
ARE YOU SURE ABOUT THIS?
I'D ALWAYS WONDERED IF SAKURA MIGHT BE GAY THOUGH.
ALL THAT STUFF ABO "DISCRIM NATION" AND "BEIN NORMAL."
IF THAT GUY HADN'T SUGGESTED HE WAS YOUR BOYFRIEND, I MIGHT HAVE NEVER CONSIDERED IT THOUGH.
SORRY, SAKURA. I TRIED TO KEEP IT AS VAGUE AS I COULD.
IT'S FINE. I'M THE ONE WHO DIDN'T STOP YOU.
I'M ALWAYS THIS WAY.
NOTHING'S CHANGED.
WHEN I WANT TO RUN AWAY, ALL THINKING STOPS WHILE I LOOK FOR A PLACE TO HIDE.
AND MISTAKES HAPPEN.
HUH.
SO I HIT THE NAIL ON THE HEAD.

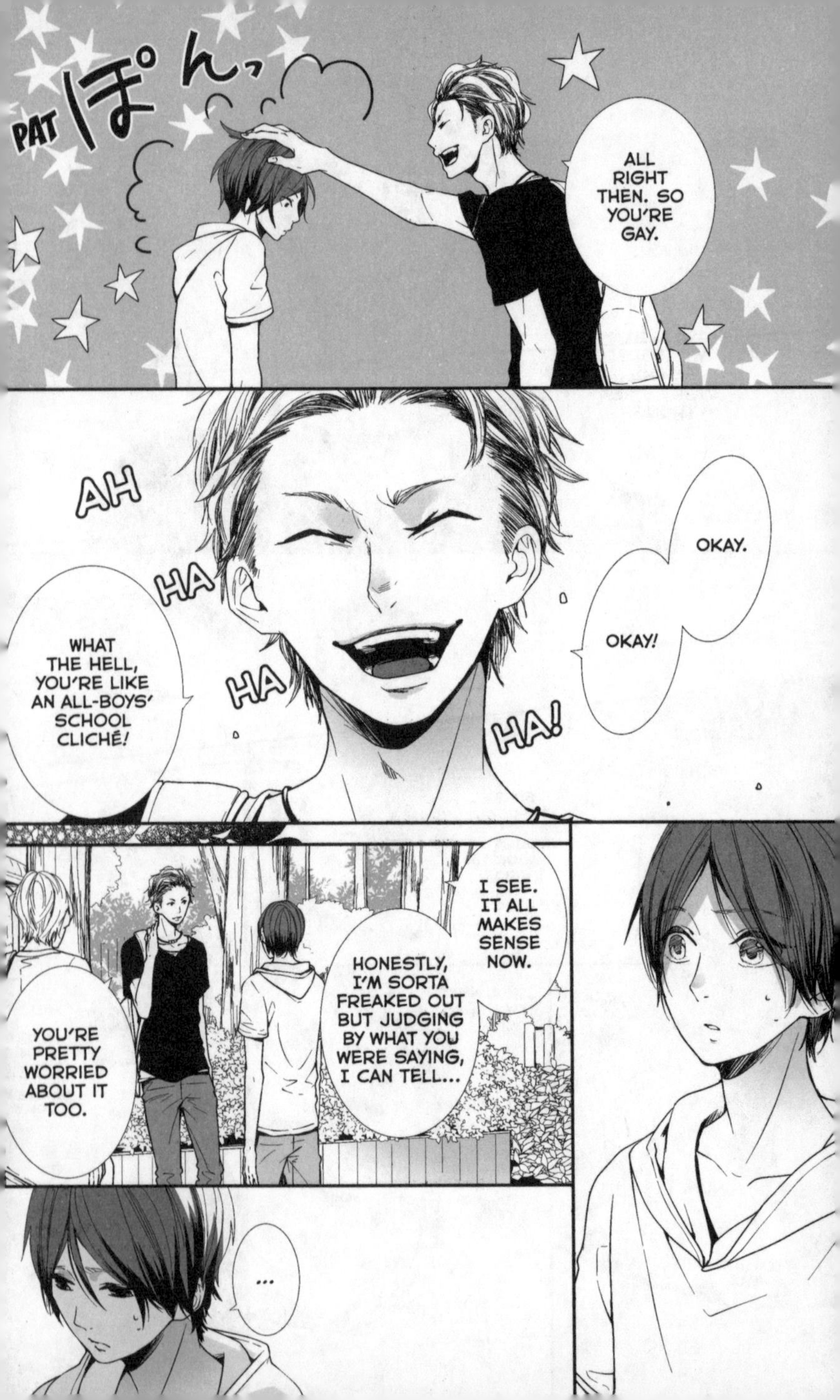
PAT
ぽんっ
ALL RIGHT THEN. SO YOU'RE GAY.
OKAY.
OKAY!
AH
HA
HA
HA!
WHAT THE HELL, YOU'RE LIKE AN ALL-BOYS' SCHOOL CLICHÉ!
I SEE. IT ALL MAKES SENSE NOW.
HONESTLY, I'M SORTA FREAKED OUT BUT JUDGING BY WHAT YOU WERE SAYING, I CAN TELL...
YOU'RE PRETTY WORRIED ABOUT IT TOO.
...

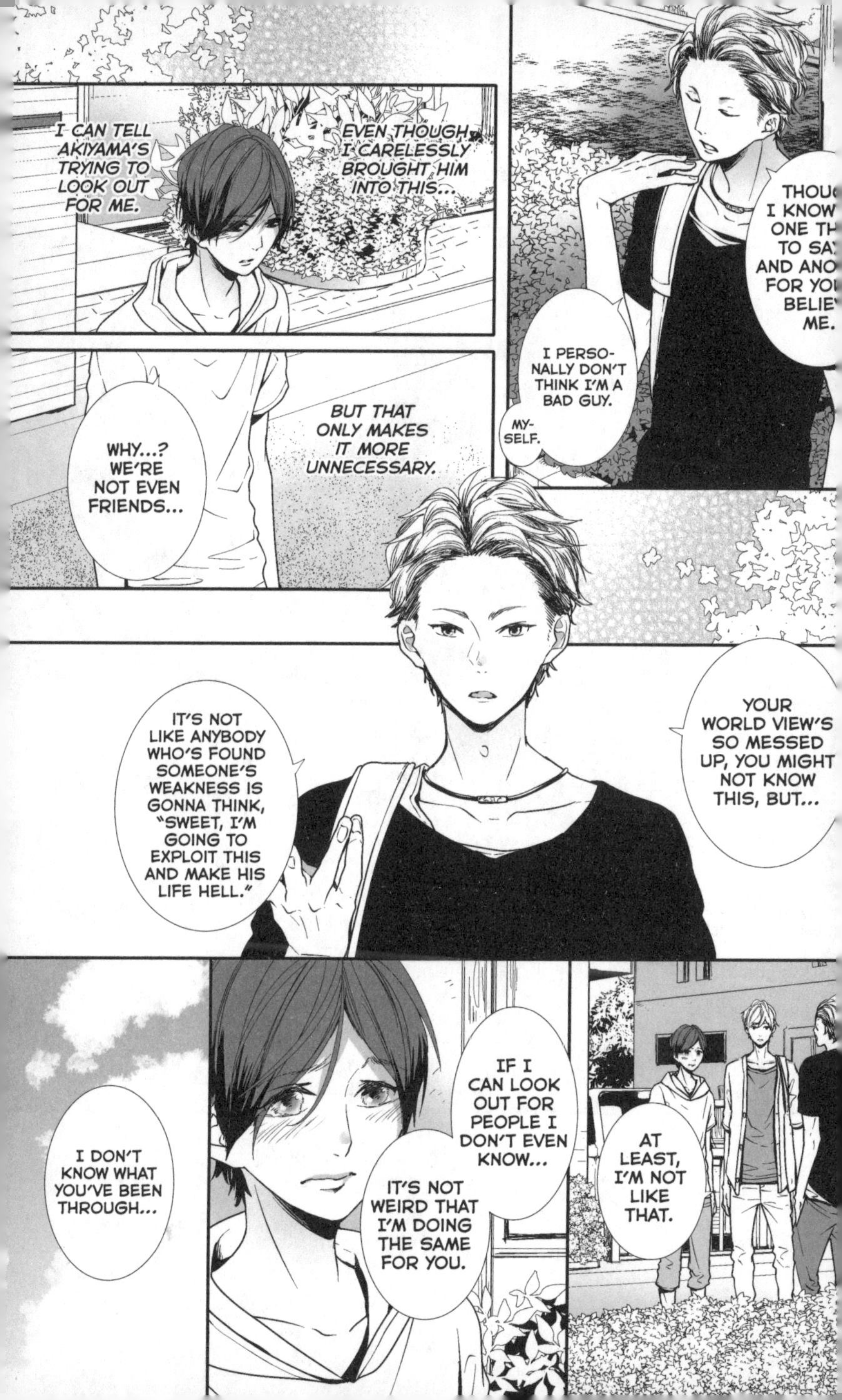
THOU I KNOW ONE TH TO SA AND ANO FOR YOU BELIE ME.
I PERSONALLY DON'T THINK I'M A BAD GUY.
MYSELF.
EVEN THOUGH I CARELESSLY BROUGHT HIM INTO THIS...
I CAN TELL AKIYAMA'S TRYING TO LOOK OUT FOR ME.
BUT THAT ONLY MAKES IT MORE UNNECESSARY.
WHY...? WE'RE NOT EVEN FRIENDS...
YOUR WORLD VIEW'S SO MESSED UP, YOU MIGHT NOT KNOW THIS, BUT...
IT'S NOT LIKE ANYBODY WHO'S FOUND SOMEONE'S WEAKNESS IS GONNA THINK, "SWEET, I'M GOING TO EXPLOIT THIS AND MAKE HIS LIFE HELL."
AT LEAST, I'M NOT LIKE THAT.
IF I CAN LOOK OUT FOR PEOPLE I DON'T EVEN KNOW...
IT'S NOT WEIRD THAT I'M DOING THE SAME FOR YOU.
I DON'T KNOW WHAT YOU'VE BEEN THROUGH...

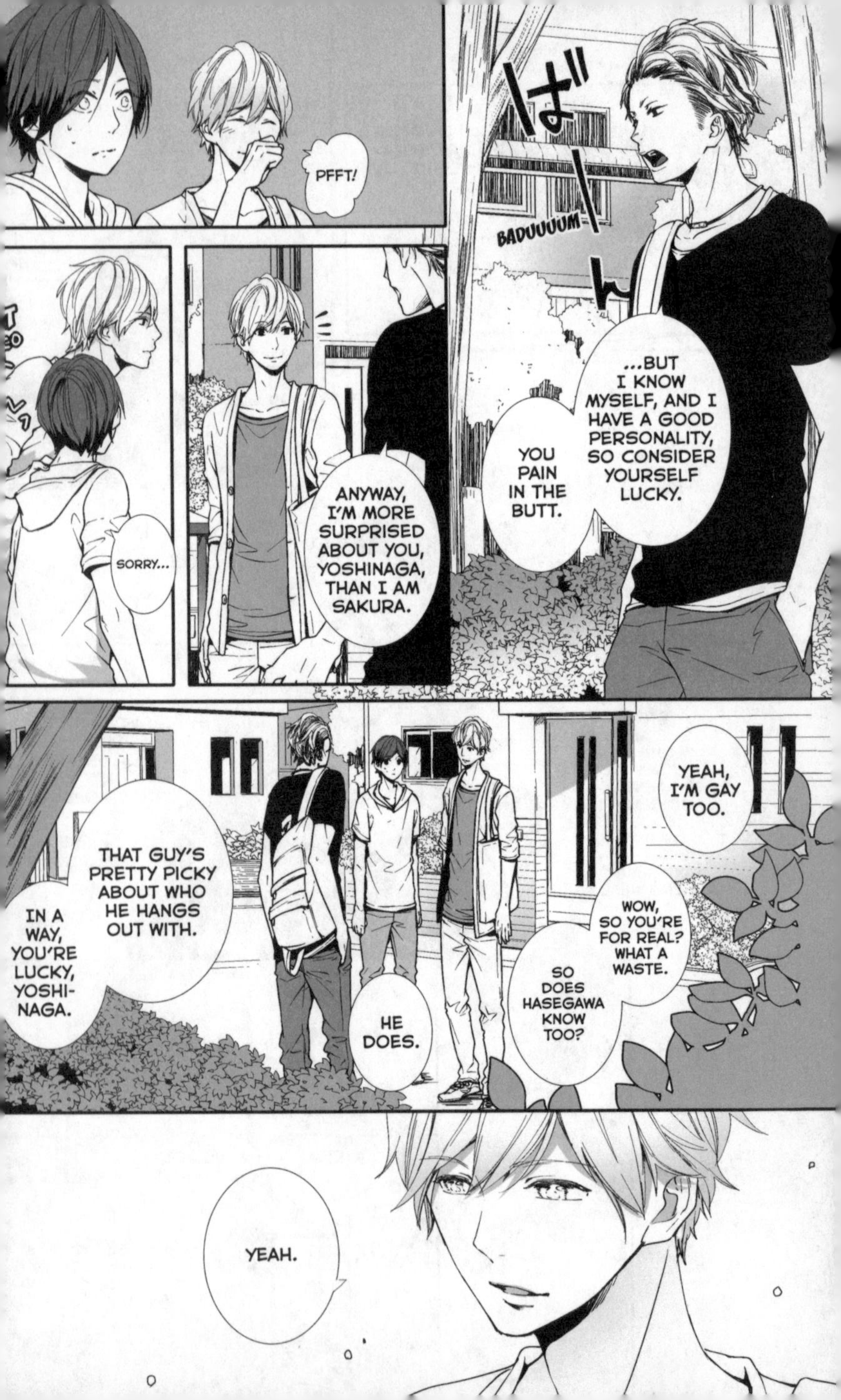
BADUUUUM
...BUT I KNOW MYSELF, AND I HAVE A GOOD PERSONALITY, SO CONSIDER YOURSELF LUCKY.
YOU PAIN IN THE BUTT.
PFFT!
ANYWAY, I'M MORE SURPRISED ABOUT YOU, YOSHINAGA, THAN I AM SAKURA.
SORRY...
YEAH, I'M GAY TOO.
WOW, SO YOU'RE FOR REAL? WHAT A WASTE.
SO DOES HASEGAWA KNOW TOO?
HE DOES.
THAT GUY'S PRETTY PICKY ABOUT WHO HE HANGS OUT WITH.
IN A WAY, YOU'RE LUCKY, YOSHI-NAGA.
YEAH.

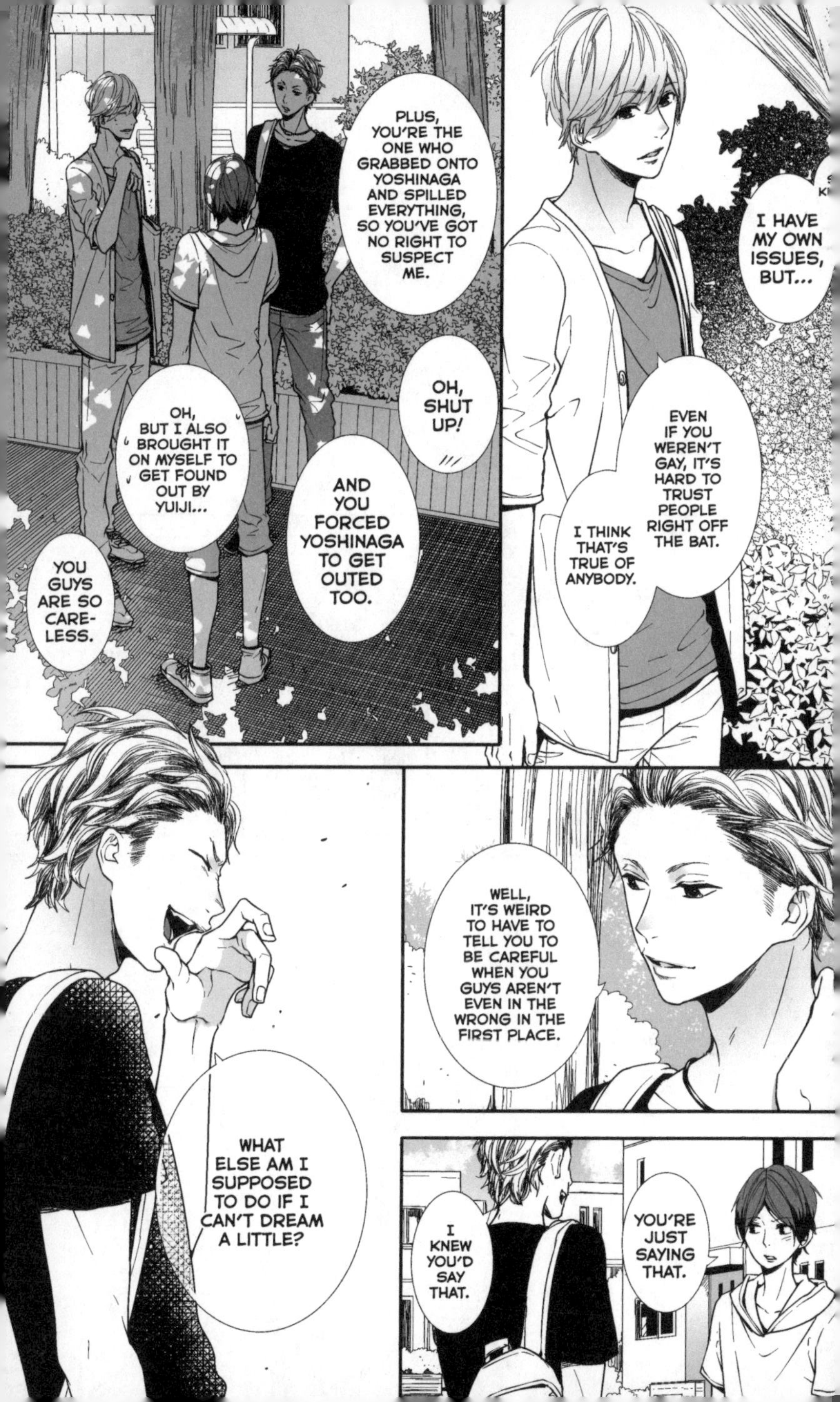
I HAVE MY OWN ISSUES, BUT...
EVEN IF YOU WEREN'T GAY, IT'S HARD TO TRUST PEOPLE RIGHT OFF THE BAT.
I THINK THAT'S TRUE OF ANYBODY.
PLUS, YOU'RE THE ONE WHO GRABBED ONTO YOSHINAGA AND SPILLED EVERYTHING, SO YOU'VE GOT NO RIGHT TO SUSPECT ME.
OH, SHUT UP!
AND YOU FORCED YOSHINAGA TO GET OUTED TOO.
OH, BUT I ALSO BROUGHT IT ON MYSELF TO GET FOUND OUT BY YUIJI...
YOU GUYS ARE SO CARE-LESS.
WELL, IT'S WEIRD TO HAVE TO TELL YOU TO BE CAREFUL WHEN YOU GUYS AREN'T EVEN IN THE WRONG IN THE FIRST PLACE.
YOU'RE JUST SAYING THAT.
I KNEW YOU'D SAY THAT.
WHAT ELSE AM I SUPPOSED TO DO IF I CAN'T DREAM A LITTLE?

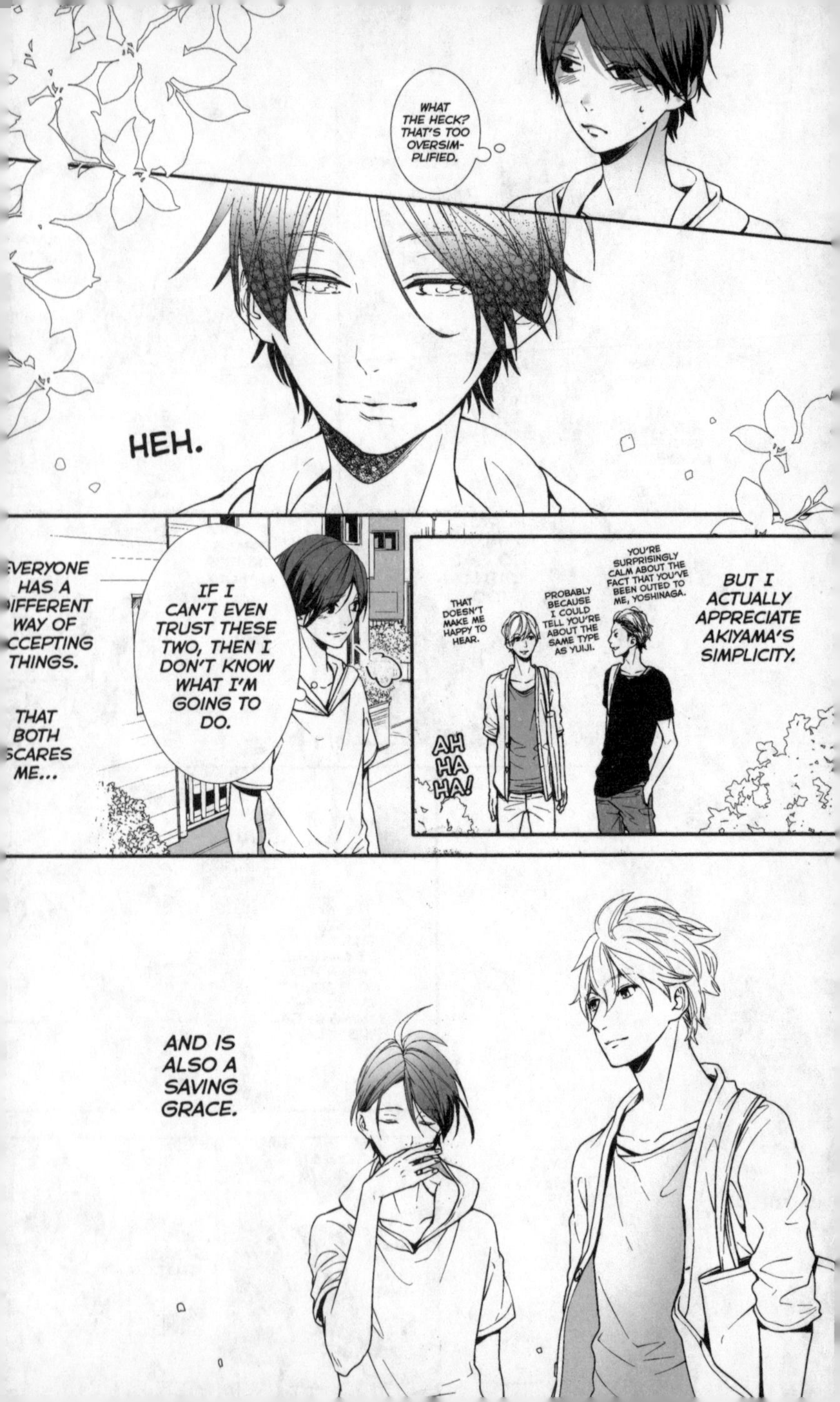
WHAT THE HECK? THAT'S TOO OVERSIM-PLIFIED.
HEH.
BUT I ACTUALLY APPRECIATE AKIYAMA'S SIMPLICITY.
YOU'RE SURPRISINGLY CALM ABOUT THE FACT THAT YOU'VE BEEN OUTED TO ME, YOSHINAGA.
PROBABLY BECAUSE I COULD TELL YOU'RE ABOUT THE SAME TYPE AS YUIJI.
THAT DOESN'T MAKE ME HAPPY TO HEAR.
AH HA HA!
IF I CAN'T EVEN TRUST THESE TWO, THEN I DON'T KNOW WHAT I'M GOING TO DO.
EVERYONE HAS A DIFFERENT WAY OF ACCEPTING THINGS.
THAT BOTH SCARES ME...
AND IS ALSO A SAVING GRACE.

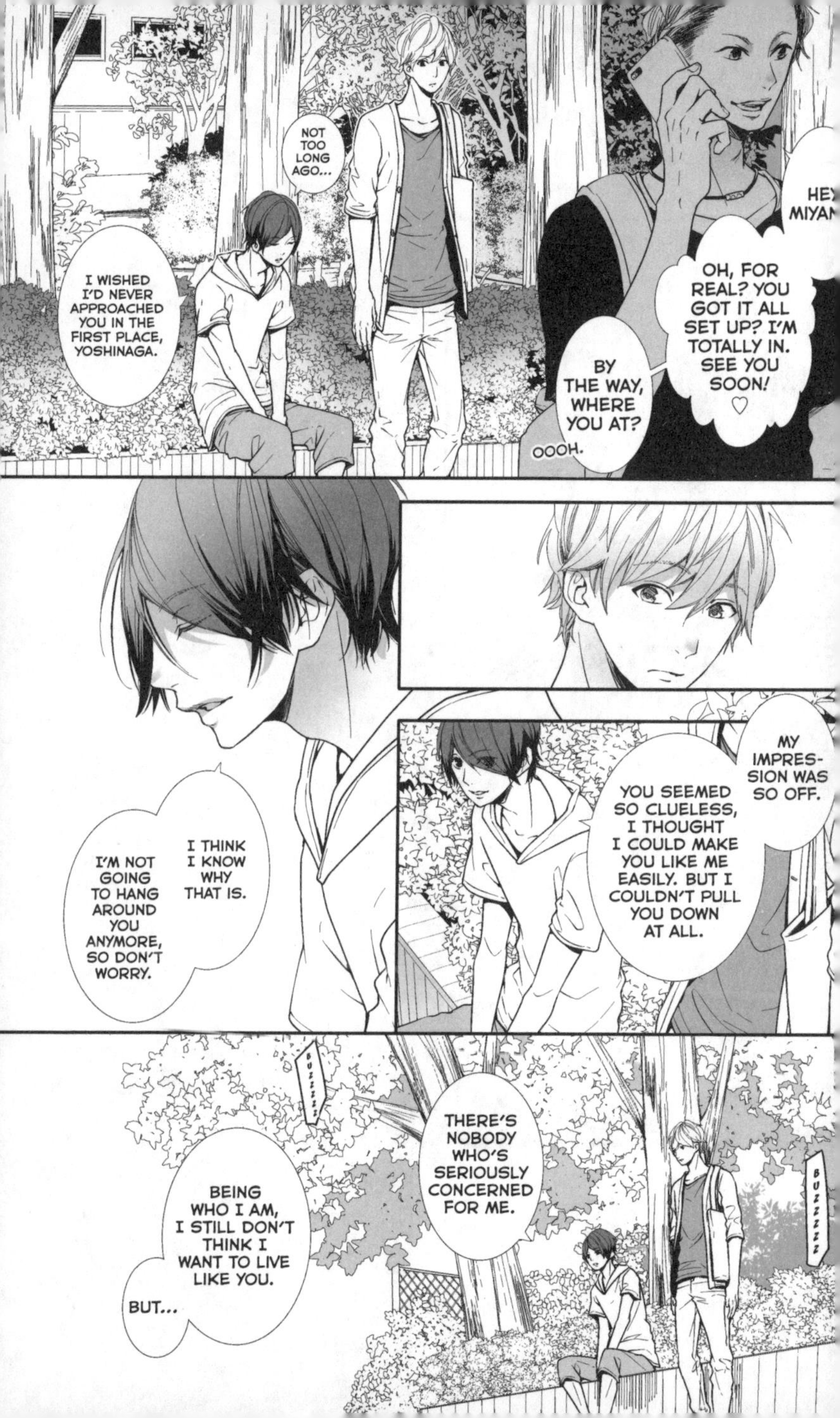

HEY MIYAN
OH, FOR REAL? YOU GOT IT ALL SET UP? I'M TOTALLY IN. SEE YOU SOON! ♡
BY THE WAY, WHERE YOU AT?
OOOH.
NOT TOO LONG AGO...
I WISHED I'D NEVER APPROACHED YOU IN THE FIRST PLACE, YOSHINAGA.
MY IMPRES-SION WAS SO OFF.
YOU SEEMED SO CLUELESS, I THOUGHT I COULD MAKE YOU LIKE ME EASILY. BUT I COULDN'T PULL YOU DOWN AT ALL.
I THINK I KNOW WHY THAT IS.
I'M NOT GOING TO HANG AROUND YOU ANYMORE, SO DON'T WORRY.
BUZZZZ
THERE'S NOBODY WHO'S SERIOUSLY CONCERNED FOR ME.
BUZZZZ
BEING WHO I AM, I STILL DON'T THINK I WANT TO LIVE LIKE YOU.
BUT...

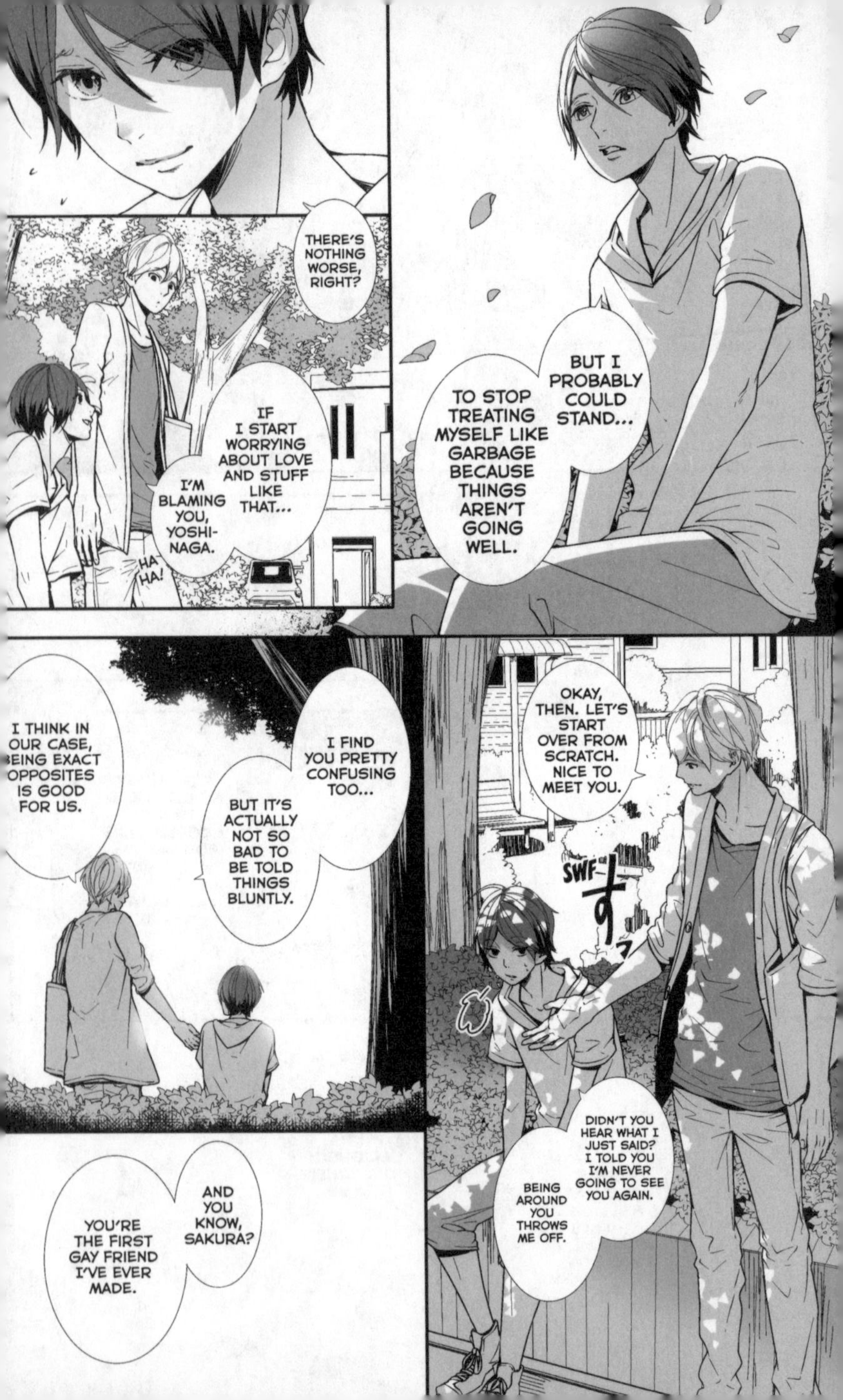
BUT I PROBABLY COULD STAND...
TO STOP TREATING MYSELF LIKE GARBAGE BECAUSE THINGS AREN'T GOING WELL.
THERE'S NOTHING WORSE, RIGHT?
IF I START WORRYING ABOUT LOVE AND STUFF LIKE THAT...
I'M BLAMING YOU, YOSHI-NAGA.
HA HA!
OKAY, THEN. LET'S START OVER FROM SCRATCH. NICE TO MEET YOU.
SWF-
DIDN'T YOU HEAR WHAT I JUST SAID? I TOLD YOU I'M NEVER GOING TO SEE YOU AGAIN.
BEING AROUND YOU THROWS ME OFF.
I FIND YOU PRETTY CONFUSING TOO...
BUT IT'S ACTUALLY NOT SO BAD TO BE TOLD THINGS BLUNTLY.
I THINK IN OUR CASE, BEING EXACT OPPOSITES IS GOOD FOR US.
AND YOU KNOW, SAKURA?
YOU'RE THE FIRST GAY FRIEND I'VE EVER MADE.

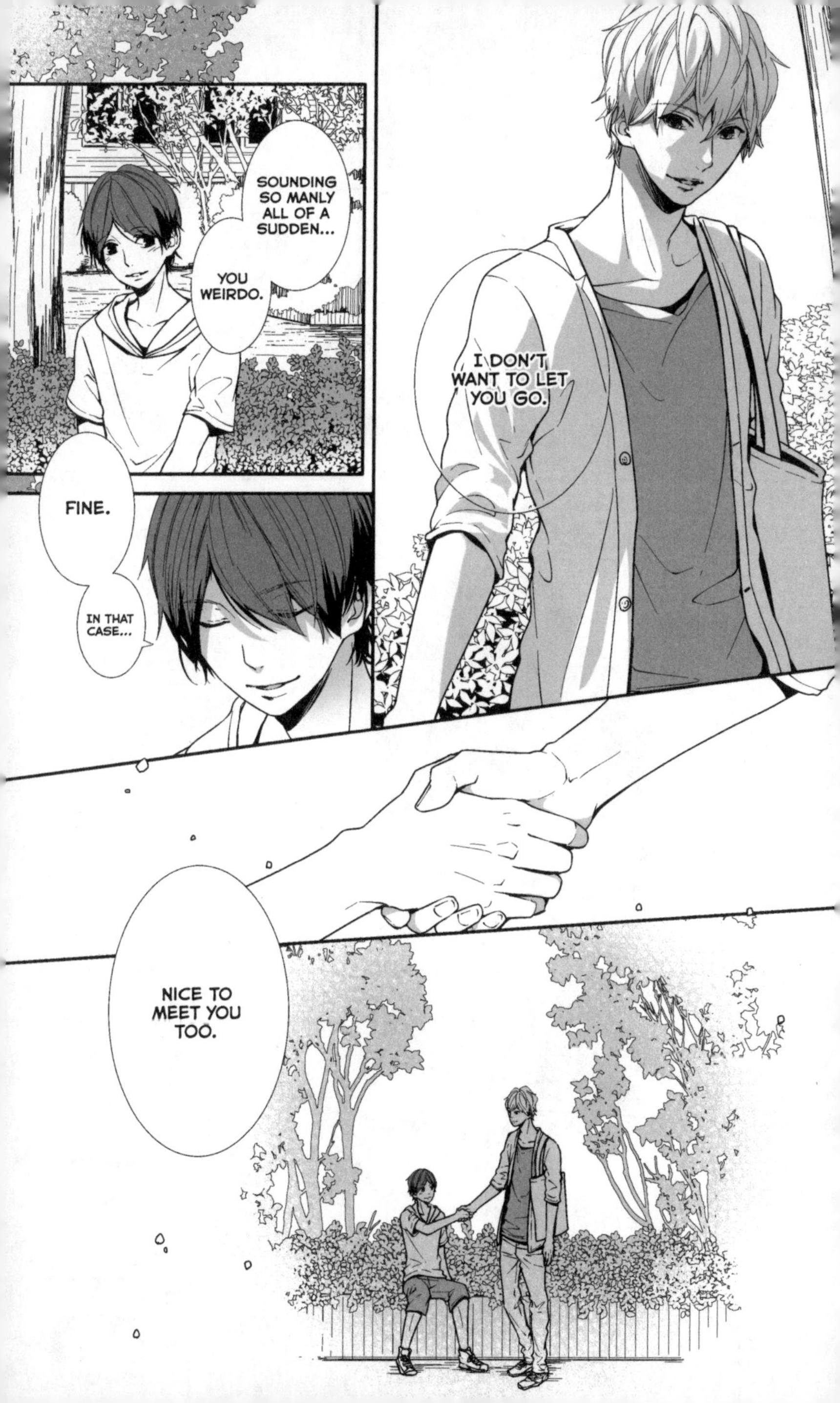
I DON'T WANT TO LET YOU GO.
SOUNDING SO MANLY ALL OF A SUDDEN...
YOU WEIRDO.
FINE.
IN THAT CASE...
NICE TO MEET YOU TOO.

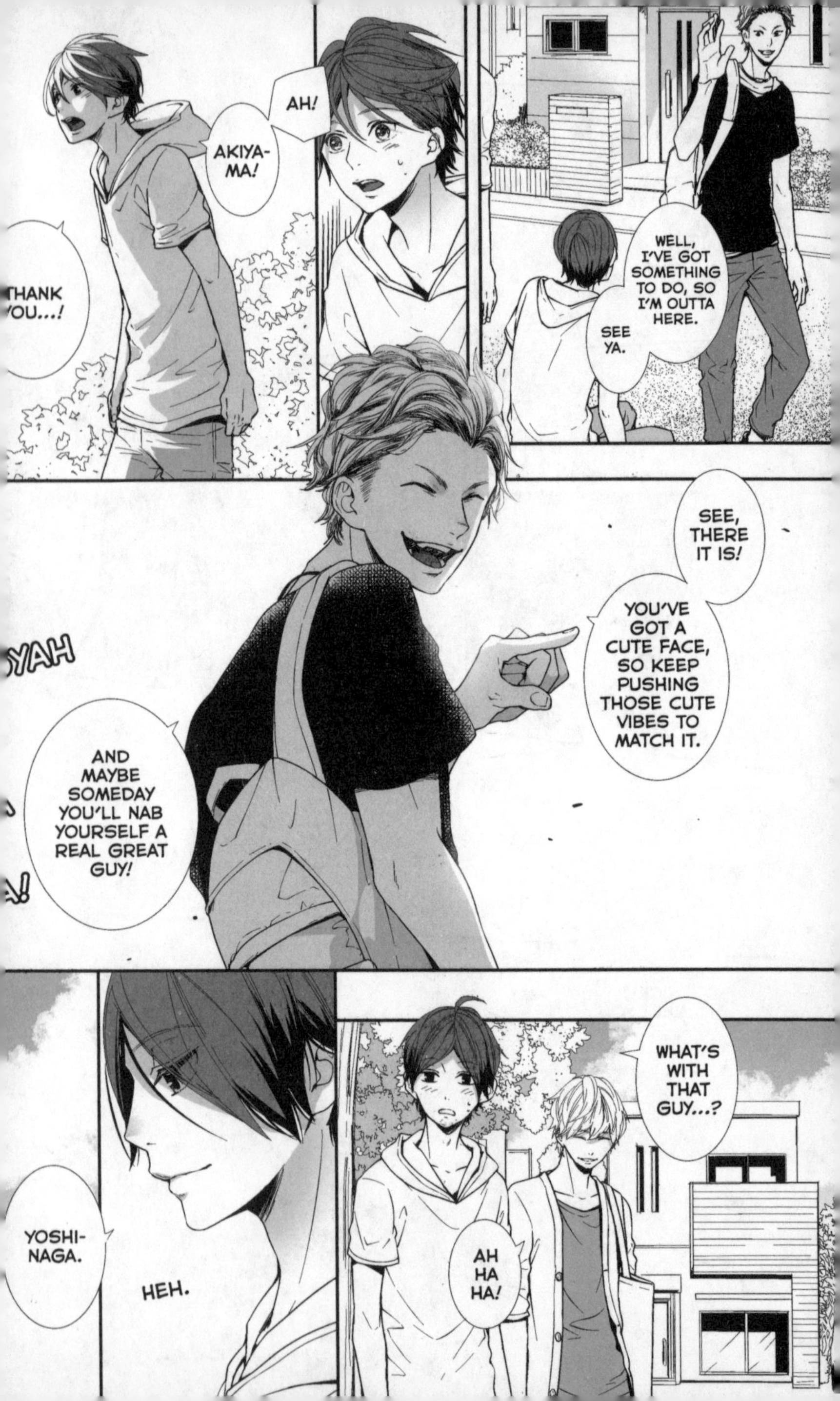
WELL, I'VE GOT SOMETHING TO DO, SO I'M OUTTA HERE.
SEE YA.
AH!
AKIYAMA!
THANK YOU...!
SEE, THERE IT IS!
YOU'VE GOT A CUTE FACE, SO KEEP PUSHING THOSE CUTE VIBES TO MATCH IT.
AND MAYBE SOMEDAY YOU'LL NAB YOURSELF A REAL GREAT GUY!
WHAT'S WITH THAT GUY...?
AH HA HA!
YOSHI-NAGA.
HEH.

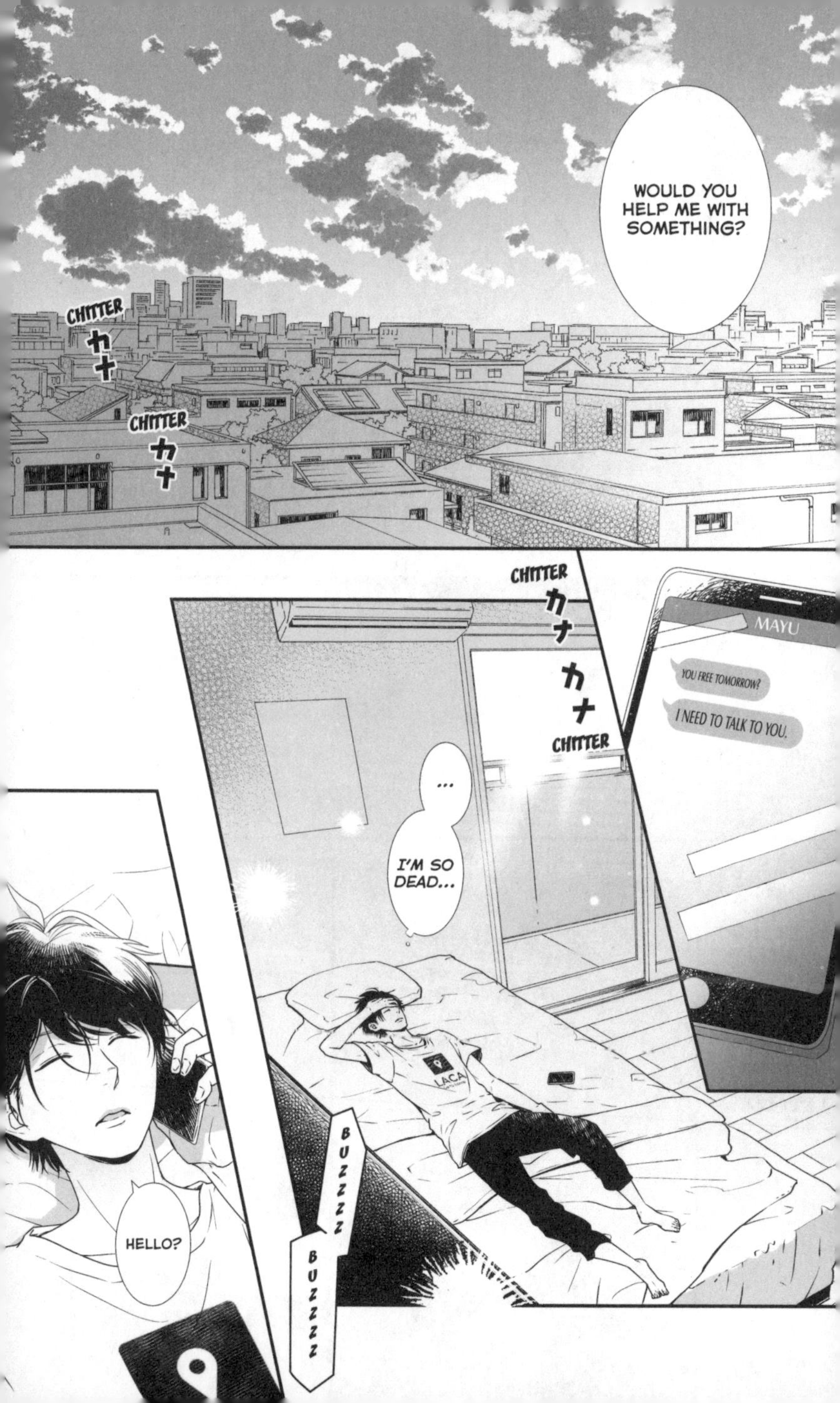
WOULD YOU HELP ME WITH SOMETHING?
CHITTER
カナ
CHITTER
カナ
MAYU
YOU FREE TOMORROW?
I NEED TO TALK TO YOU.
CHITTER
カナ
カナ
CHITTER
...
I'M SO DEAD...
BUZZZZ
BUZZZZ
HELLO?

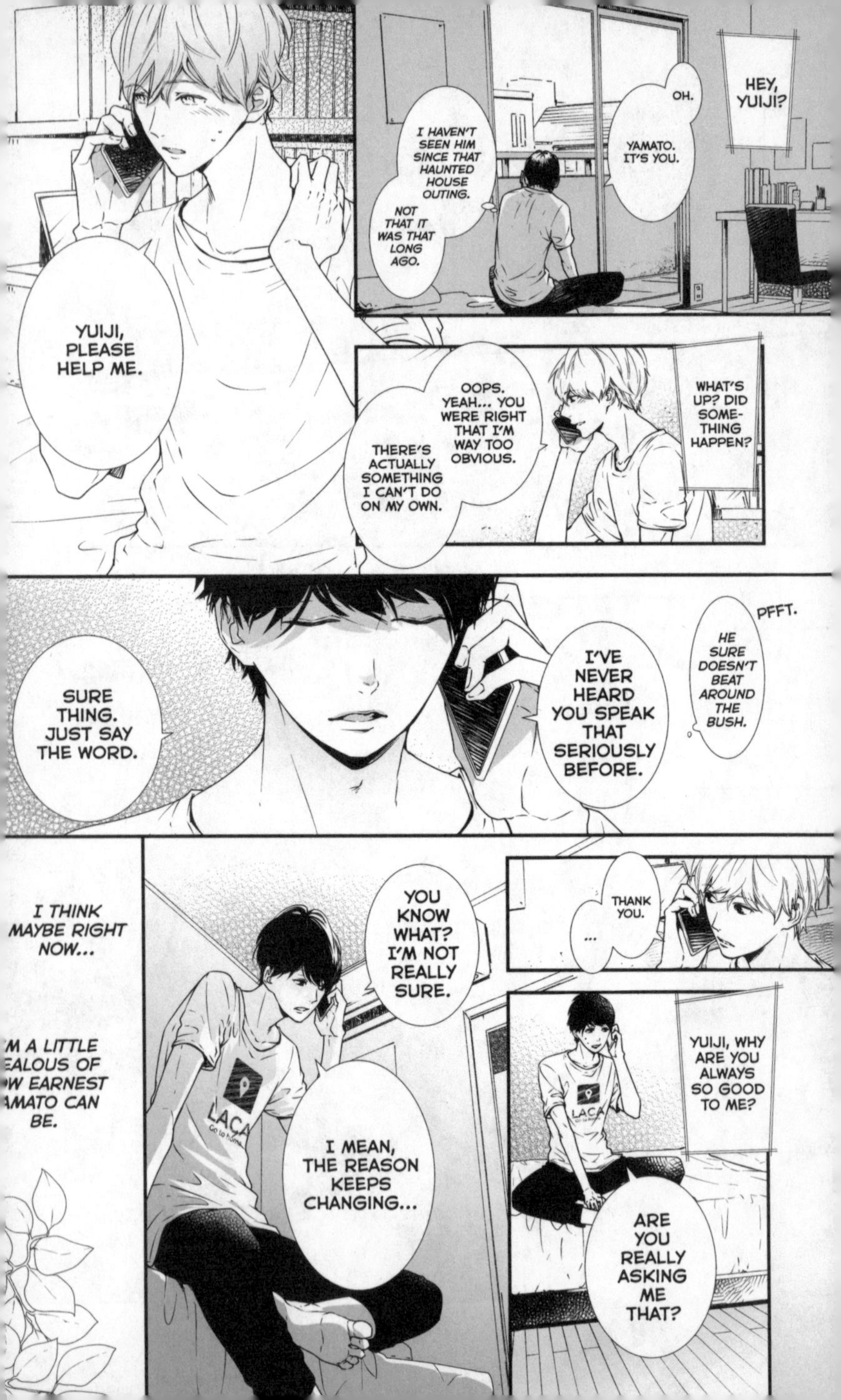
HEY, YUIJI?
OH.
YAMATO. IT'S YOU.
I HAVEN'T SEEN HIM SINCE THAT HAUNTED HOUSE OUTING.
NOT THAT IT WAS THAT LONG AGO.
WHAT'S UP? DID SOME-THING HAPPEN?
OOPS. YEAH... YOU WERE RIGHT THAT I'M WAY TOO OBVIOUS.
THERE'S ACTUALLY SOMETHING I CAN'T DO ON MY OWN.
YUIJI, PLEASE HELP ME.
PFFT.
HE SURE DOESN'T BEAT AROUND THE BUSH.
I'VE NEVER HEARD YOU SPEAK THAT SERIOUSLY BEFORE.
SURE THING. JUST SAY THE WORD.
THANK YOU.
...
YUIJI, WHY ARE YOU ALWAYS SO GOOD TO ME?
ARE YOU REALLY ASKING ME THAT?
YOU KNOW WHAT? I'M NOT REALLY SURE.
I MEAN, THE REASON KEEPS CHANGING...
I THINK MAYBE RIGHT NOW...
M A LITTLE EALOUS OF W EARNEST AMATO CAN BE.

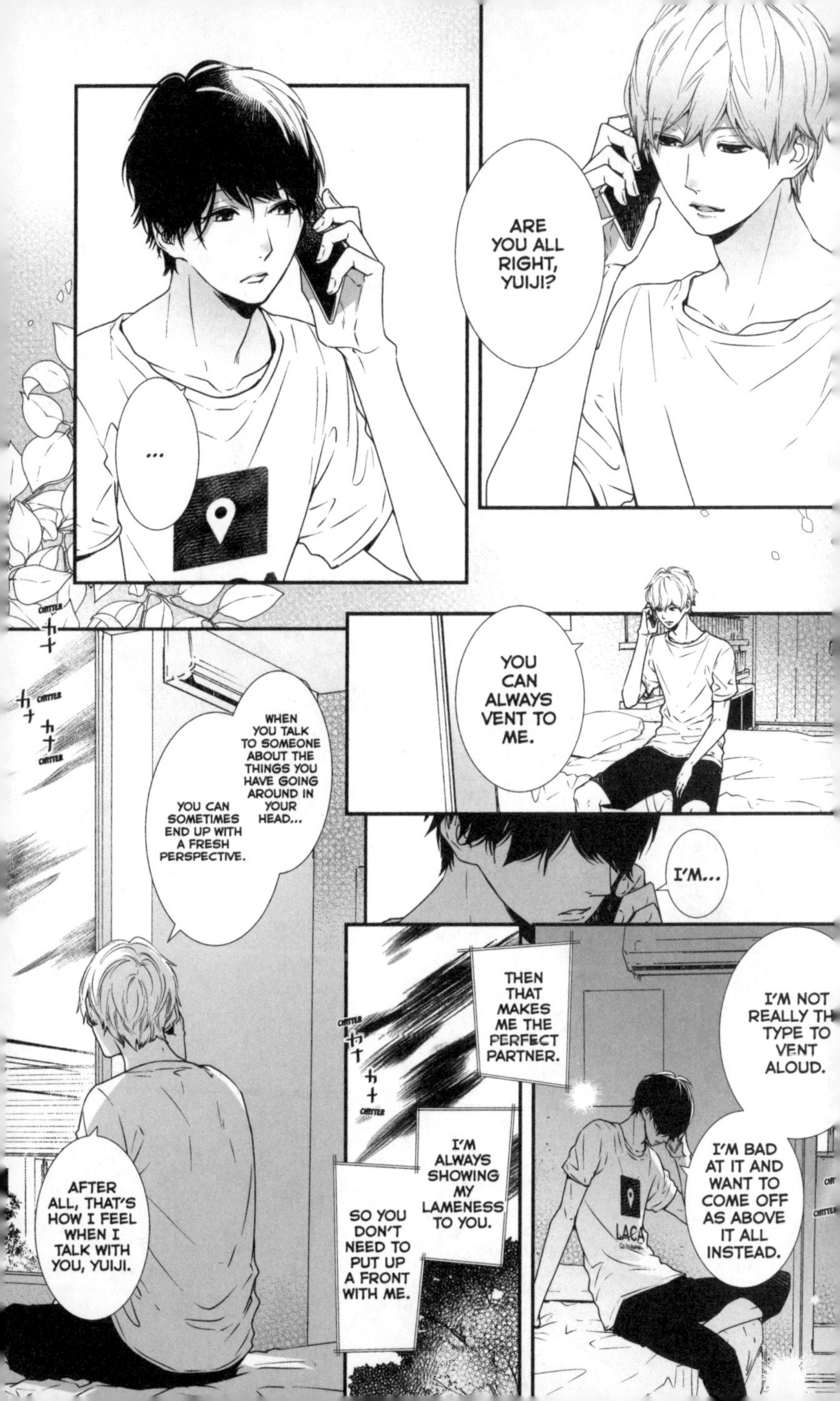
ARE YOU ALL RIGHT, YUIJI?
...
YOU CAN ALWAYS VENT TO ME.
I'M...
I'M NOT REALLY TH TYPE TO VENT ALOUD.
I'M BAD AT IT AND WANT TO COME OFF AS ABOVE IT ALL INSTEAD.
THEN THAT MAKES ME THE PERFECT PARTNER.
I'M ALWAYS SHOWING MY LAMENESS TO YOU.
SO YOU DON'T NEED TO PUT UP A FRONT WITH ME.
WHEN YOU TALK TO SOMEONE ABOUT THE THINGS YOU HAVE GOING AROUND IN YOUR HEAD...
YOU CAN SOMETIMES END UP WITH A FRESH PERSPECTIVE.
AFTER ALL, THAT'S HOW I FEEL WHEN I TALK WITH YOU, YUIJI.

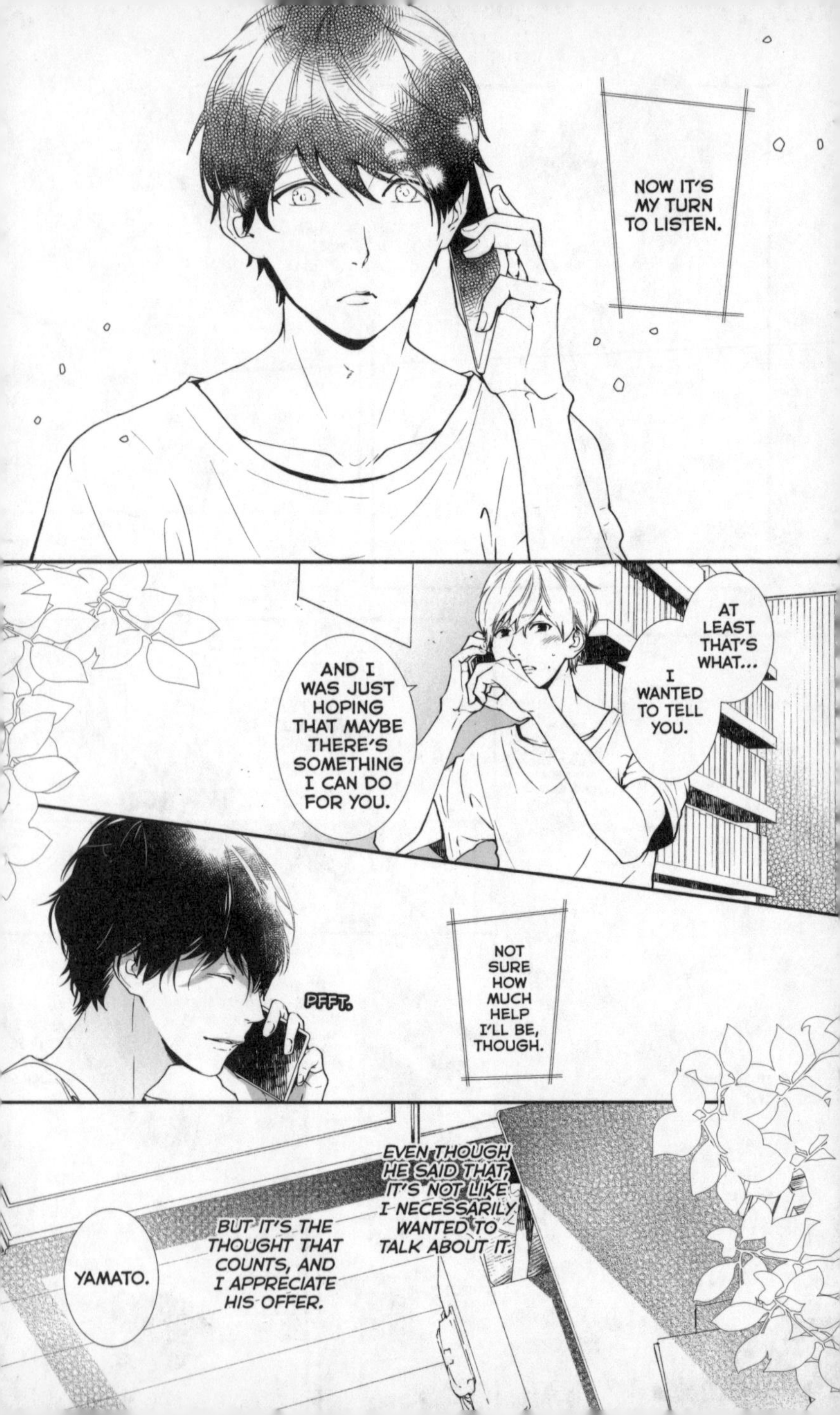
NOW IT'S MY TURN TO LISTEN.
AT LEAST THAT'S WHAT... I WANTED TO TELL YOU.
AND I WAS JUST HOPING THAT MAYBE THERE'S SOMETHING I CAN DO FOR YOU.
NOT SURE HOW MUCH HELP I'LL BE, THOUGH.
PFFT.
EVEN THOUGH HE SAID THAT, IT'S NOT LIKE I NECESSARILY WANTED TO TALK ABOUT IT.
BUT IT'S THE THOUGHT THAT COUNTS, AND I APPRECIATE HIS OFFER.
YAMATO.

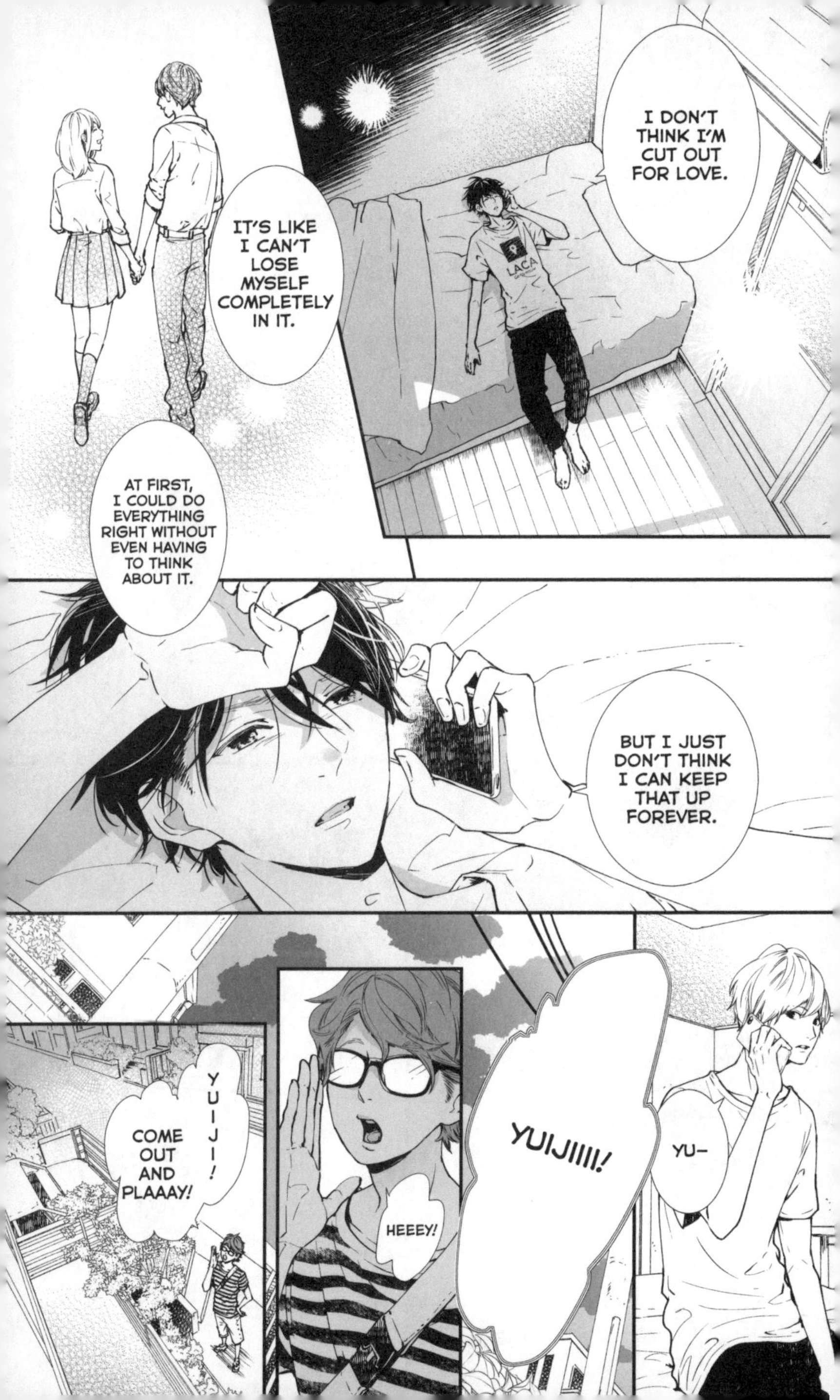
I DON'T THINK I'M CUT OUT FOR LOVE.
IT'S LIKE I CAN'T LOSE MYSELF COMPLETELY IN IT.
AT FIRST, I COULD DO EVERYTHING RIGHT WITHOUT EVEN HAVING TO THINK ABOUT IT.
BUT I JUST DON'T THINK I CAN KEEP THAT UP FOREVER.
YU–
YUIJIIII!
HEEEY!
YUIJI!
COME OUT AND PLAAAY!

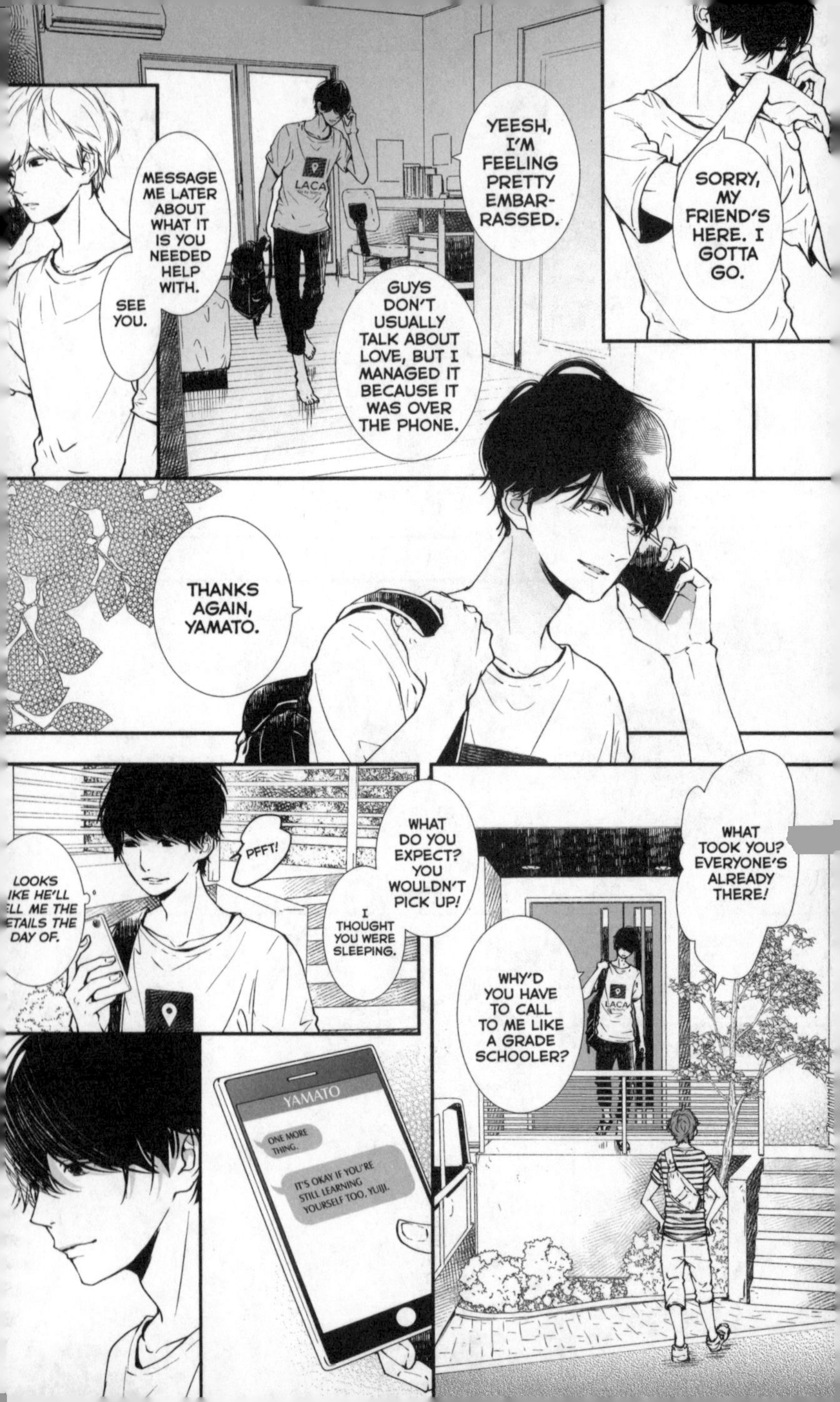

SORRY, MY FRIEND'S HERE. I GOTTA GO.
YEESH, I'M FEELING PRETTY EMBARRASSED.
GUYS DON'T USUALLY TALK ABOUT LOVE, BUT I MANAGED IT BECAUSE IT WAS OVER THE PHONE.
MESSAGE ME LATER ABOUT WHAT IT IS YOU NEEDED HELP WITH.
SEE YOU.
THANKS AGAIN, YAMATO.
WHAT TOOK YOU? EVERYONE'S ALREADY THERE!
WHY'D YOU HAVE TO CALL TO ME LIKE A GRADE SCHOOLER?
WHAT DO YOU EXPECT? YOU WOULDN'T PICK UP!
I THOUGHT YOU WERE SLEEPING.
PFFT!
LOOKS IKE HE'LL ELL ME THE ETAILS THE DAY OF.
YAMATO
ONE MORE THING.
IT'S OKAY IF YOU'RE STILL LEARNING YOURSELF TOO, YUJI.

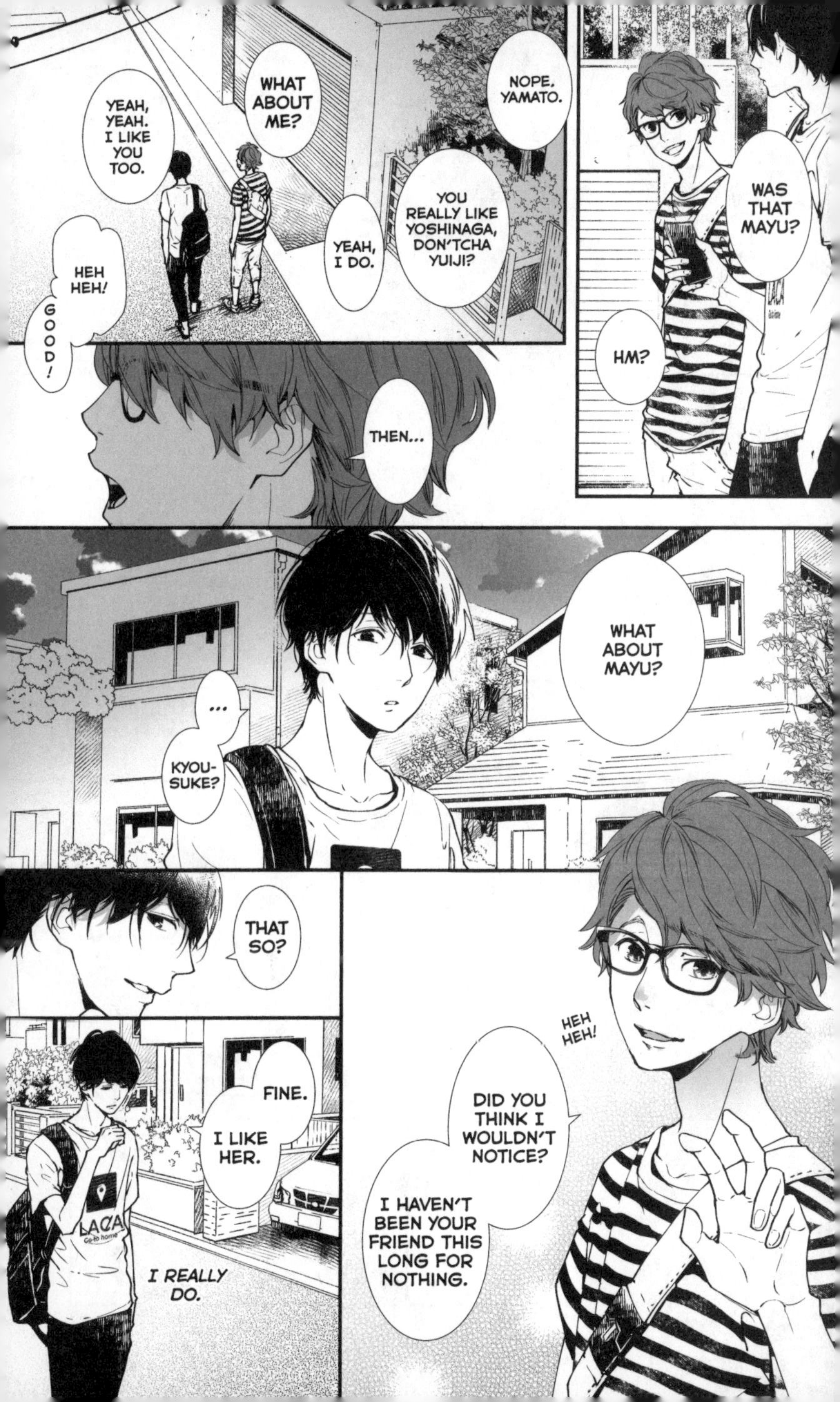
WAS THAT MAYU?
HM?
NOPE, YAMATO.
WHAT ABOUT ME?
YOU REALLY LIKE YOSHINAGA, DON'TCHA YUIJI?
YEAH, I DO.
YEAH, YEAH. I LIKE YOU TOO.
HEH HEH!
GOOD!
THEN...
WHAT ABOUT MAYU?
...
KYOU-SUKE?
HEH HEH!
DID YOU THINK I WOULDN'T NOTICE?
I HAVEN'T BEEN YOUR FRIEND THIS LONG FOR NOTHING.
THAT SO?
FINE.
I LIKE HER.
I REALLY DO.

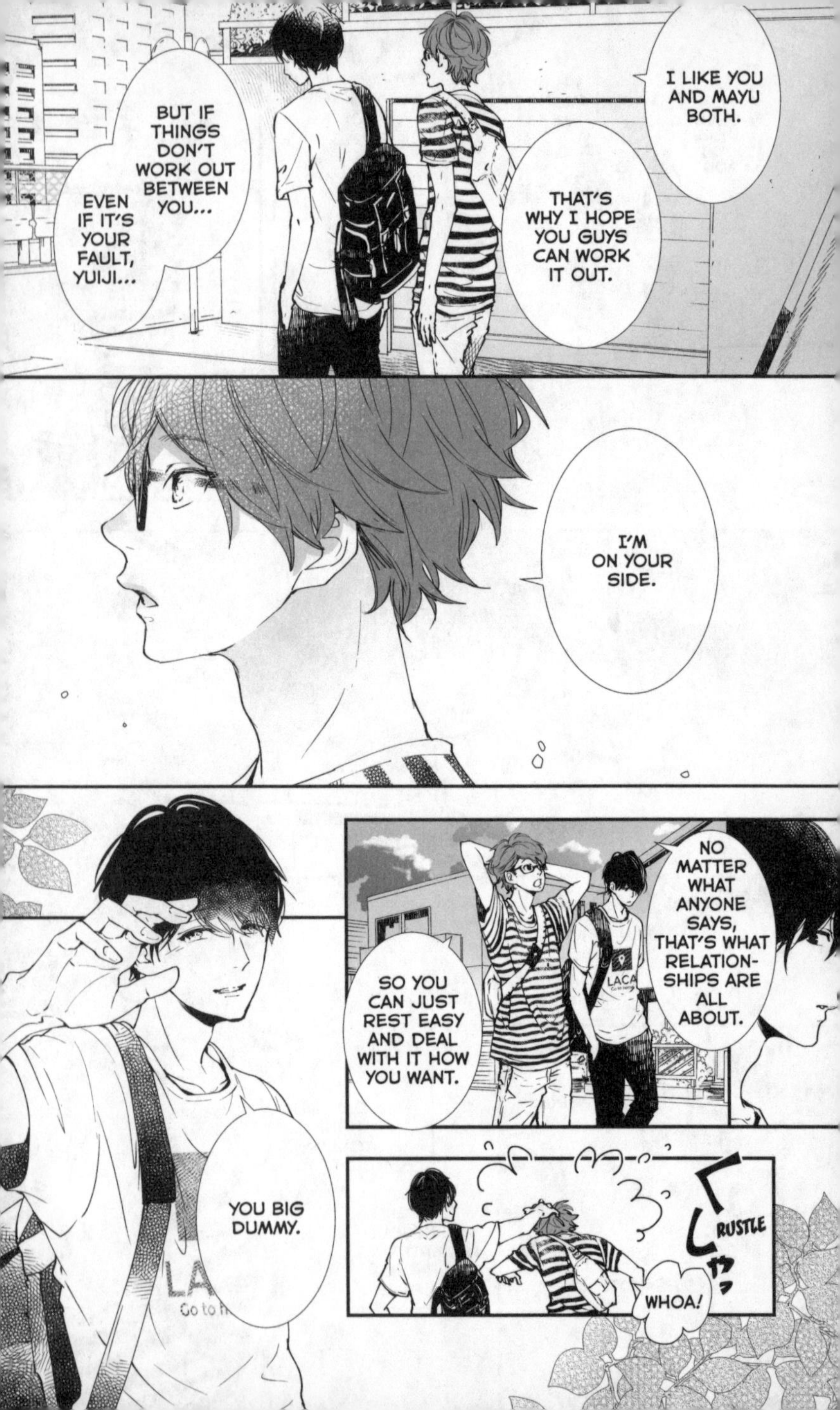
I LIKE YOU AND MAYU BOTH.
THAT'S WHY I HOPE YOU GUYS CAN WORK IT OUT.
BUT IF THINGS DON'T WORK OUT BETWEEN YOU...
EVEN IF IT'S YOUR FAULT, YUIJI...
I'M ON YOUR SIDE.
NO MATTER WHAT ANYONE SAYS, THAT'S WHAT RELATION-SHIPS ARE ALL ABOUT.
SO YOU CAN JUST REST EASY AND DEAL WITH IT HOW YOU WANT.
RUSTLE
WHOA!
YOU BIG DUMMY.

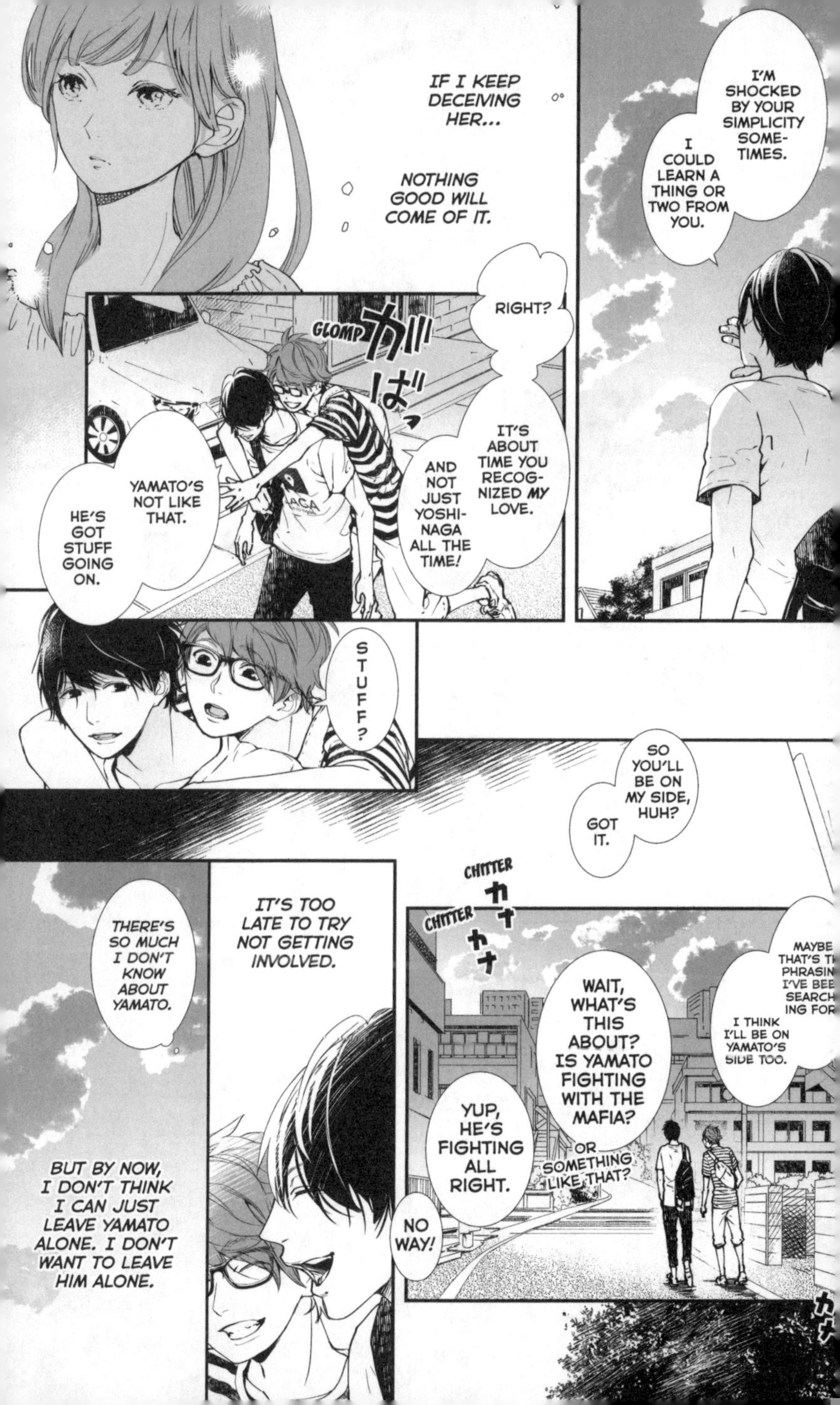
I'M SHOCKED BY YOUR SIMPLICITY SOME-TIMES.
I COULD LEARN A THING OR TWO FROM YOU.
IF I KEEP DECEIVING HER...
NOTHING GOOD WILL COME OF IT.
RIGHT?
IT'S ABOUT TIME YOU RECOG-NIZED MY LOVE.
AND NOT JUST YOSHI-NAGA ALL THE TIME!
GLOMP
YAMATO'S NOT LIKE THAT.
HE'S GOT STUFF GOING ON.
STUFF?
SO YOU'LL BE ON MY SIDE, HUH?
GOT IT.
I THINK I'LL BE ON YAMATO'S SIDE TOO.
WAIT, WHAT'S THIS ABOUT? IS YAMATO FIGHTING WITH THE MAFIA?
OR SOMETHING LIKE THAT?
YUP, HE'S FIGHTING ALL RIGHT.
NO WAY!
CHITTER
CHITTER
IT'S TOO LATE TO TRY NOT GETTING INVOLVED.
THERE'S SO MUCH I DON'T KNOW ABOUT YAMATO.
BUT BY NOW, I DON'T THINK I CAN JUST LEAVE YAMATO ALONE. I DON'T WANT TO LEAVE HIM ALONE.

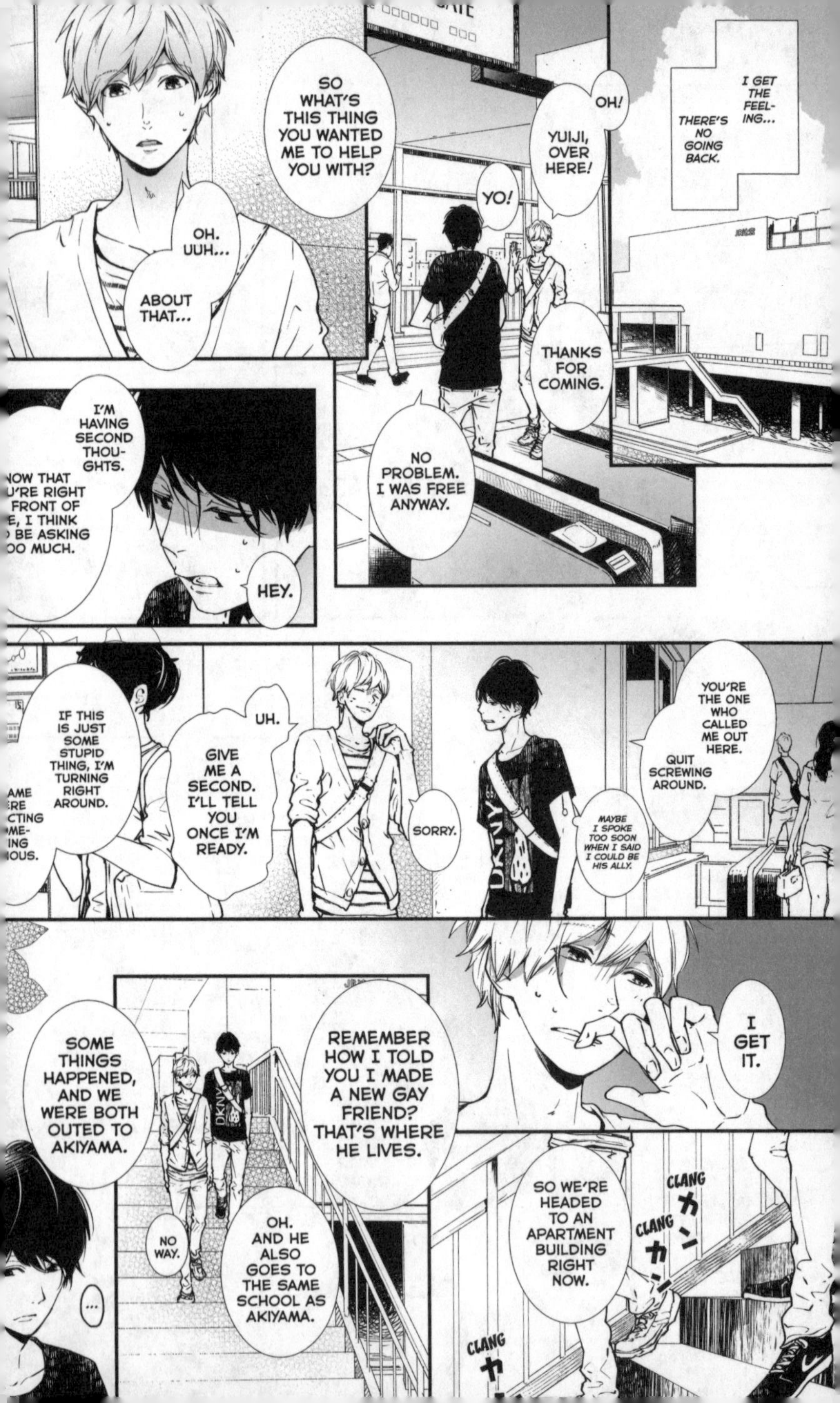
I GET THE FEELING...
THERE'S NO GOING BACK.
OH!
YUIJI, OVER HERE!
YO!
THANKS FOR COMING.
NO PROBLEM. I WAS FREE ANYWAY.
SO WHAT'S THIS THING YOU WANTED ME TO HELP YOU WITH?
OH. UUH...
ABOUT THAT...
I'M HAVING SECOND THOUGHTS.
HEY.
YOU'RE THE ONE WHO CALLED ME OUT HERE.
QUIT SCREWING AROUND.
MAYBE I SPOKE TOO SOON WHEN I SAID I COULD BE HIS ALLY.
SORRY.
UH.
GIVE ME A SECOND. I'LL TELL YOU ONCE I'M READY.
IF THIS IS JUST SOME STUPID THING, I'M TURNING RIGHT AROUND.
I GET IT.
REMEMBER HOW I TOLD YOU I MADE A NEW GAY FRIEND? THAT'S WHERE HE LIVES.
SOME THINGS HAPPENED, AND WE WERE BOTH OUTED TO AKIYAMA.
CLANG カン
CLANG カン
SO WE'RE HEADED TO AN APARTMENT BUILDING RIGHT NOW.
CLANG
OH. AND HE ALSO GOES TO THE SAME SCHOOL AS AKIYAMA.
NO WAY.
...

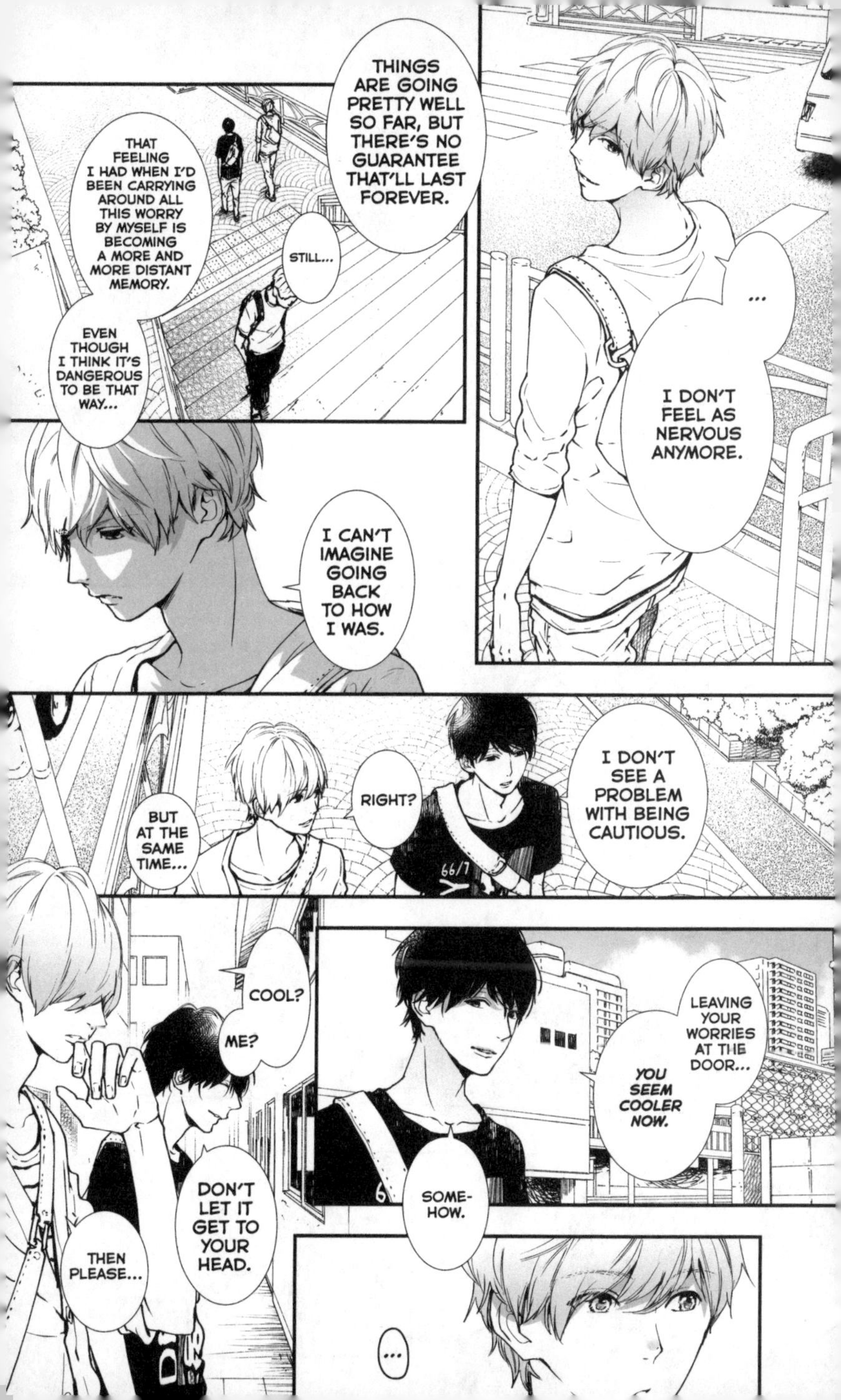
THINGS ARE GOING PRETTY WELL SO FAR, BUT THERE'S NO GUARANTEE THAT'LL LAST FOREVER.
STILL...
...
I DON'T FEEL AS NERVOUS ANYMORE.
THAT FEELING I HAD WHEN I'D BEEN CARRYING AROUND ALL THIS WORRY BY MYSELF IS BECOMING A MORE AND MORE DISTANT MEMORY.
EVEN THOUGH I THINK IT'S DANGEROUS TO BE THAT WAY...
I CAN'T IMAGINE GOING BACK TO HOW I WAS.
I DON'T SEE A PROBLEM WITH BEING CAUTIOUS.
RIGHT?
BUT AT THE SAME TIME...
LEAVING YOUR WORRIES AT THE DOOR...
YOU SEEM COOLER NOW.
SOME-HOW.
COOL?
ME?
DON'T LET IT GET TO YOUR HEAD.
THEN PLEASE...
...

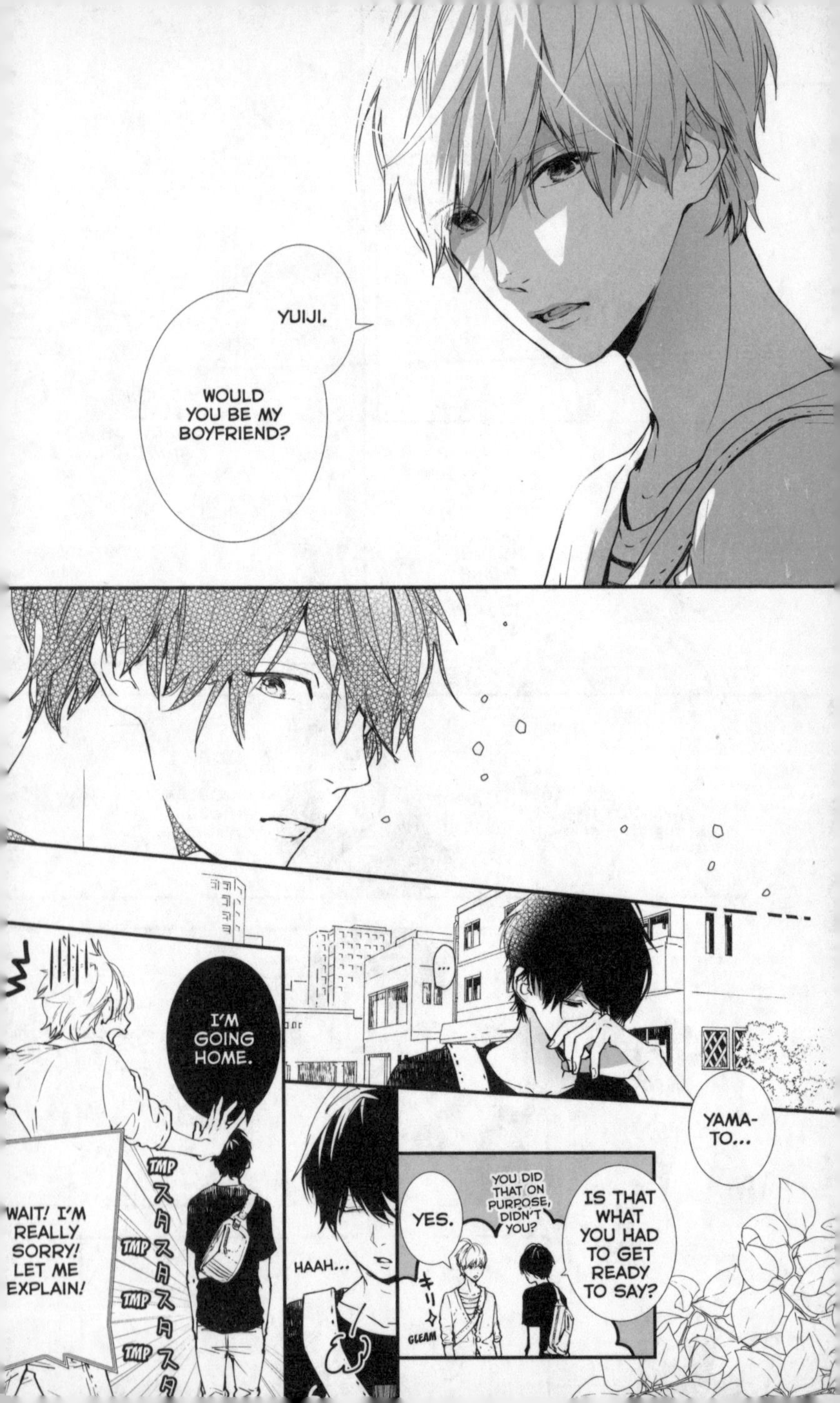

YUIJI.
WOULD YOU BE MY BOYFRIEND?
...
YAMA-TO...
IS THAT WHAT YOU HAD TO GET READY TO SAY?
YOU DID THAT ON PURPOSE, DIDN'T YOU?
YES.
キリッ
GLEAM
HAAH...
I'M GOING HOME.
TMP
TMP
TMP
TMP
スタスタスタスタ
WAIT! I'M REALLY SORRY! LET ME EXPLAIN!

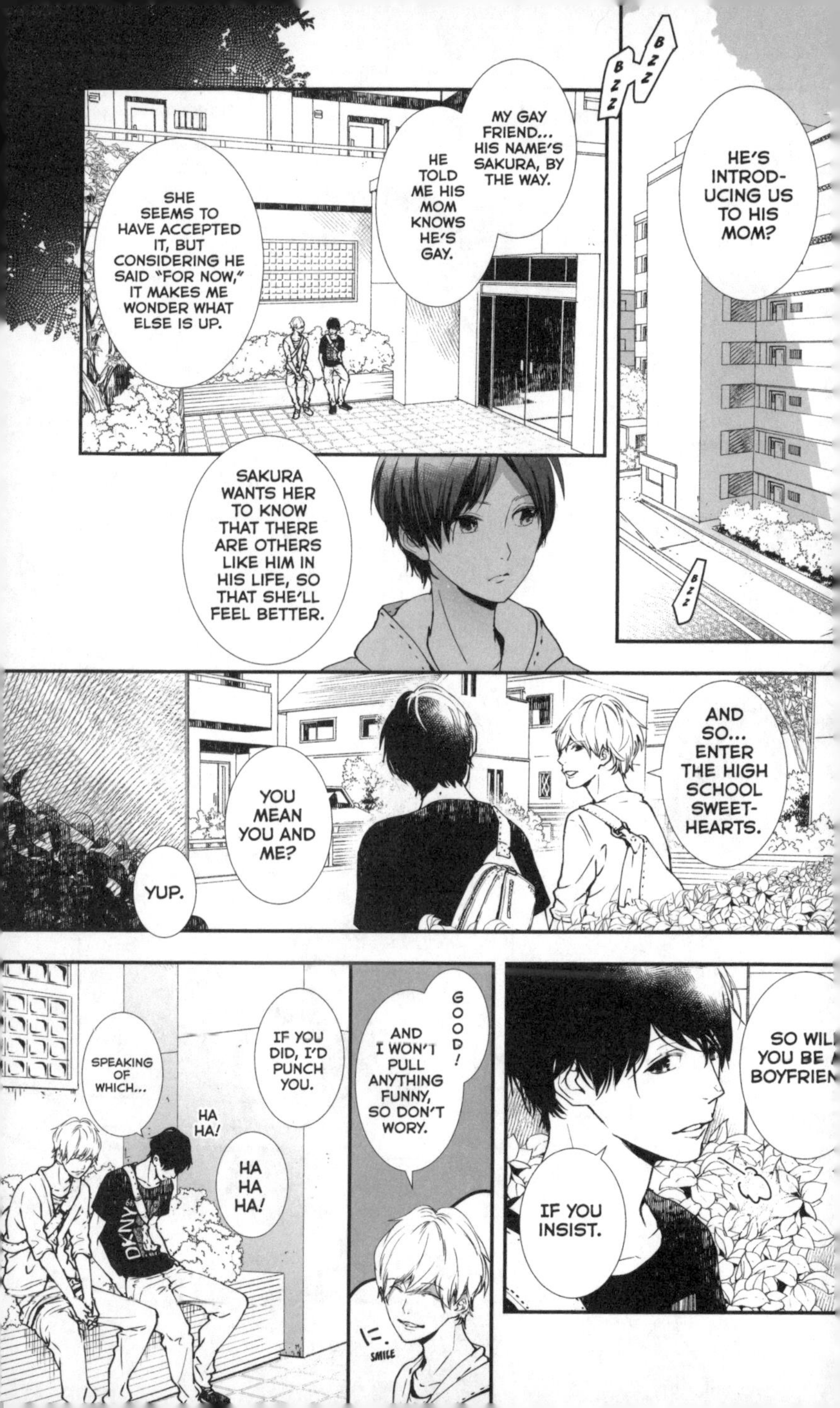

BZZ
BZZ
HE'S INTRODUCING US TO HIS MOM?
BZZ
MY GAY FRIEND... HIS NAME'S SAKURA, BY THE WAY.
HE TOLD ME HIS MOM KNOWS HE'S GAY.
SHE SEEMS TO HAVE ACCEPTED IT, BUT CONSIDERING HE SAID "FOR NOW," IT MAKES ME WONDER WHAT ELSE IS UP.
SAKURA WANTS HER TO KNOW THAT THERE ARE OTHERS LIKE HIM IN HIS LIFE, SO THAT SHE'LL FEEL BETTER.
AND SO... ENTER THE HIGH SCHOOL SWEET-HEARTS.
YOU MEAN YOU AND ME?
YUP.
SO WIL YOU BE A BOYFRIEN
IF YOU INSIST.
GOOD!
AND I WON'T PULL ANYTHING FUNNY, SO DON'T WORY.
SMILE
IF YOU DID, I'D PUNCH YOU.
HA HA!
HA HA HA!
SPEAKING OF WHICH...
DKNY

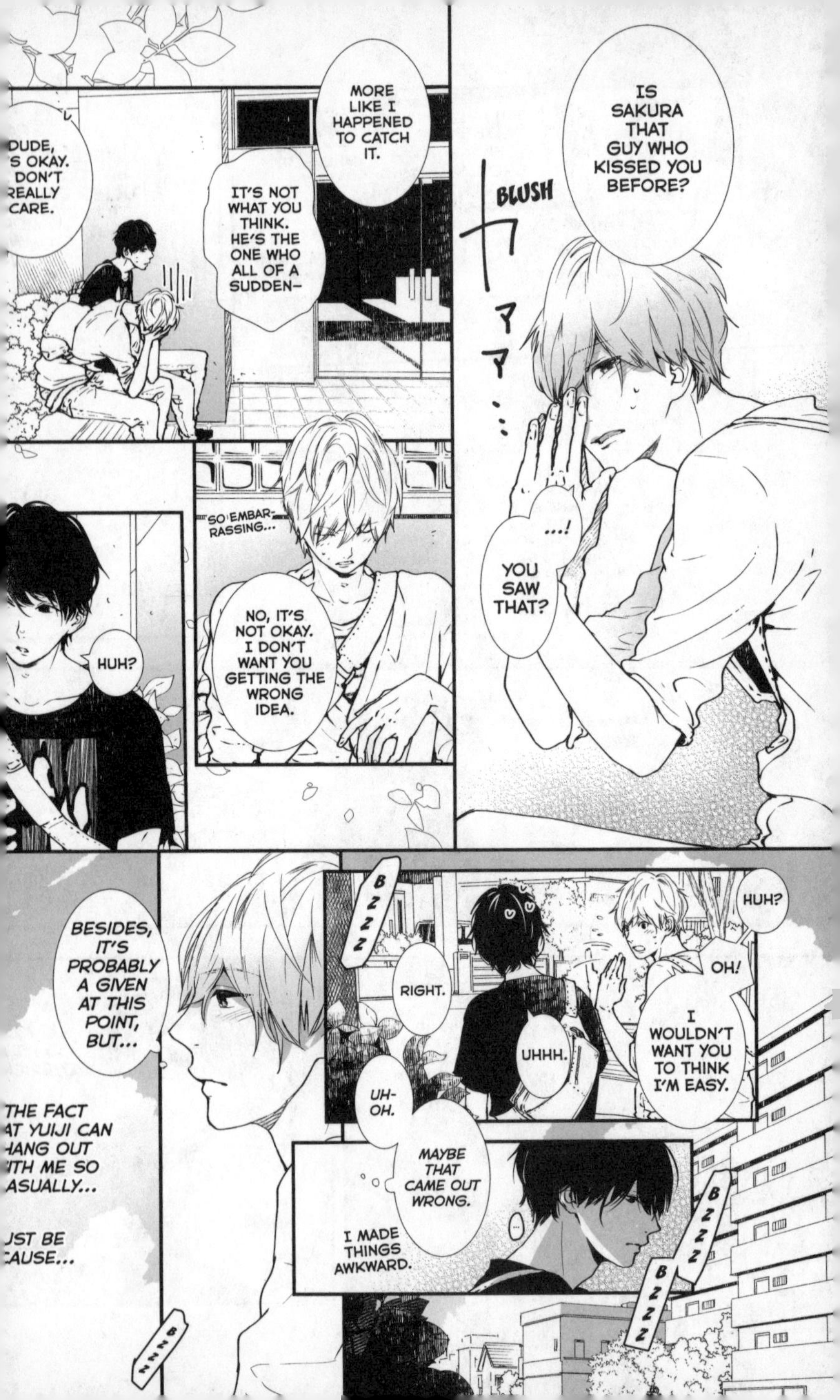
IS SAKURA THAT GUY WHO KISSED YOU BEFORE?
BLUSH
...!
YOU SAW THAT?
MORE LIKE I HAPPENED TO CATCH IT.
IT'S NOT WHAT YOU THINK. HE'S THE ONE WHO ALL OF A SUDDEN—
DUDE, 'S OKAY. DON'T REALLY CARE.
SO EMBARRASSING...
NO, IT'S NOT OKAY. I DON'T WANT YOU GETTING THE WRONG IDEA.
HUH?
HUH?
OH!
I WOULDN'T WANT YOU TO THINK I'M EASY.
UHHH.
RIGHT.
BZZZ
UH-OH.
BZZZ
BZZZ
...
MAYBE THAT CAME OUT WRONG.
I MADE THINGS AWKWARD.
BESIDES, IT'S PROBABLY A GIVEN AT THIS POINT, BUT...
THE FACT AT YUIJI CAN HANG OUT ITH ME SO ASUALLY...
UST BE CAUSE...
BNNN

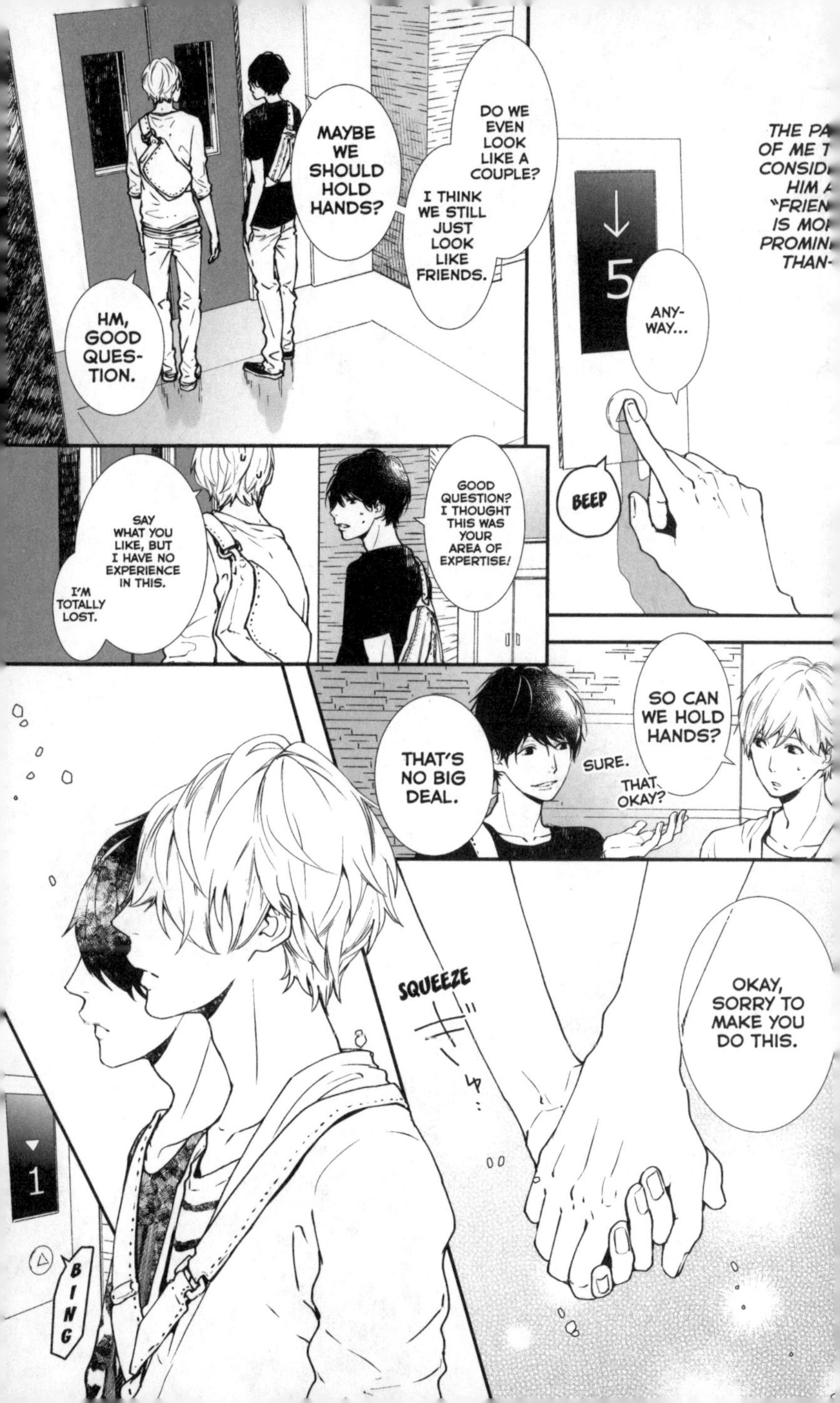
THE PA
OF ME T
CONSID
HIM A
"FRIEN
IS MO
PROMIN
THAN-
ANY-WAY...
BEEP
DO WE EVEN LOOK LIKE A COUPLE?
I THINK WE STILL JUST LOOK LIKE FRIENDS.
MAYBE WE SHOULD HOLD HANDS?
HM, GOOD QUES-TION.
GOOD QUESTION? I THOUGHT THIS WAS YOUR AREA OF EXPERTISE!
SAY WHAT YOU LIKE, BUT I HAVE NO EXPERIENCE IN THIS.
I'M TOTALLY LOST.
SO CAN WE HOLD HANDS?
SURE.
THAT OKAY?
THAT'S NO BIG DEAL.
OKAY, SORRY TO MAKE YOU DO THIS.
SQUEEZE
BING

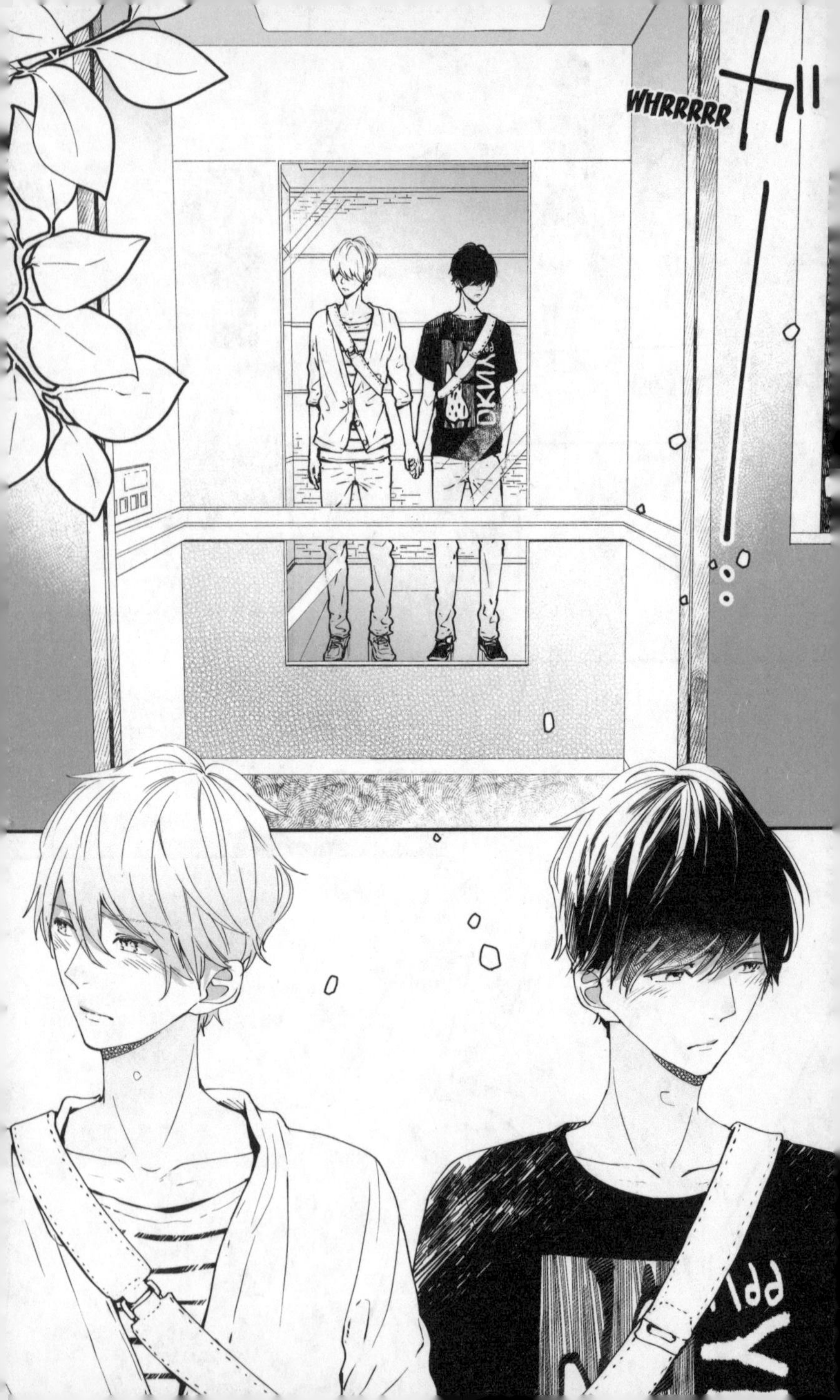
ガー
WHRRRRR

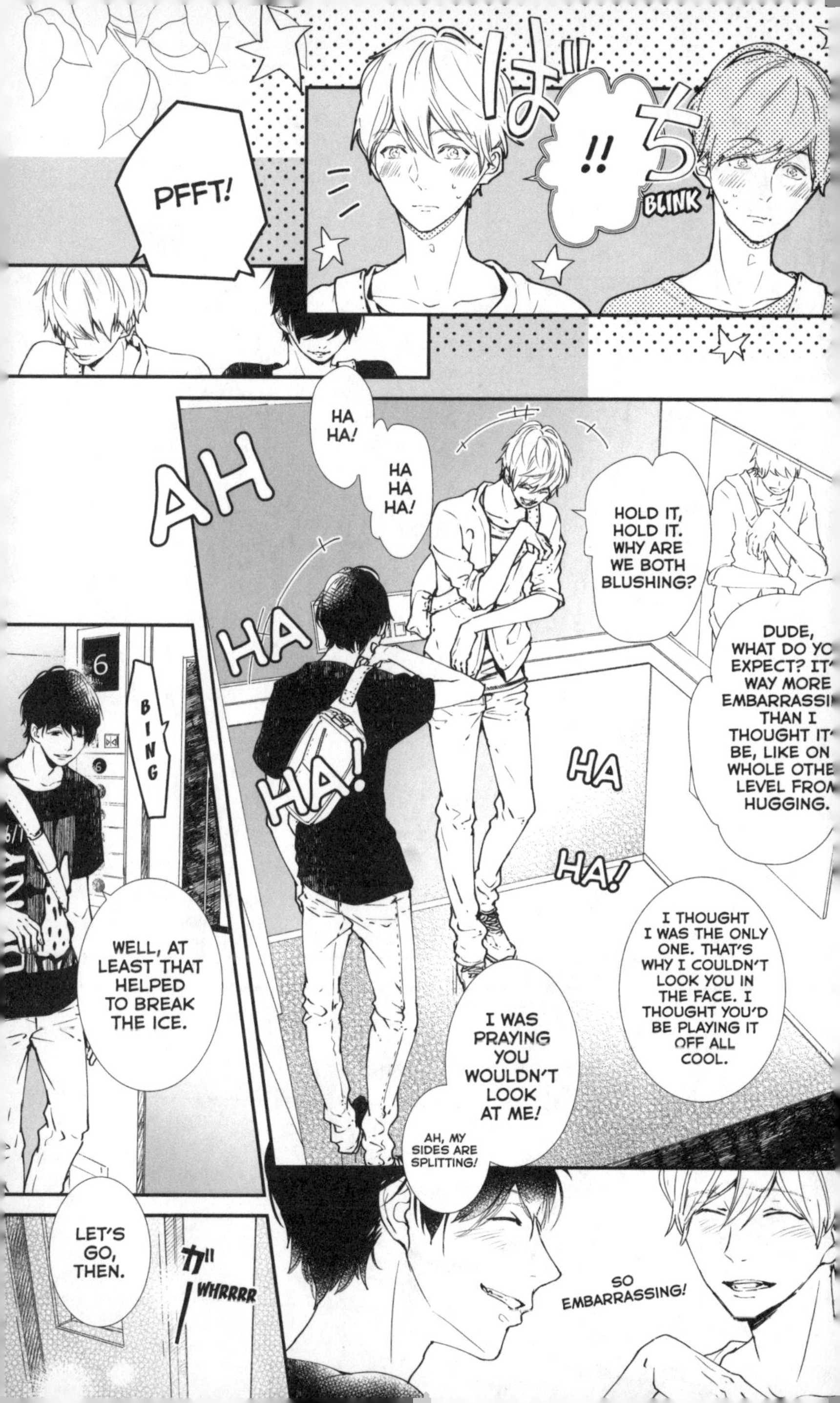

ばち
!!
BLINK
PFFT!
HOLD IT, HOLD IT. WHY ARE WE BOTH BLUSHING?
DUDE, WHAT DO YO EXPECT? IT WAY MORE EMBARRASSI THAN I THOUGHT IT BE, LIKE ON WHOLE OTHE LEVEL FRO HUGGING.
HA HA!
HA HA HA!
AH
HA
HA!
HA
HA!
I THOUGHT I WAS THE ONLY ONE. THAT'S WHY I COULDN'T LOOK YOU IN THE FACE. I THOUGHT YOU'D BE PLAYING IT OFF ALL COOL.
I WAS PRAYING YOU WOULDN'T LOOK AT ME!
BING
WELL, AT LEAST THAT HELPED TO BREAK THE ICE.
AH, MY SIDES ARE SPLITTING!
SO EMBARRASSING!
LET'S GO, THEN.
ガ
WHRRRR

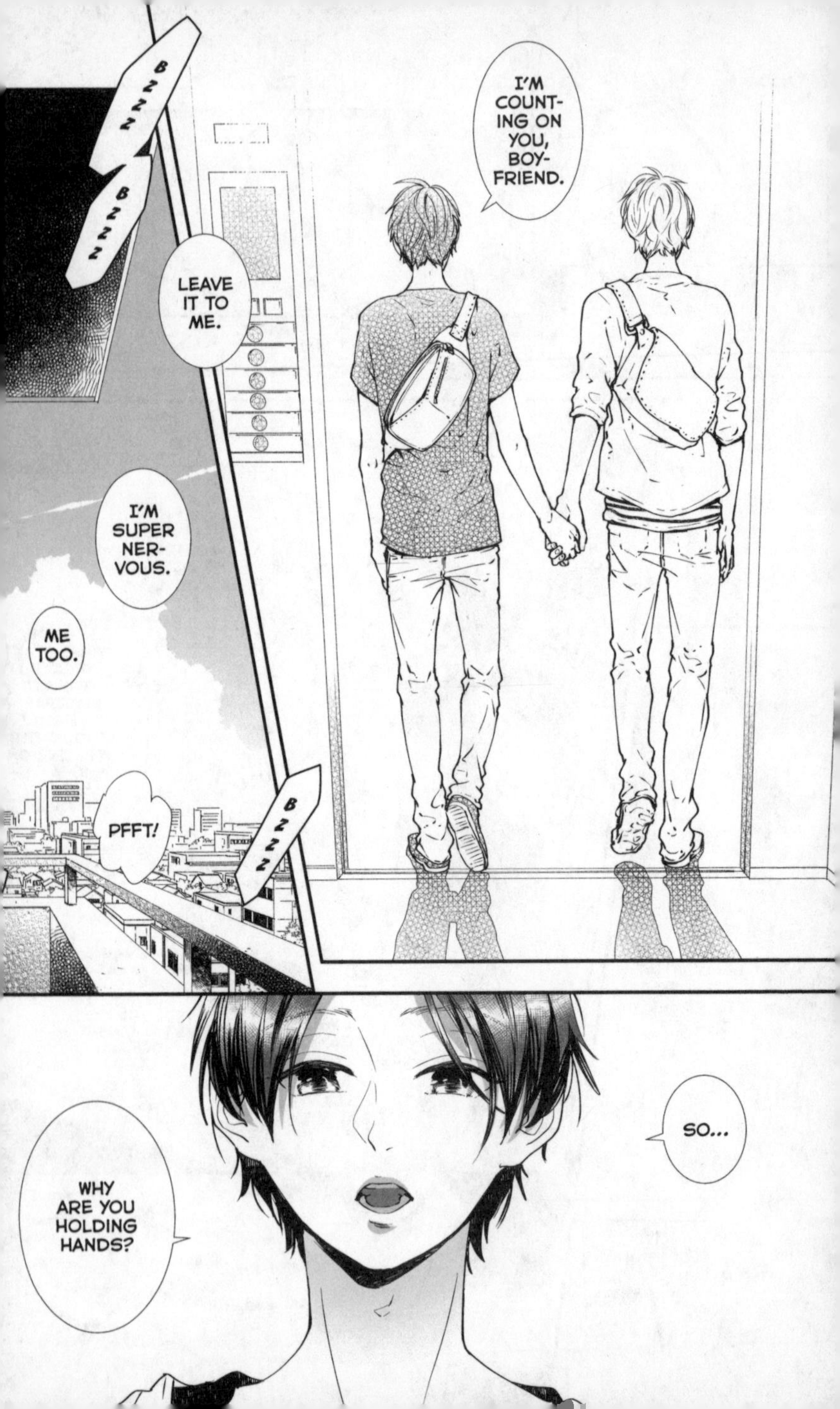
I'M COUNTING ON YOU, BOYFRIEND.
BZZZ
BZZZ
LEAVE IT TO ME.
I'M SUPER NERVOUS.
ME TOO.
PFFT!
BZZZ
SO...
WHY ARE YOU HOLDING HANDS?

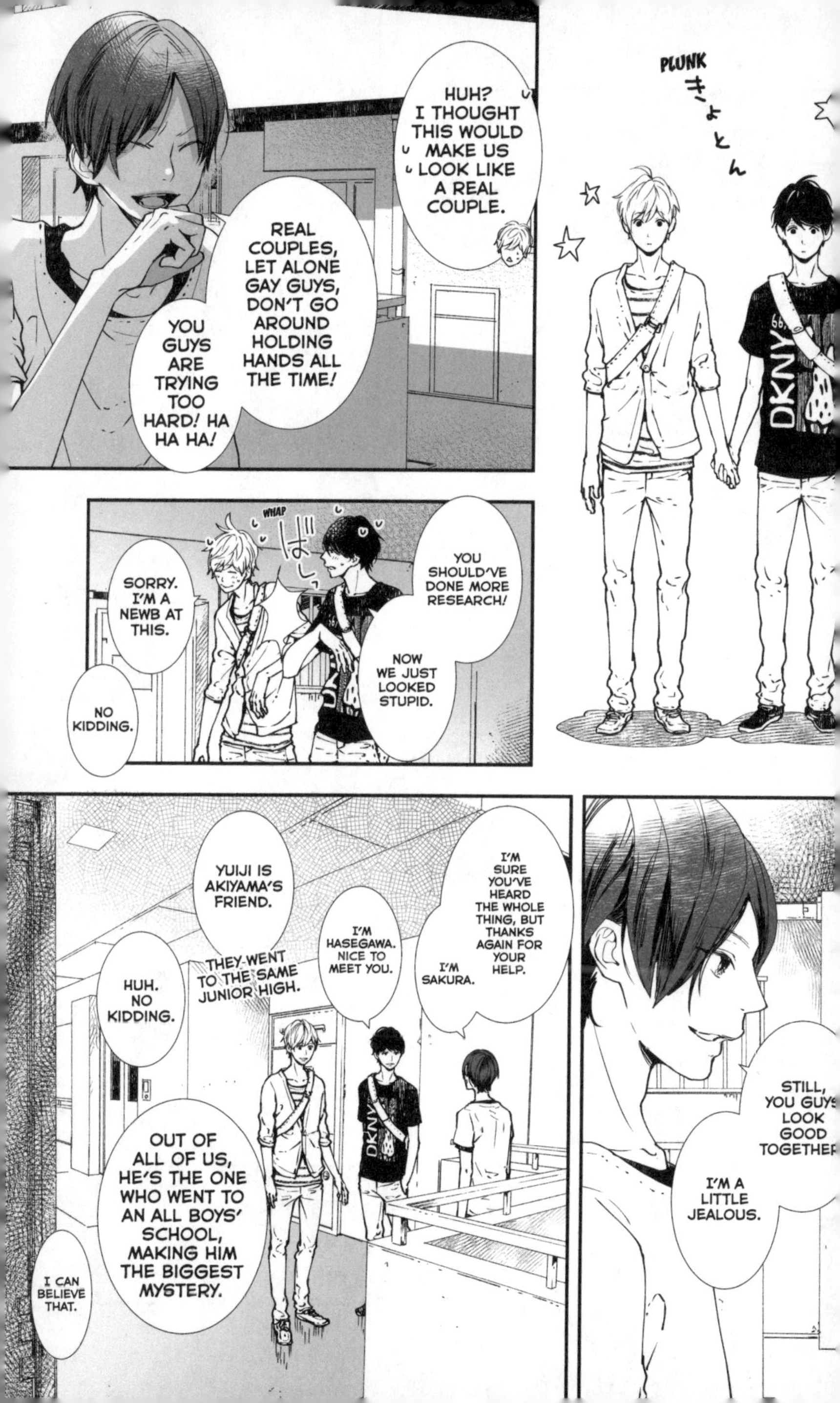
PLUNK
きょとん
HUH? I THOUGHT THIS WOULD MAKE US LOOK LIKE A REAL COUPLE.
REAL COUPLES, LET ALONE GAY GUYS, DON'T GO AROUND HOLDING HANDS ALL THE TIME!
YOU GUYS ARE TRYING TOO HARD! HA HA HA!
WHAP
ばしっ
YOU SHOULD'VE DONE MORE RESEARCH!
NOW WE JUST LOOKED STUPID.
SORRY. I'M A NEWB AT THIS.
NO KIDDING.
STILL, YOU GUYS LOOK GOOD TOGETHER
I'M A LITTLE JEALOUS.
I'M SURE YOU'VE HEARD THE WHOLE THING, BUT THANKS AGAIN FOR YOUR HELP.
I'M SAKURA.
I'M HASEGAWA. NICE TO MEET YOU.
YUIJI IS AKIYAMA'S FRIEND.
THEY WENT TO THE SAME JUNIOR HIGH.
HUH. NO KIDDING.
OUT OF ALL OF US, HE'S THE ONE WHO WENT TO AN ALL BOYS' SCHOOL, MAKING HIM THE BIGGEST MYSTERY.
I CAN BELIEVE THAT.

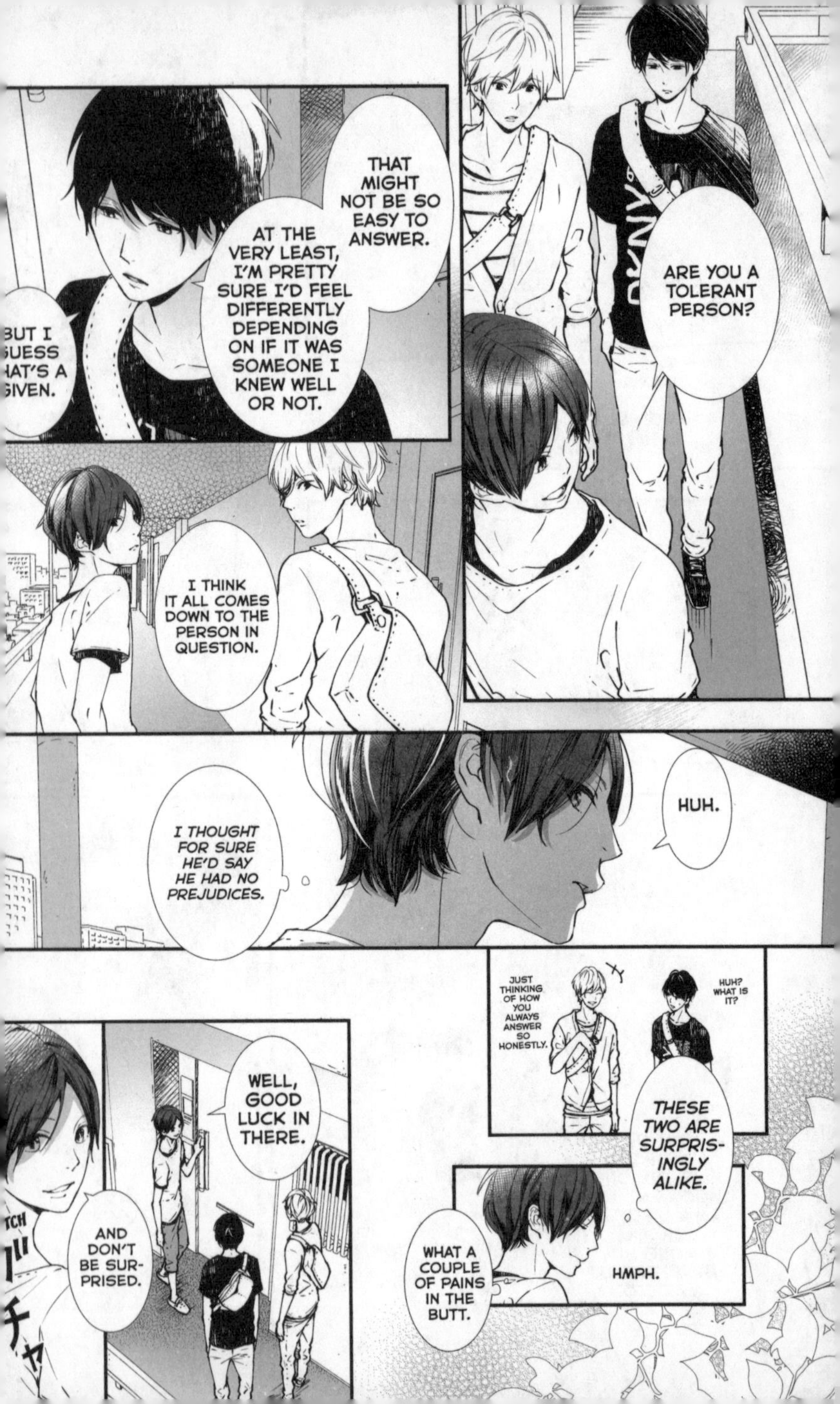
ARE YOU A TOLERANT PERSON?
THAT MIGHT NOT BE SO EASY TO ANSWER.
AT THE VERY LEAST, I'M PRETTY SURE I'D FEEL DIFFERENTLY DEPENDING ON IF IT WAS SOMEONE I KNEW WELL OR NOT.
BUT I UESS HAT'S A IVEN.
I THINK IT ALL COMES DOWN TO THE PERSON IN QUESTION.
HUH.
I THOUGHT FOR SURE HE'D SAY HE HAD NO PREJUDICES.
HUH? WHAT IS IT?
JUST THINKING OF HOW YOU ALWAYS ANSWER SO HONESTLY.
THESE TWO ARE SURPRIS-INGLY ALIKE.
HMPH.
WHAT A COUPLE OF PAINS IN THE BUTT.
WELL, GOOD LUCK IN THERE.
AND DON'T BE SUR-PRISED.

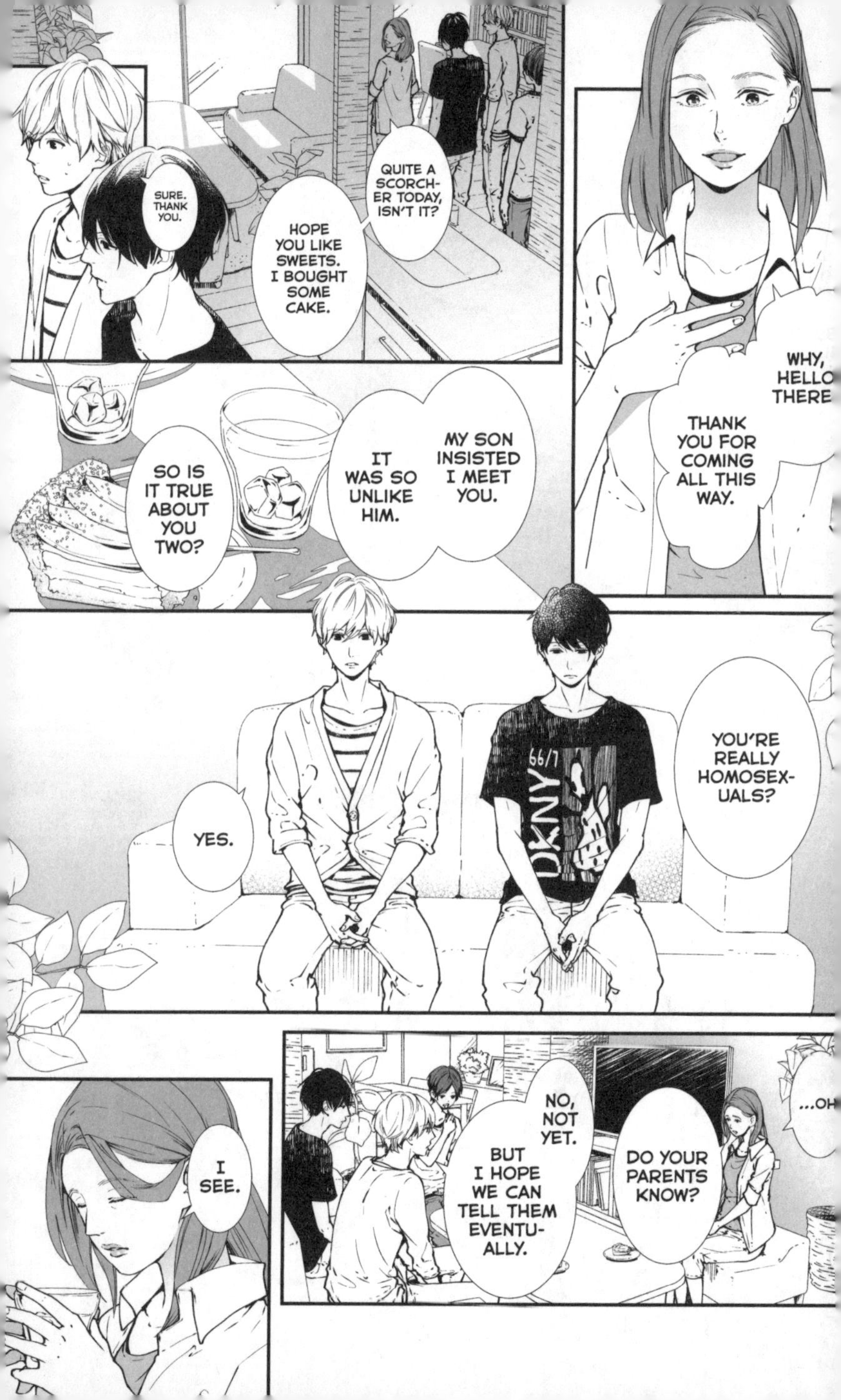
WHY, HELLO THERE
THANK YOU FOR COMING ALL THIS WAY.
QUITE A SCORCHER TODAY, ISN'T IT?
HOPE YOU LIKE SWEETS. I BOUGHT SOME CAKE.
SURE. THANK YOU.
MY SON INSISTED I MEET YOU.
IT WAS SO UNLIKE HIM.
SO IS IT TRUE ABOUT YOU TWO?
YOU'RE REALLY HOMOSEXUALS?
YES.
...OH
DO YOUR PARENTS KNOW?
NO, NOT YET.
BUT I HOPE WE CAN TELL THEM EVENTUALLY.
I SEE.

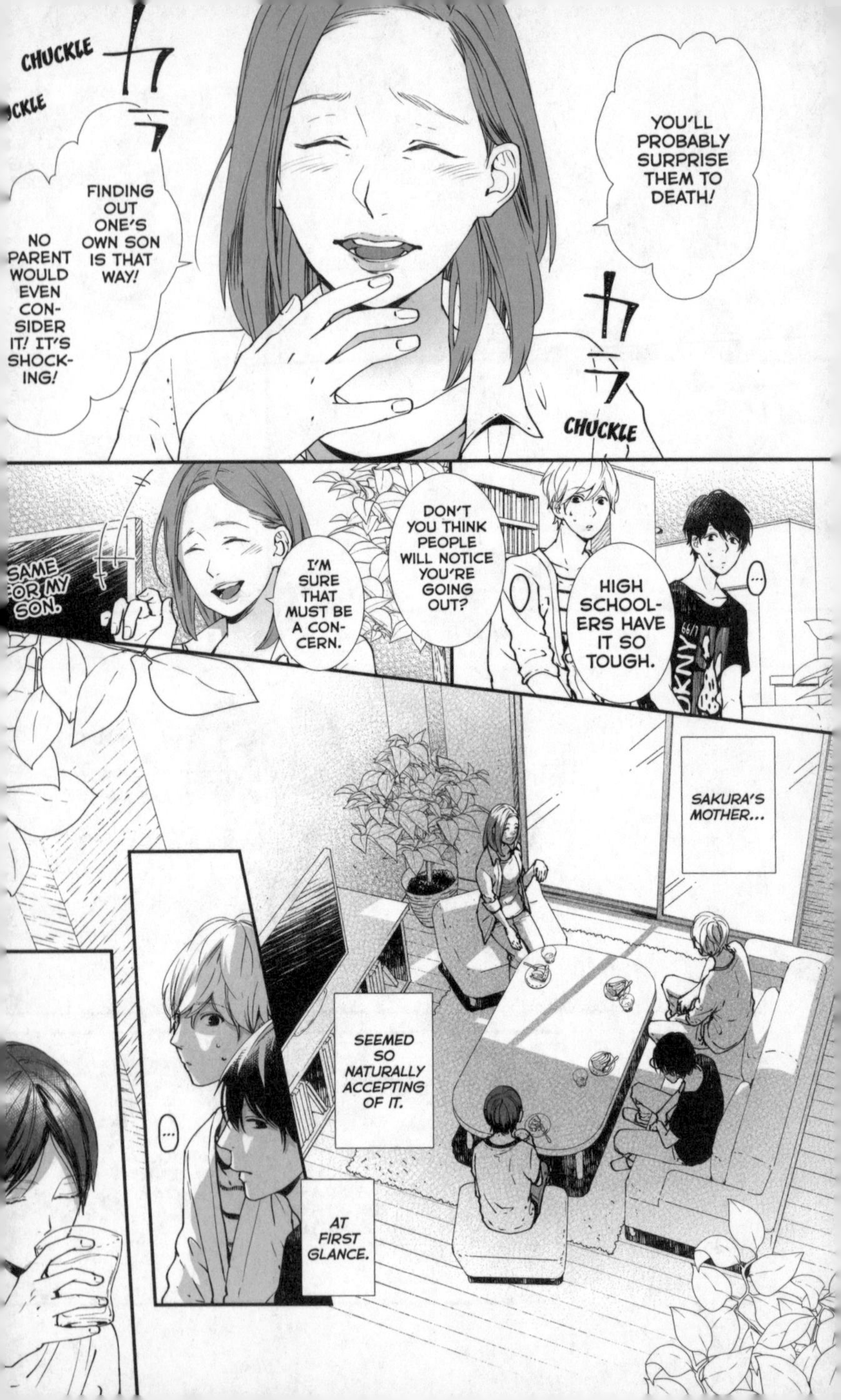
YOU'LL PROBABLY SURPRISE THEM TO DEATH!
CHUCKLE
FINDING OUT ONE'S OWN SON IS THAT WAY!
NO PARENT WOULD EVEN CONSIDER IT! IT'S SHOCKING!
CHUCKLE
CKLE
...
HIGH SCHOOLERS HAVE IT SO TOUGH.
DON'T YOU THINK PEOPLE WILL NOTICE YOU'RE GOING OUT?
I'M SURE THAT MUST BE A CONCERN.
SAME FOR MY SON.
SAKURA'S MOTHER...
SEEMED SO NATURALLY ACCEPTING OF IT.
AT FIRST GLANCE.
...

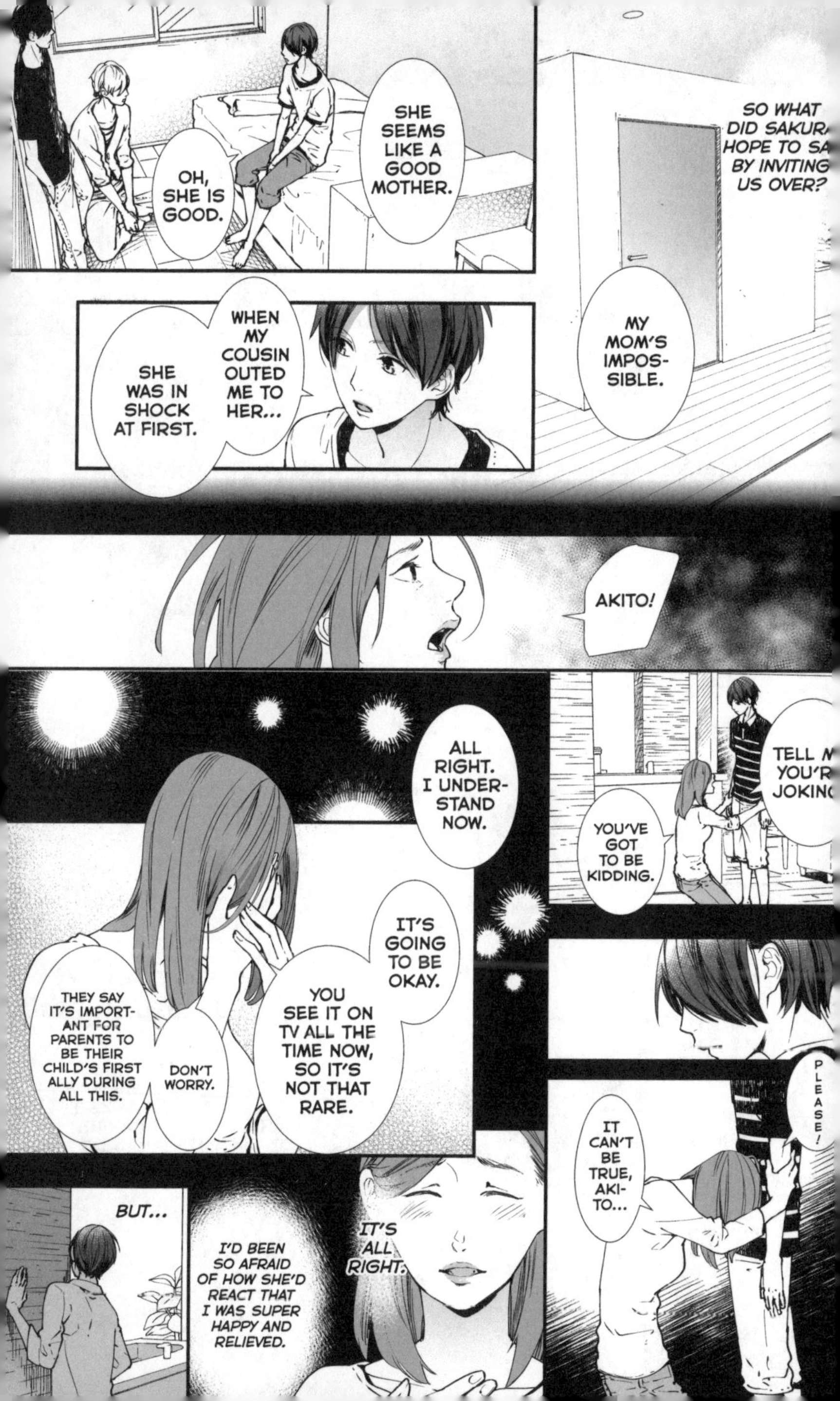
SO WHAT DID SAKUR HOPE TO SA BY INVITING US OVER?
MY MOM'S IMPOSSIBLE.
SHE SEEMS LIKE A GOOD MOTHER.
OH, SHE IS GOOD.
WHEN MY COUSIN OUTED ME TO HER...
SHE WAS IN SHOCK AT FIRST.
AKITO!
TELL M YOU'R JOKIN
YOU'VE GOT TO BE KIDDING.
PLEASE!
IT CAN'T BE TRUE, AKITO...
ALL RIGHT. I UNDERSTAND NOW.
IT'S GOING TO BE OKAY.
YOU SEE IT ON TV ALL THE TIME NOW, SO IT'S NOT THAT RARE.
DON'T WORRY.
THEY SAY IT'S IMPORTANT FOR PARENTS TO BE THEIR CHILD'S FIRST ALLY DURING ALL THIS.
IT'S ALL RIGHT.
I'D BEEN SO AFRAID OF HOW SHE'D REACT THAT I WAS SUPER HAPPY AND RELIEVED.
BUT...

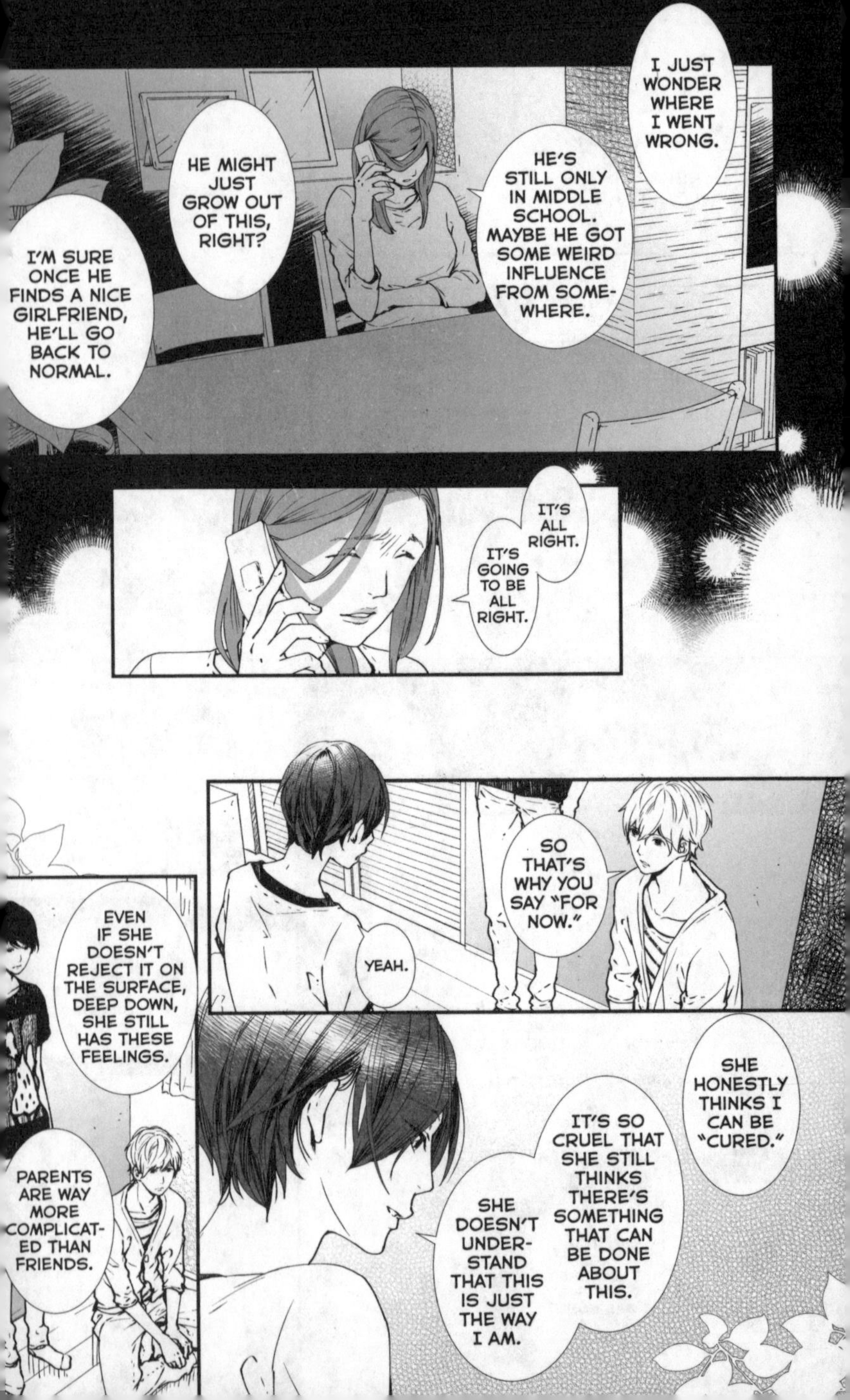

I JUST WONDER WHERE I WENT WRONG.
HE'S STILL ONLY IN MIDDLE SCHOOL. MAYBE HE GOT SOME WEIRD INFLUENCE FROM SOME-WHERE.
HE MIGHT JUST GROW OUT OF THIS, RIGHT?
I'M SURE ONCE HE FINDS A NICE GIRLFRIEND, HE'LL GO BACK TO NORMAL.
IT'S ALL RIGHT.
IT'S GOING TO BE ALL RIGHT.
SO THAT'S WHY YOU SAY "FOR NOW."
YEAH.
SHE HONESTLY THINKS I CAN BE "CURED."
IT'S SO CRUEL THAT SHE STILL THINKS THERE'S SOMETHING THAT CAN BE DONE ABOUT THIS.
SHE DOESN'T UNDER-STAND THAT THIS IS JUST THE WAY I AM.
EVEN IF SHE DOESN'T REJECT IT ON THE SURFACE, DEEP DOWN, SHE STILL HAS THESE FEELINGS.
PARENTS ARE WAY MORE COMPLICAT-ED THAN FRIENDS.

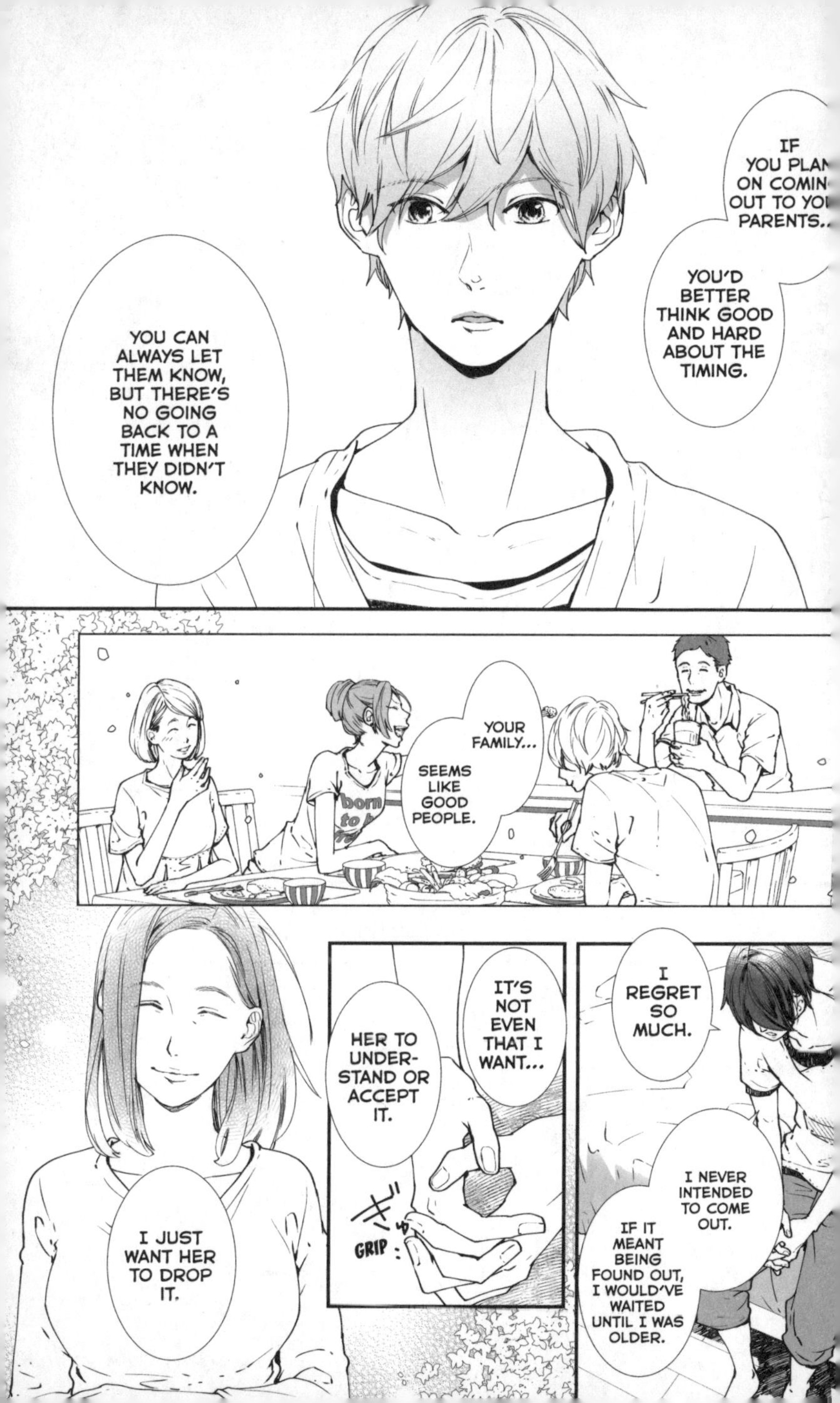
IF YOU PLAN ON COMIN OUT TO YO PARENTS...
YOU'D BETTER THINK GOOD AND HARD ABOUT THE TIMING.
YOU CAN ALWAYS LET THEM KNOW, BUT THERE'S NO GOING BACK TO A TIME WHEN THEY DIDN'T KNOW.
YOUR FAMILY...
SEEMS LIKE GOOD PEOPLE.
I REGRET SO MUCH.
I NEVER INTENDED TO COME OUT.
IF IT MEANT BEING FOUND OUT, I WOULD'VE WAITED UNTIL I WAS OLDER.
IT'S NOT EVEN THAT I WANT...
HER TO UNDER-STAND OR ACCEPT IT.
GRIP
I JUST WANT HER TO DROP IT.

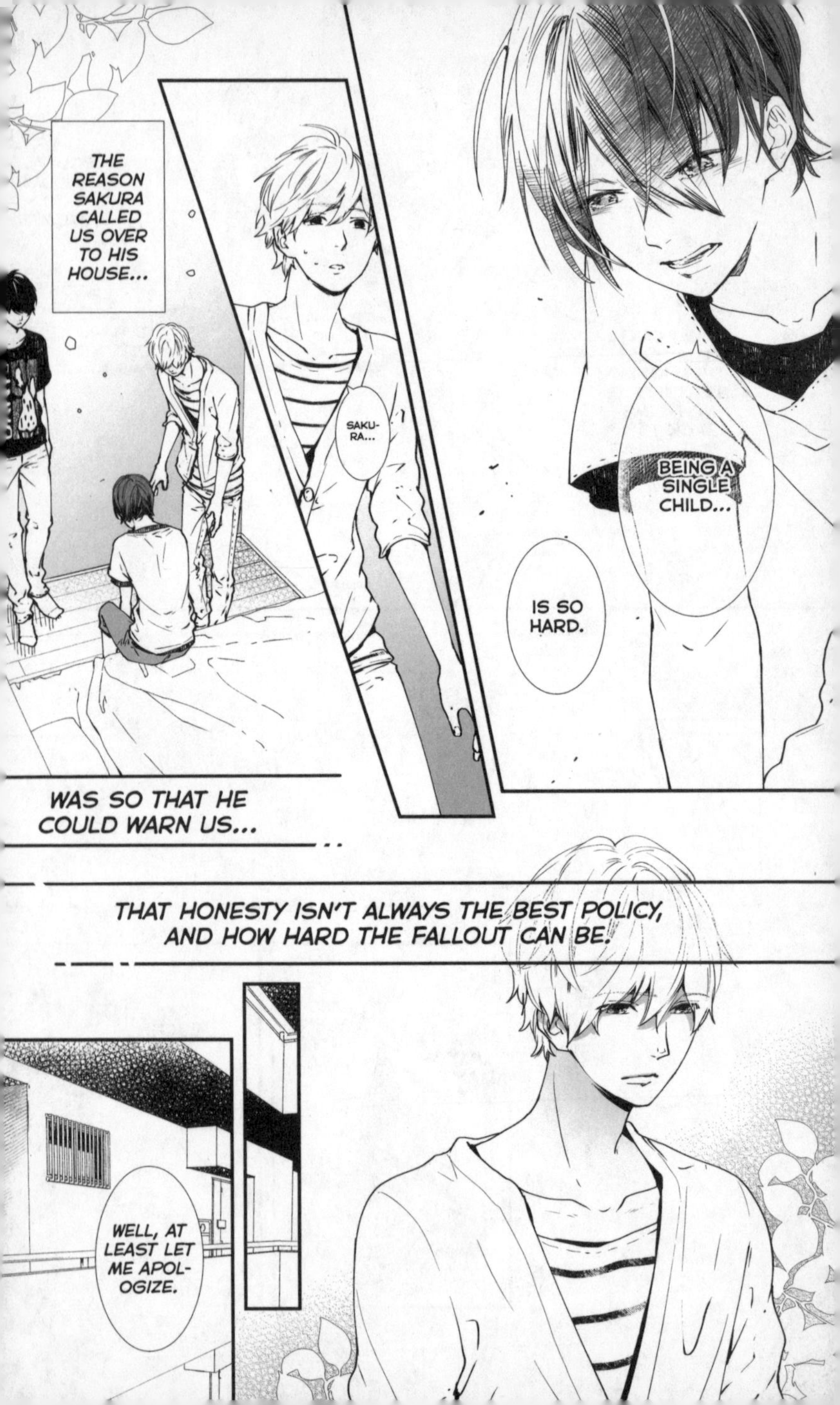
BEING A SINGLE CHILD...
IS SO HARD.
SAKU-RA...
THE REASON SAKURA CALLED US OVER TO HIS HOUSE...
WAS SO THAT HE COULD WARN US...
THAT HONESTY ISN'T ALWAYS THE BEST POLICY, AND HOW HARD THE FALLOUT CAN BE.
WELL, AT LEAST LET ME APOLO-GIZE.

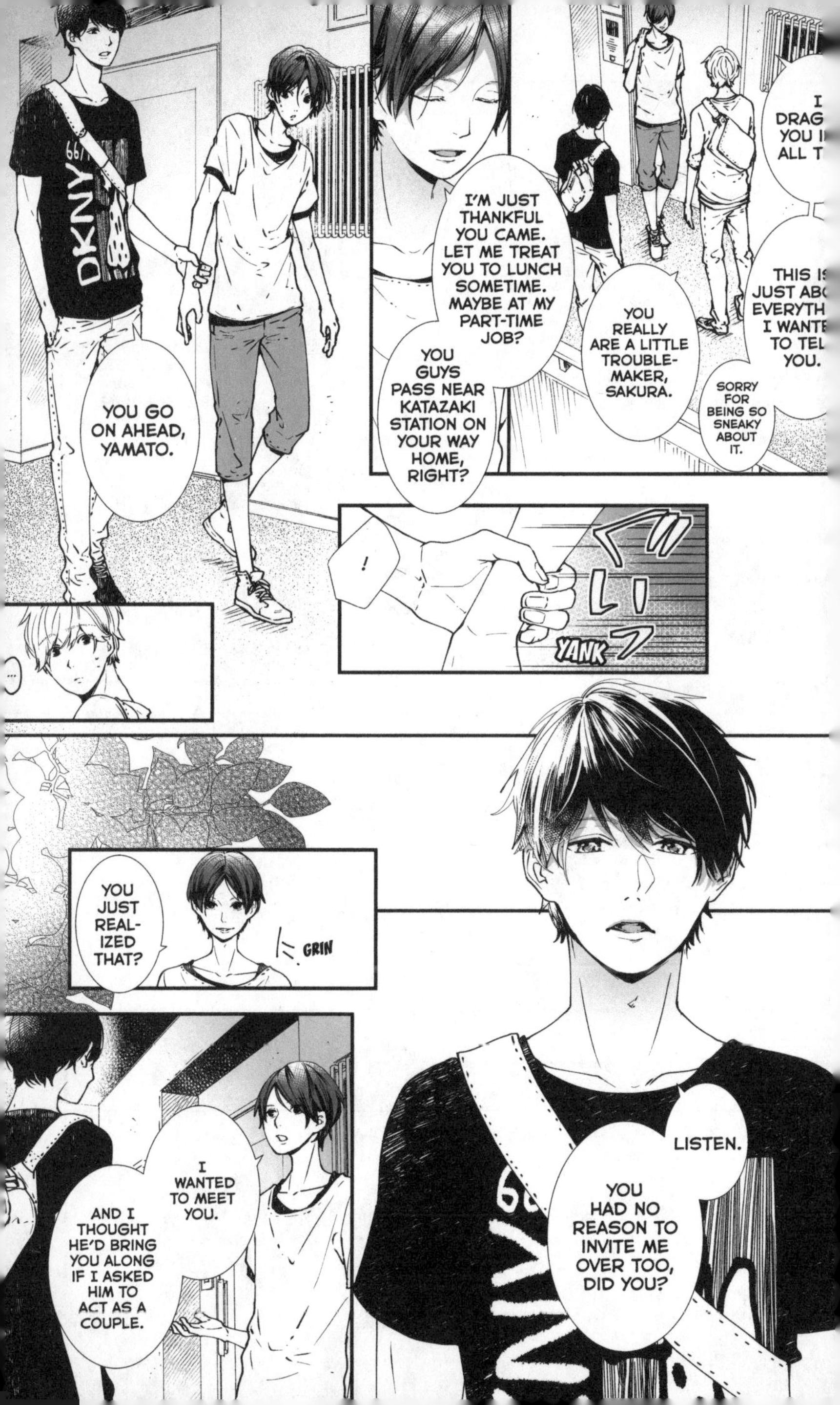
I DRAG YOU I ALL T
THIS IS JUST ABO EVERYTH I WANTE TO TEL YOU.
SORRY FOR BEING SO SNEAKY ABOUT IT.
YOU REALLY ARE A LITTLE TROUBLE-MAKER, SAKURA.
I'M JUST THANKFUL YOU CAME. LET ME TREAT YOU TO LUNCH SOMETIME. MAYBE AT MY PART-TIME JOB?
YOU GUYS PASS NEAR KATAZAKI STATION ON YOUR WAY HOME, RIGHT?
!
YANK
YOU GO ON AHEAD, YAMATO.
...
LISTEN.
YOU HAD NO REASON TO INVITE ME OVER TOO, DID YOU?
YOU JUST REAL-IZED THAT?
GRIN
I WANTED TO MEET YOU.
AND I THOUGHT HE'D BRING YOU ALONG IF I ASKED HIM TO ACT AS A COUPLE.

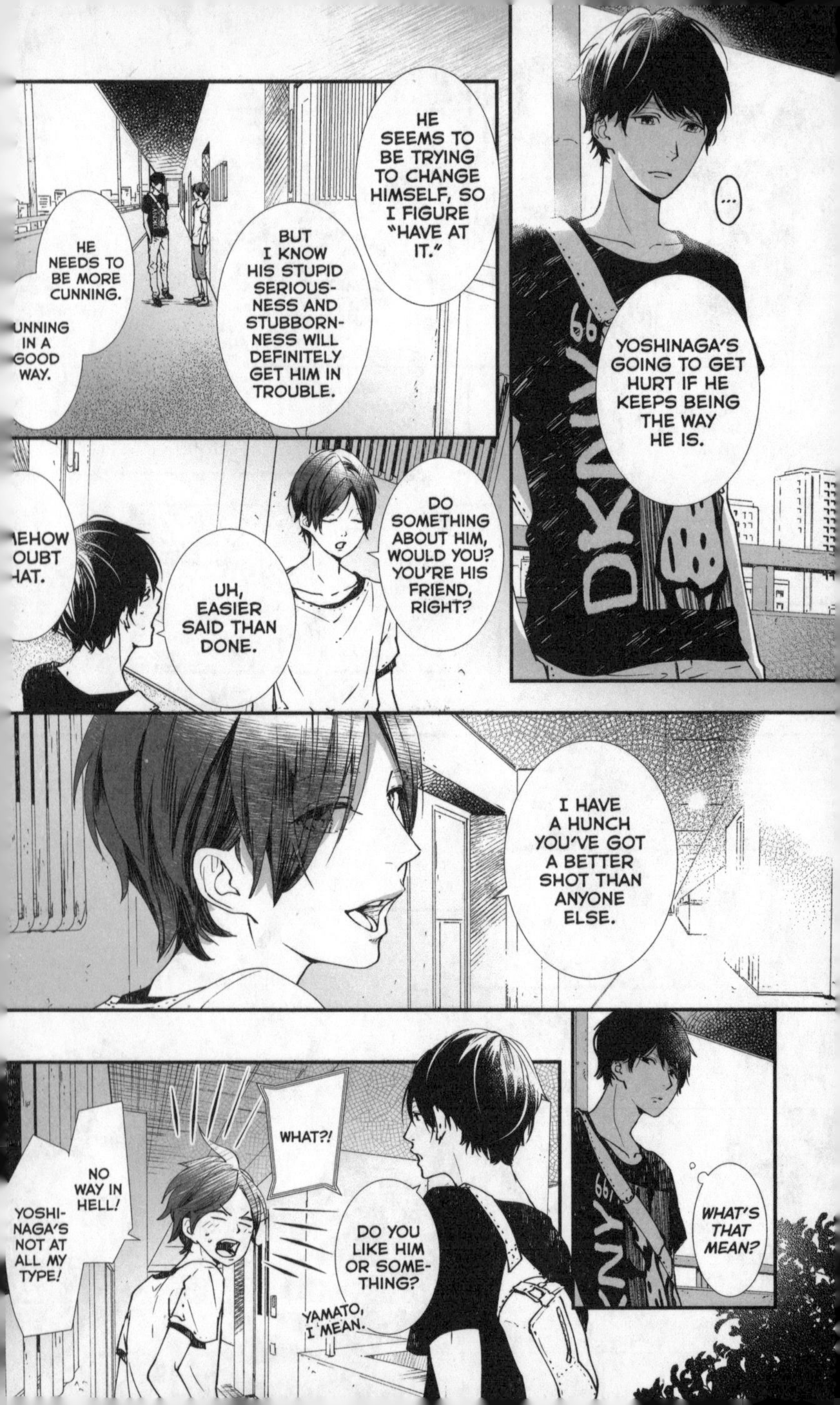
...
YOSHINAGA'S GOING TO GET HURT IF HE KEEPS BEING THE WAY HE IS.
HE SEEMS TO BE TRYING TO CHANGE HIMSELF, SO I FIGURE "HAVE AT IT."
BUT I KNOW HIS STUPID SERIOUS-NESS AND STUBBORN-NESS WILL DEFINITELY GET HIM IN TROUBLE.
HE NEEDS TO BE MORE CUNNING.
UNNING IN A GOOD WAY.
DO SOMETHING ABOUT HIM, WOULD YOU? YOU'RE HIS FRIEND, RIGHT?
UH, EASIER SAID THAN DONE.
EHOW OUBT HAT.
I HAVE A HUNCH YOU'VE GOT A BETTER SHOT THAN ANYONE ELSE.
WHAT'S THAT MEAN?
DO YOU LIKE HIM OR SOME-THING?
YAMATO, I MEAN.
WHAT?!
NO WAY IN HELL!
YOSHI-NAGA'S NOT AT ALL MY TYPE!

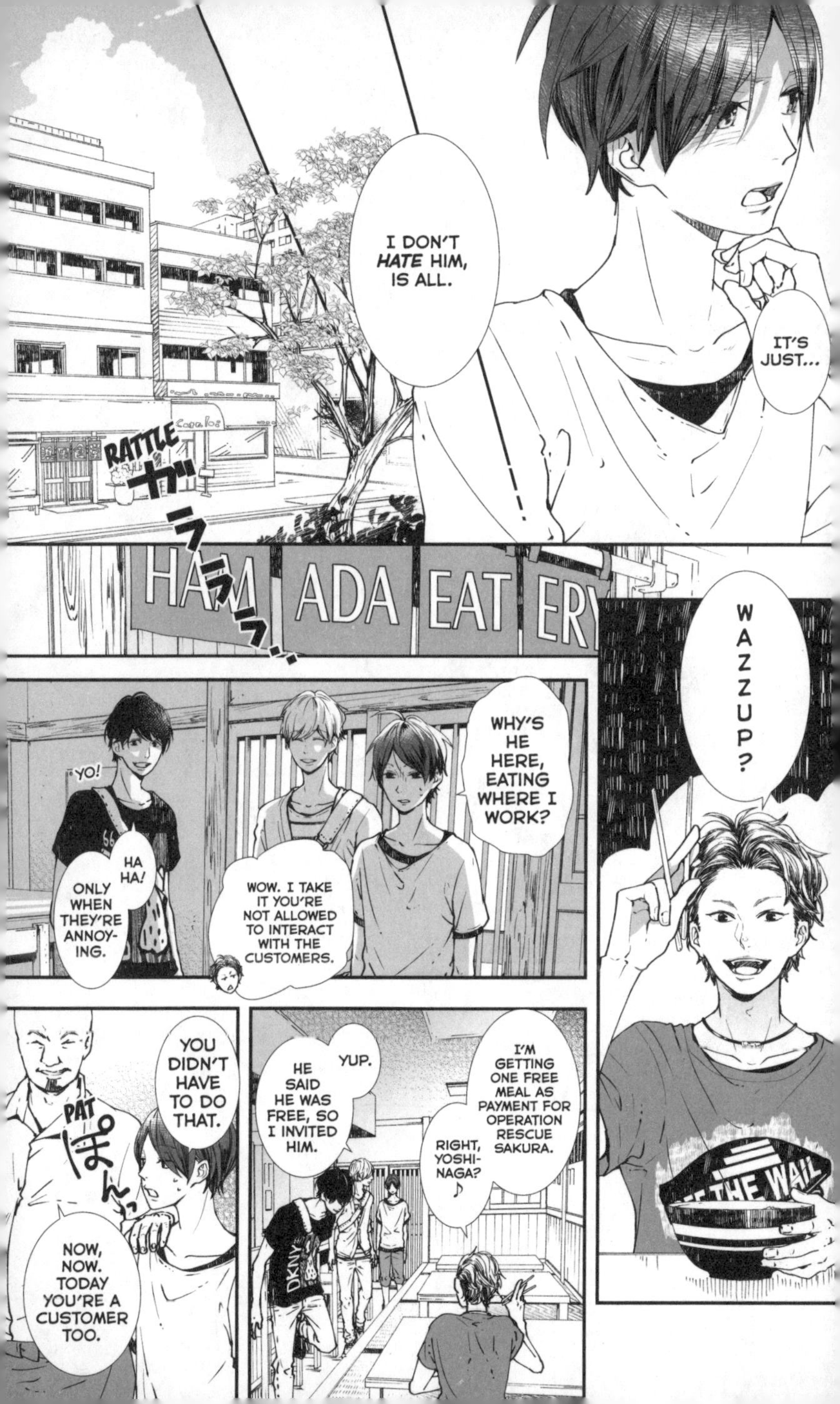
I DON'T *HATE* HIM, IS ALL.
IT'S JUST...
RATTLE
WAZZUP?
HAMADA EATERY
WHY'S HE HERE, EATING WHERE I WORK?
WOW. I TAKE IT YOU'RE NOT ALLOWED TO INTERACT WITH THE CUSTOMERS.
HA HA! ONLY WHEN THEY'RE ANNOY-ING.
YO!
I'M GETTING ONE FREE MEAL AS PAYMENT FOR OPERATION RESCUE SAKURA.
RIGHT, YOSHI-NAGA? ♪
YUP.
HE SAID HE WAS FREE, SO I INVITED HIM.
YOU DIDN'T HAVE TO DO THAT.
PAT
NOW, NOW. TODAY YOU'RE A CUSTOMER TOO.

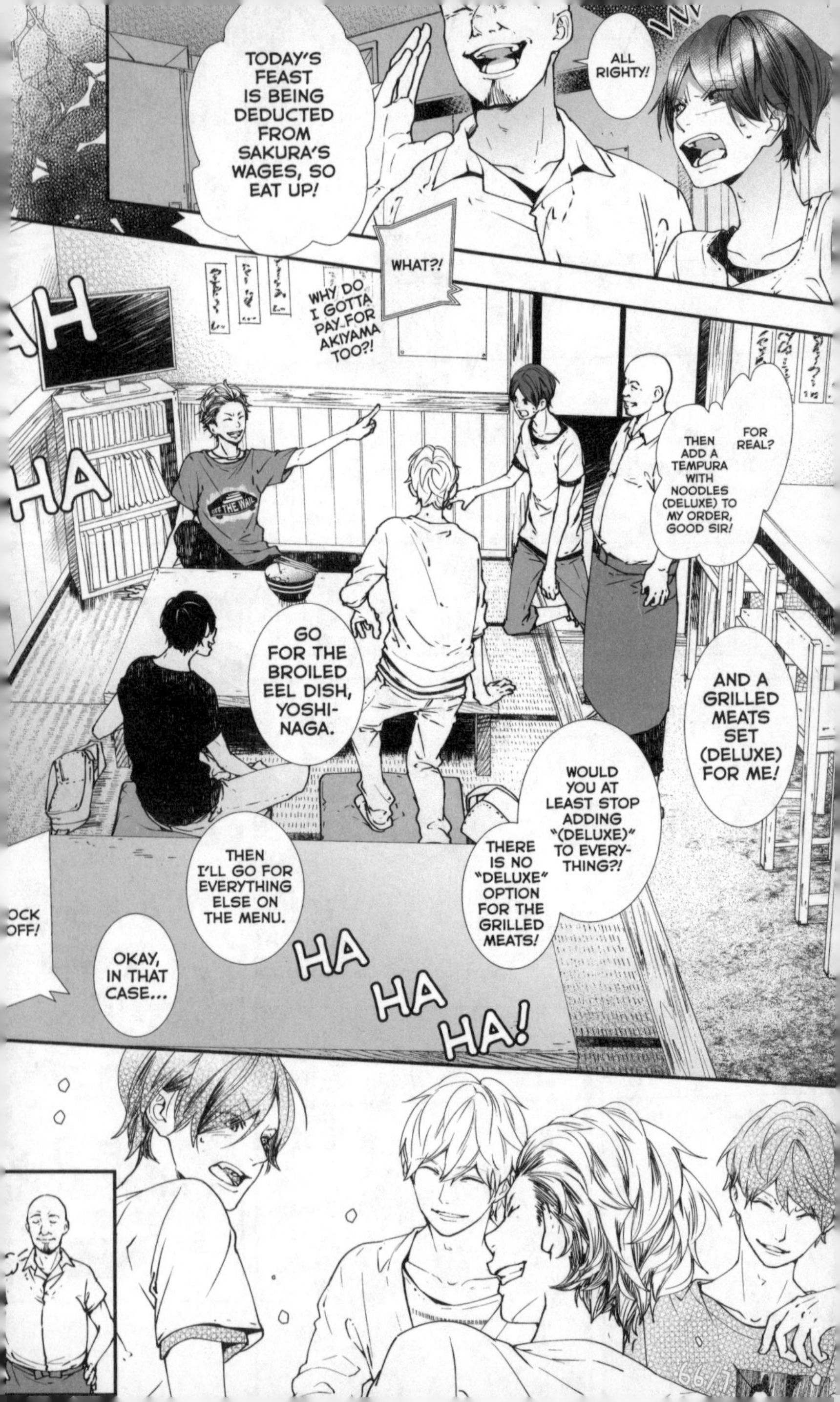
ALL RIGHTY!
TODAY'S FEAST IS BEING DEDUCTED FROM SAKURA'S WAGES, SO EAT UP!
WHAT?!
WHY DO I GOTTA PAY FOR AKIYAMA TOO?!
FOR REAL?
THEN ADD A TEMPURA WITH NOODLES (DELUXE) TO MY ORDER, GOOD SIR!
AH
HA
AND A GRILLED MEATS SET (DELUXE) FOR ME!
WOULD YOU AT LEAST STOP ADDING "(DELUXE)" TO EVERY-THING?!
THERE IS NO "DELUXE" OPTION FOR THE GRILLED MEATS!
GO FOR THE BROILED EEL DISH, YOSHI-NAGA.
THEN I'LL GO FOR EVERYTHING ELSE ON THE MENU.
OKAY, IN THAT CASE...
HA HA HA!
OCK OFF!

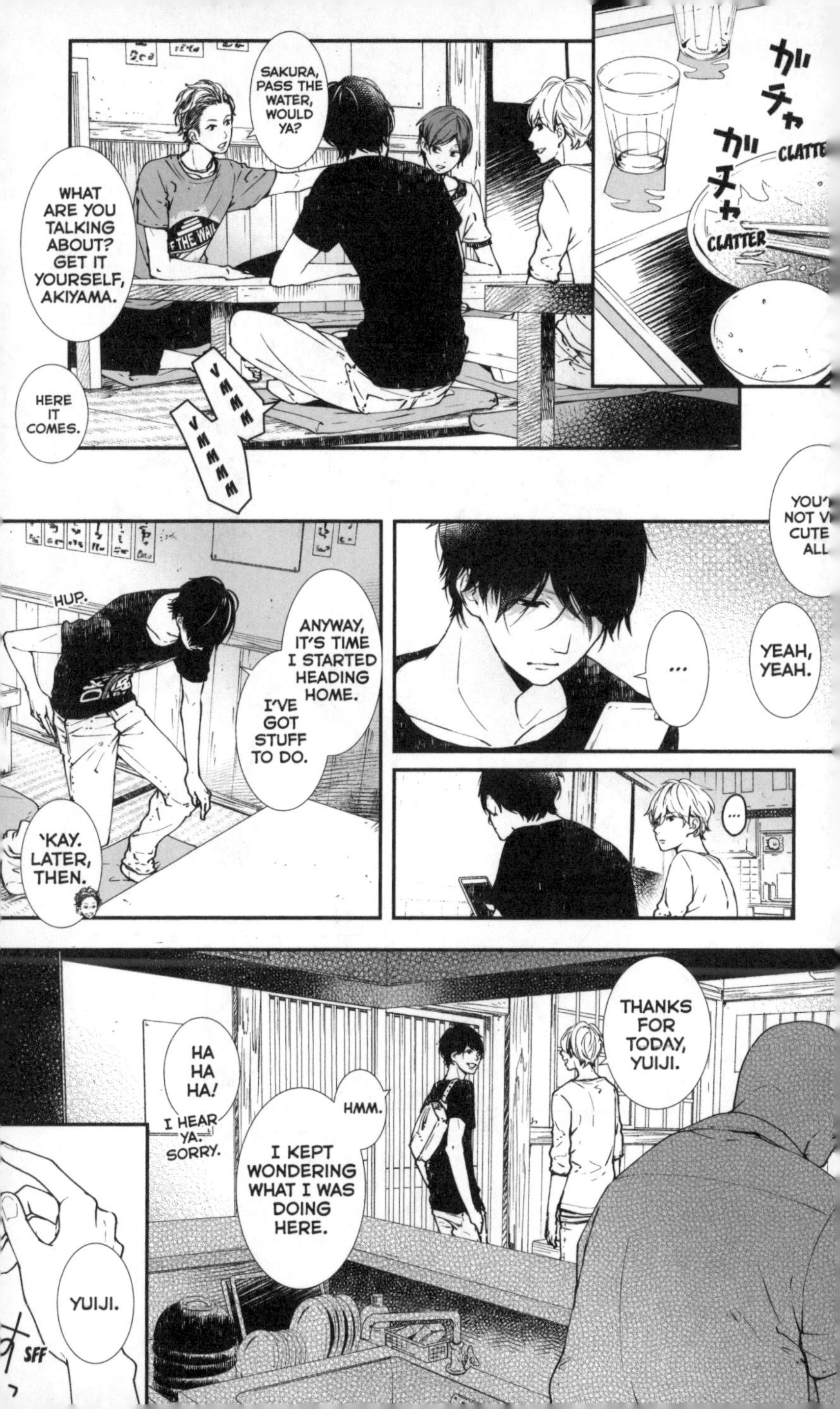

ガチャ
CLATTER
ガチャ
CLATTER
SAKURA, PASS THE WATER, WOULD YA?
WHAT ARE YOU TALKING ABOUT? GET IT YOURSELF, AKIYAMA.
HERE IT COMES.
VMMM
VMMMM
...
YEAH, YEAH.
...
HUP.
ANYWAY, IT'S TIME I STARTED HEADING HOME.
I'VE GOT STUFF TO DO.
'KAY. LATER, THEN.
THANKS FOR TODAY, YUIJI.
HMM.
I KEPT WONDERING WHAT I WAS DOING HERE.
HA HA HA!
I HEAR YA. SORRY.
YUIJI.
SFF

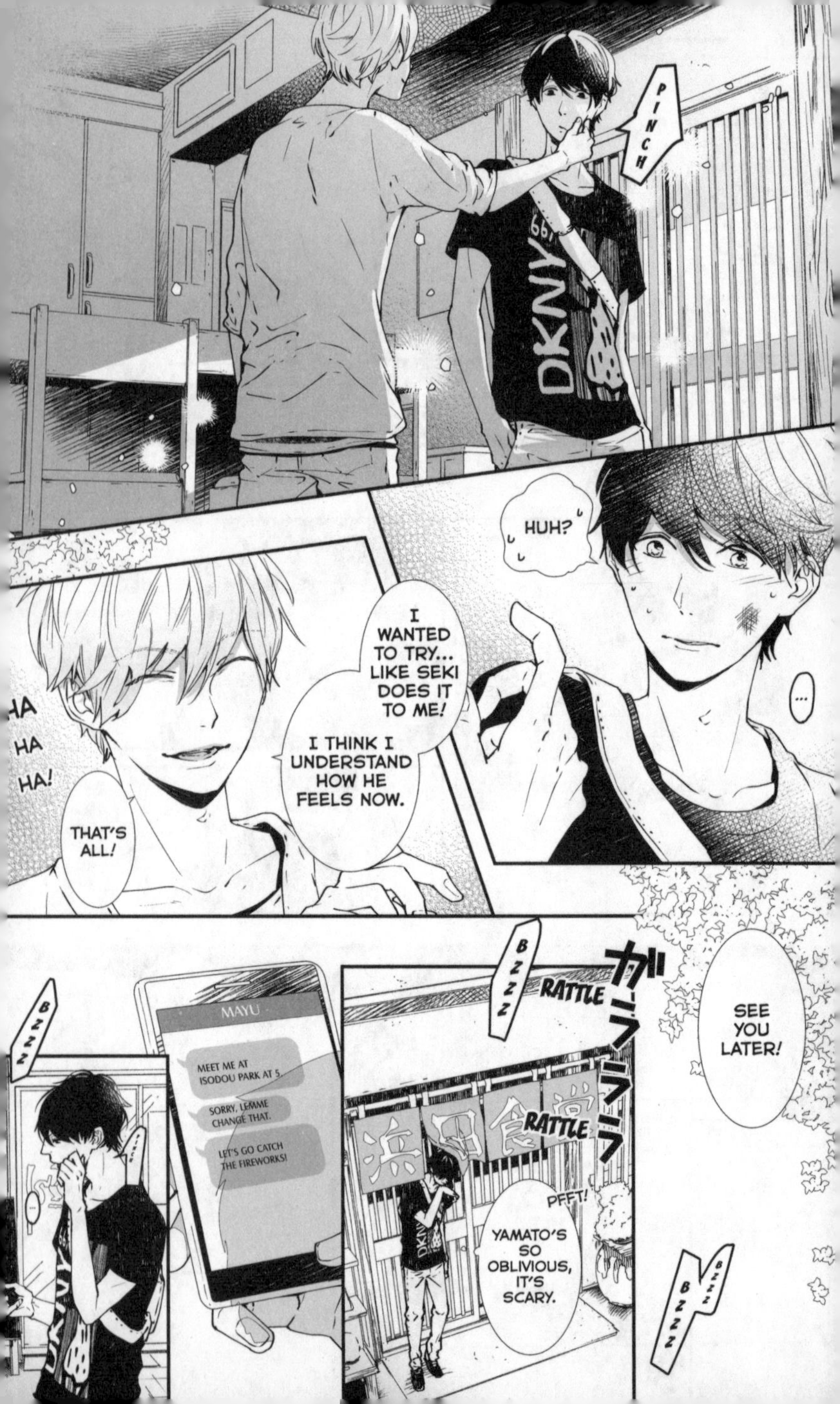
PINCH
HUH?
...
I WANTED TO TRY... LIKE SEKI DOES IT TO ME!
I THINK I UNDERSTAND HOW HE FEELS NOW.
HA HA HA!
THAT'S ALL!
SEE YOU LATER!
BZZZ
RATTLE
RATTLE
PFFT!
YAMATO'S SO OBLIVIOUS, IT'S SCARY.
BZZZ
BZZZ
MAYU
MEET ME AT ISODOU PARK AT 5.
SORRY, LEMME CHANGE THAT.
LET'S GO CATCH THE FIREWORKS!
BZZZ

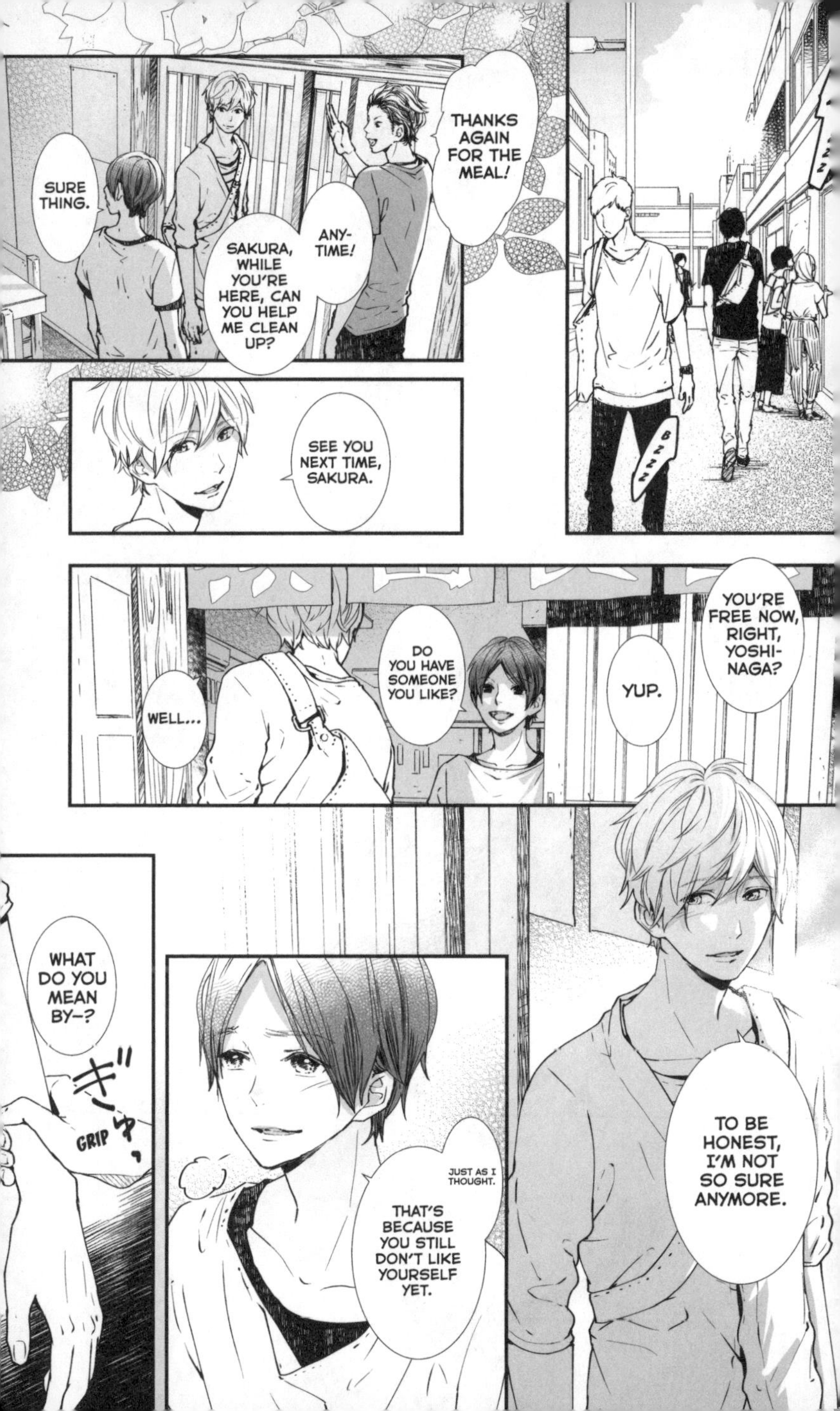
BZZZ
THANKS AGAIN FOR THE MEAL!
ANY-TIME!
SAKURA, WHILE YOU'RE HERE, CAN YOU HELP ME CLEAN UP?
SURE THING.
SEE YOU NEXT TIME, SAKURA.
YOU'RE FREE NOW, RIGHT, YOSHI-NAGA?
YUP.
DO YOU HAVE SOMEONE YOU LIKE?
WELL...
TO BE HONEST, I'M NOT SO SURE ANYMORE.
JUST AS I THOUGHT.
THAT'S BECAUSE YOU STILL DON'T LIKE YOURSELF YET.
WHAT DO YOU MEAN BY–?
GRIP

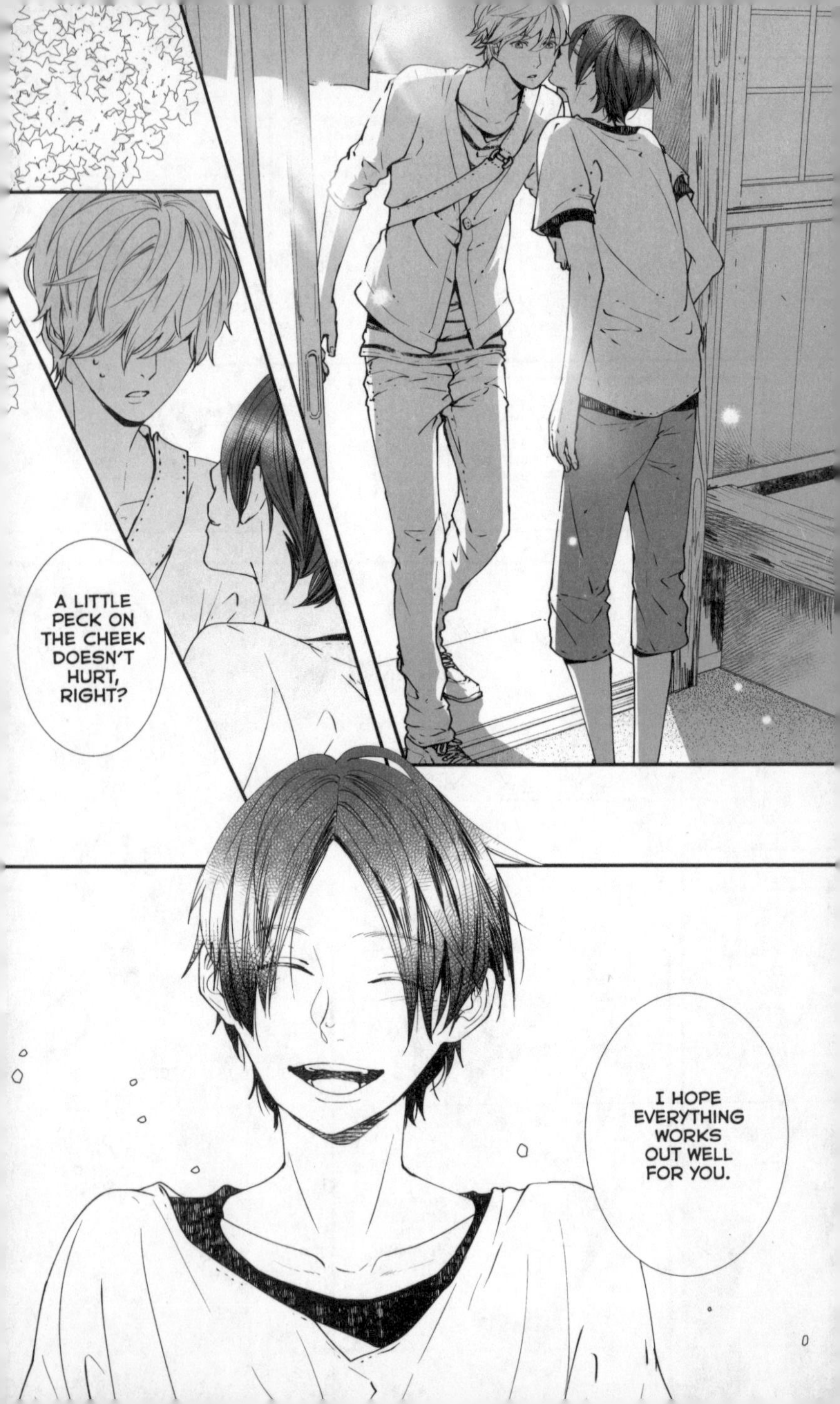
A LITTLE PECK ON THE CHEEK DOESN'T HURT, RIGHT?
I HOPE EVERYTHING WORKS OUT WELL FOR YOU.

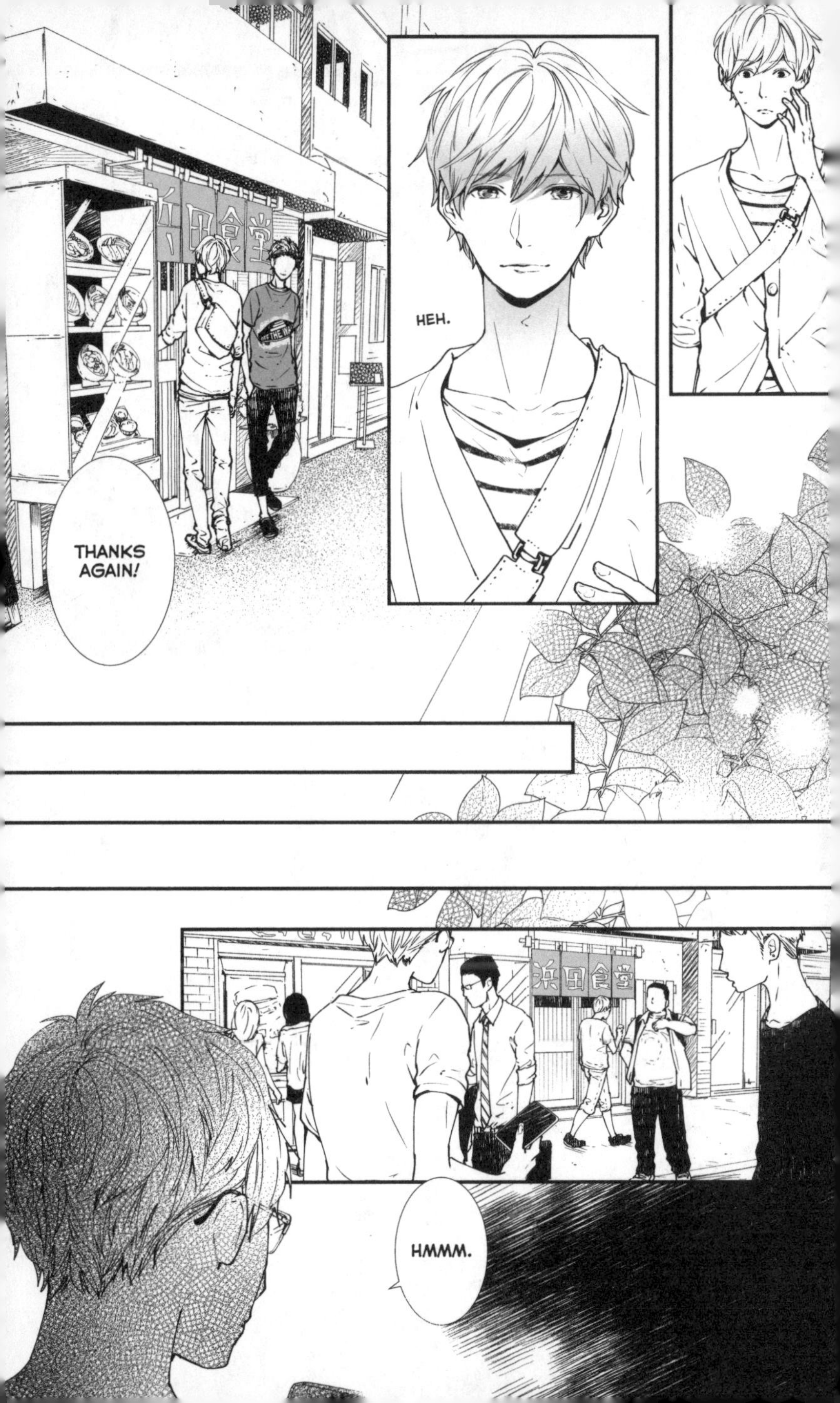
HEH.
THANKS AGAIN!
浜田食堂
HMMM.

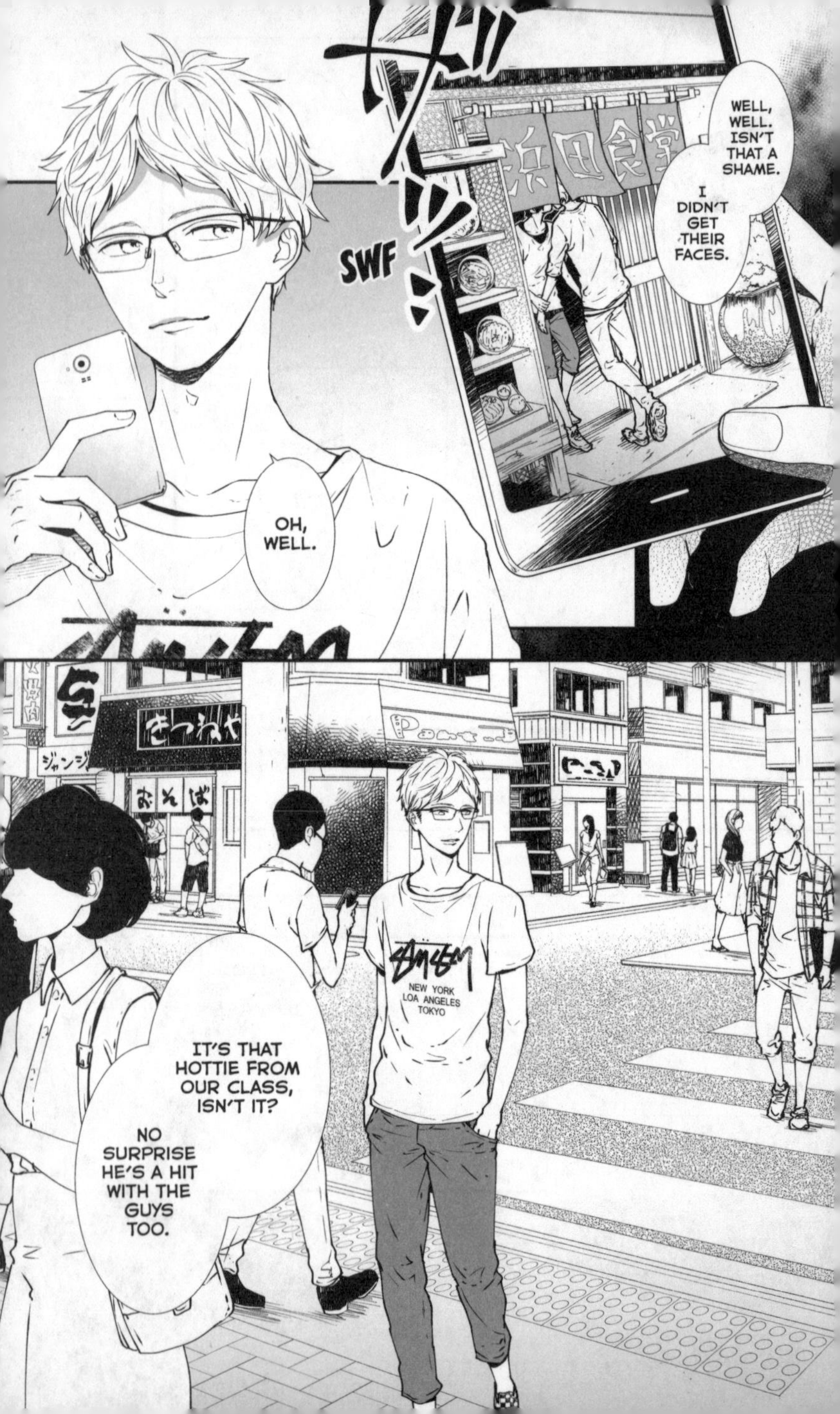

浜田食堂
WELL, WELL. ISN'T THAT A SHAME.
I DIDN'T GET THEIR FACES.
SWF
OH, WELL.
きつねや
おそば
NEW YORK
LOA ANGELES
TOKYO
IT'S THAT HOTTIE FROM OUR CLASS, ISN'T IT?
NO SURPRISE HE'S A HIT WITH THE GUYS TOO.

KOIMONOGATARI:
LOVE STORIES

2

LOVE STORIES.2 / TAGURA TOHRU

Chapter 7

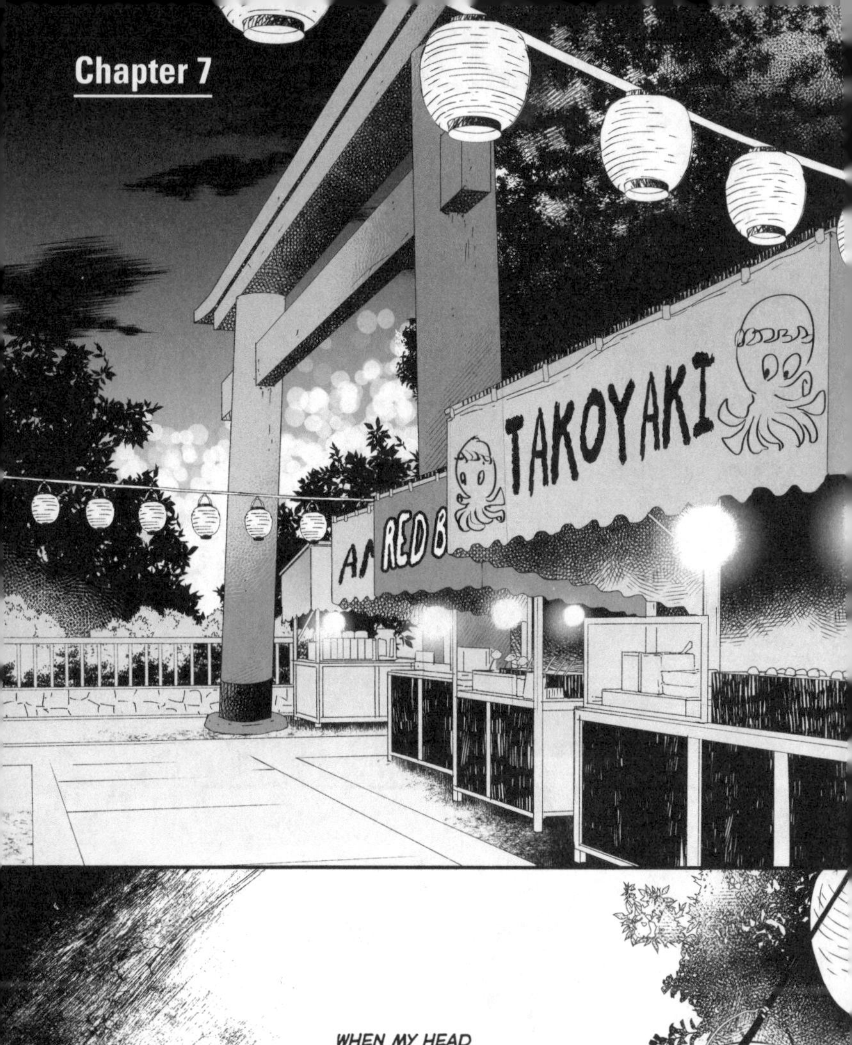
TAKOYAKI
RED B

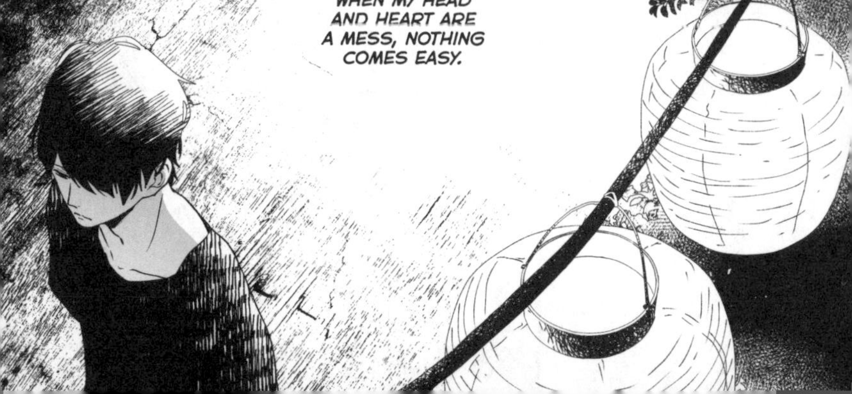
WHEN MY HEAD AND HEART ARE A MESS, NOTHING COMES EASY.

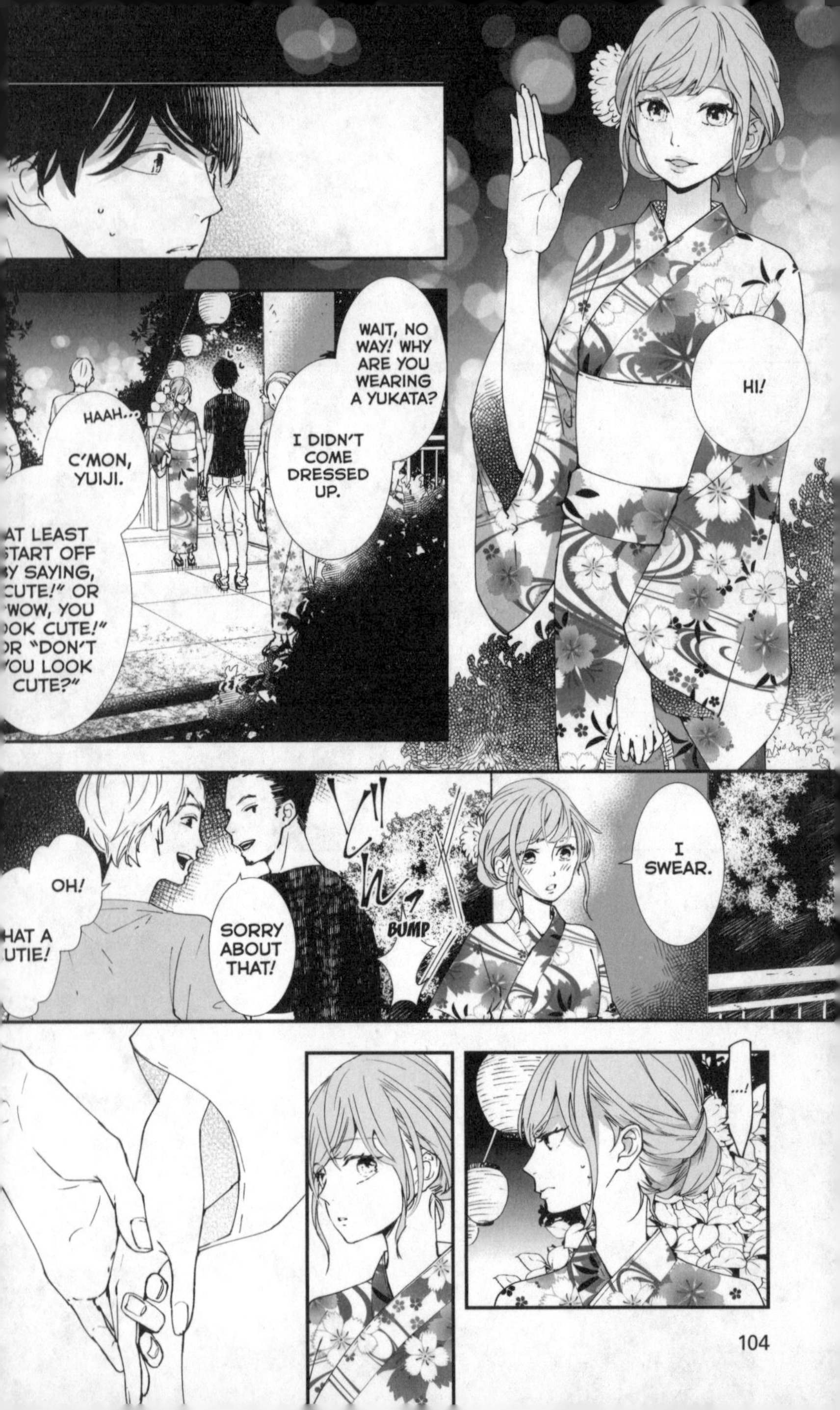
HI!
WAIT, NO WAY! WHY ARE YOU WEARING A YUKATA?
I DIDN'T COME DRESSED UP.
HAAH...
C'MON, YUIJI.
AT LEAST START OFF BY SAYING, "CUTE!" OR "WOW, YOU LOOK CUTE!" OR "DON'T YOU LOOK CUTE?"
I SWEAR.
BUMP
SORRY ABOUT THAT!
OH!
HAT A UTIE!
...!

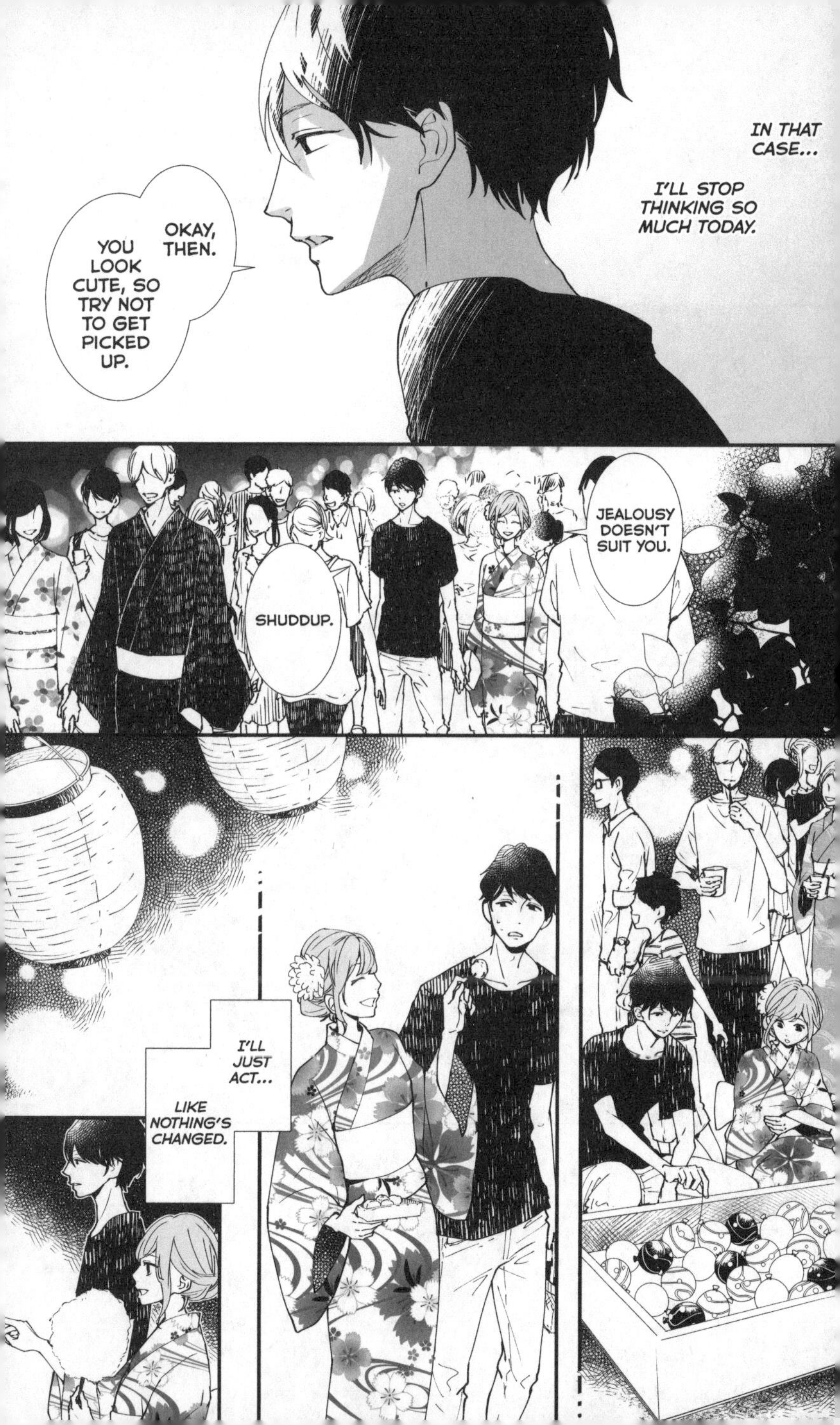
IN THAT CASE...
I'LL STOP THINKING SO MUCH TODAY.
OKAY, THEN.
YOU LOOK CUTE, SO TRY NOT TO GET PICKED UP.
JEALOUSY DOESN'T SUIT YOU.
SHUDDUP.
I'LL JUST ACT...
LIKE NOTHING'S CHANGED.

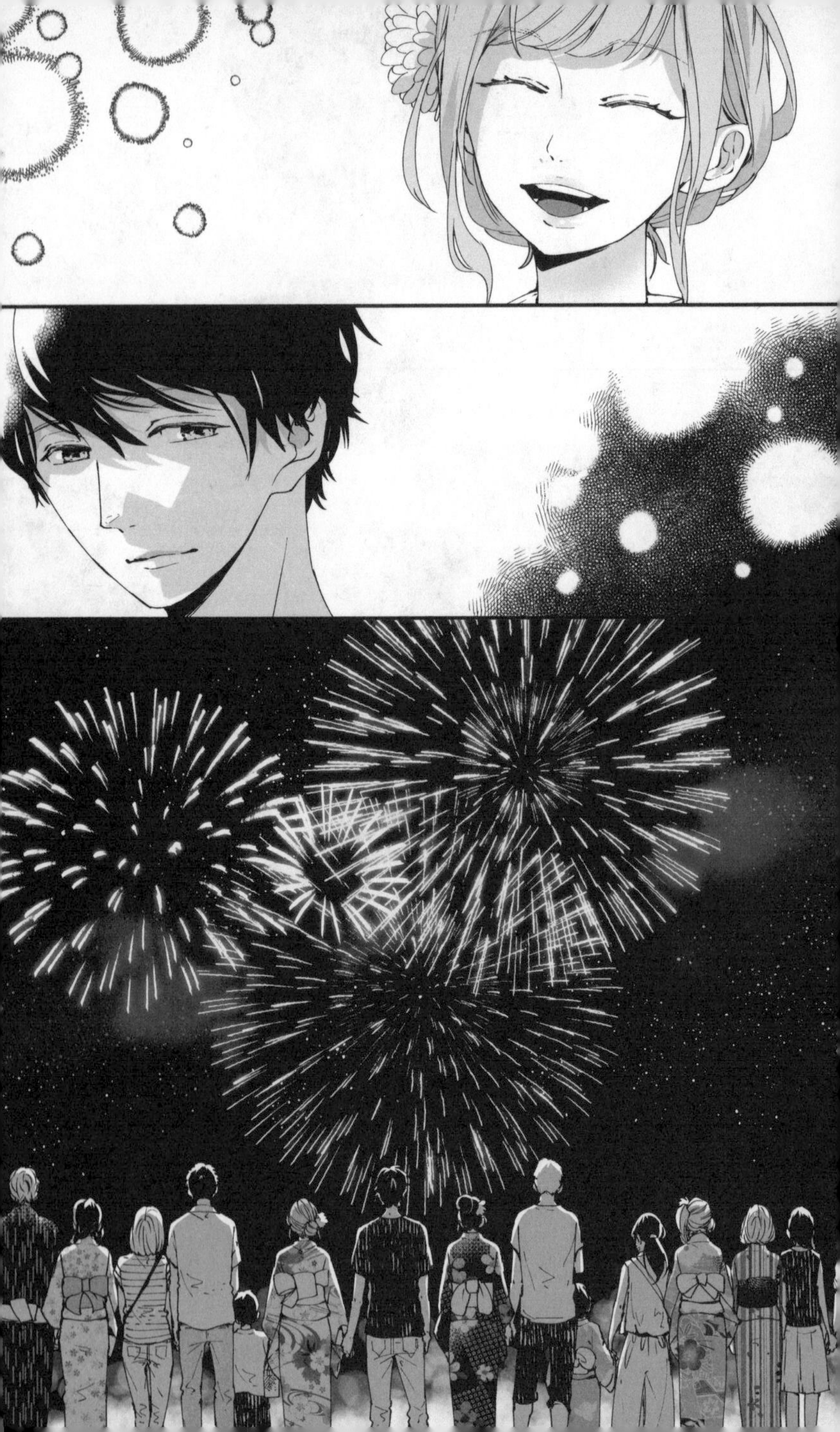

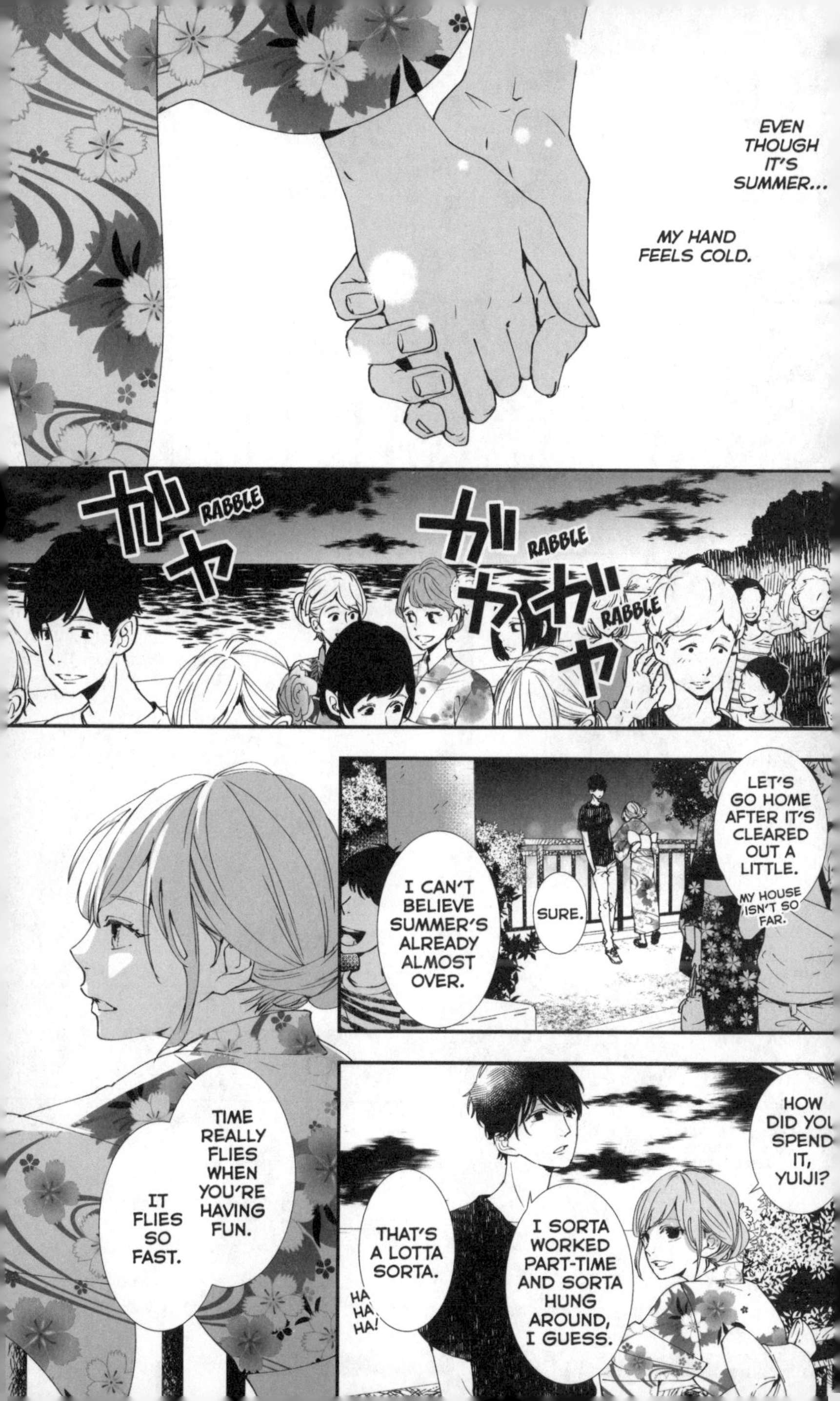

EVEN THOUGH IT'S SUMMER...
MY HAND FEELS COLD.
ガヤ
RABBLE
ガヤ
RABBLE
ガヤ
RABBLE
LET'S GO HOME AFTER IT'S CLEARED OUT A LITTLE.
MY HOUSE ISN'T SO FAR.
SURE.
I CAN'T BELIEVE SUMMER'S ALREADY ALMOST OVER.
HOW DID YOU SPEND IT, YUIJI?
I SORTA WORKED PART-TIME AND SORTA HUNG AROUND, I GUESS.
THAT'S A LOTTA SORTA.
HA HA HA!
TIME REALLY FLIES WHEN YOU'RE HAVING FUN.
IT FLIES SO FAST.

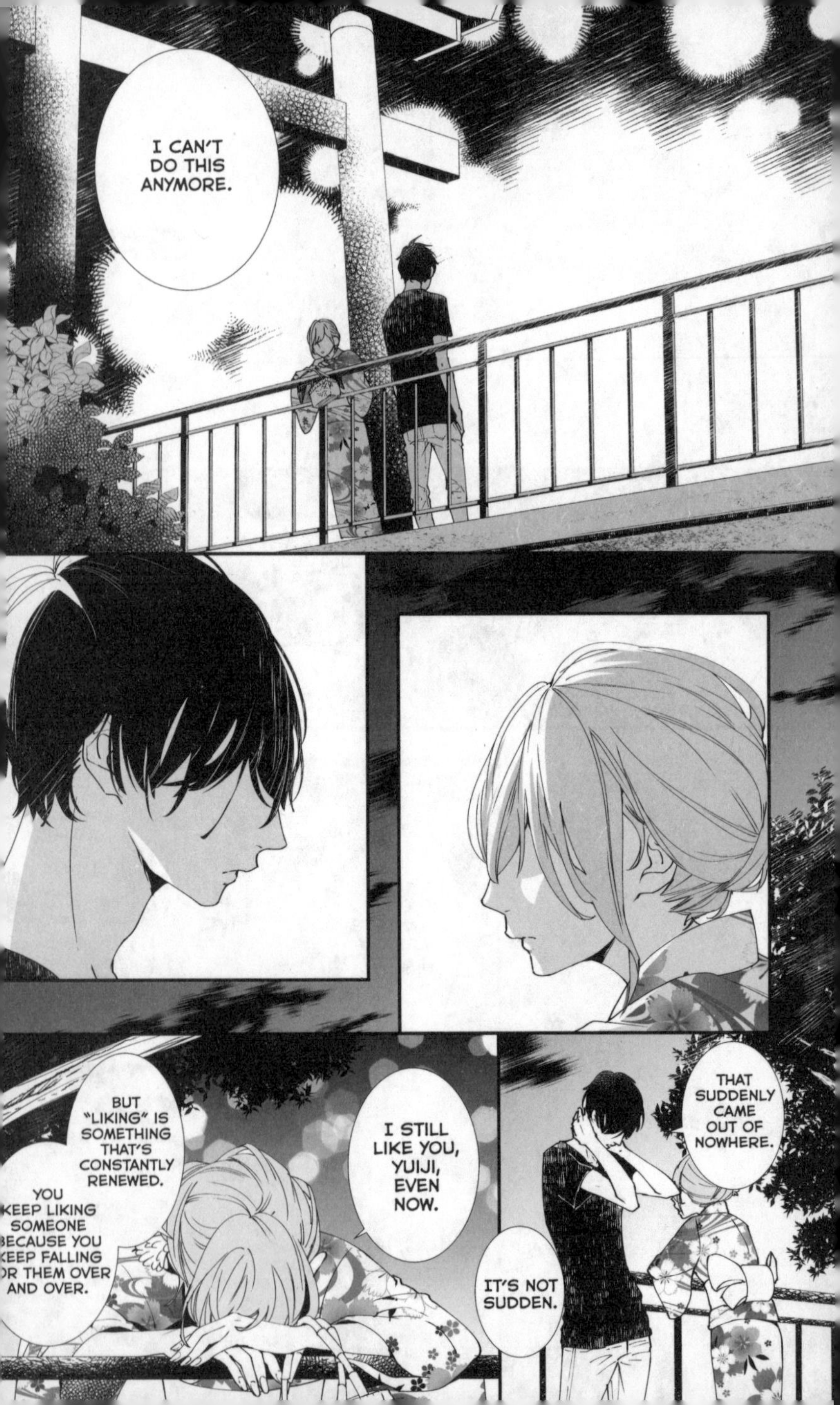
I CAN'T DO THIS ANYMORE.
THAT SUDDENLY CAME OUT OF NOWHERE.
IT'S NOT SUDDEN.
I STILL LIKE YOU, YUIJI, EVEN NOW.
BUT "LIKING" IS SOMETHING THAT'S CONSTANTLY RENEWED.
YOU KEEP LIKING SOMEONE BECAUSE YOU KEEP FALLING FOR THEM OVER AND OVER.

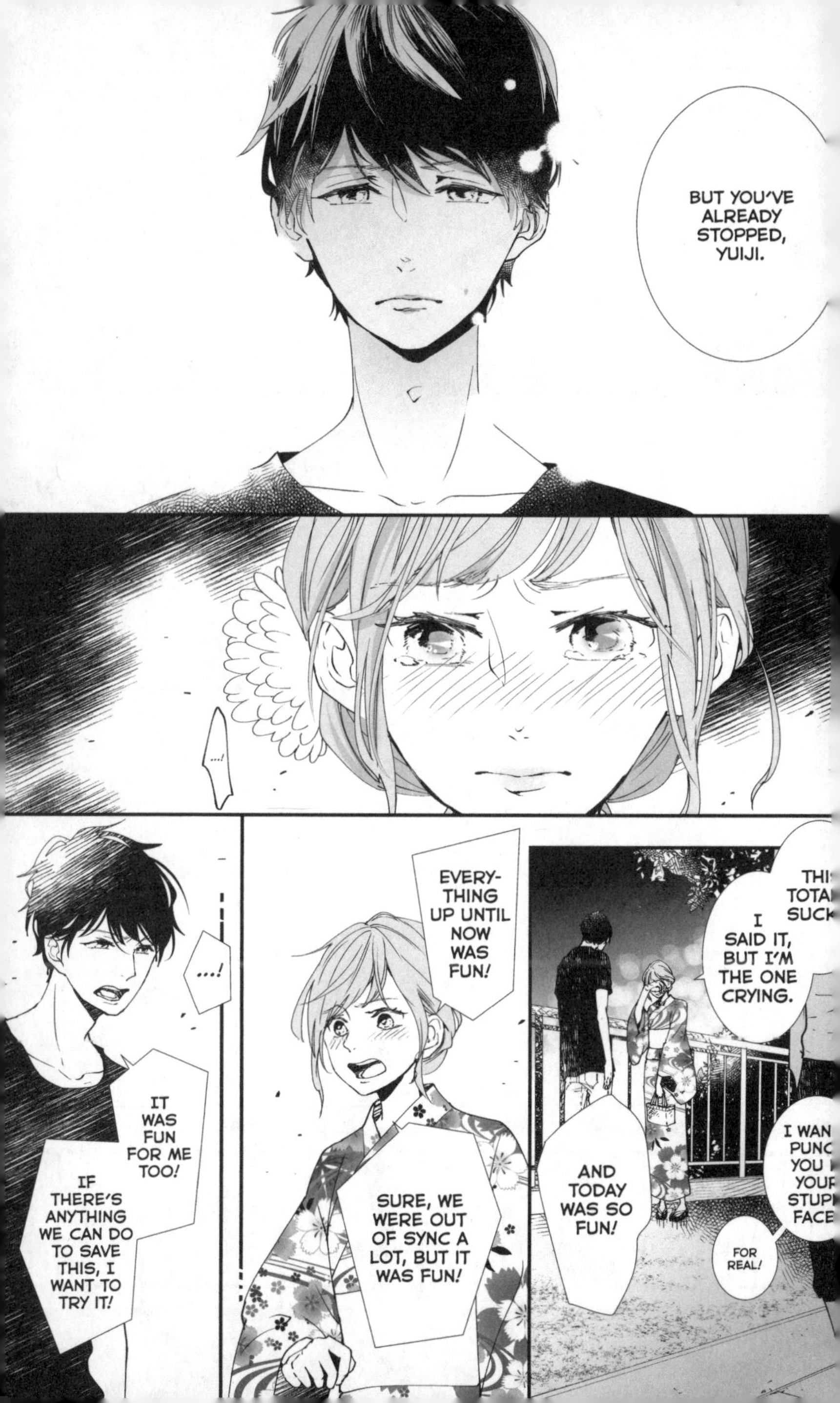
BUT YOU'VE ALREADY STOPPED, YUIJI.
...!
THIS TOTAL SUCK
I SAID IT, BUT I'M THE ONE CRYING.
I WAN PUNC YOU YOUR STUPI FACE
FOR REAL!
AND TODAY WAS SO FUN!
EVERY-THING UP UNTIL NOW WAS FUN!
SURE, WE WERE OUT OF SYNC A LOT, BUT IT WAS FUN!
...!
IT WAS FUN FOR ME TOO!
IF THERE'S ANYTHING WE CAN DO TO SAVE THIS, I WANT TO TRY IT!

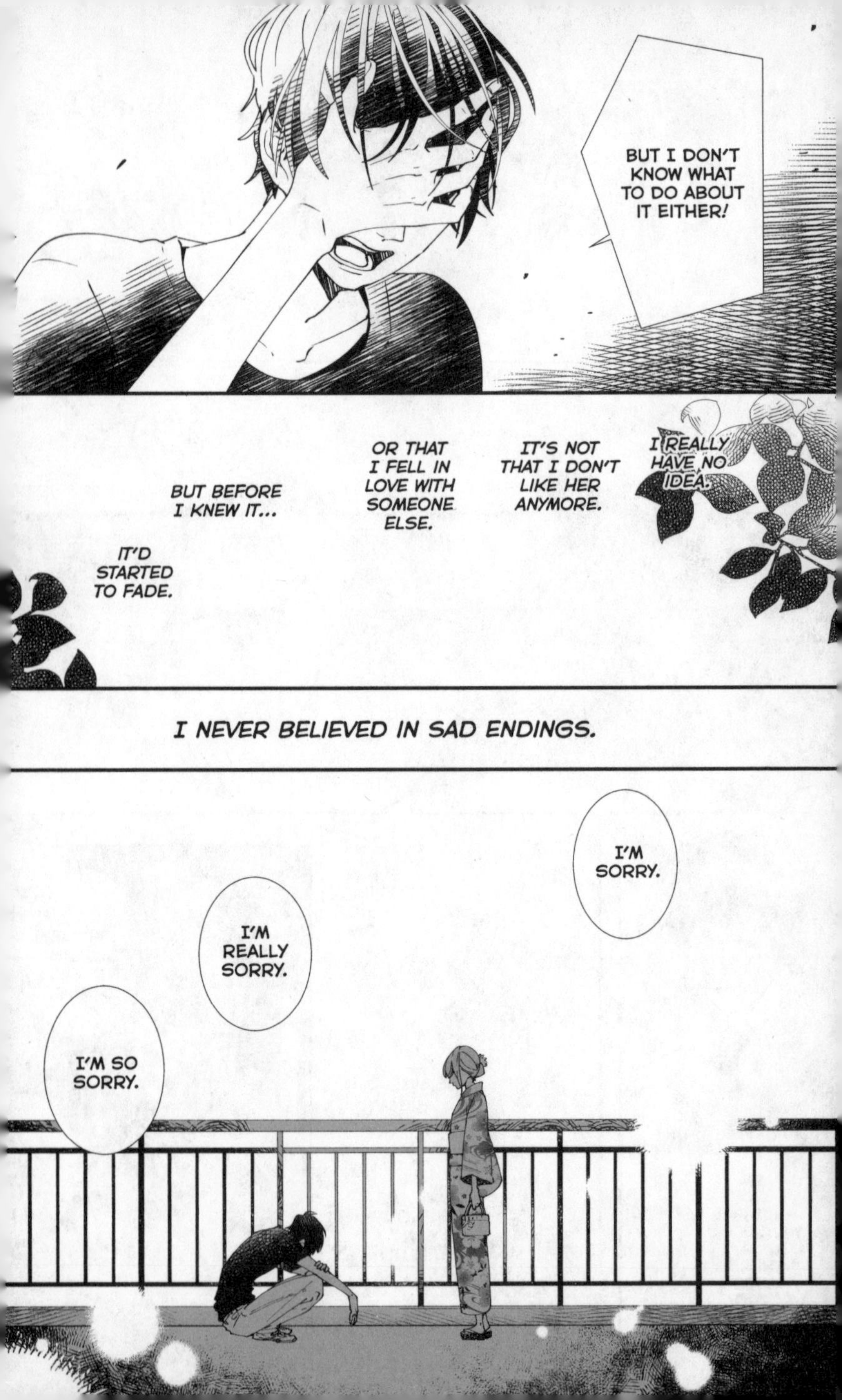
BUT I DON'T KNOW WHAT TO DO ABOUT IT EITHER!
I REALLY HAVE NO IDEA.
IT'S NOT THAT I DON'T LIKE HER ANYMORE.
OR THAT I FELL IN LOVE WITH SOMEONE ELSE.
BUT BEFORE I KNEW IT...
IT'D STARTED TO FADE.
I NEVER BELIEVED IN SAD ENDINGS.
I'M SORRY.
I'M REALLY SORRY.
I'M SO SORRY.

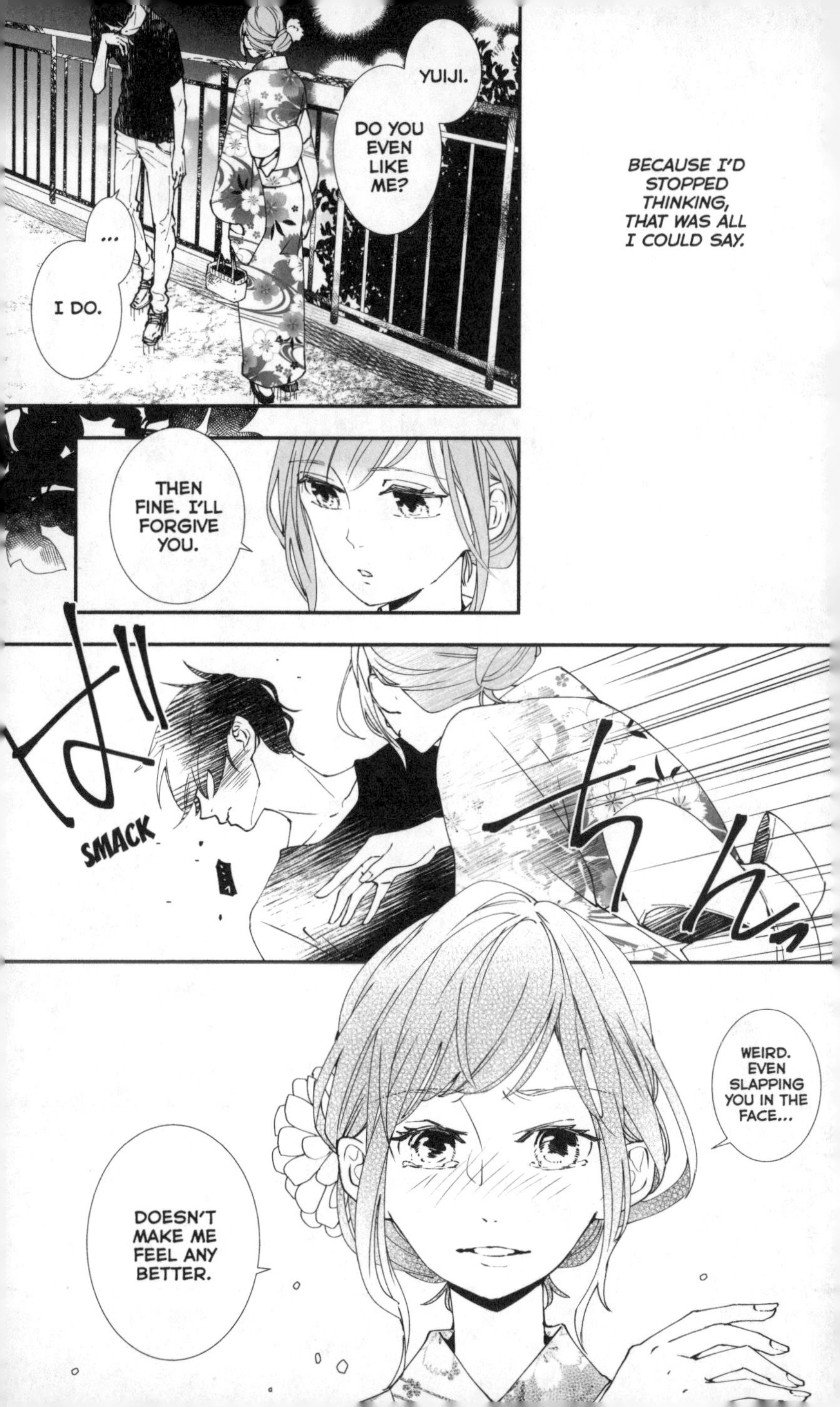
BECAUSE I'D STOPPED THINKING, THAT WAS ALL I COULD SAY.
YUIJI.
DO YOU EVEN LIKE ME?
...
I DO.
THEN FINE. I'LL FORGIVE YOU.
ぱちん
SMACK
WEIRD. EVEN SLAPPING YOU IN THE FACE...
DOESN'T MAKE ME FEEL ANY BETTER.

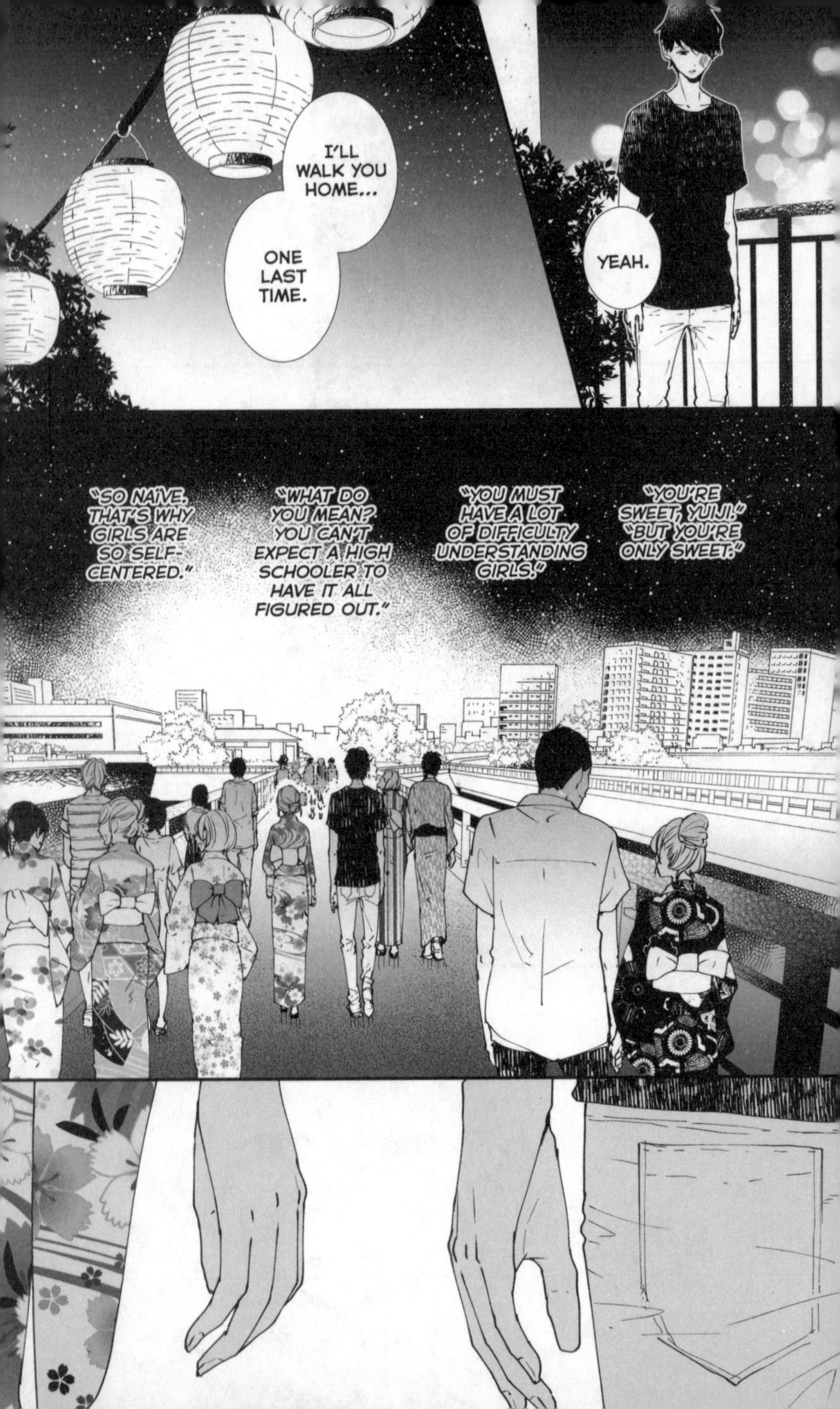
YEAH.
I'LL WALK YOU HOME...
ONE LAST TIME.
"YOU'RE SWEET, YUJI." "BUT YOU'RE ONLY SWEET."
"YOU MUST HAVE A LOT OF DIFFICULTY UNDERSTANDING GIRLS."
"WHAT DO YOU MEAN? YOU CAN'T EXPECT A HIGH SCHOOLER TO HAVE IT ALL FIGURED OUT."
"SO NAÏVE. THAT'S WHY GIRLS ARE SO SELF-CENTERED."

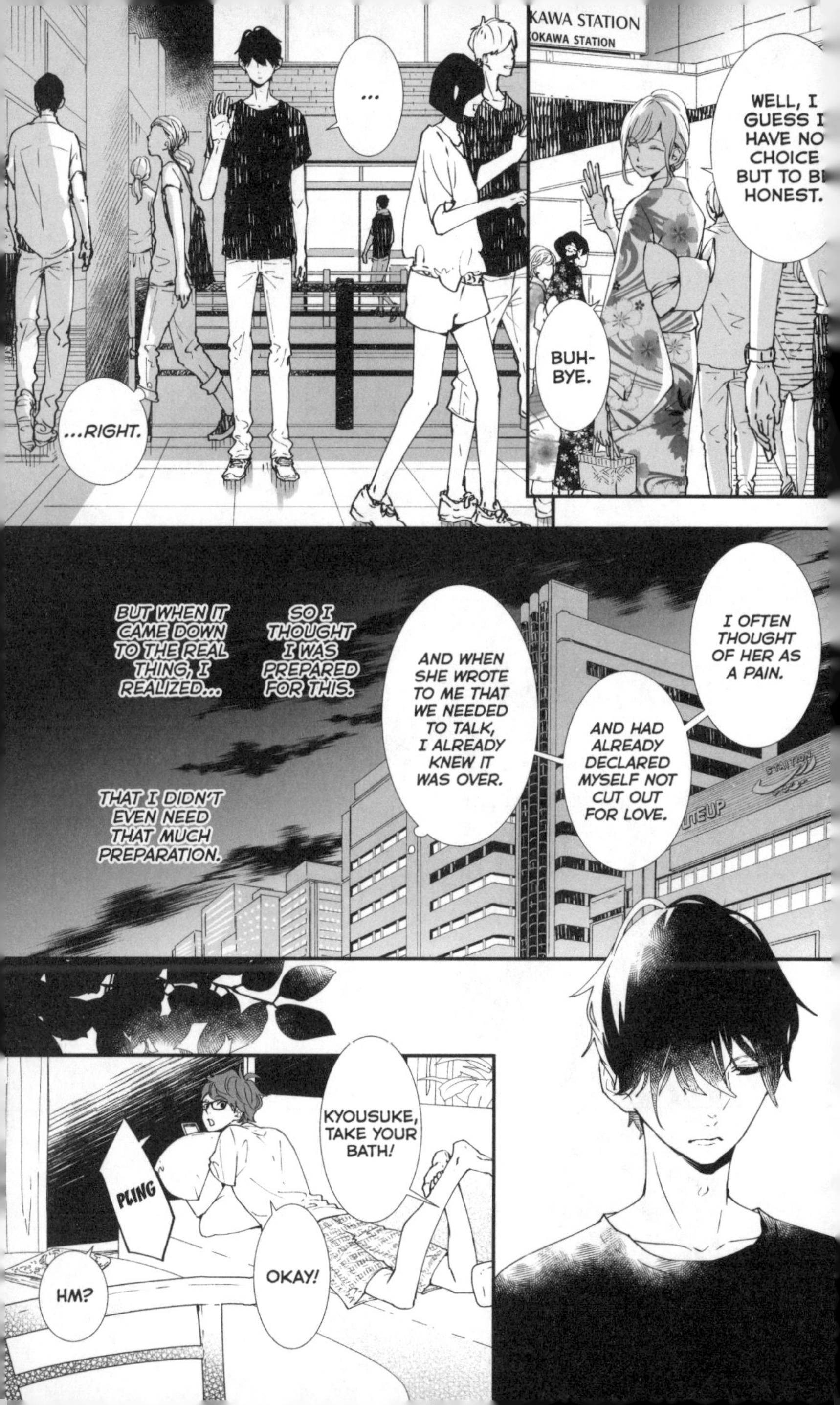
KAWA STATION
OKAWA STATION
WELL, I GUESS I HAVE NO CHOICE BUT TO B
BUH-BYE.
...
...RIGHT.
I OFTEN THOUGHT OF HER AS A PAIN.
AND HAD ALREADY DECLARED MYSELF NOT CUT OUT FOR LOVE.
AND WHEN SHE WROTE TO ME THAT WE NEEDED TO TALK, I ALREADY KNEW IT WAS OVER.
SO I THOUGHT I WAS PREPARED FOR THIS.
BUT WHEN IT CAME DOWN TO THE REAL THING, I REALIZED...
THAT I DIDN'T EVEN NEED THAT MUCH PREPARATION.
KYOUSUKE, TAKE YOUR BATH!
OKAY!
PLING
HM?

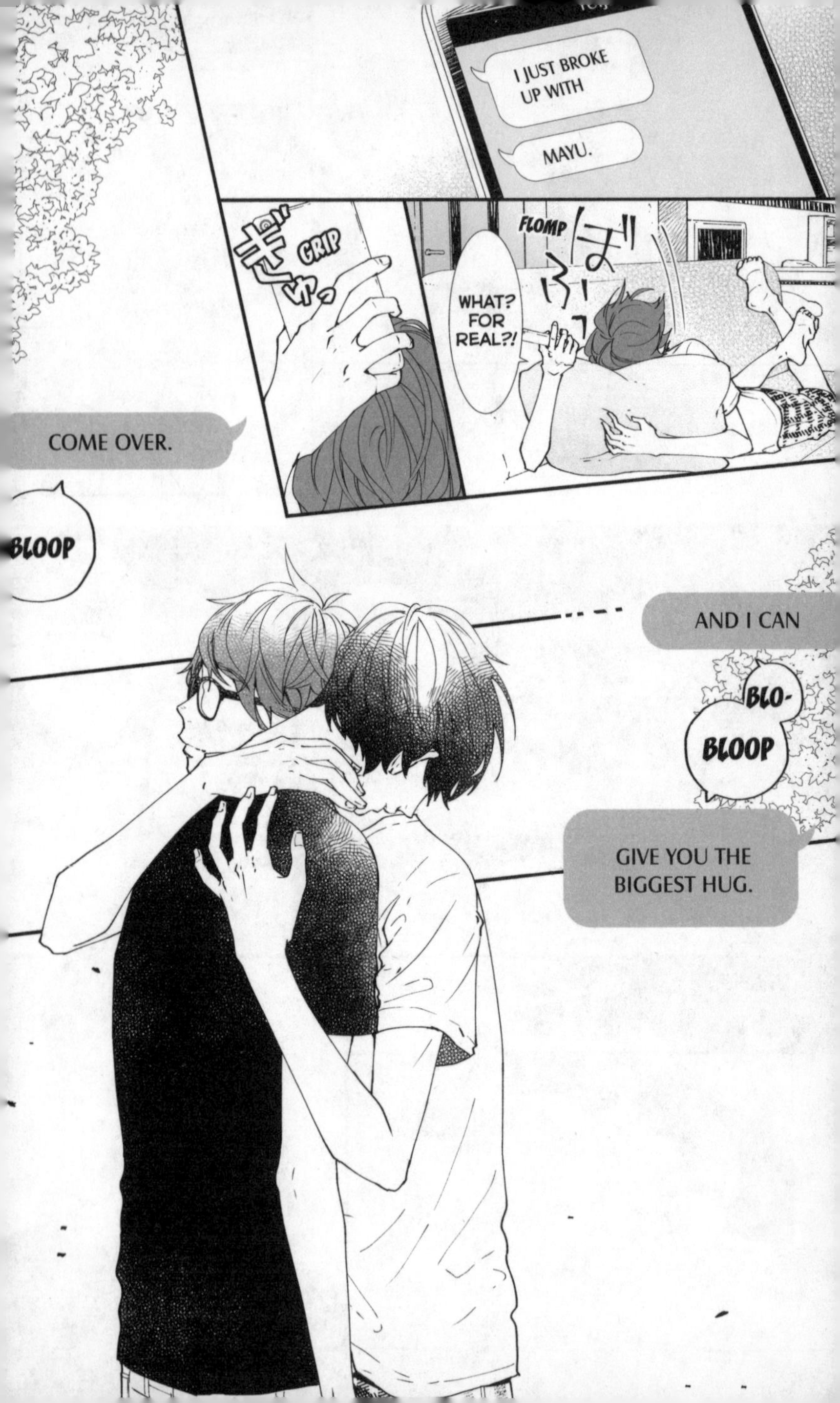
I JUST BROKE UP WITH
MAYU.
FLOMP
ばふっ
WHAT? FOR REAL?!
ぎゅっ
GRIP
COME OVER.
BLOOP
AND I CAN
BLO-BLOOP
GIVE YOU THE BIGGEST HUG.

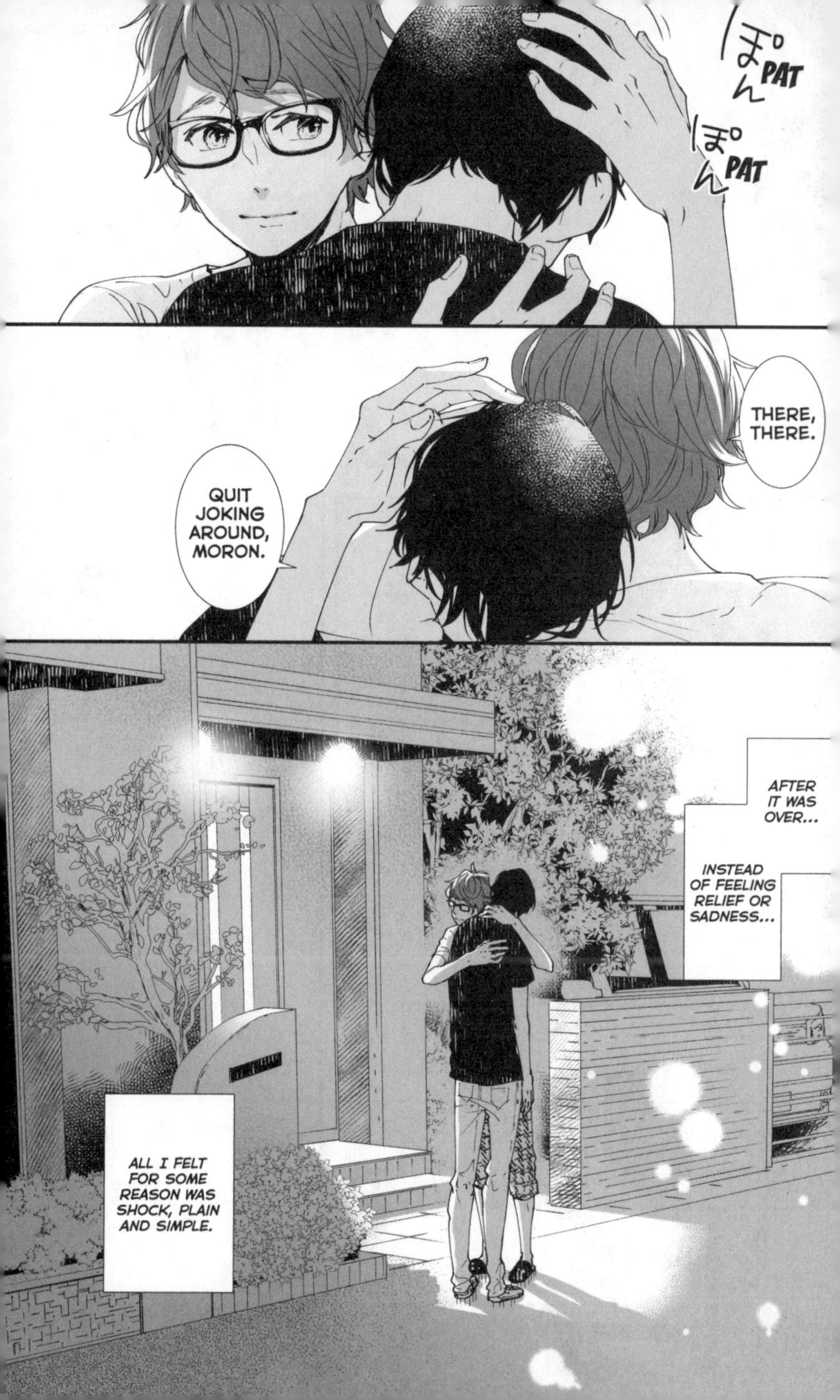
ぽん PAT
ぽん PAT
THERE, THERE.
QUIT JOKING AROUND, MORON.
AFTER IT WAS OVER...
INSTEAD OF FEELING RELIEF OR SADNESS...
ALL I FELT FOR SOME REASON WAS SHOCK, PLAIN AND SIMPLE.

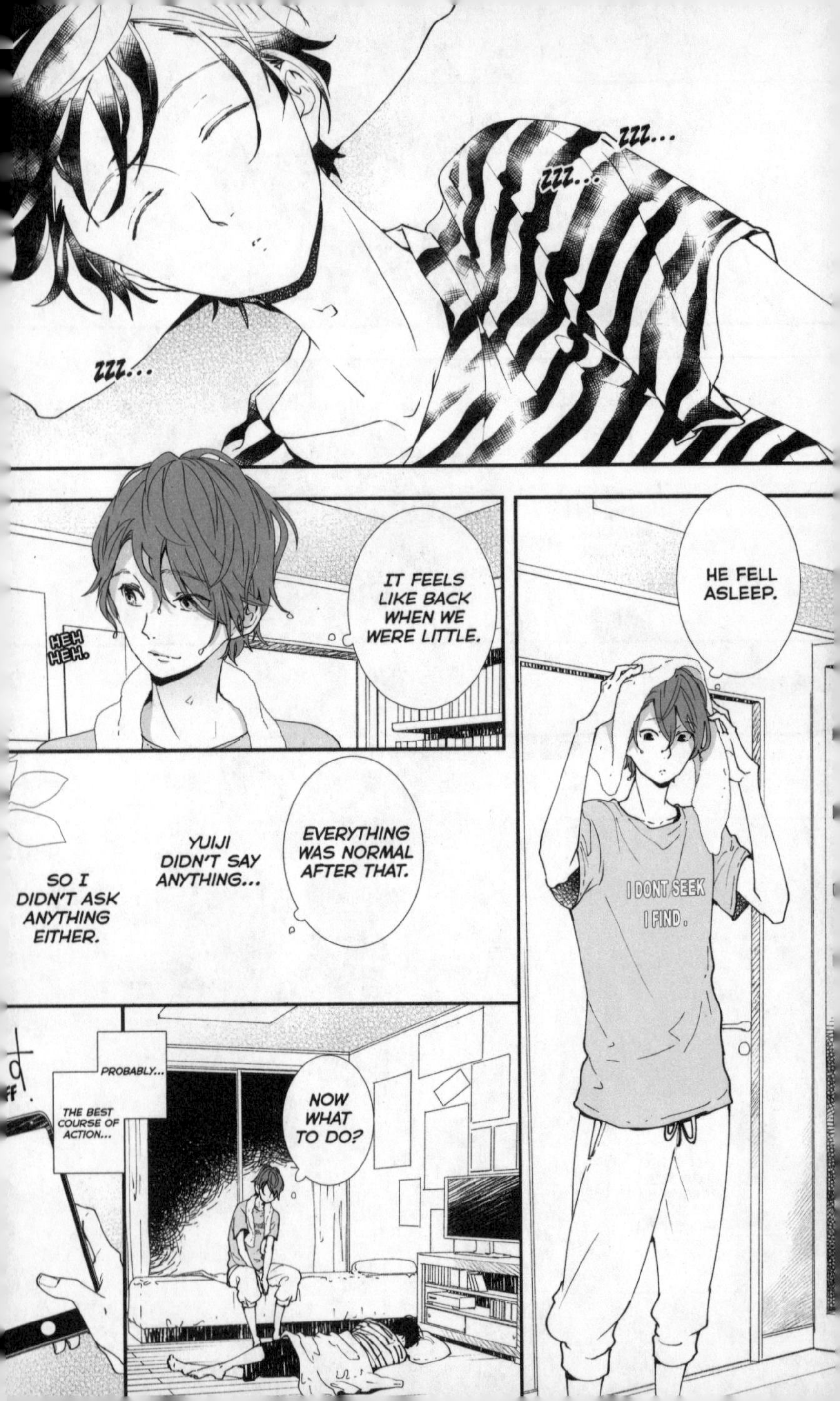
ZZZ...
ZZZ...
ZZZ...
HE FELL ASLEEP.
I DONT SEEK I FIND.
IT FEELS LIKE BACK WHEN WE WERE LITTLE.
HEH HEH.
EVERYTHING WAS NORMAL AFTER THAT.
YUIJI DIDN'T SAY ANYTHING...
SO I DIDN'T ASK ANYTHING EITHER.
NOW WHAT TO DO?
PROBABLY...
THE BEST COURSE OF ACTION...

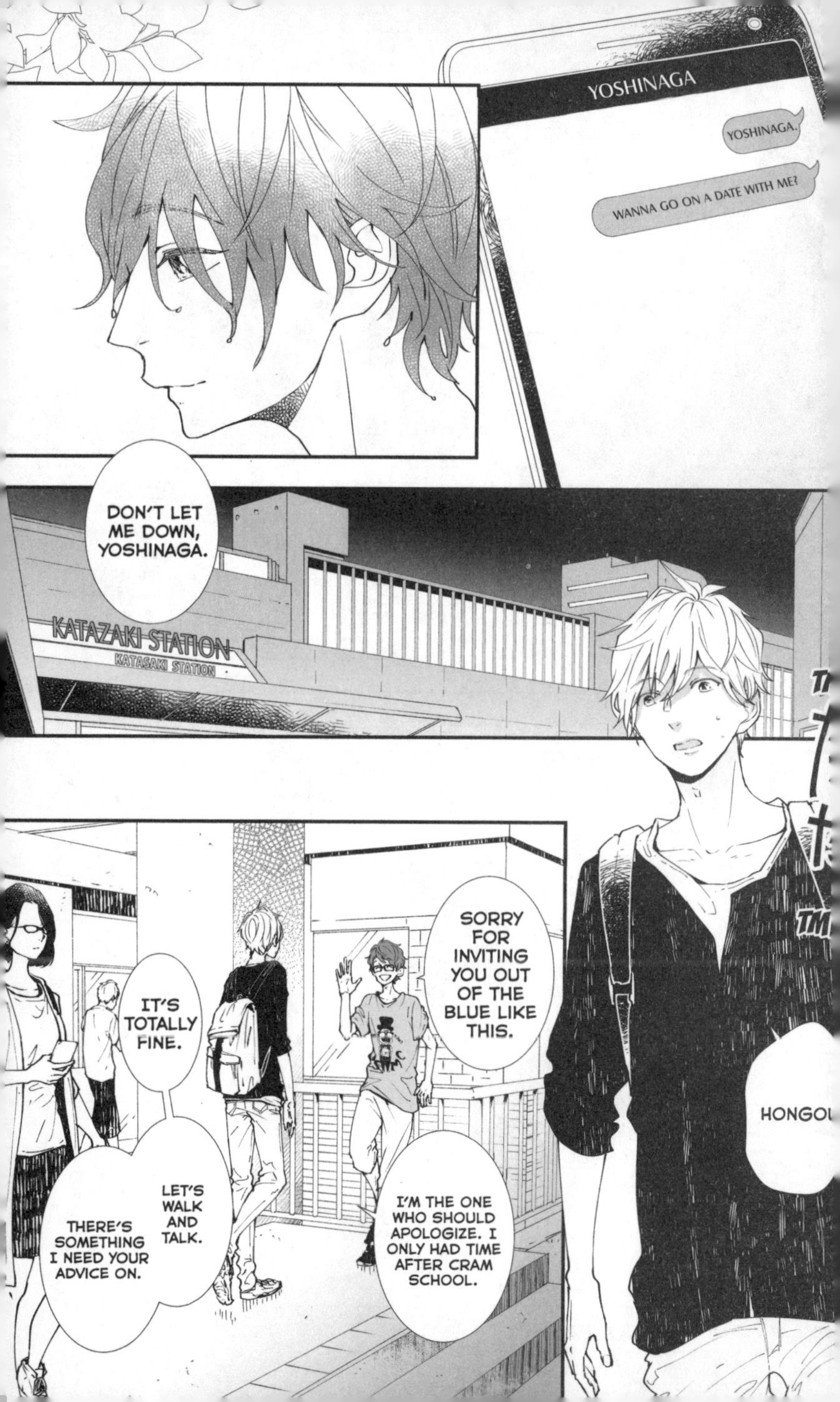
YOSHINAGA
YOSHINAGA.
WANNA GO ON A DATE WITH ME?
DON'T LET ME DOWN, YOSHINAGA.
KATAZAKI STATION
KATASAKI STATION
HONGOU
SORRY FOR INVITING YOU OUT OF THE BLUE LIKE THIS.
IT'S TOTALLY FINE.
I'M THE ONE WHO SHOULD APOLOGIZE. I ONLY HAD TIME AFTER CRAM SCHOOL.
LET'S WALK AND TALK.
THERE'S SOMETHING I NEED YOUR ADVICE ON.

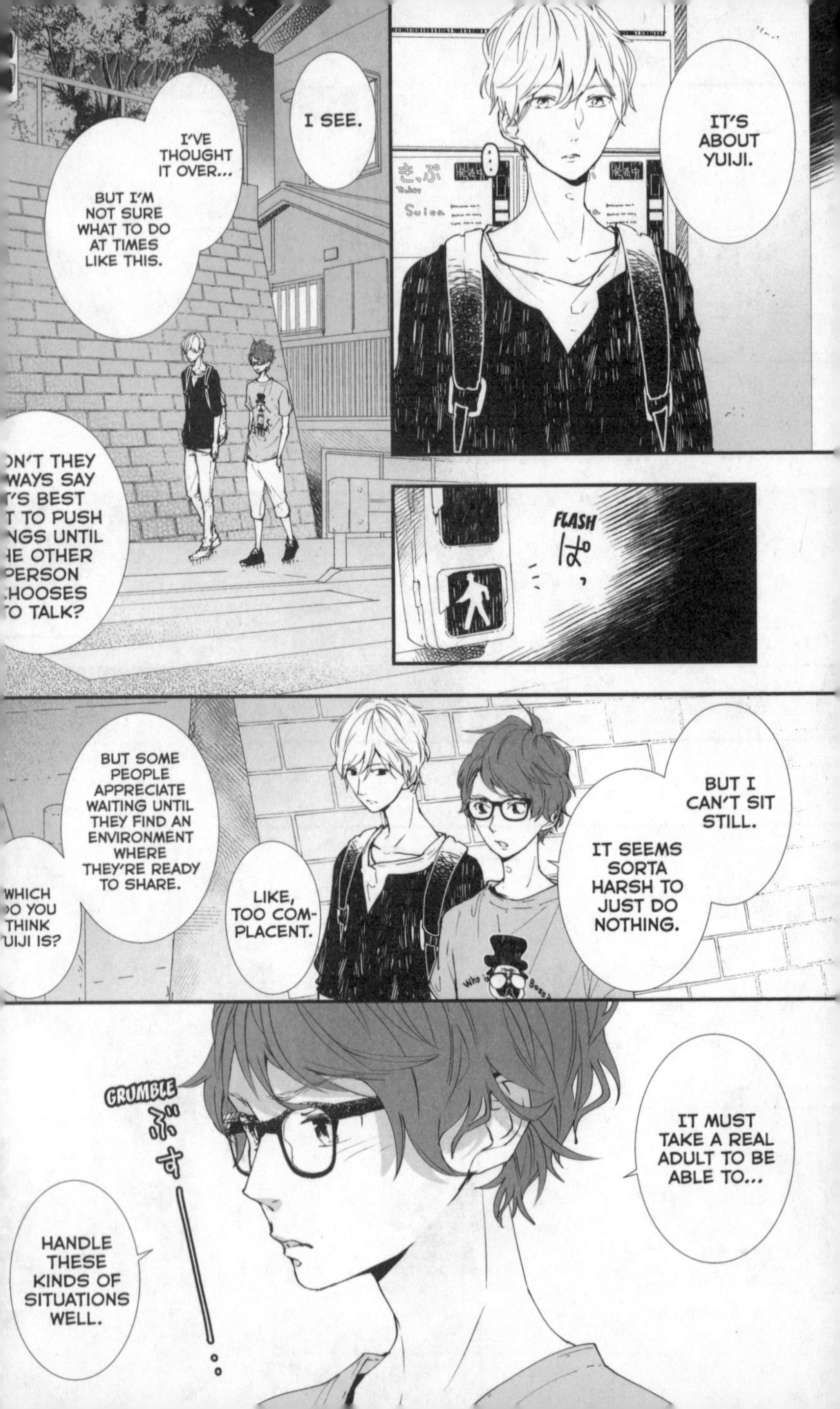
IT'S ABOUT YUIJI.
…
FLASH
ぱっ
I SEE.
I'VE THOUGHT IT OVER... BUT I'M NOT SURE WHAT TO DO AT TIMES LIKE THIS.
ON'T THEY WAYS SAY T'S BEST T TO PUSH NGS UNTIL HE OTHER PERSON CHOOSES TO TALK?
BUT I CAN'T SIT STILL.
IT SEEMS SORTA HARSH TO JUST DO NOTHING.
LIKE, TOO COM-PLACENT.
BUT SOME PEOPLE APPRECIATE WAITING UNTIL THEY FIND AN ENVIRONMENT WHERE THEY'RE READY TO SHARE.
WHICH DO YOU THINK UIJI IS?
IT MUST TAKE A REAL ADULT TO BE ABLE TO...
GRUMBLE
ぶすー…
HANDLE THESE KINDS OF SITUATIONS WELL.

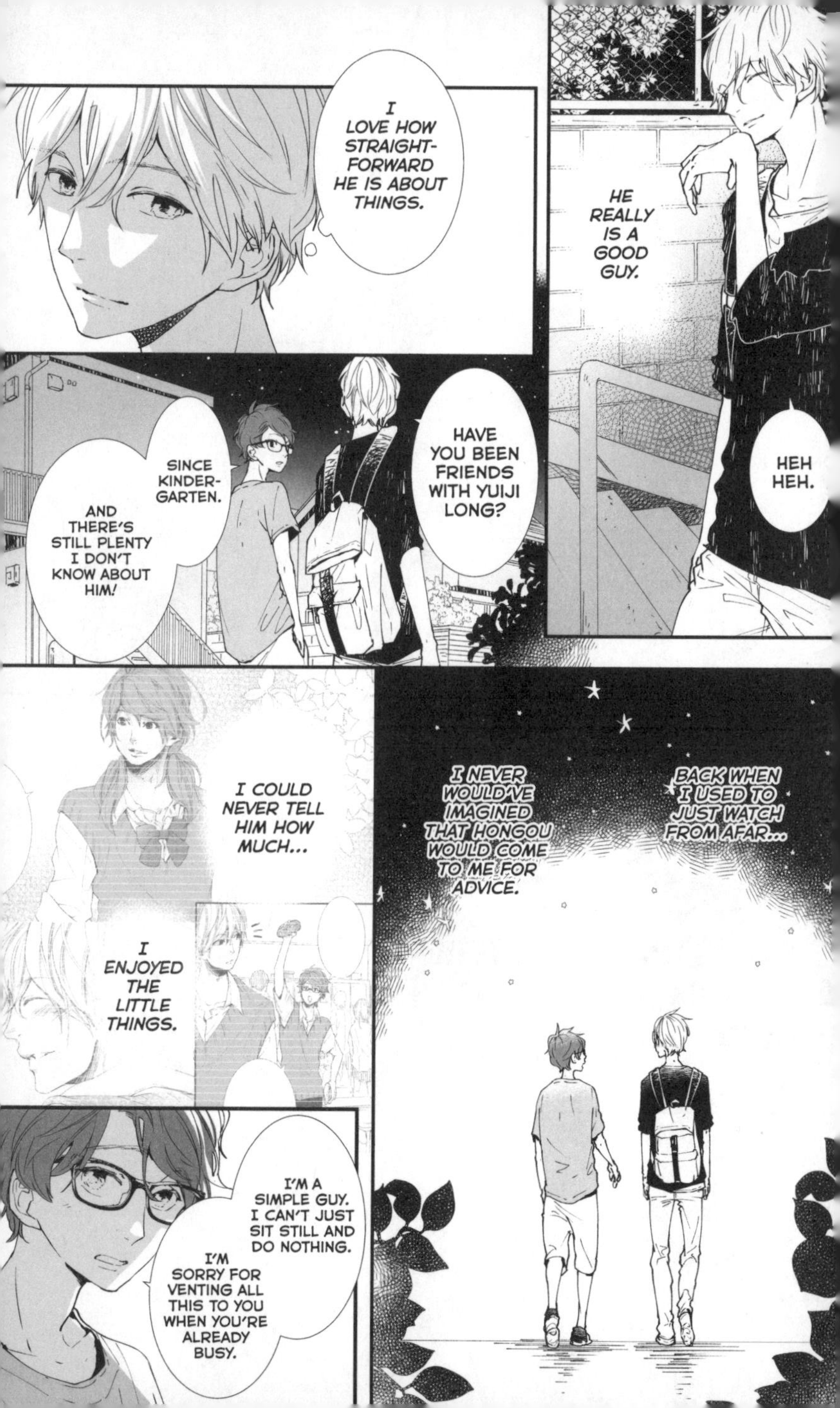

HE REALLY IS A GOOD GUY.
HEH HEH.
I LOVE HOW STRAIGHT-FORWARD HE IS ABOUT THINGS.
HAVE YOU BEEN FRIENDS WITH YUIJI LONG?
SINCE KINDER-GARTEN.
AND THERE'S STILL PLENTY I DON'T KNOW ABOUT HIM!
BACK WHEN I USED TO JUST WATCH FROM AFAR...
I NEVER WOULD'VE IMAGINED THAT HONGOU WOULD COME TO ME FOR ADVICE.
I COULD NEVER TELL HIM HOW MUCH...
I ENJOYED THE LITTLE THINGS.
I'M A SIMPLE GUY. I CAN'T JUST SIT STILL AND DO NOTHING.
I'M SORRY FOR VENTING ALL THIS TO YOU WHEN YOU'RE ALREADY BUSY.

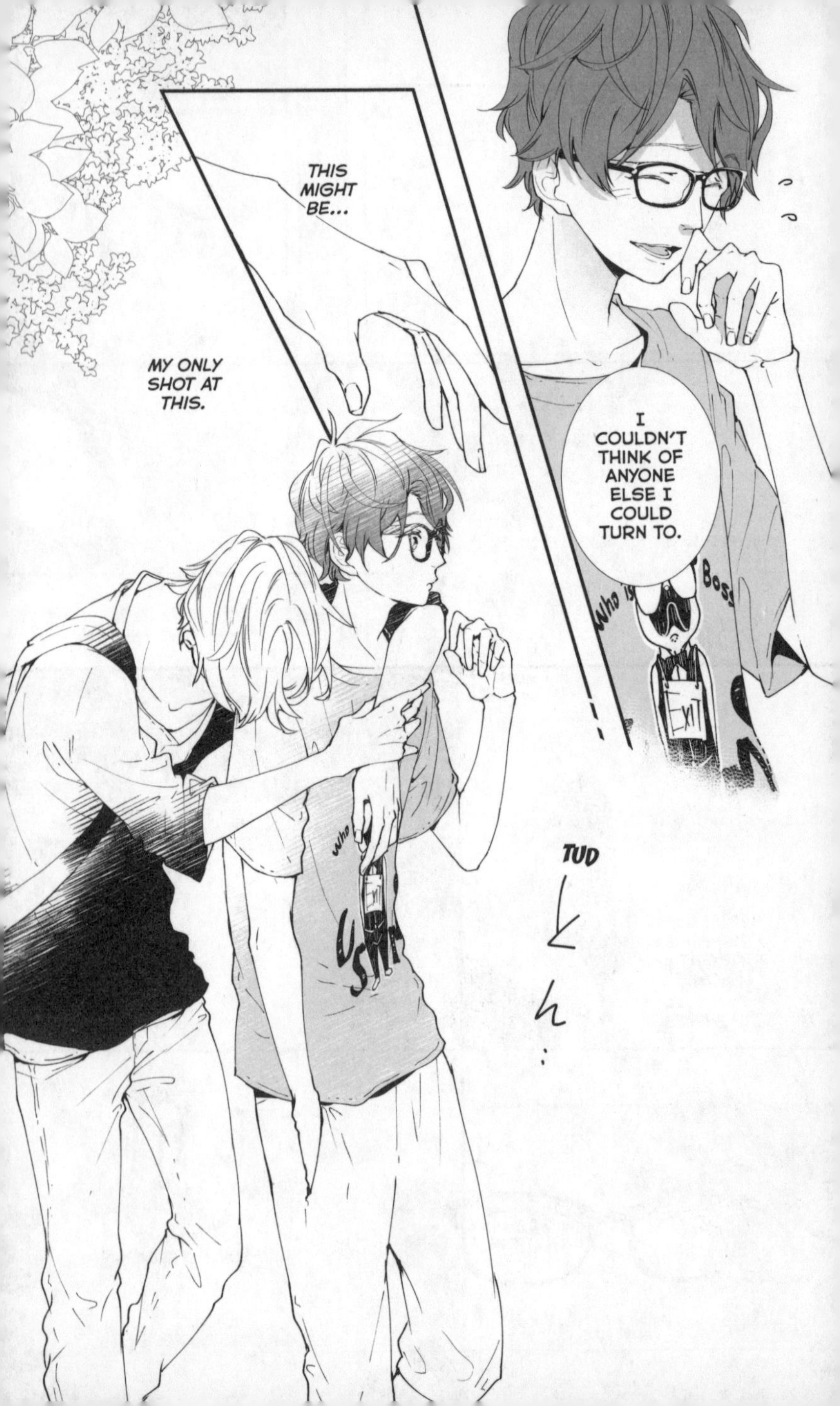
I COULDN'T THINK OF ANYONE ELSE I COULD TURN TO.
THIS MIGHT BE...
MY ONLY SHOT AT THIS.
TUD

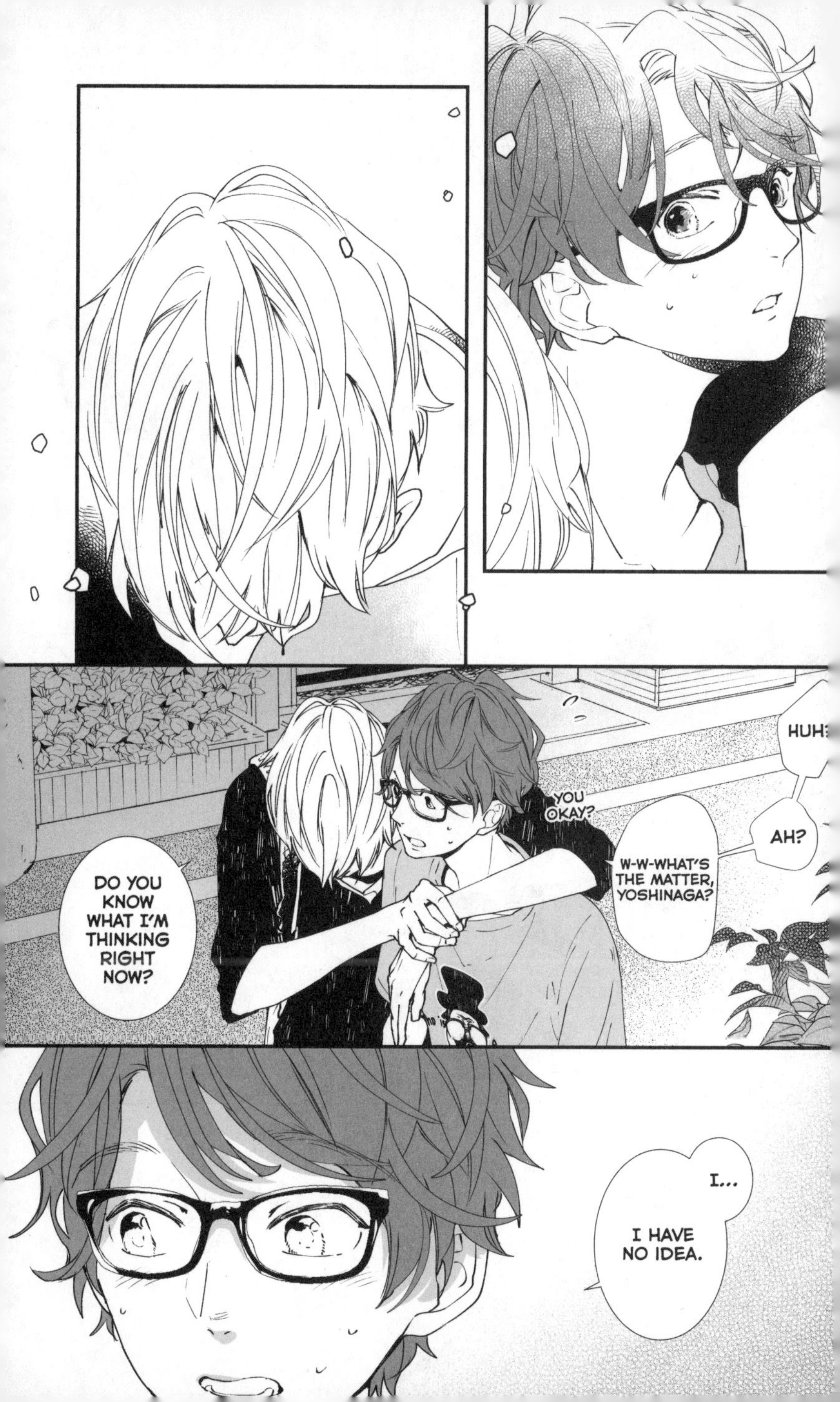
HUH?
AH?
W-W-WHAT'S THE MATTER, YOSHINAGA?
YOU OKAY?
DO YOU KNOW WHAT I'M THINKING RIGHT NOW?
I...
I HAVE NO IDEA.

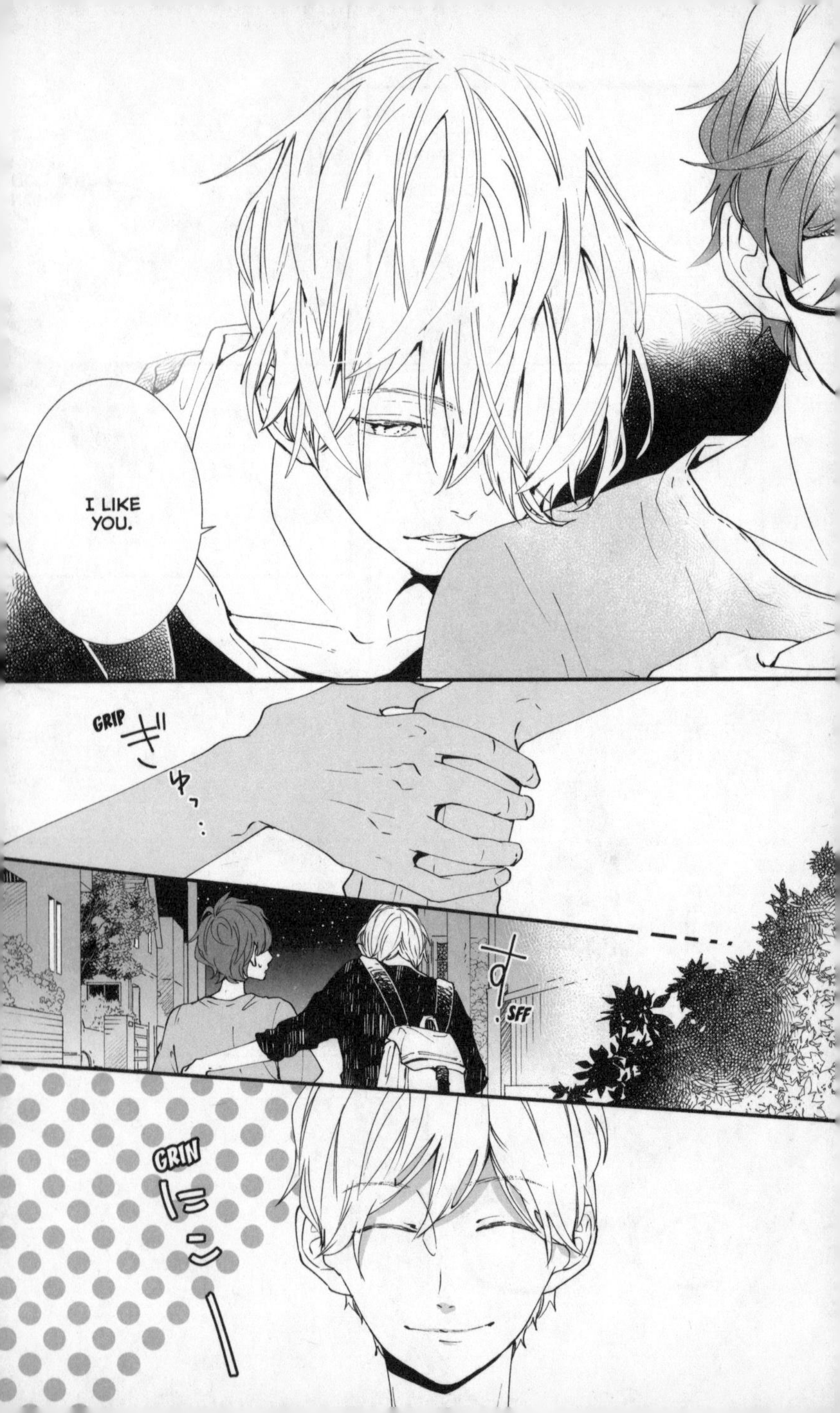
I LIKE YOU.
GRIP
ぎゅっ..
す
SFF
GRIN
にこー

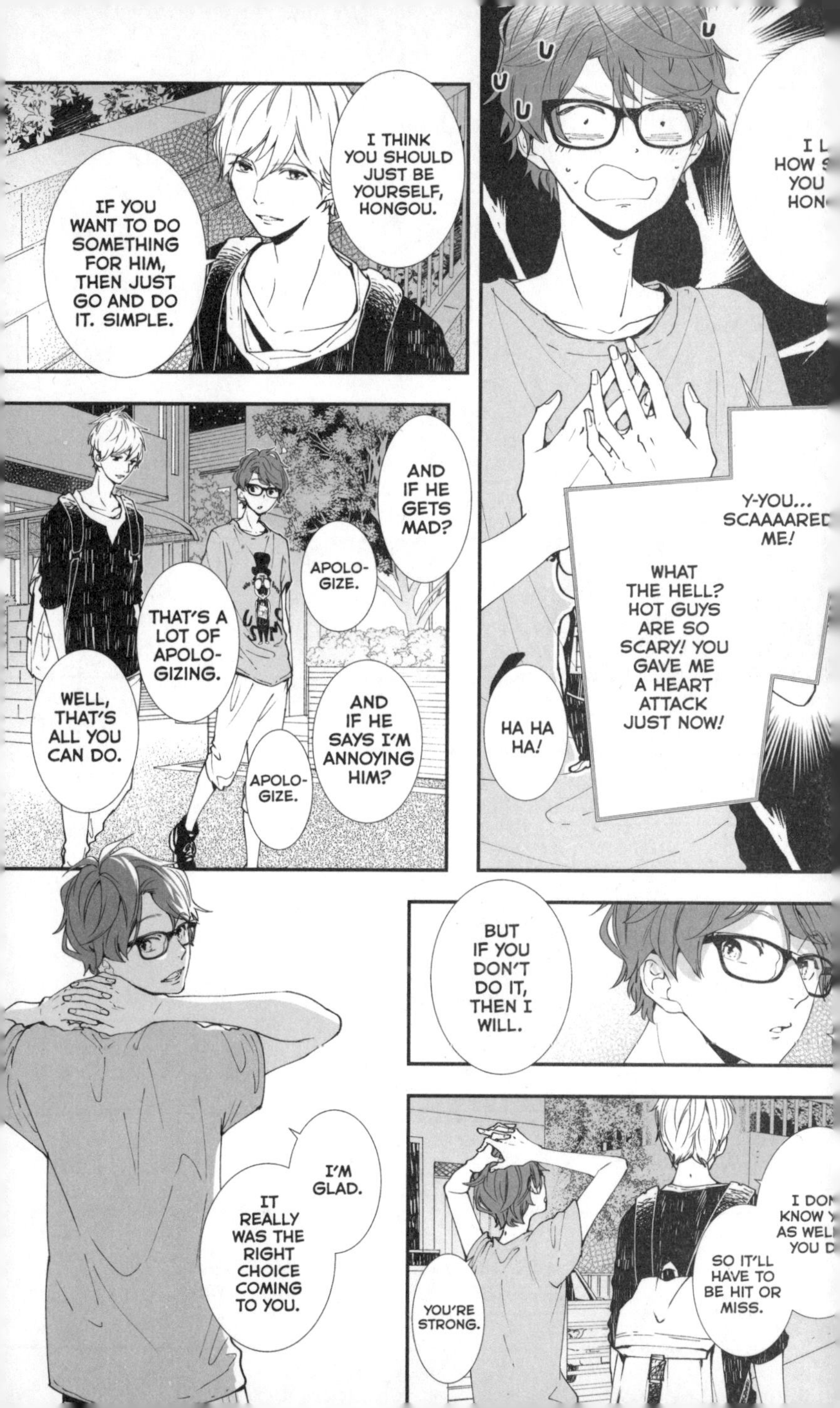
U U U U U
I L
HOW S
YOU
HON
Y-YOU... SCAAAARED ME!
WHAT THE HELL? HOT GUYS ARE SO SCARY! YOU GAVE ME A HEART ATTACK JUST NOW!
HA HA HA!
I THINK YOU SHOULD JUST BE YOURSELF, HONGOU.
IF YOU WANT TO DO SOMETHING FOR HIM, THEN JUST GO AND DO IT. SIMPLE.
AND IF HE GETS MAD?
APOLO-GIZE.
THAT'S A LOT OF APOLO-GIZING.
AND IF HE SAYS I'M ANNOYING HIM?
APOLO-GIZE.
WELL, THAT'S ALL YOU CAN DO.
BUT IF YOU DON'T DO IT, THEN I WILL.
I DON
KNOW Y
AS WEL
YOU D
SO IT'LL HAVE TO BE HIT OR MISS.
YOU'RE STRONG.
I'M GLAD.
IT REALLY WAS THE RIGHT CHOICE COMING TO YOU.

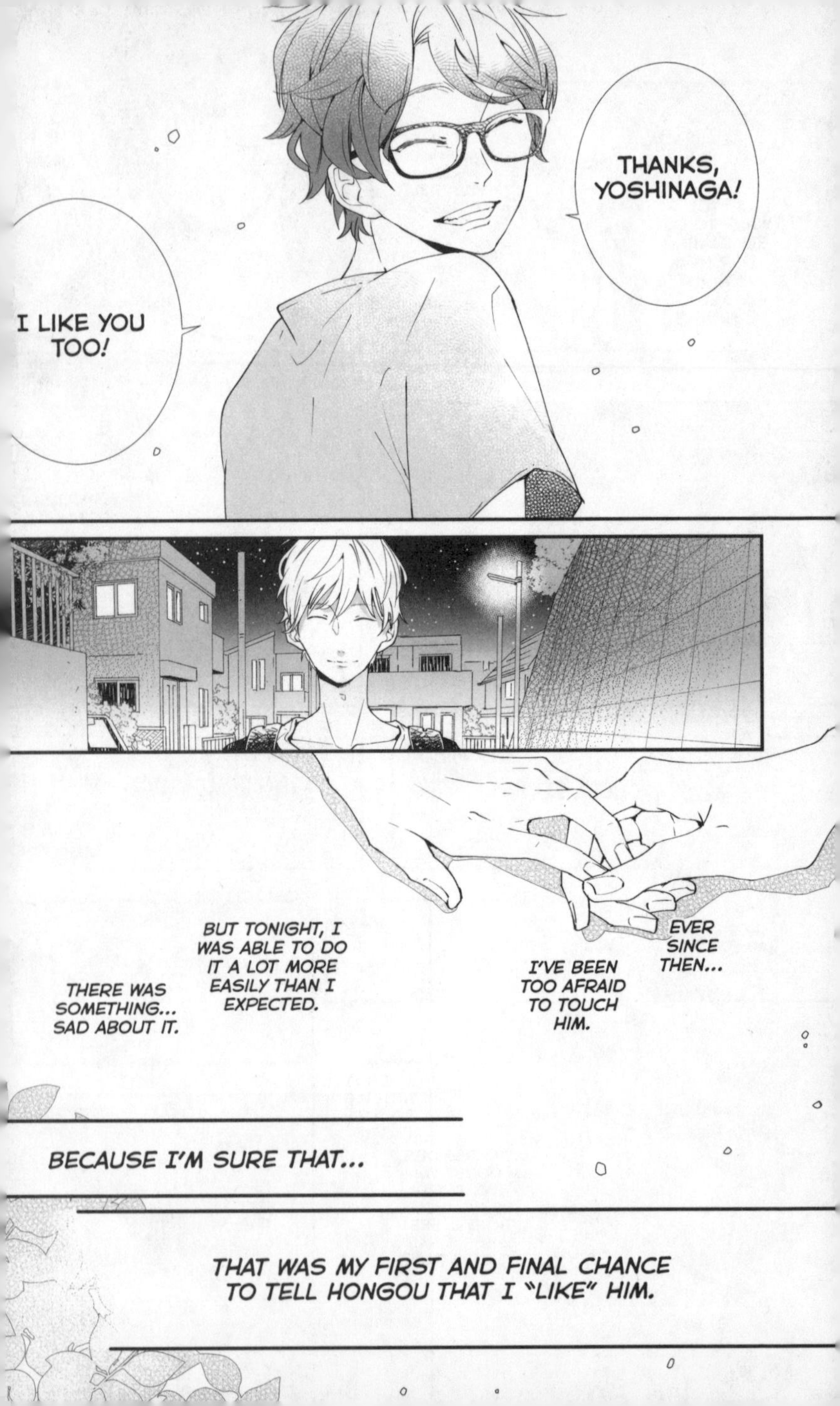
THANKS, YOSHINAGA!
I LIKE YOU TOO!
EVER SINCE THEN...
I'VE BEEN TOO AFRAID TO TOUCH HIM.
BUT TONIGHT, I WAS ABLE TO DO IT A LOT MORE EASILY THAN I EXPECTED.
THERE WAS SOMETHING... SAD ABOUT IT.
BECAUSE I'M SURE THAT...
THAT WAS MY FIRST AND FINAL CHANCE TO TELL HONGOU THAT I "LIKE" HIM.

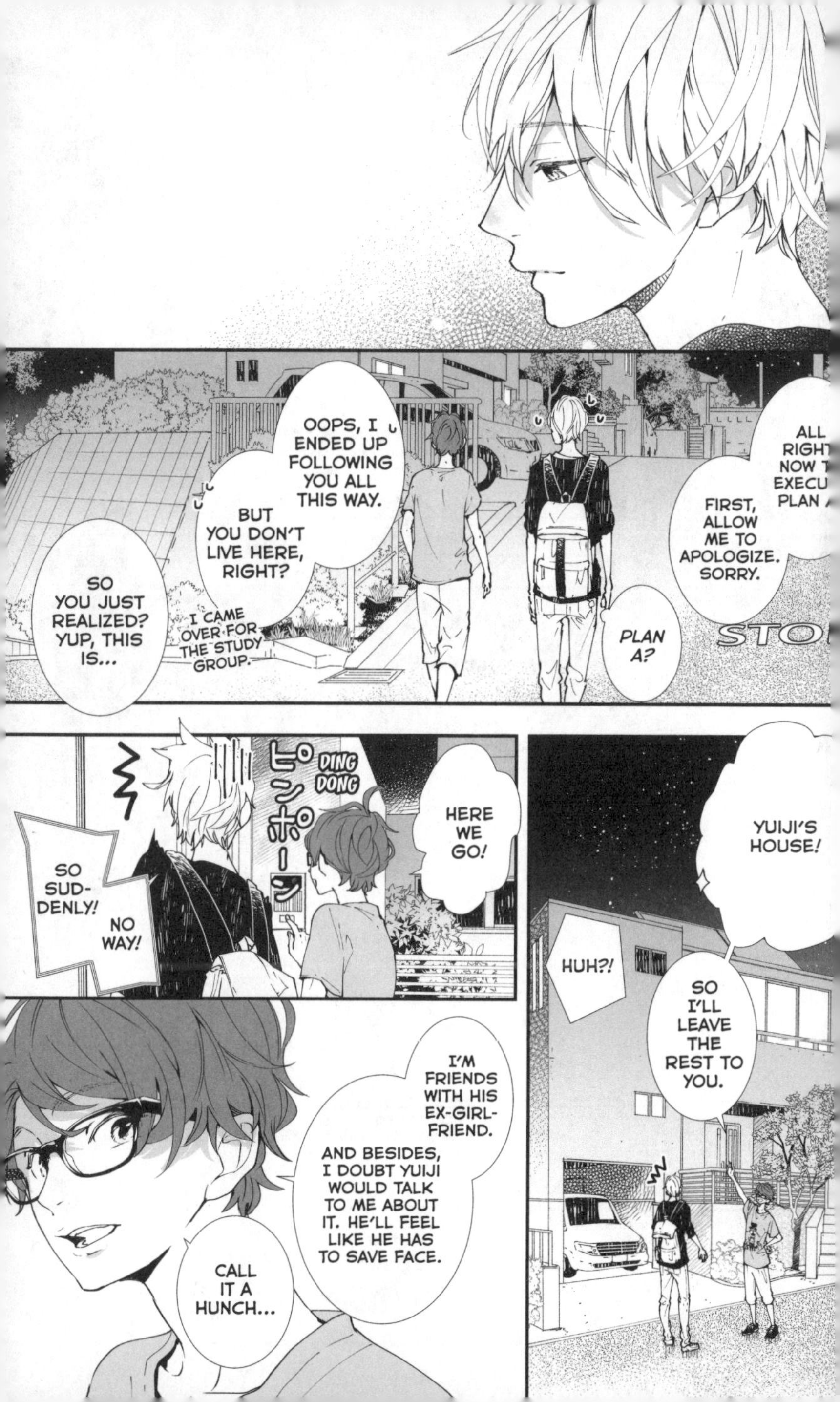
ALL RIGHT NOW T EXECU PLAN
FIRST, ALLOW ME TO APOLOGIZE. SORRY.
STO
PLAN A?
OOPS, I ENDED UP FOLLOWING YOU ALL THIS WAY.
BUT YOU DON'T LIVE HERE, RIGHT?
I CAME OVER FOR THE STUDY GROUP.
SO YOU JUST REALIZED? YUP, THIS IS...
YUIJI'S HOUSE!
HUH?!
SO I'LL LEAVE THE REST TO YOU.
HERE WE GO!
ピンポーン
DING DONG
SO SUD-DENLY!
NO WAY!
I'M FRIENDS WITH HIS EX-GIRL-FRIEND.
AND BESIDES, I DOUBT YUIJI WOULD TALK TO ME ABOUT IT. HE'LL FEEL LIKE HE HAS TO SAVE FACE.
CALL IT A HUNCH...

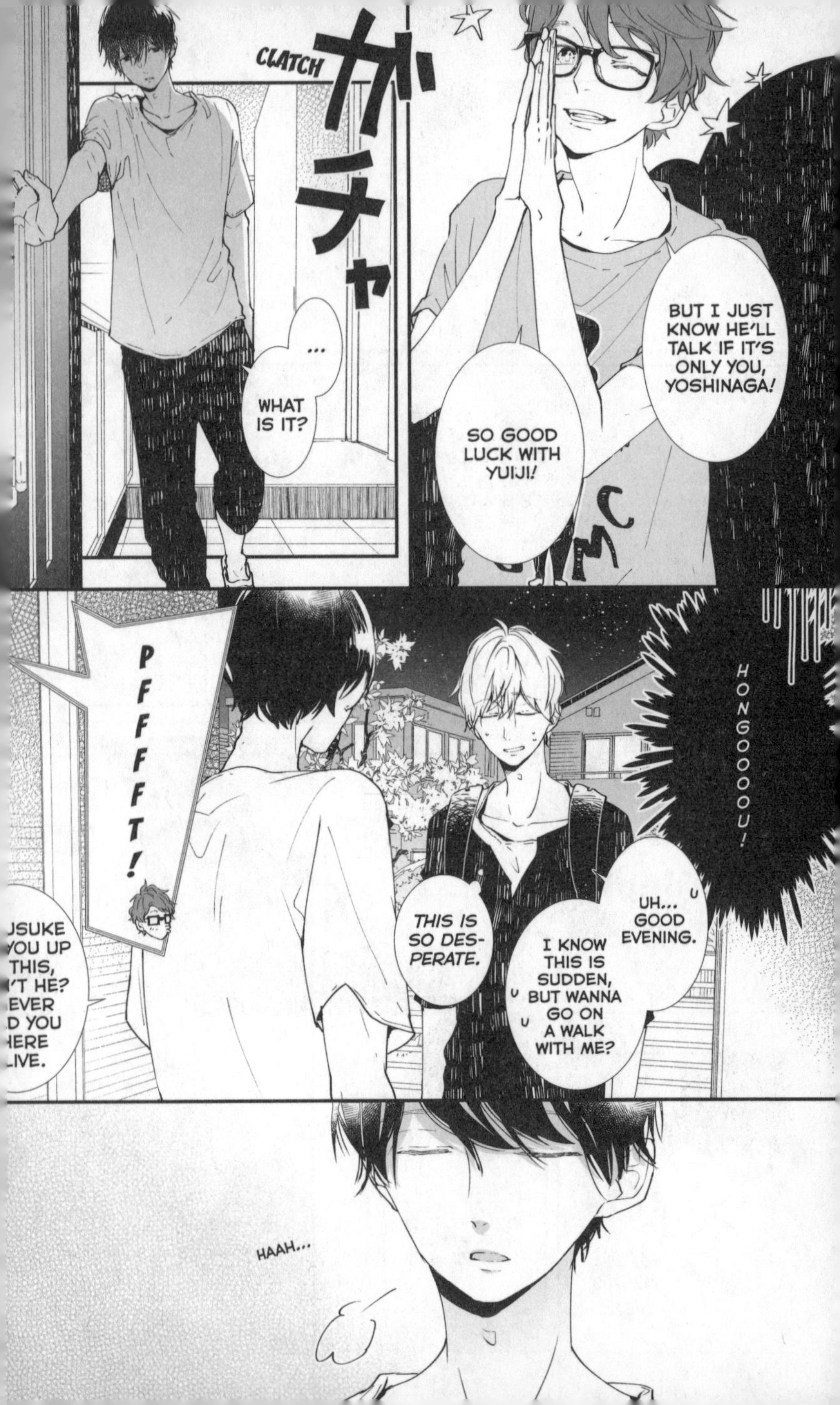
BUT I JUST KNOW HE'LL TALK IF IT'S ONLY YOU, YOSHINAGA!
SO GOOD LUCK WITH YUIJI!
CLATCH
ガチャ
...
WHAT IS IT?
HONGOOOOU!
UH... GOOD EVENING.
I KNOW THIS IS SUDDEN, BUT WANNA GO ON A WALK WITH ME?
THIS IS SO DES-PERATE.
PFFFFT!
USUKE YOU UP THIS, 'T HE? EVER D YOU HERE LIVE.
HAAH...

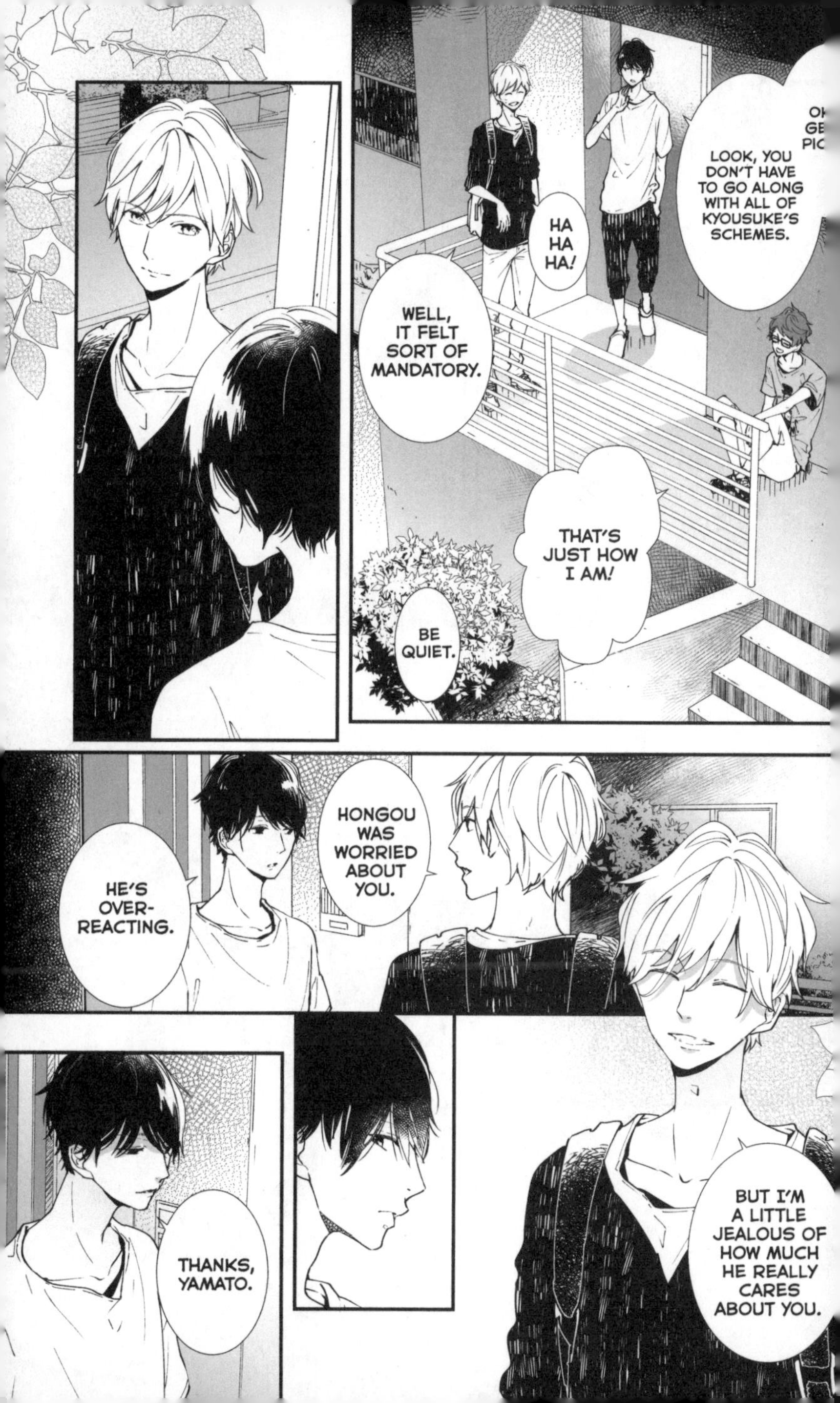
LOOK, YOU DON'T HAVE TO GO ALONG WITH ALL OF KYOUSUKE'S SCHEMES.
HA HA HA!
WELL, IT FELT SORT OF MANDATORY.
THAT'S JUST HOW I AM!
BE QUIET.
HONGOU WAS WORRIED ABOUT YOU.
HE'S OVER-REACTING.
BUT I'M A LITTLE JEALOUS OF HOW MUCH HE REALLY CARES ABOUT YOU.
THANKS, YAMATO.

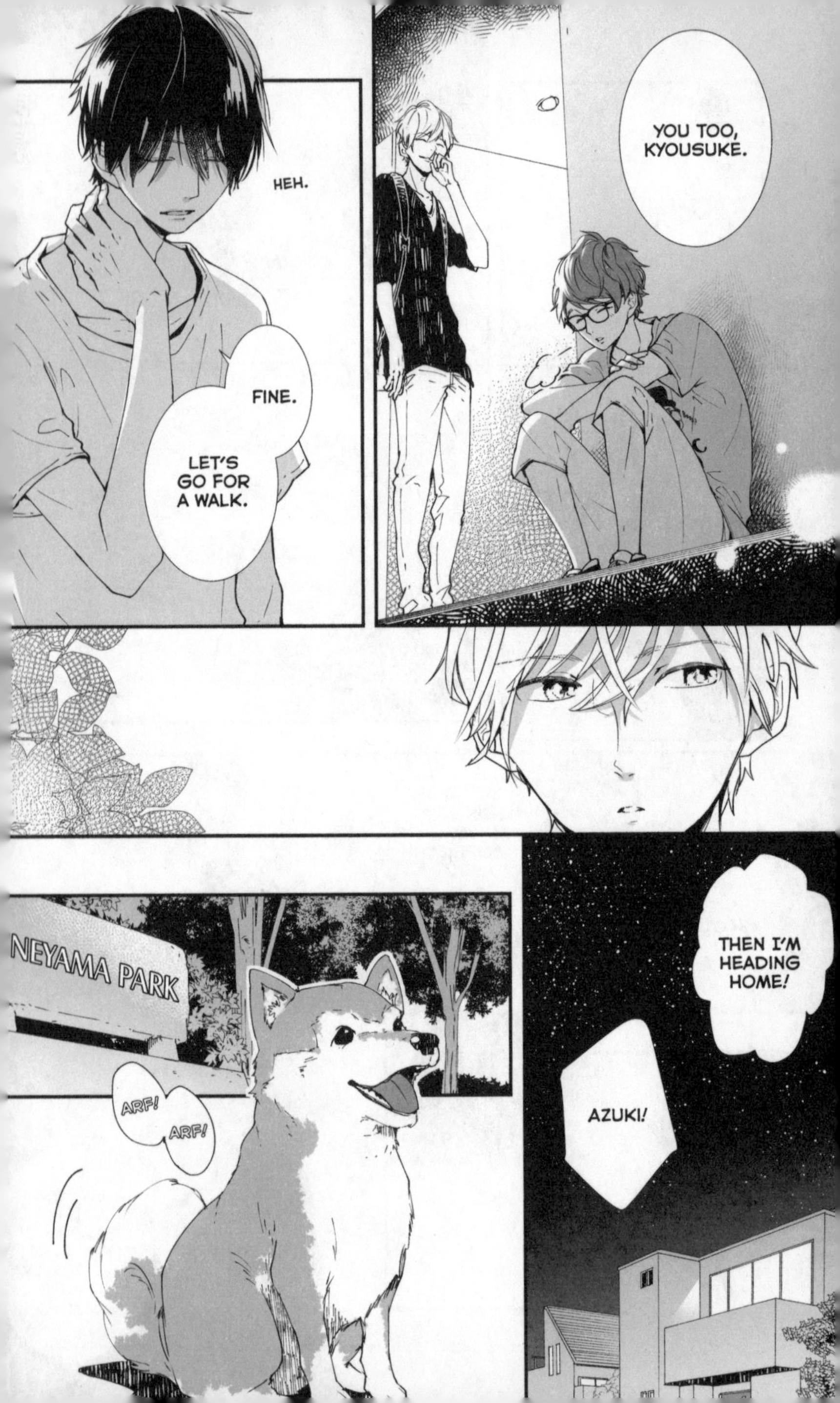
YOU TOO, KYOUSUKE.
HEH.
FINE.
LET'S GO FOR A WALK.
THEN I'M HEADING HOME!
AZUKI!
NEYAMA PARK
ARF!
ARF!

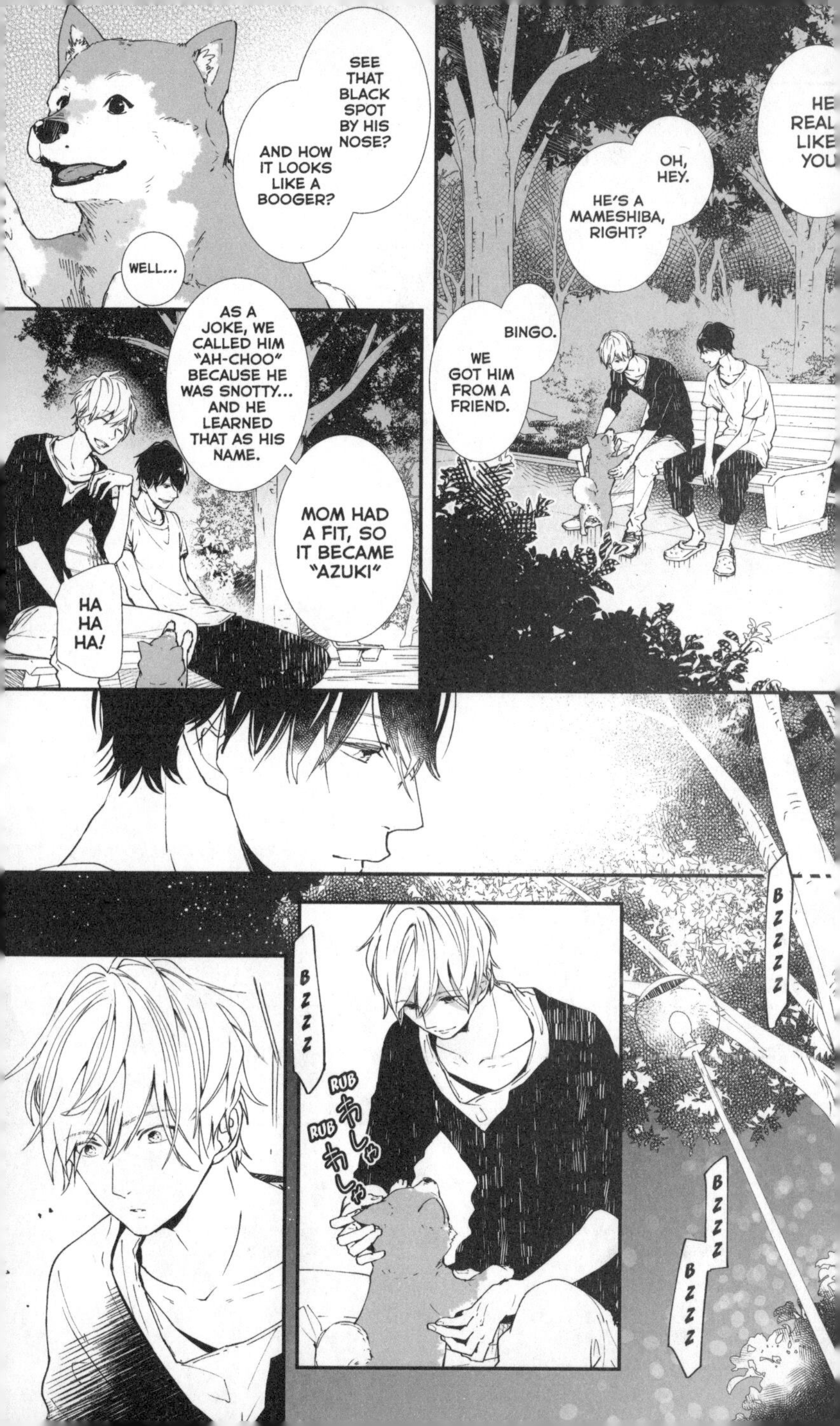
HE REAL LIKE YOU
OH, HEY.
HE'S A MAMESHIBA, RIGHT?
BINGO.
WE GOT HIM FROM A FRIEND.
SEE THAT BLACK SPOT BY HIS NOSE?
AND HOW IT LOOKS LIKE A BOOGER?
WELL...
AS A JOKE, WE CALLED HIM "AH-CHOO" BECAUSE HE WAS SNOTTY... AND HE LEARNED THAT AS HIS NAME.
MOM HAD A FIT, SO IT BECAME "AZUKI"
HA HA HA!
BZZZZ
BZZZ
BZZZ
BZZZ
RUB わしゃ
RUB わしゃ

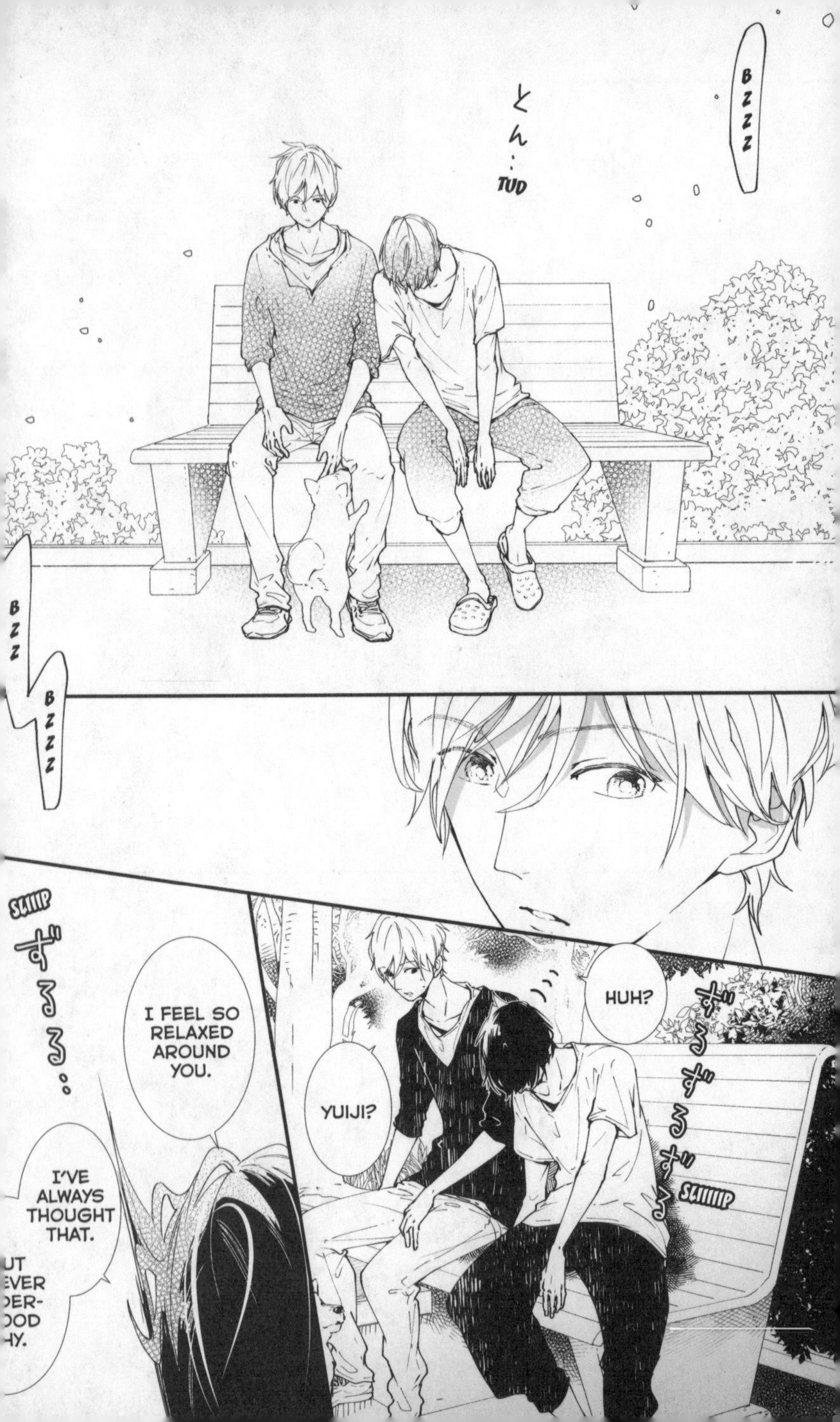

BZZZ
とん…
TUD
BZZ
BZZZ
HUH?
YUIJI?
ずるずるずる
SLIIIIIP
SLIIIP
ずる。
I FEEL SO RELAXED AROUND YOU.
I'VE ALWAYS THOUGHT THAT.
UT EVER DER- OOD HY.

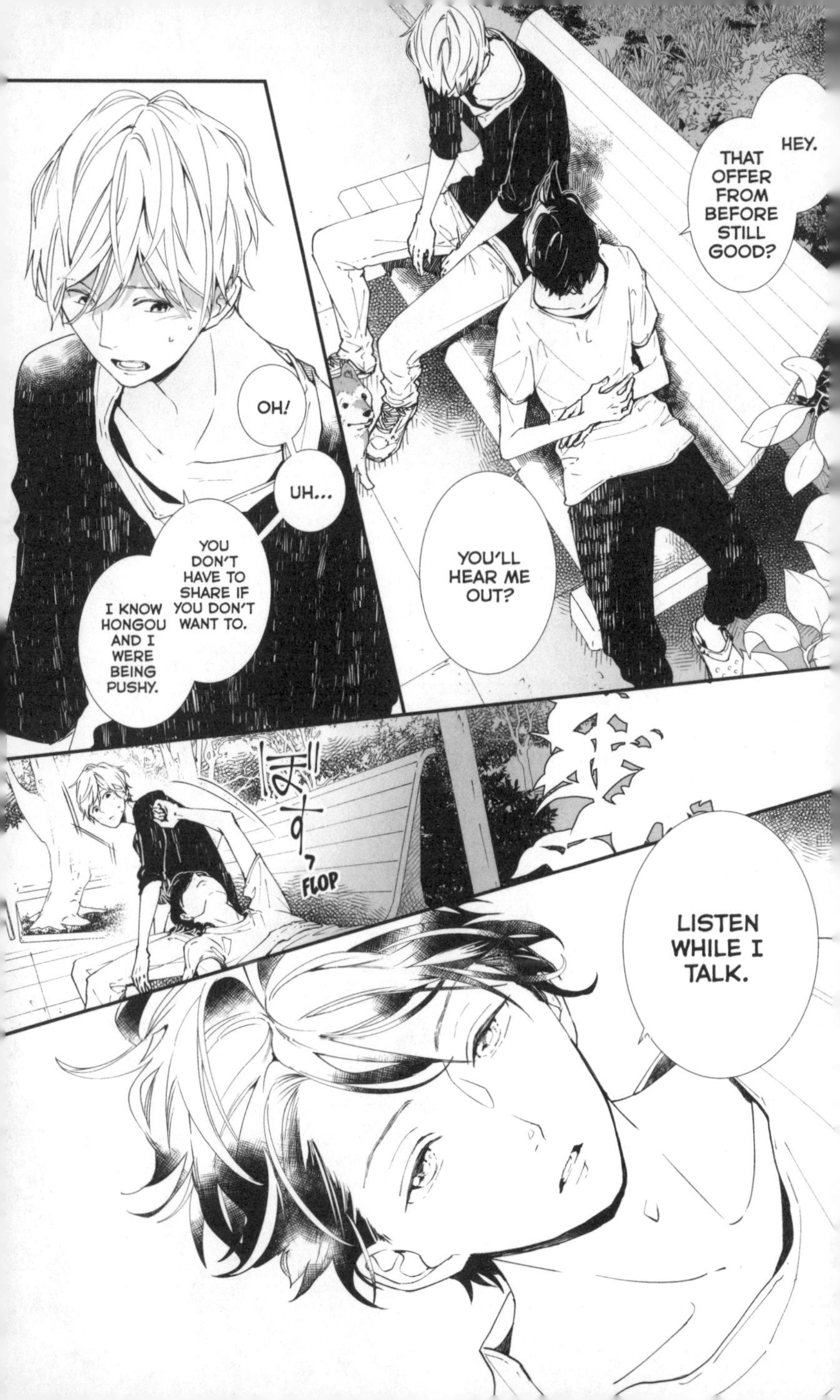
HEY.
THAT OFFER FROM BEFORE STILL GOOD?
YOU'LL HEAR ME OUT?
OH!
UH...
YOU DON'T HAVE TO SHARE IF YOU DON'T WANT TO.
I KNOW HONGOU AND I WERE BEING PUSHY.
ぼすっ
FLOP
LISTEN WHILE I TALK.

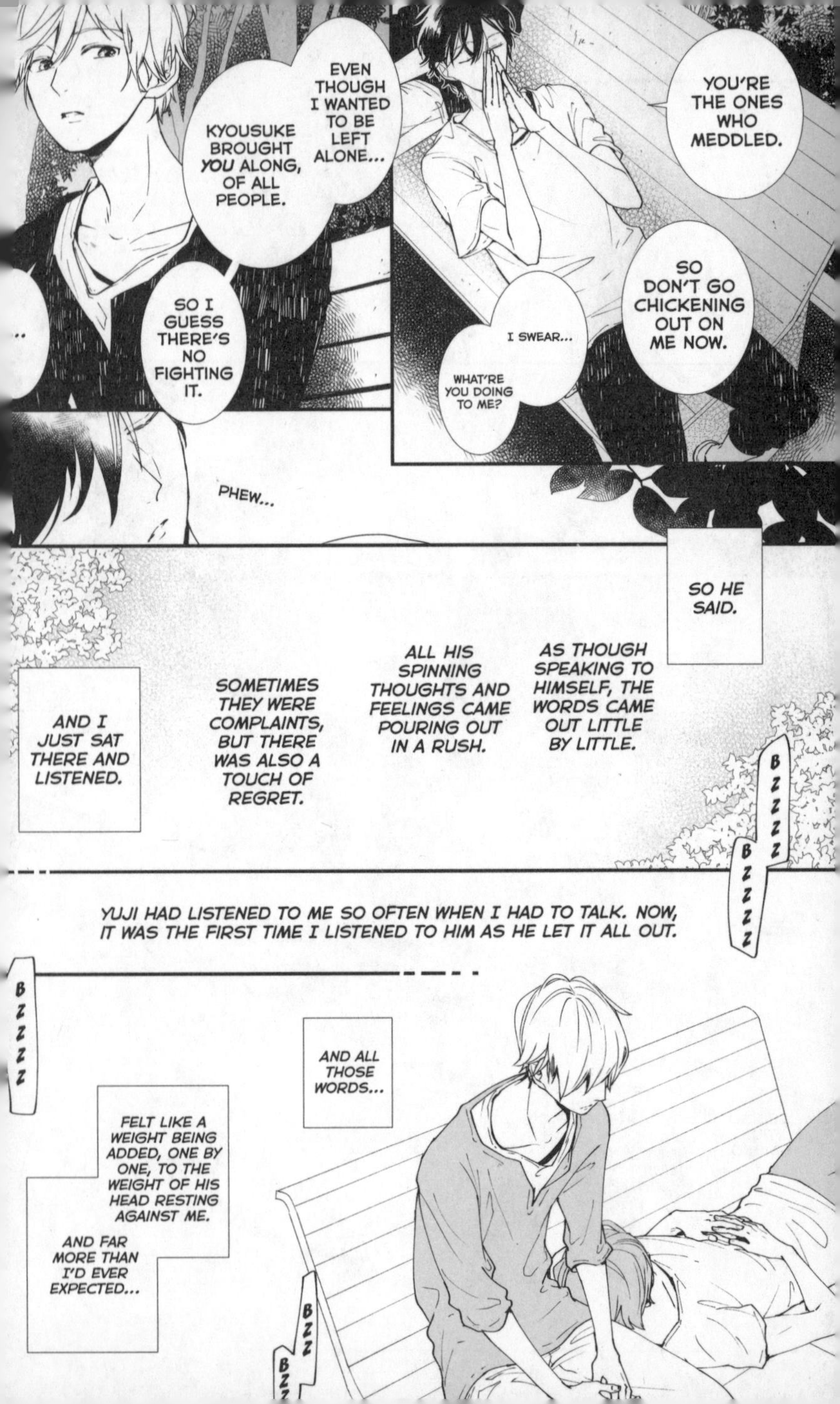
YOU'RE THE ONES WHO MEDDLED.
SO DON'T GO CHICKENING OUT ON ME NOW.
I SWEAR...
WHAT'RE YOU DOING TO ME?
EVEN THOUGH I WANTED TO BE LEFT ALONE...
KYOUSUKE BROUGHT *YOU* ALONG, OF ALL PEOPLE.
SO I GUESS THERE'S NO FIGHTING IT.
..
PHEW...
SO HE SAID.
AS THOUGH SPEAKING TO HIMSELF, THE WORDS CAME OUT LITTLE BY LITTLE.
ALL HIS SPINNING THOUGHTS AND FEELINGS CAME POURING OUT IN A RUSH.
SOMETIMES THEY WERE COMPLAINTS, BUT THERE WAS ALSO A TOUCH OF REGRET.
AND I JUST SAT THERE AND LISTENED.
BZZZ
BZZZ
YUJI HAD LISTENED TO ME SO OFTEN WHEN I HAD TO TALK. NOW, IT WAS THE FIRST TIME I LISTENED TO HIM AS HE LET IT ALL OUT.
BZZZ
AND ALL THOSE WORDS...
FELT LIKE A WEIGHT BEING ADDED, ONE BY ONE, TO THE WEIGHT OF HIS HEAD RESTING AGAINST ME.
AND FAR MORE THAN I'D EVER EXPECTED...
BZZ
BZZ

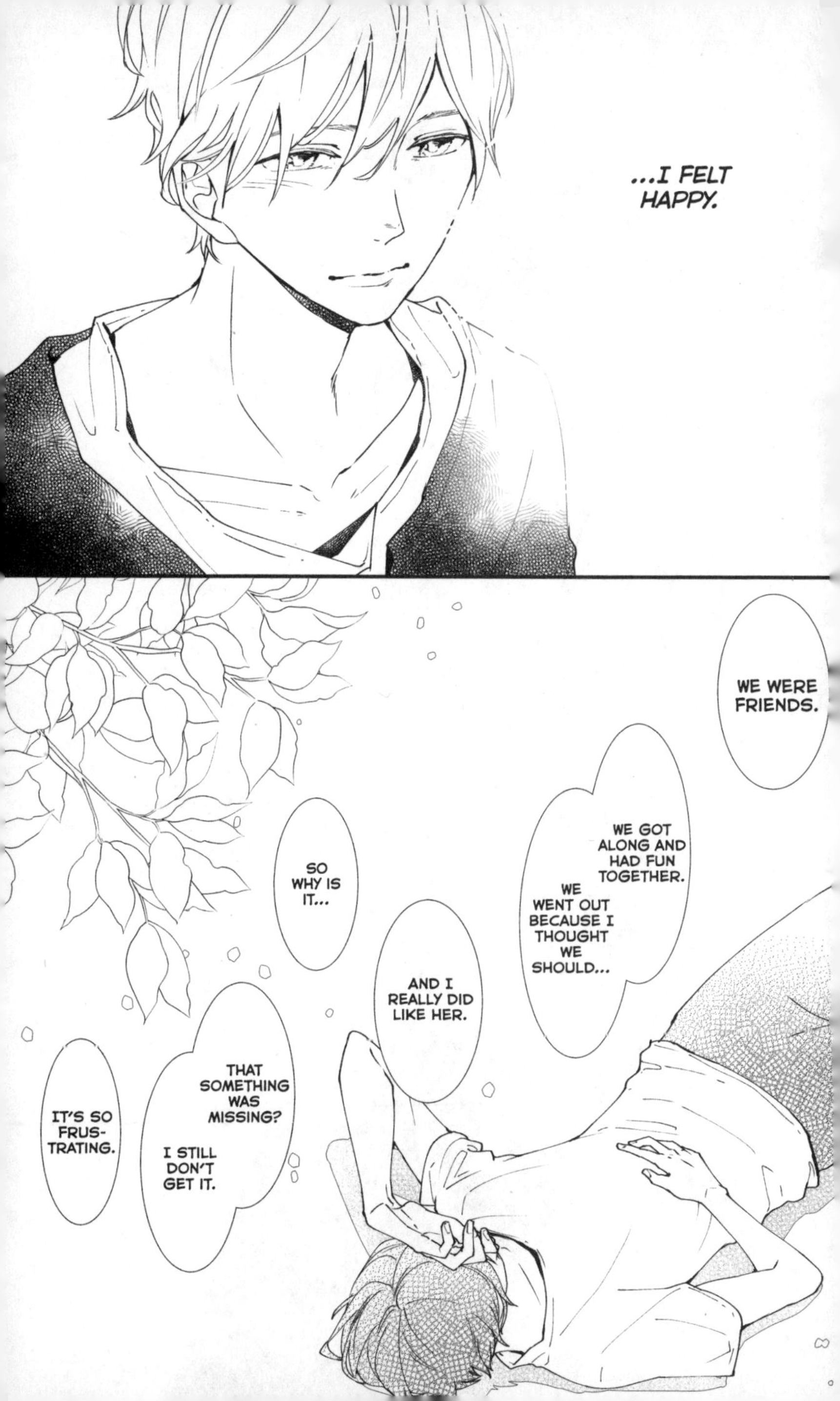
...I FELT HAPPY.
WE WERE FRIENDS.
WE GOT ALONG AND HAD FUN TOGETHER.
WE WENT OUT BECAUSE I THOUGHT WE SHOULD...
AND I REALLY DID LIKE HER.
SO WHY IS IT...
THAT SOMETHING WAS MISSING?
I STILL DON'T GET IT.
IT'S SO FRUS-TRATING.

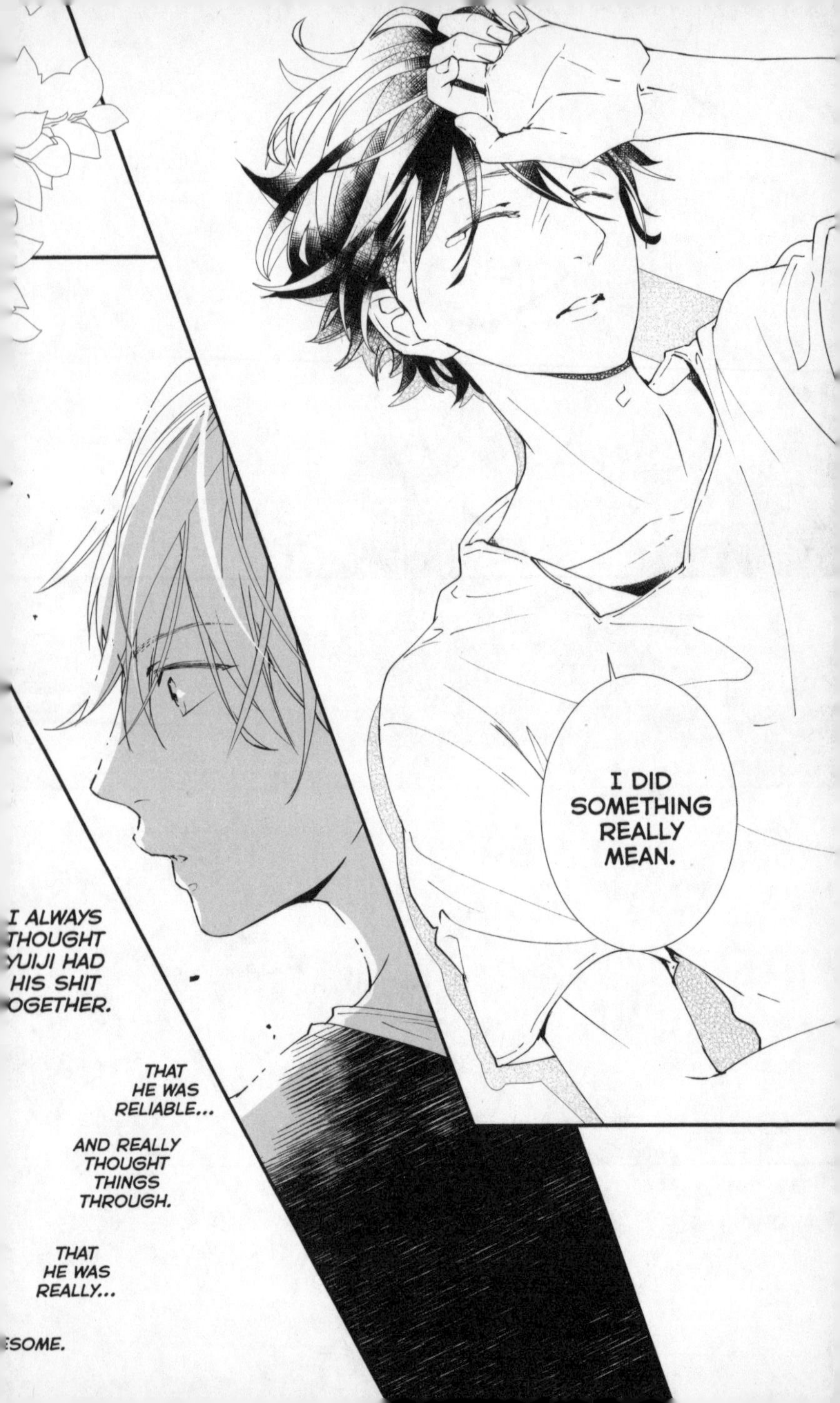
I DID SOMETHING REALLY MEAN.
I ALWAYS THOUGHT YUIJI HAD HIS SHIT OGETHER.
THAT HE WAS RELIABLE...
AND REALLY THOUGHT THINGS THROUGH.
THAT HE WAS REALLY...
ESOME.

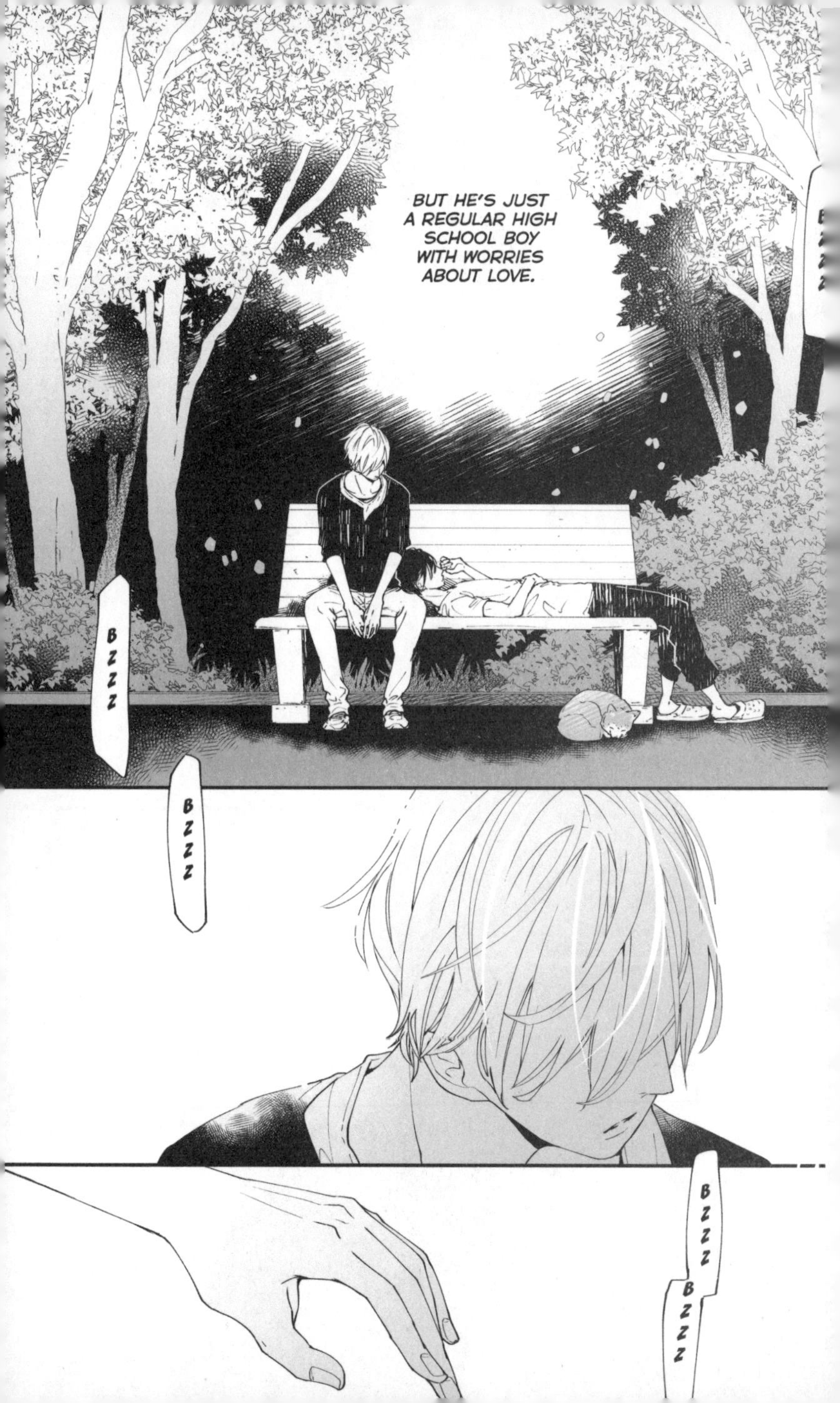
BZZZ
BUT HE'S JUST A REGULAR HIGH SCHOOL BOY WITH WORRIES ABOUT LOVE.
BZZZ
BZZZ
BZZZ
BZZZ

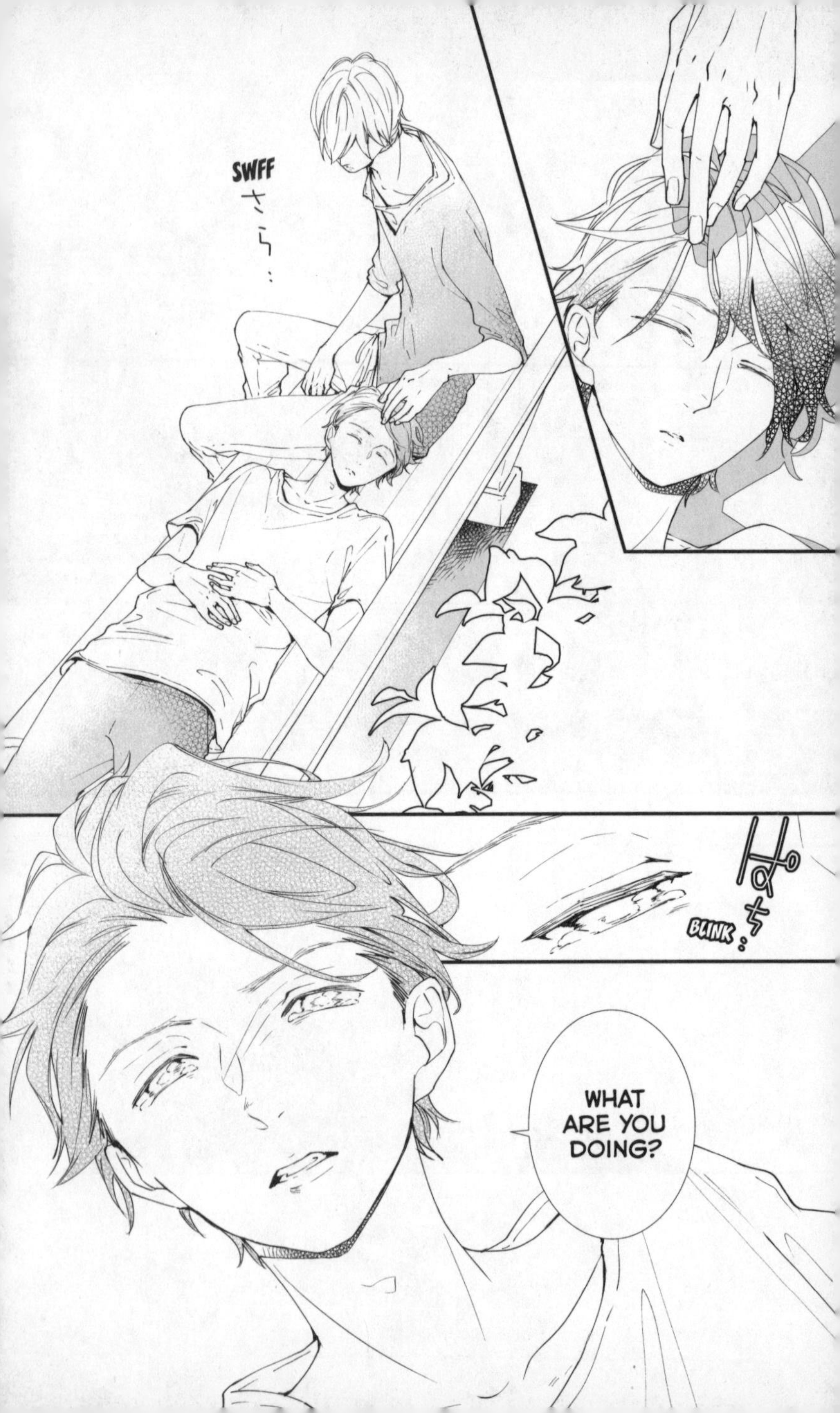
SWFF
さら…
BLINK
ぱち
WHAT ARE YOU DOING?

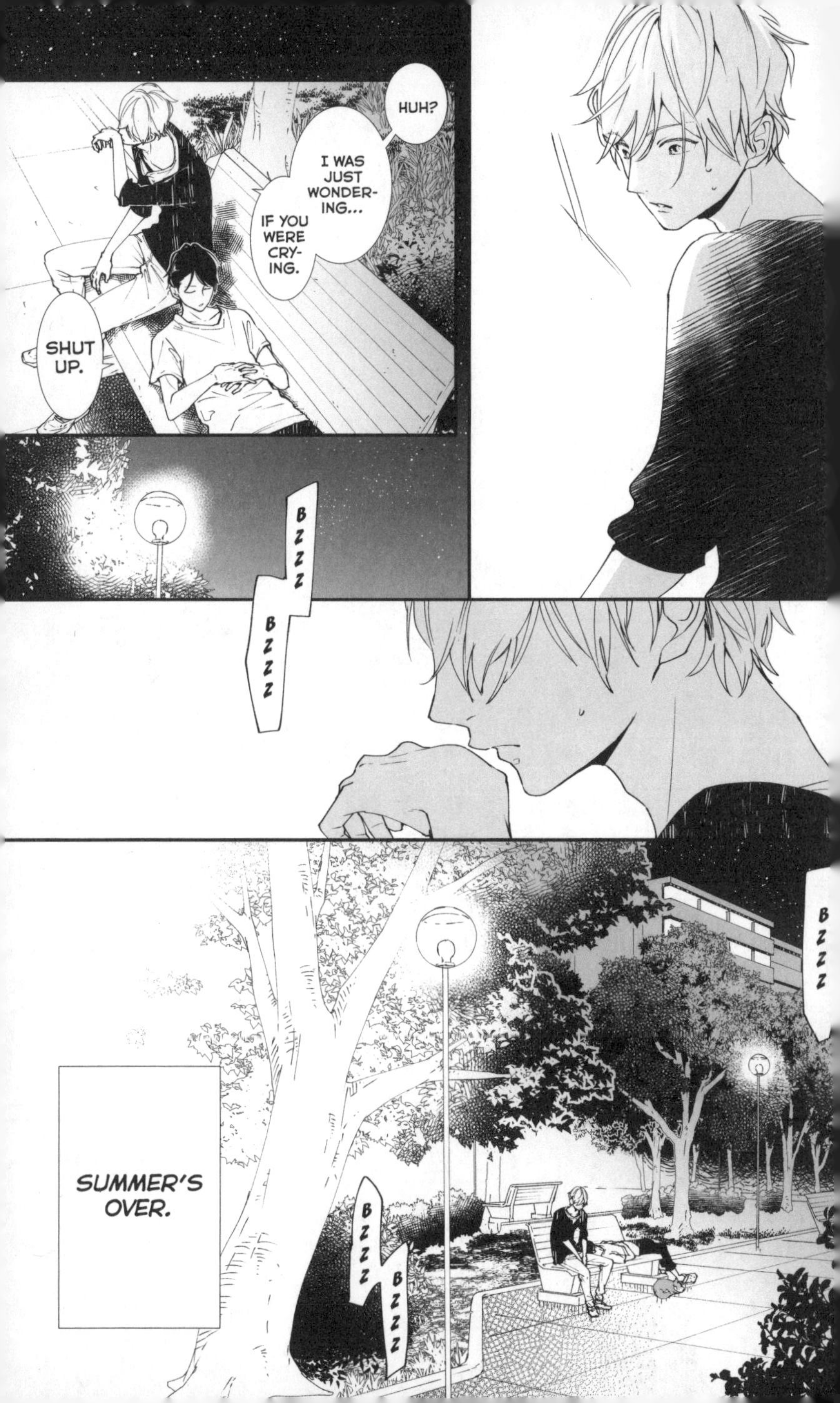
HUH?
I WAS JUST WONDER-ING...
IF YOU WERE CRY-ING.
SHUT UP.
BZZZ
BZZZ
BZZZ
SUMMER'S OVER.
BZZZ
BZZZ

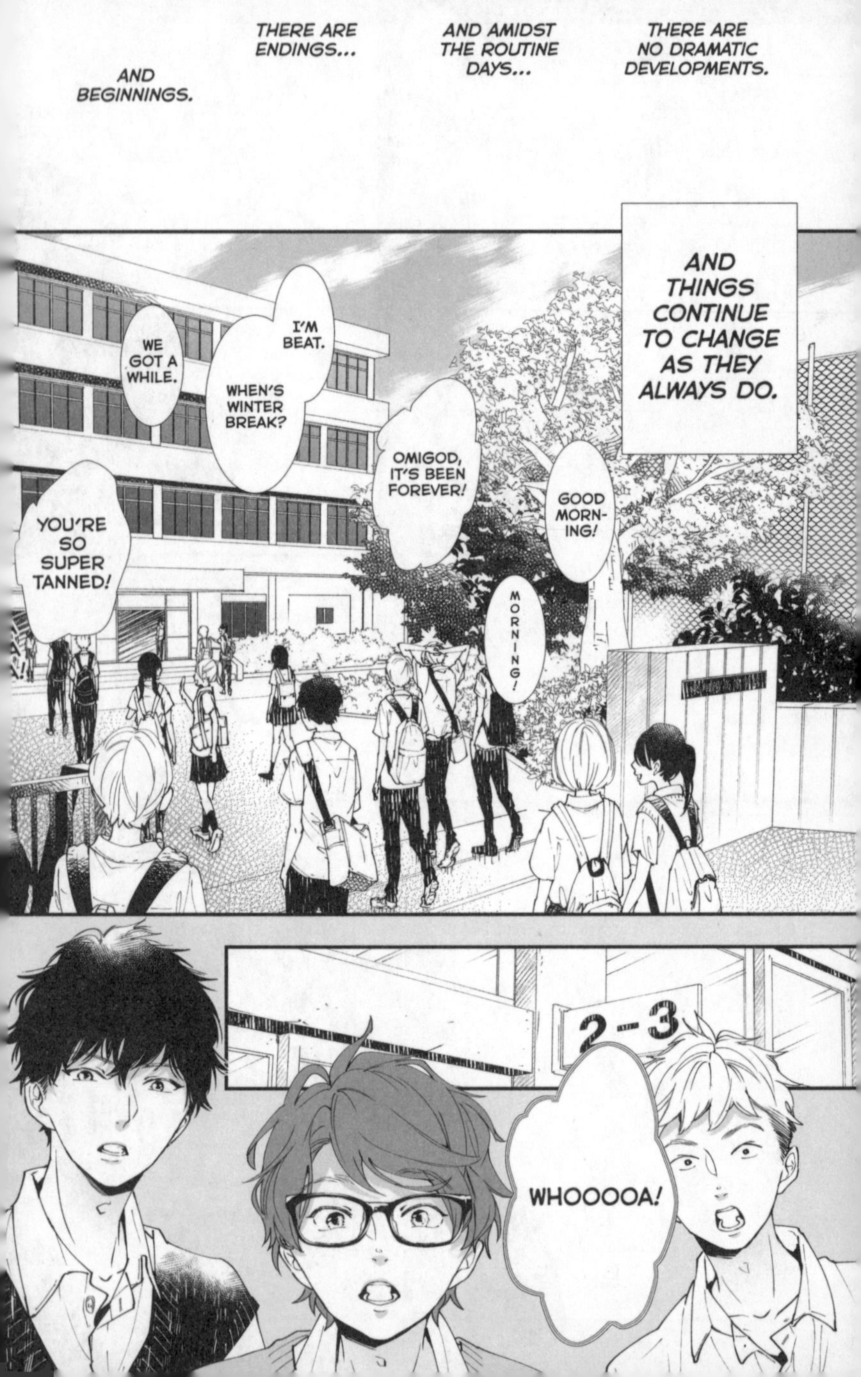
THERE ARE NO DRAMATIC DEVELOPMENTS.
AND AMIDST THE ROUTINE DAYS...
THERE ARE ENDINGS...
AND BEGINNINGS.
AND THINGS CONTINUE TO CHANGE AS THEY ALWAYS DO.
GOOD MORN-ING!
MORNING!
OMIGOD, IT'S BEEN FOREVER!
I'M BEAT.
WHEN'S WINTER BREAK?
WE GOT A WHILE.
YOU'RE SO SUPER TANNED!
2-3
WHOOOOA!

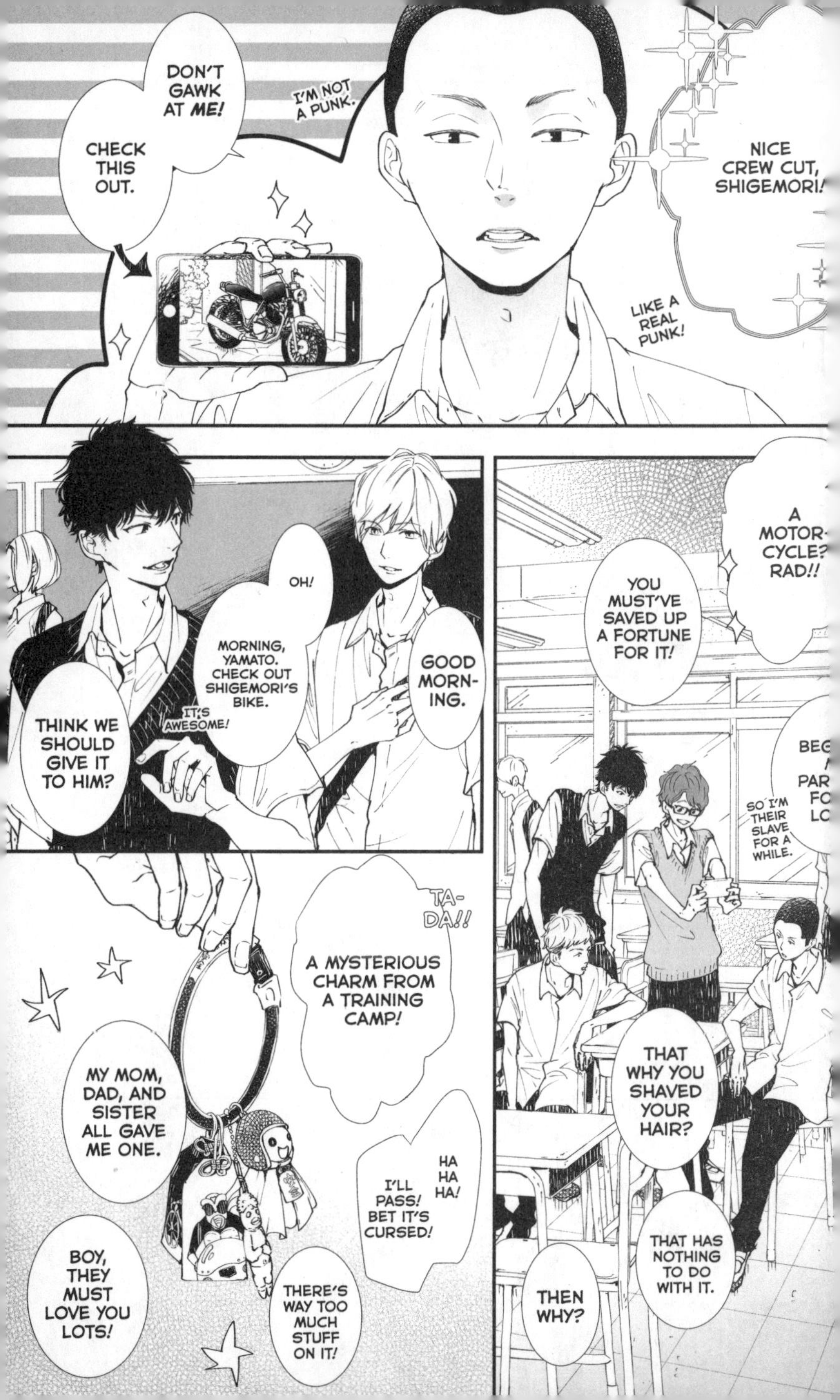

NICE CREW CUT, SHIGEMORI!
LIKE A REAL PUNK!
I'M NOT A PUNK.
DON'T GAWK AT *ME*!
CHECK THIS OUT.
A MOTOR-CYCLE? RAD!!
YOU MUST'VE SAVED UP A FORTUNE FOR IT!
BEG PAR FO LO
SO I'M THEIR SLAVE FOR A WHILE.
THAT WHY YOU SHAVED YOUR HAIR?
THAT HAS NOTHING TO DO WITH IT.
THEN WHY?
GOOD MORNING.
OH!
MORNING, YAMATO. CHECK OUT SHIGEMORI'S BIKE.
IT'S AWESOME!
THINK WE SHOULD GIVE IT TO HIM?
TA-DA!!
A MYSTERIOUS CHARM FROM A TRAINING CAMP!
HA HA HA!
I'LL PASS! BET IT'S CURSED!
MY MOM, DAD, AND SISTER ALL GAVE ME ONE.
THERE'S WAY TOO MUCH STUFF ON IT!
BOY, THEY MUST LOVE YOU LOTS!

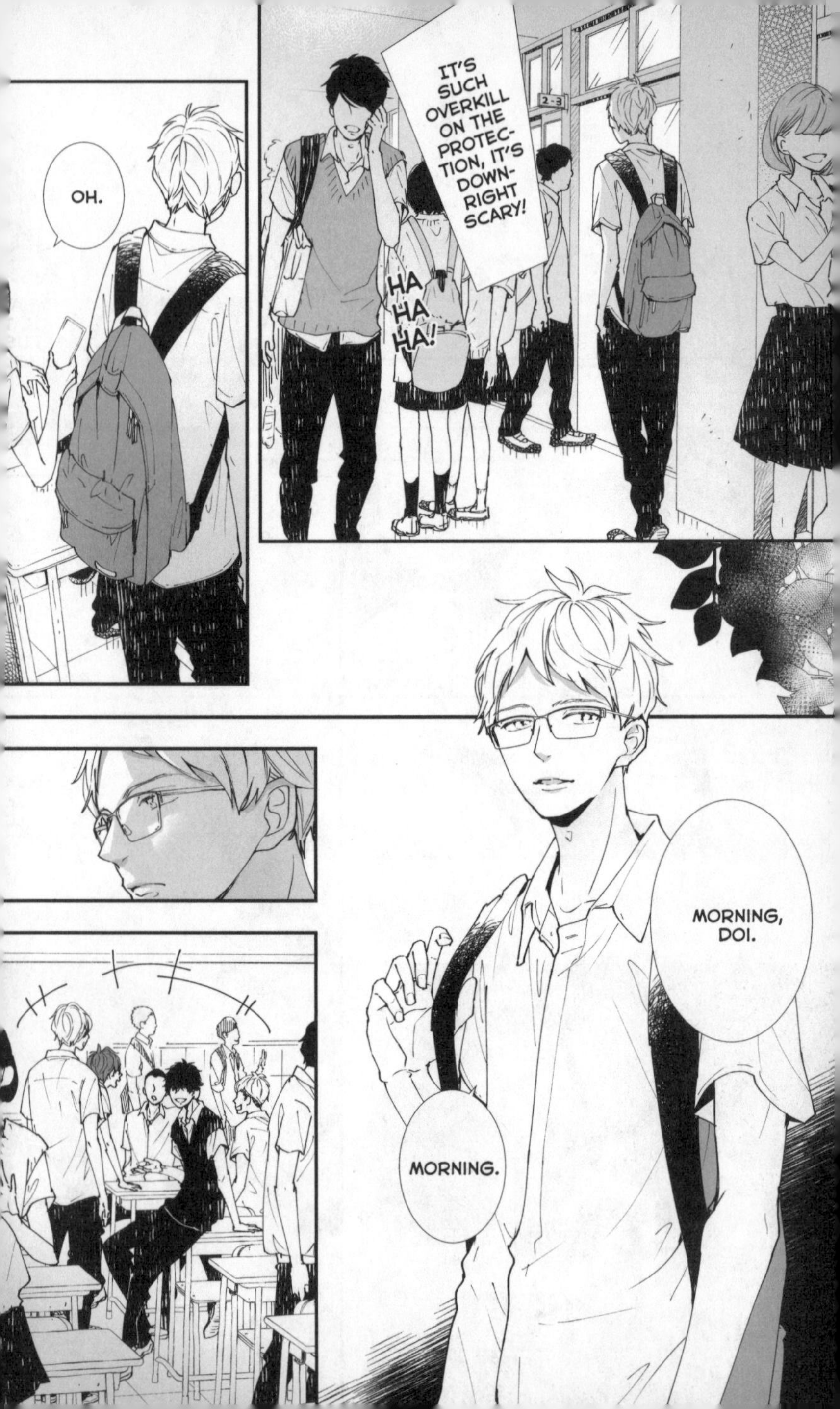
IT'S SUCH OVERKILL ON THE PROTECTION, IT'S DOWN-RIGHT SCARY!
HA HA HA!
OH.
MORNING, DOI.
MORNING.

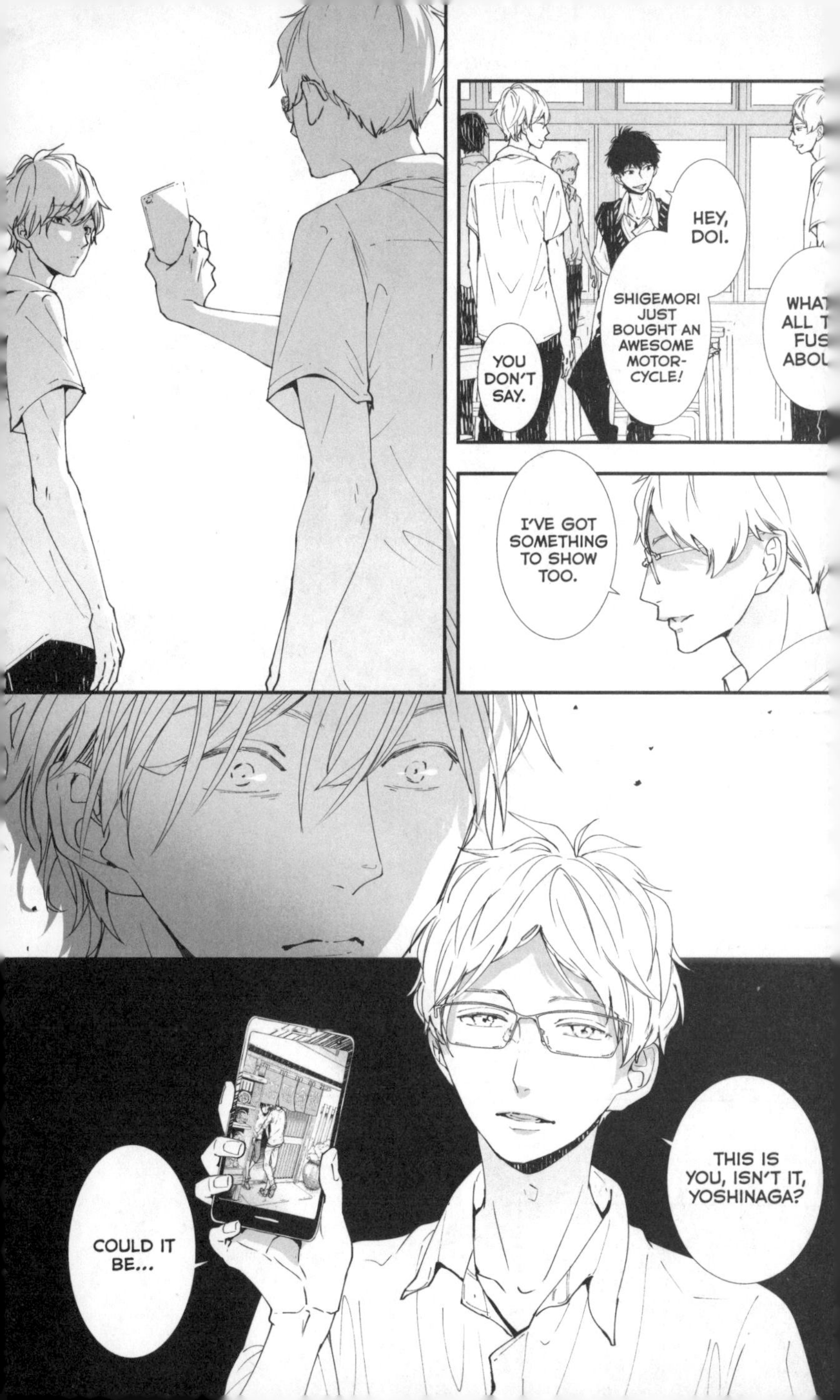
HEY, DOI.
SHIGEMORI JUST BOUGHT AN AWESOME MOTOR-CYCLE!
YOU DON'T SAY.
I'VE GOT SOMETHING TO SHOW TOO.
THIS IS YOU, ISN'T IT, YOSHINAGA?
COULD IT BE...

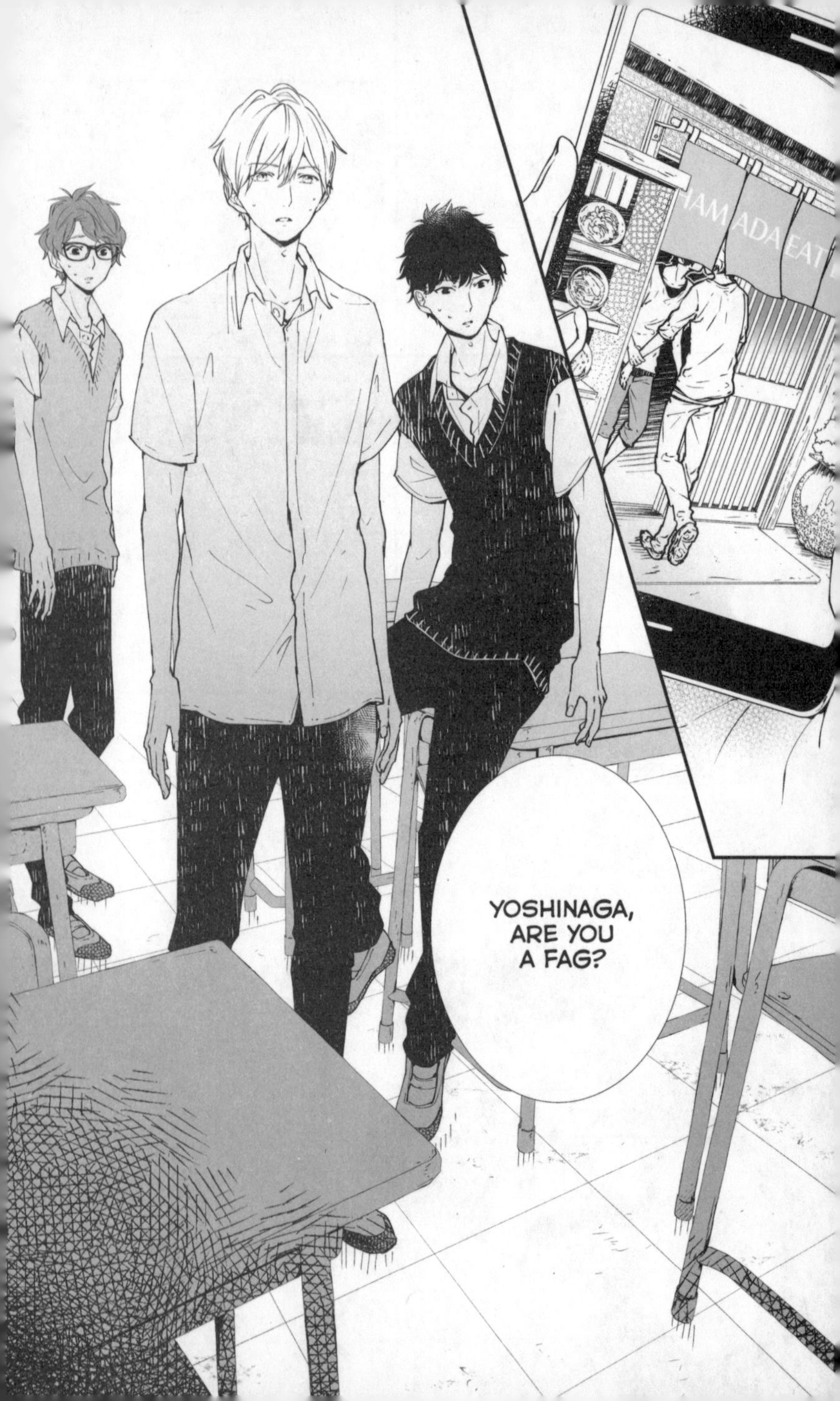
HAMADA EAT
YOSHINAGA, ARE YOU A FAG?

KOIMONOGATARI:
LOVE STORIES

2

LOVE STORIES.2 / TAGURA TOHRU

Chapter 8

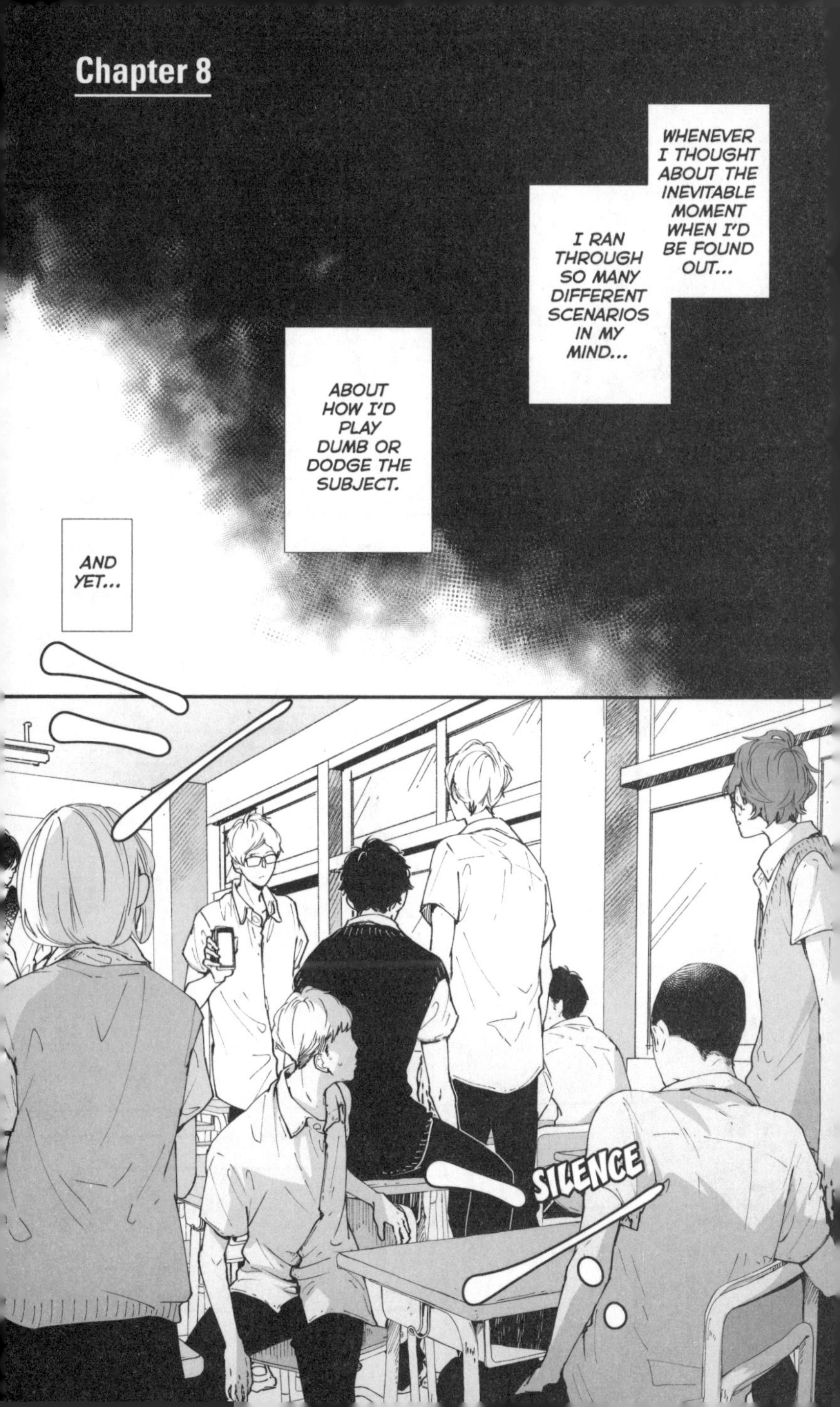
WHENEVER I THOUGHT ABOUT THE INEVITABLE MOMENT WHEN I'D BE FOUND OUT...
I RAN THROUGH SO MANY DIFFERENT SCENARIOS IN MY MIND...
ABOUT HOW I'D PLAY DUMB OR DODGE THE SUBJECT.
AND YET...
SILENCE

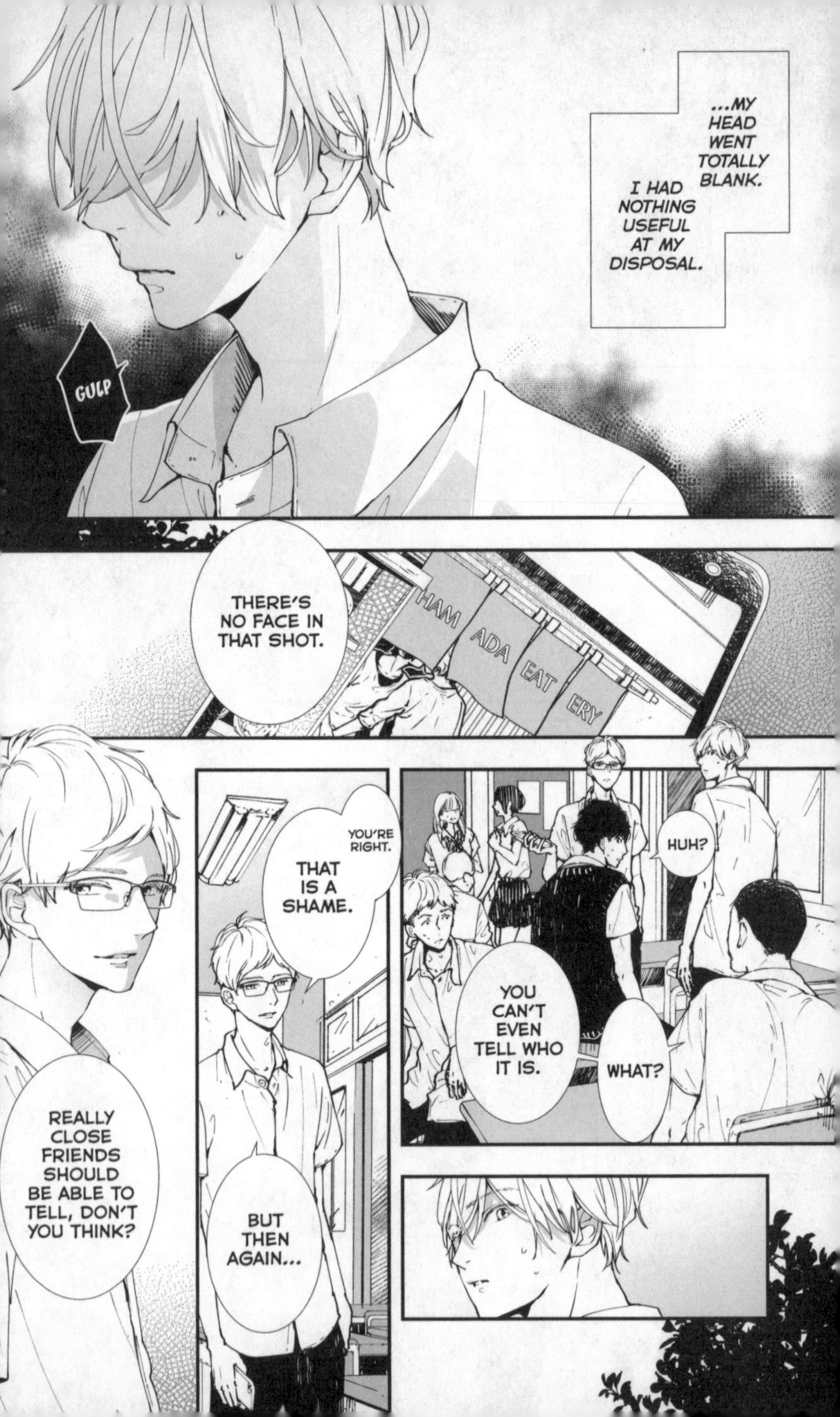
...MY HEAD WENT TOTALLY BLANK.
I HAD NOTHING USEFUL AT MY DISPOSAL.
GULP
THERE'S NO FACE IN THAT SHOT.
HAM ADA EAT ERY
HUH?
YOU CAN'T EVEN TELL WHO IT IS.
WHAT?
YOU'RE RIGHT.
THAT IS A SHAME.
BUT THEN AGAIN...
REALLY CLOSE FRIENDS SHOULD BE ABLE TO TELL, DON'T YOU THINK?

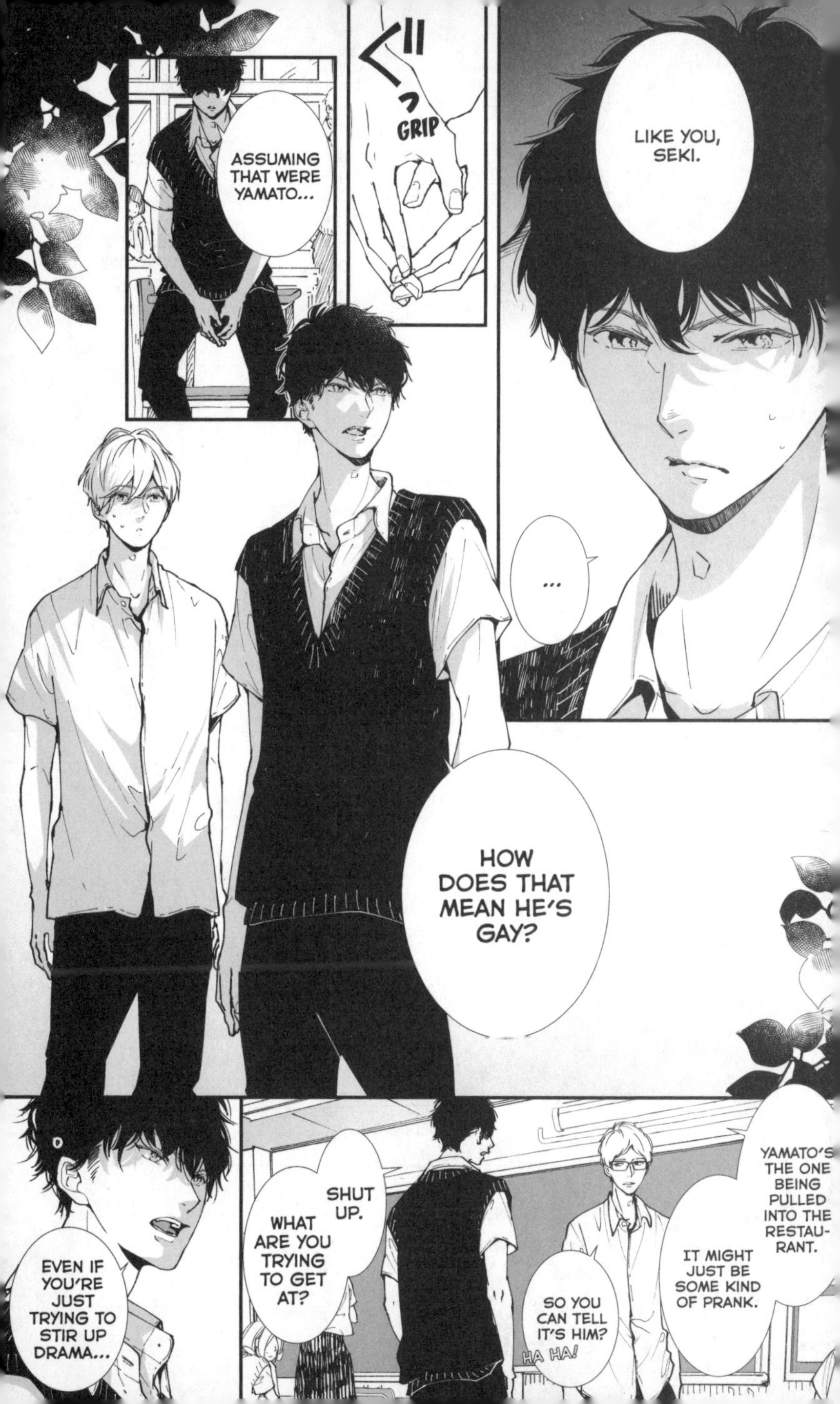

LIKE YOU, SEKI.
...
ぐっ
GRIP
ASSUMING THAT WERE YAMATO...
HOW DOES THAT MEAN HE'S GAY?
YAMATO'S THE ONE BEING PULLED INTO THE RESTAURANT.
IT MIGHT JUST BE SOME KIND OF PRANK.
SO YOU CAN TELL IT'S HIM?
HA HA!
SHUT UP.
WHAT ARE YOU TRYING TO GET AT?
EVEN IF YOU'RE JUST TRYING TO STIR UP DRAMA...

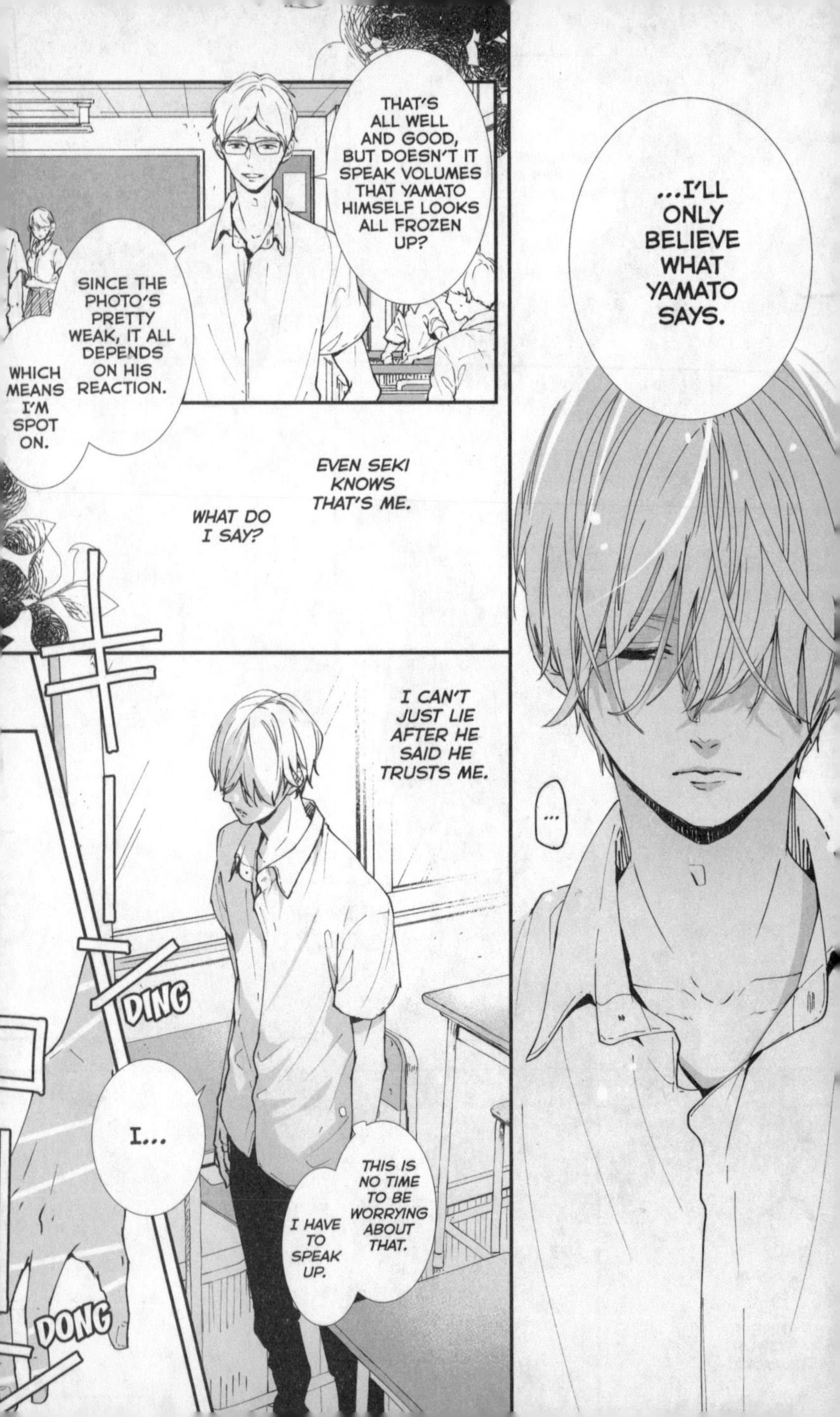
...I'LL ONLY BELIEVE WHAT YAMATO SAYS.
...
THAT'S ALL WELL AND GOOD, BUT DOESN'T IT SPEAK VOLUMES THAT YAMATO HIMSELF LOOKS ALL FROZEN UP?
SINCE THE PHOTO'S PRETTY WEAK, IT ALL DEPENDS ON HIS REACTION.
WHICH MEANS I'M SPOT ON.
EVEN SEKI KNOWS THAT'S ME.
WHAT DO I SAY?
I CAN'T JUST LIE AFTER HE SAID HE TRUSTS ME.
DING
THIS IS NO TIME TO BE WORRYING ABOUT THAT.
I HAVE TO SPEAK UP.
I...
DONG

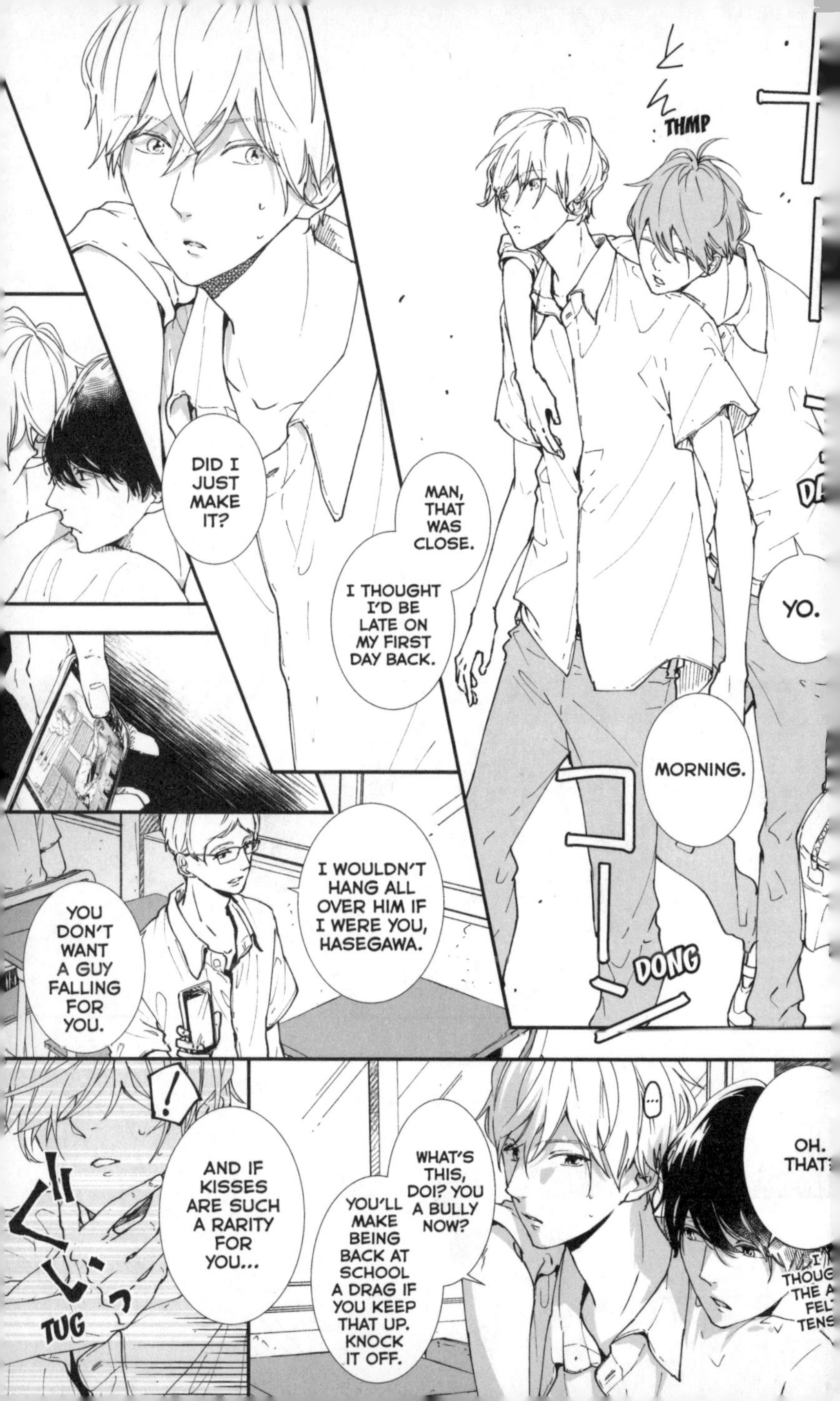
THMP
YO.
MORNING.
DONG
MAN, THAT WAS CLOSE.
I THOUGHT I'D BE LATE ON MY FIRST DAY BACK.
DID I JUST MAKE IT?
I WOULDN'T HANG ALL OVER HIM IF I WERE YOU, HASEGAWA.
YOU DON'T WANT A GUY FALLING FOR YOU.
OH.
...
WHAT'S THIS, DOI? YOU A BULLY NOW?
YOU'LL MAKE BEING BACK AT SCHOOL A DRAG IF YOU KEEP THAT UP. KNOCK IT OFF.
!
AND IF KISSES ARE SUCH A RARITY FOR YOU...
TUG

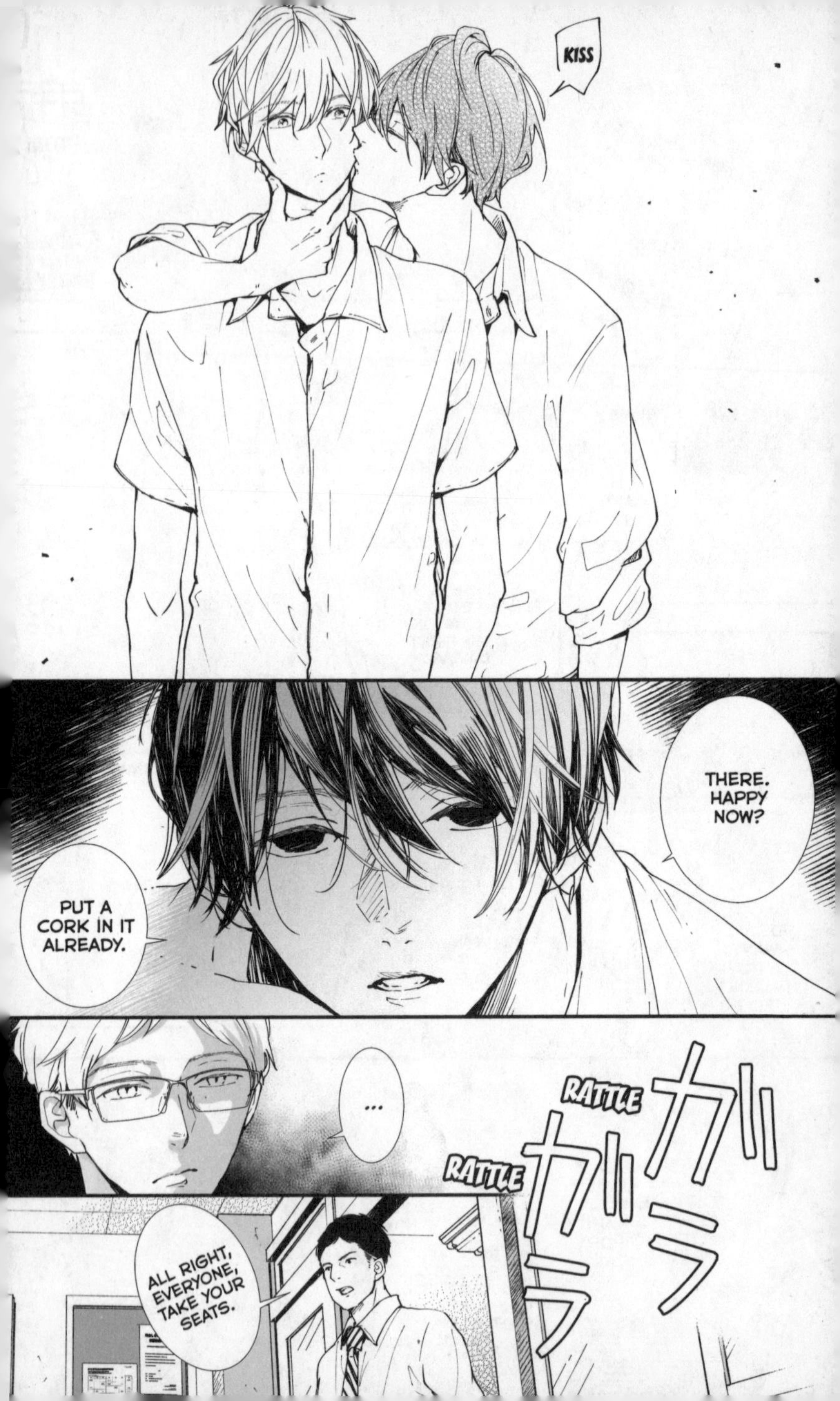
KISS
THERE. HAPPY NOW?
PUT A CORK IN IT ALREADY.
RATTLE ガラ
RATTLE ガラ
...
ALL RIGHT, EVERYONE, TAKE YOUR SEATS.

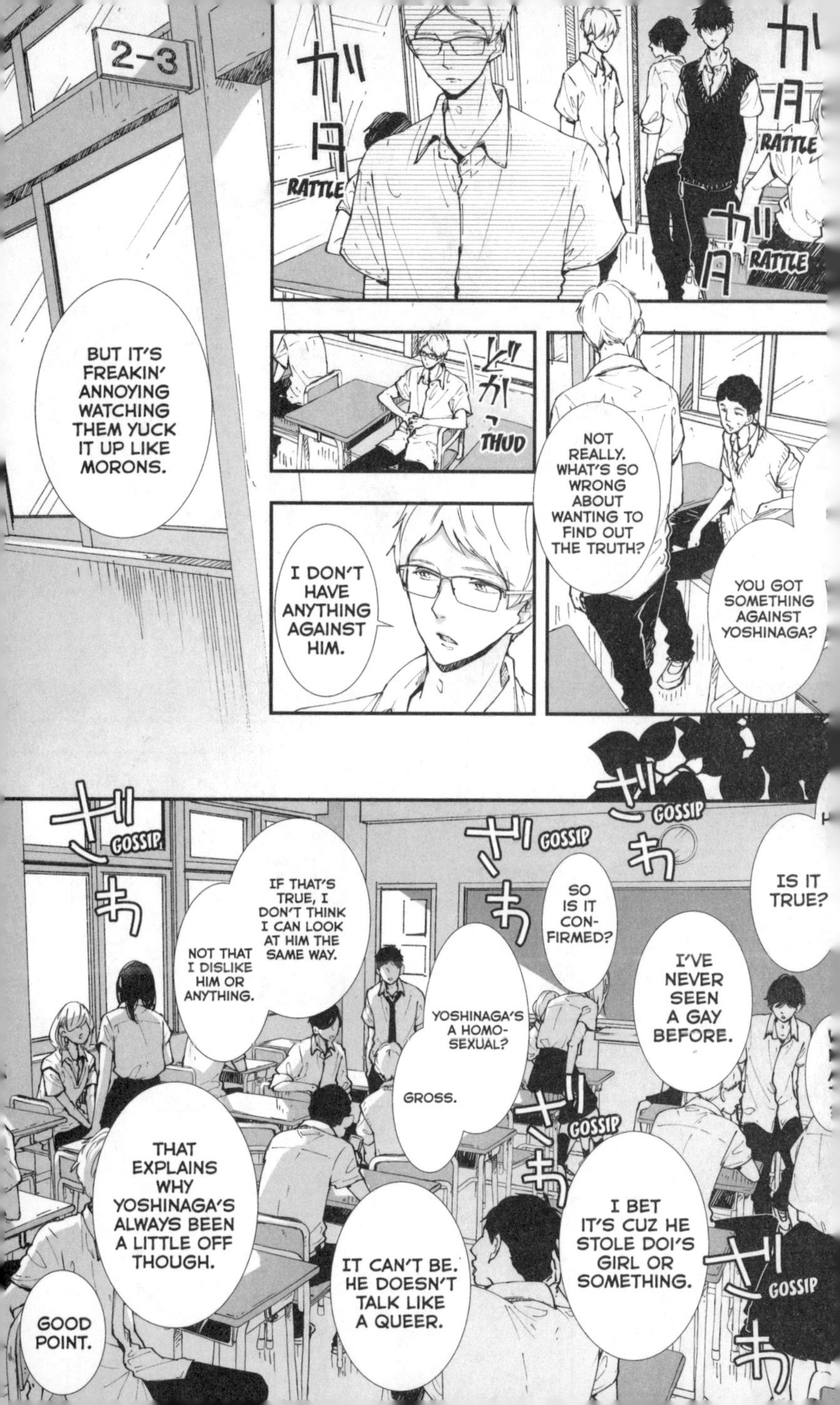

ガタ
RATTLE
ガタ
RATTLE
ガタ
RATTLE
YOU GOT SOMETHING AGAINST YOSHINAGA?
NOT REALLY. WHAT'S SO WRONG ABOUT WANTING TO FIND OUT THE TRUTH?
どがっ
THUD
I DON'T HAVE ANYTHING AGAINST HIM.
BUT IT'S FREAKIN' ANNOYING WATCHING THEM YUCK IT UP LIKE MORONS.
IS IT TRUE?
ざわ
GOSSIP
SO IS IT CONFIRMED?
I'VE NEVER SEEN A GAY BEFORE.
ざわ
GOSSIP
YOSHINAGA'S A HOMOSEXUAL?
GROSS.
IF THAT'S TRUE, I DON'T THINK I CAN LOOK AT HIM THE SAME WAY.
NOT THAT I DISLIKE HIM OR ANYTHING.
ざわ
GOSSIP
ざわ
GOSSIP
ざわ
GOSSIP
I BET IT'S CUZ HE STOLE DOI'S GIRL OR SOMETHING.
IT CAN'T BE. HE DOESN'T TALK LIKE A QUEER.
THAT EXPLAINS WHY YOSHINAGA'S ALWAYS BEEN A LITTLE OFF THOUGH.
GOOD POINT.

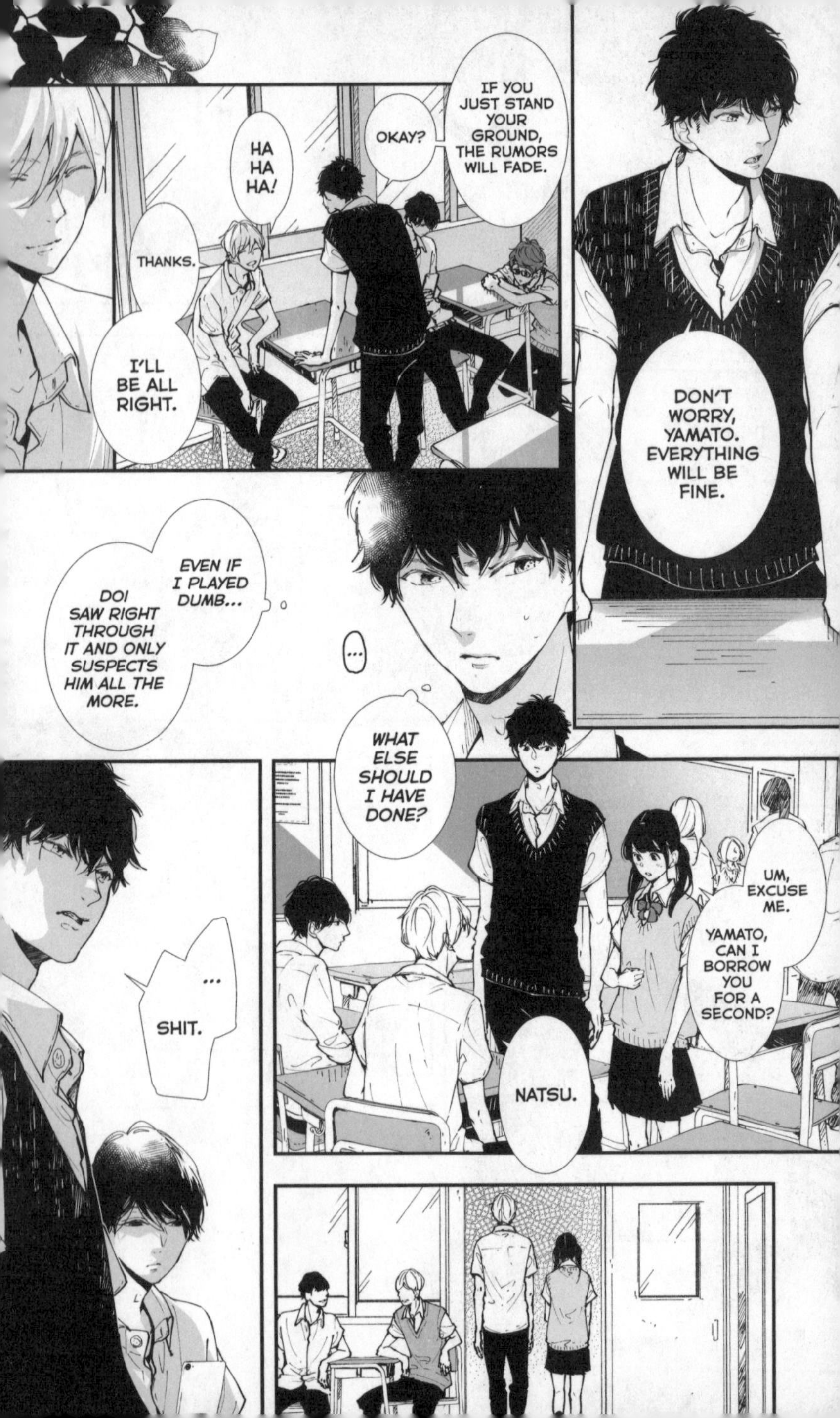
DON'T WORRY, YAMATO. EVERYTHING WILL BE FINE.
IF YOU JUST STAND YOUR GROUND, THE RUMORS WILL FADE.
OKAY?
HA HA HA!
THANKS.
I'LL BE ALL RIGHT.
...
EVEN IF I PLAYED DUMB...
DOI SAW RIGHT THROUGH IT AND ONLY SUSPECTS HIM ALL THE MORE.
WHAT ELSE SHOULD I HAVE DONE?
UM, EXCUSE ME.
YAMATO, CAN I BORROW YOU FOR A SECOND?
NATSU.
... SHIT.

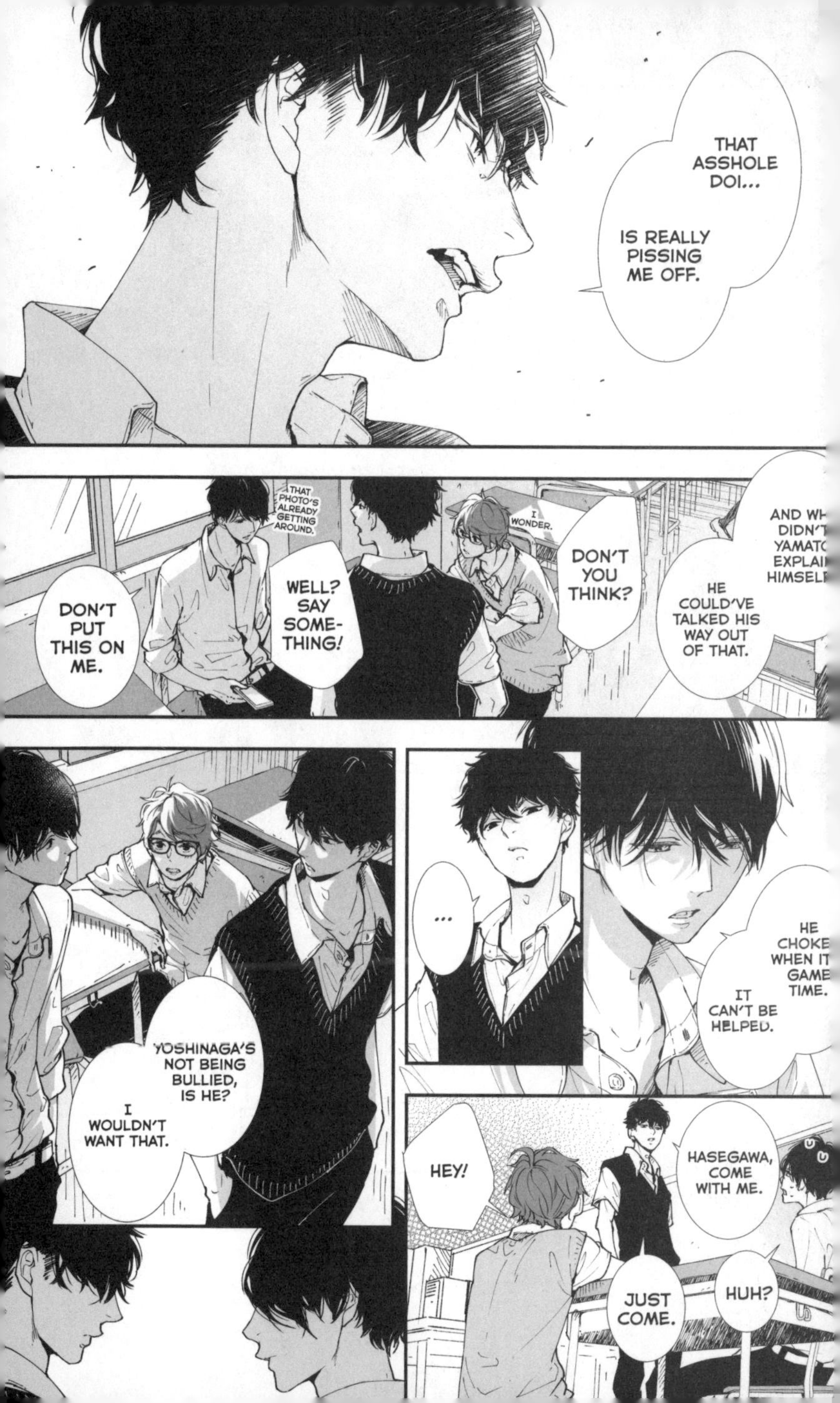
THAT ASSHOLE DOI...
IS REALLY PISSING ME OFF.
AND WH DIDN'T YAMATO EXPLAI HIMSEL
HE COULD'VE TALKED HIS WAY OUT OF THAT.
DON'T YOU THINK?
I WONDER.
WELL? SAY SOME-THING!
THAT PHOTO'S ALREADY GETTING AROUND.
DON'T PUT THIS ON ME.
HE CHOKE WHEN IT GAME TIME.
IT CAN'T BE HELPED.
...
HASEGAWA, COME WITH ME.
HEY!
HUH?
JUST COME.
YOSHINAGA'S NOT BEING BULLIED, IS HE?
I WOULDN'T WANT THAT.

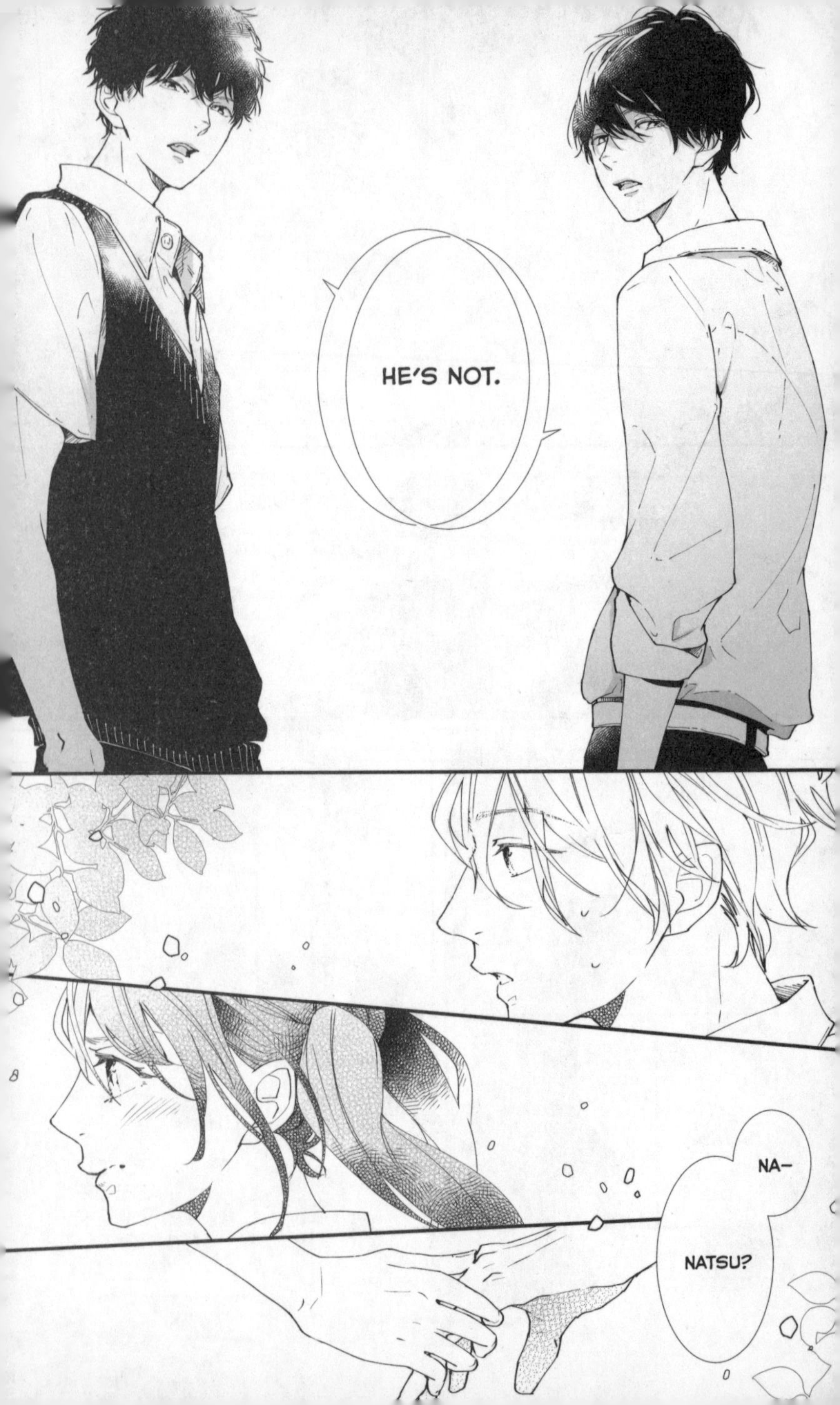
HE'S NOT.
NA–
NATSU?

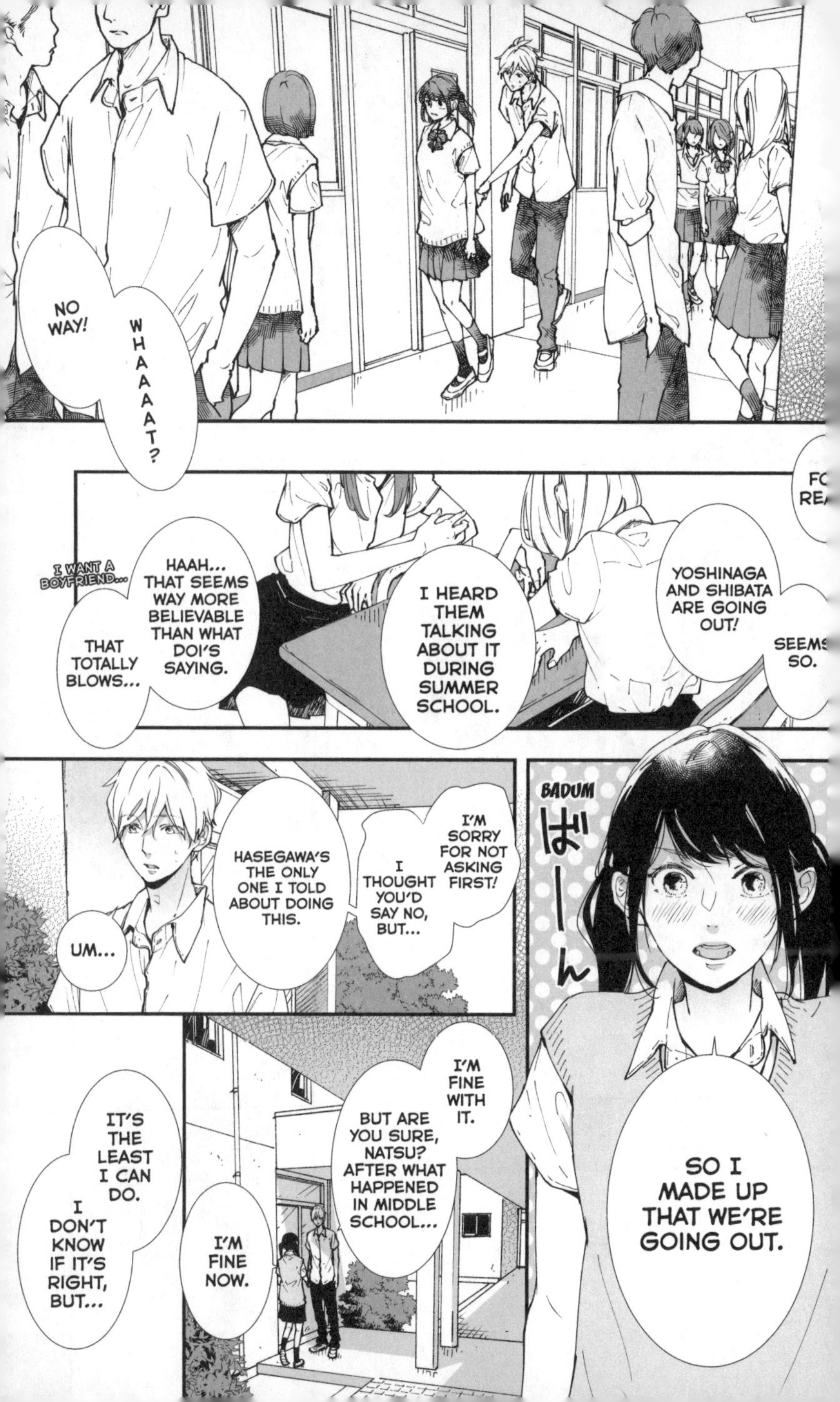
WHAAAAT?
NO WAY!
YOSHINAGA AND SHIBATA ARE GOING OUT!
SEEMS SO.
I HEARD THEM TALKING ABOUT IT DURING SUMMER SCHOOL.
HAAH... THAT SEEMS WAY MORE BELIEVABLE THAN WHAT DOI'S SAYING.
THAT TOTALLY BLOWS...
I WANT A BOYFRIEND...
BADUM
ばーん
SO I MADE UP THAT WE'RE GOING OUT.
I'M SORRY FOR NOT ASKING FIRST!
I THOUGHT YOU'D SAY NO, BUT...
HASEGAWA'S THE ONLY ONE I TOLD ABOUT DOING THIS.
UM...
I'M FINE WITH IT.
BUT ARE YOU SURE, NATSU? AFTER WHAT HAPPENED IN MIDDLE SCHOOL...
I'M FINE NOW.
IT'S THE LEAST I CAN DO.
I DON'T KNOW IF IT'S RIGHT, BUT...

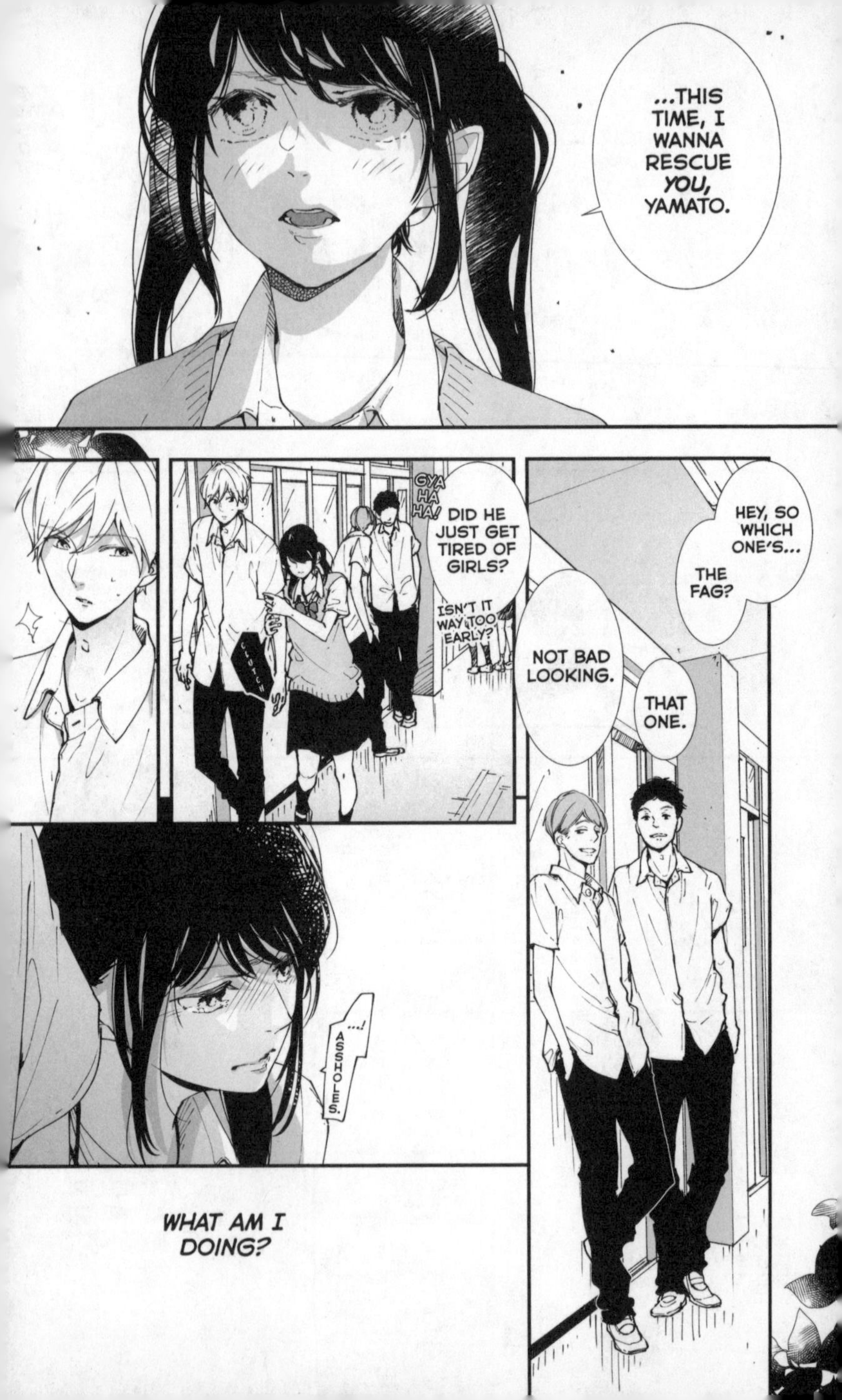
...THIS TIME, I WANNA RESCUE *YOU*, YAMATO.
HEY, SO WHICH ONE'S...
THE FAG?
NOT BAD LOOKING.
THAT ONE.
GYA HA HA!
DID HE JUST GET TIRED OF GIRLS?
ISN'T IT WAY TOO EARLY?
CLUTCH
...! ASSHOLES.
WHAT AM I DOING?

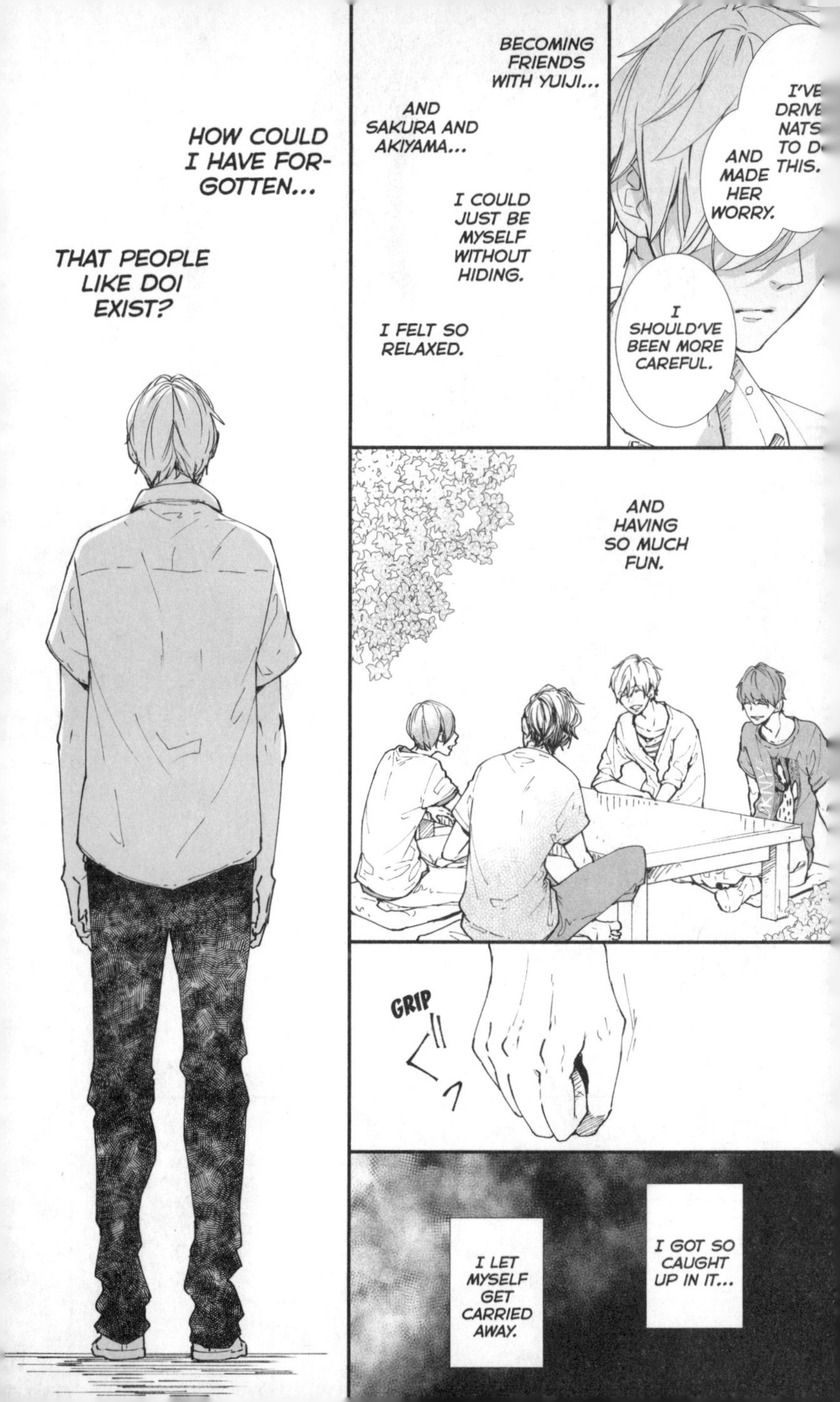

I'VE DRIVE NATS TO D THIS.
AND MADE HER WORRY.
I SHOULD'VE BEEN MORE CAREFUL.
BECOMING FRIENDS WITH YUIJI...
AND SAKURA AND AKIYAMA...
I COULD JUST BE MYSELF WITHOUT HIDING.
I FELT SO RELAXED.
AND HAVING SO MUCH FUN.
GRIP
I GOT SO CAUGHT UP IN IT...
I LET MYSELF GET CARRIED AWAY.
HOW COULD I HAVE FOR-GOTTEN...
THAT PEOPLE LIKE DOI EXIST?

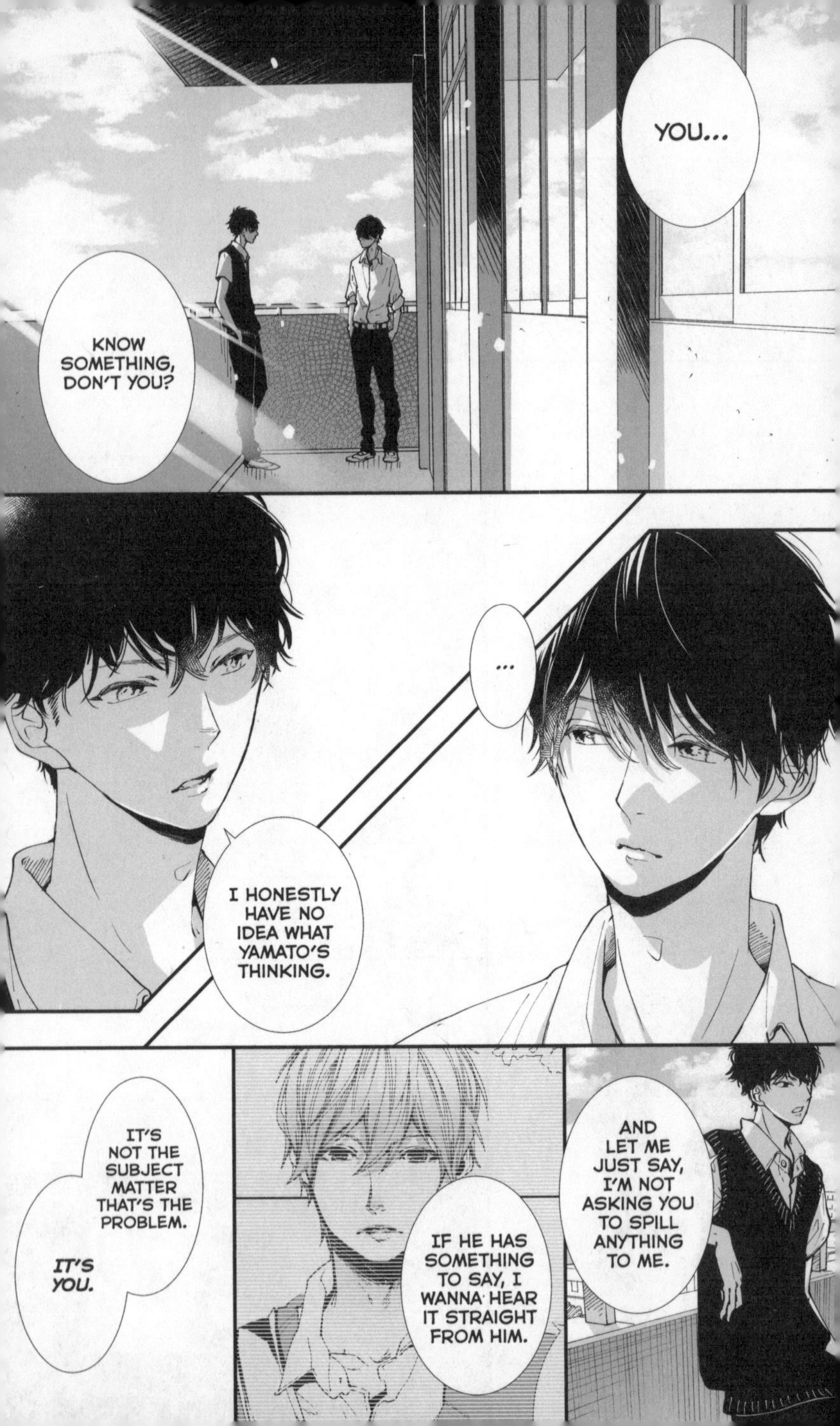
YOU...
KNOW SOMETHING, DON'T YOU?
...
I HONESTLY HAVE NO IDEA WHAT YAMATO'S THINKING.
AND LET ME JUST SAY, I'M NOT ASKING YOU TO SPILL ANYTHING TO ME.
IF HE HAS SOMETHING TO SAY, I WANNA HEAR IT STRAIGHT FROM HIM.
IT'S NOT THE SUBJECT MATTER THAT'S THE PROBLEM.
IT'S YOU.

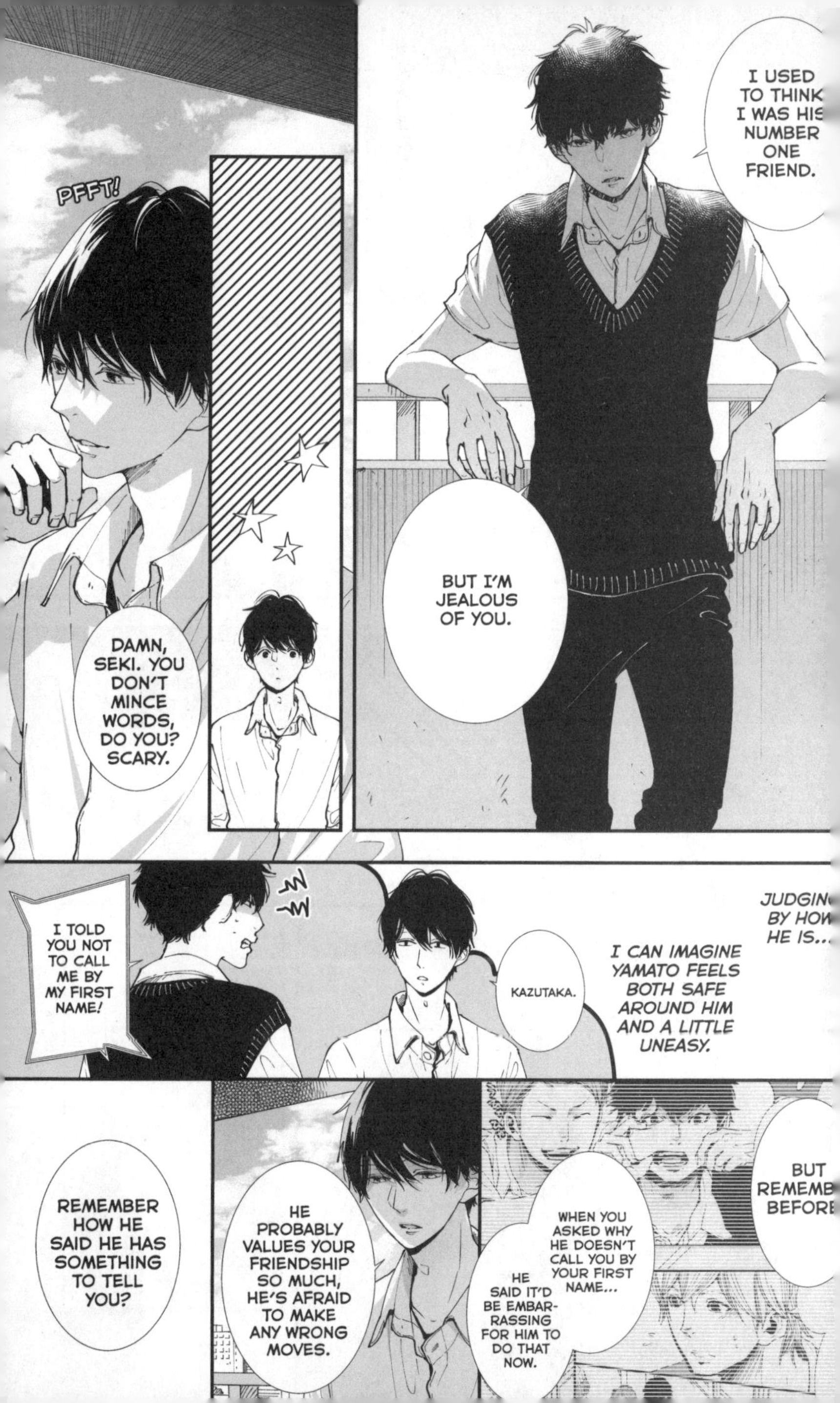
I USED TO THINK I WAS HIS NUMBER ONE FRIEND.
BUT I'M JEALOUS OF YOU.
PFFT!
DAMN, SEKI. YOU DON'T MINCE WORDS, DO YOU? SCARY.
JUDGIN BY HOW HE IS...
I CAN IMAGINE YAMATO FEELS BOTH SAFE AROUND HIM AND A LITTLE UNEASY.
KAZUTAKA.
I TOLD YOU NOT TO CALL ME BY MY FIRST NAME!
BUT REMEMB BEFORE
WHEN YOU ASKED WHY HE DOESN'T CALL YOU BY YOUR FIRST NAME...
HE SAID IT'D BE EMBAR-RASSING FOR HIM TO DO THAT NOW.
HE PROBABLY VALUES YOUR FRIENDSHIP SO MUCH, HE'S AFRAID TO MAKE ANY WRONG MOVES.
REMEMBER HOW HE SAID HE HAS SOMETHING TO TELL YOU?

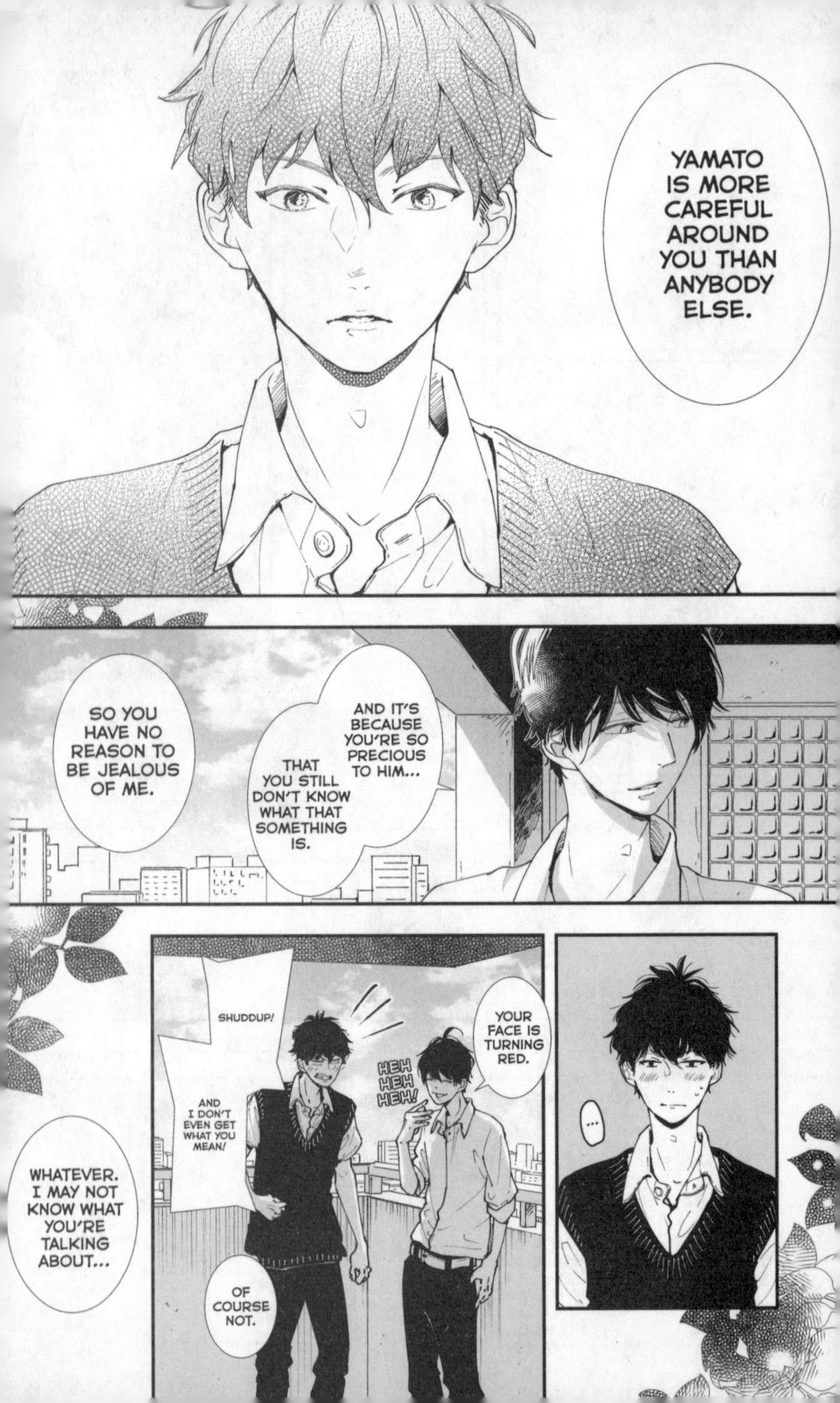
YAMATO IS MORE CAREFUL AROUND YOU THAN ANYBODY ELSE.
AND IT'S BECAUSE YOU'RE SO PRECIOUS TO HIM...
THAT YOU STILL DON'T KNOW WHAT THAT SOMETHING IS.
SO YOU HAVE NO REASON TO BE JEALOUS OF ME.
...
YOUR FACE IS TURNING RED.
HEH HEH HEH!
SHUDDUP!
AND I DON'T EVEN GET WHAT YOU MEAN!
WHATEVER. I MAY NOT KNOW WHAT YOU'RE TALKING ABOUT...
OF COURSE NOT.

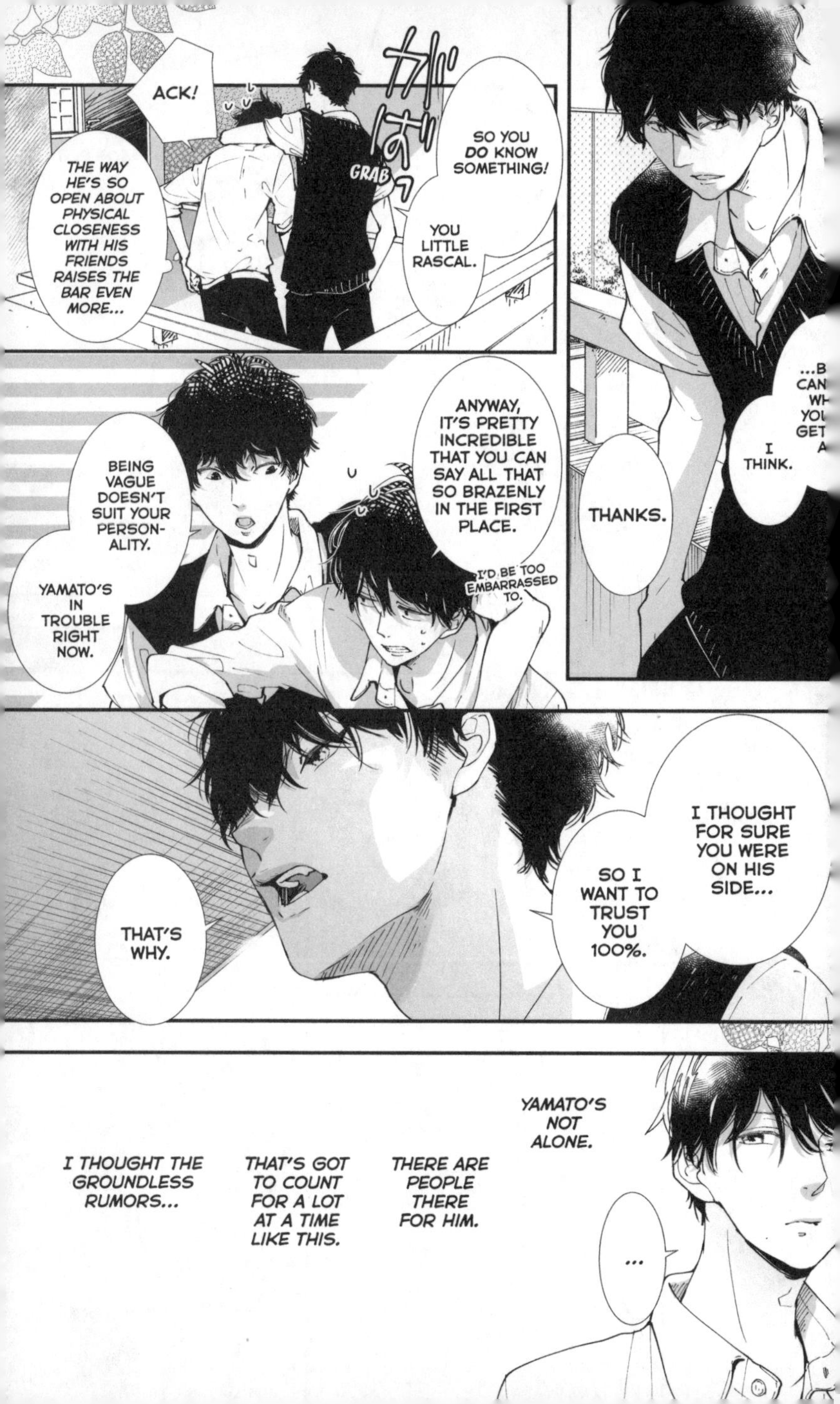
...B
CAN
WH
YOU
GET
A
I THINK.
THANKS.
SO YOU DO KNOW SOMETHING!
GRAB
YOU LITTLE RASCAL.
ACK!
THE WAY HE'S SO OPEN ABOUT PHYSICAL CLOSENESS WITH HIS FRIENDS RAISES THE BAR EVEN MORE...
ANYWAY, IT'S PRETTY INCREDIBLE THAT YOU CAN SAY ALL THAT SO BRAZENLY IN THE FIRST PLACE.
I'D BE TOO EMBARRASSED TO.
BEING VAGUE DOESN'T SUIT YOUR PERSON-ALITY.
YAMATO'S IN TROUBLE RIGHT NOW.
I THOUGHT FOR SURE YOU WERE ON HIS SIDE...
SO I WANT TO TRUST YOU 100%.
THAT'S WHY.
...
YAMATO'S NOT ALONE.
THERE ARE PEOPLE THERE FOR HIM.
THAT'S GOT TO COUNT FOR A LOT AT A TIME LIKE THIS.
I THOUGHT THE GROUNDLESS RUMORS...

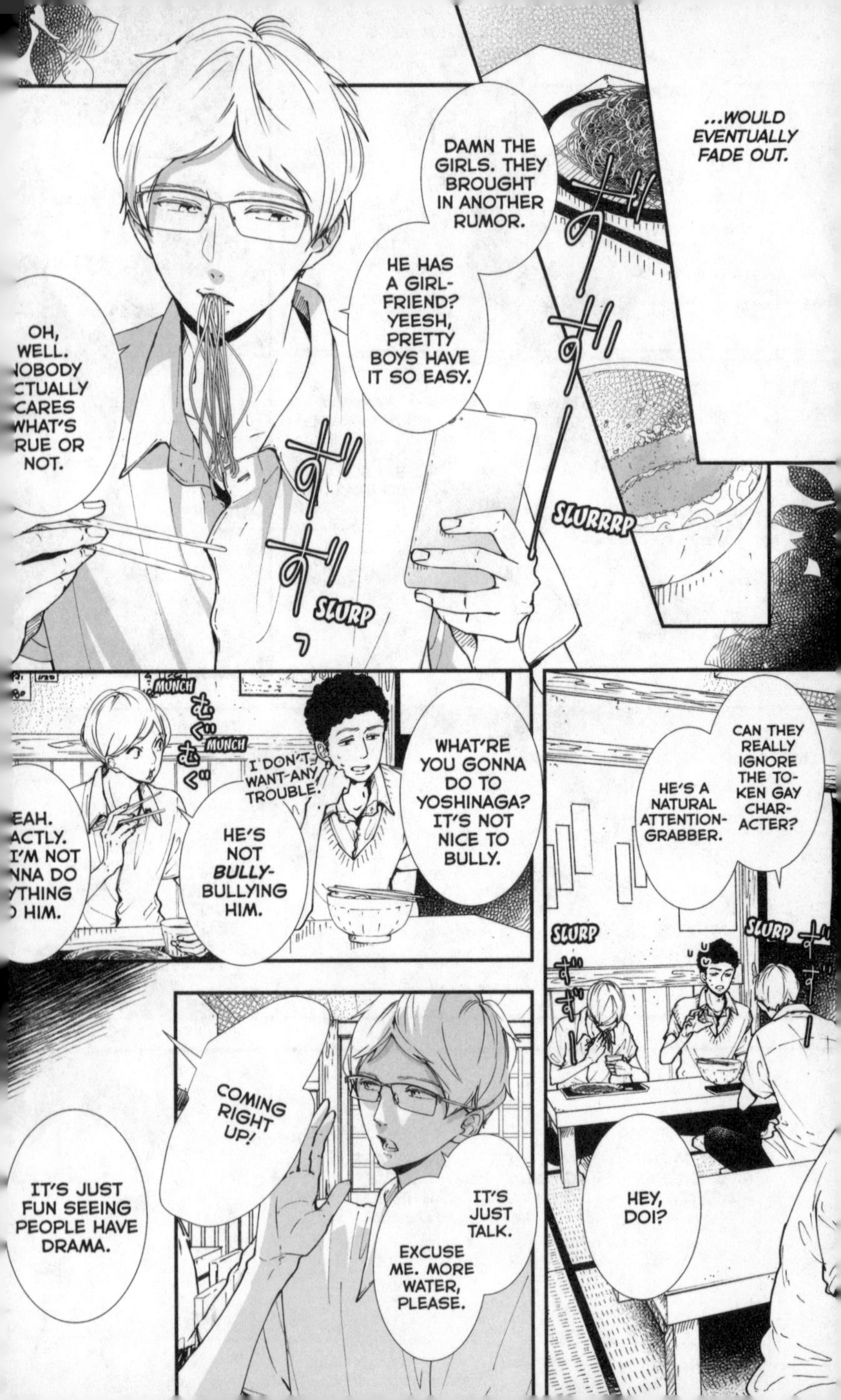
...WOULD EVENTUALLY FADE OUT.
SLURRRP
DAMN THE GIRLS. THEY BROUGHT IN ANOTHER RUMOR.
HE HAS A GIRL-FRIEND? YEESH, PRETTY BOYS HAVE IT SO EASY.
SLURP
OH, WELL. NOBODY CTUALLY CARES WHAT'S RUE OR NOT.
CAN THEY REALLY IGNORE THE TO-KEN GAY CHAR-ACTER?
HE'S A NATURAL ATTENTION-GRABBER.
SLURP
SLURP
HEY, DOI?
MUNCH
MUNCH
WHAT'RE YOU GONNA DO TO YOSHINAGA? IT'S NOT NICE TO BULLY.
I DON'T WANT ANY TROUBLE.
HE'S NOT *BULLY*-BULLYING HIM.
EAH. ACTLY. I'M NOT NNA DO YTHING HIM.
IT'S JUST TALK.
EXCUSE ME. MORE WATER, PLEASE.
COMING RIGHT UP!
IT'S JUST FUN SEEING PEOPLE HAVE DRAMA.

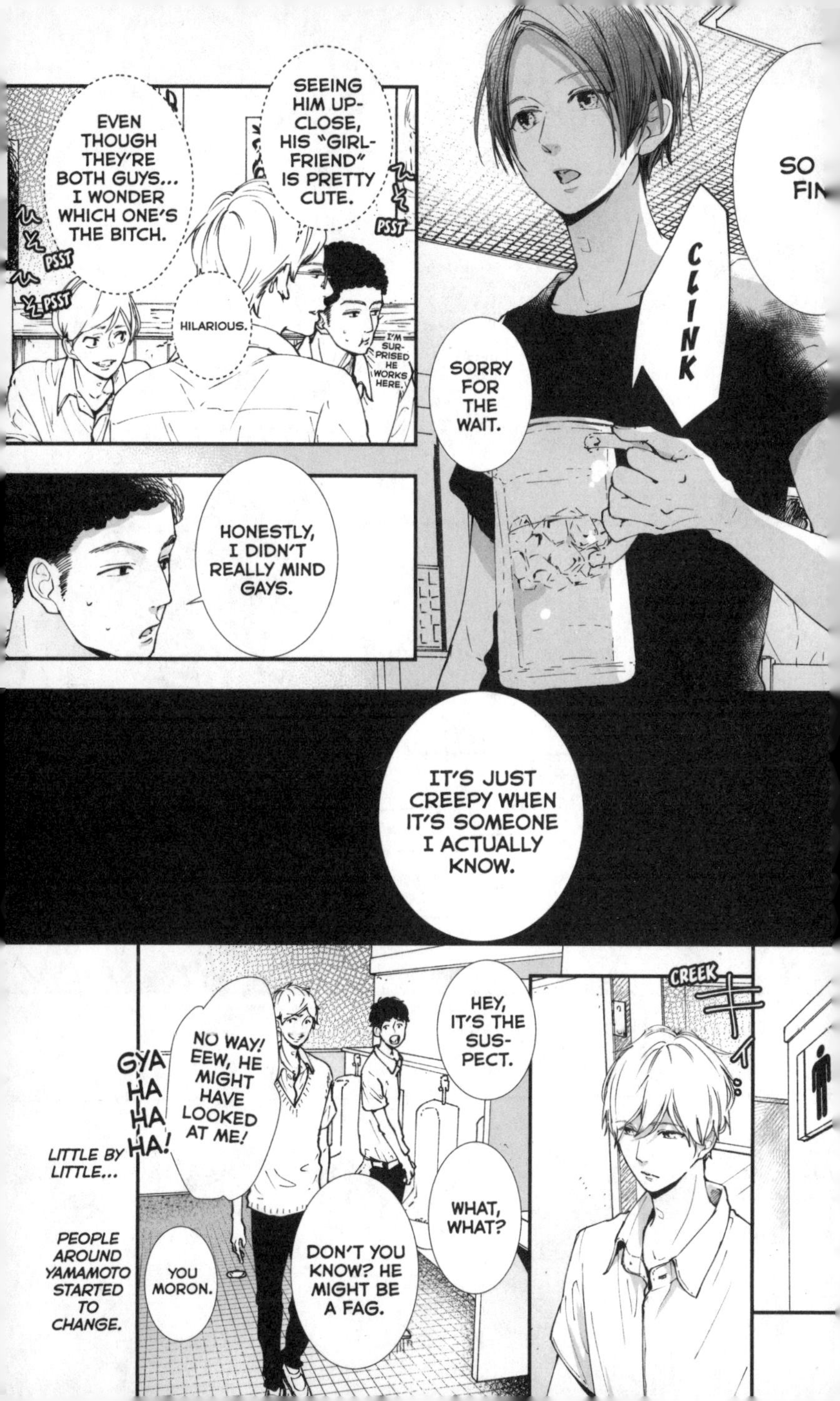

SO FIN
CLINK
SORRY FOR THE WAIT.
SEEING HIM UP-CLOSE, HIS "GIRL-FRIEND" IS PRETTY CUTE.
PSST
EVEN THOUGH THEY'RE BOTH GUYS... I WONDER WHICH ONE'S THE BITCH.
PSST
PSST
I'M SURPRISED HE WORKS HERE.
HILARIOUS.
HONESTLY, I DIDN'T REALLY MIND GAYS.
IT'S JUST CREEPY WHEN IT'S SOMEONE I ACTUALLY KNOW.
CREEK
HEY, IT'S THE SUS-PECT.
WHAT, WHAT?
DON'T YOU KNOW? HE MIGHT BE A FAG.
NO WAY! EEW, HE MIGHT HAVE LOOKED AT ME!
YOU MORON.
GYA HA HA HA!
LITTLE BY LITTLE...
PEOPLE AROUND YAMAMOTO STARTED TO CHANGE.

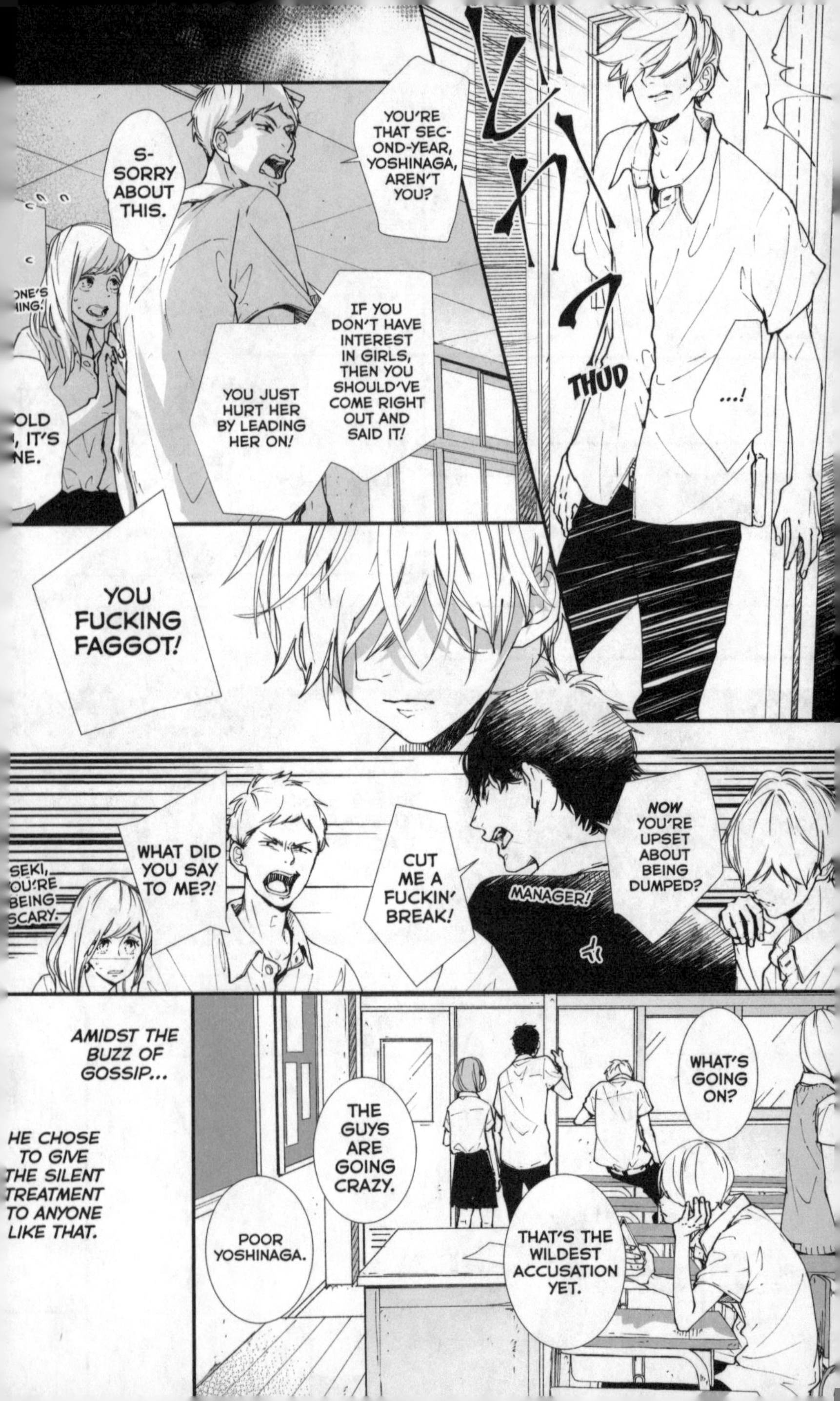
THUD
...!
YOU'RE THAT SEC-OND-YEAR, YOSHINAGA, AREN'T YOU?
S-SORRY ABOUT THIS.
IF YOU DON'T HAVE INTEREST IN GIRLS, THEN YOU SHOULD'VE COME RIGHT OUT AND SAID IT!
YOU JUST HURT HER BY LEADING HER ON!
YOU FUCKING FAGGOT!
NOW YOU'RE UPSET ABOUT BEING DUMPED?
CUT ME A FUCKIN' BREAK!
MANAGER!
WHAT DID YOU SAY TO ME?!
SEKI, YOU'RE BEING SCARY.
WHAT'S GOING ON?
THE GUYS ARE GOING CRAZY.
THAT'S THE WILDEST ACCUSATION YET.
POOR YOSHINAGA.
AMIDST THE BUZZ OF GOSSIP...
HE CHOSE TO GIVE THE SILENT TREATMENT TO ANYONE LIKE THAT.

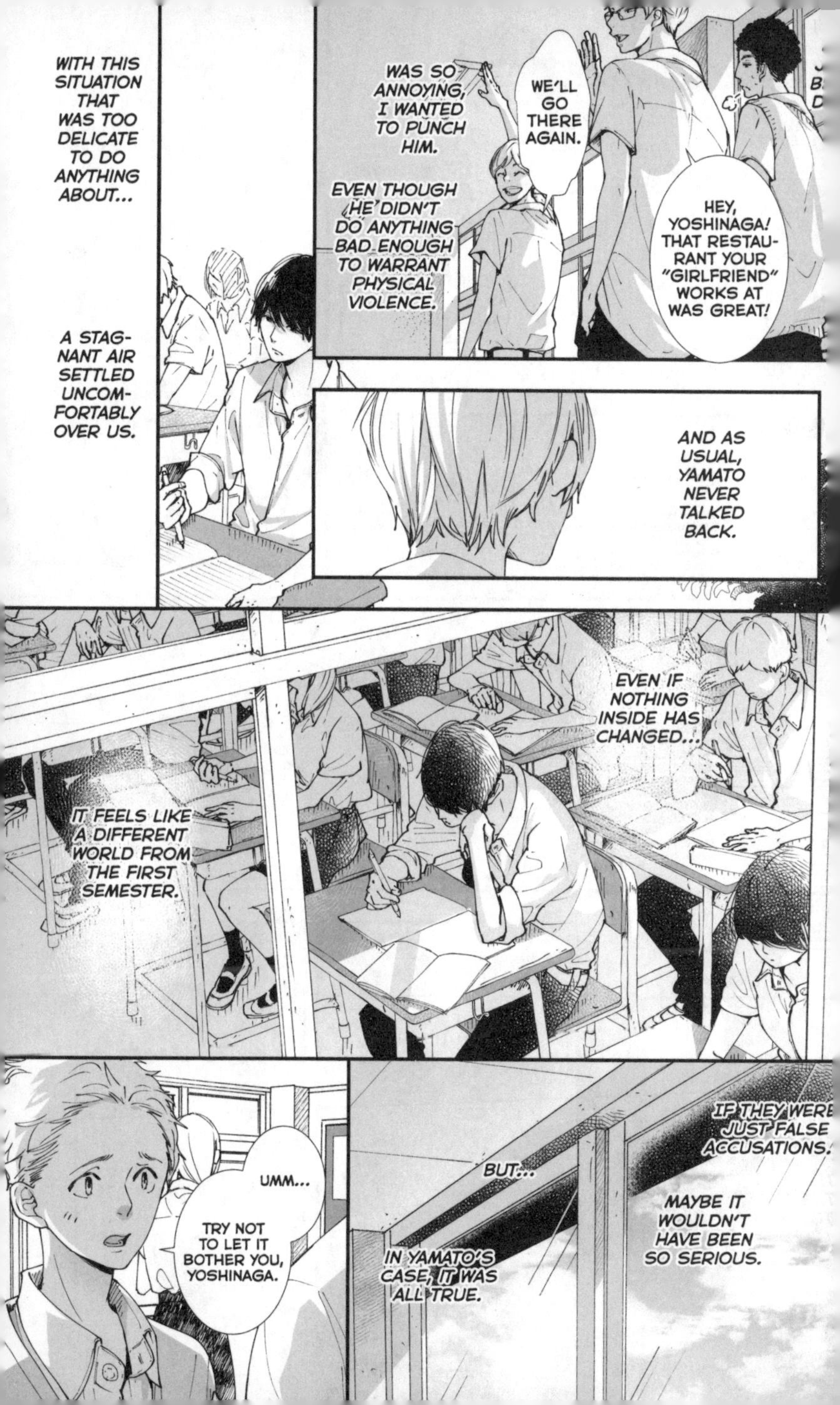
HEY, YOSHINAGA! THAT RESTAU-RANT YOUR "GIRLFRIEND" WORKS AT WAS GREAT!
WE'LL GO THERE AGAIN.
WAS SO ANNOYING, I WANTED TO PUNCH HIM.
EVEN THOUGH HE DIDN'T DO ANYTHING BAD ENOUGH TO WARRANT PHYSICAL VIOLENCE.
AND AS USUAL, YAMATO NEVER TALKED BACK.
WITH THIS SITUATION THAT WAS TOO DELICATE TO DO ANYTHING ABOUT...
A STAG-NANT AIR SETTLED UNCOM-FORTABLY OVER US.
EVEN IF NOTHING INSIDE HAS CHANGED...
IT FEELS LIKE A DIFFERENT WORLD FROM THE FIRST SEMESTER.
IF THEY WERE JUST FALSE ACCUSATIONS.
MAYBE IT WOULDN'T HAVE BEEN SO SERIOUS.
BUT...
IN YAMATO'S CASE, IT WAS ALL TRUE.
UMM...
TRY NOT TO LET IT BOTHER YOU, YOSHINAGA.

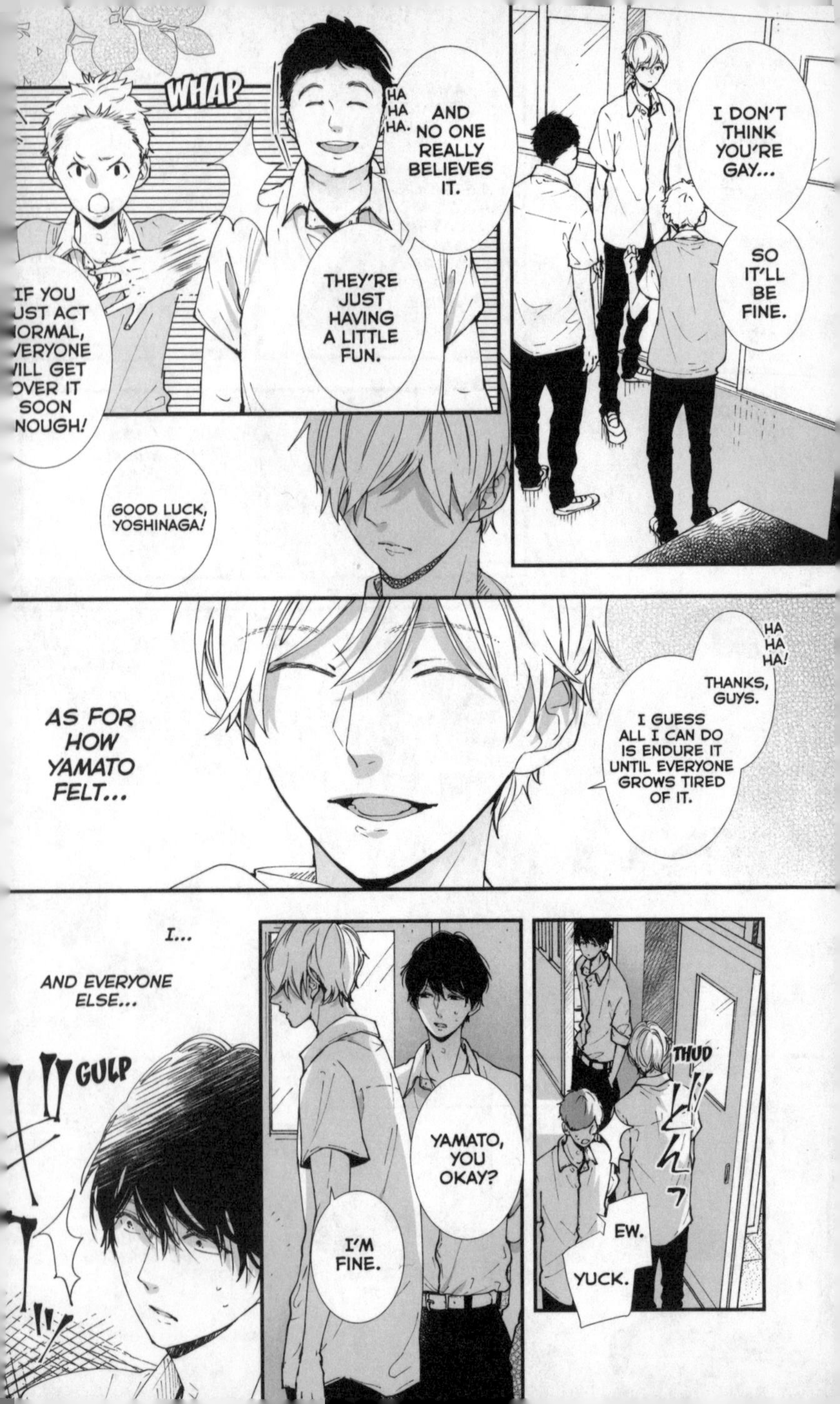
I DON'T THINK YOU'RE GAY...
SO IT'LL BE FINE.
HA HA HA.
AND NO ONE REALLY BELIEVES IT.
THEY'RE JUST HAVING A LITTLE FUN.
WHAP
IF YOU UST ACT ORMAL, VERYONE VILL GET OVER IT SOON NOUGH!
GOOD LUCK, YOSHINAGA!
HA HA HA!
THANKS, GUYS.
I GUESS ALL I CAN DO IS ENDURE IT UNTIL EVERYONE GROWS TIRED OF IT.
AS FOR HOW YAMATO FELT...
THUD
EW.
YUCK.
YAMATO, YOU OKAY?
I'M FINE.
I...
AND EVERYONE ELSE...
GULP

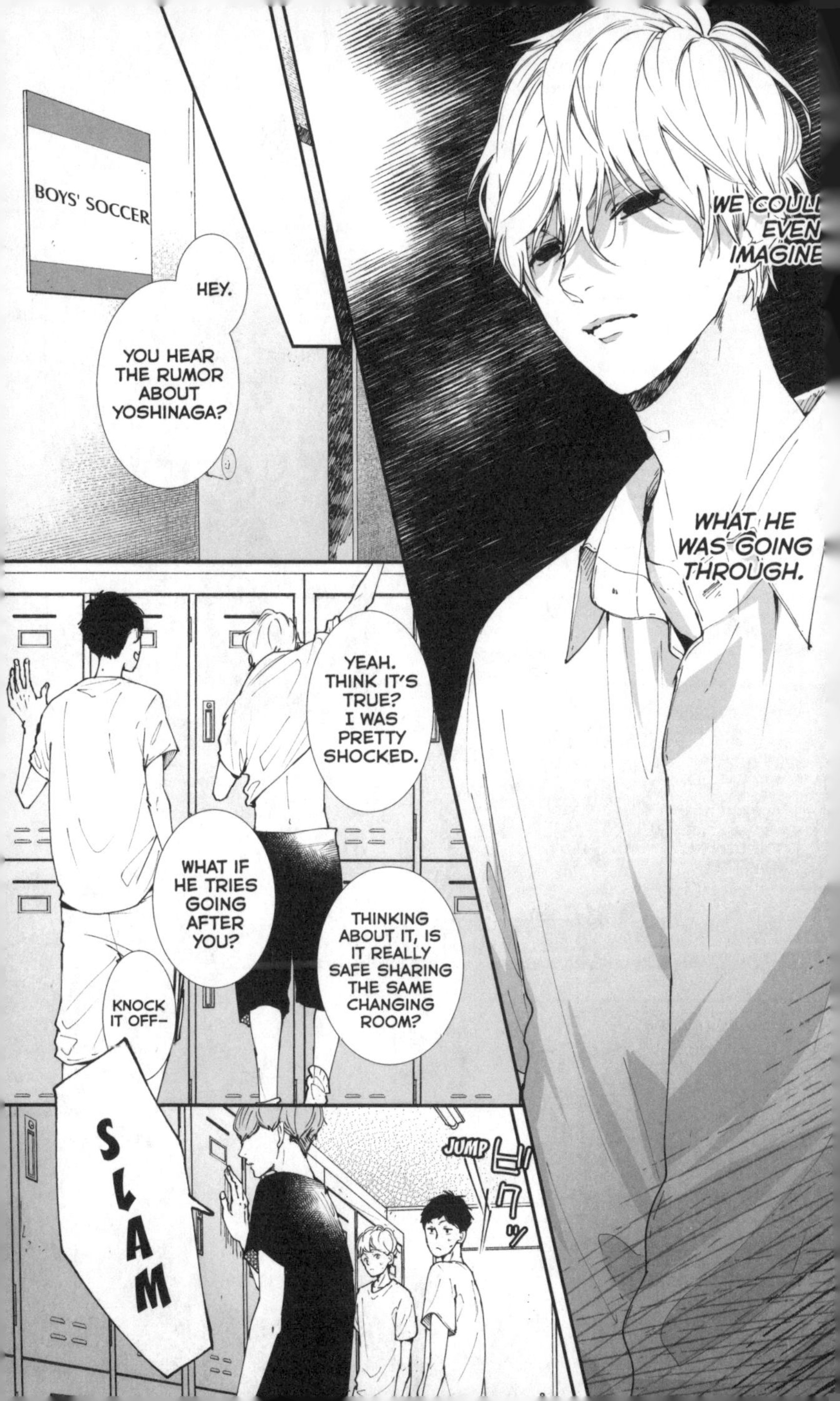
WE COULD EVEN IMAGINE
WHAT HE WAS GOING THROUGH.
BOYS' SOCCER
HEY.
YOU HEAR THE RUMOR ABOUT YOSHINAGA?
YEAH. THINK IT'S TRUE? I WAS PRETTY SHOCKED.
WHAT IF HE TRIES GOING AFTER YOU?
THINKING ABOUT IT, IS IT REALLY SAFE SHARING THE SAME CHANGING ROOM?
KNOCK IT OFF—
SLAM
JUMP

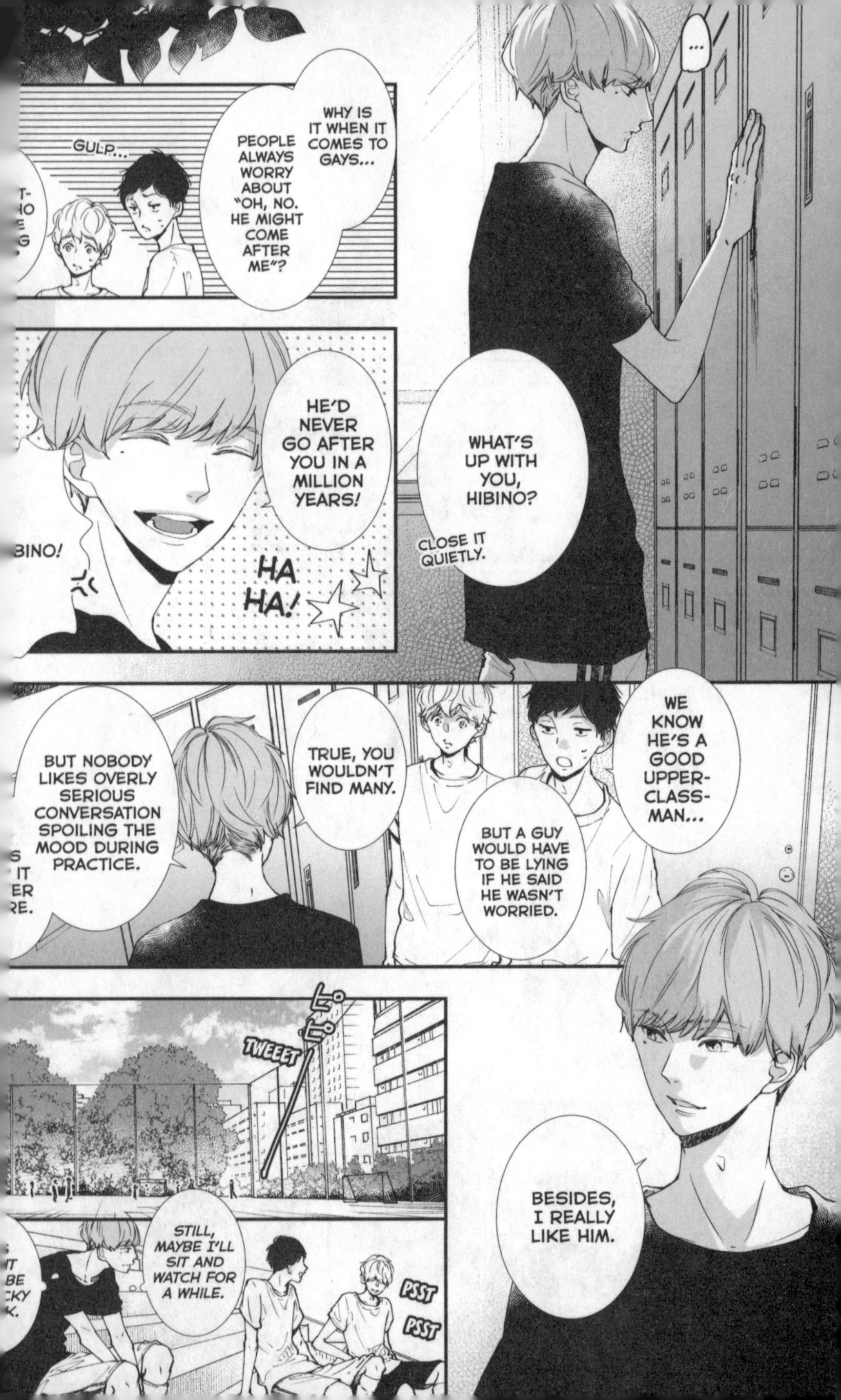
...
WHAT'S UP WITH YOU, HIBINO?
CLOSE IT QUIETLY.
WHY IS IT WHEN IT COMES TO GAYS... PEOPLE ALWAYS WORRY ABOUT "OH, NO. HE MIGHT COME AFTER ME"?
GULP...
HE'D NEVER GO AFTER YOU IN A MILLION YEARS!
HA HA!
WE KNOW HE'S A GOOD UPPER-CLASS-MAN...
BUT A GUY WOULD HAVE TO BE LYING IF HE SAID HE WASN'T WORRIED.
TRUE, YOU WOULDN'T FIND MANY.
BUT NOBODY LIKES OVERLY SERIOUS CONVERSATION SPOILING THE MOOD DURING PRACTICE.
BESIDES, I REALLY LIKE HIM.
TWEEET
STILL, MAYBE I'LL SIT AND WATCH FOR A WHILE.
PSST
PSST

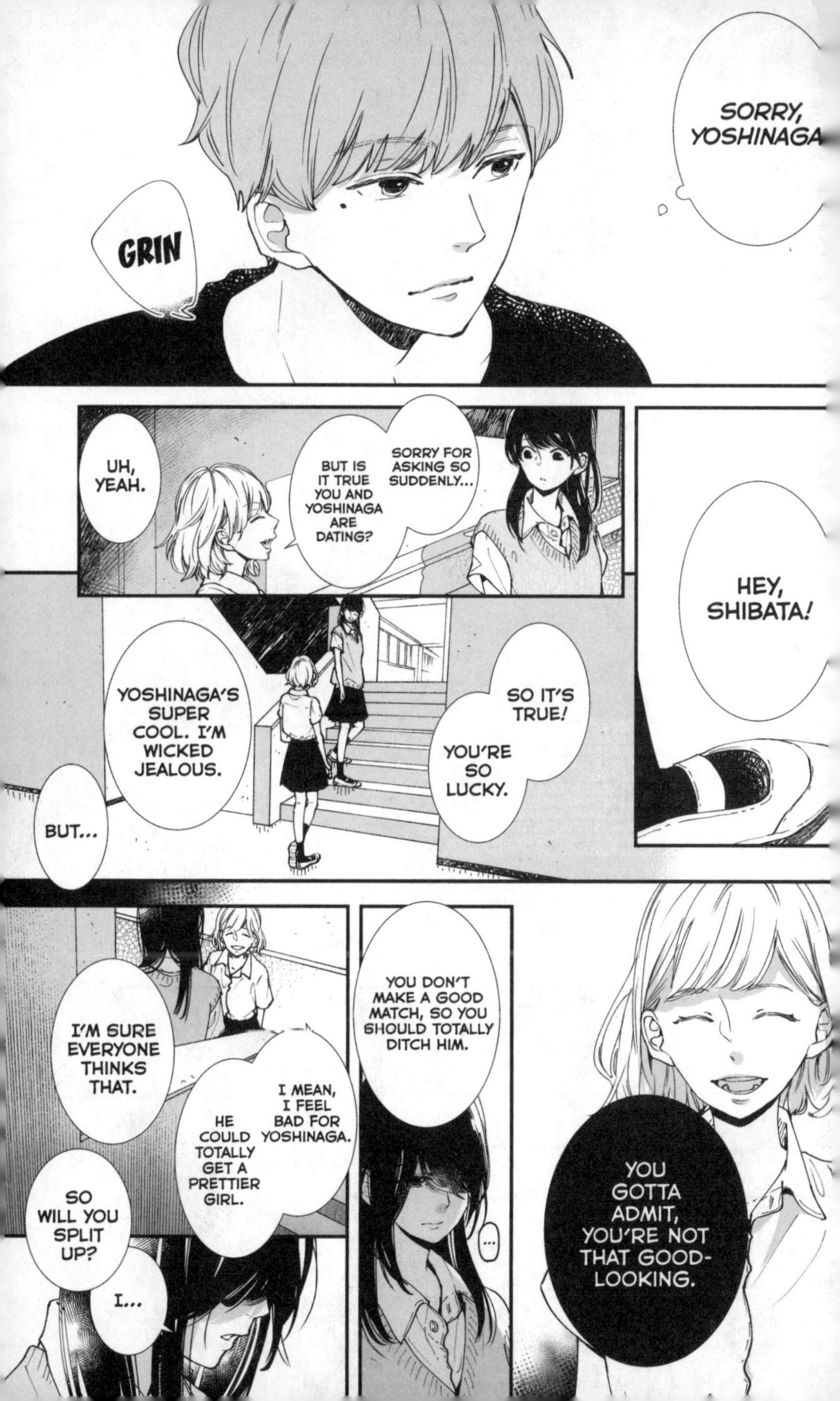
SORRY, YOSHINAGA
GRIN
HEY, SHIBATA!
SORRY FOR ASKING SO SUDDENLY...
BUT IS IT TRUE YOU AND YOSHINAGA ARE DATING?
UH, YEAH.
SO IT'S TRUE!
YOU'RE SO LUCKY.
YOSHINAGA'S SUPER COOL. I'M WICKED JEALOUS.
BUT...
YOU GOTTA ADMIT, YOU'RE NOT THAT GOOD-LOOKING.
YOU DON'T MAKE A GOOD MATCH, SO YOU SHOULD TOTALLY DITCH HIM.
...
I MEAN, I FEEL BAD FOR YOSHINAGA.
HE COULD TOTALLY GET A PRETTIER GIRL.
I'M SURE EVERYONE THINKS THAT.
SO WILL YOU SPLIT UP?
I...

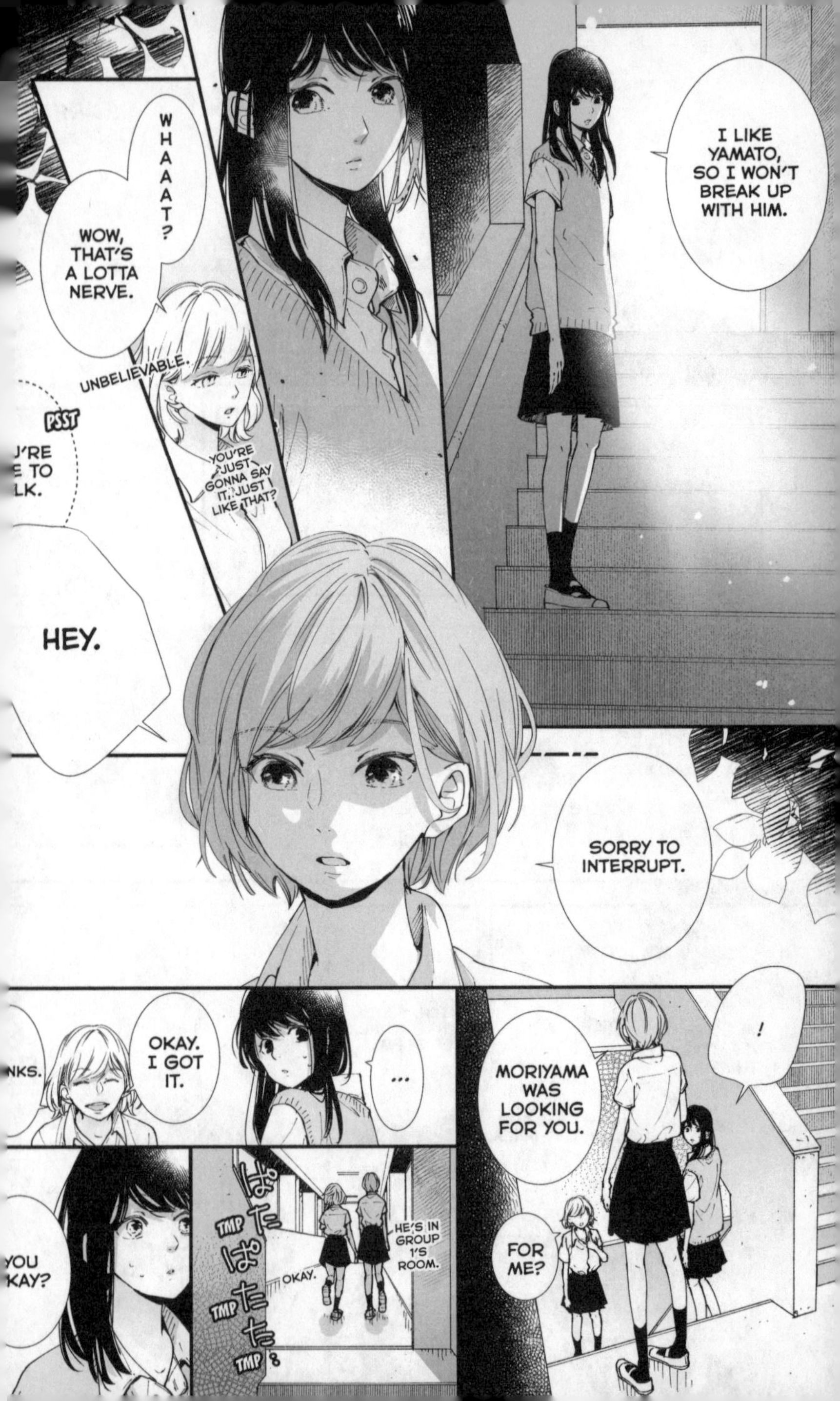
I LIKE YAMATO, SO I WON'T BREAK UP WITH HIM.
WHAAAAT?
WOW, THAT'S A LOTTA NERVE.
UNBELIEVABLE.
YOU'RE JUST GONNA SAY IT, JUST LIKE THAT?
PSST
HEY.
SORRY TO INTERRUPT.
!
MORIYAMA WAS LOOKING FOR YOU.
FOR ME?
...
OKAY. I GOT IT.
HE'S IN GROUP 1'S ROOM.
OKAY.
ぱたぱたた
TMP TMP TMP

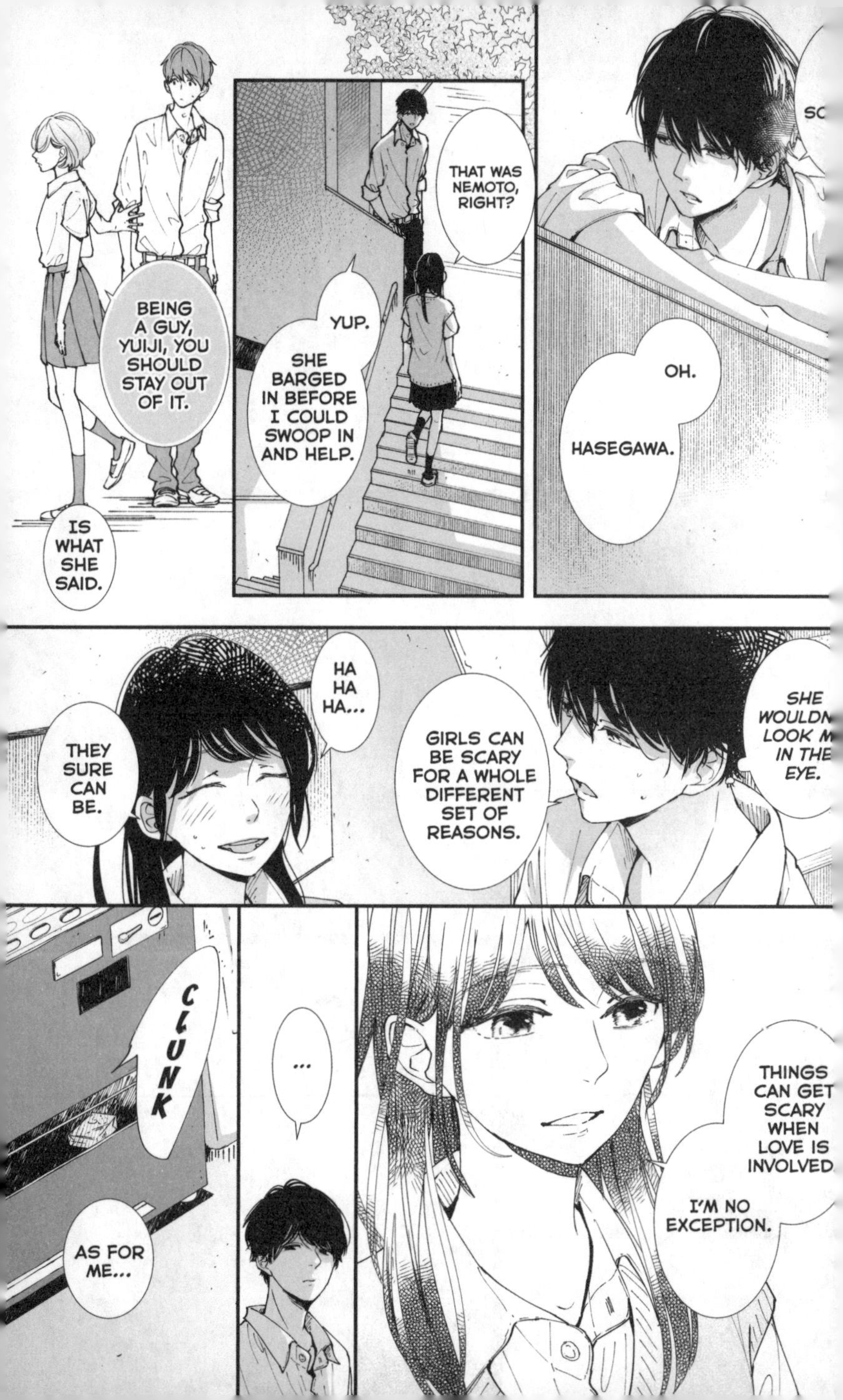

OH.
HASEGAWA.
THAT WAS NEMOTO, RIGHT?
YUP.
SHE BARGED IN BEFORE I COULD SWOOP IN AND HELP.
BEING A GUY, YUIJI, YOU SHOULD STAY OUT OF IT.
IS WHAT SHE SAID.
SHE WOULDN LOOK M IN THE EYE.
GIRLS CAN BE SCARY FOR A WHOLE DIFFERENT SET OF REASONS.
HA HA HA...
THEY SURE CAN BE.
THINGS CAN GET SCARY WHEN LOVE IS INVOLVED.
I'M NO EXCEPTION.
...
CLUNK
AS FOR ME...

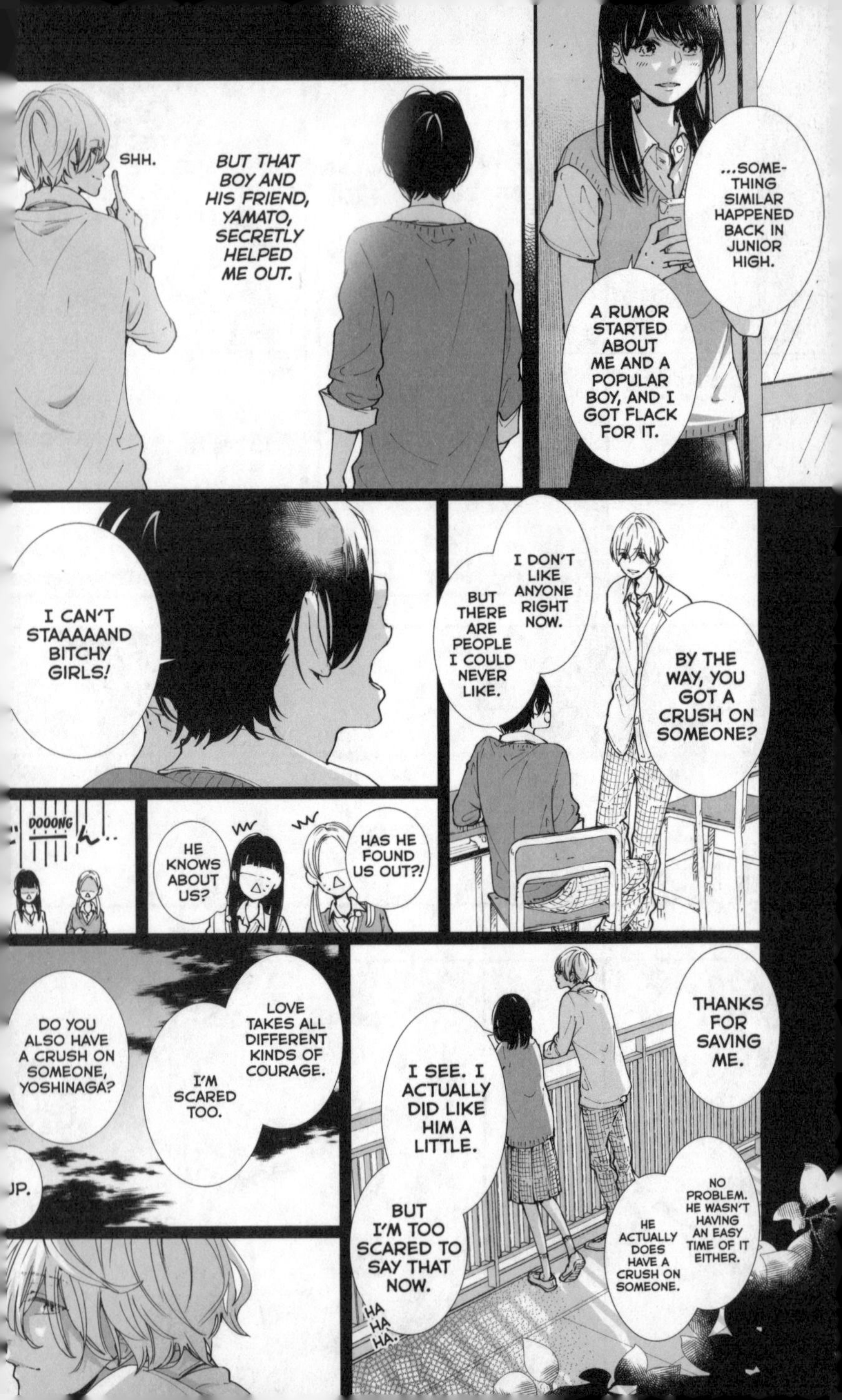
...SOME-THING SIMILAR HAPPENED BACK IN JUNIOR HIGH.
A RUMOR STARTED ABOUT ME AND A POPULAR BOY, AND I GOT FLACK FOR IT.
BUT THAT BOY AND HIS FRIEND, YAMATO, SECRETLY HELPED ME OUT.
SHH.
BY THE WAY, YOU GOT A CRUSH ON SOMEONE?
I DON'T LIKE ANYONE RIGHT NOW.
BUT THERE ARE PEOPLE I COULD NEVER LIKE.
I CAN'T STAAAAAND BITCHY GIRLS!
HAS HE FOUND US OUT?!
HE KNOWS ABOUT US?
DOOONG
THANKS FOR SAVING ME.
NO PROBLEM. HE WASN'T HAVING AN EASY TIME OF IT EITHER.
HE ACTUALLY DOES HAVE A CRUSH ON SOMEONE.
I SEE. I ACTUALLY DID LIKE HIM A LITTLE.
BUT I'M TOO SCARED TO SAY THAT NOW.
HA HA HA.
LOVE TAKES ALL DIFFERENT KINDS OF COURAGE.
I'M SCARED TOO.
DO YOU ALSO HAVE A CRUSH ON SOMEONE, YOSHINAGA?
UP.

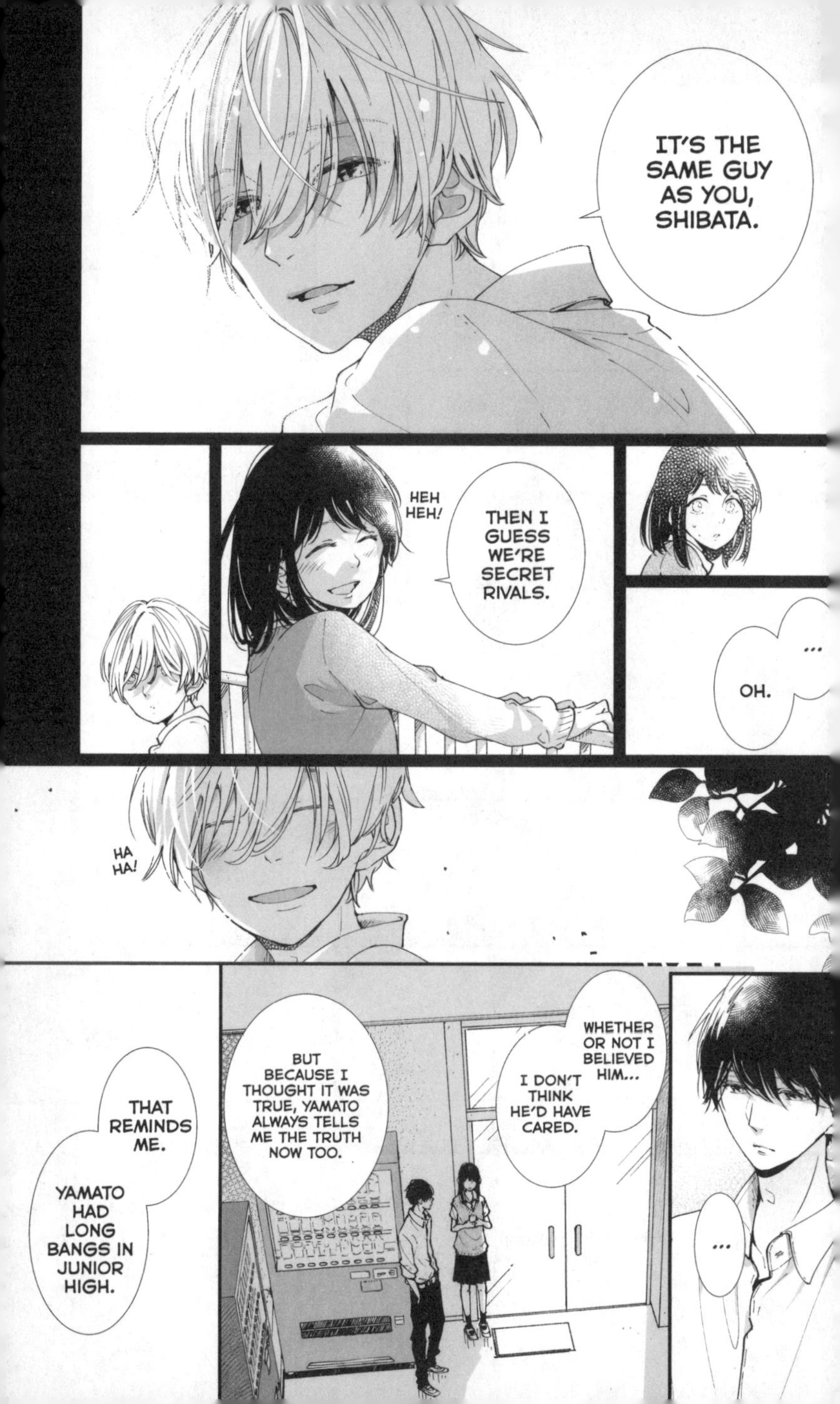
IT'S THE SAME GUY AS YOU, SHIBATA.
... OH.
THEN I GUESS WE'RE SECRET RIVALS.
HEH HEH!
HA HA!
...
WHETHER OR NOT I BELIEVED HIM...
I DON'T THINK HE'D HAVE CARED.
BUT BECAUSE I THOUGHT IT WAS TRUE, YAMATO ALWAYS TELLS ME THE TRUTH NOW TOO.
THAT REMINDS ME.
YAMATO HAD LONG BANGS IN JUNIOR HIGH.

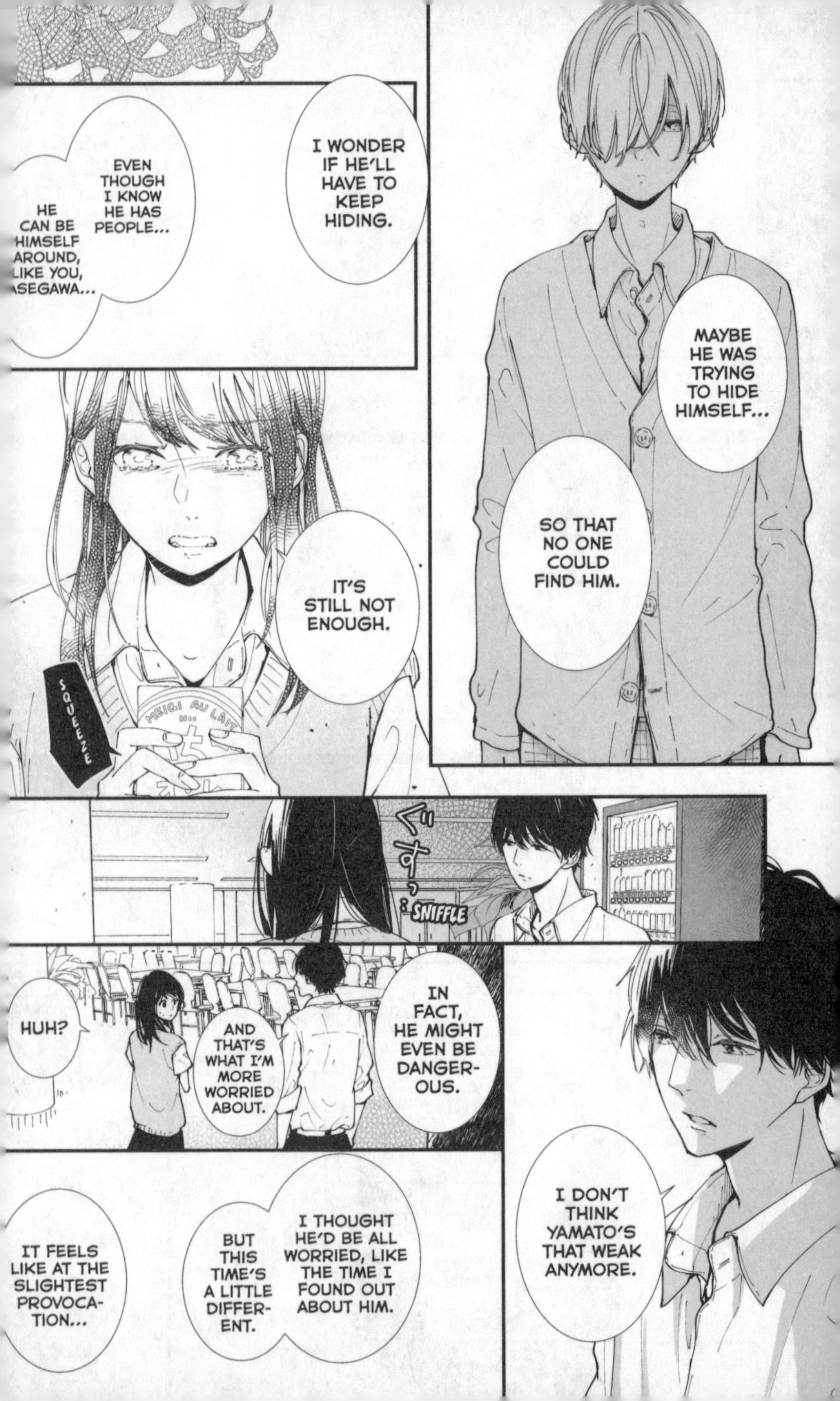

MAYBE HE WAS TRYING TO HIDE HIMSELF...
SO THAT NO ONE COULD FIND HIM.
I WONDER IF HE'LL HAVE TO KEEP HIDING.
EVEN THOUGH I KNOW HE HAS PEOPLE...
HE CAN BE HIMSELF AROUND, LIKE YOU, ASEGAWA...
IT'S STILL NOT ENOUGH.
SQUEEZE
MEIGI AU LAIT
SNIFFLE
I DON'T THINK YAMATO'S THAT WEAK ANYMORE.
IN FACT, HE MIGHT EVEN BE DANGER-OUS.
AND THAT'S WHAT I'M MORE WORRIED ABOUT.
HUH?
I THOUGHT HE'D BE ALL WORRIED, LIKE THE TIME I FOUND OUT ABOUT HIM.
BUT THIS TIME'S A LITTLE DIFFER-ENT.
IT FEELS LIKE AT THE SLIGHTEST PROVOCA-TION...

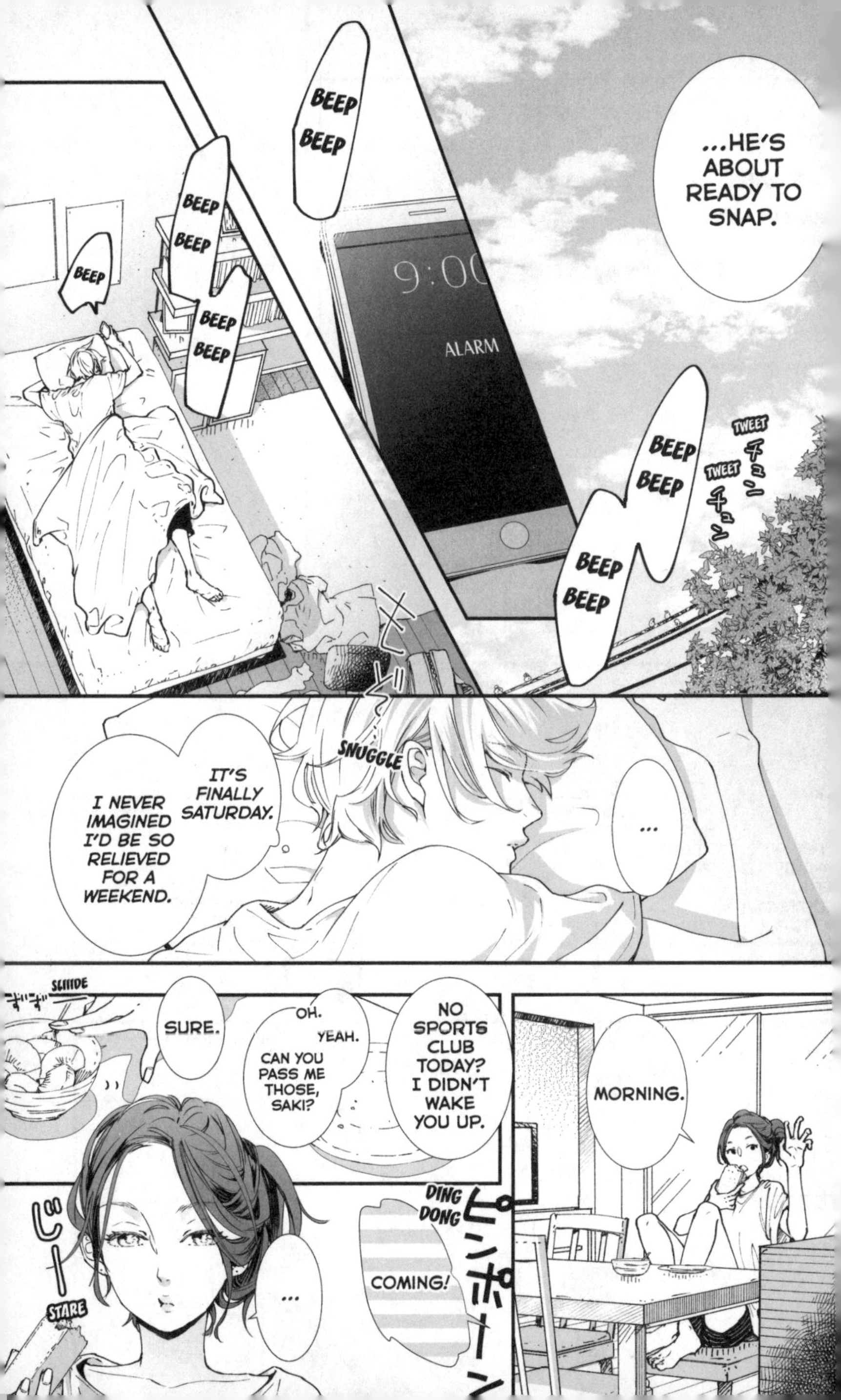

...HE'S ABOUT READY TO SNAP.
TWEET TWEET
チュン チュン
BEEP BEEP
BEEP BEEP
BEEP BEEP
BEEP BEEP
BEEP BEEP
BEEP
...
SNUGGLE
IT'S FINALLY SATURDAY.
I NEVER IMAGINED I'D BE SO RELIEVED FOR A WEEKEND.
MORNING.
NO SPORTS CLUB TODAY? I DIDN'T WAKE YOU UP.
OH.
YEAH.
CAN YOU PASS ME THOSE, SAKI?
SURE.
SLIIIDE
DING DONG
ピンポーン
COMING!
...
STARE

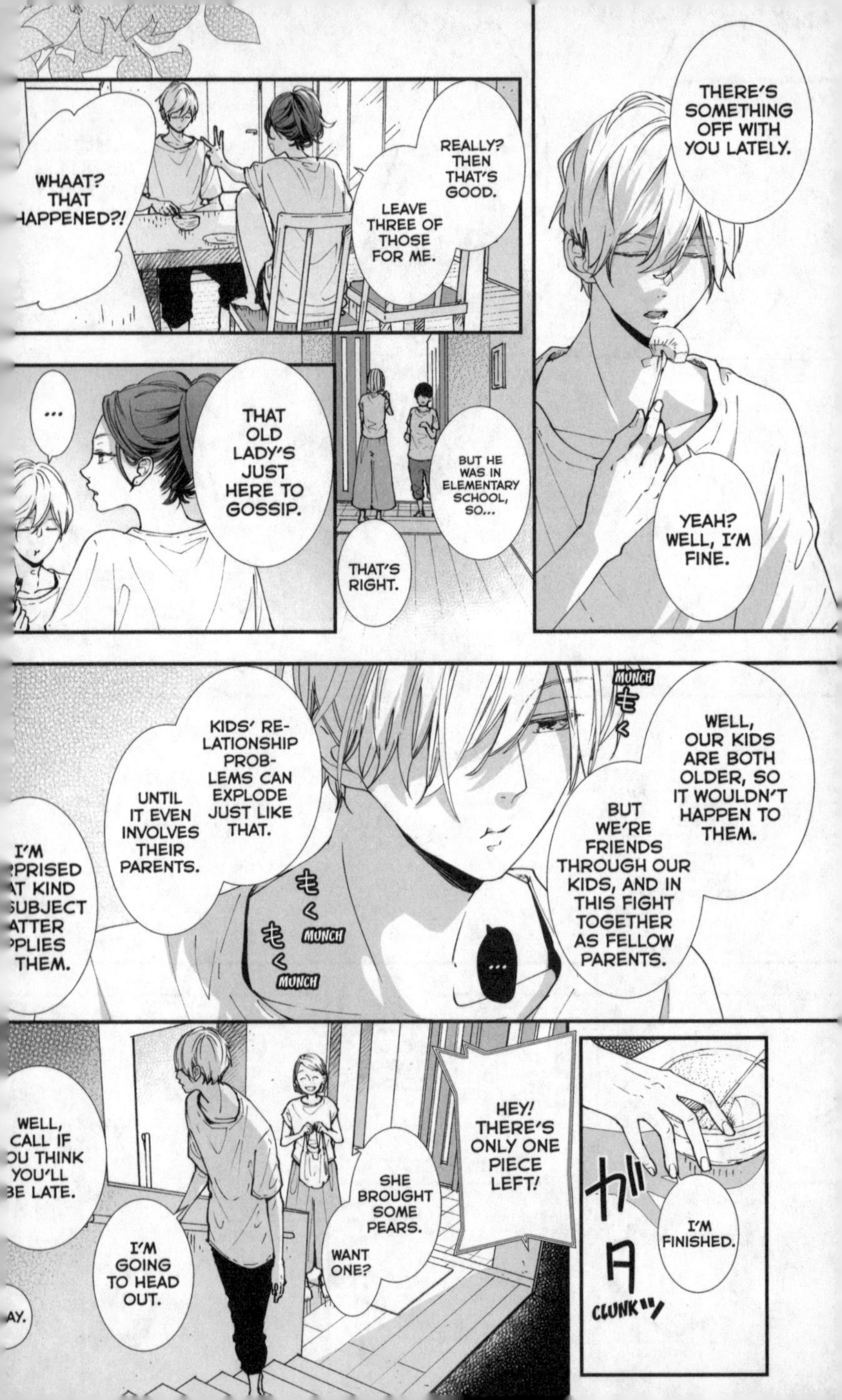
THERE'S SOMETHING OFF WITH YOU LATELY.
YEAH? WELL, I'M FINE.
REALLY? THEN THAT'S GOOD.
LEAVE THREE OF THOSE FOR ME.
WHAAT? THAT HAPPENED?!
BUT HE WAS IN ELEMENTARY SCHOOL, SO...
THAT'S RIGHT.
THAT OLD LADY'S JUST HERE TO GOSSIP.
...
MUNCH もく
WELL, OUR KIDS ARE BOTH OLDER, SO IT WOULDN'T HAPPEN TO THEM.
BUT WE'RE FRIENDS THROUGH OUR KIDS, AND IN THIS FIGHT TOGETHER AS FELLOW PARENTS.
...
もく MUNCH
もく MUNCH
KIDS' RE-LATIONSHIP PROB-LEMS CAN EXPLODE JUST LIKE THAT.
UNTIL IT EVEN INVOLVES THEIR PARENTS.
I'M RPRISED AT KIND SUBJECT ATTER PPLIES THEM.
ガタ CLUNK
I'M FINISHED.
HEY! THERE'S ONLY ONE PIECE LEFT!
SHE BROUGHT SOME PEARS.
WANT ONE?
I'M GOING TO HEAD OUT.
WELL, CALL IF OU THINK YOU'LL BE LATE.
AY.

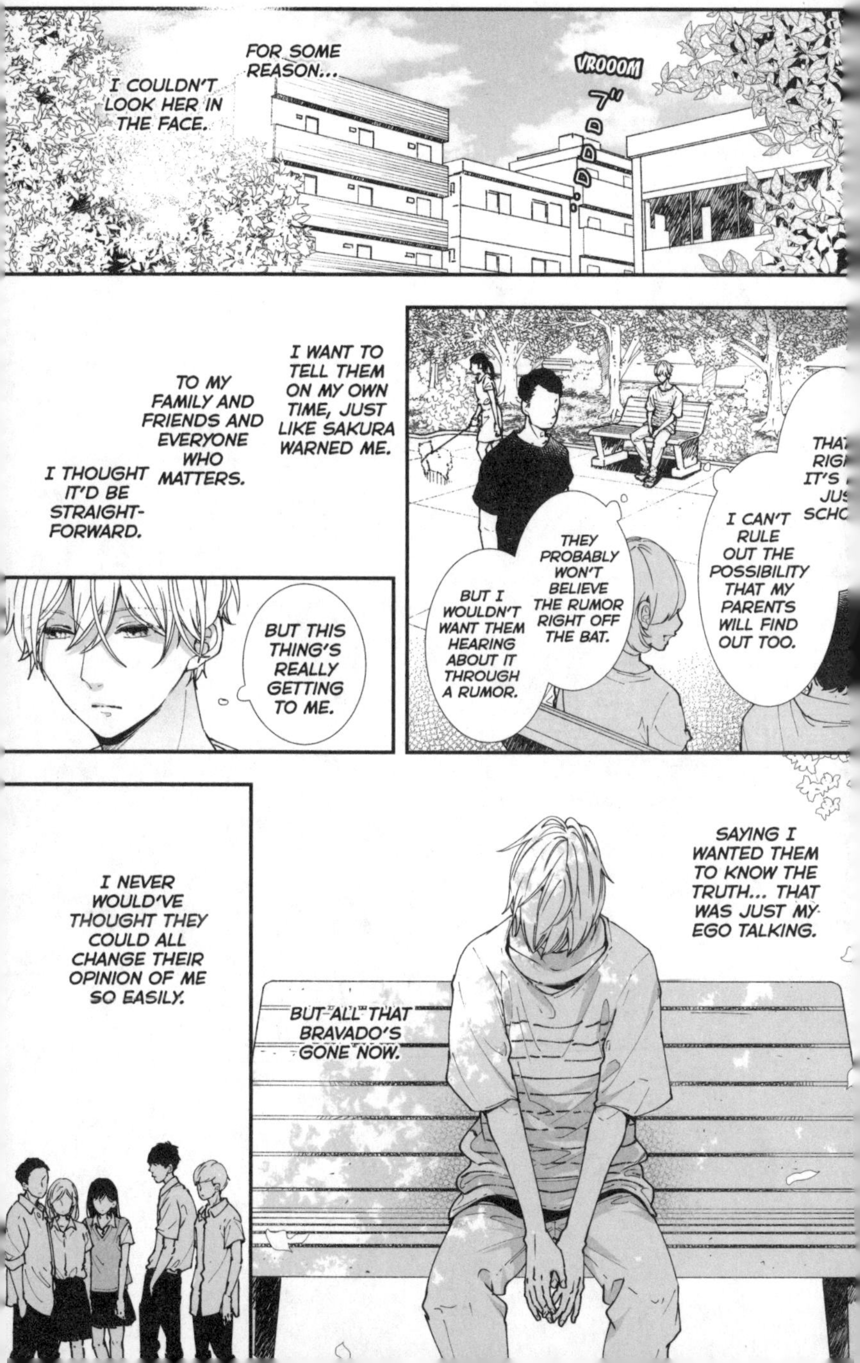
VROOOM
FOR SOME REASON...
I COULDN'T LOOK HER IN THE FACE.
I CAN'T RULE OUT THE POSSIBILITY THAT MY PARENTS WILL FIND OUT TOO.
THEY PROBABLY WON'T BELIEVE THE RUMOR RIGHT OFF THE BAT.
BUT I WOULDN'T WANT THEM HEARING ABOUT IT THROUGH A RUMOR.
I WANT TO TELL THEM ON MY OWN TIME, JUST LIKE SAKURA WARNED ME.
TO MY FAMILY AND FRIENDS AND EVERYONE WHO MATTERS.
I THOUGHT IT'D BE STRAIGHT-FORWARD.
BUT THIS THING'S REALLY GETTING TO ME.
SAYING I WANTED THEM TO KNOW THE TRUTH... THAT WAS JUST MY EGO TALKING.
BUT ALL THAT BRAVADO'S GONE NOW.
I NEVER WOULD'VE THOUGHT THEY COULD ALL CHANGE THEIR OPINION OF ME SO EASILY.

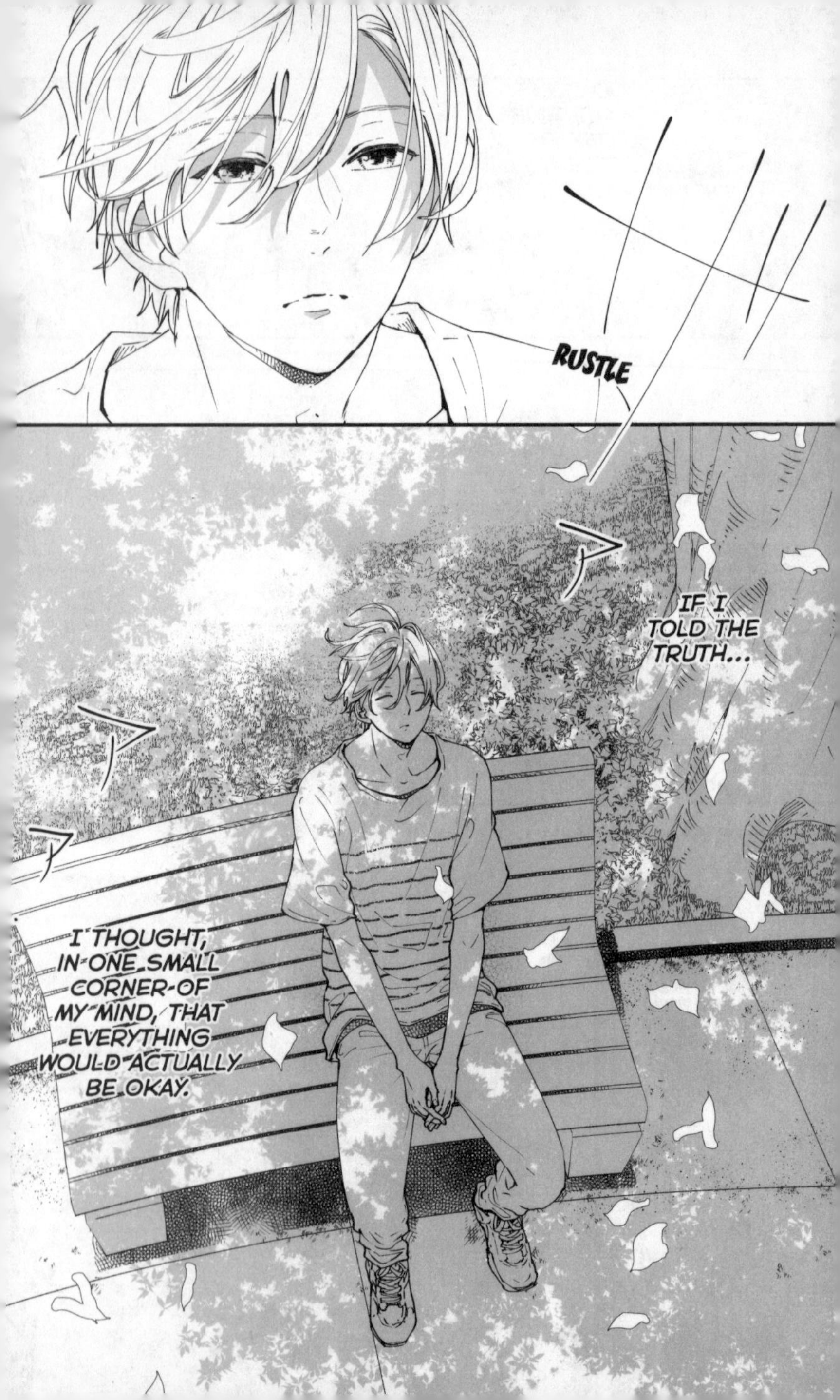
RUSTLE
IF I TOLD THE TRUTH...
I THOUGHT, IN ONE SMALL CORNER OF MY MIND, THAT EVERYTHING WOULD ACTUALLY BE OKAY.

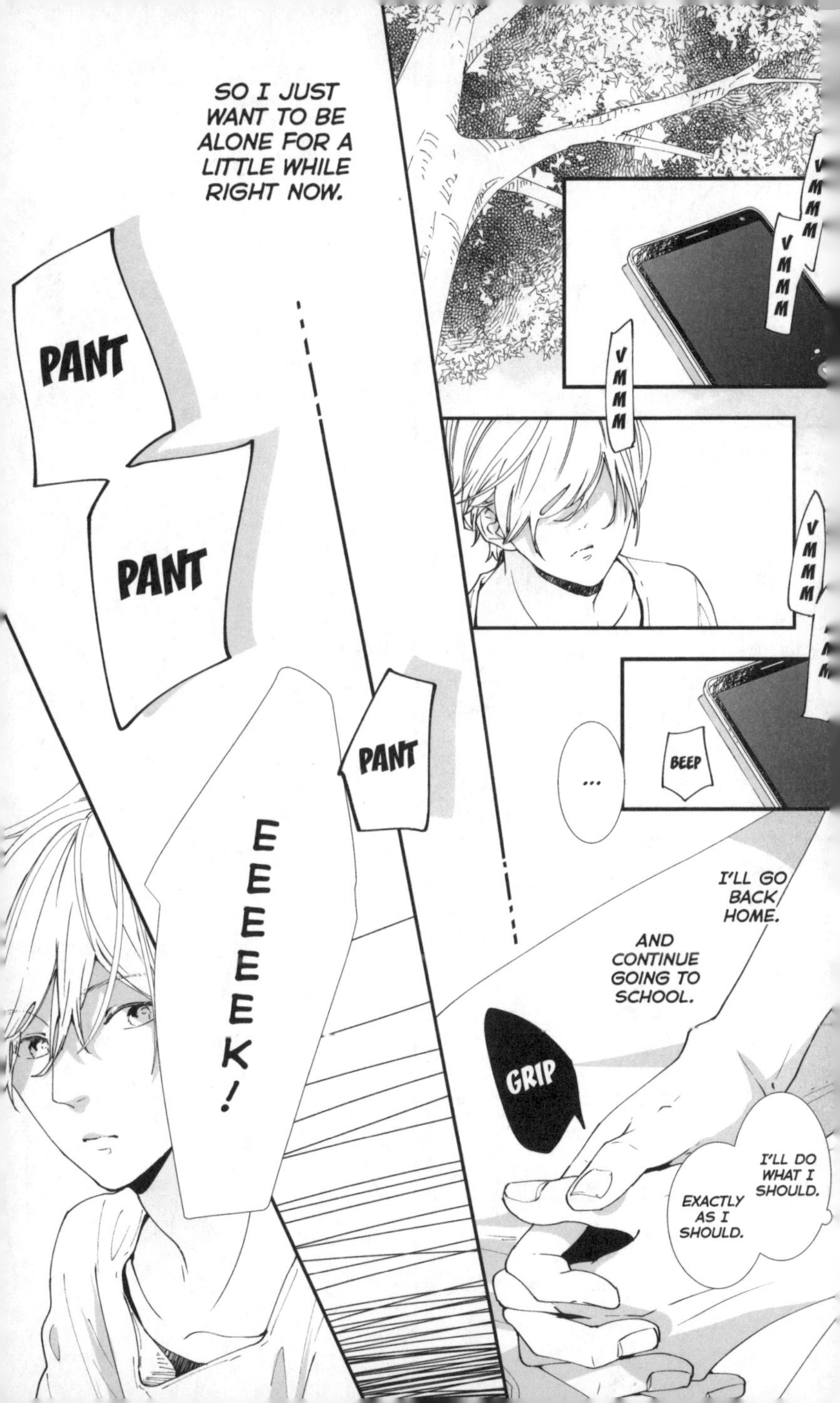
VMMM
VMMM
VMMM
VMMM
BEEP
...
I'LL GO BACK HOME.
AND CONTINUE GOING TO SCHOOL.
GRIP
I'LL DO WHAT I SHOULD.
EXACTLY AS I SHOULD.
SO I JUST WANT TO BE ALONE FOR A LITTLE WHILE RIGHT NOW.
PANT
PANT
PANT
EEEEEK!

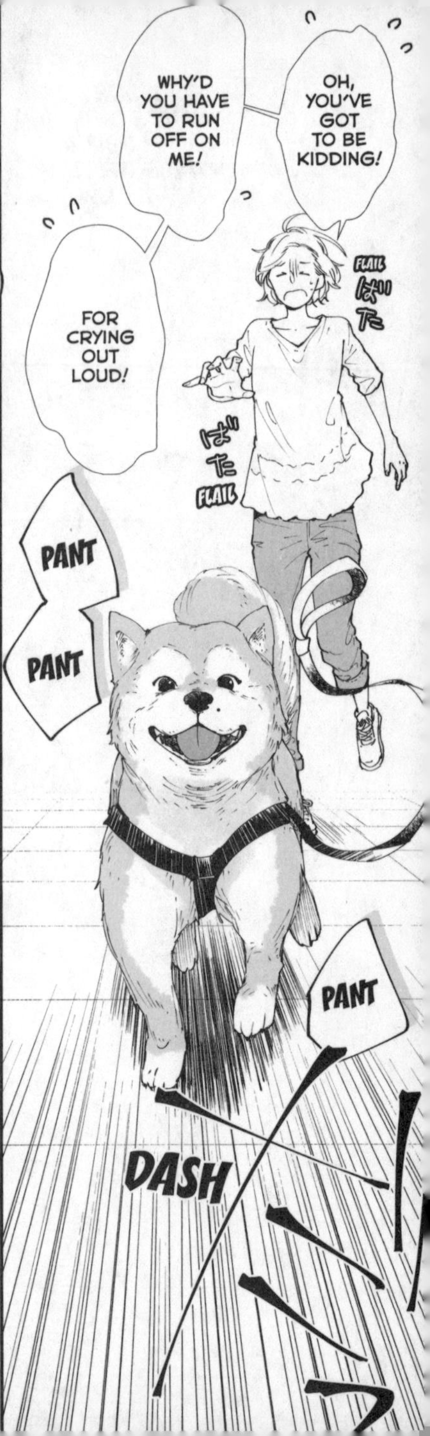
OH, YOU'VE GOT TO BE KIDDING!
WHY'D YOU HAVE TO RUN OFF ON ME!
FOR CRYING OUT LOUD!
FLAIL
ばた
ばた
FLAIL
PANT
PANT
PANT
DASH

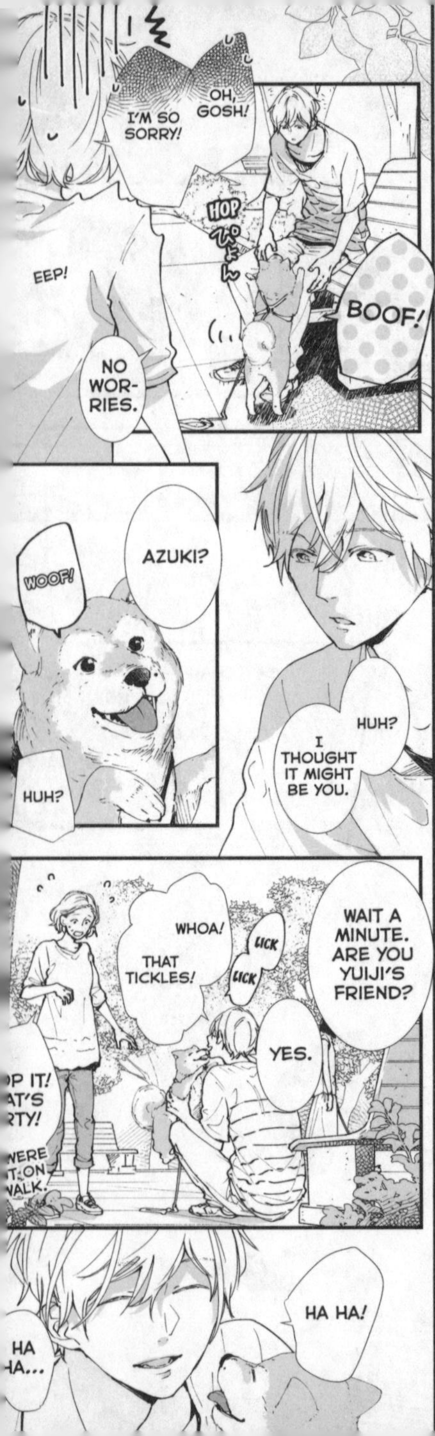
OH, GOSH!
I'M SO SORRY!
HOP
ぴょん
BOOF!
EEP!
NO WORRIES.
HUH?
I THOUGHT IT MIGHT BE YOU.
AZUKI?
WOOF!
HUH?
WAIT A MINUTE. ARE YOU YUIJI'S FRIEND?
YES.
LICK
LICK
WHOA!
THAT TICKLES!
P IT! AT'S RTY!
WERE T ON WALK.
HA HA!
HA HA...

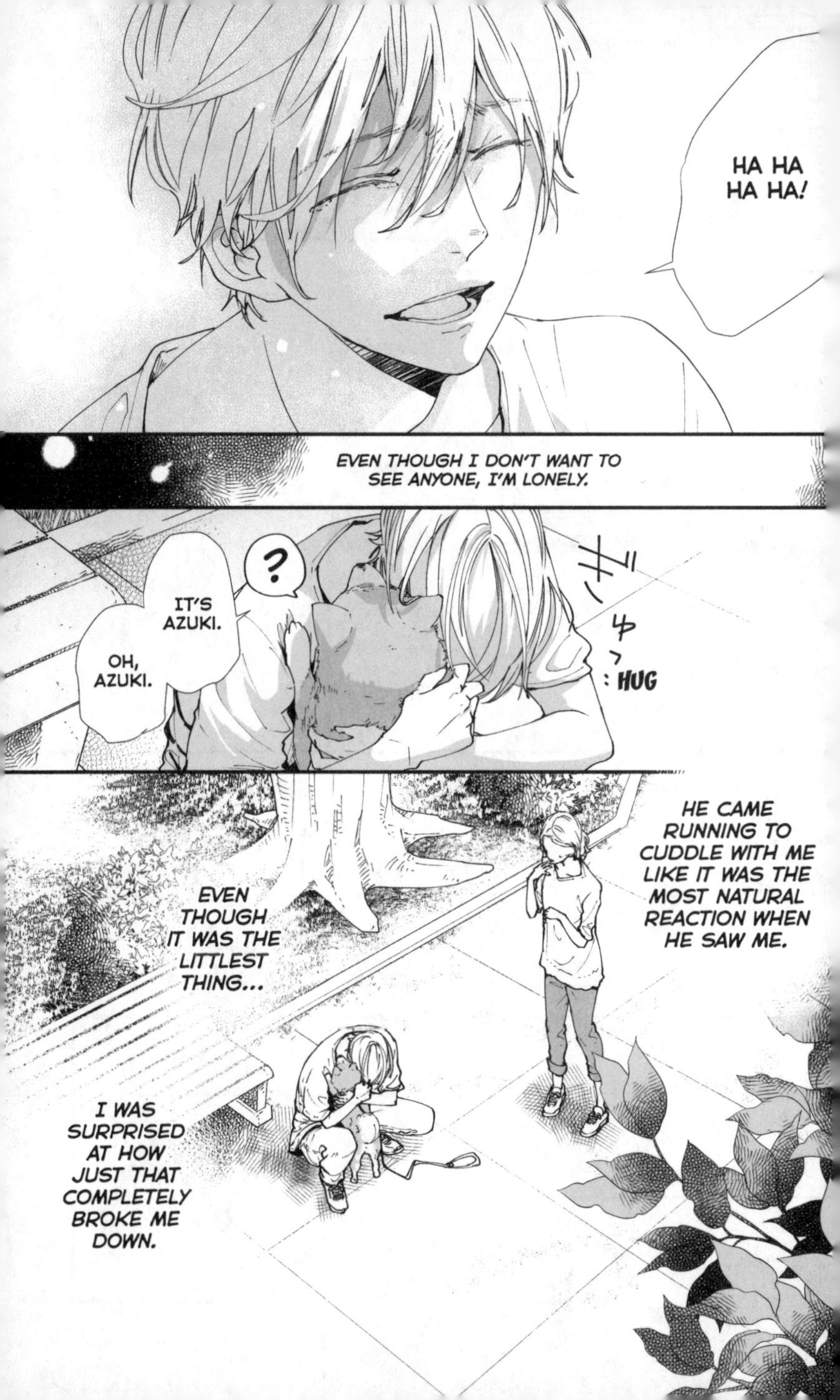
HA HA
HA HA!
EVEN THOUGH I DON'T WANT TO SEE ANYONE, I'M LONELY.
ぎゅっ
: HUG
?
IT'S AZUKI.
OH, AZUKI.
HE CAME RUNNING TO CUDDLE WITH ME LIKE IT WAS THE MOST NATURAL REACTION WHEN HE SAW ME.
EVEN THOUGH IT WAS THE LITTLEST THING...
I WAS SURPRISED AT HOW JUST THAT COMPLETELY BROKE ME DOWN.

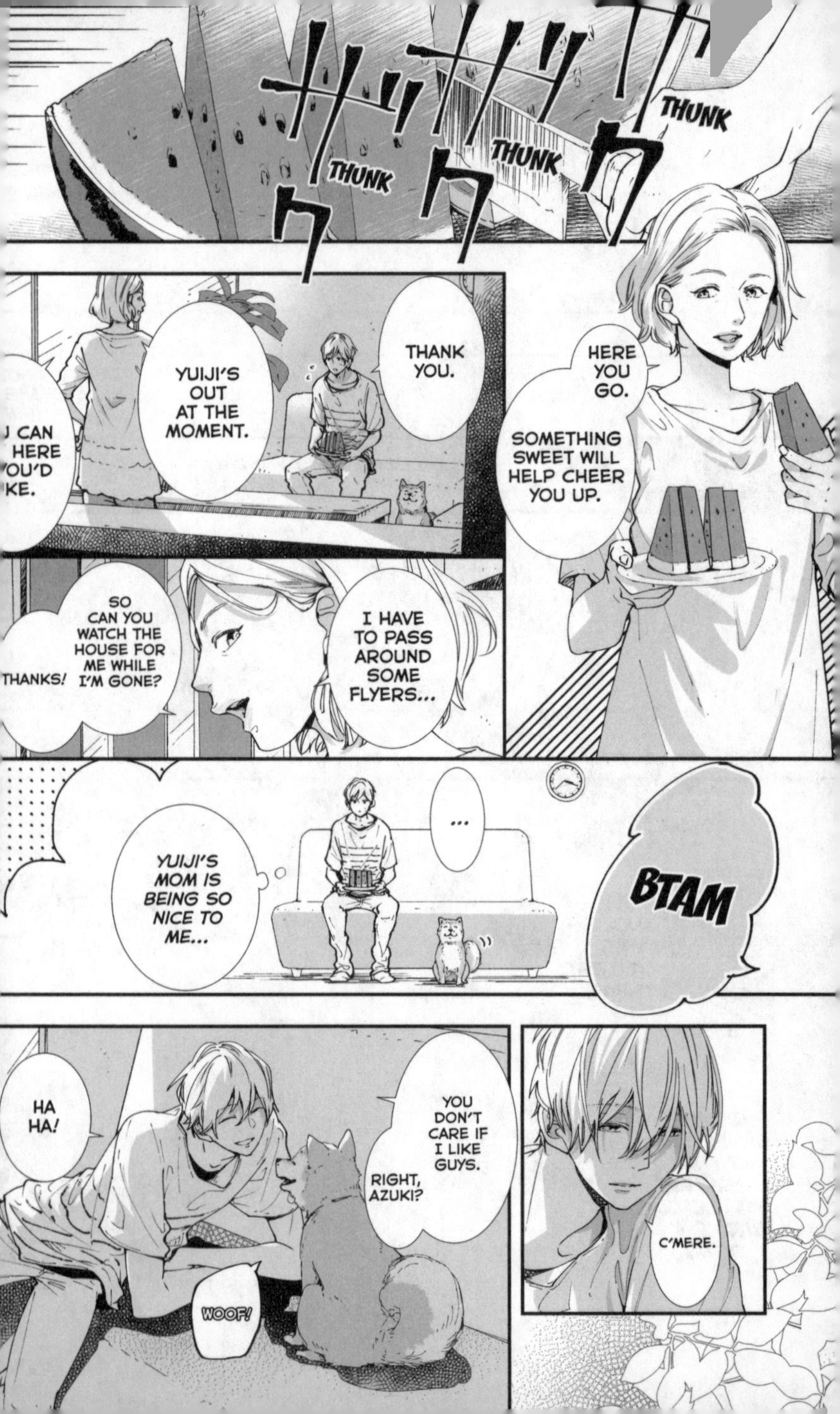
THUNK
THUNK
THUNK
HERE YOU GO.
SOMETHING SWEET WILL HELP CHEER YOU UP.
THANK YOU.
YUIJI'S OUT AT THE MOMENT.
I HAVE TO PASS AROUND SOME FLYERS...
SO CAN YOU WATCH THE HOUSE FOR ME WHILE I'M GONE?
THANKS!
BTAM
...
YUIJI'S MOM IS BEING SO NICE TO ME...
C'MERE.
YOU DON'T CARE IF I LIKE GUYS.
RIGHT, AZUKI?
HA HA!
WOOF!

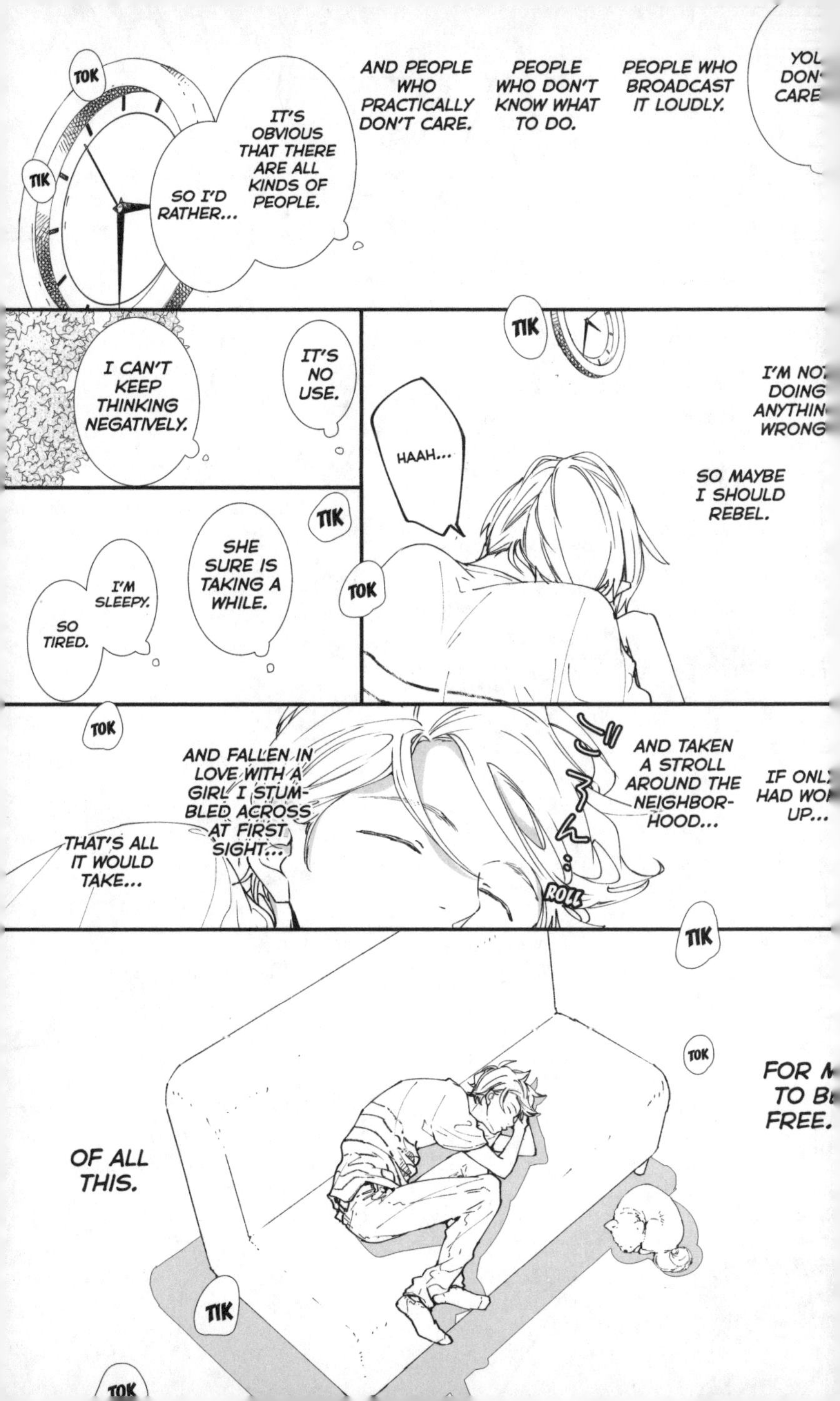
YOU DON CARE
PEOPLE WHO BROADCAST IT LOUDLY.
PEOPLE WHO DON'T KNOW WHAT TO DO.
AND PEOPLE WHO PRACTICALLY DON'T CARE.
IT'S OBVIOUS THAT THERE ARE ALL KINDS OF PEOPLE.
SO I'D RATHER...
TOK
TIK
I'M NO DOING ANYTHIN WRONG
SO MAYBE I SHOULD REBEL.
TIK
HAAH...
TOK
IT'S NO USE.
I CAN'T KEEP THINKING NEGATIVELY.
TIK
SHE SURE IS TAKING A WHILE.
I'M SLEEPY.
SO TIRED.
IF ONL HAD WO UP...
AND TAKEN A STROLL AROUND THE NEIGHBOR-HOOD...
ROLL
AND FALLEN IN LOVE WITH A GIRL I STUM-BLED ACROSS AT FIRST SIGHT...
TOK
THAT'S ALL IT WOULD TAKE...
TIK
TOK
FOR M TO B FREE.
OF ALL THIS.
TIK
TOK

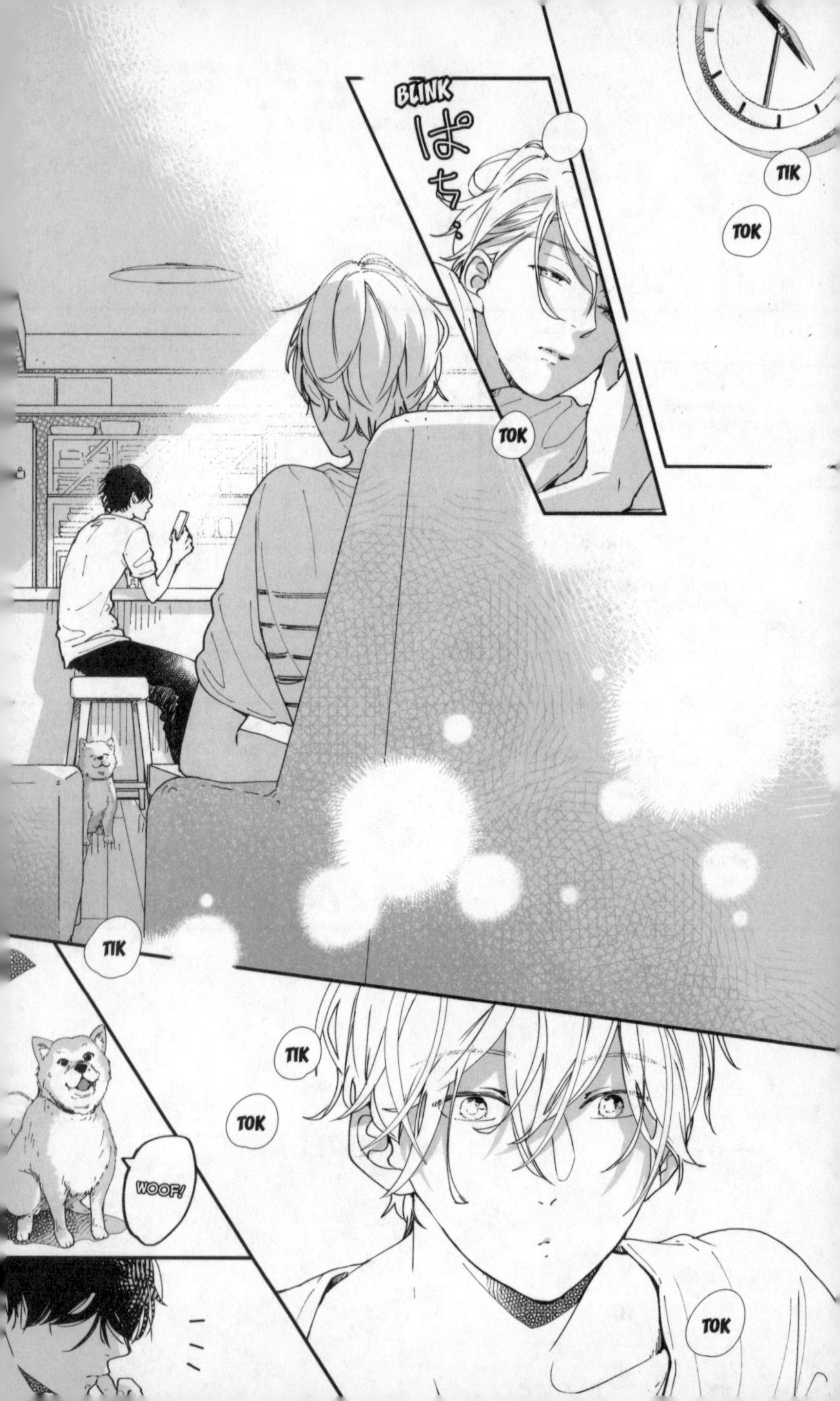
TIK
TOK
BLINK
ぱち
TOK
TIK
TIK
TOK
TOK
WOOF!

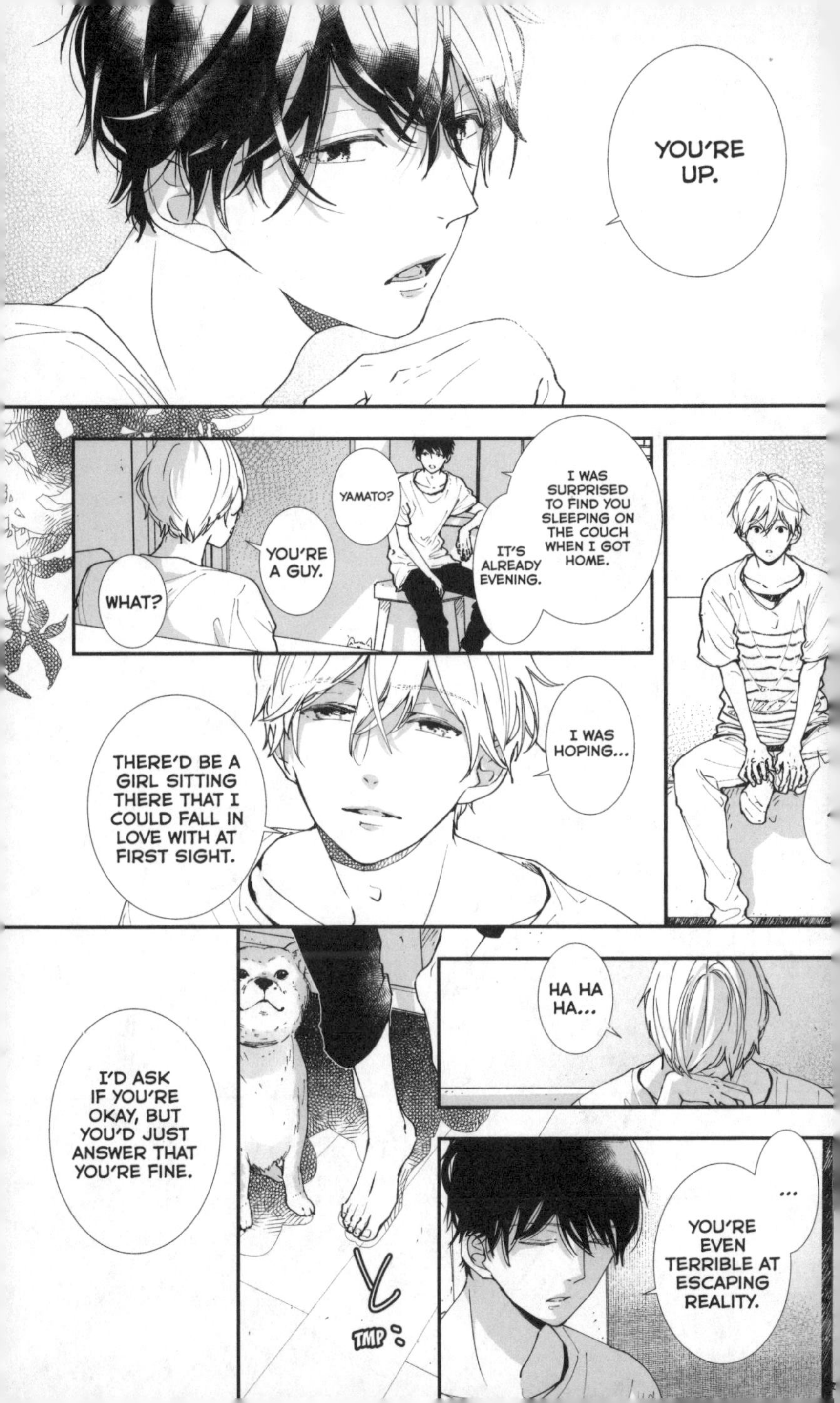
YOU'RE UP.
I WAS SURPRISED TO FIND YOU SLEEPING ON THE COUCH WHEN I GOT HOME.
IT'S ALREADY EVENING.
YAMATO?
YOU'RE A GUY.
WHAT?
I WAS HOPING...
THERE'D BE A GIRL SITTING THERE THAT I COULD FALL IN LOVE WITH AT FIRST SIGHT.
HA HA HA...
...
YOU'RE EVEN TERRIBLE AT ESCAPING REALITY.
I'D ASK IF YOU'RE OKAY, BUT YOU'D JUST ANSWER THAT YOU'RE FINE.
TMP

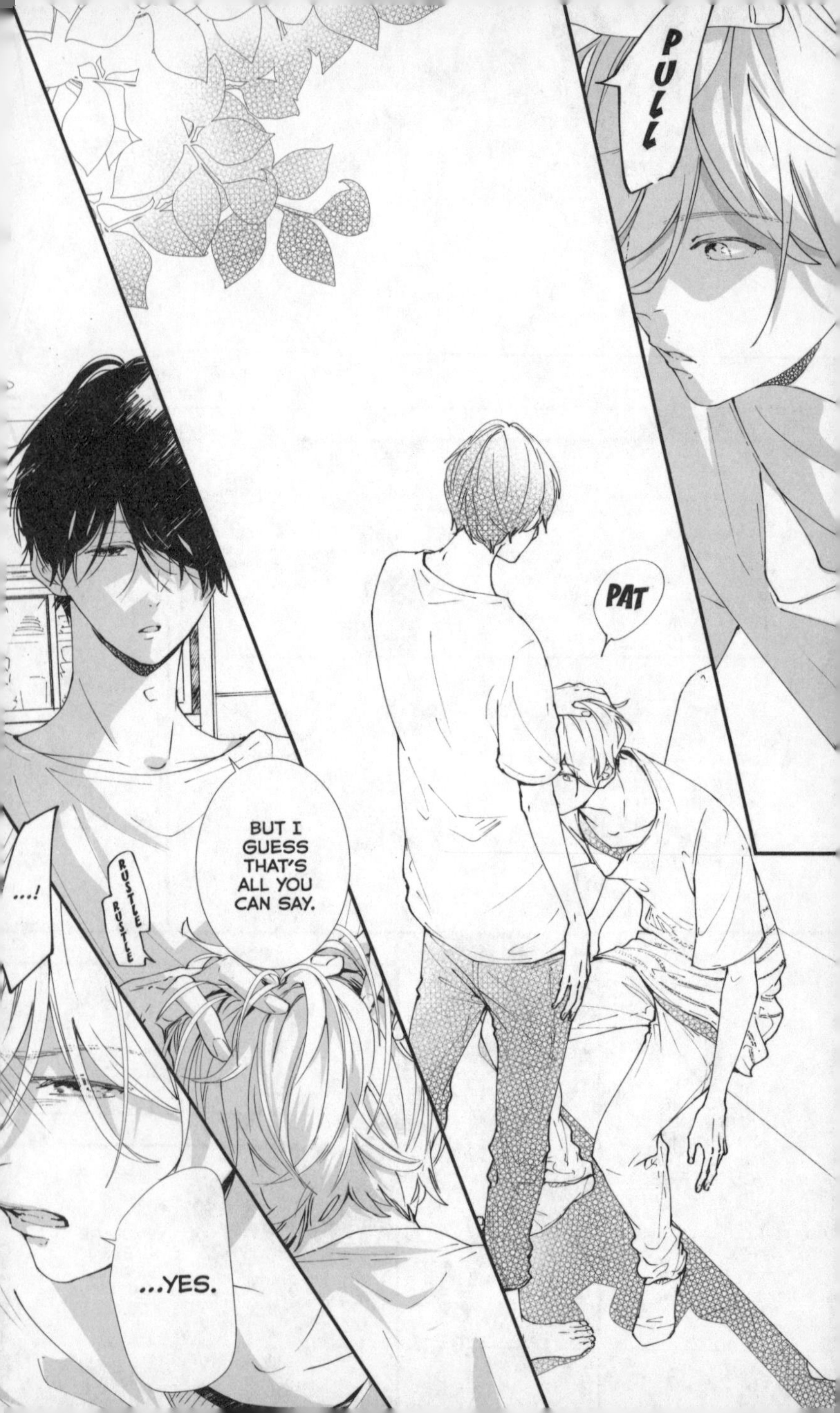
PULL
PAT
BUT I GUESS THAT'S ALL YOU CAN SAY.
RUSTLE RUSTLE
...!
...YES.

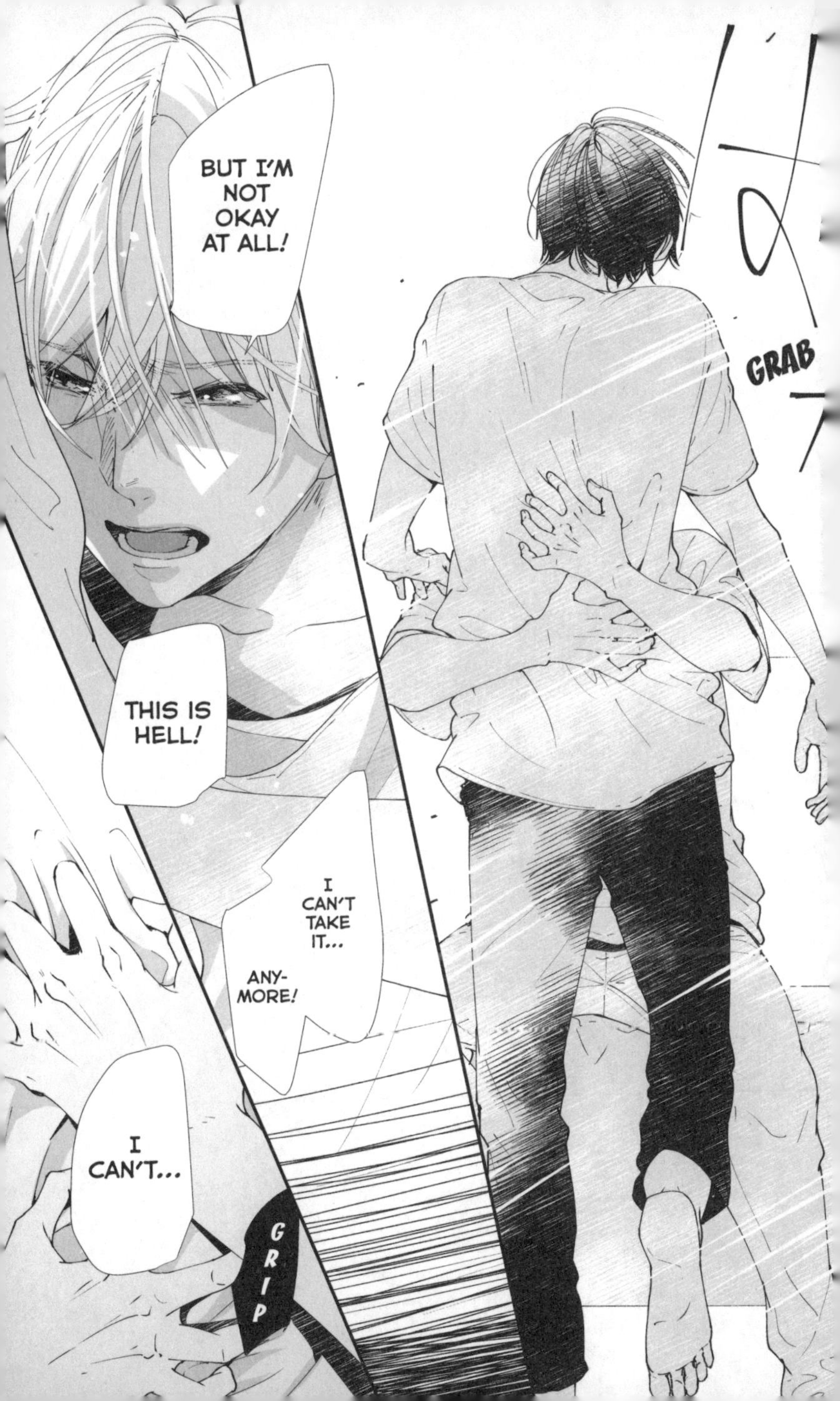
GRAB
BUT I'M NOT OKAY AT ALL!
THIS IS HELL!
I CAN'T TAKE IT...
ANY-MORE!
I CAN'T...
GRIP

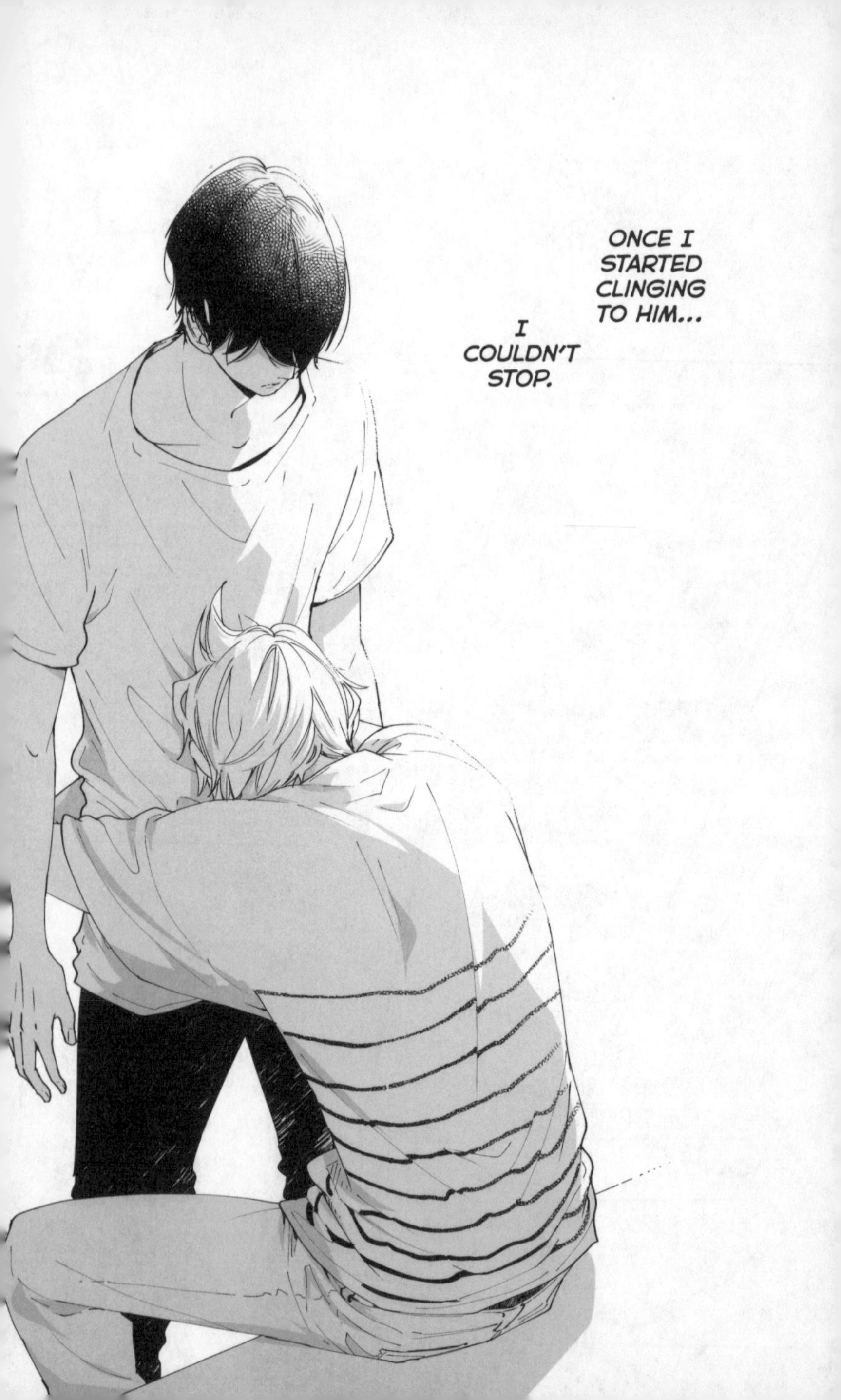
ONCE I STARTED CLINGING TO HIM...
I COULDN'T STOP.

KOIMONOGATARI:
LOVE STORIES

2

KOIMONOGATARI

LOVE STORIES

• Character Intro (5) •

Hibino

• Yamato's underclassman

Doi

• A classmate of Yuiji and Yamato's.

Chapter 9

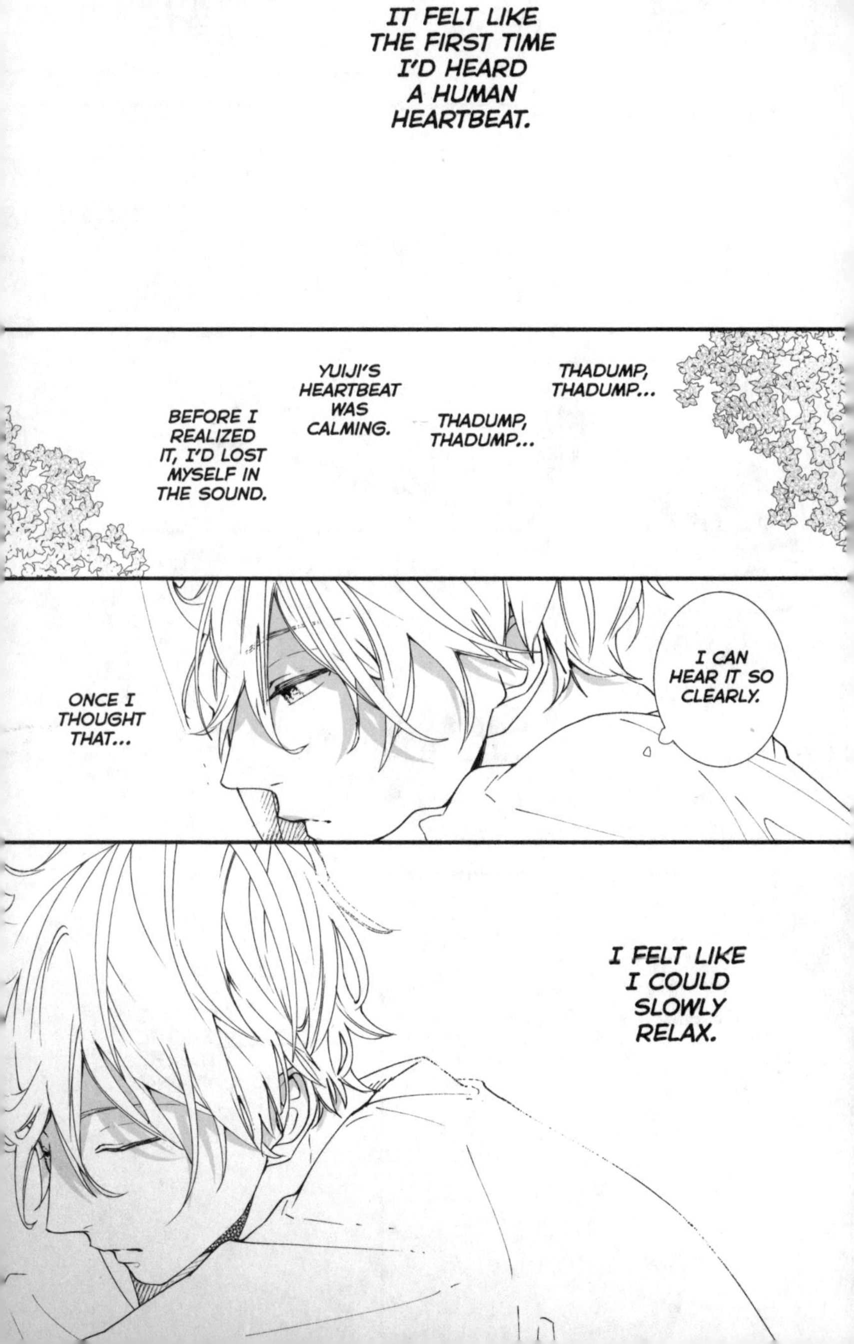
IT FELT LIKE THE FIRST TIME I'D HEARD A HUMAN HEARTBEAT.
THADUMP, THADUMP...
THADUMP, THADUMP...
YUIJI'S HEARTBEAT WAS CALMING.
BEFORE I REALIZED IT, I'D LOST MYSELF IN THE SOUND.
I CAN HEAR IT SO CLEARLY.
ONCE I THOUGHT THAT...
I FELT LIKE I COULD SLOWLY RELAX.

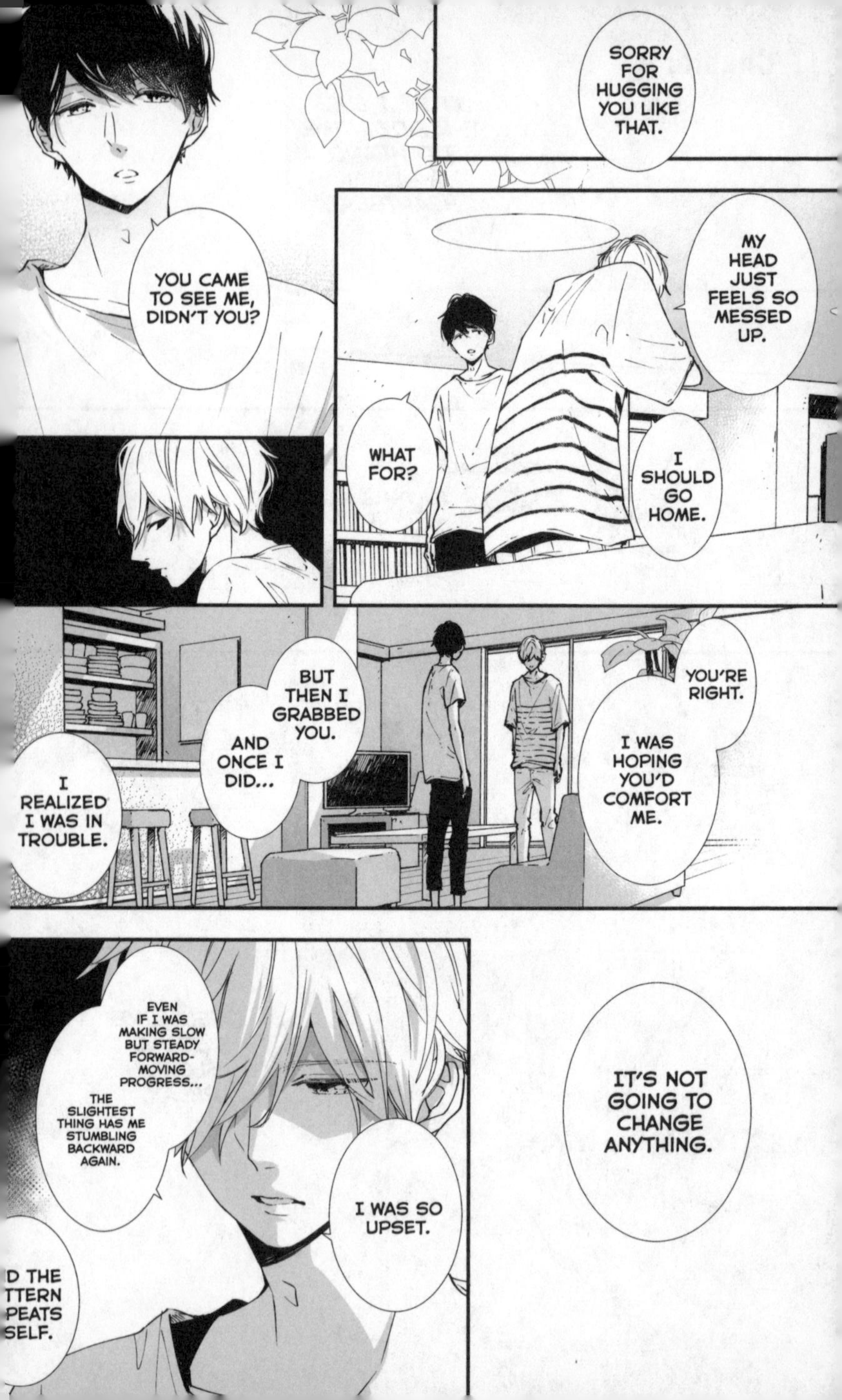
SORRY FOR HUGGING YOU LIKE THAT.
MY HEAD JUST FEELS SO MESSED UP.
I SHOULD GO HOME.
WHAT FOR?
YOU CAME TO SEE ME, DIDN'T YOU?
YOU'RE RIGHT.
I WAS HOPING YOU'D COMFORT ME.
BUT THEN I GRABBED YOU.
AND ONCE I DID...
I REALIZED I WAS IN TROUBLE.
IT'S NOT GOING TO CHANGE ANYTHING.
I WAS SO UPSET.
EVEN IF I WAS MAKING SLOW BUT STEADY FORWARD-MOVING PROGRESS...
THE SLIGHTEST THING HAS ME STUMBLING BACKWARD AGAIN.
D THE TTERN PEATS SELF.

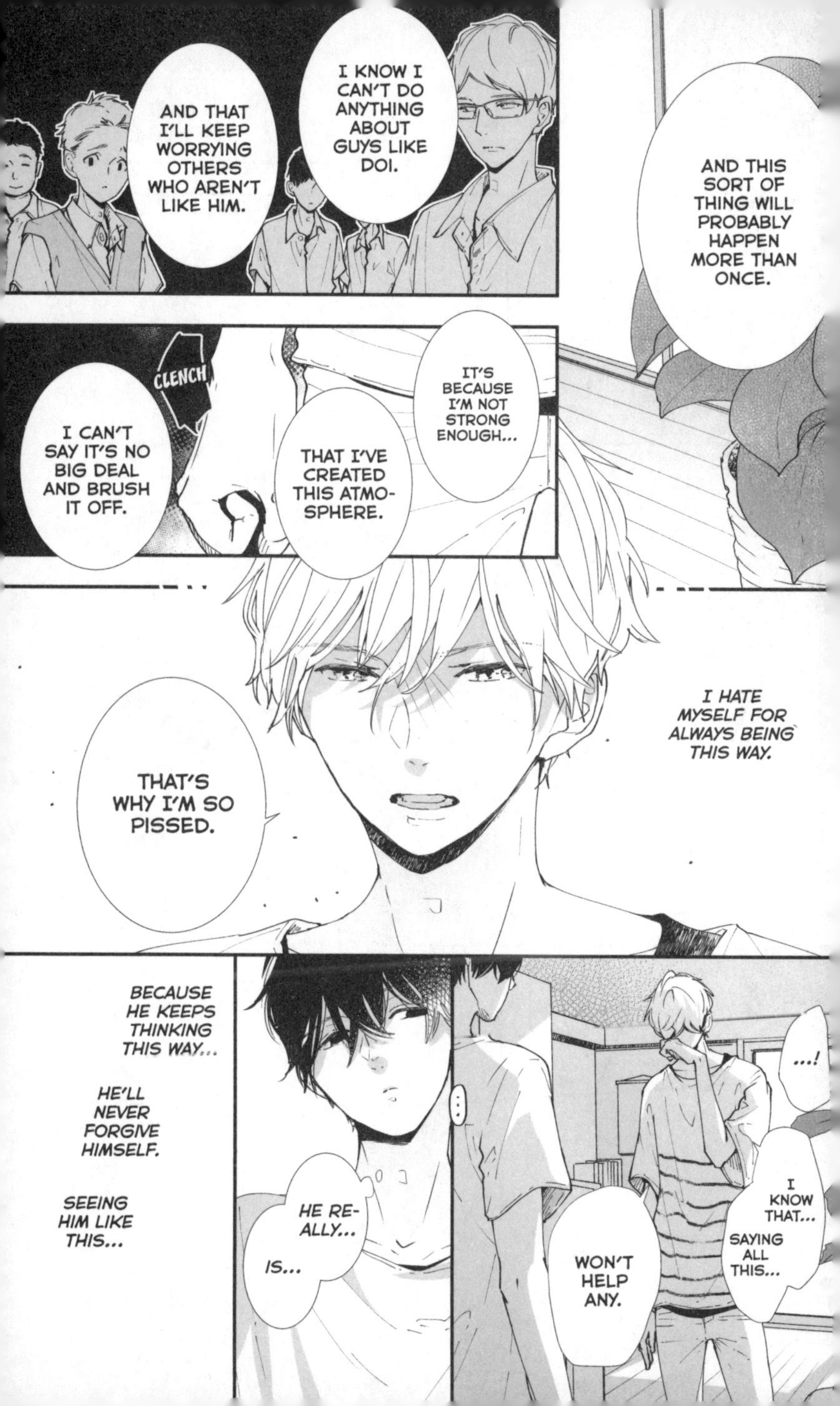
AND THIS SORT OF THING WILL PROBABLY HAPPEN MORE THAN ONCE.
I KNOW I CAN'T DO ANYTHING ABOUT GUYS LIKE DOI.
AND THAT I'LL KEEP WORRYING OTHERS WHO AREN'T LIKE HIM.
IT'S BECAUSE I'M NOT STRONG ENOUGH...
THAT I'VE CREATED THIS ATMO-SPHERE.
CLENCH
I CAN'T SAY IT'S NO BIG DEAL AND BRUSH IT OFF.
I HATE MYSELF FOR ALWAYS BEING THIS WAY.
THAT'S WHY I'M SO PISSED.
...!
I KNOW THAT...
SAYING ALL THIS...
WON'T HELP ANY.
...
HE RE-ALLY...
IS...
BECAUSE HE KEEPS THINKING THIS WAY...
HE'LL NEVER FORGIVE HIMSELF.
SEEING HIM LIKE THIS...

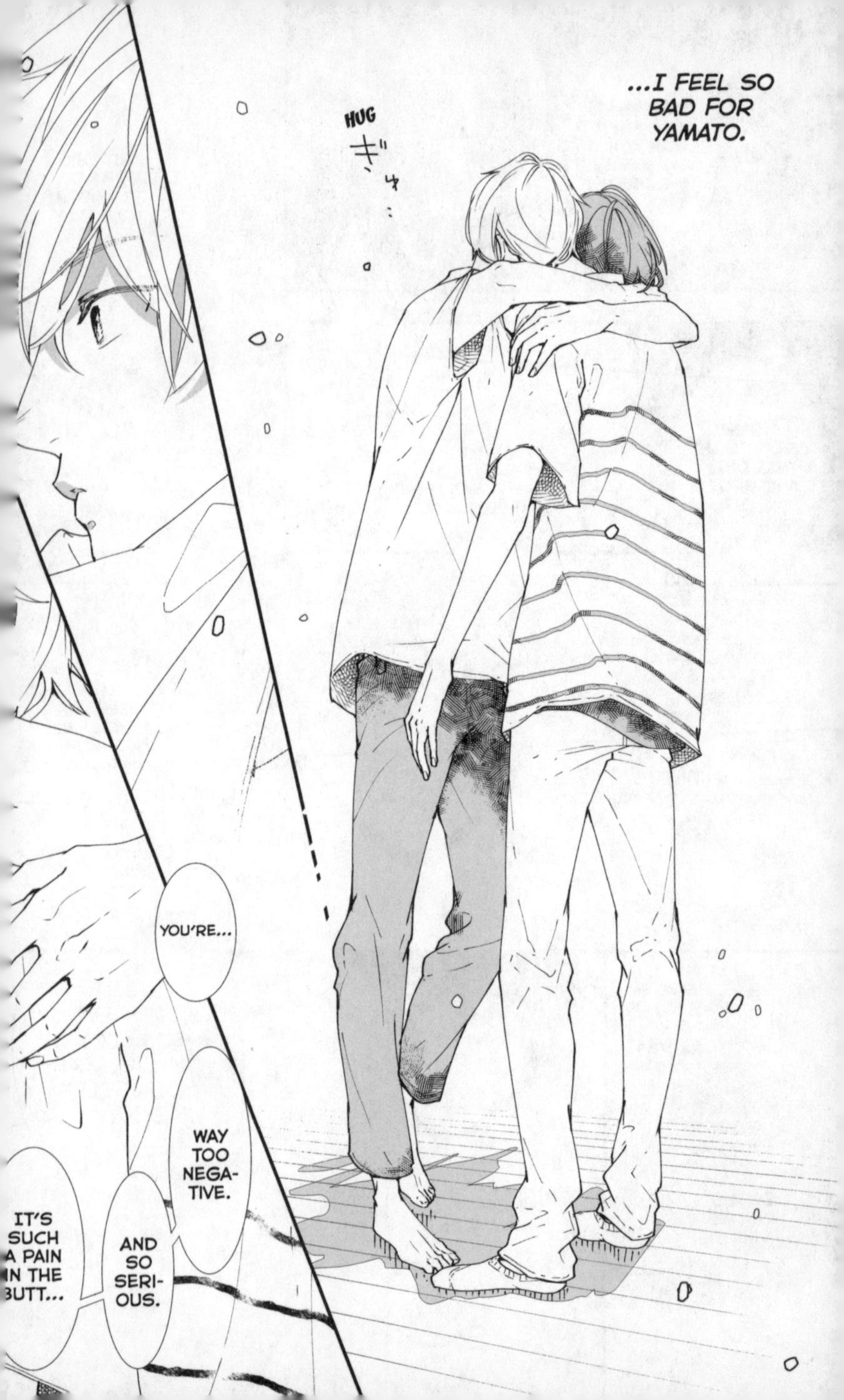
...I FEEL SO BAD FOR YAMATO.
HUG
YOU'RE...
WAY TOO NEGATIVE.
AND SO SERIOUS.
IT'S SUCH A PAIN IN THE BUTT...

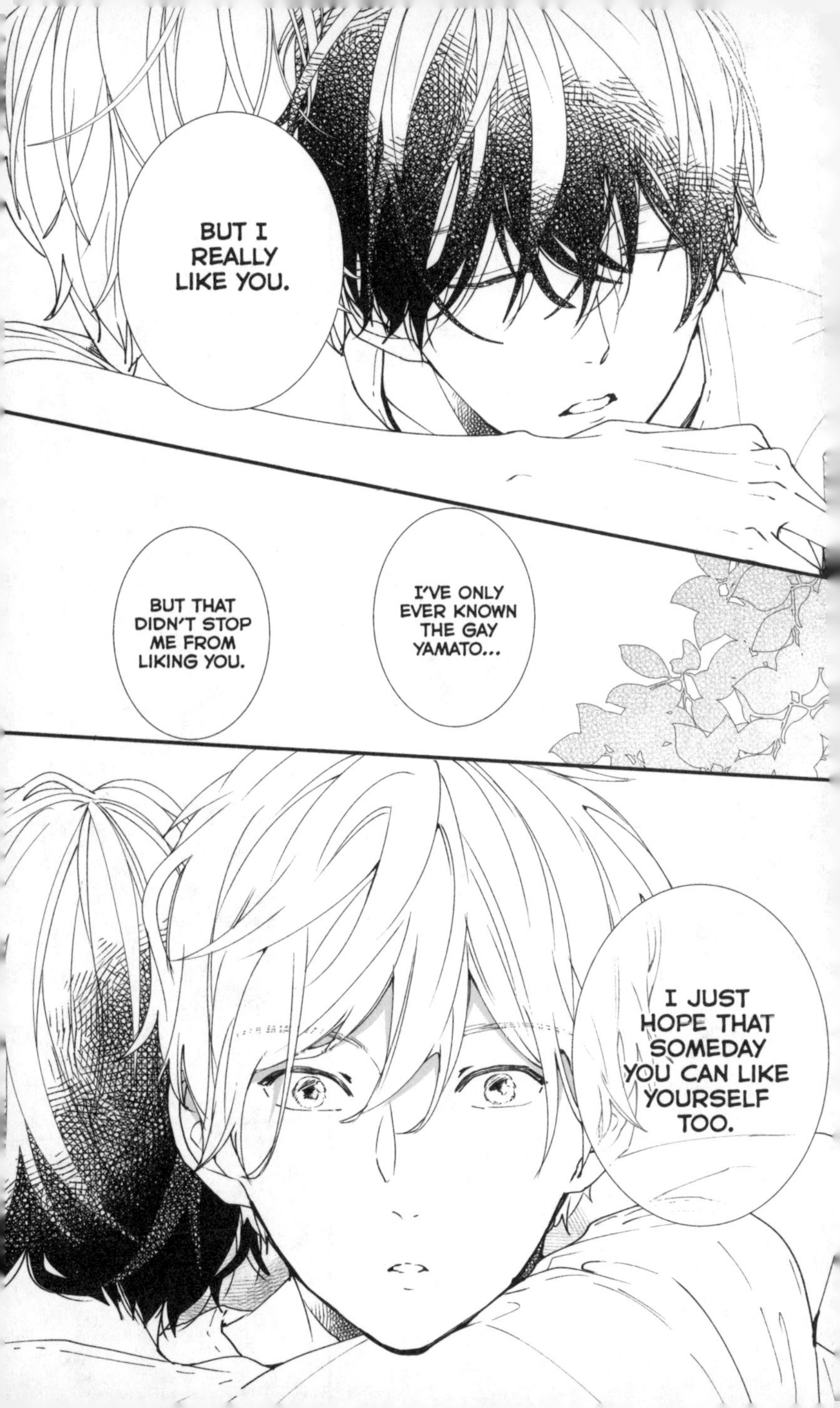
BUT I REALLY LIKE YOU.
I'VE ONLY EVER KNOWN THE GAY YAMATO...
BUT THAT DIDN'T STOP ME FROM LIKING YOU.
I JUST HOPE THAT SOMEDAY YOU CAN LIKE YOURSELF TOO.

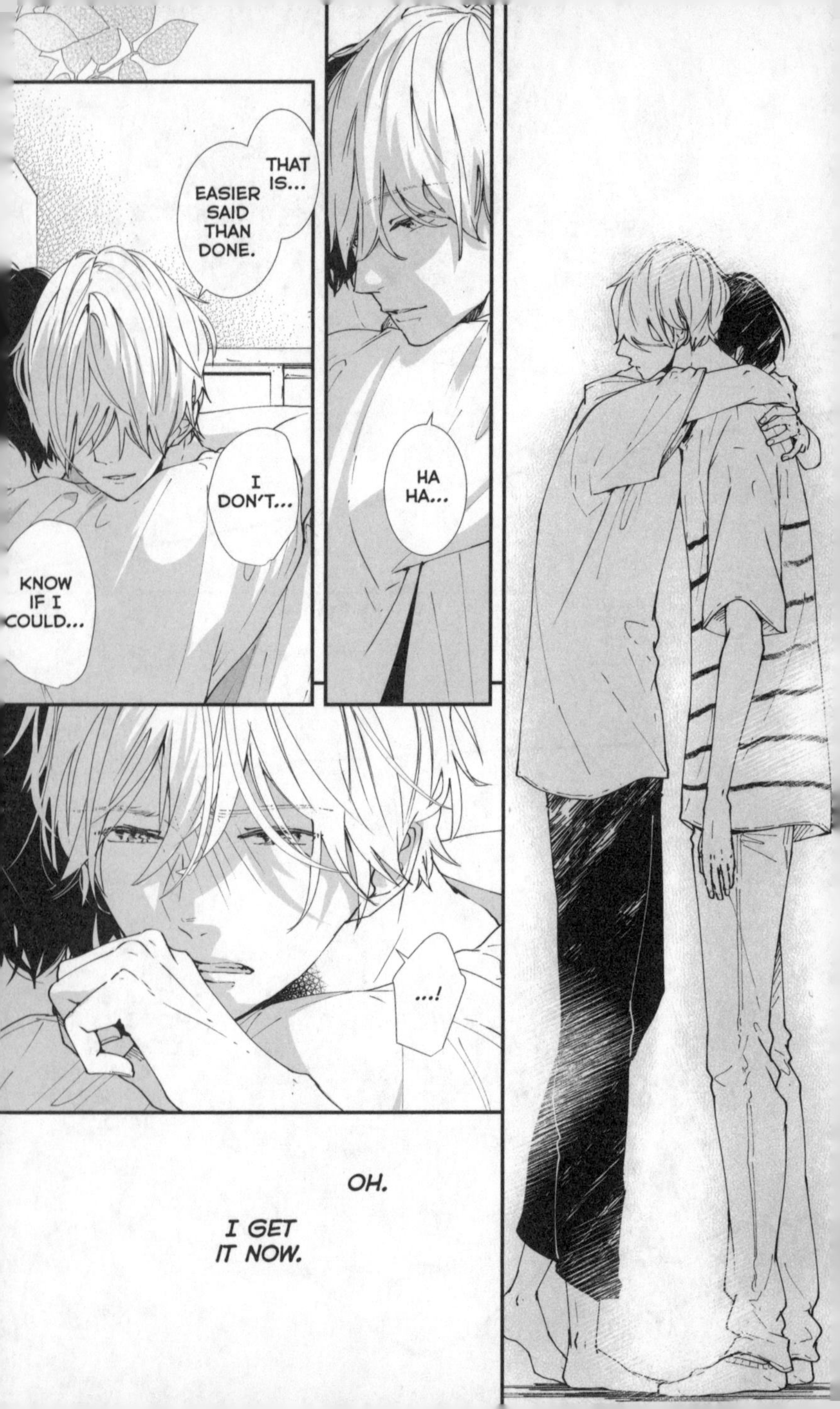
HA HA...
THAT IS... EASIER SAID THAN DONE.
I DON'T...
KNOW IF I COULD...
...!
OH.
I GET IT NOW.

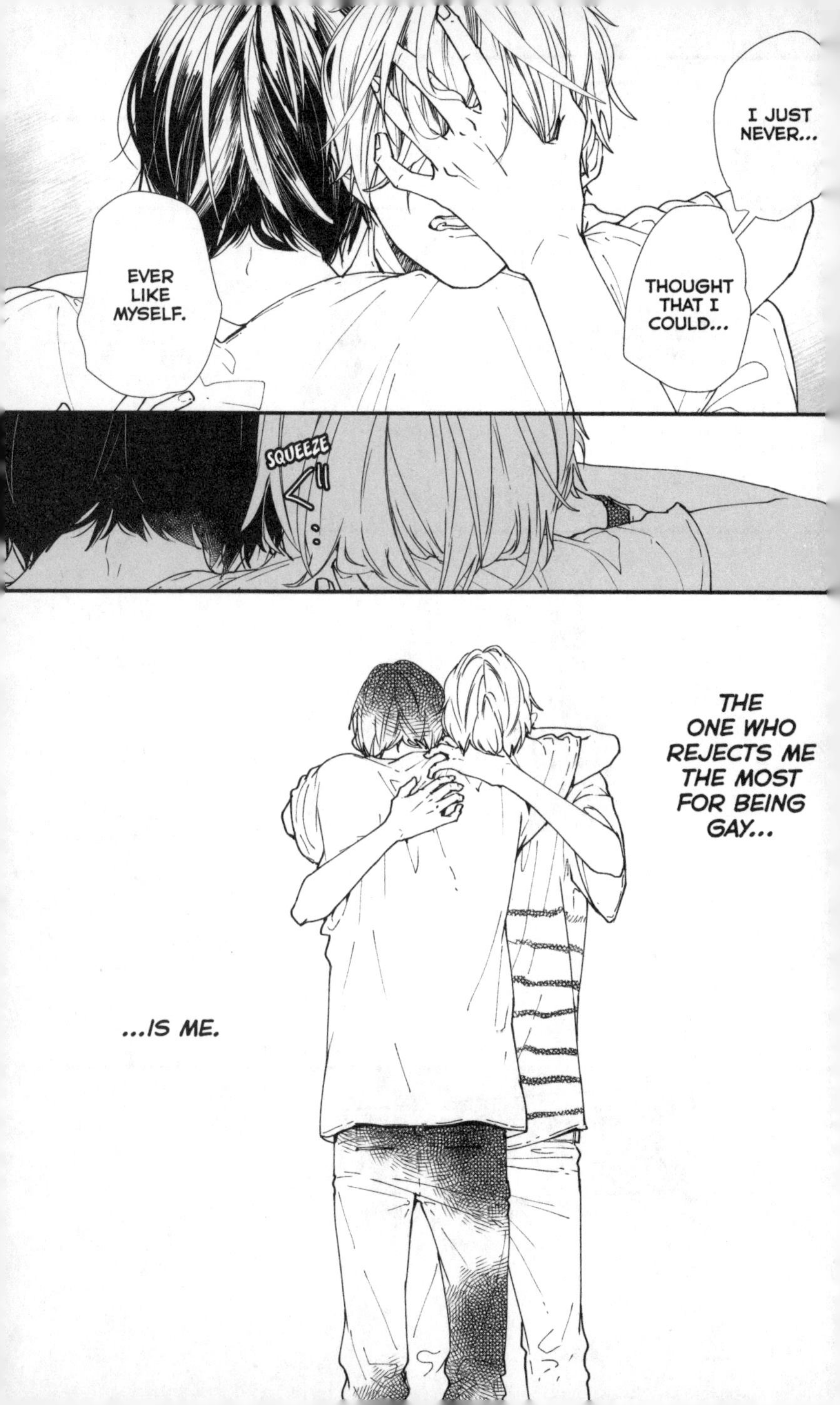
I JUST NEVER...
THOUGHT THAT I COULD...
EVER LIKE MYSELF.
SQUEEZE
THE ONE WHO REJECTS ME THE MOST FOR BEING GAY...
...IS ME.

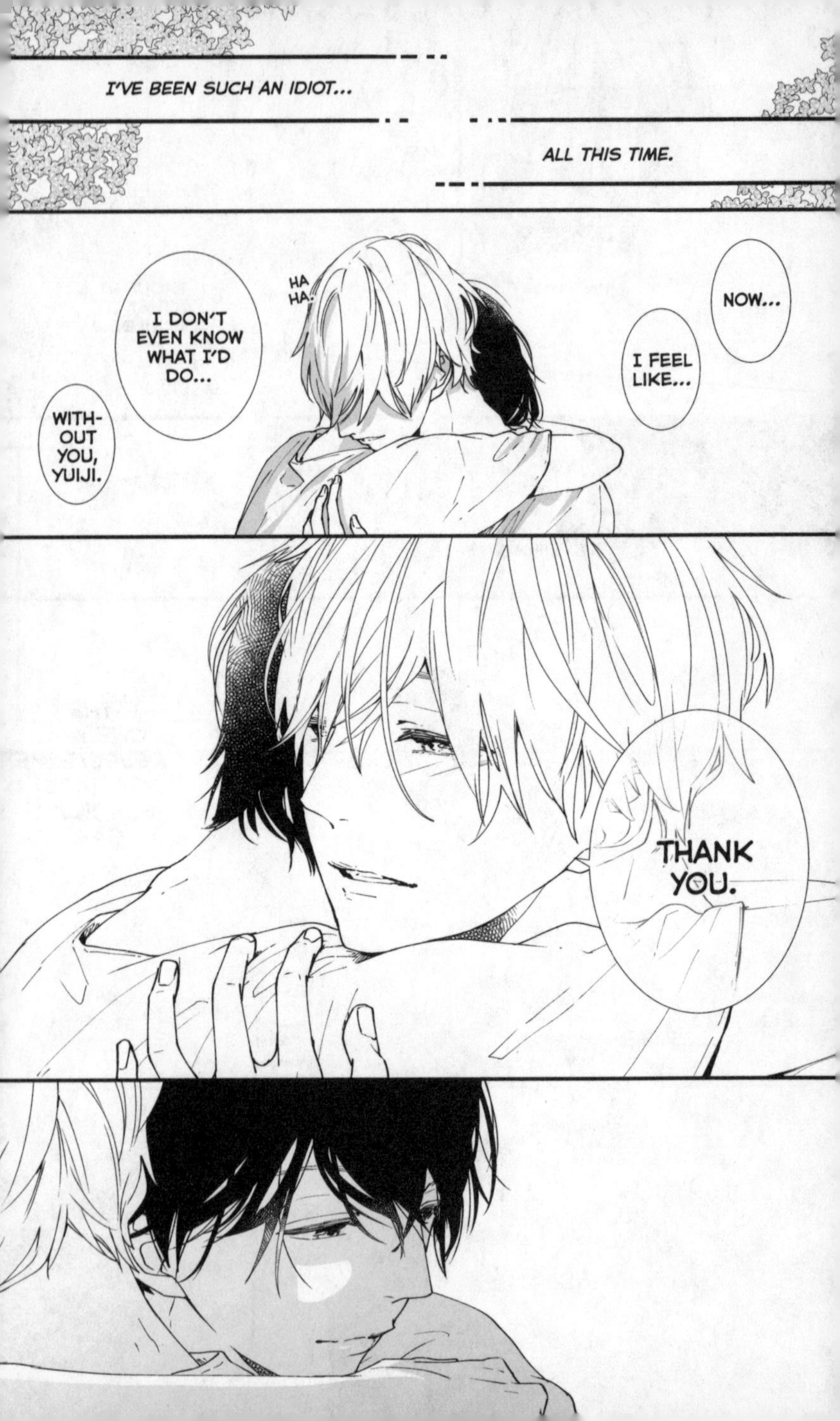
I'VE BEEN SUCH AN IDIOT...
ALL THIS TIME.
NOW...
I FEEL LIKE...
HA HA.
I DON'T EVEN KNOW WHAT I'D DO...
WITH-OUT YOU, YUIJI.
THANK YOU.

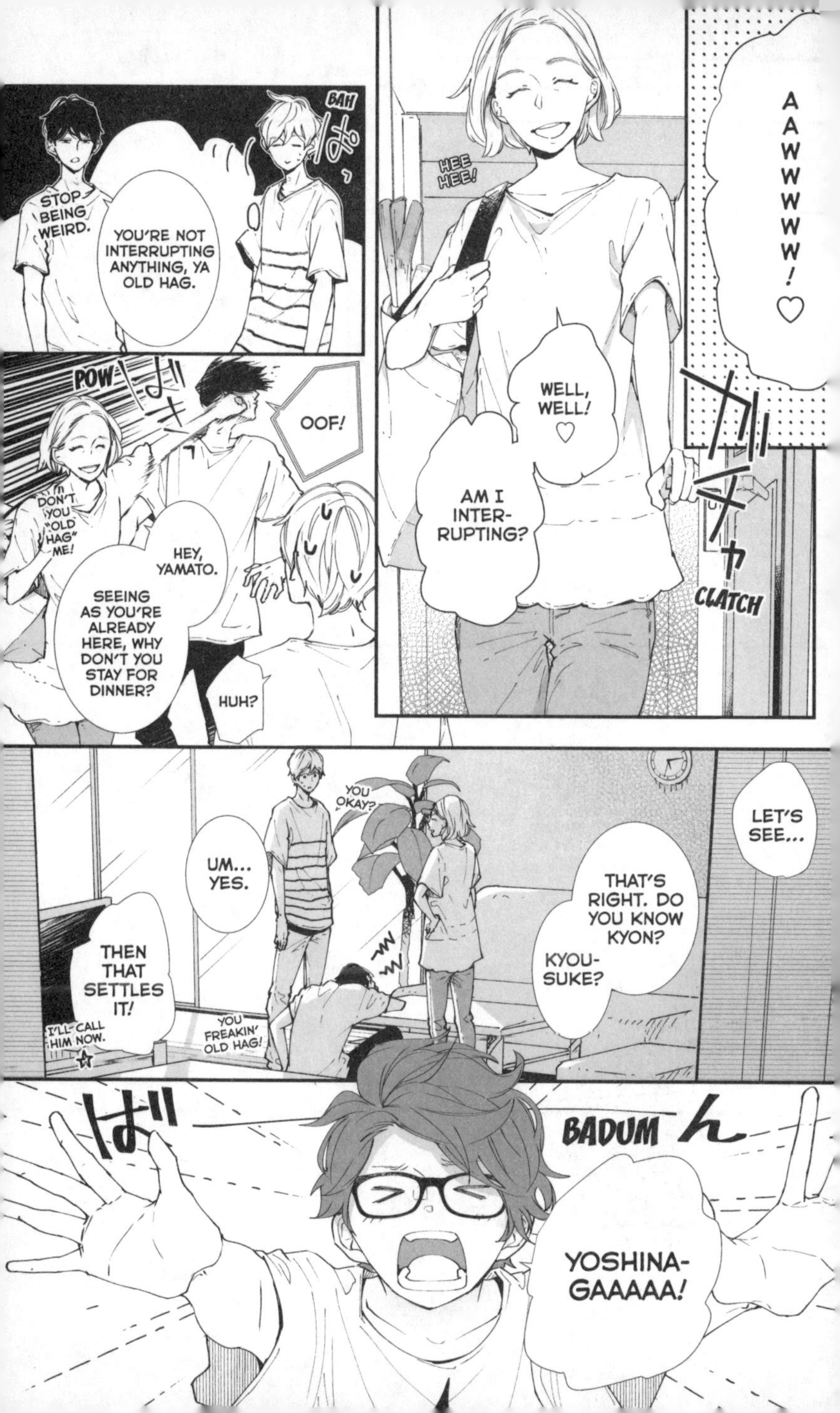

AAWWWWWW! ♡
CLATCH
HEE HEE!
WELL, WELL! ♡
AM I INTER-RUPTING?
BAH
YOU'RE NOT INTERRUPTING ANYTHING, YA OLD HAG.
STOP BEING WEIRD.
POW
OOF!
DON'T YOU "OLD HAG" ME!
HEY, YAMATO.
SEEING AS YOU'RE ALREADY HERE, WHY DON'T YOU STAY FOR DINNER?
HUH?
LET'S SEE...
THAT'S RIGHT. DO YOU KNOW KYON?
KYOU-SUKE?
YOU OKAY?
UM... YES.
THEN THAT SETTLES IT!
YOU FREAKIN' OLD HAG!
I'LL CALL HIM NOW. ☆
BADUM
YOSHINA-GAAAAA!

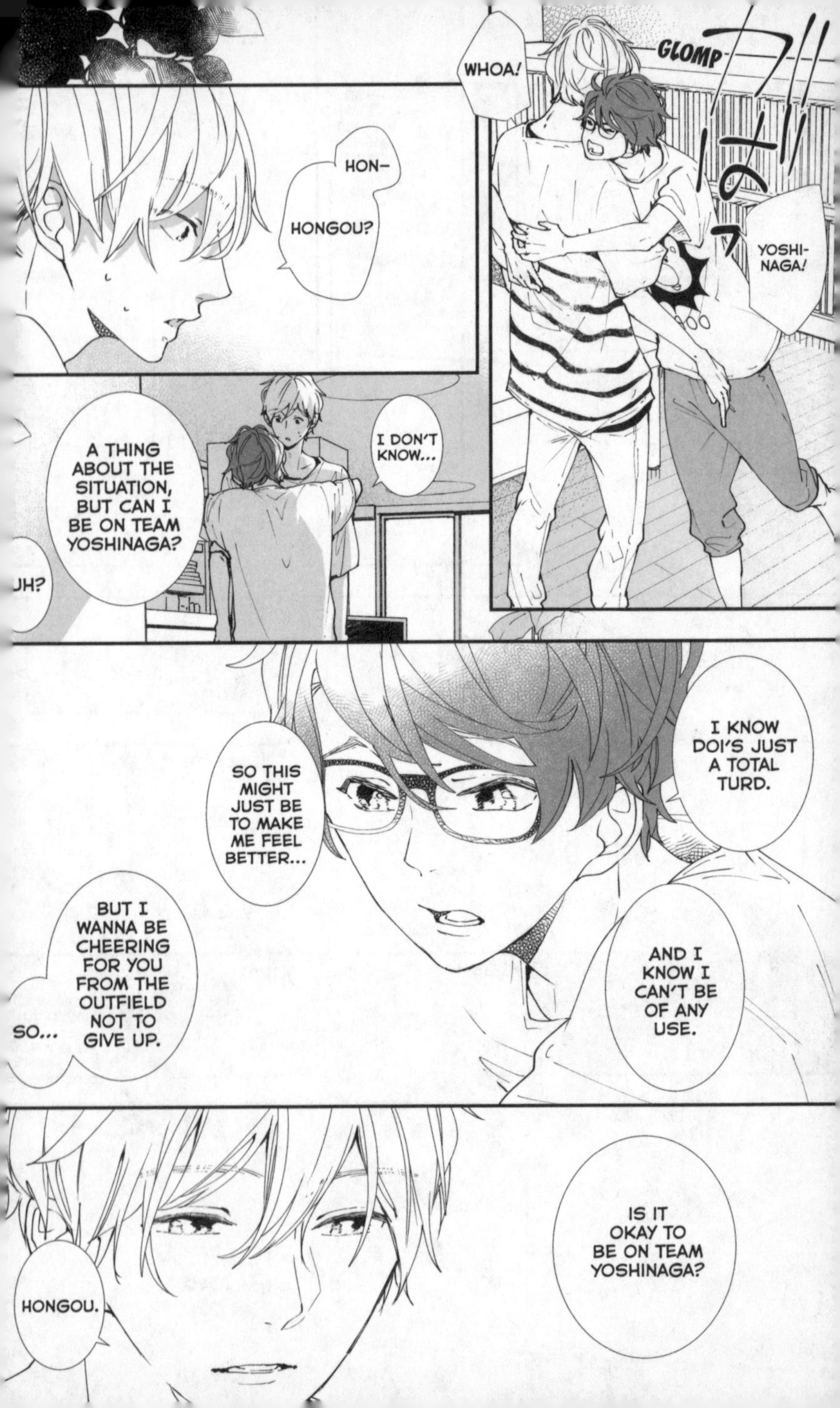
GLOMP
WHOA!
YOSHI-NAGA!
HON-
HONGOU?
I DON'T KNOW...
A THING ABOUT THE SITUATION, BUT CAN I BE ON TEAM YOSHINAGA?
UH?
I KNOW DOI'S JUST A TOTAL TURD.
AND I KNOW I CAN'T BE OF ANY USE.
SO THIS MIGHT JUST BE TO MAKE ME FEEL BETTER...
BUT I WANNA BE CHEERING FOR YOU FROM THE OUTFIELD NOT TO GIVE UP.
SO...
IS IT OKAY TO BE ON TEAM YOSHINAGA?
HONGOU.

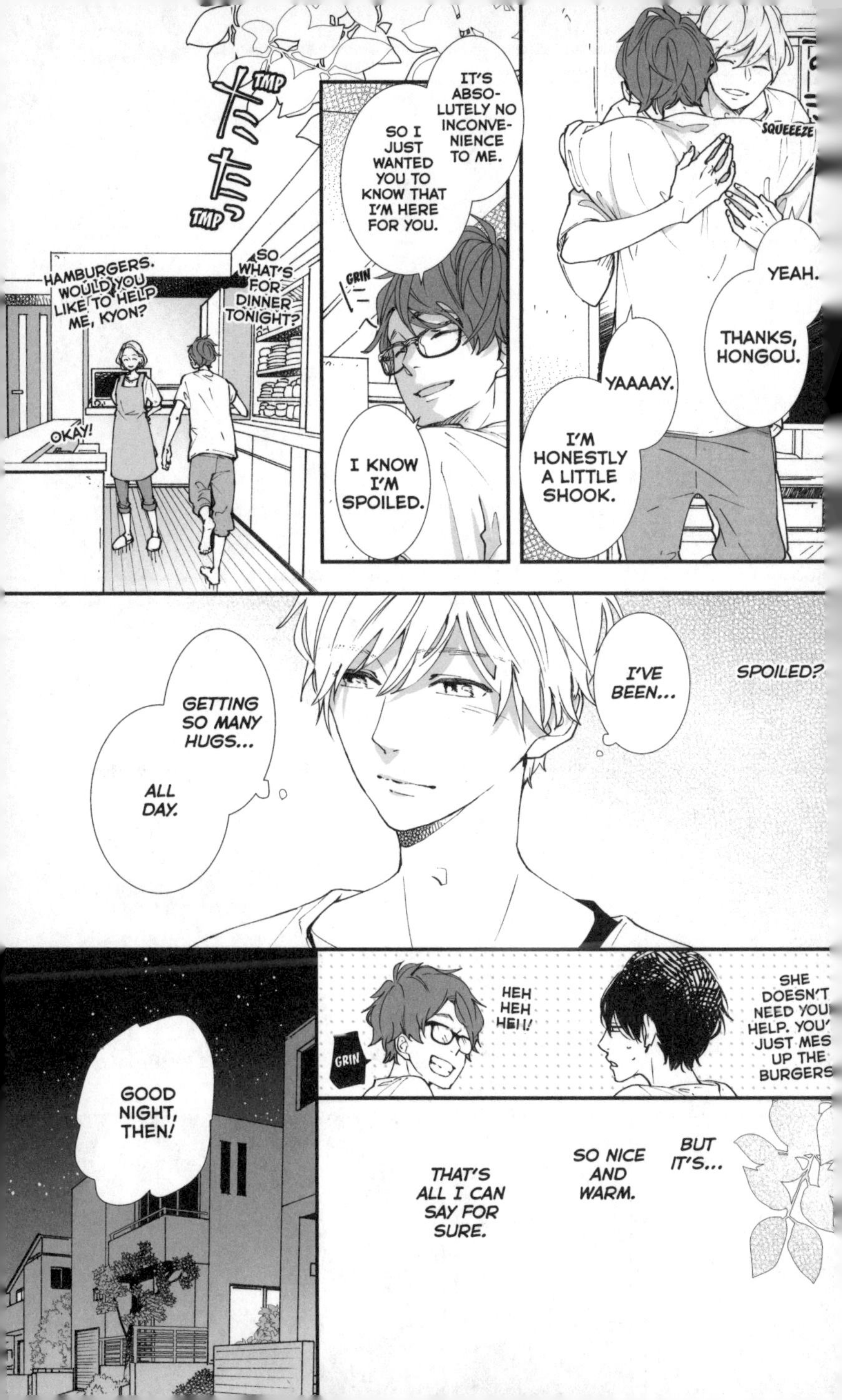
SQUEEEZE
YEAH.
THANKS, HONGOU.
YAAAAY.
I'M HONESTLY A LITTLE SHOOK.
IT'S ABSOLUTELY NO INCONVENIENCE TO ME.
SO I JUST WANTED YOU TO KNOW THAT I'M HERE FOR YOU.
GRIN
I KNOW I'M SPOILED.
TMP
TMP
SO WHAT'S FOR DINNER TONIGHT?
HAMBURGERS. WOULD YOU LIKE TO HELP ME, KYON?
OKAY!
SPOILED?
I'VE BEEN...
GETTING SO MANY HUGS...
ALL DAY.
SHE DOESN'T NEED YOU HELP. YOU' JUST MES UP THE BURGERS
HEH HEH HEH!
GRIN
BUT IT'S...
SO NICE AND WARM.
THAT'S ALL I CAN SAY FOR SURE.
GOOD NIGHT, THEN!

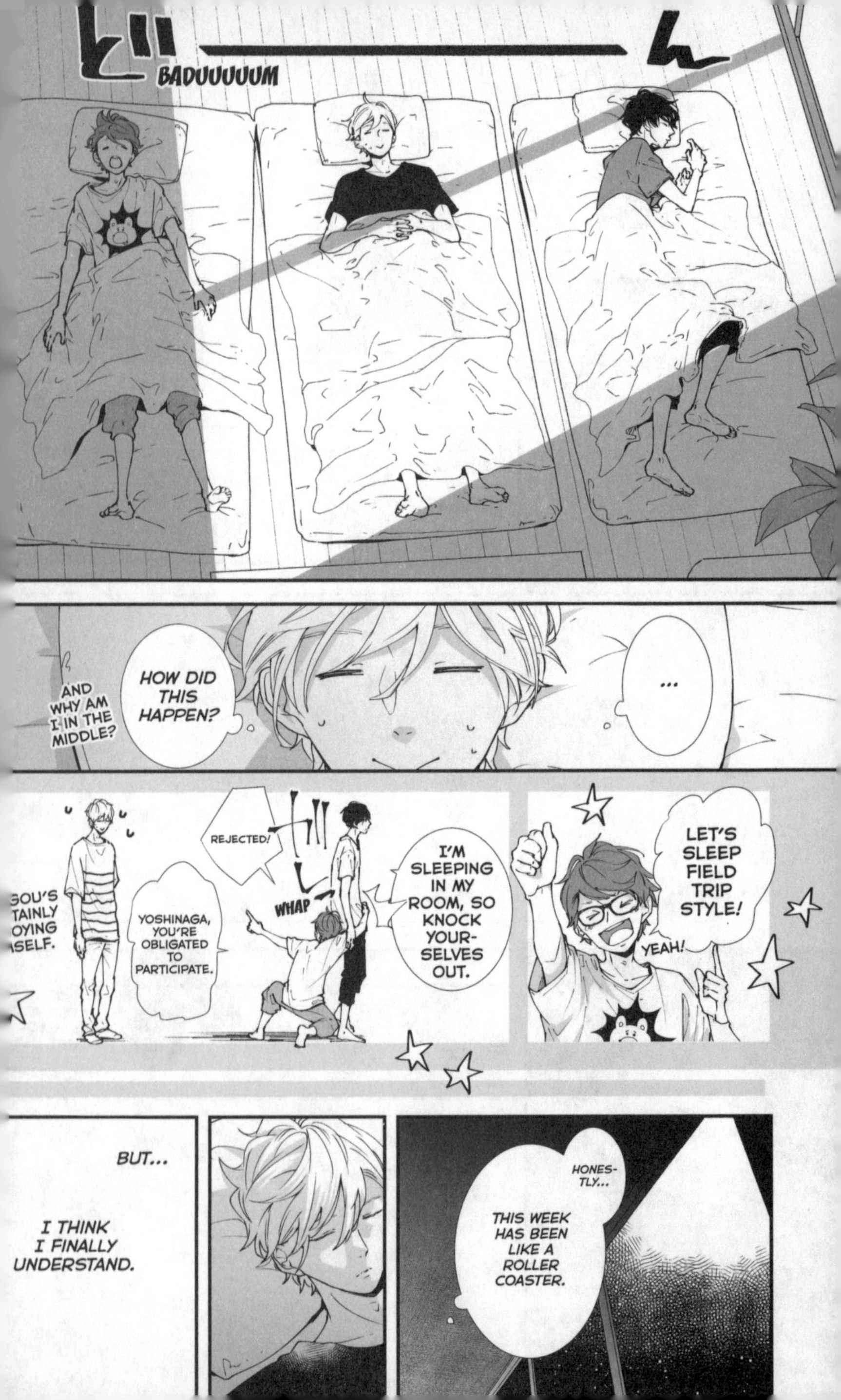
BADUUUUUM
...
HOW DID THIS HAPPEN?
AND WHY AM I IN THE MIDDLE?
LET'S SLEEP FIELD TRIP STYLE!
YEAH!
I'M SLEEPING IN MY ROOM, SO KNOCK YOURSELVES OUT.
REJECTED!
WHAP
YOSHINAGA, YOU'RE OBLIGATED TO PARTICIPATE.
GOU'S TAINLY OYING SELF.
HONESTLY...
THIS WEEK HAS BEEN LIKE A ROLLER COASTER.
BUT...
I THINK I FINALLY UNDERSTAND.

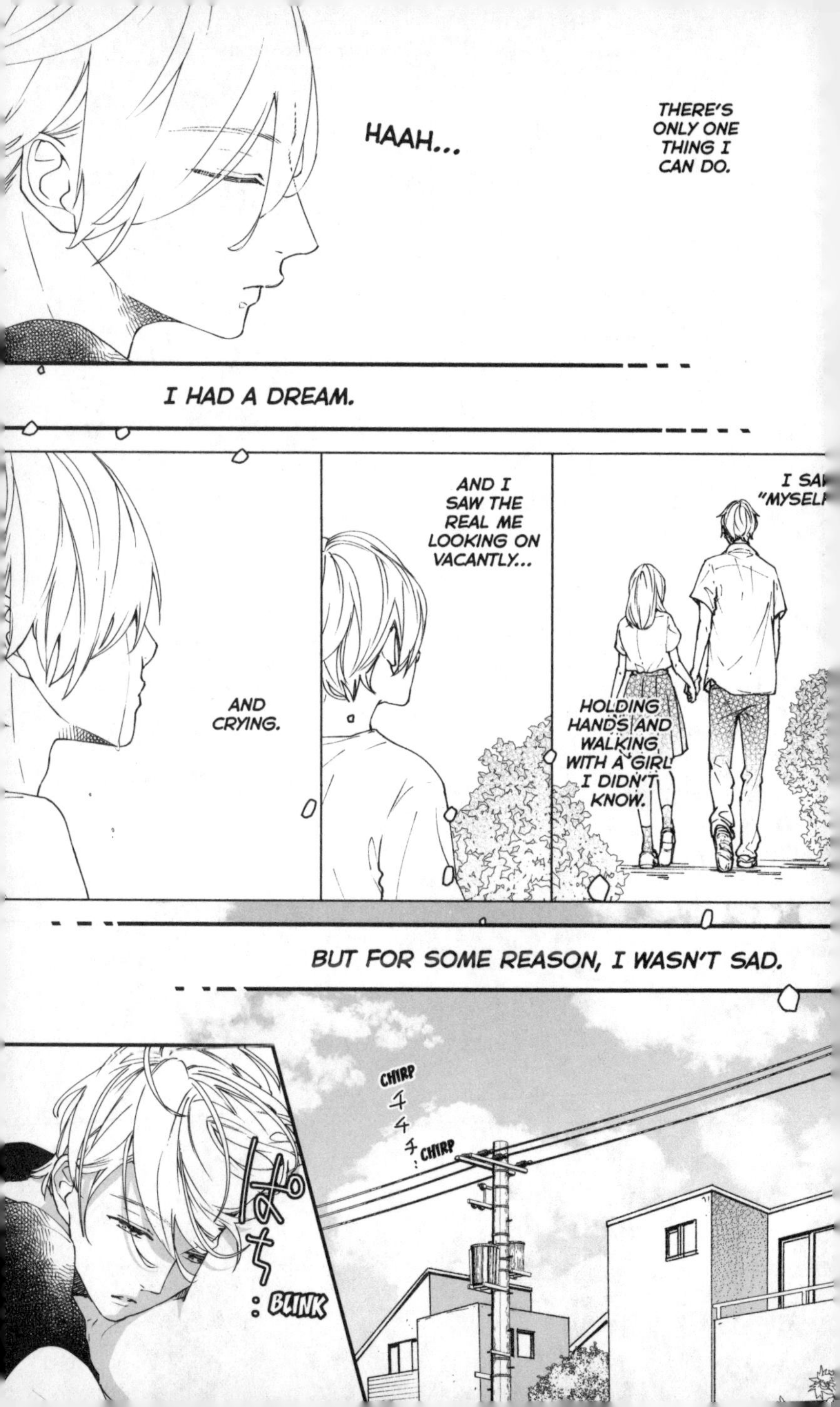

THERE'S ONLY ONE THING I CAN DO.
HAAH...
I HAD A DREAM.
I SA "MYSEL
HOLDING HANDS AND WALKING WITH A GIRL I DIDN'T KNOW.
AND I SAW THE REAL ME LOOKING ON VACANTLY...
AND CRYING.
BUT FOR SOME REASON, I WASN'T SAD.
CHIRP
チチチ
CHIRP
ぱち
BLINK

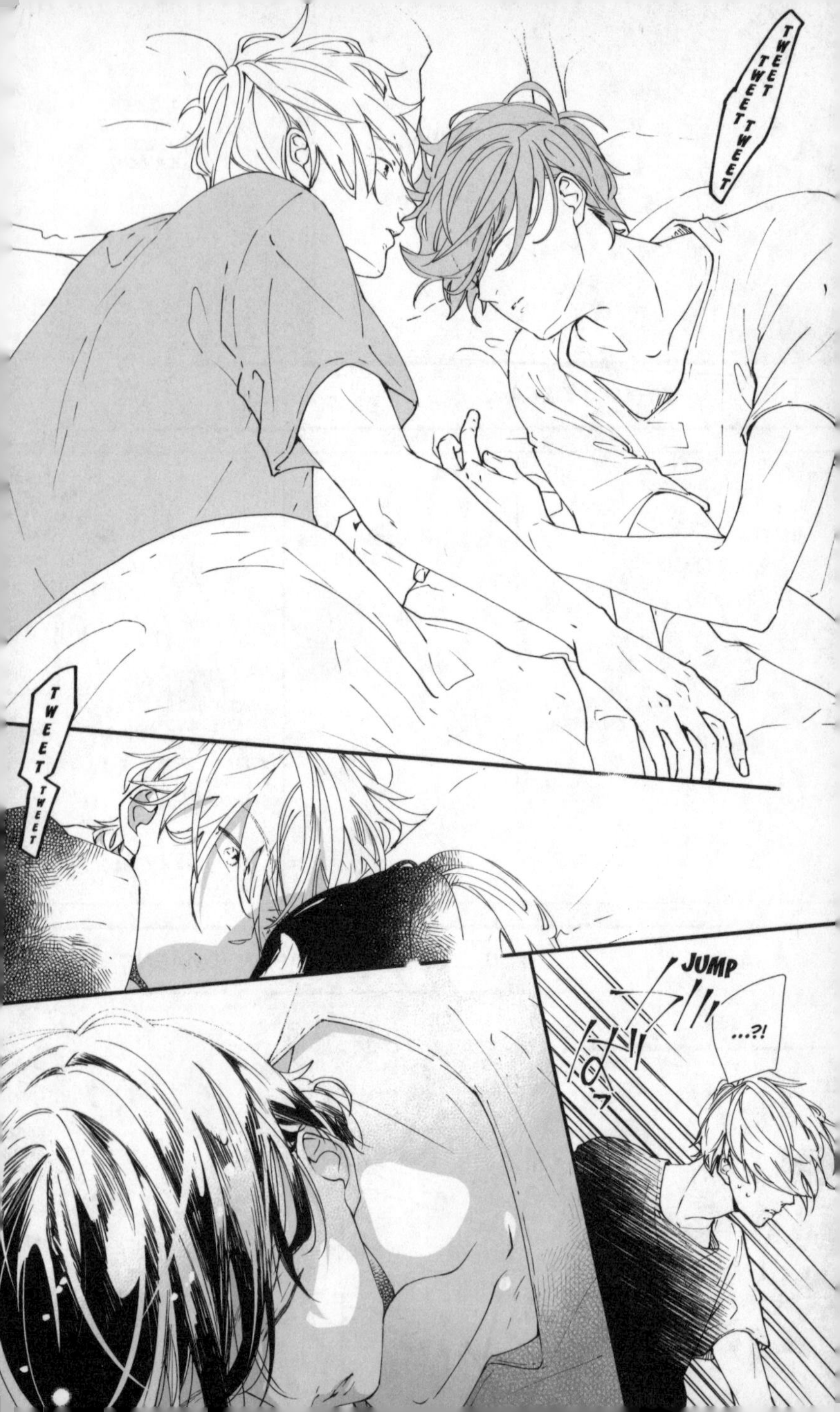
TWEET TWEET TWEET TWEET
TWEET TWEET
JUMP
...?!

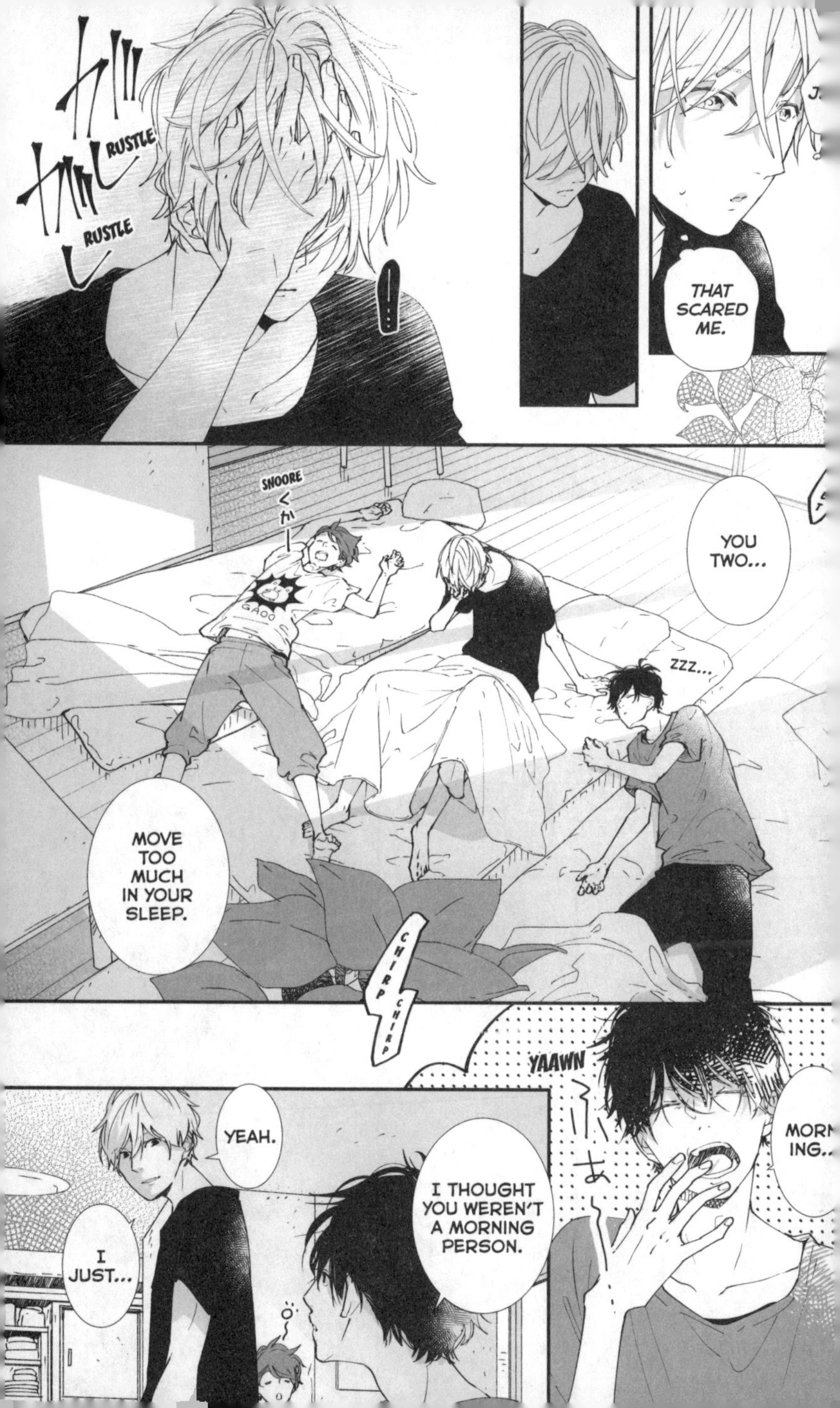
THAT SCARED ME.
RUSTLE
RUSTLE
!...
YOU TWO...
MOVE TOO MUCH IN YOUR SLEEP.
SNOORE
くかー
ZZZ...
CHIRP CHIRP
YAAWN
MORNING...
I THOUGHT YOU WEREN'T A MORNING PERSON.
YEAH.
I JUST...

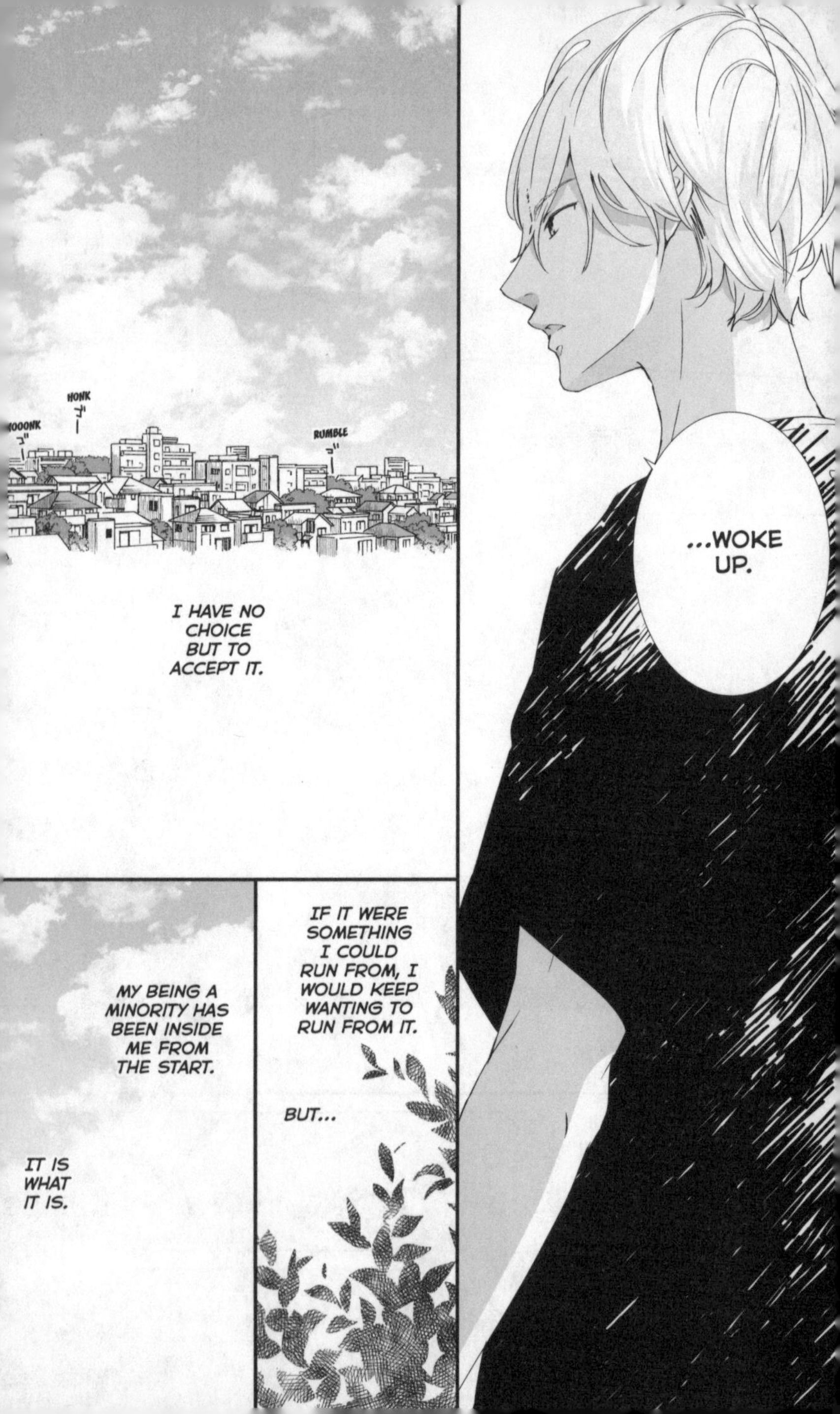
...WOKE UP.
RUMBLE
HONK
I HAVE NO CHOICE BUT TO ACCEPT IT.
IF IT WERE SOMETHING I COULD RUN FROM, I WOULD KEEP WANTING TO RUN FROM IT.
BUT...
MY BEING A MINORITY HAS BEEN INSIDE ME FROM THE START.
IT IS WHAT IT IS.

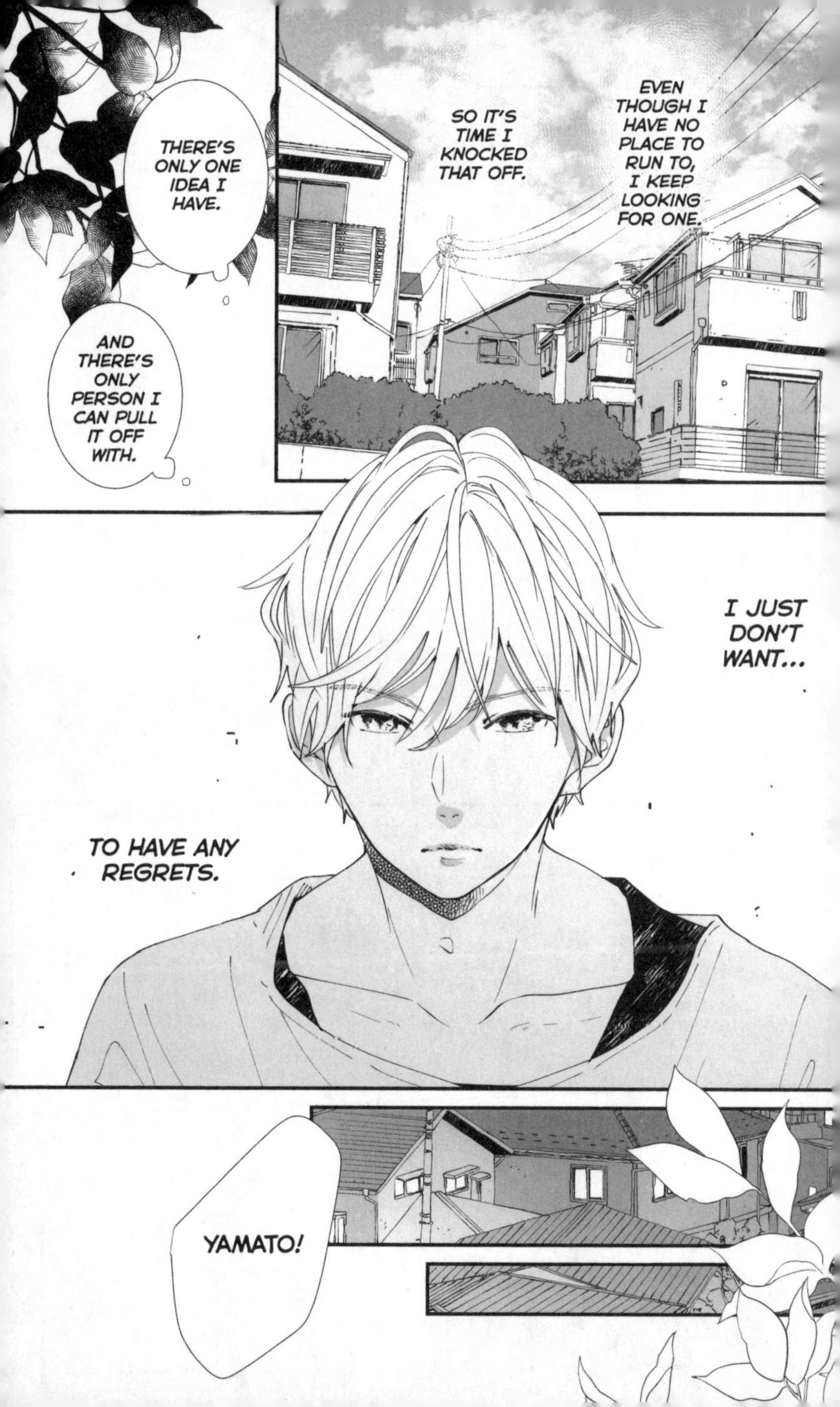
EVEN THOUGH I HAVE NO PLACE TO RUN TO, I KEEP LOOKING FOR ONE.
SO IT'S TIME I KNOCKED THAT OFF.
THERE'S ONLY ONE IDEA I HAVE.
AND THERE'S ONLY PERSON I CAN PULL IT OFF WITH.
I JUST DON'T WANT...
TO HAVE ANY REGRETS.
YAMATO!

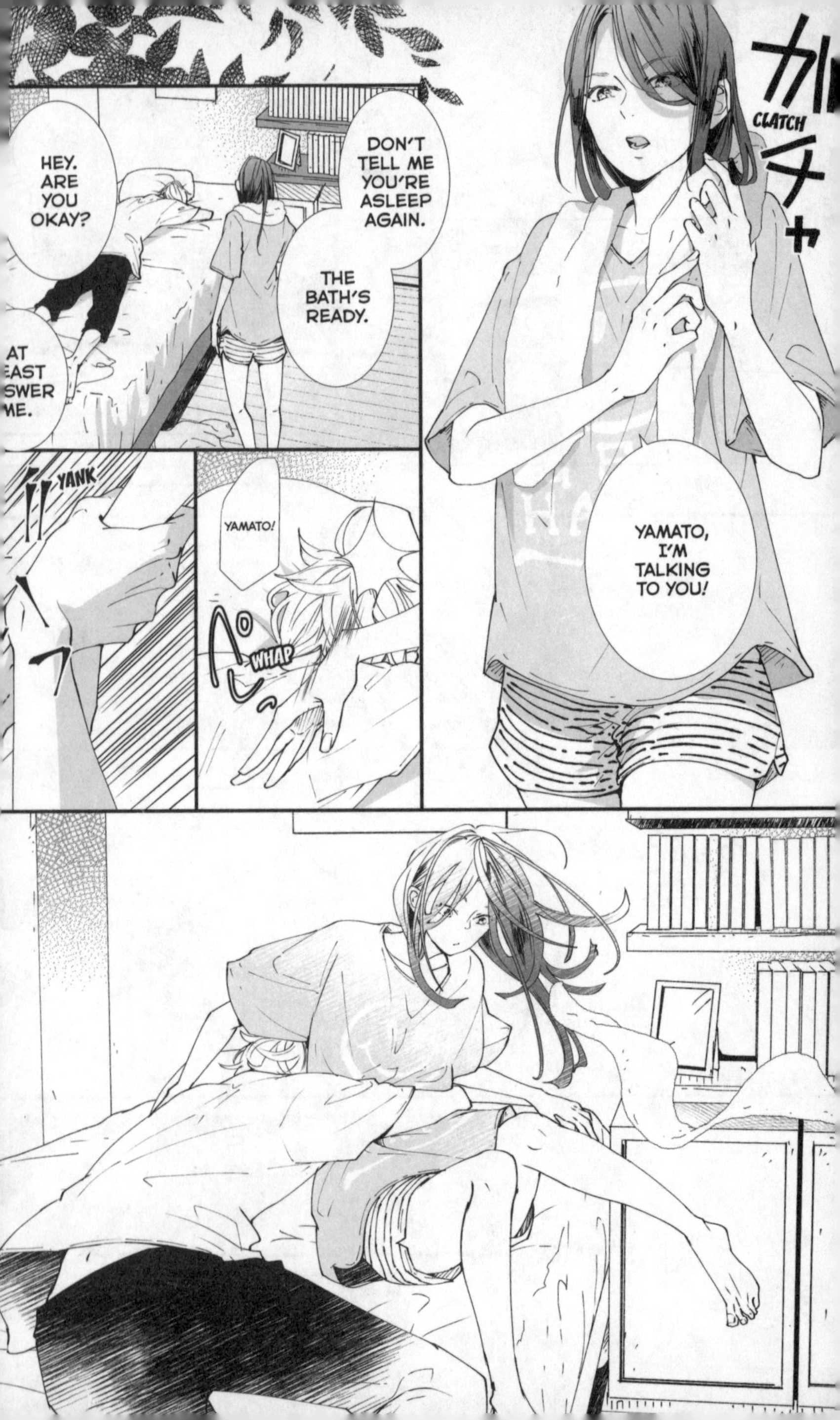
カチャ
CLATCH
YAMATO, I'M TALKING TO YOU!
DON'T TELL ME YOU'RE ASLEEP AGAIN.
THE BATH'S READY.
HEY. ARE YOU OKAY?
AT EAST SWER ME.
YAMATO!
WHAP
YANK

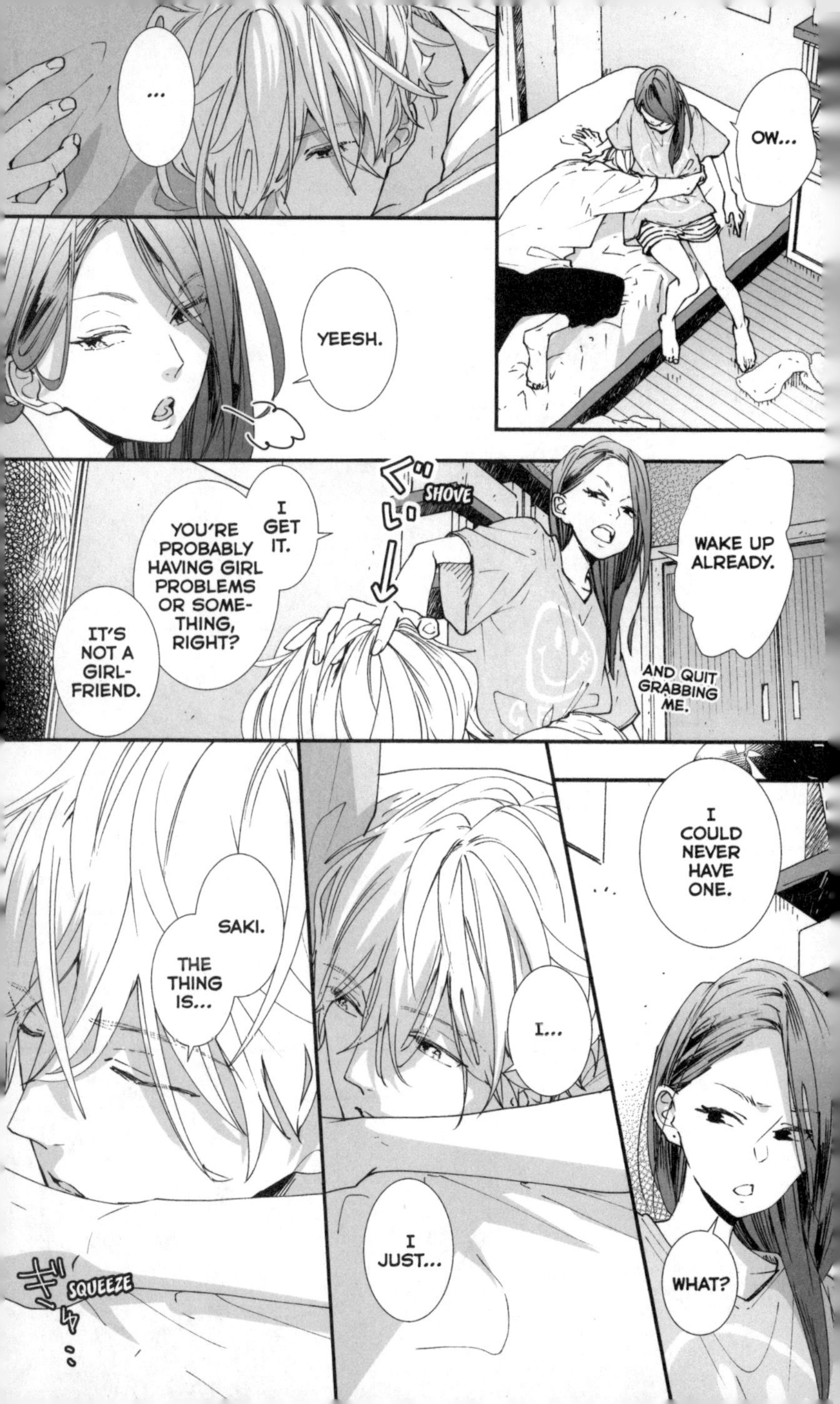
OW...
...
YEESH.
WAKE UP ALREADY.
AND QUIT GRABBING ME.
SHOVE
I GET IT.
YOU'RE PROBABLY HAVING GIRL PROBLEMS OR SOME-THING, RIGHT?
IT'S NOT A GIRL-FRIEND.
I COULD NEVER HAVE ONE.
...
WHAT?
I...
I JUST...
SAKI.
THE THING IS...
SQUEEZE

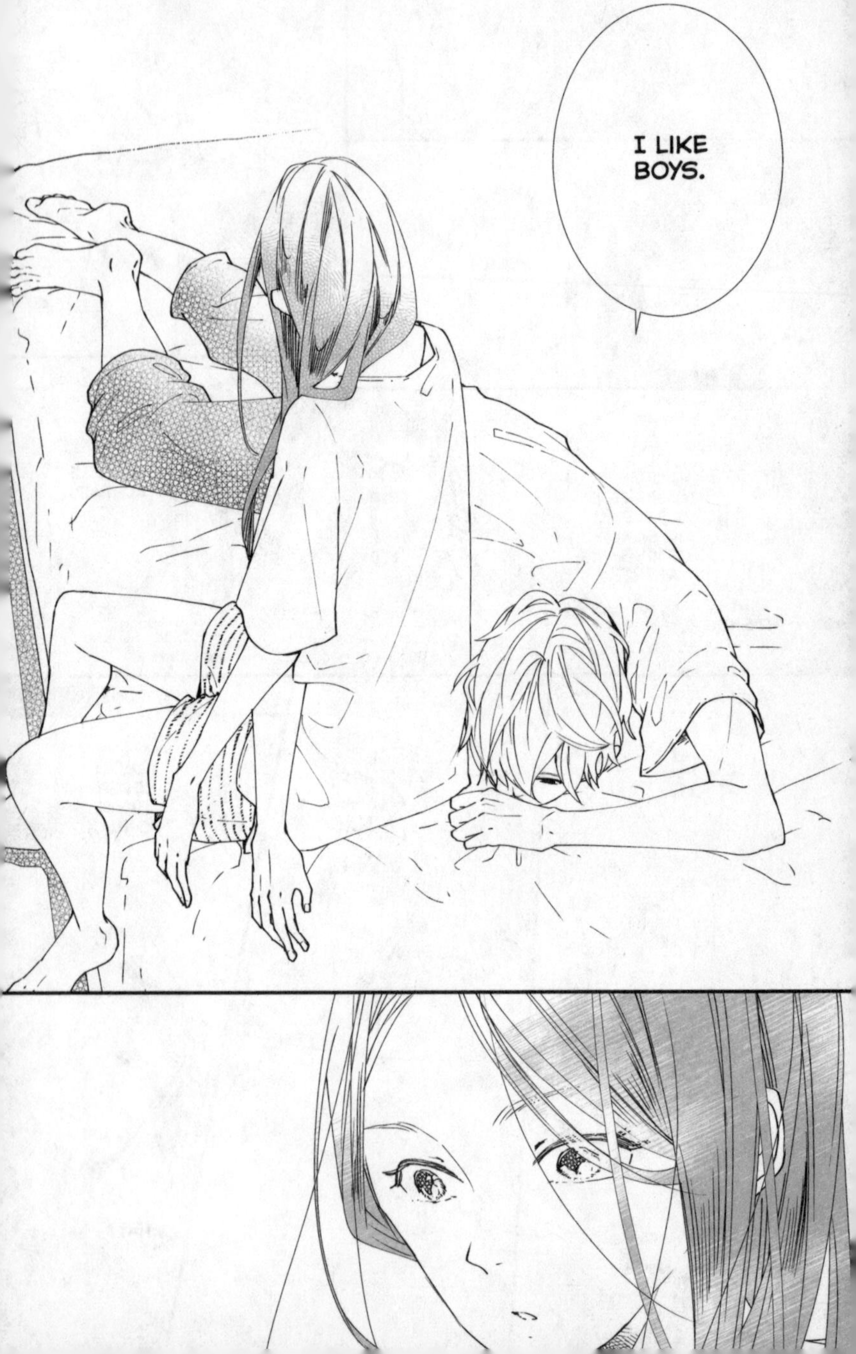
I LIKE BOYS.

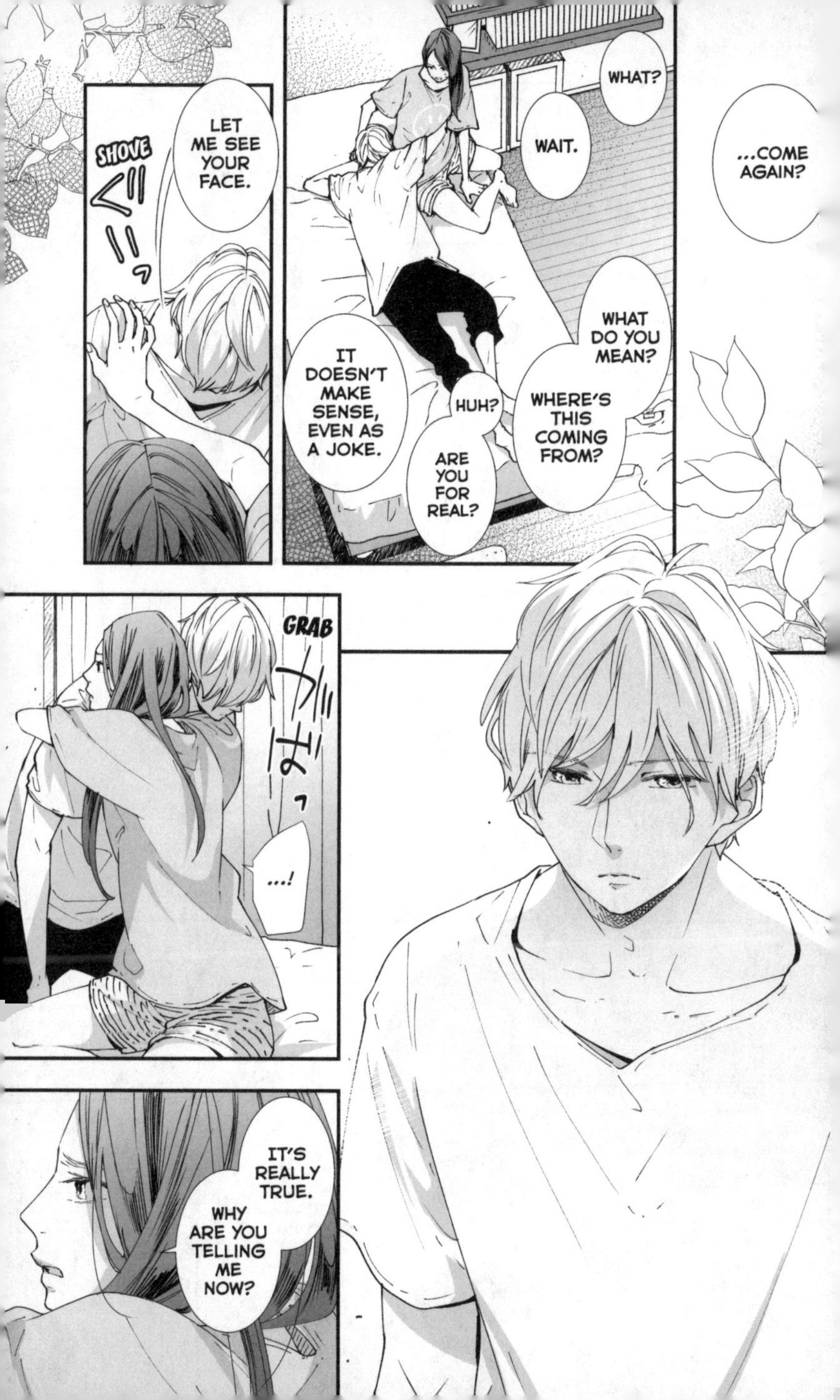
...COME AGAIN?
WHAT?
WAIT.
WHAT DO YOU MEAN?
WHERE'S THIS COMING FROM?
HUH?
ARE YOU FOR REAL?
IT DOESN'T MAKE SENSE, EVEN AS A JOKE.
LET ME SEE YOUR FACE.
SHOVE
GRAB
...!
IT'S REALLY TRUE.
WHY ARE YOU TELLING ME NOW?

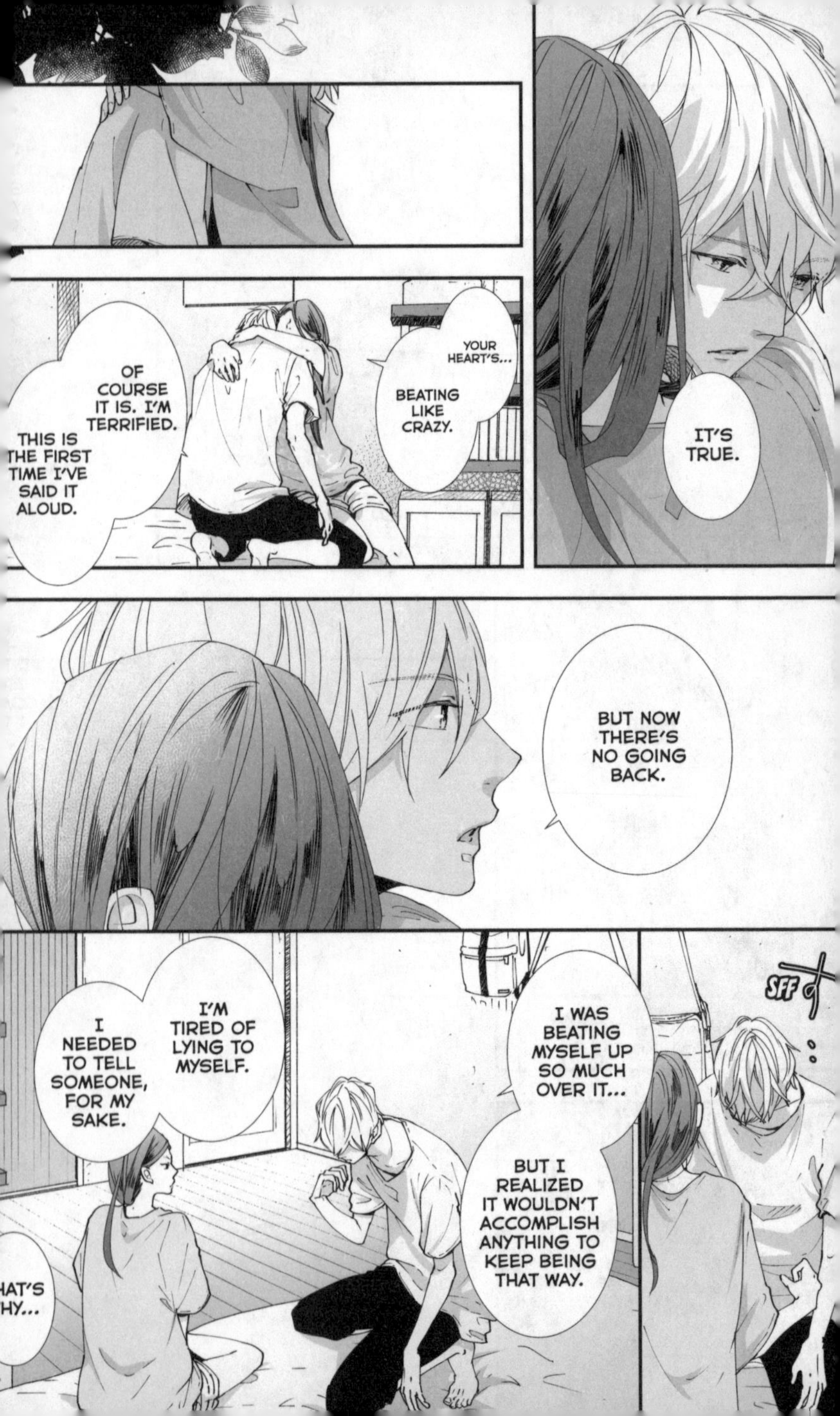
IT'S TRUE.
YOUR HEART'S... BEATING LIKE CRAZY.
OF COURSE IT IS. I'M TERRIFIED. THIS IS THE FIRST TIME I'VE SAID IT ALOUD.
BUT NOW THERE'S NO GOING BACK.
SFF
...
I WAS BEATING MYSELF UP SO MUCH OVER IT...
BUT I REALIZED IT WOULDN'T ACCOMPLISH ANYTHING TO KEEP BEING THAT WAY.
I'M TIRED OF LYING TO MYSELF.
I NEEDED TO TELL SOMEONE, FOR MY SAKE.
HAT'S HY...

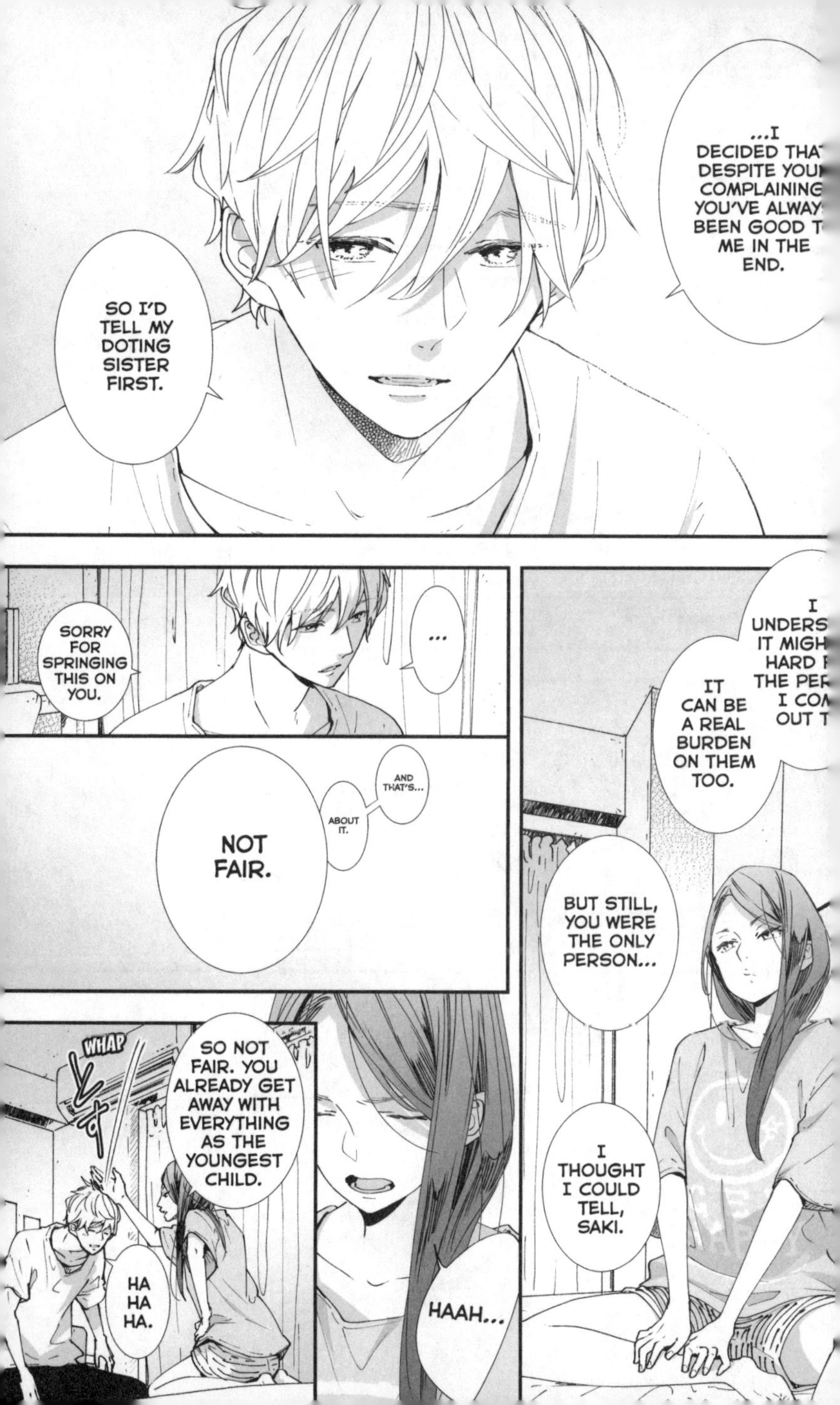

...I DECIDED THA DESPITE YOU COMPLAINING YOU'VE ALWAY BEEN GOOD T ME IN THE END.
SO I'D TELL MY DOTING SISTER FIRST.
I UNDERS IT MIGH HARD THE PER I COM OUT T
IT CAN BE A REAL BURDEN ON THEM TOO.
BUT STILL, YOU WERE THE ONLY PERSON...
I THOUGHT I COULD TELL, SAKI.
HAAH...
...
SORRY FOR SPRINGING THIS ON YOU.
AND THAT'S...
ABOUT IT.
NOT FAIR.
SO NOT FAIR. YOU ALREADY GET AWAY WITH EVERYTHING AS THE YOUNGEST CHILD.
WHAP
HA HA HA.

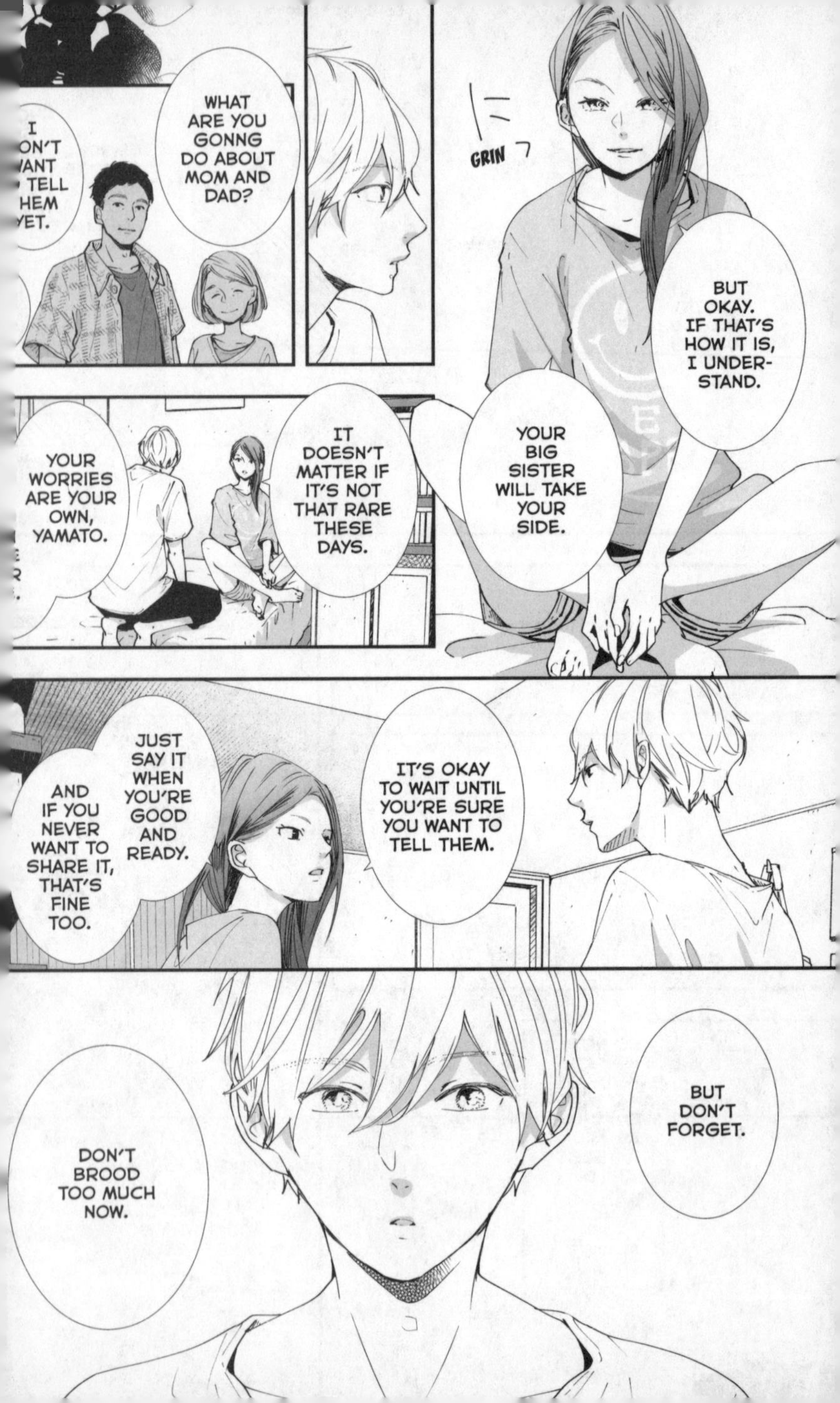
GRIN
BUT OKAY. IF THAT'S HOW IT IS, I UNDER-STAND.
YOUR BIG SISTER WILL TAKE YOUR SIDE.
WHAT ARE YOU GONNG DO ABOUT MOM AND DAD?
I ON'T ANT TELL HEM YET.
IT DOESN'T MATTER IF IT'S NOT THAT RARE THESE DAYS.
YOUR WORRIES ARE YOUR OWN, YAMATO.
IT'S OKAY TO WAIT UNTIL YOU'RE SURE YOU WANT TO TELL THEM.
JUST SAY IT WHEN YOU'RE GOOD AND READY.
AND IF YOU NEVER WANT TO SHARE IT, THAT'S FINE TOO.
BUT DON'T FORGET.
DON'T BROOD TOO MUCH NOW.

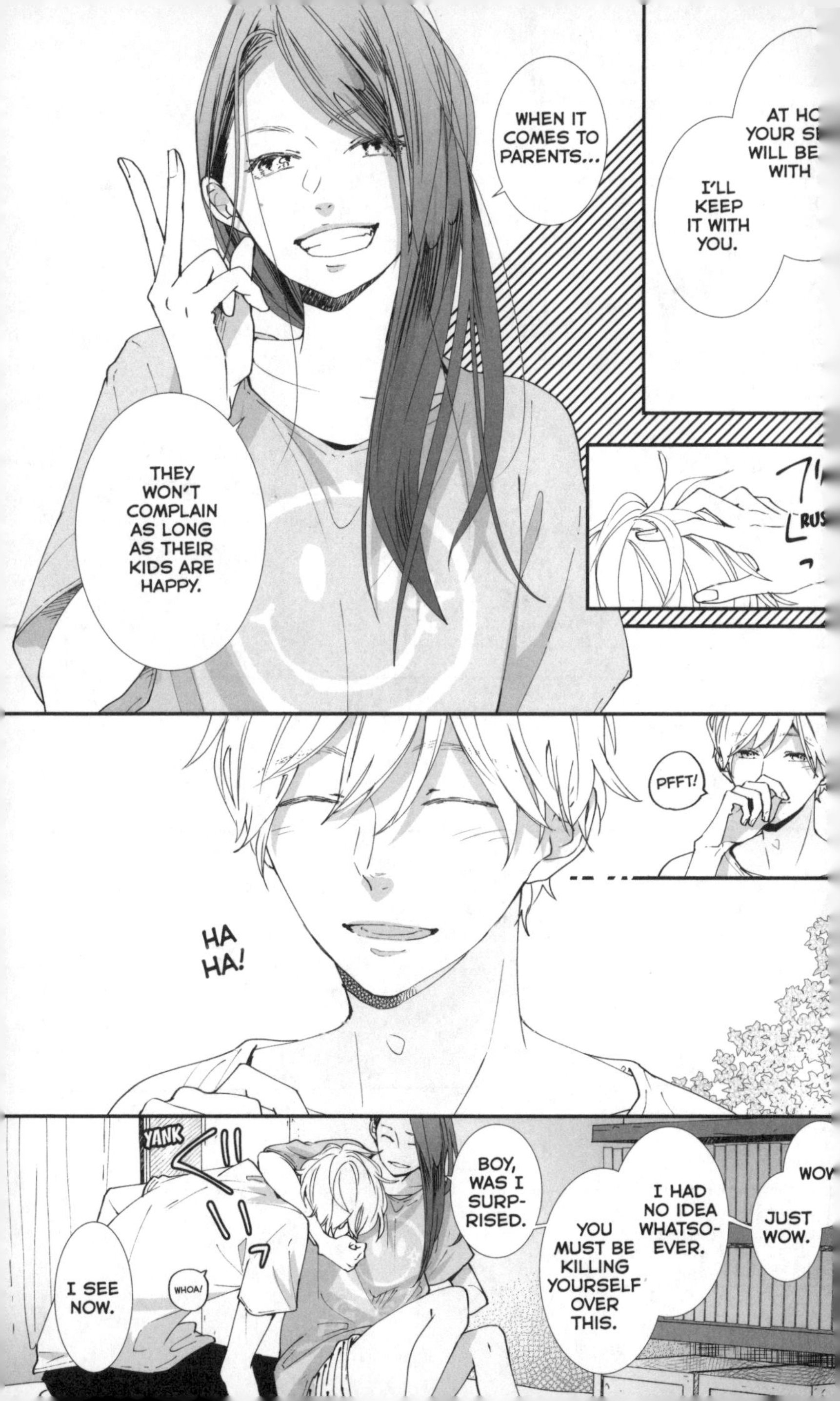
I'LL KEEP IT WITH YOU.
WHEN IT COMES TO PARENTS...
THEY WON'T COMPLAIN AS LONG AS THEIR KIDS ARE HAPPY.
PFFT!
HA HA!
WOW
JUST WOW.
I HAD NO IDEA WHATSO-EVER.
YOU MUST BE KILLING YOURSELF OVER THIS.
BOY, WAS I SURP-RISED.
YANK
WHOA!
I SEE NOW.

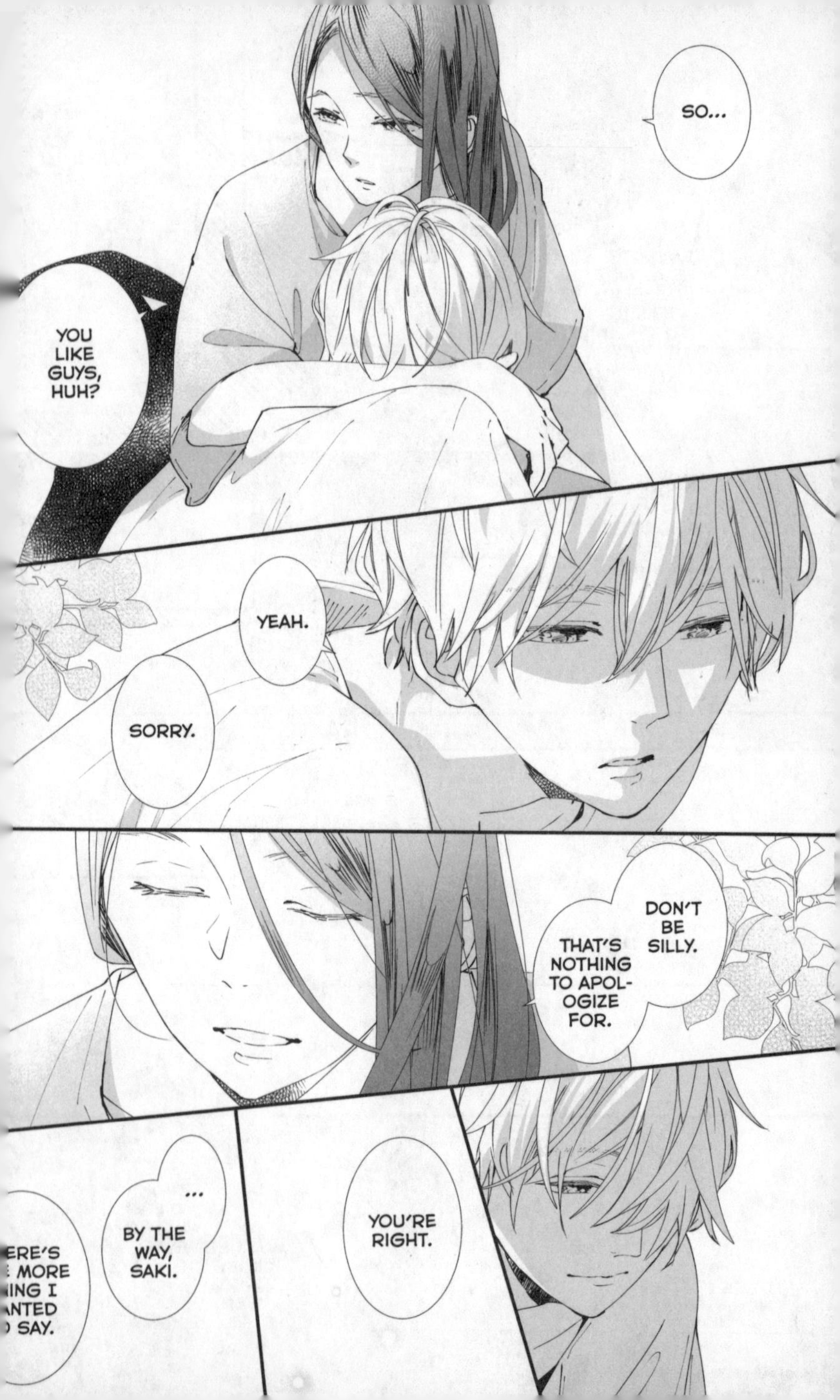
SO...
YOU LIKE GUYS, HUH?
YEAH.
SORRY.
DON'T BE SILLY.
THAT'S NOTHING TO APOLOGIZE FOR.
YOU'RE RIGHT.
... BY THE WAY, SAKI.

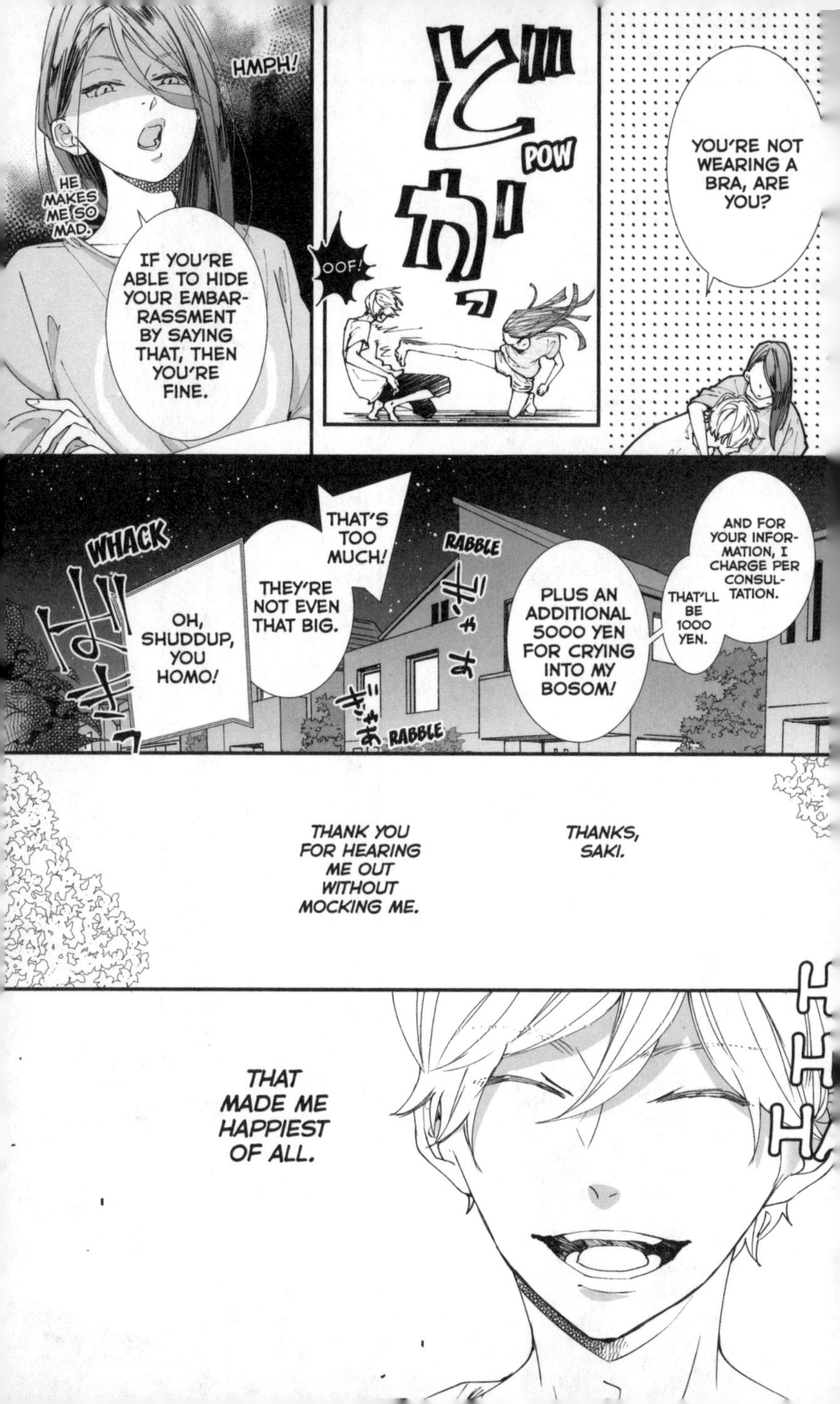
YOU'RE NOT WEARING A BRA, ARE YOU?
POW
OOF!
HMPH!
IF YOU'RE ABLE TO HIDE YOUR EMBARRASSMENT BY SAYING THAT, THEN YOU'RE FINE.
HE MAKES ME SO MAD.
AND FOR YOUR INFORMATION, I CHARGE PER CONSULTATION.
THAT'LL BE 1000 YEN.
PLUS AN ADDITIONAL 5000 YEN FOR CRYING INTO MY BOSOM!
RABBLE
RABBLE
THAT'S TOO MUCH!
THEY'RE NOT EVEN THAT BIG.
OH, SHUDDUP, YOU HOMO!
WHACK
THANKS, SAKI.
THANK YOU FOR HEARING ME OUT WITHOUT MOCKING ME.
HHH
THAT MADE ME HAPPIEST OF ALL.

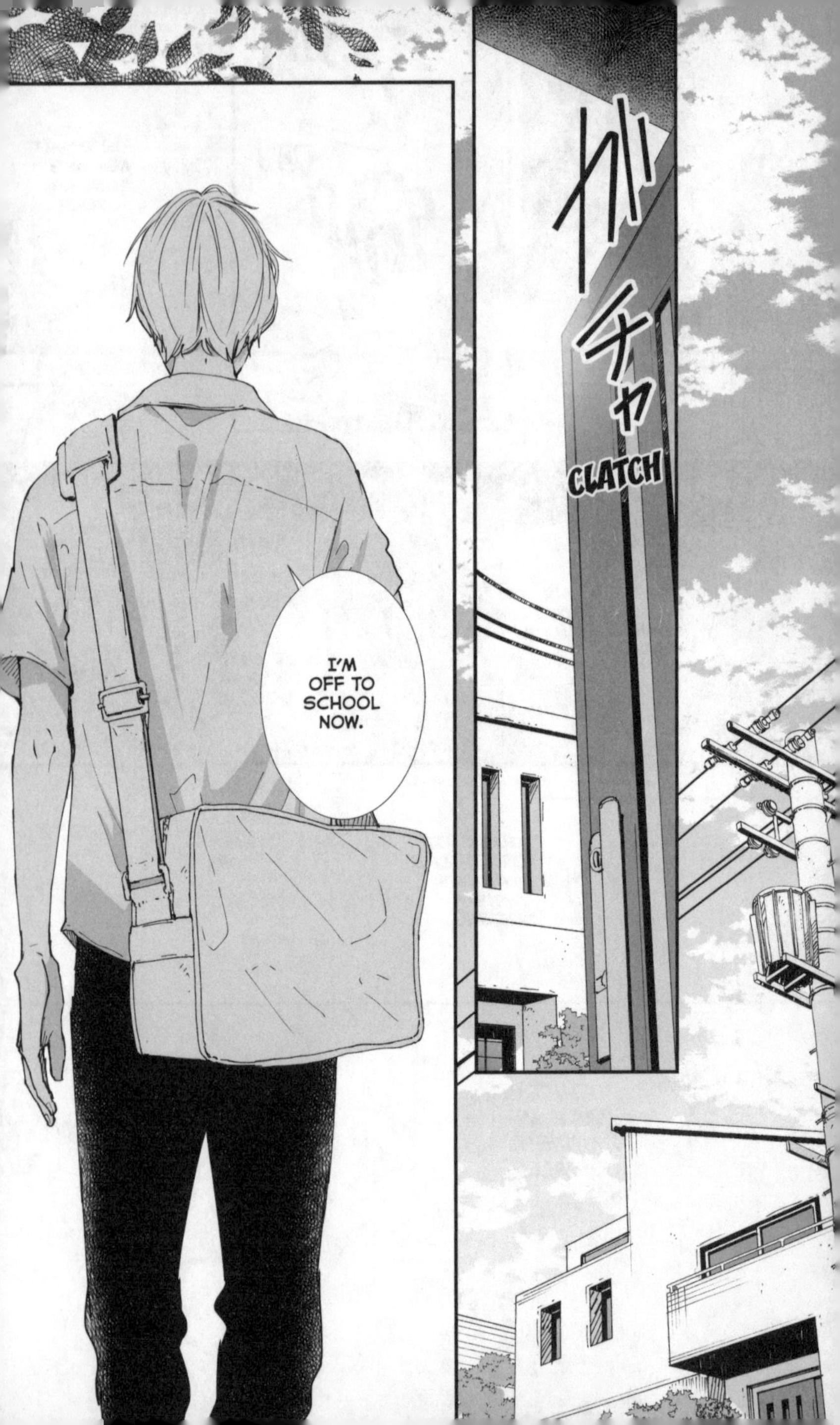
ガチャ
CLATCH
I'M OFF TO SCHOOL NOW.

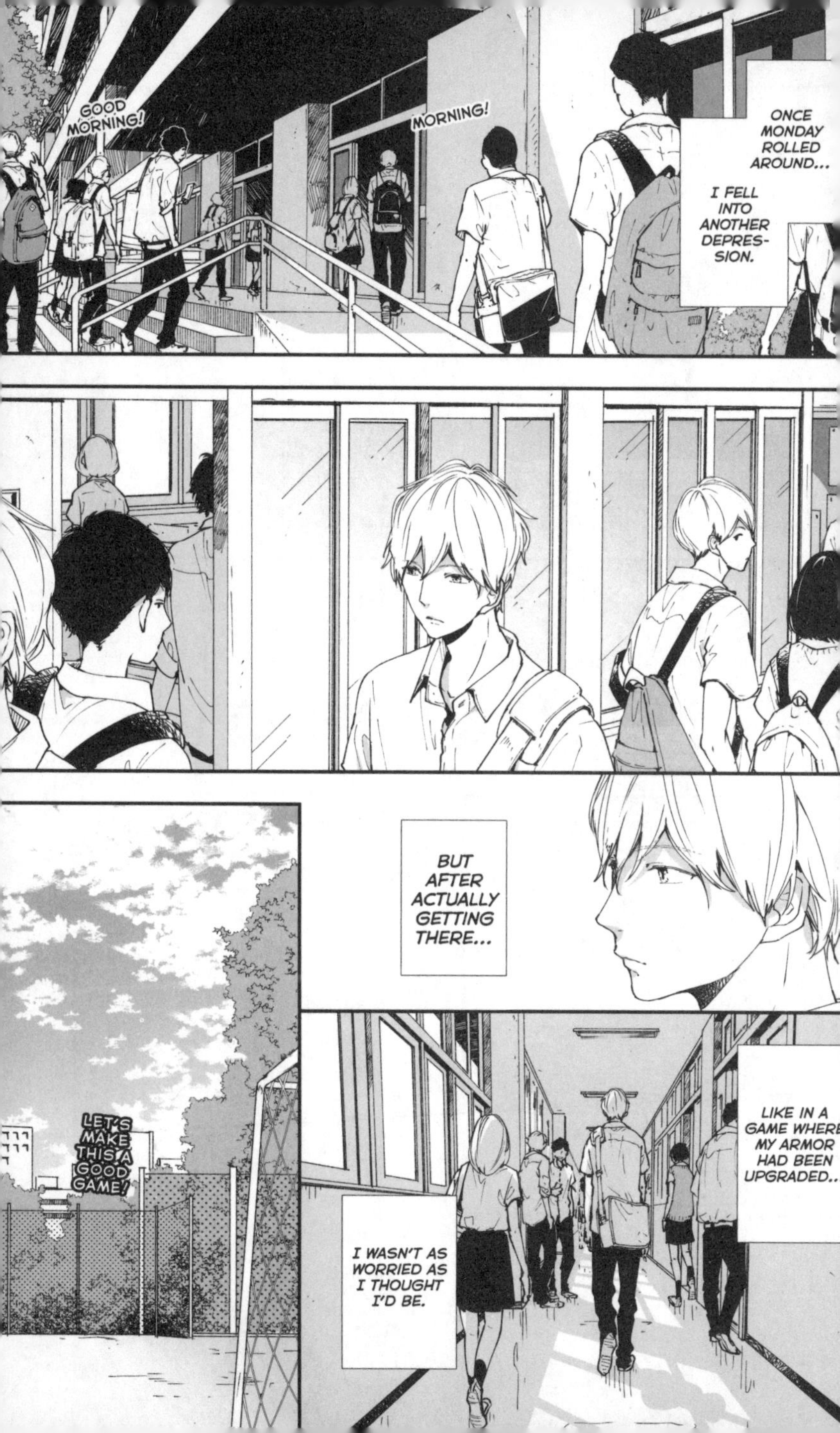
ONCE MONDAY ROLLED AROUND...
I FELL INTO ANOTHER DEPRES-SION.
MORNING!
GOOD MORNING!
BUT AFTER ACTUALLY GETTING THERE...
LIKE IN A GAME WHERE MY ARMOR HAD BEEN UPGRADED...
I WASN'T AS WORRIED AS I THOUGHT I'D BE.
LET'S MAKE THIS A GOOD GAME!

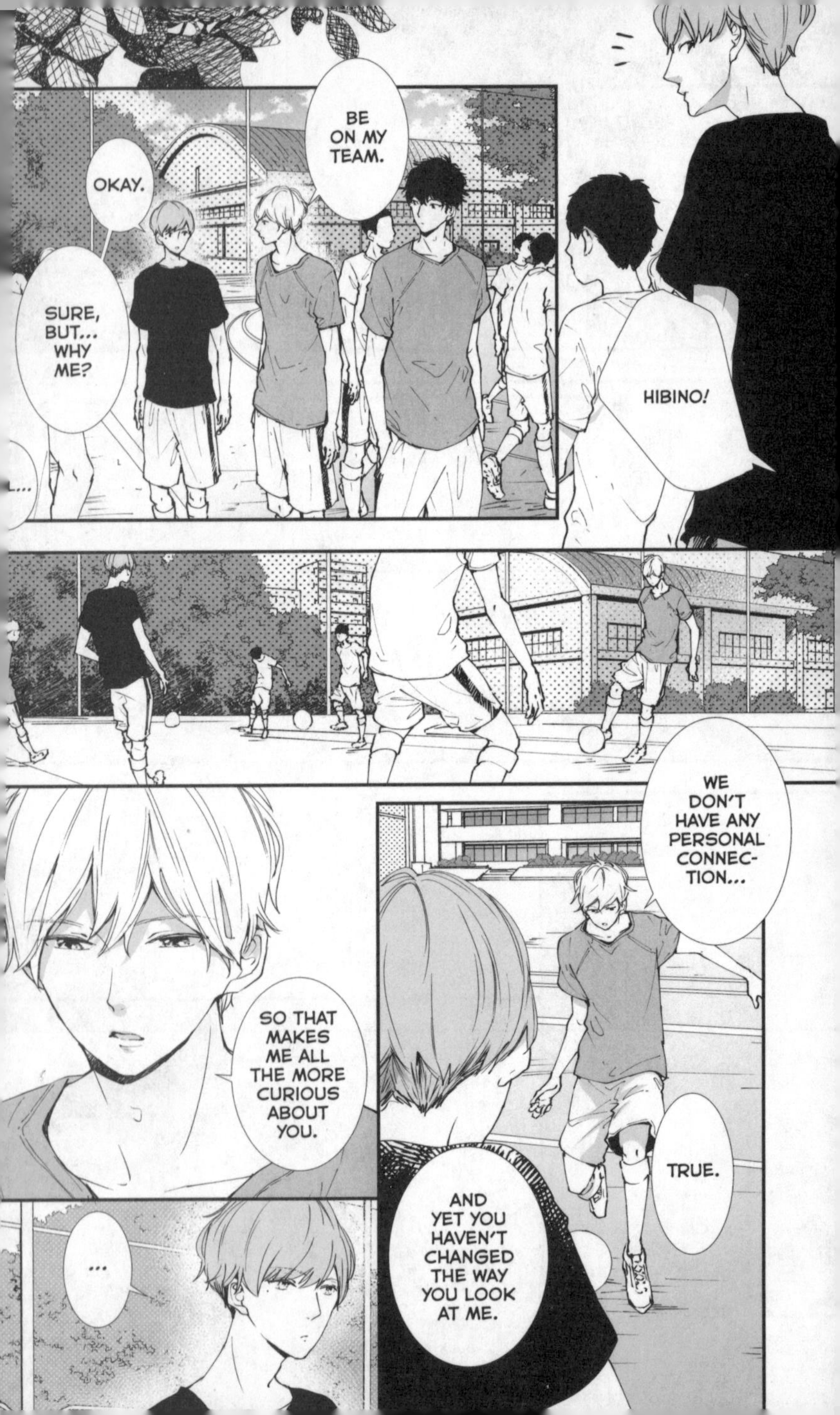
HIBINO!
BE ON MY TEAM.
OKAY.
SURE, BUT... WHY ME?
....
WE DON'T HAVE ANY PERSONAL CONNEC- TION...
TRUE.
AND YET YOU HAVEN'T CHANGED THE WAY YOU LOOK AT ME.
SO THAT MAKES ME ALL THE MORE CURIOUS ABOUT YOU.
...

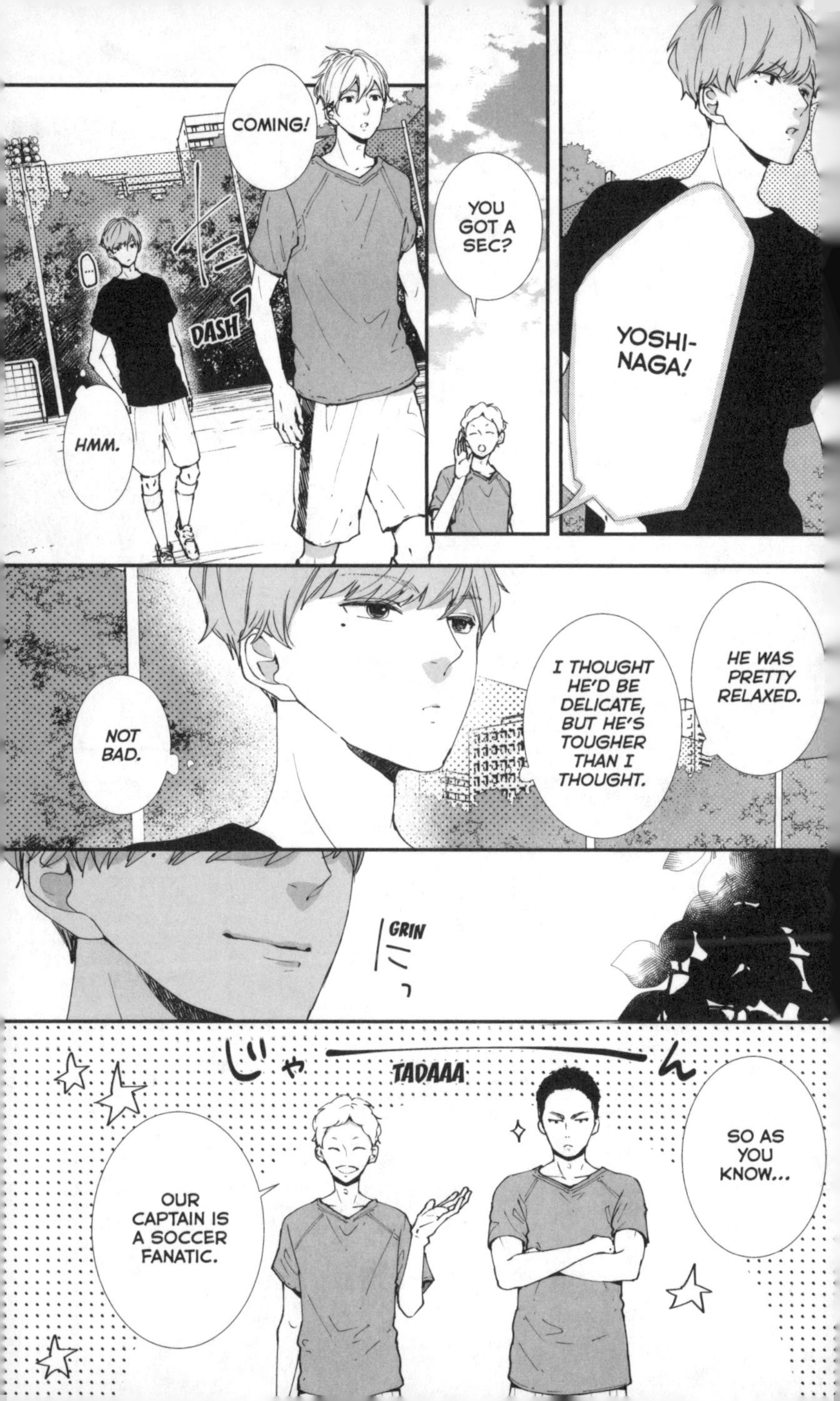
YOSHI-NAGA!
YOU GOT A SEC?
COMING!
DASH
...
HMM.
HE WAS PRETTY RELAXED.
I THOUGHT HE'D BE DELICATE, BUT HE'S TOUGHER THAN I THOUGHT.
NOT BAD.
GRIN
じゃーーん
TADAAA
SO AS YOU KNOW...
OUR CAPTAIN IS A SOCCER FANATIC.

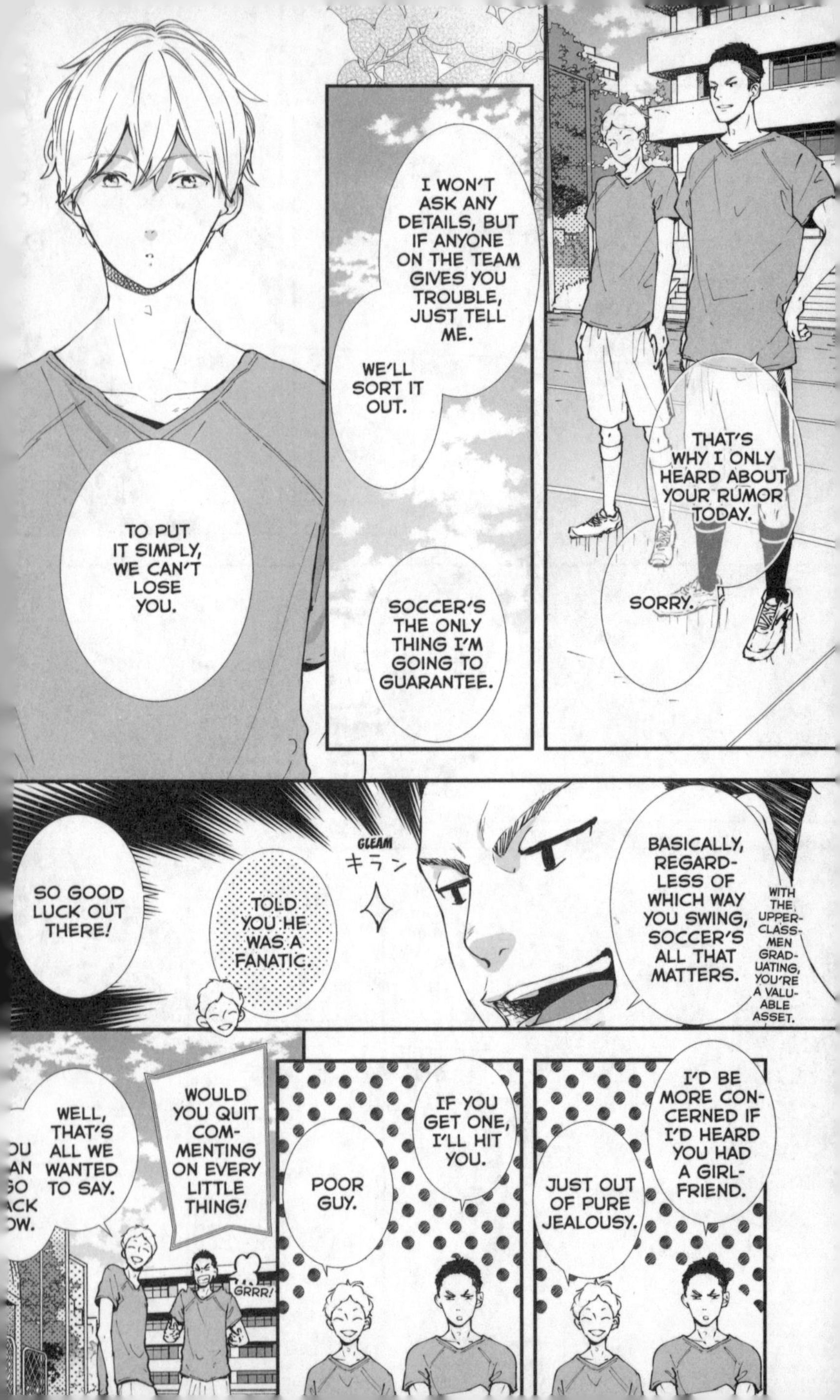
THAT'S WHY I ONLY HEARD ABOUT YOUR RUMOR TODAY.
SORRY.
I WON'T ASK ANY DETAILS, BUT IF ANYONE ON THE TEAM GIVES YOU TROUBLE, JUST TELL ME.
WE'LL SORT IT OUT.
SOCCER'S THE ONLY THING I'M GOING TO GUARANTEE.
TO PUT IT SIMPLY, WE CAN'T LOSE YOU.
WITH THE UPPERCLASSMEN GRADUATING, YOU'RE A VALUABLE ASSET.
BASICALLY, REGARDLESS OF WHICH WAY YOU SWING, SOCCER'S ALL THAT MATTERS.
GLEAM
キラン
TOLD YOU HE WAS A FANATIC.
SO GOOD LUCK OUT THERE!
I'D BE MORE CONCERNED IF I'D HEARD YOU HAD A GIRLFRIEND.
JUST OUT OF PURE JEALOUSY.
IF YOU GET ONE, I'LL HIT YOU.
POOR GUY.
WOULD YOU QUIT COMMENTING ON EVERY LITTLE THING!
GRRR!
WELL, THAT'S ALL WE WANTED TO SAY.

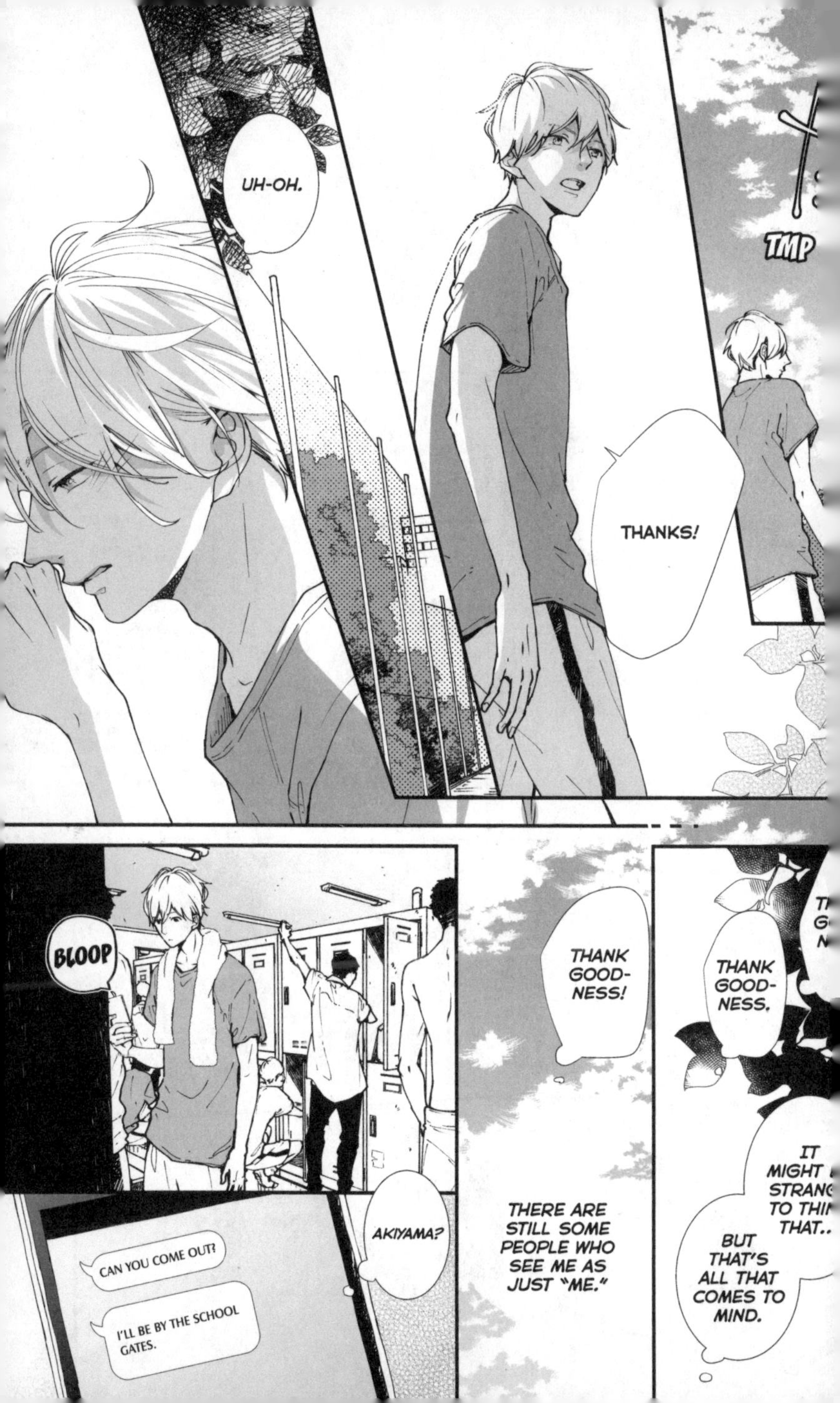
TMP
THANKS!
UH-OH.
THANK GOODNESS.
IT MIGHT STRANG TO THI THAT..
BUT THAT'S ALL THAT COMES TO MIND.
THANK GOOD-NESS!
THERE ARE STILL SOME PEOPLE WHO SEE ME AS JUST "ME."
BLOOP
AKIYAMA?
CAN YOU COME OUT?
I'LL BE BY THE SCHOOL GATES.

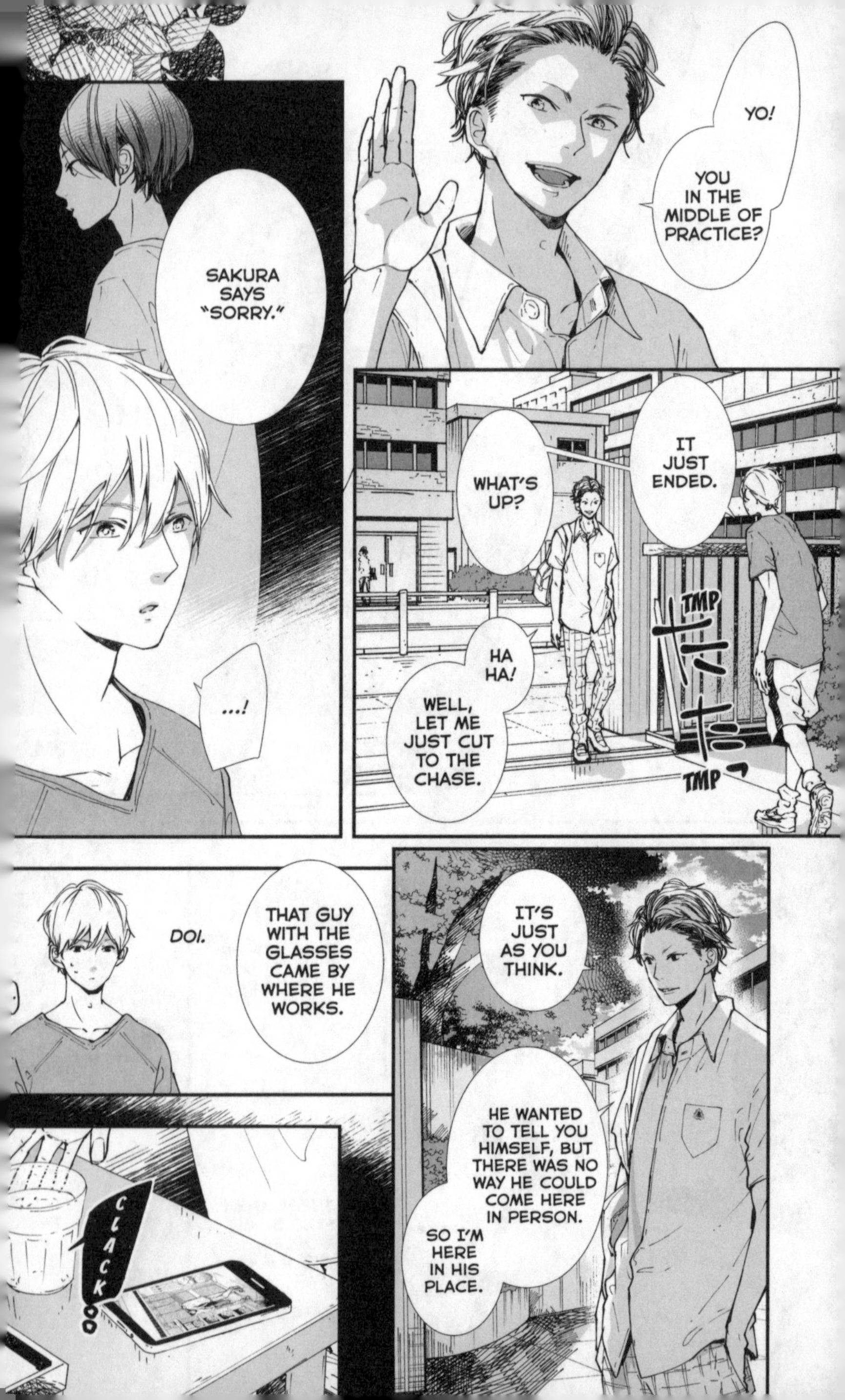
YO!
YOU IN THE MIDDLE OF PRACTICE?
IT JUST ENDED.
WHAT'S UP?
TMP
TMP
HA HA!
WELL, LET ME JUST CUT TO THE CHASE.
SAKURA SAYS "SORRY."
...!
IT'S JUST AS YOU THINK.
HE WANTED TO TELL YOU HIMSELF, BUT THERE WAS NO WAY HE COULD COME HERE IN PERSON.
SO I'M HERE IN HIS PLACE.
THAT GUY WITH THE GLASSES CAME BY WHERE HE WORKS.
DOI.
CLACK

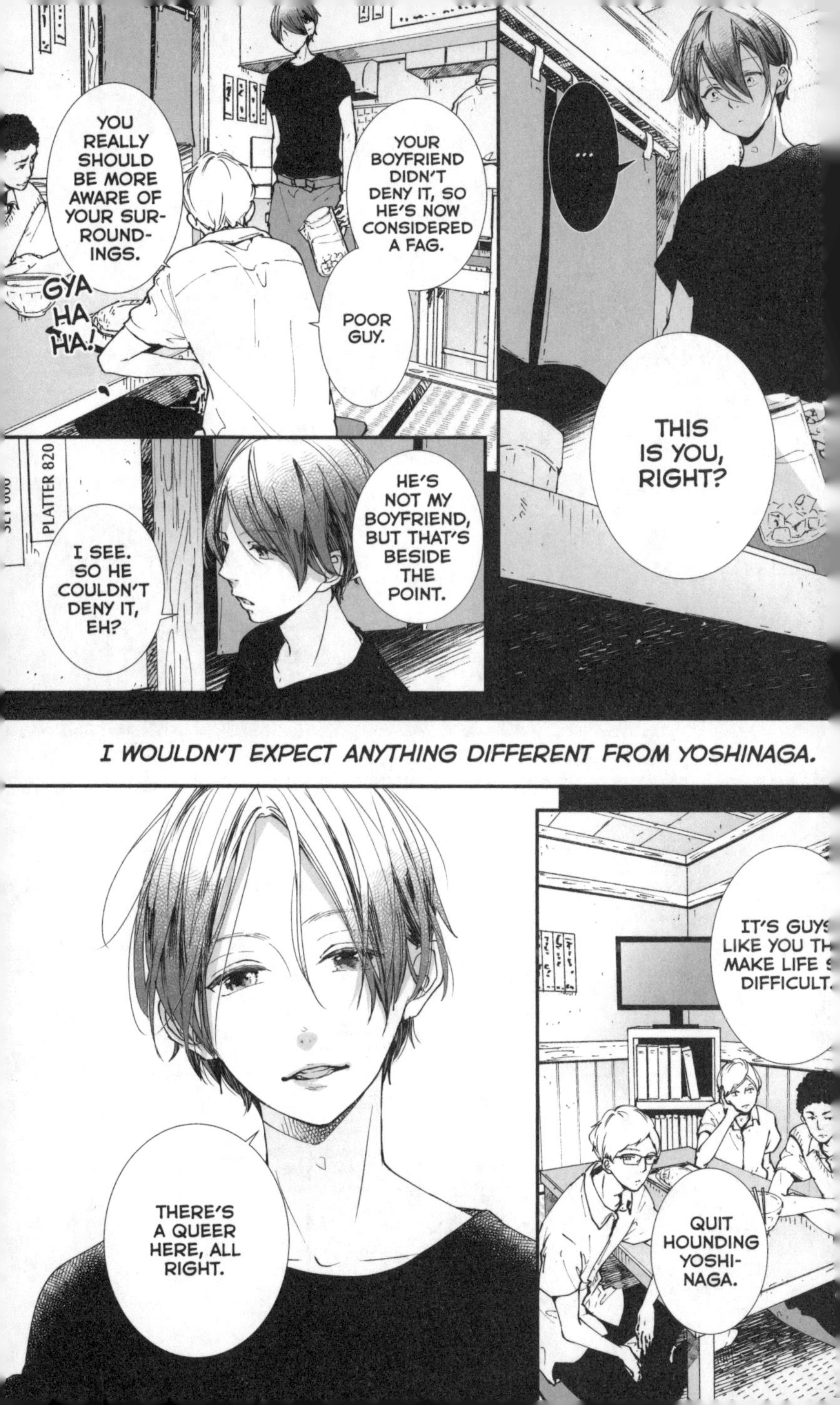
...
THIS IS YOU, RIGHT?
YOUR BOYFRIEND DIDN'T DENY IT, SO HE'S NOW CONSIDERED A FAG.
POOR GUY.
YOU REALLY SHOULD BE MORE AWARE OF YOUR SUR-ROUNDINGS.
GYA HA HA!
PLATTER 820
HE'S NOT MY BOYFRIEND, BUT THAT'S BESIDE THE POINT.
I SEE. SO HE COULDN'T DENY IT, EH?
I WOULDN'T EXPECT ANYTHING DIFFERENT FROM YOSHINAGA.
IT'S GUYS LIKE YOU TH MAKE LIFE S DIFFICULT.
QUIT HOUNDING YOSHI-NAGA.
THERE'S A QUEER HERE, ALL RIGHT.

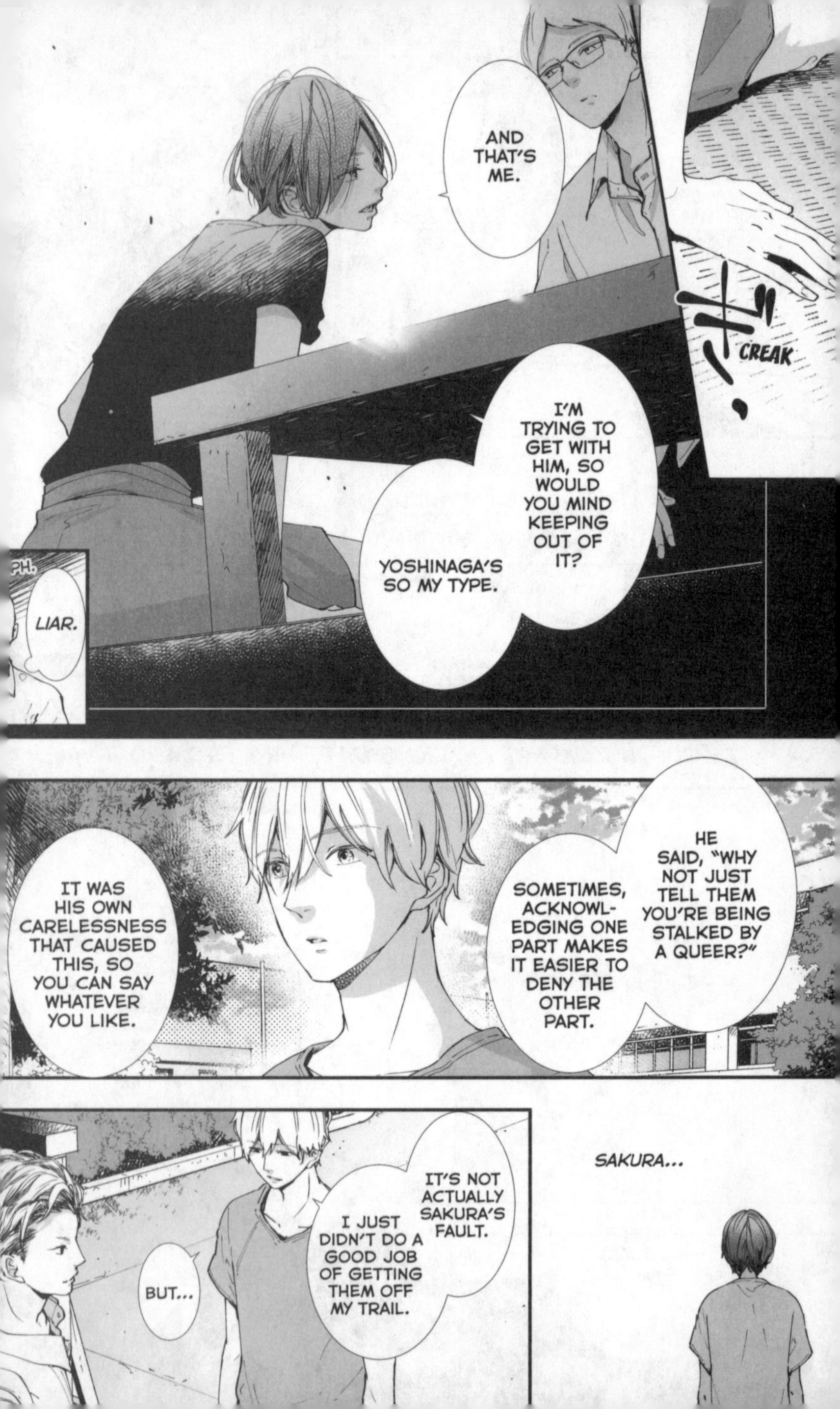
CREAK
AND THAT'S ME.
I'M TRYING TO GET WITH HIM, SO WOULD YOU MIND KEEPING OUT OF IT?
YOSHINAGA'S SO MY TYPE.
LIAR.
HE SAID, "WHY NOT JUST TELL THEM YOU'RE BEING STALKED BY A QUEER?"
SOMETIMES, ACKNOWL-EDGING ONE PART MAKES IT EASIER TO DENY THE OTHER PART.
IT WAS HIS OWN CARELESSNESS THAT CAUSED THIS, SO YOU CAN SAY WHATEVER YOU LIKE.
SAKURA...
IT'S NOT ACTUALLY SAKURA'S FAULT.
I JUST DIDN'T DO A GOOD JOB OF GETTING THEM OFF MY TRAIL.
BUT...

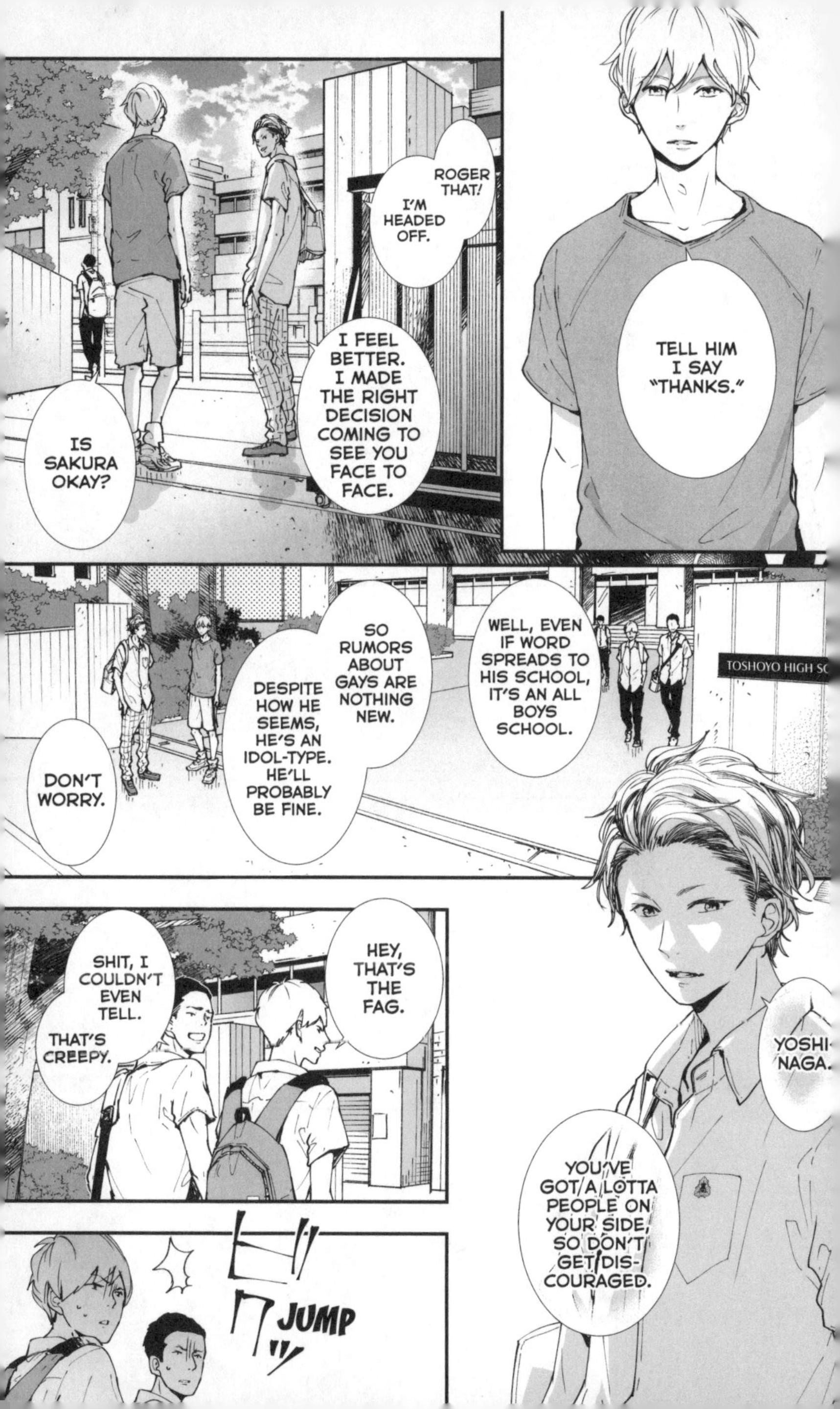
TELL HIM I SAY "THANKS."
ROGER THAT!
I'M HEADED OFF.
I FEEL BETTER. I MADE THE RIGHT DECISION COMING TO SEE YOU FACE TO FACE.
IS SAKURA OKAY?
TOSHOYO HIGH SC
WELL, EVEN IF WORD SPREADS TO HIS SCHOOL, IT'S AN ALL BOYS SCHOOL.
SO RUMORS ABOUT GAYS ARE NOTHING NEW.
DESPITE HOW HE SEEMS, HE'S AN IDOL-TYPE. HE'LL PROBABLY BE FINE.
DON'T WORRY.
YOSHI-NAGA.
YOU'VE GOT A LOTTA PEOPLE ON YOUR SIDE, SO DON'T GET DIS-COURAGED.
HEY, THAT'S THE FAG.
SHIT, I COULDN'T EVEN TELL.
THAT'S CREEPY.
JUMP

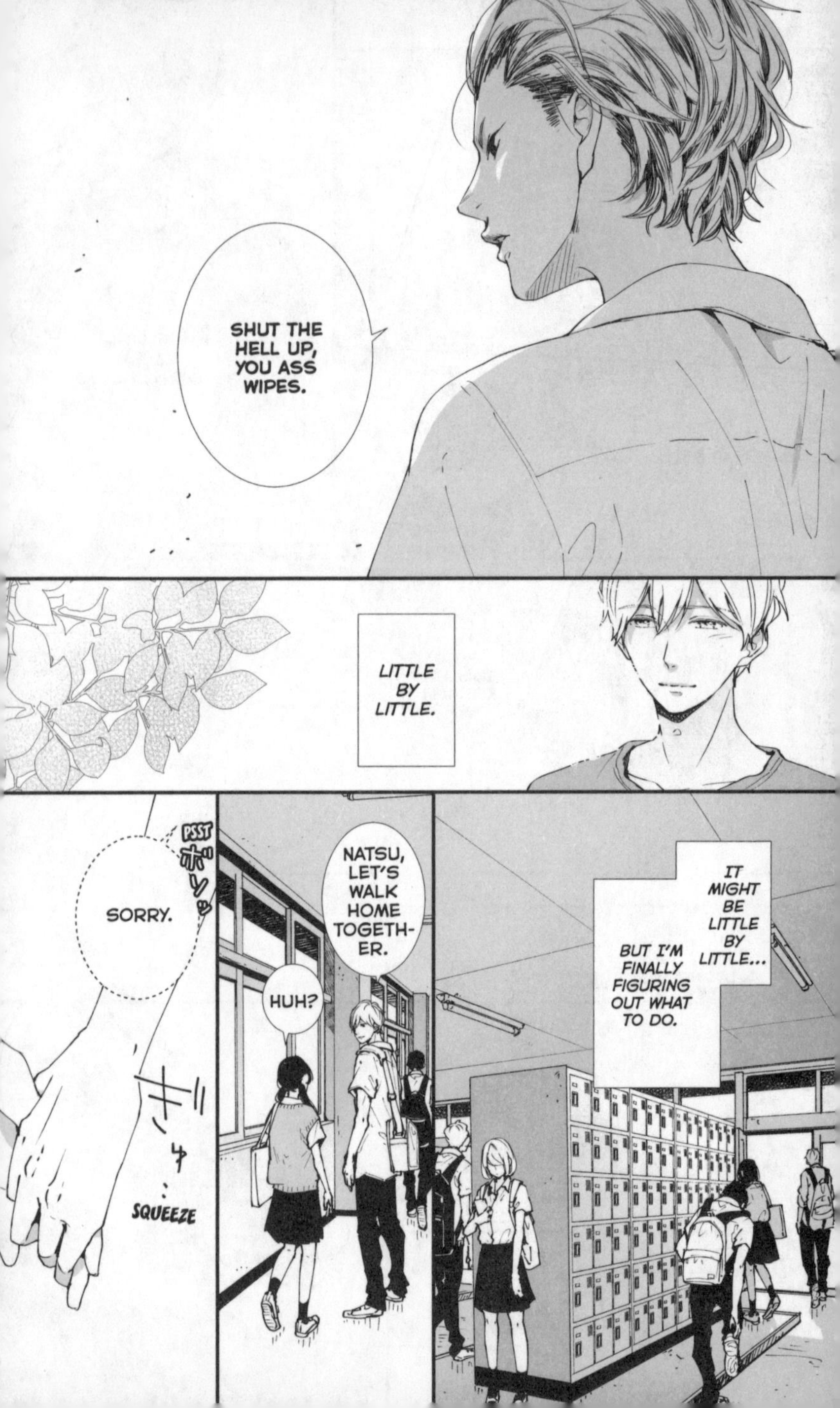
SHUT THE HELL UP, YOU ASS WIPES.
LITTLE BY LITTLE.
IT MIGHT BE LITTLE BY LITTLE...
BUT I'M FINALLY FIGURING OUT WHAT TO DO.
NATSU, LET'S WALK HOME TOGETH-ER.
HUH?
PSST
ボソッ
SORRY.
SQUEEZE

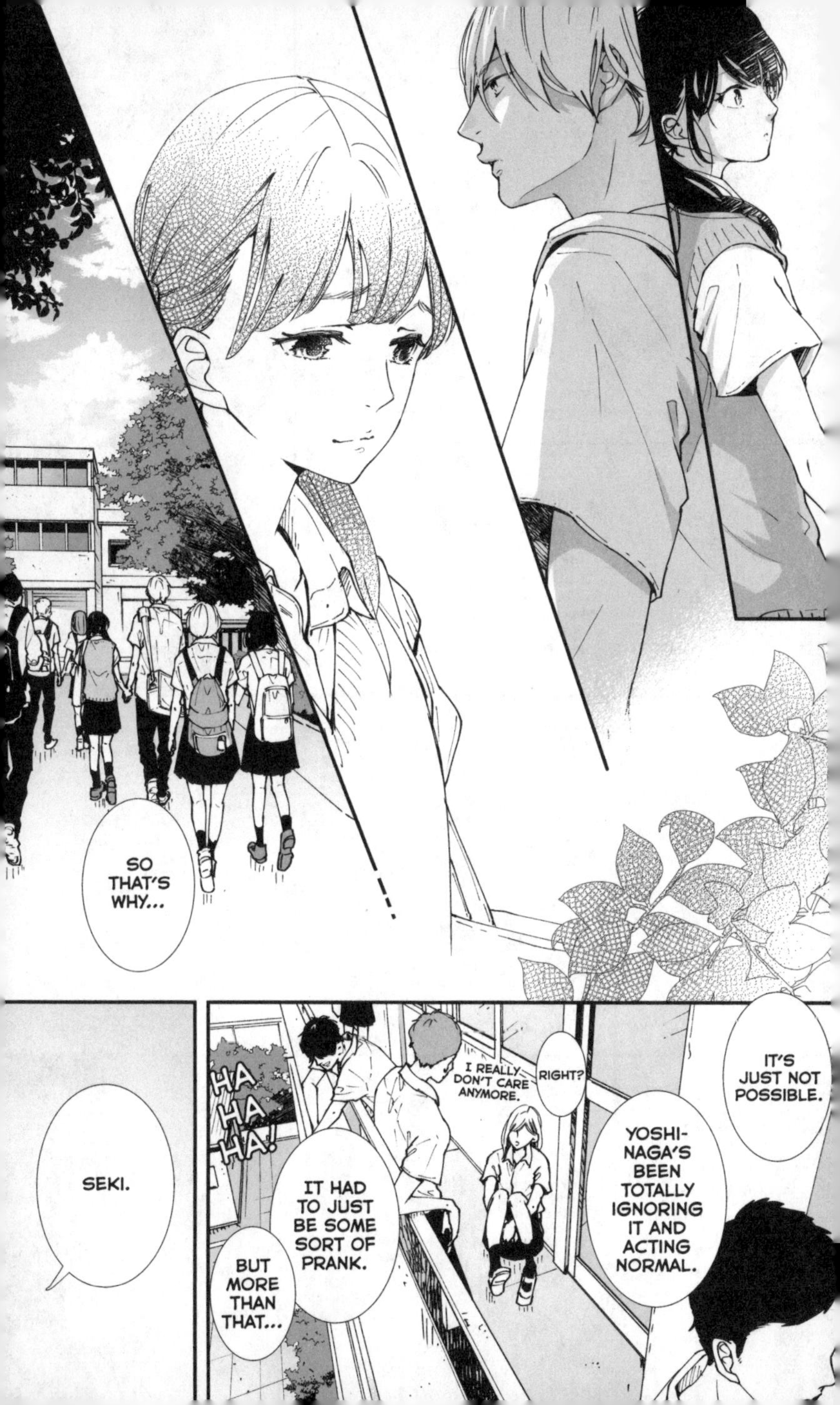
SO THAT'S WHY...
IT'S JUST NOT POSSIBLE.
YOSHI-NAGA'S BEEN TOTALLY IGNORING IT AND ACTING NORMAL.
RIGHT?
I REALLY DON'T CARE ANYMORE.
HA HA HA!
IT HAD TO JUST BE SOME SORT OF PRANK.
BUT MORE THAN THAT...
SEKI.

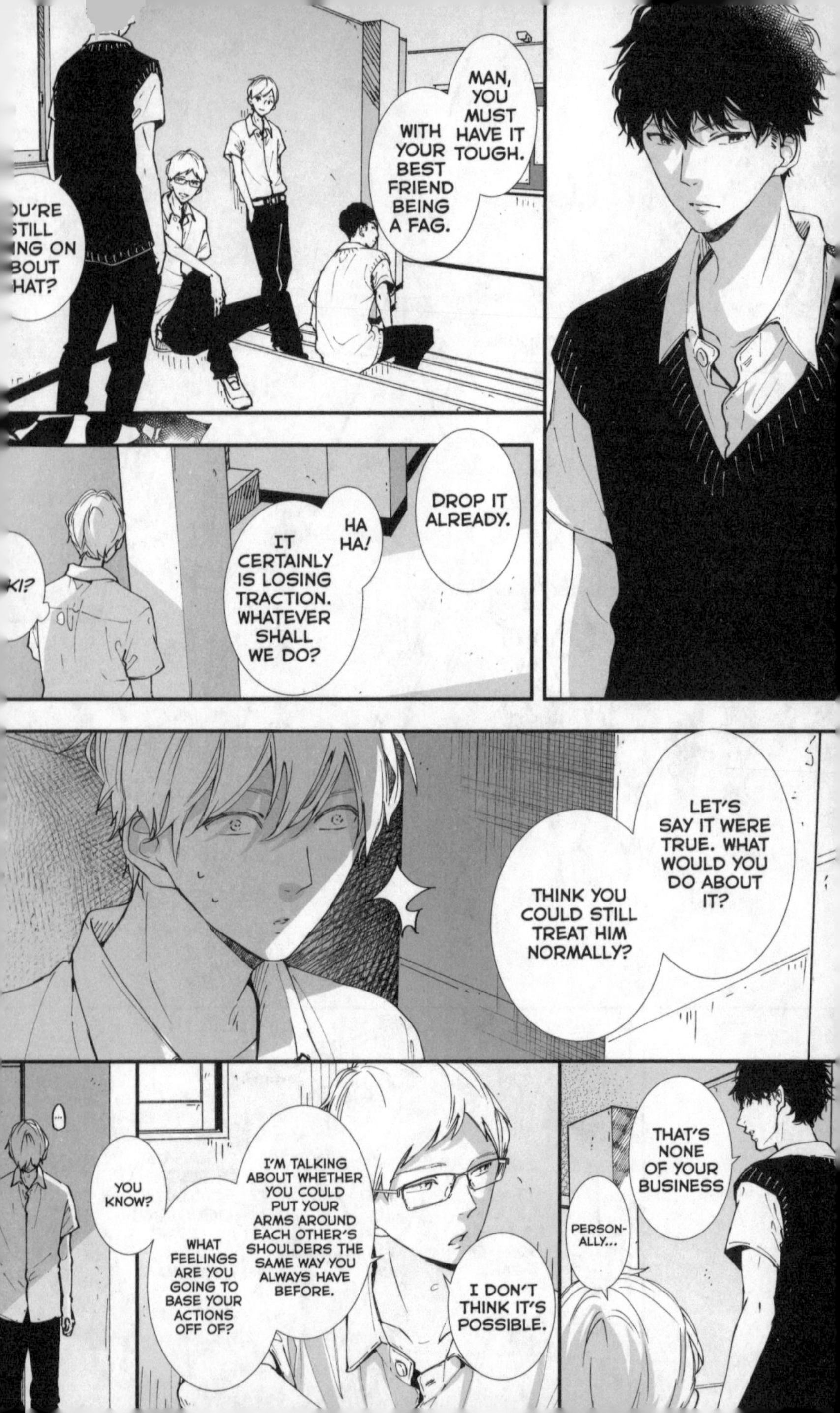
MAN, YOU MUST HAVE IT TOUGH.
WITH YOUR BEST FRIEND BEING A FAG.
U'RE TILL ING ON BOUT HAT?
DROP IT ALREADY.
HA HA!
IT CERTAINLY IS LOSING TRACTION. WHATEVER SHALL WE DO?
KI?
LET'S SAY IT WERE TRUE. WHAT WOULD YOU DO ABOUT IT?
THINK YOU COULD STILL TREAT HIM NORMALLY?
THAT'S NONE OF YOUR BUSINESS
PERSON-ALLY...
I'M TALKING ABOUT WHETHER YOU COULD PUT YOUR ARMS AROUND EACH OTHER'S SHOULDERS THE SAME WAY YOU ALWAYS HAVE BEFORE.
I DON'T THINK IT'S POSSIBLE.
WHAT FEELINGS ARE YOU GOING TO BASE YOUR ACTIONS OFF OF?
YOU KNOW?
...

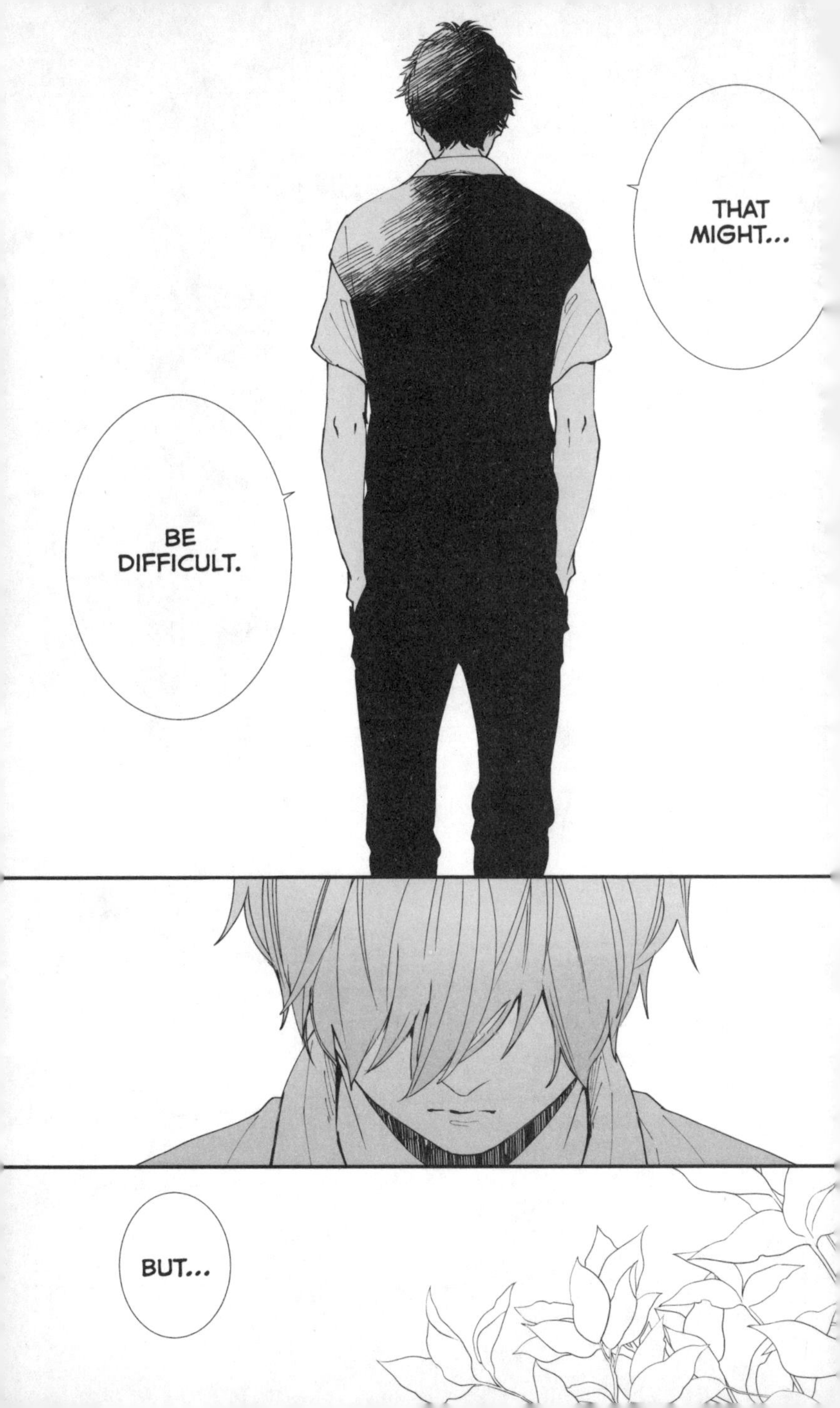
THAT MIGHT...
BE DIFFICULT.
BUT...

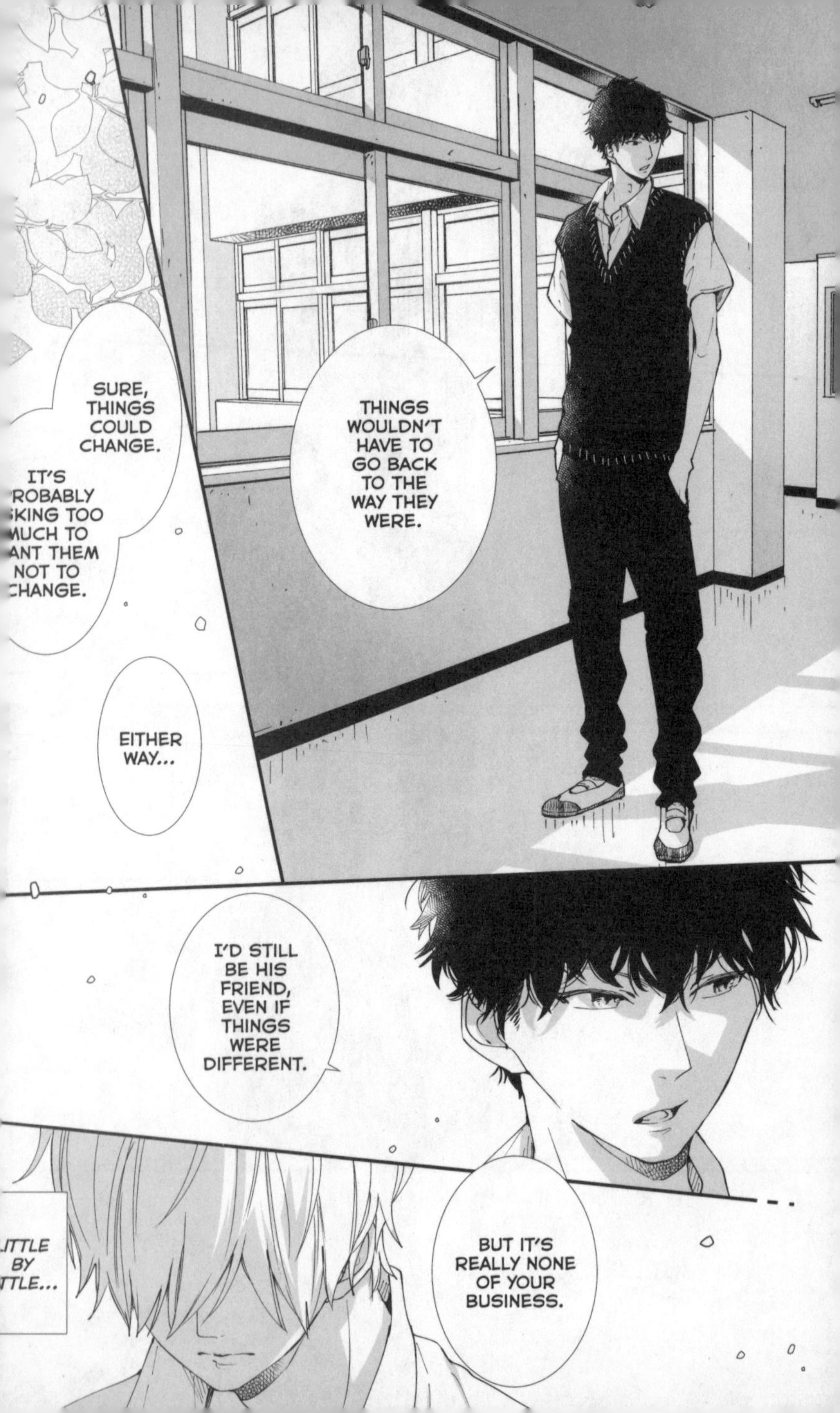
THINGS WOULDN'T HAVE TO GO BACK TO THE WAY THEY WERE.
SURE, THINGS COULD CHANGE.
IT'S ROBABLY KING TOO MUCH TO ANT THEM NOT TO HANGE.
EITHER WAY...
I'D STILL BE HIS FRIEND, EVEN IF THINGS WERE DIFFERENT.
BUT IT'S REALLY NONE OF YOUR BUSINESS.
ITTLE BY TTLE...

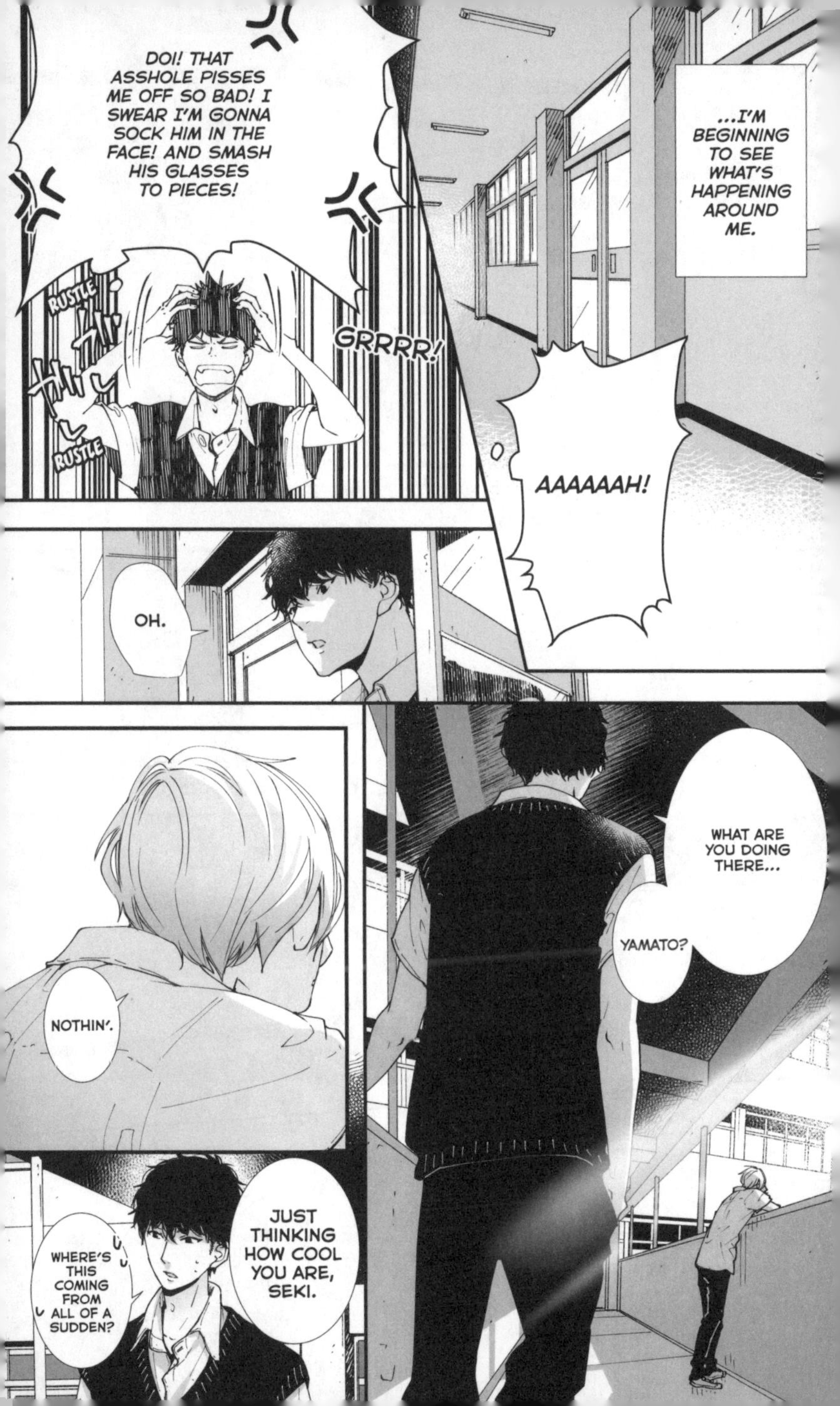
...I'M BEGINNING TO SEE WHAT'S HAPPENING AROUND ME.
AAAAAAH!
DOI! THAT ASSHOLE PISSES ME OFF SO BAD! I SWEAR I'M GONNA SOCK HIM IN THE FACE! AND SMASH HIS GLASSES TO PIECES!
GRRRR!
RUSTLE
RUSTLE
OH.
WHAT ARE YOU DOING THERE...
YAMATO?
NOTHIN'.
JUST THINKING HOW COOL YOU ARE, SEKI.
WHERE'S THIS COMING FROM ALL OF A SUDDEN?

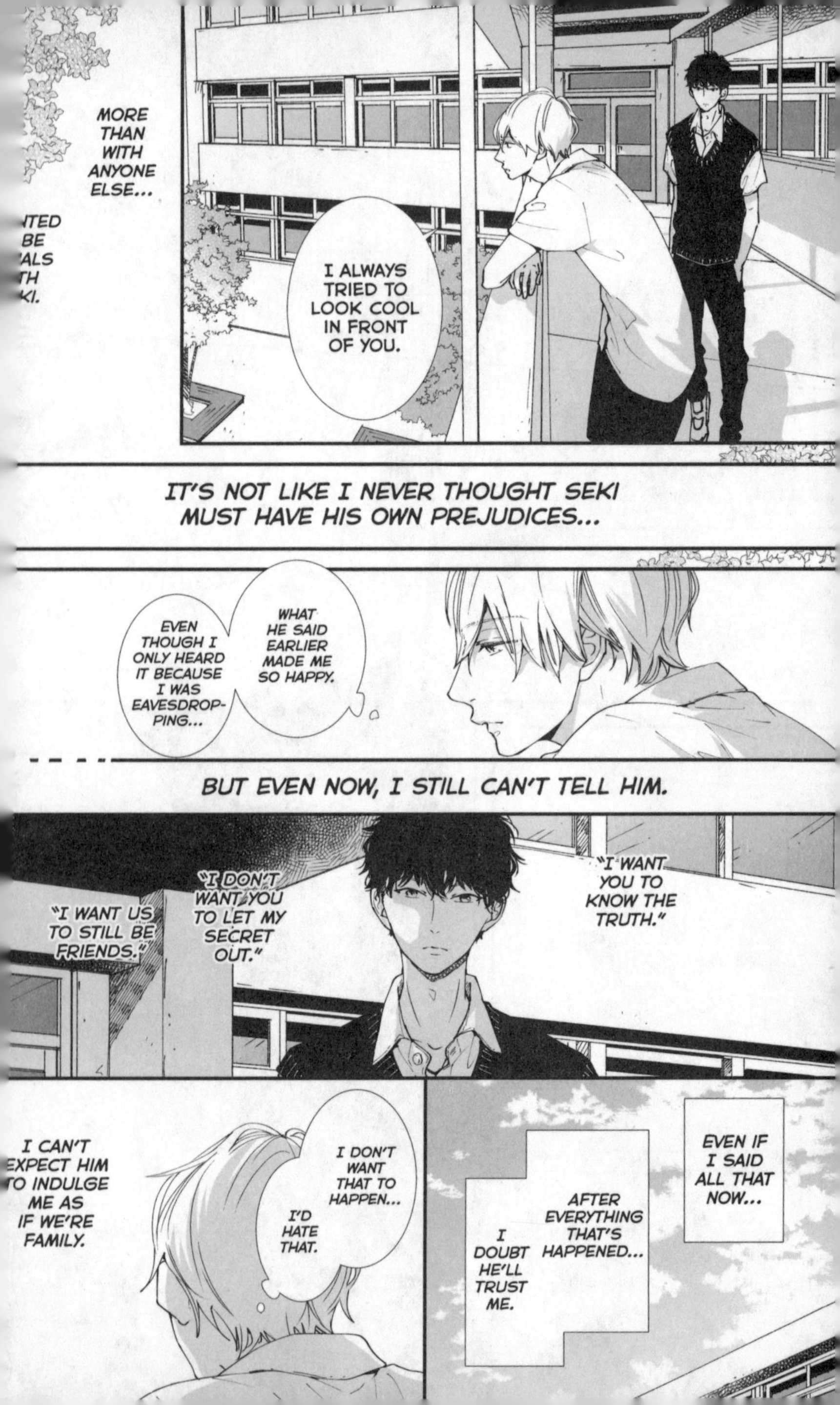
I ALWAYS TRIED TO LOOK COOL IN FRONT OF YOU.
MORE THAN WITH ANYONE ELSE...
IT'S NOT LIKE I NEVER THOUGHT SEKI MUST HAVE HIS OWN PREJUDICES...
WHAT HE SAID EARLIER MADE ME SO HAPPY.
EVEN THOUGH I ONLY HEARD IT BECAUSE I WAS EAVESDROPPING...
BUT EVEN NOW, I STILL CAN'T TELL HIM.
"I WANT YOU TO KNOW THE TRUTH."
"I DON'T WANT YOU TO LET MY SECRET OUT."
"I WANT US TO STILL BE FRIENDS."
EVEN IF I SAID ALL THAT NOW...
AFTER EVERYTHING THAT'S HAPPENED...
I DOUBT HE'LL TRUST ME.
I DON'T WANT THAT TO HAPPEN...
I'D HATE THAT.
I CAN'T EXPECT HIM TO INDULGE ME AS IF WE'RE FAMILY.

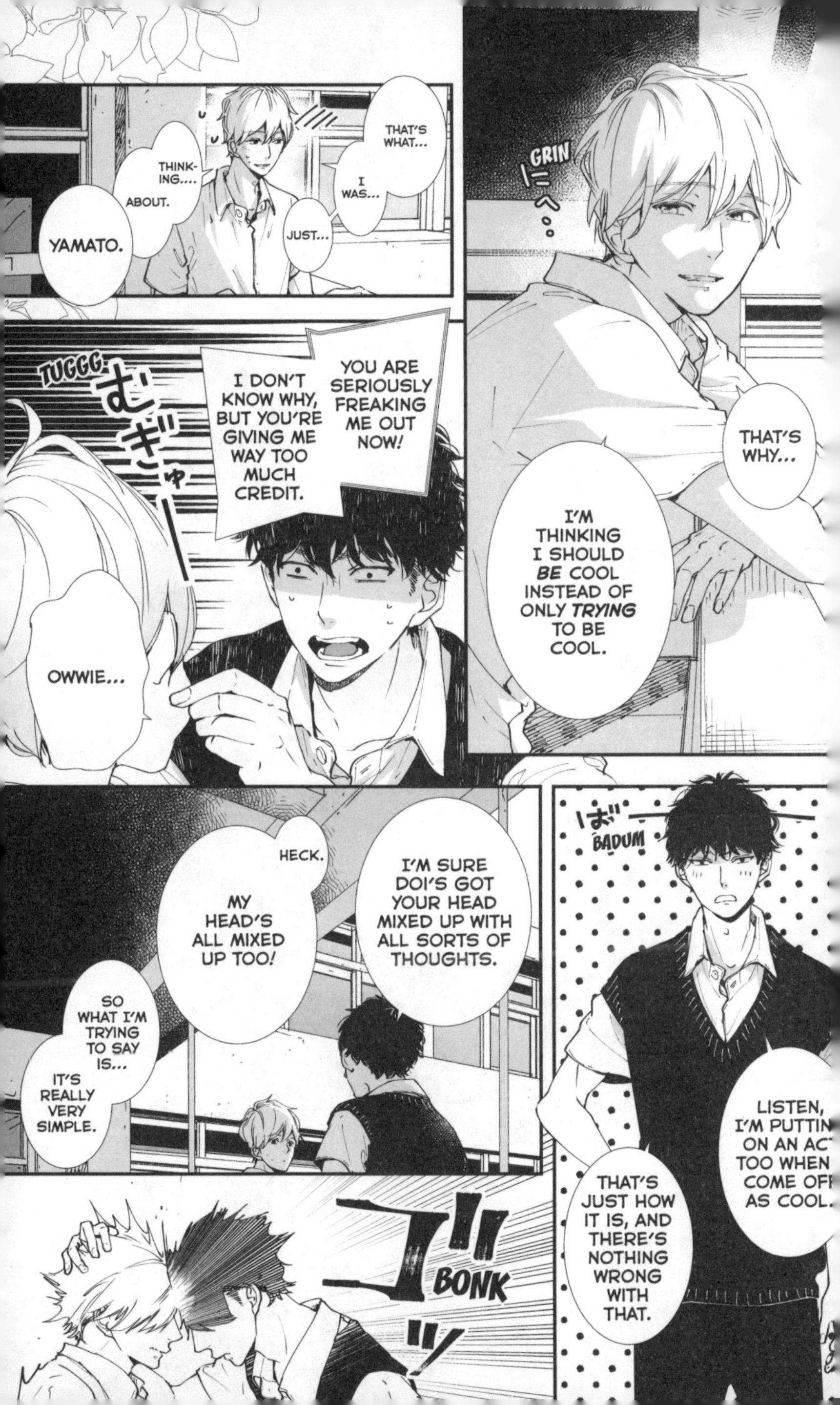
GRIN にへ。。
THAT'S WHY...
I'M THINKING I SHOULD BE COOL INSTEAD OF ONLY TRYING TO BE COOL.
THAT'S WHAT...
I WAS...
JUST...
THINKING....
ABOUT.
YAMATO.
YOU ARE SERIOUSLY FREAKING ME OUT NOW!
I DON'T KNOW WHY, BUT YOU'RE GIVING ME WAY TOO MUCH CREDIT.
TUGGG むぎゅー
OWWIE...
ば" BADUM
LISTEN, I'M PUTTIN ON AN AC TOO WHEN COME OF AS COOL.
THAT'S JUST HOW IT IS, AND THERE'S NOTHING WRONG WITH THAT.
I'M SURE DOI'S GOT YOUR HEAD MIXED UP WITH ALL SORTS OF THOUGHTS.
HECK.
MY HEAD'S ALL MIXED UP TOO!
SO WHAT I'M TRYING TO SAY IS...
IT'S REALLY VERY SIMPLE.
ゴッ BONK

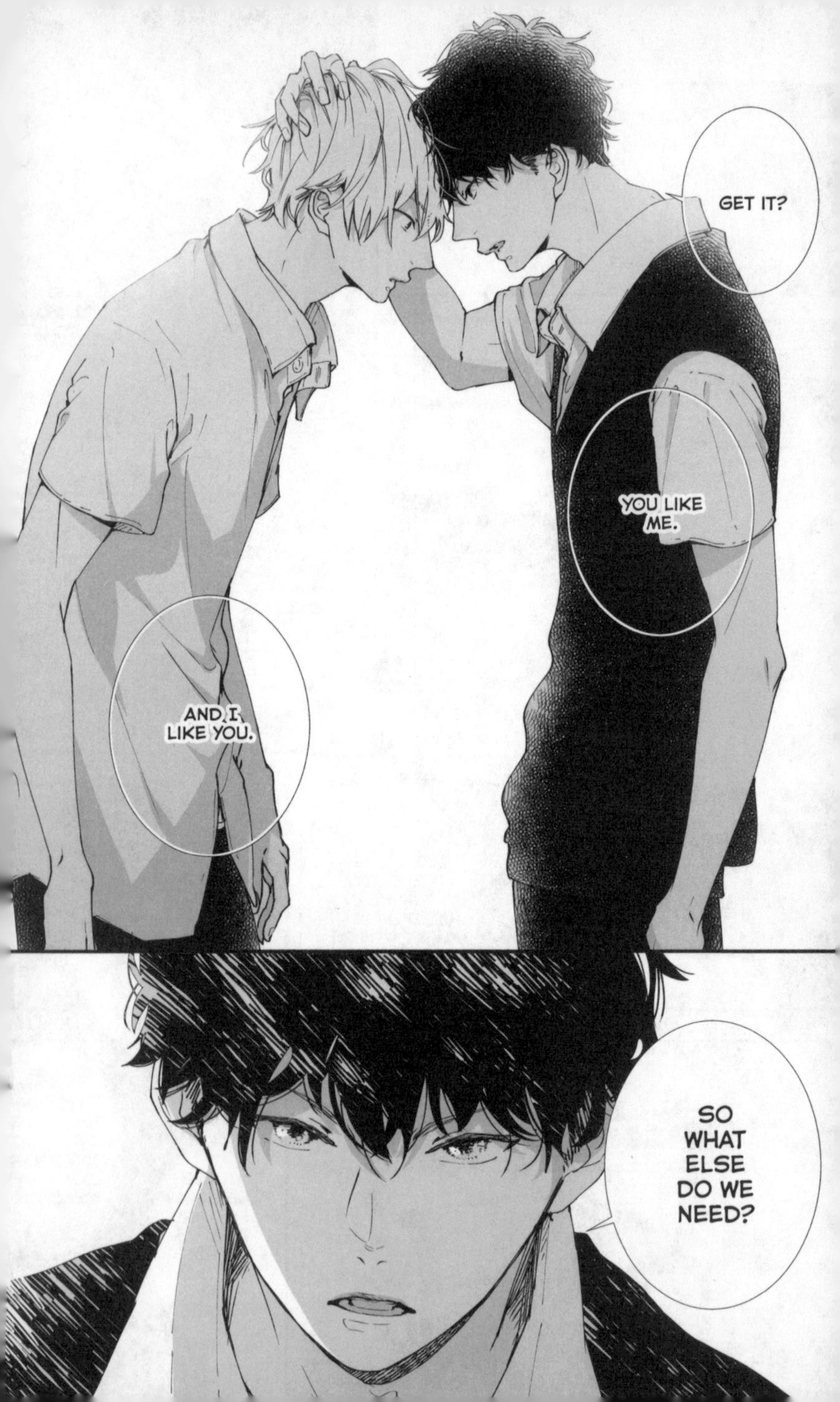
GET IT?
YOU LIKE ME.
AND I LIKE YOU.
SO WHAT ELSE DO WE NEED?

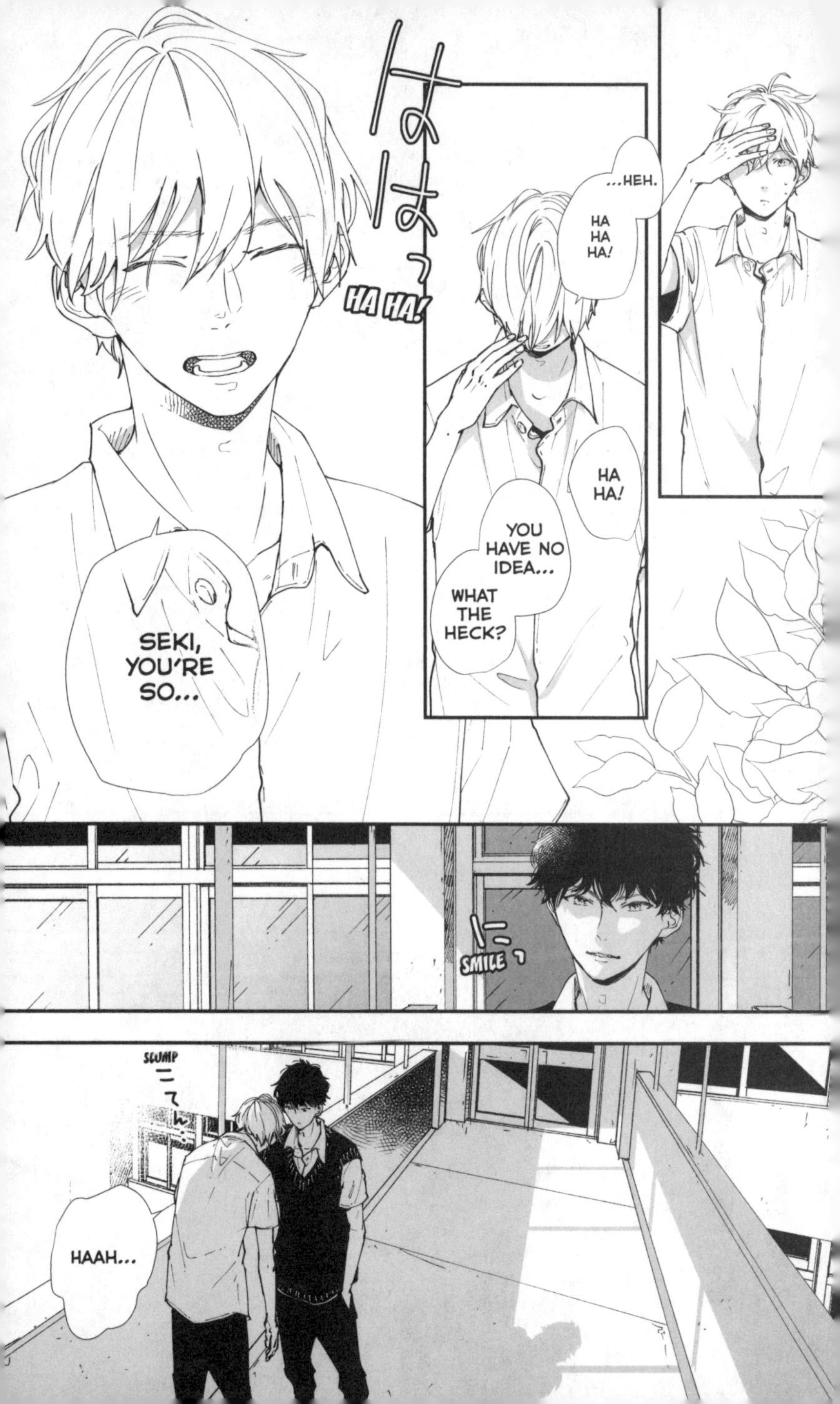
...HEH.
HA HA HA!
HA HA!
YOU HAVE NO IDEA...
WHAT THE HECK?
ははっ
HA HA!
SEKI, YOU'RE SO...
SMILE
こてん
SLUMP
HAAH...

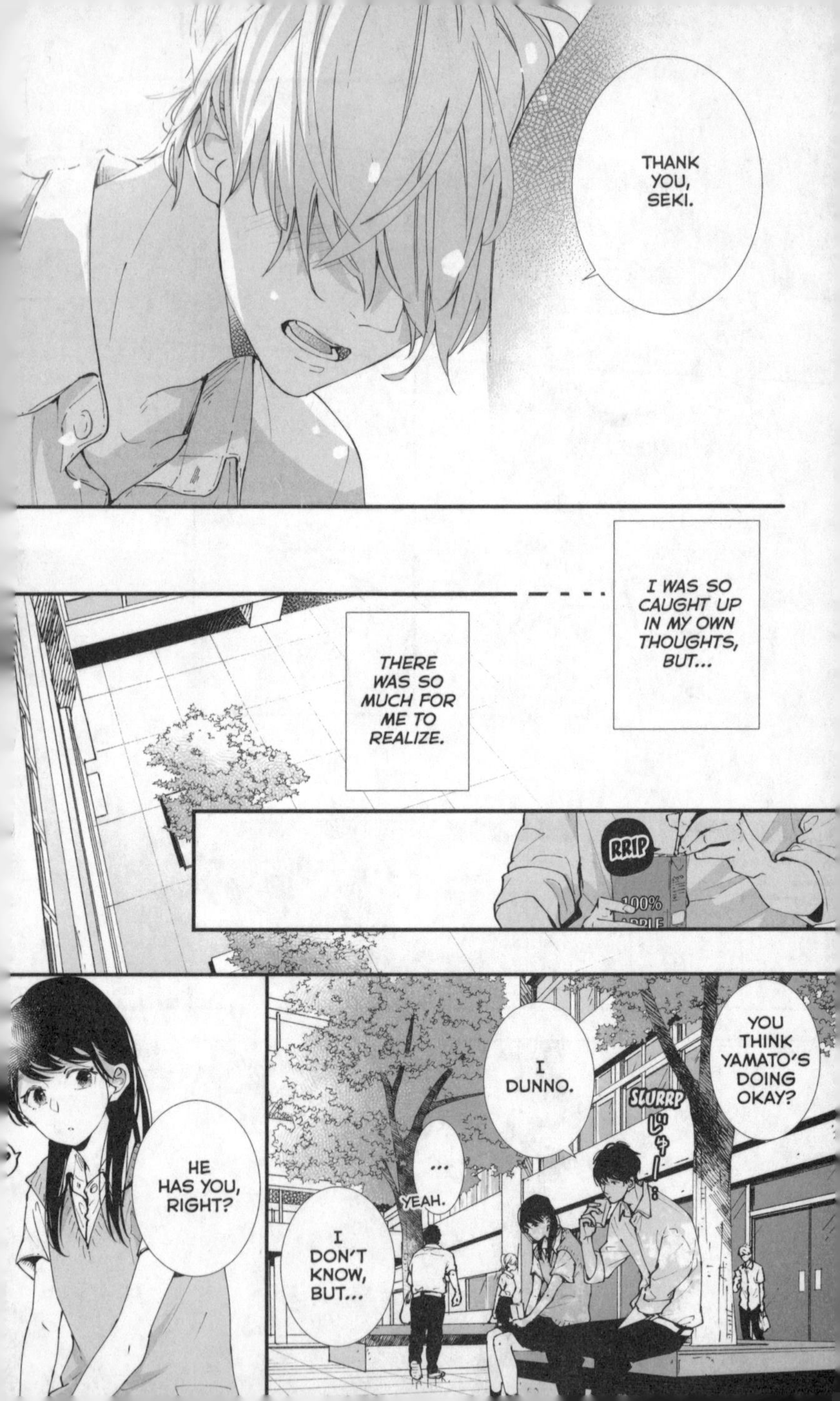
THANK YOU, SEKI.
I WAS SO CAUGHT UP IN MY OWN THOUGHTS, BUT...
THERE WAS SO MUCH FOR ME TO REALIZE.
RRIP
100%
YOU THINK YAMATO'S DOING OKAY?
I DUNNO.
SLURRP
...
YEAH.
I DON'T KNOW, BUT...
HE HAS YOU, RIGHT?

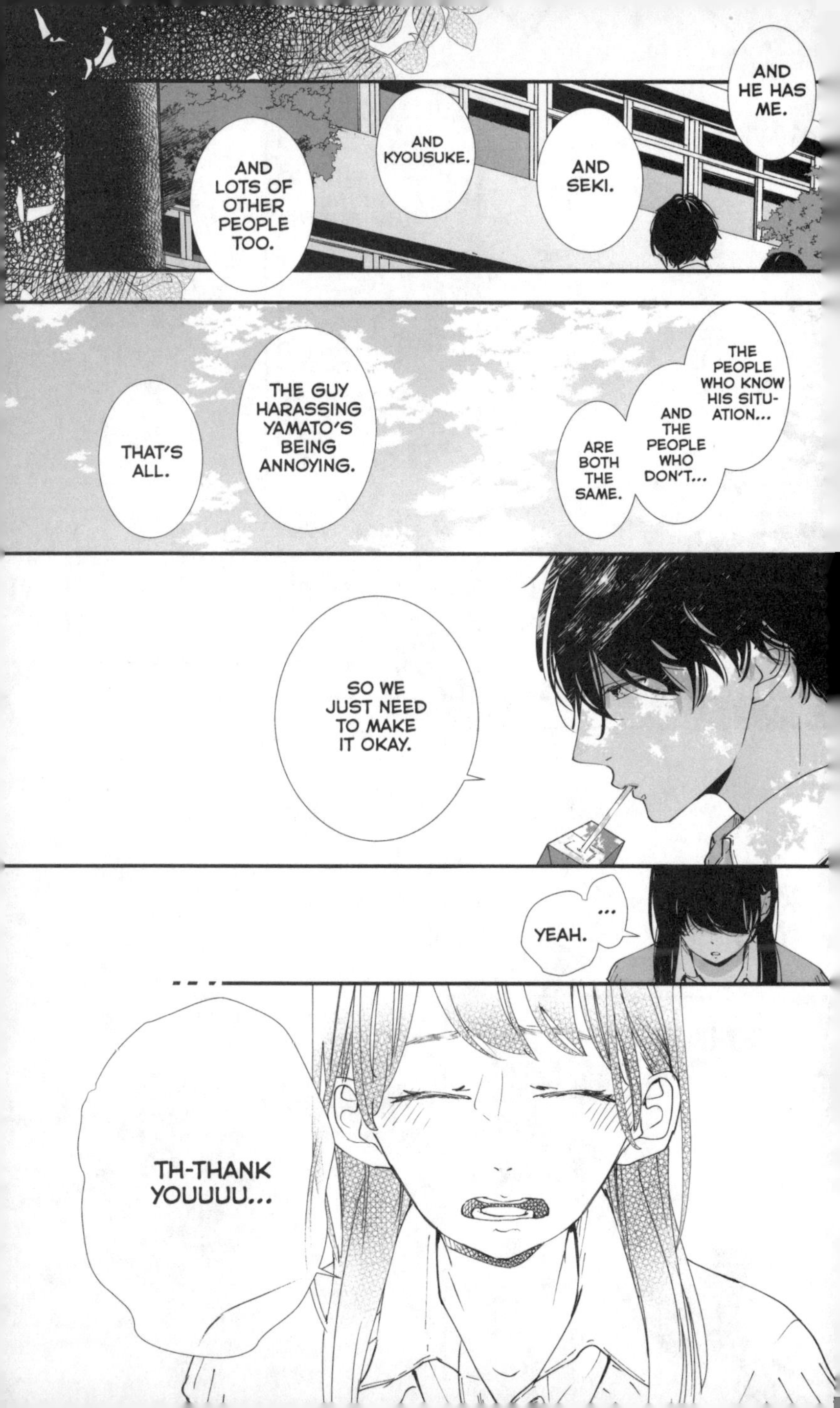
AND HE HAS ME.
AND SEKI.
AND KYOUSUKE.
AND LOTS OF OTHER PEOPLE TOO.
THE PEOPLE WHO KNOW HIS SITU-ATION...
AND THE PEOPLE WHO DON'T...
ARE BOTH THE SAME.
THE GUY HARASSING YAMATO'S BEING ANNOYING.
THAT'S ALL.
SO WE JUST NEED TO MAKE IT OKAY.
... YEAH.
TH-THANK YOUUUU...

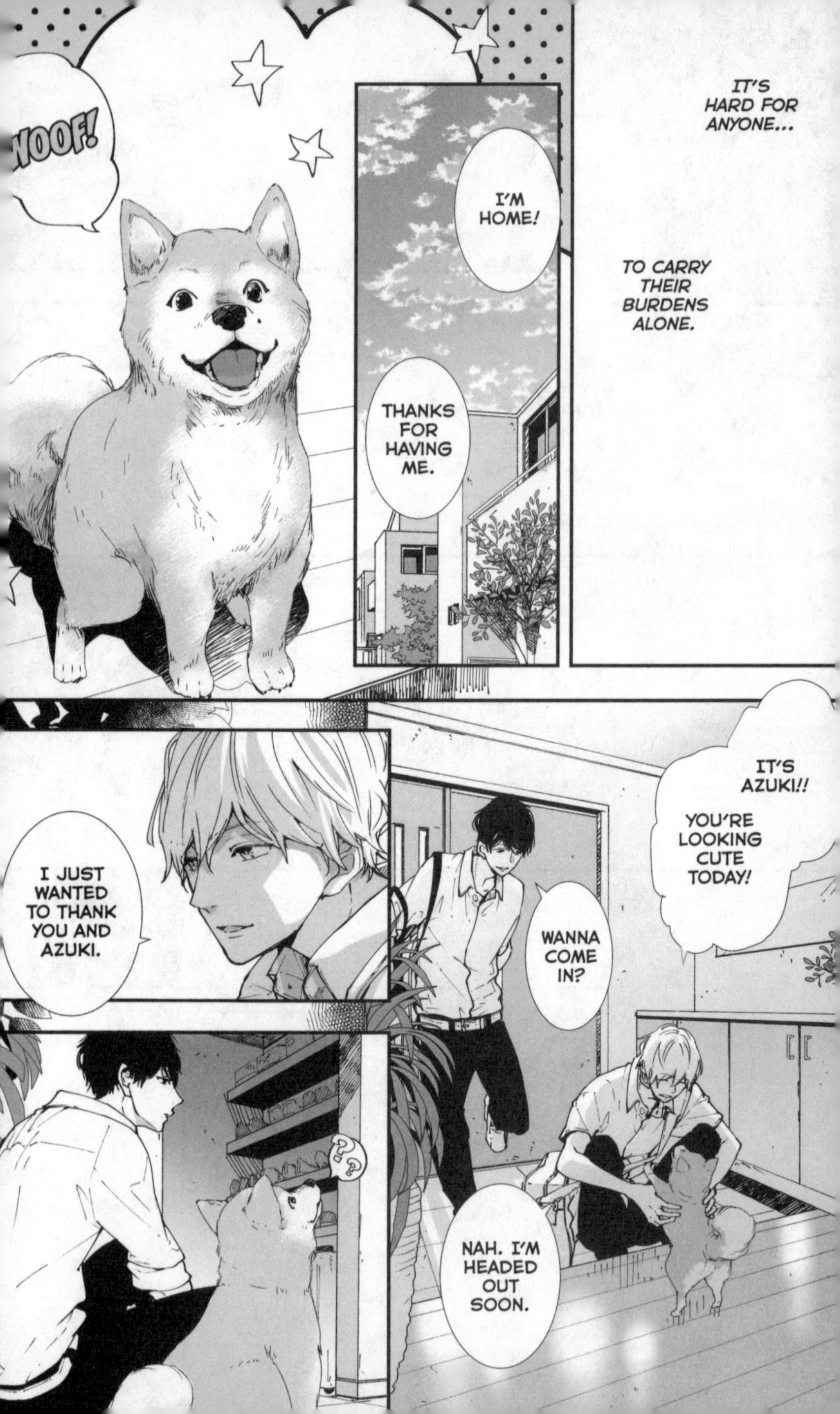
IT'S HARD FOR ANYONE...
TO CARRY THEIR BURDENS ALONE.
I'M HOME!
THANKS FOR HAVING ME.
WOOF!
IT'S AZUKI!!
YOU'RE LOOKING CUTE TODAY!
WANNA COME IN?
NAH. I'M HEADED OUT SOON.
I JUST WANTED TO THANK YOU AND AZUKI.

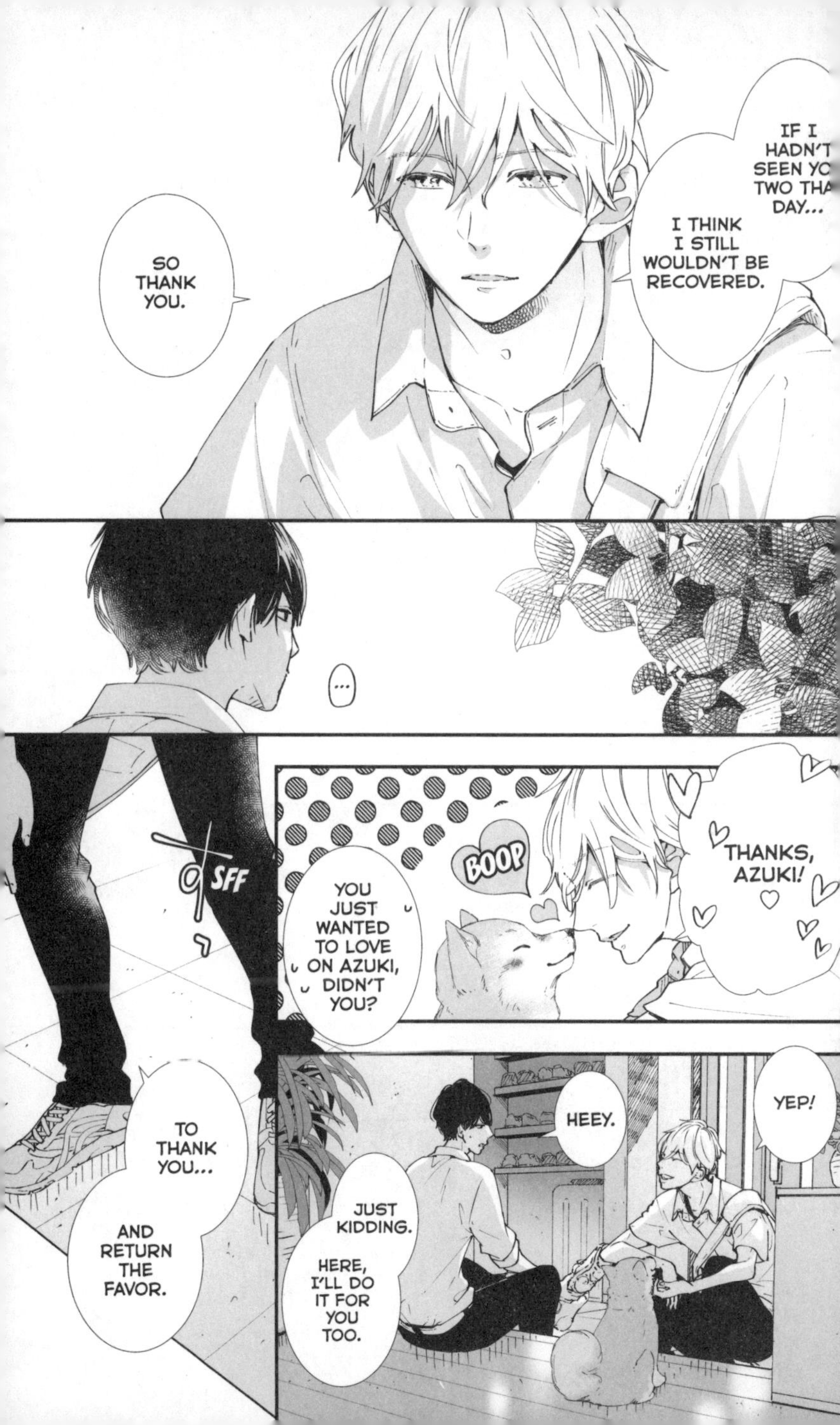

IF I HADN'T SEEN YO TWO THA DAY...
I THINK I STILL WOULDN'T BE RECOVERED.
SO THANK YOU.
...
THANKS, AZUKI!
BOOP
YOU JUST WANTED TO LOVE ON AZUKI, DIDN'T YOU?
YEP!
HEEY.
JUST KIDDING.
HERE, I'LL DO IT FOR YOU TOO.
SFF
TO THANK YOU...
AND RETURN THE FAVOR.

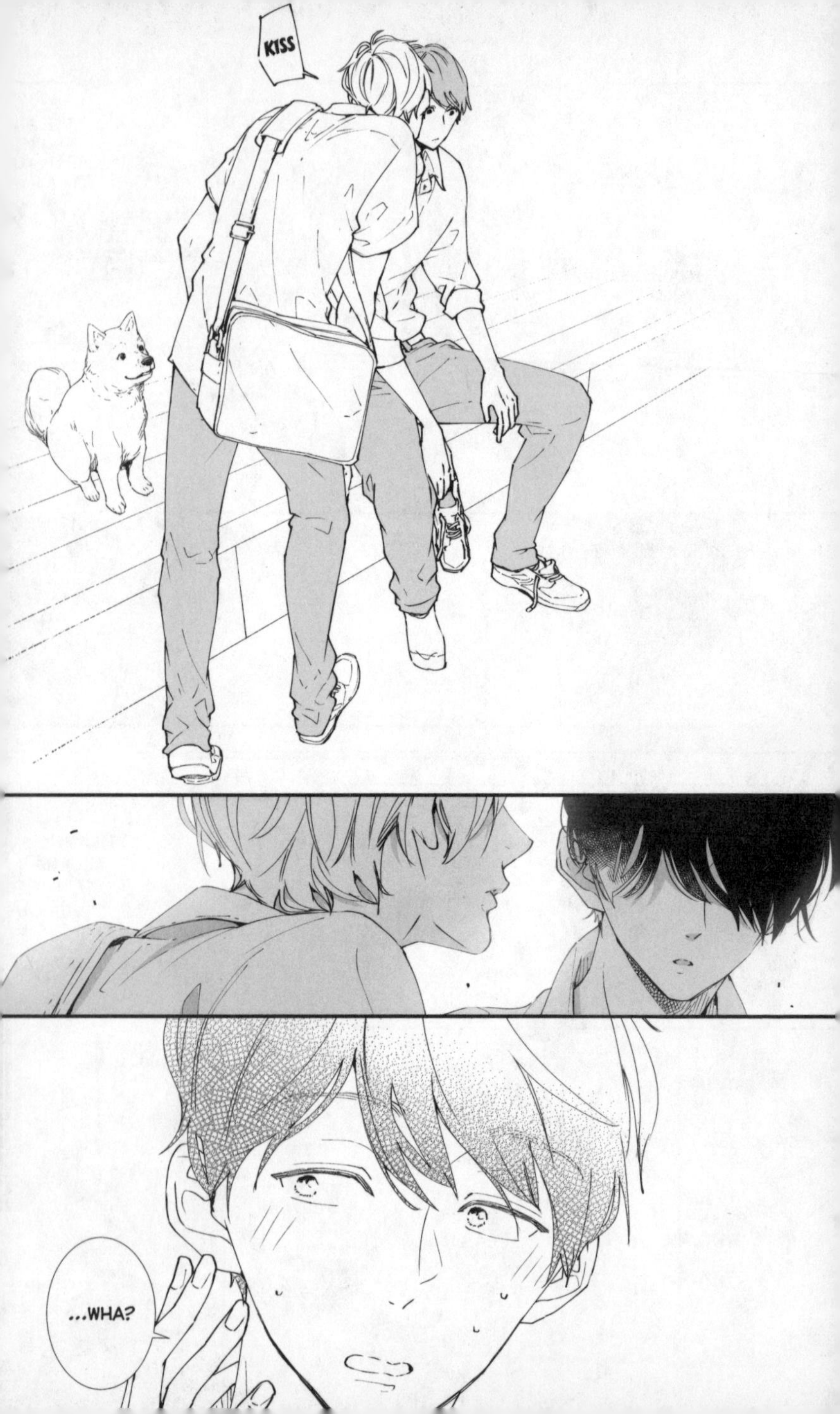
KISS
...WHA?

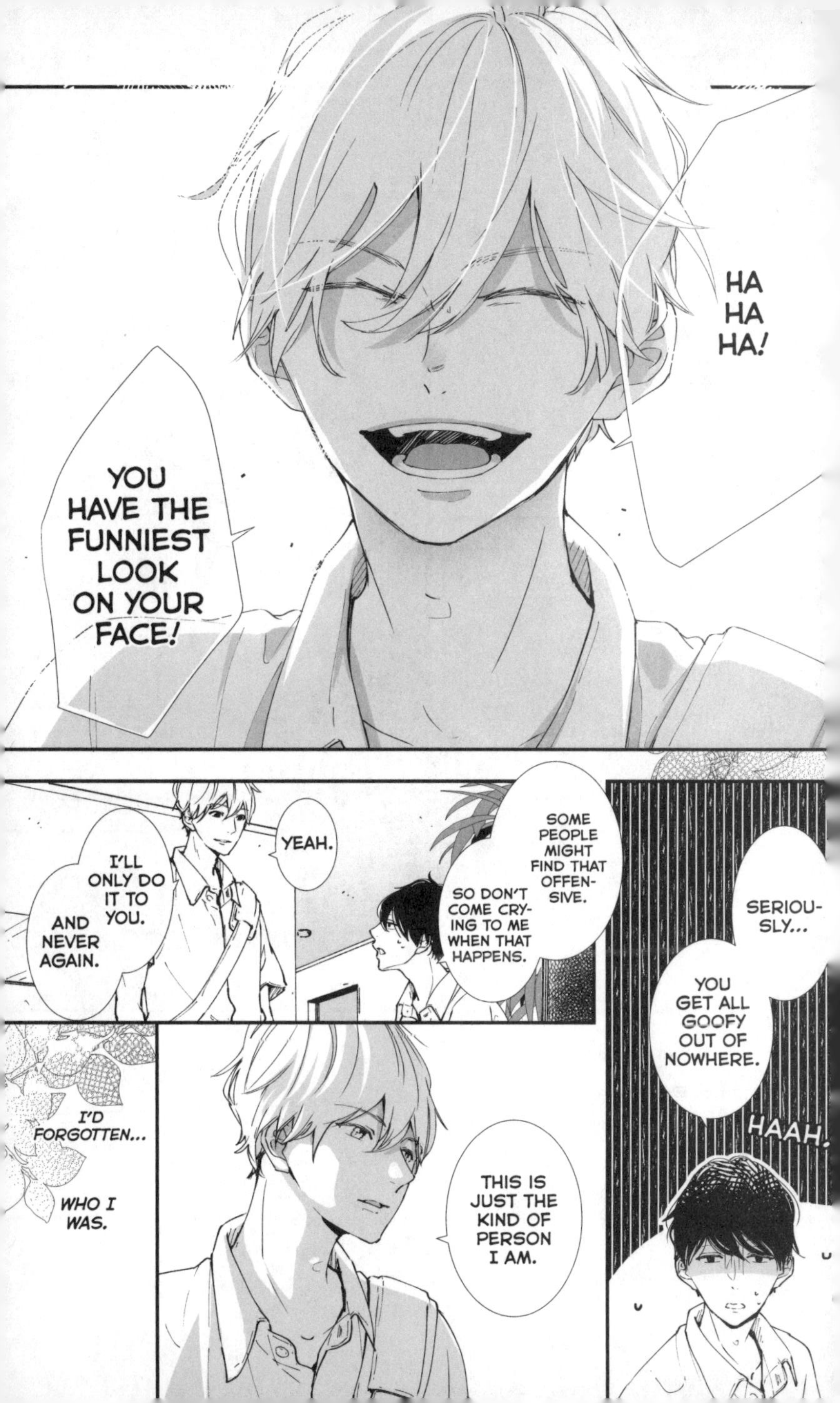
HA HA HA!
YOU HAVE THE FUNNIEST LOOK ON YOUR FACE!
SERIOU-SLY...
YOU GET ALL GOOFY OUT OF NOWHERE.
HAAH.
SOME PEOPLE MIGHT FIND THAT OFFEN-SIVE.
SO DON'T COME CRY-ING TO ME WHEN THAT HAPPENS.
YEAH.
I'LL ONLY DO IT TO YOU.
AND NEVER AGAIN.
THIS IS JUST THE KIND OF PERSON I AM.
I'D FORGOTTEN...
WHO I WAS.

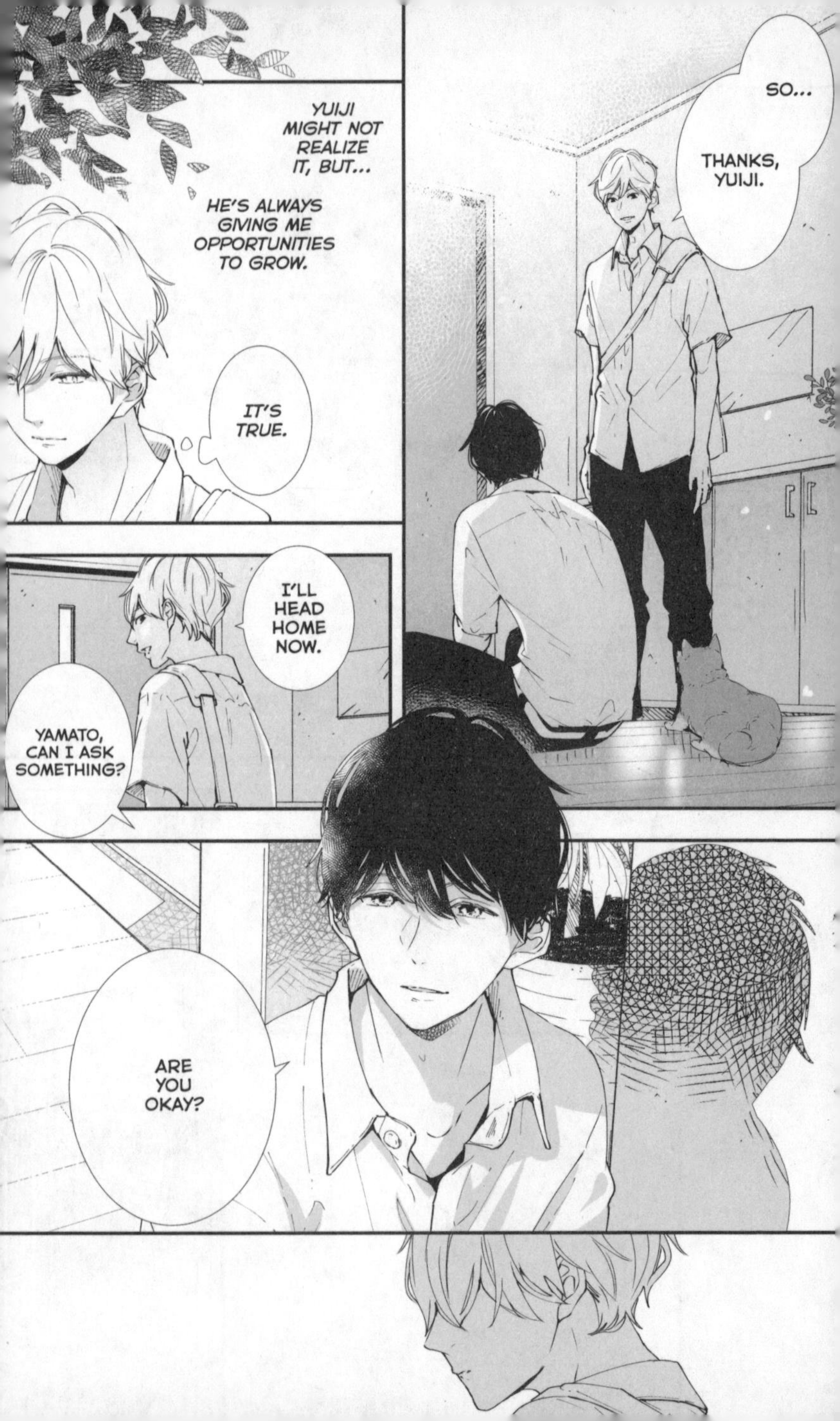
SO...
THANKS, YUIJI.
YUIJI MIGHT NOT REALIZE IT, BUT...
HE'S ALWAYS GIVING ME OPPORTUNITIES TO GROW.
IT'S TRUE.
I'LL HEAD HOME NOW.
YAMATO, CAN I ASK SOMETHING?
ARE YOU OKAY?

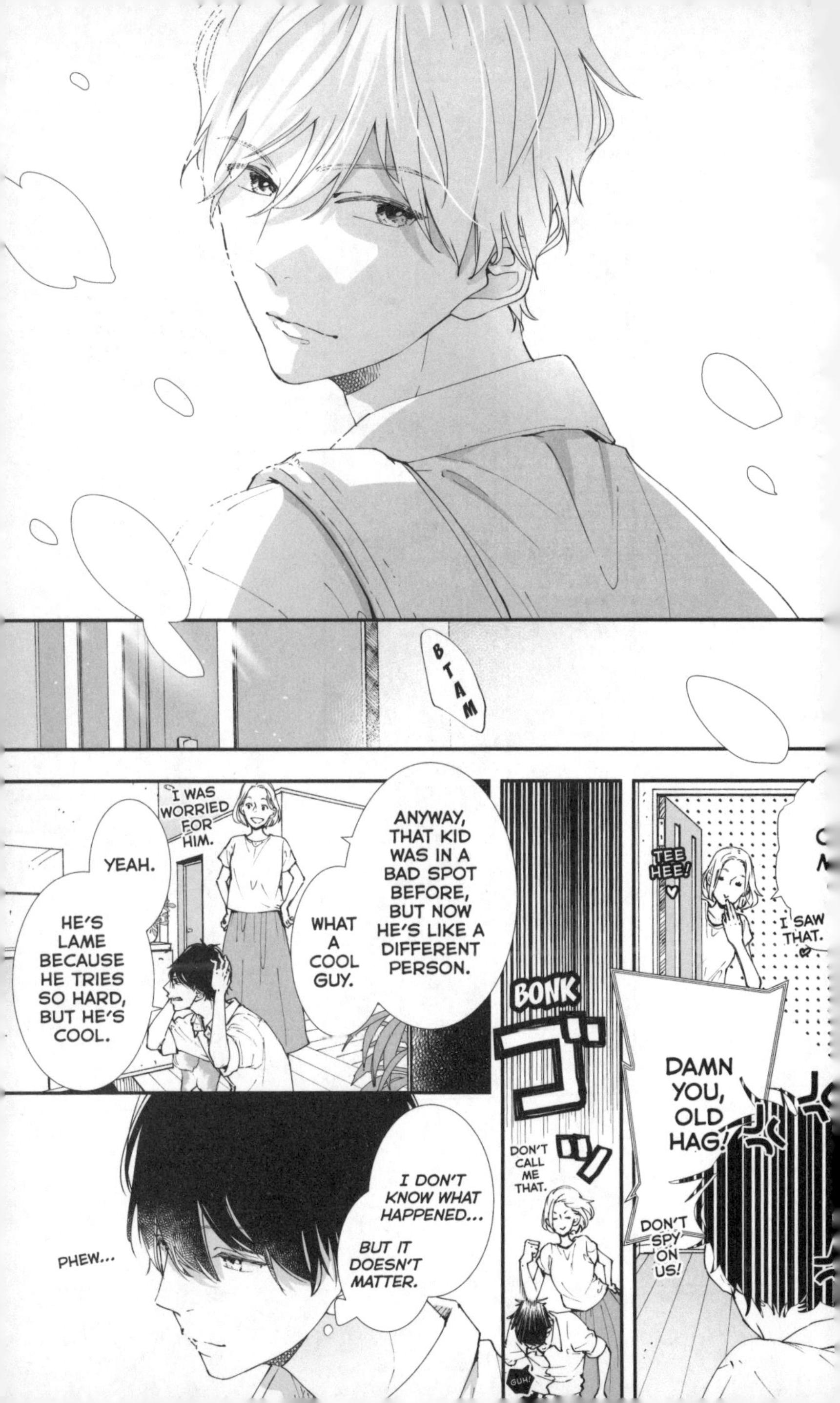

BTAM
TEE HEE!
I SAW THAT.
DAMN YOU, OLD HAG!
DON'T SPY ON US!
BONK
ゴッ
DON'T CALL ME THAT.
GUH!
ANYWAY, THAT KID WAS IN A BAD SPOT BEFORE, BUT NOW HE'S LIKE A DIFFERENT PERSON.
WHAT A COOL GUY.
I WAS WORRIED FOR HIM.
YEAH.
HE'S LAME BECAUSE HE TRIES SO HARD, BUT HE'S COOL.
I DON'T KNOW WHAT HAPPENED...
BUT IT DOESN'T MATTER.
PHEW...

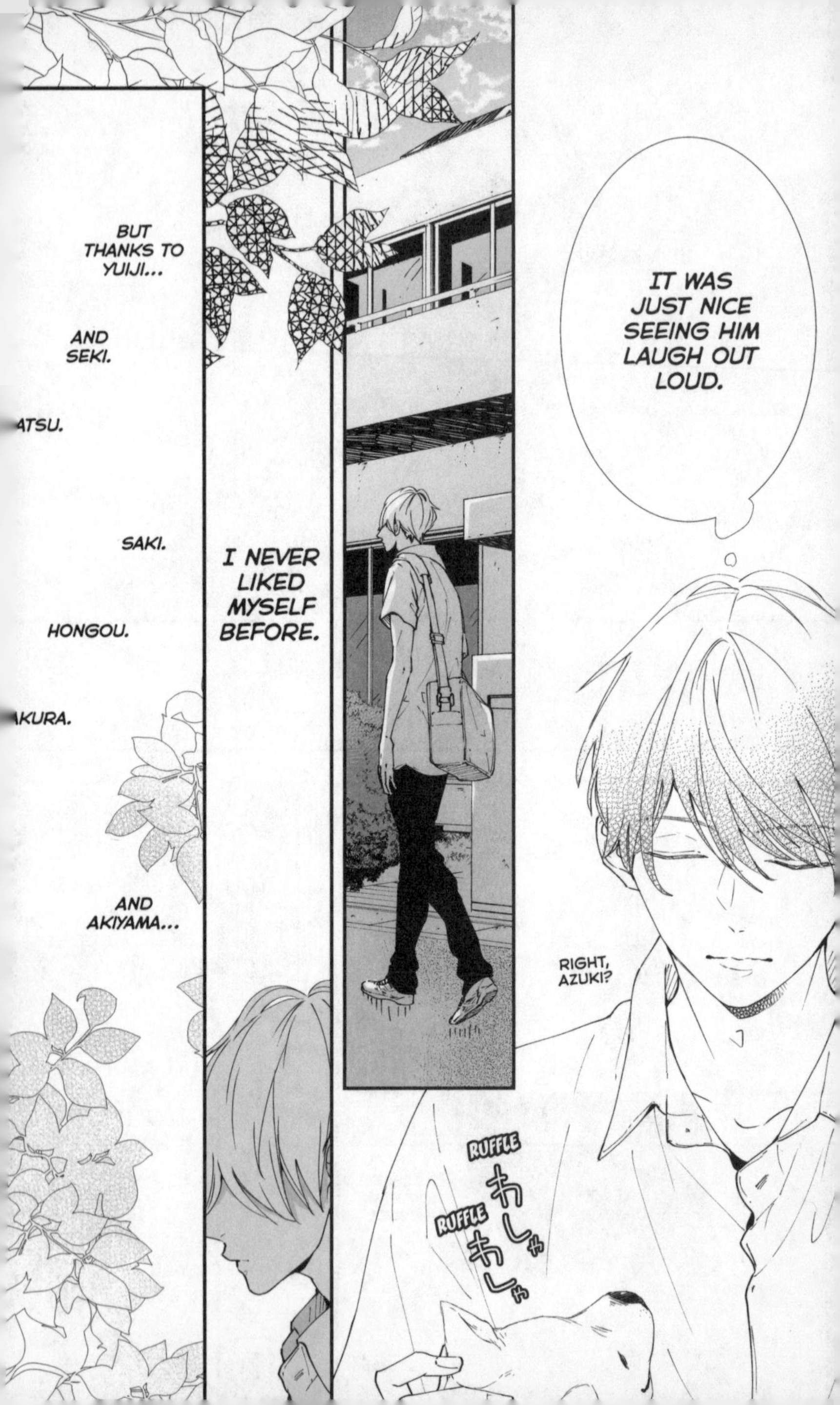
IT WAS JUST NICE SEEING HIM LAUGH OUT LOUD.
RIGHT, AZUKI?
RUFFLE
わしゃ
RUFFLE
わしゃ
I NEVER LIKED MYSELF BEFORE.
BUT THANKS TO YUIJI...
AND SEKI.
ATSU.
SAKI.
HONGOU.
AKURA.
AND AKIYAMA...

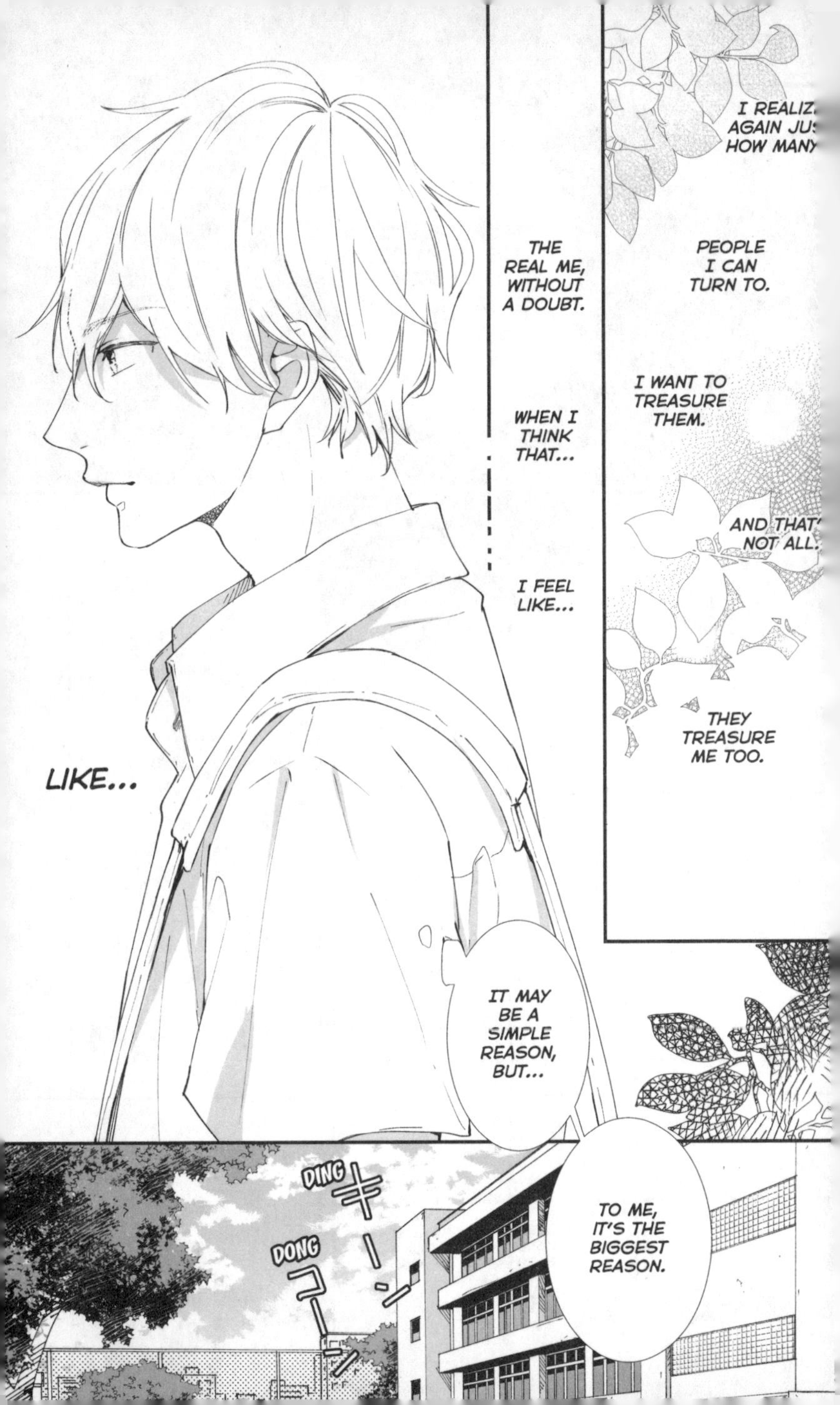
I REALIZ
AGAIN JUS
HOW MANY
PEOPLE I CAN TURN TO.
I WANT TO TREASURE THEM.
AND THAT'S NOT ALL.
THEY TREASURE ME TOO.
THE REAL ME, WITHOUT A DOUBT.
WHEN I THINK THAT...
I FEEL LIKE...
LIKE...
IT MAY BE A SIMPLE REASON, BUT...
TO ME, IT'S THE BIGGEST REASON.
DING
DONG

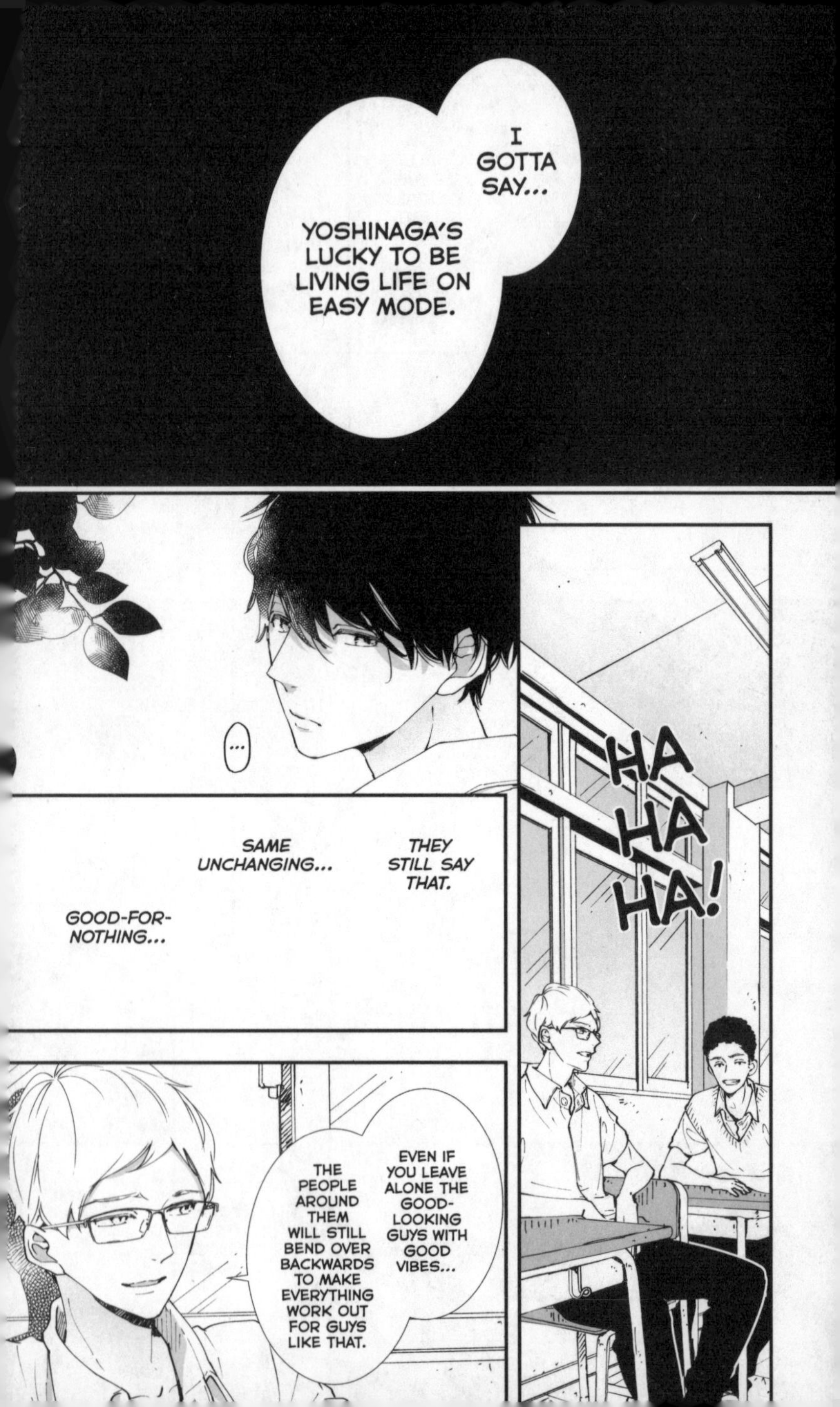
I GOTTA SAY...
YOSHINAGA'S LUCKY TO BE LIVING LIFE ON EASY MODE.
HA HA HA!
...
THEY STILL SAY THAT.
SAME UNCHANGING...
GOOD-FOR-NOTHING...
EVEN IF YOU LEAVE ALONE THE GOOD-LOOKING GUYS WITH GOOD VIBES...
THE PEOPLE AROUND THEM WILL STILL BEND OVER BACKWARDS TO MAKE EVERYTHING WORK OUT FOR GUYS LIKE THAT.

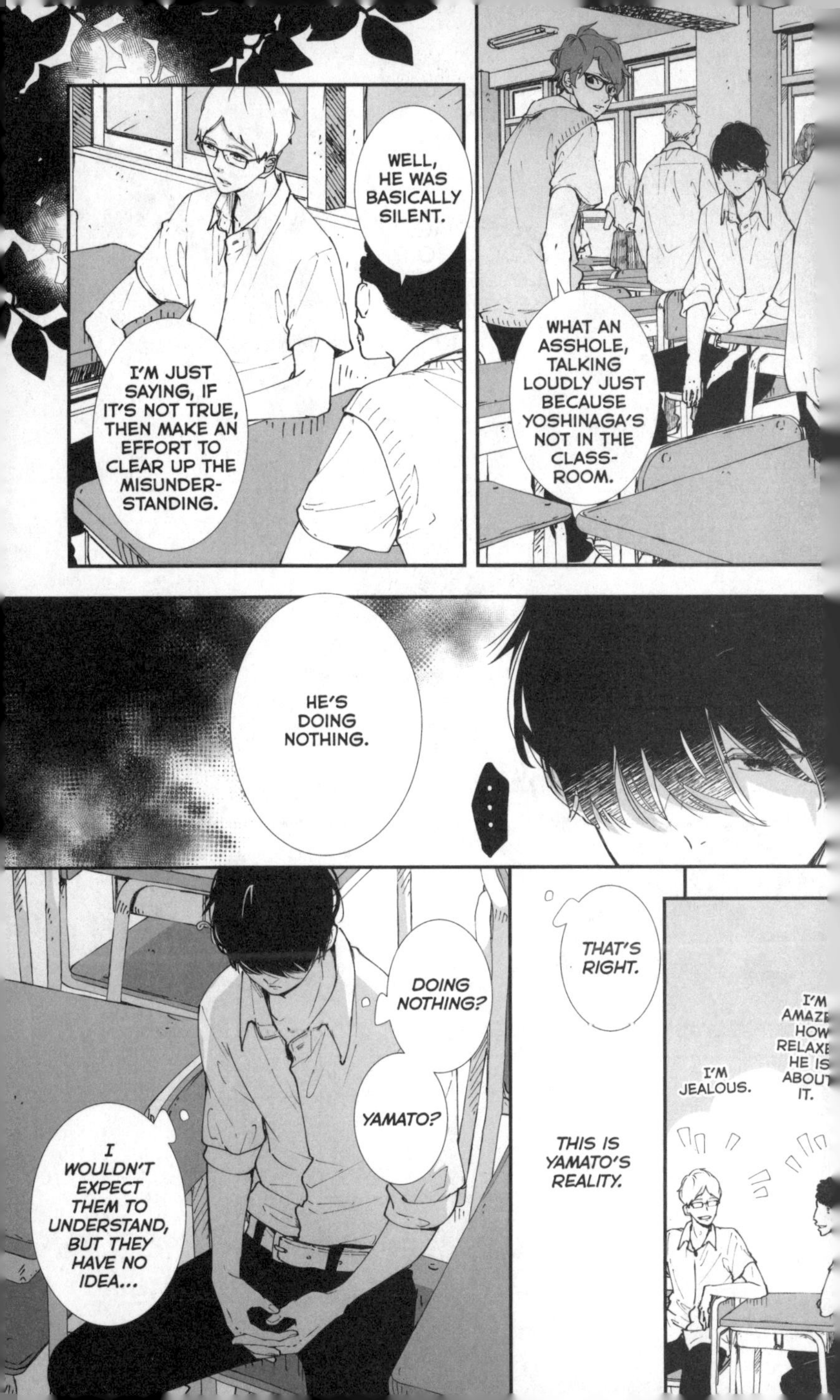
WHAT AN ASSHOLE, TALKING LOUDLY JUST BECAUSE YOSHINAGA'S NOT IN THE CLASSROOM.
WELL, HE WAS BASICALLY SILENT.
I'M JUST SAYING, IF IT'S NOT TRUE, THEN MAKE AN EFFORT TO CLEAR UP THE MISUNDERSTANDING.
...
HE'S DOING NOTHING.
I'M AMAZE HOW RELAXE HE IS ABOUT IT.
I'M JEALOUS.
THAT'S RIGHT.
THIS IS YAMATO'S REALITY.
DOING NOTHING?
YAMATO?
I WOULDN'T EXPECT THEM TO UNDERSTAND, BUT THEY HAVE NO IDEA...

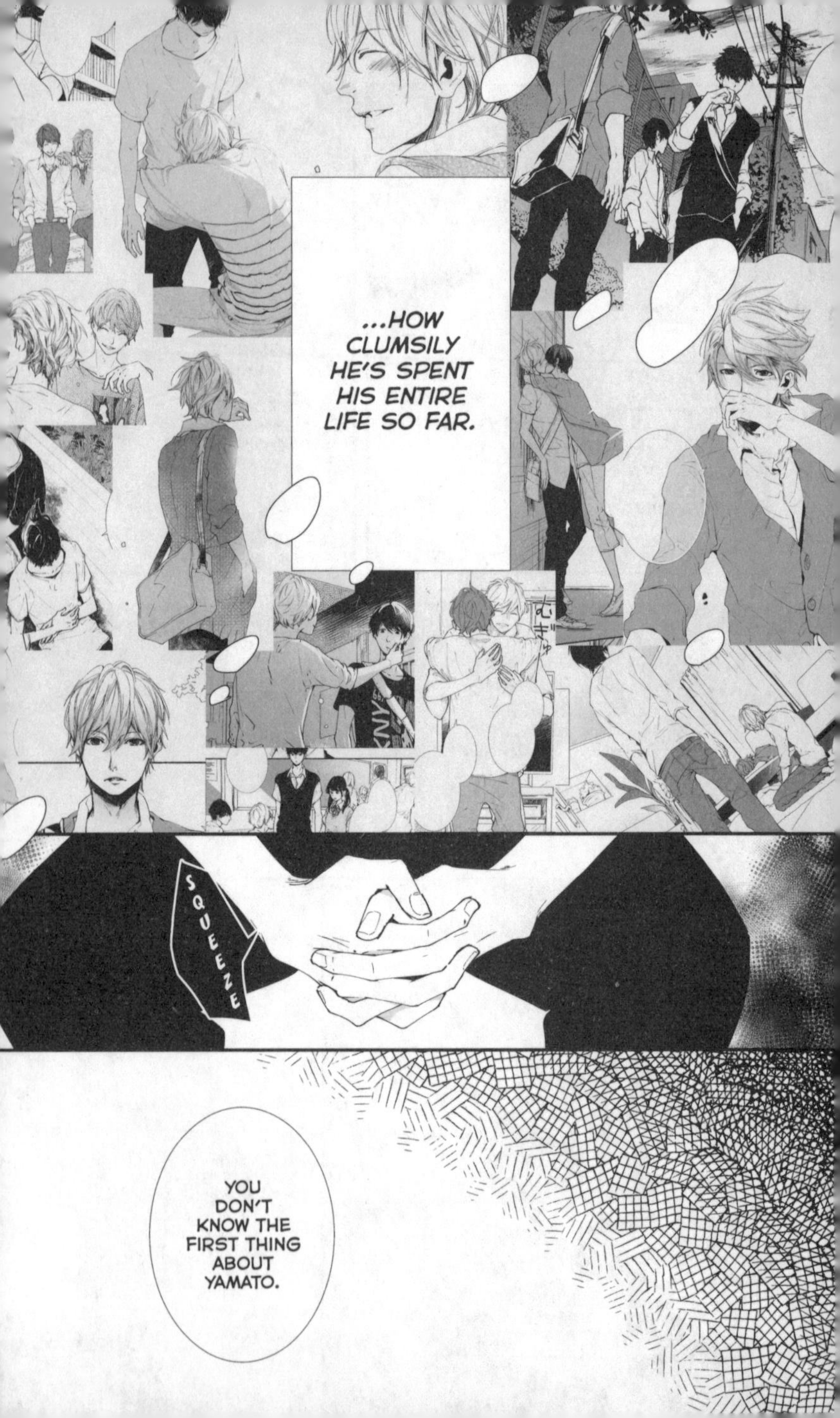
...HOW CLUMSILY HE'S SPENT HIS ENTIRE LIFE SO FAR.
SQUEEZE
YOU DON'T KNOW THE FIRST THING ABOUT YAMATO.

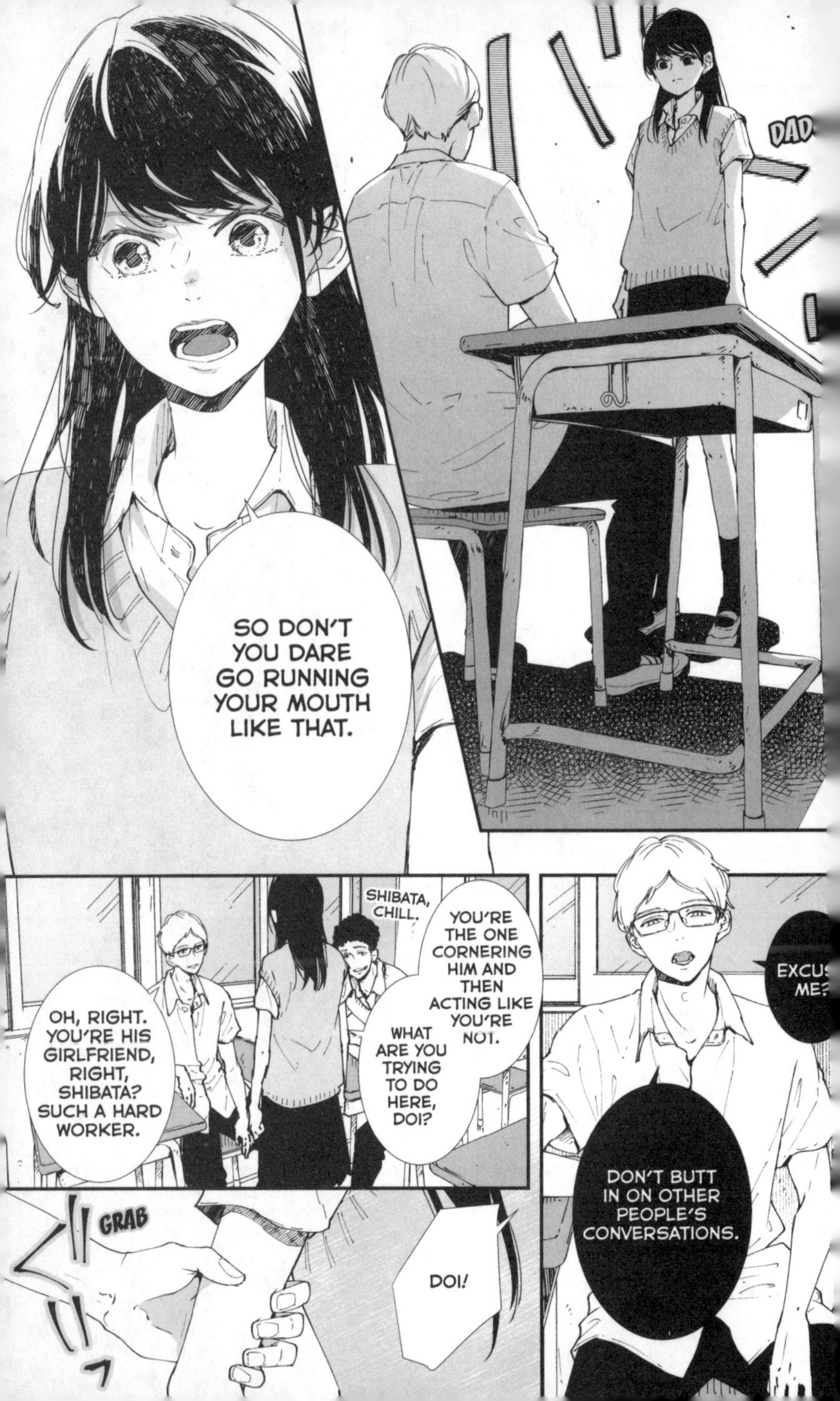

DAD
SO DON'T YOU DARE GO RUNNING YOUR MOUTH LIKE THAT.
EXCUS ME?
DON'T BUTT IN ON OTHER PEOPLE'S CONVERSATIONS.
SHIBATA, CHILL.
YOU'RE THE ONE CORNERING HIM AND THEN ACTING LIKE YOU'RE NOT.
WHAT ARE YOU TRYING TO DO HERE, DOI?
OH, RIGHT. YOU'RE HIS GIRLFRIEND, RIGHT, SHIBATA? SUCH A HARD WORKER.
DOI!
GRAB

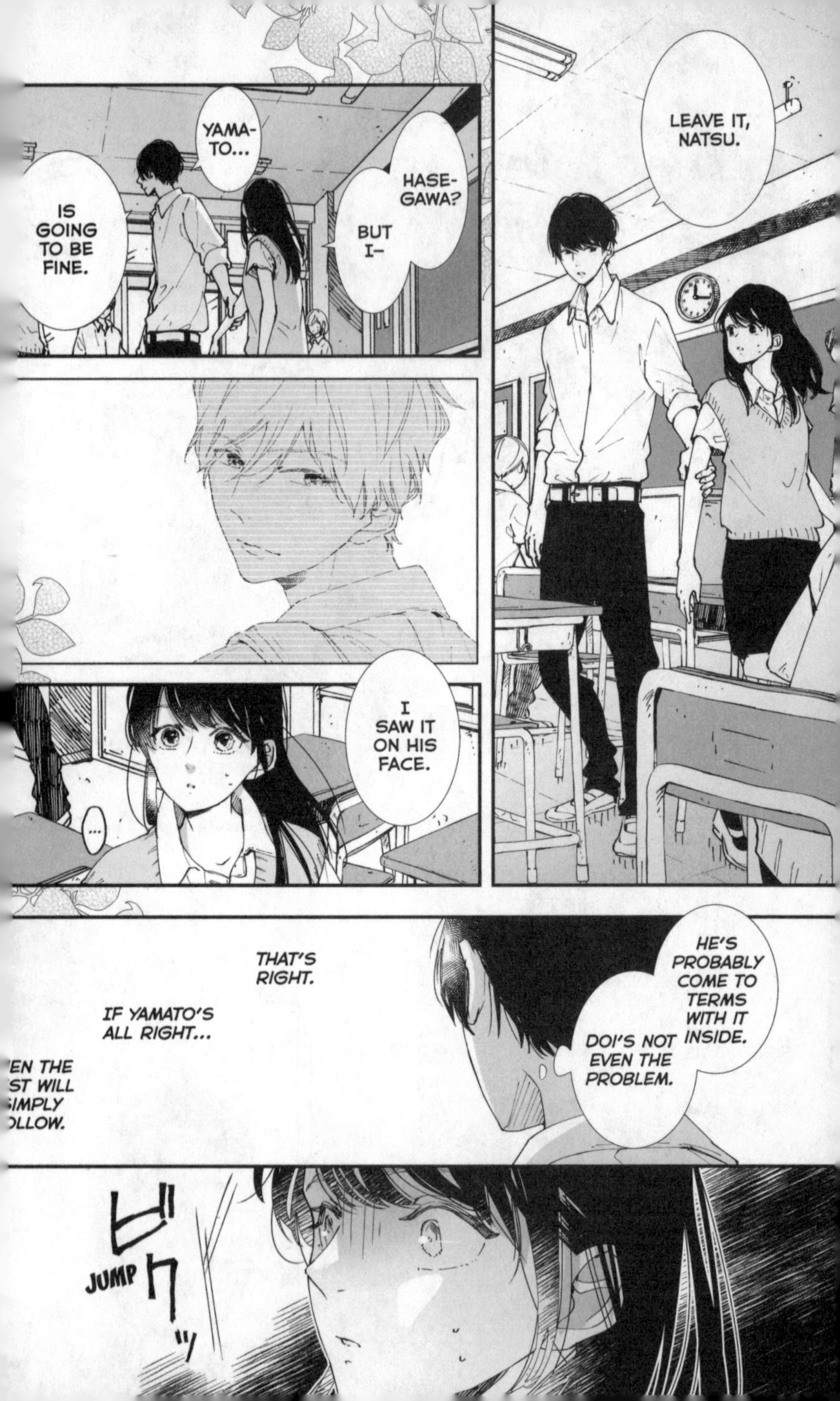
LEAVE IT, NATSU.
HASE-GAWA? BUT I—
YAMA-TO...
IS GOING TO BE FINE.
I SAW IT ON HIS FACE.
...
HE'S PROBABLY COME TO TERMS WITH IT INSIDE.
DOI'S NOT EVEN THE PROBLEM.
THAT'S RIGHT.
IF YAMATO'S ALL RIGHT...
EN THE ST WILL IMPLY OLLOW.
ビクッ
JUMP

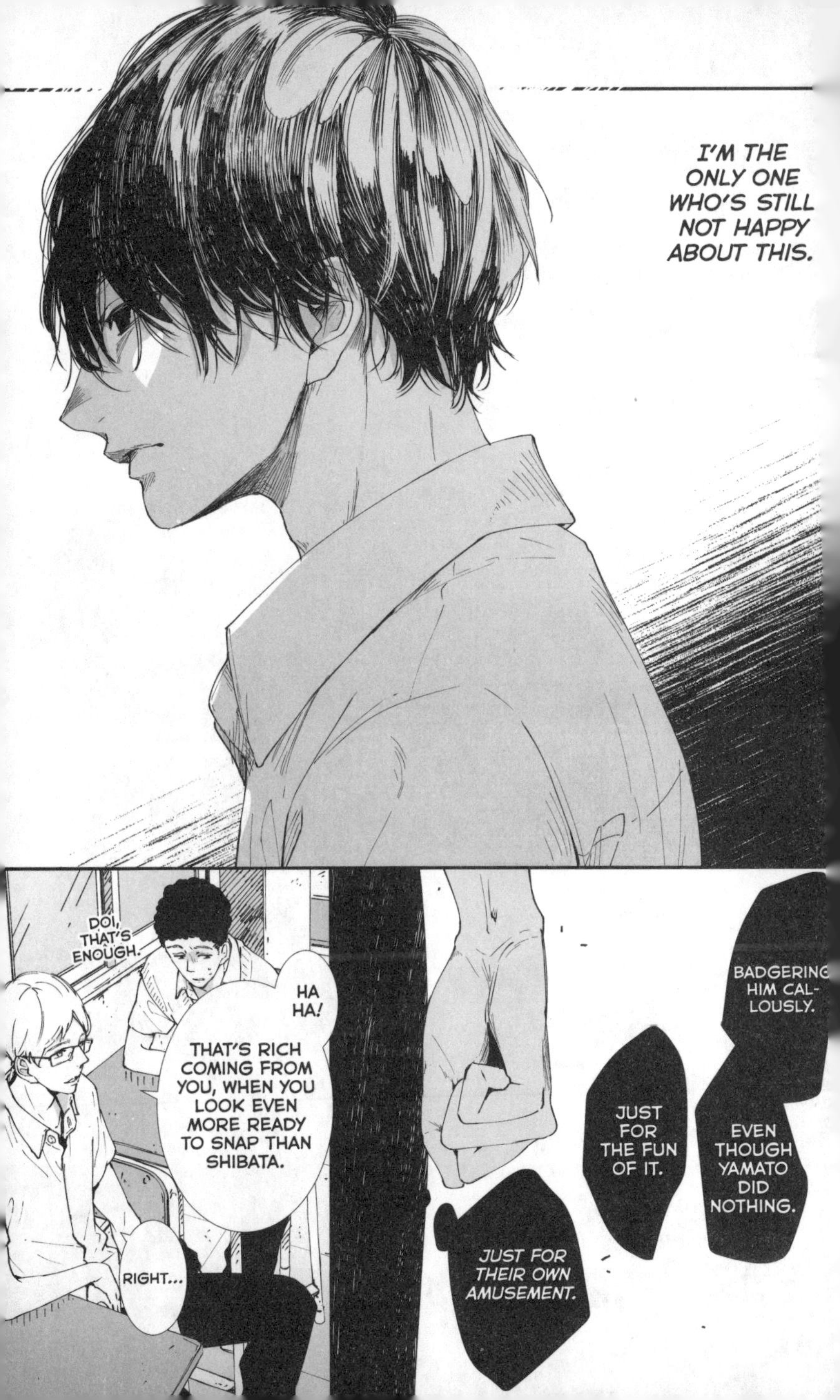
I'M THE ONLY ONE WHO'S STILL NOT HAPPY ABOUT THIS.
BADGERING HIM CAL-LOUSLY.
EVEN THOUGH YAMATO DID NOTHING.
JUST FOR THE FUN OF IT.
JUST FOR THEIR OWN AMUSEMENT.
DOI, THAT'S ENOUGH.
HA HA!
THAT'S RICH COMING FROM YOU, WHEN YOU LOOK EVEN MORE READY TO SNAP THAN SHIBATA.
RIGHT...

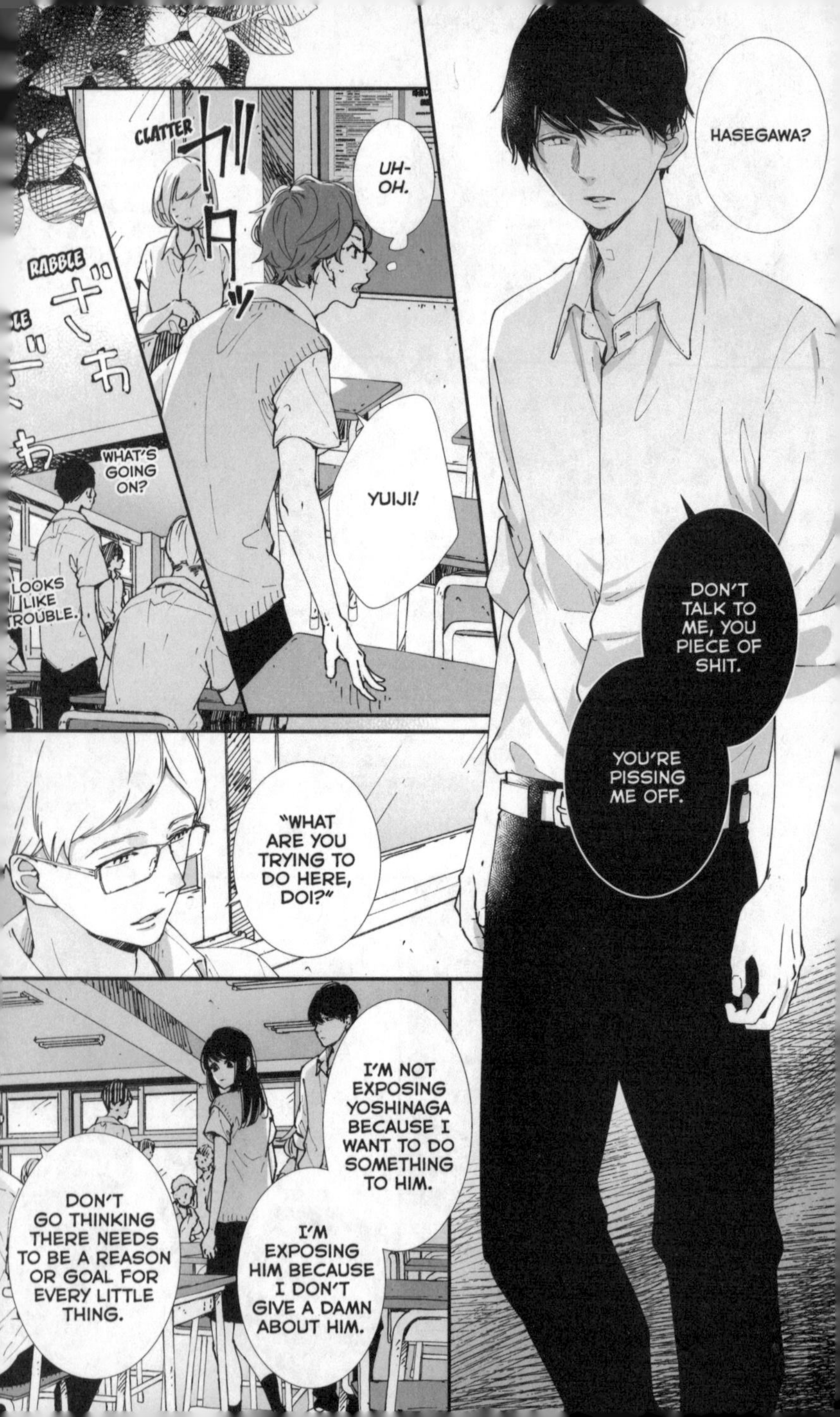
HASEGAWA?
DON'T TALK TO ME, YOU PIECE OF SHIT.
YOU'RE PISSING ME OFF.
CLATTER
UH-OH.
YUIJI!
RABBLE
WHAT'S GOING ON?
LOOKS LIKE TROUBLE.
"WHAT ARE YOU TRYING TO DO HERE, DOI?"
I'M NOT EXPOSING YOSHINAGA BECAUSE I WANT TO DO SOMETHING TO HIM.
I'M EXPOSING HIM BECAUSE I DON'T GIVE A DAMN ABOUT HIM.
DON'T GO THINKING THERE NEEDS TO BE A REASON OR GOAL FOR EVERY LITTLE THING.

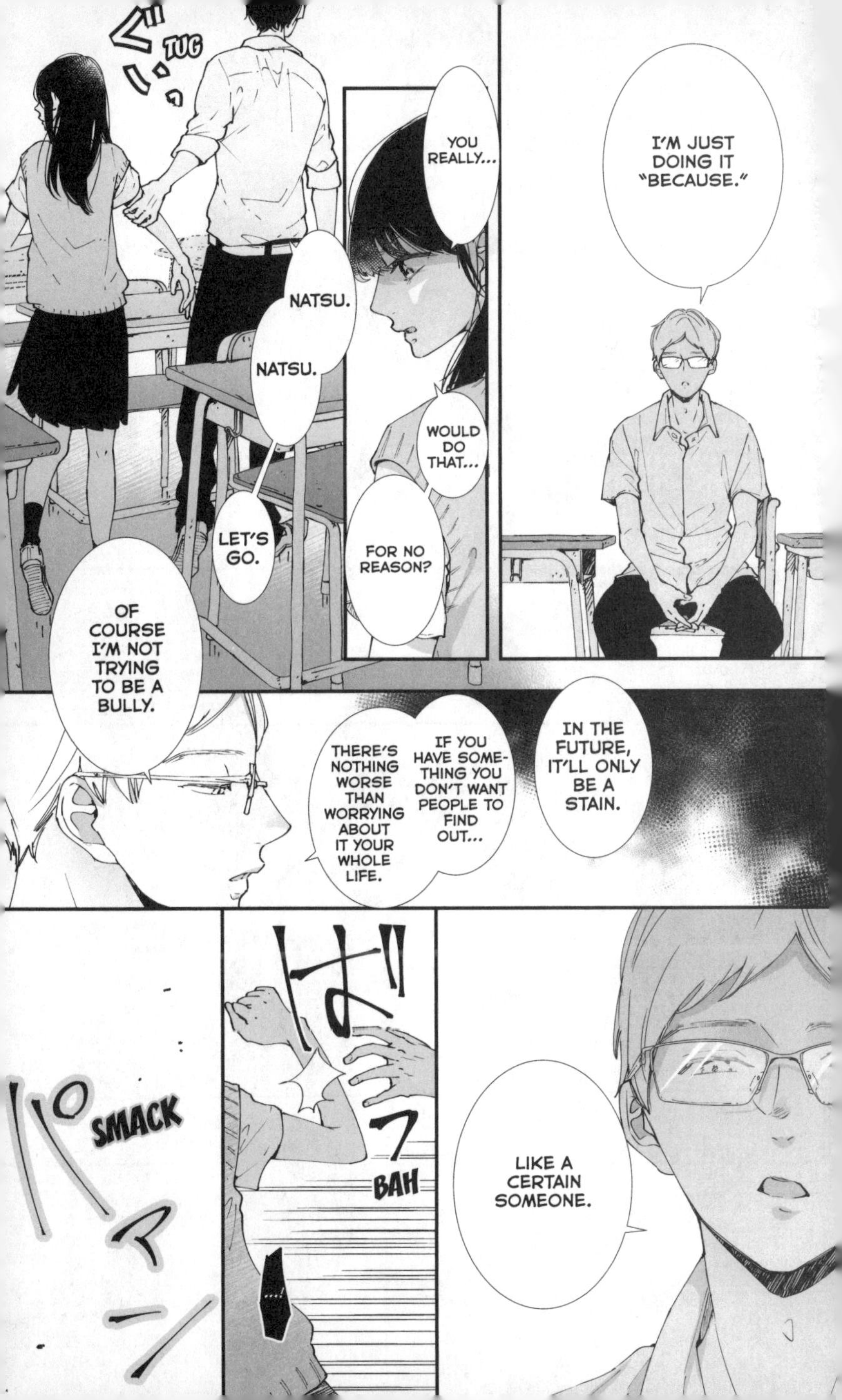
I'M JUST DOING IT "BECAUSE."
YOU REALLY...
WOULD DO THAT...
FOR NO REASON?
TUG
NATSU.
NATSU.
LET'S GO.
IN THE FUTURE, IT'LL ONLY BE A STAIN.
IF YOU HAVE SOME-THING YOU DON'T WANT PEOPLE TO FIND OUT...
THERE'S NOTHING WORSE THAN WORRYING ABOUT IT YOUR WHOLE LIFE.
OF COURSE I'M NOT TRYING TO BE A BULLY.
LIKE A CERTAIN SOMEONE.
BAH
SMACK

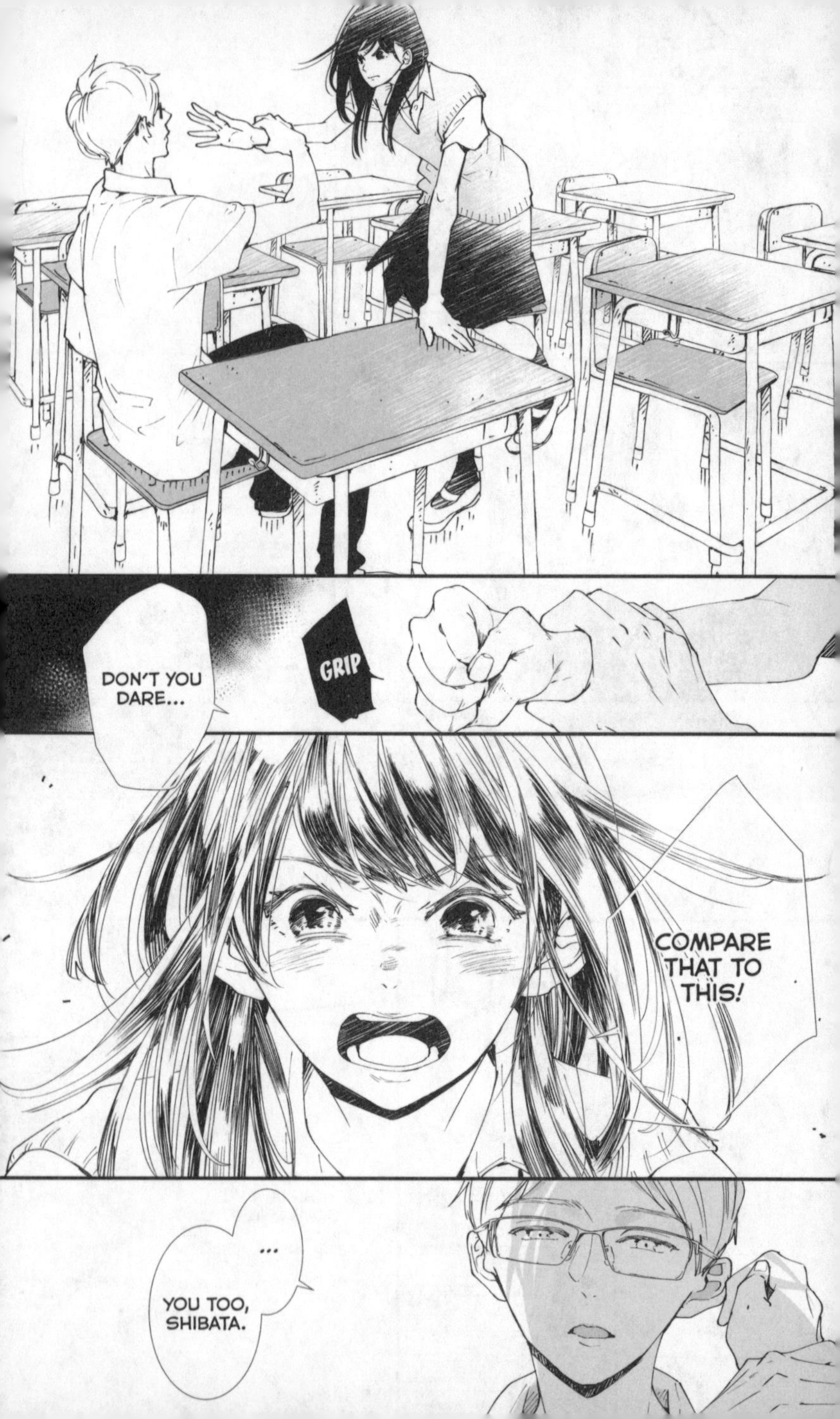
GRIP
DON'T YOU DARE...
COMPARE THAT TO THIS!
...
YOU TOO, SHIBATA.

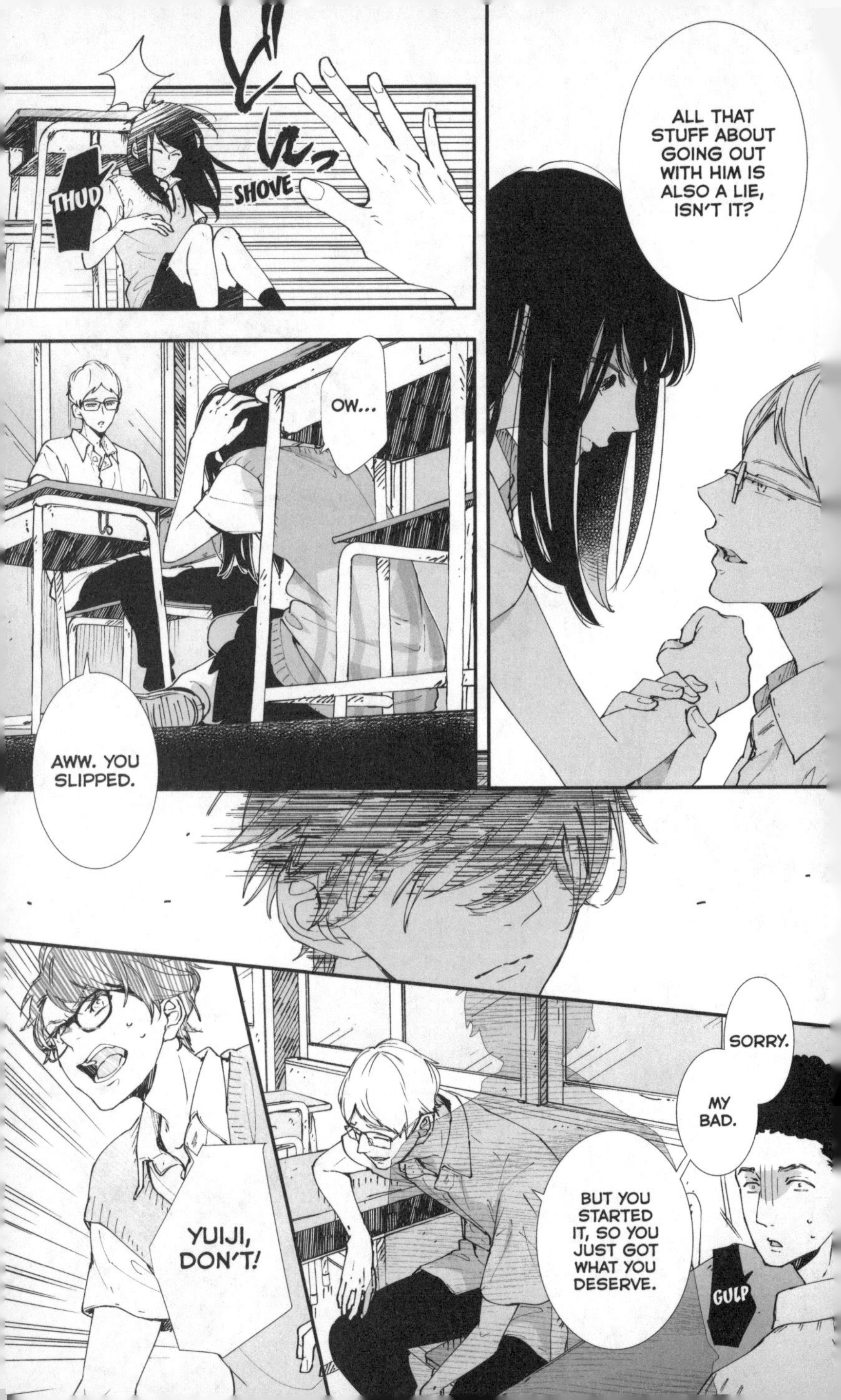
ALL THAT STUFF ABOUT GOING OUT WITH HIM IS ALSO A LIE, ISN'T IT?
SHOVE
THUD
OW...
AWW. YOU SLIPPED.
SORRY.
MY BAD.
BUT YOU STARTED IT, SO YOU JUST GOT WHAT YOU DESERVE.
GULP
YUIJI, DON'T!

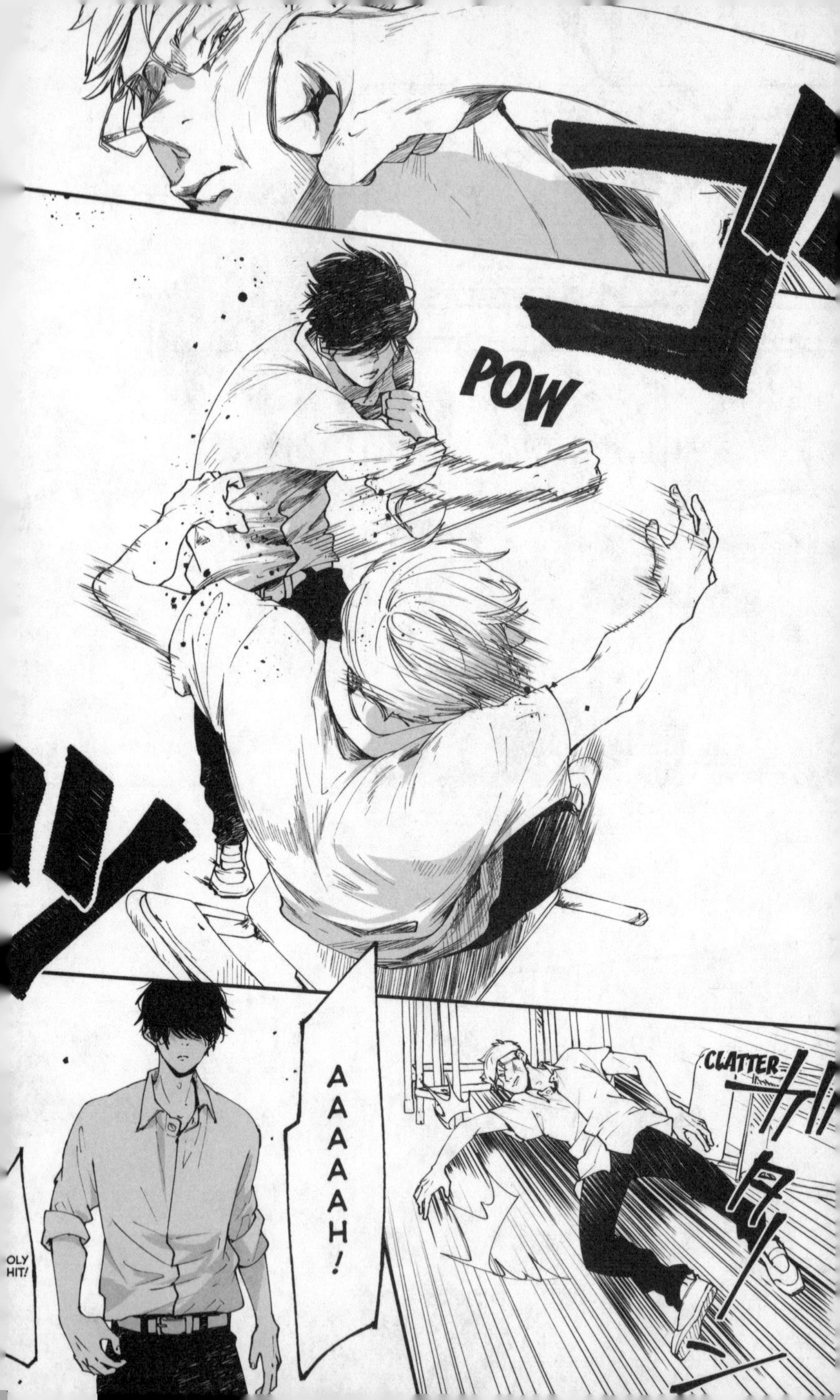

POW
CLATTER
AAAAAAH!
OLY
HIT!

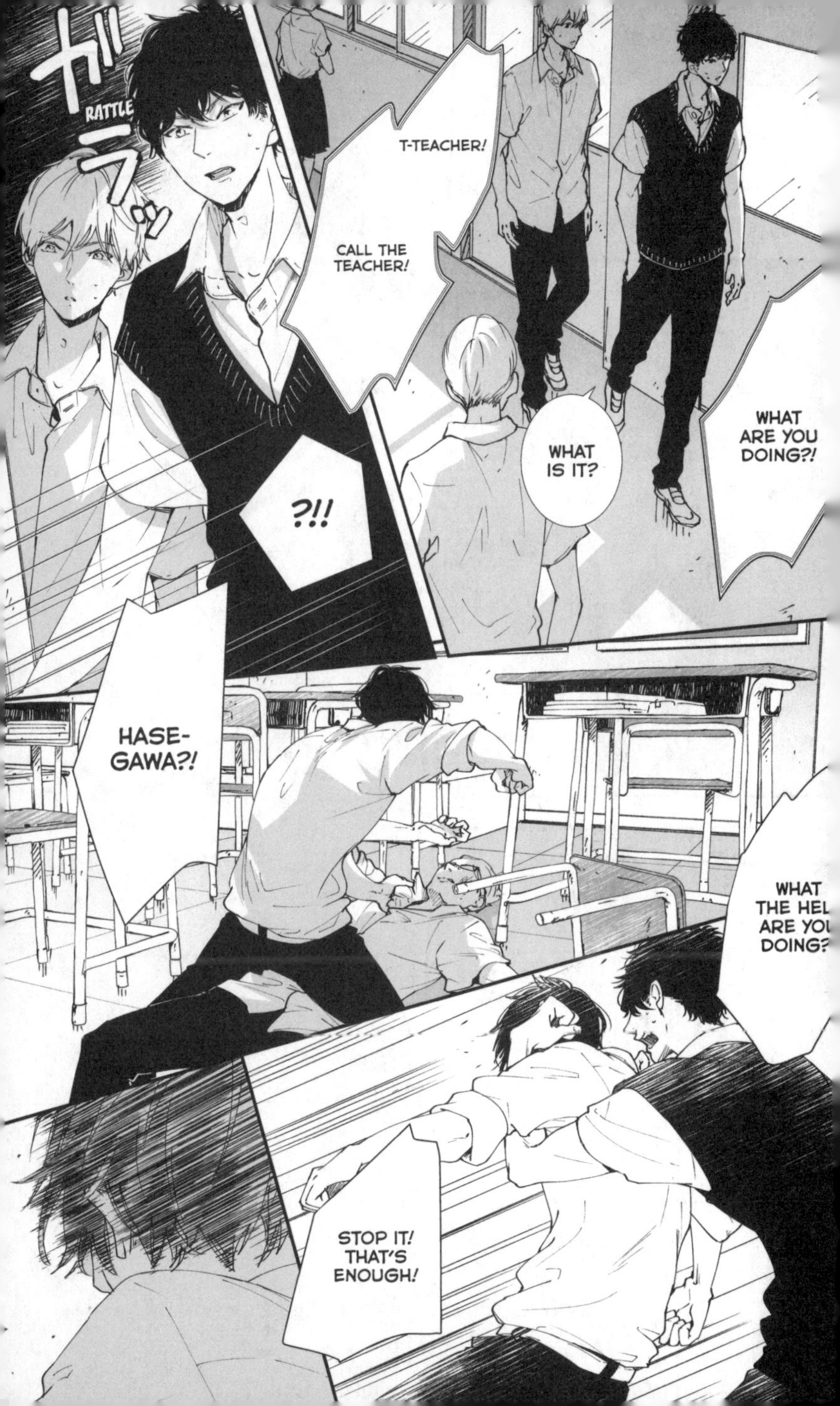
WHAT ARE YOU DOING?!
WHAT IS IT?
T-TEACHER!
CALL THE TEACHER!
ガラッ
RATTLE
?!!
HASE-GAWA?!
WHAT THE HEL ARE YOU DOING?
STOP IT! THAT'S ENOUGH!

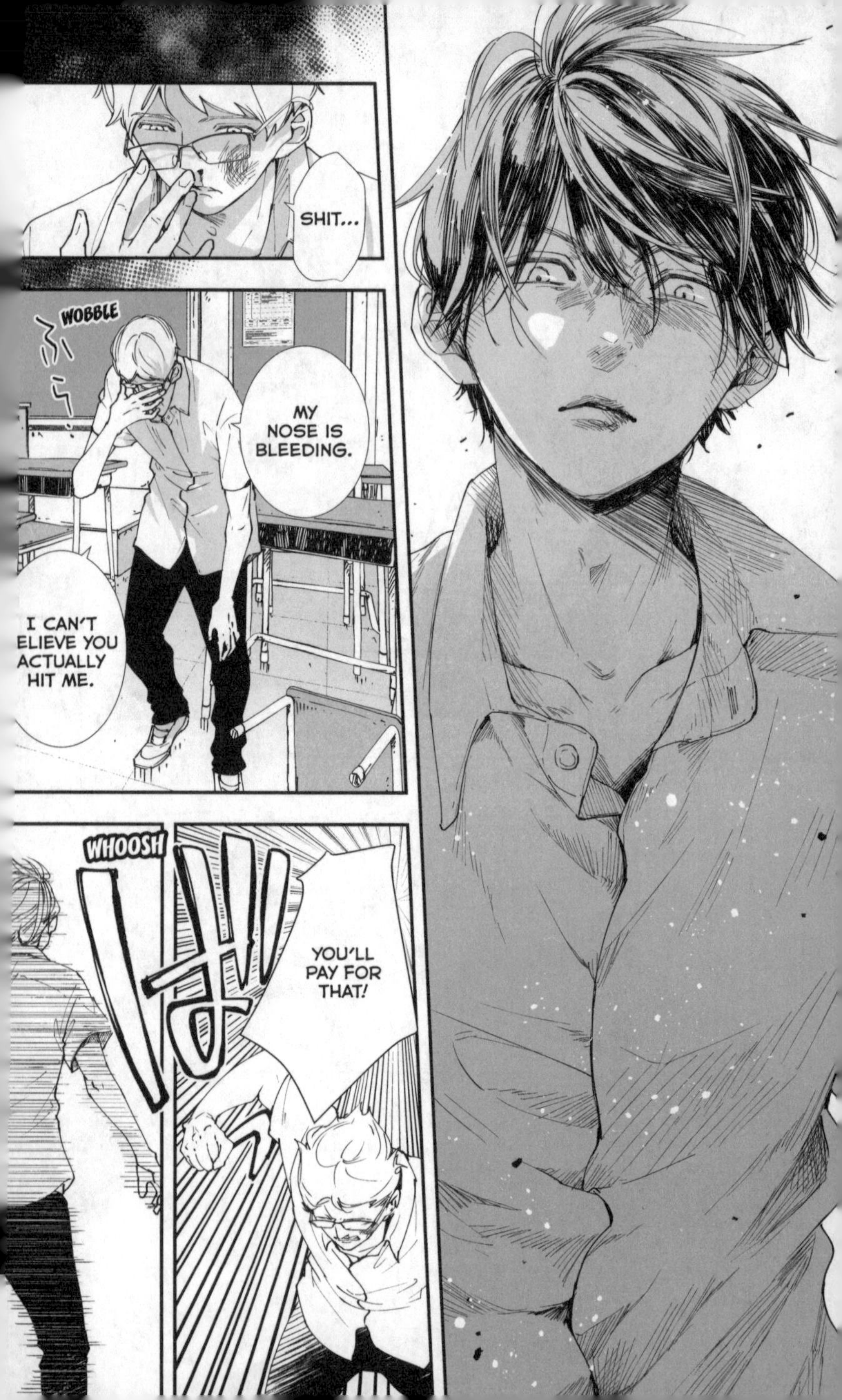
SHIT...
MY NOSE IS BLEEDING.
WOBBLE
I CAN'T ELIEVE YOU ACTUALLY HIT ME.
YOU'LL PAY FOR THAT!
WHOOSH

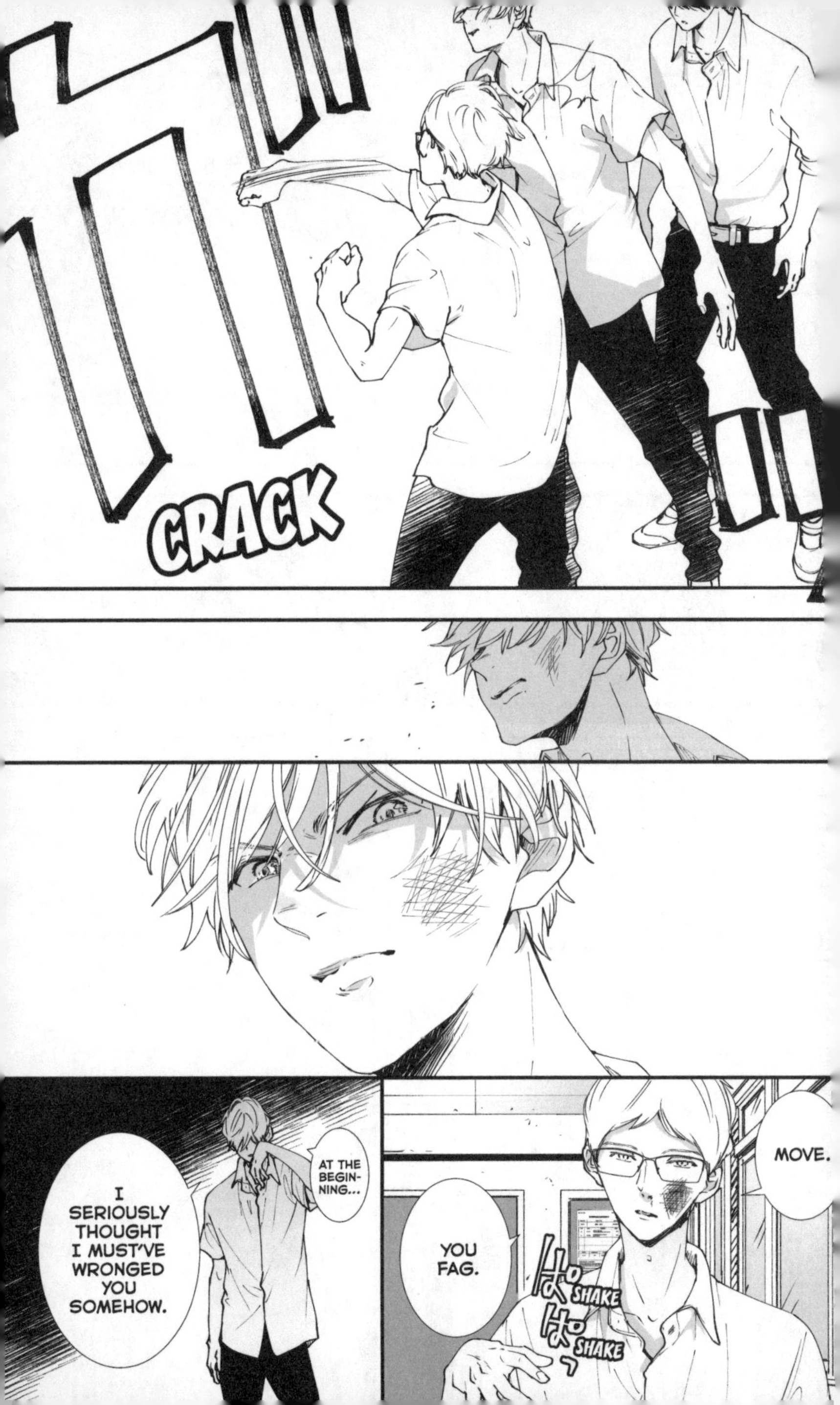
CRACK
MOVE.
YOU FAG.
SHAKE
SHAKE
AT THE BEGIN-NING...
I SERIOUSLY THOUGHT I MUST'VE WRONGED YOU SOMEHOW.

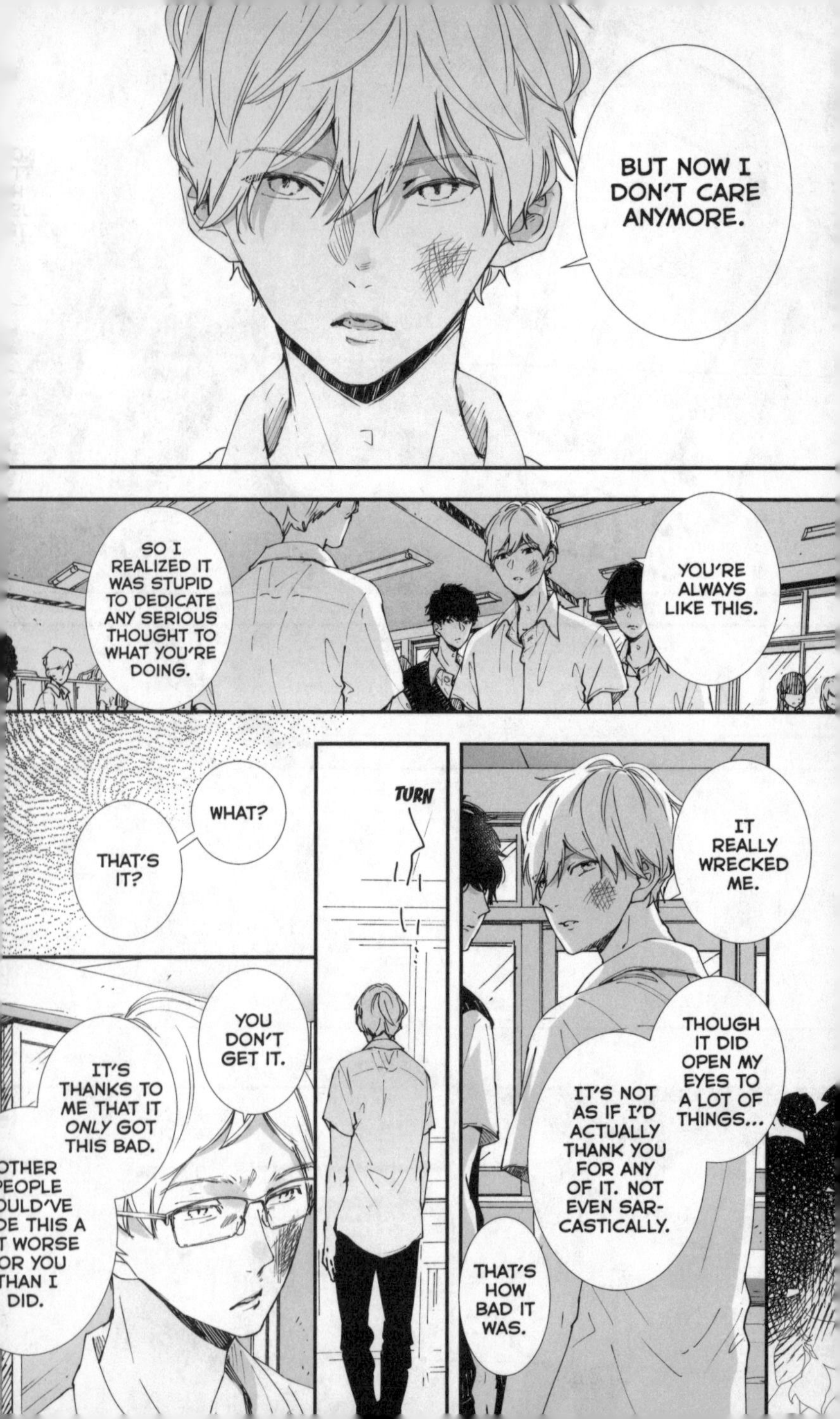
BUT NOW I DON'T CARE ANYMORE.
YOU'RE ALWAYS LIKE THIS.
SO I REALIZED IT WAS STUPID TO DEDICATE ANY SERIOUS THOUGHT TO WHAT YOU'RE DOING.
IT REALLY WRECKED ME.
THOUGH IT DID OPEN MY EYES TO A LOT OF THINGS...
IT'S NOT AS IF I'D ACTUALLY THANK YOU FOR ANY OF IT. NOT EVEN SAR-CASTICALLY.
THAT'S HOW BAD IT WAS.
TURN
WHAT?
THAT'S IT?
YOU DON'T GET IT.
IT'S THANKS TO ME THAT IT *ONLY* GOT THIS BAD.
OTHER EOPLE OULD'VE DE THIS A T WORSE OR YOU THAN I DID.

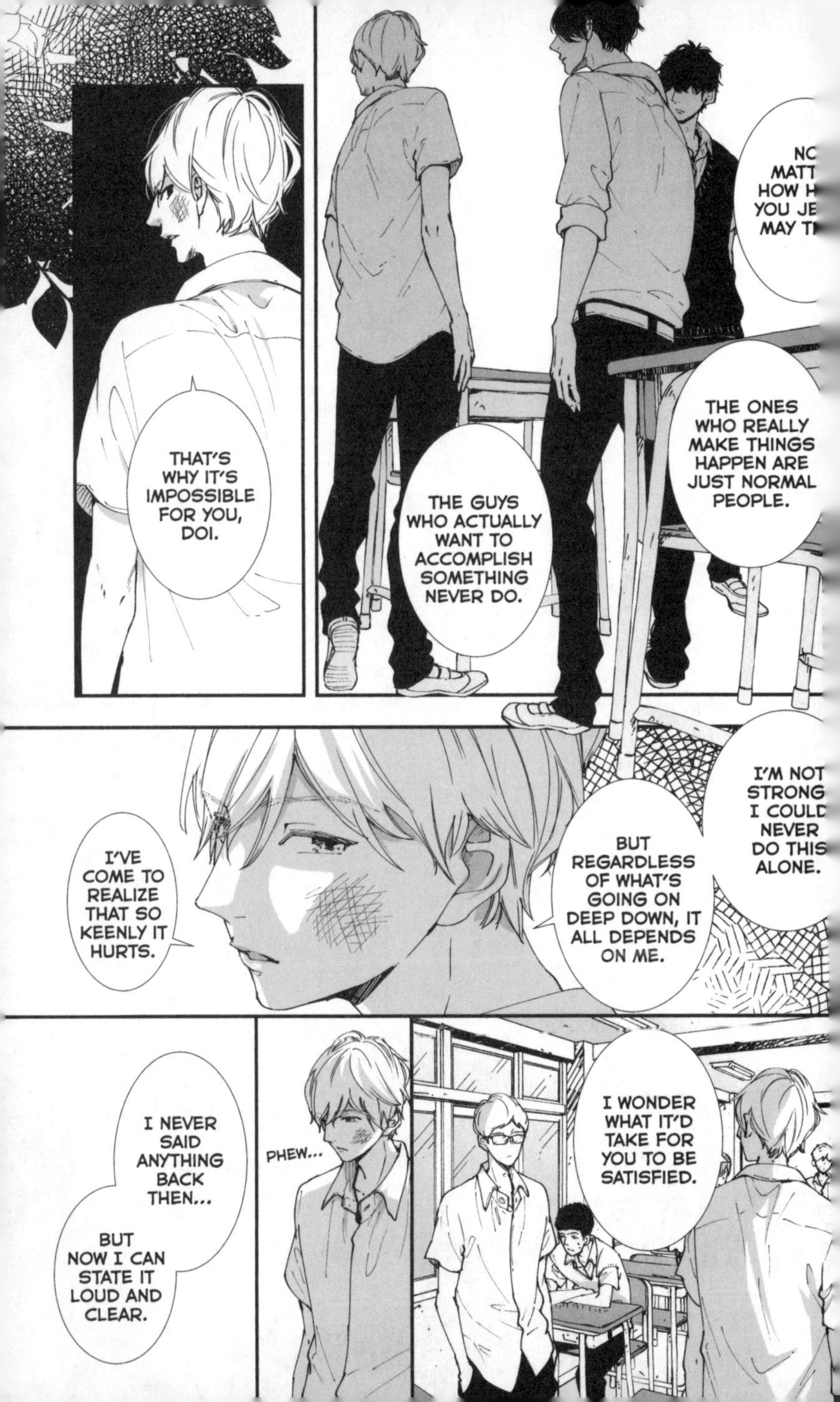
NC MATT HOW H YOU JE MAY T
THE ONES WHO REALLY MAKE THINGS HAPPEN ARE JUST NORMAL PEOPLE.
THE GUYS WHO ACTUALLY WANT TO ACCOMPLISH SOMETHING NEVER DO.
THAT'S WHY IT'S IMPOSSIBLE FOR YOU, DOI.
I'M NOT STRONG I COULD NEVER DO THIS ALONE.
BUT REGARDLESS OF WHAT'S GOING ON DEEP DOWN, IT ALL DEPENDS ON ME.
I'VE COME TO REALIZE THAT SO KEENLY IT HURTS.
I WONDER WHAT IT'D TAKE FOR YOU TO BE SATISFIED.
PHEW...
I NEVER SAID ANYTHING BACK THEN...
BUT NOW I CAN STATE IT LOUD AND CLEAR.

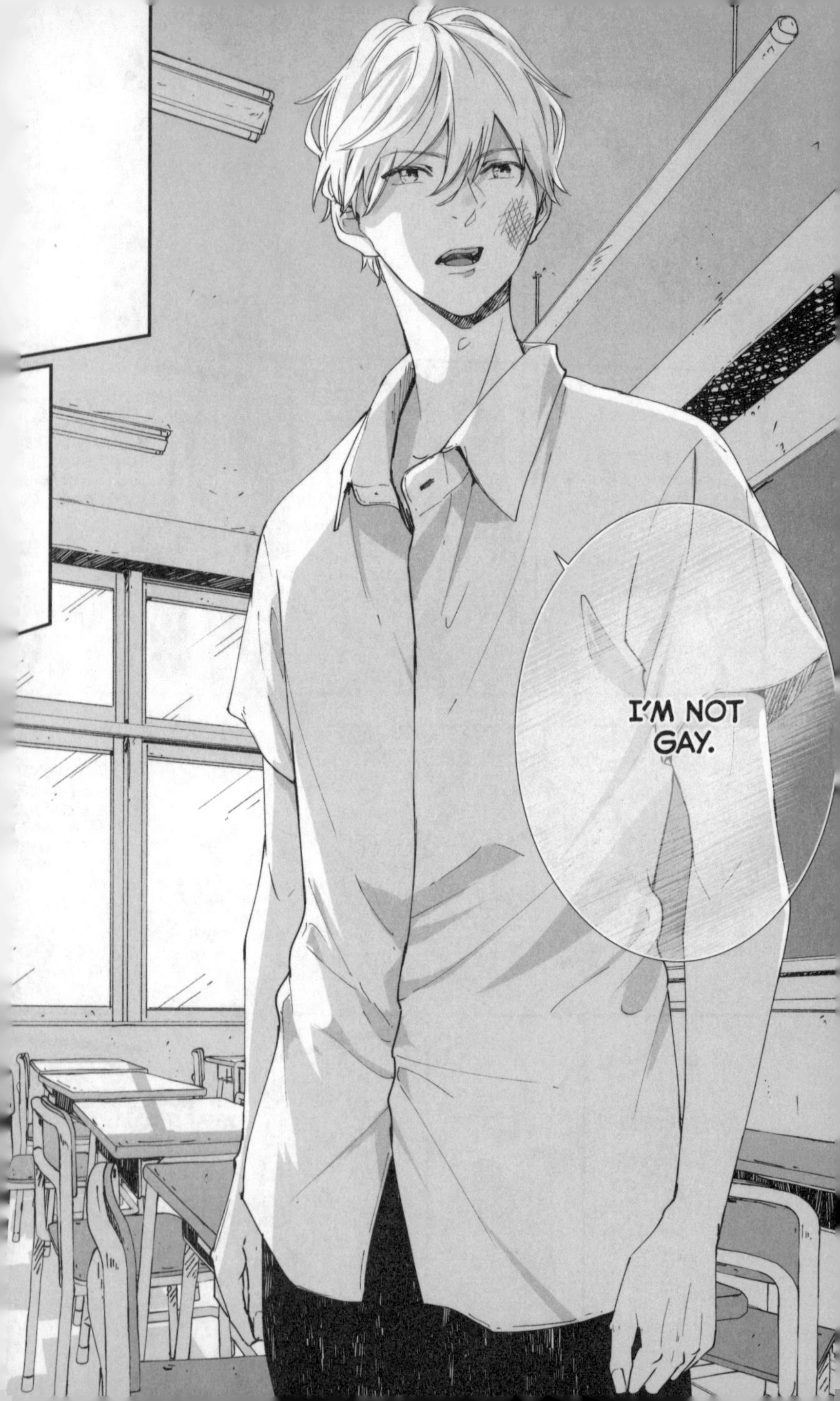
I'M NOT GAY.

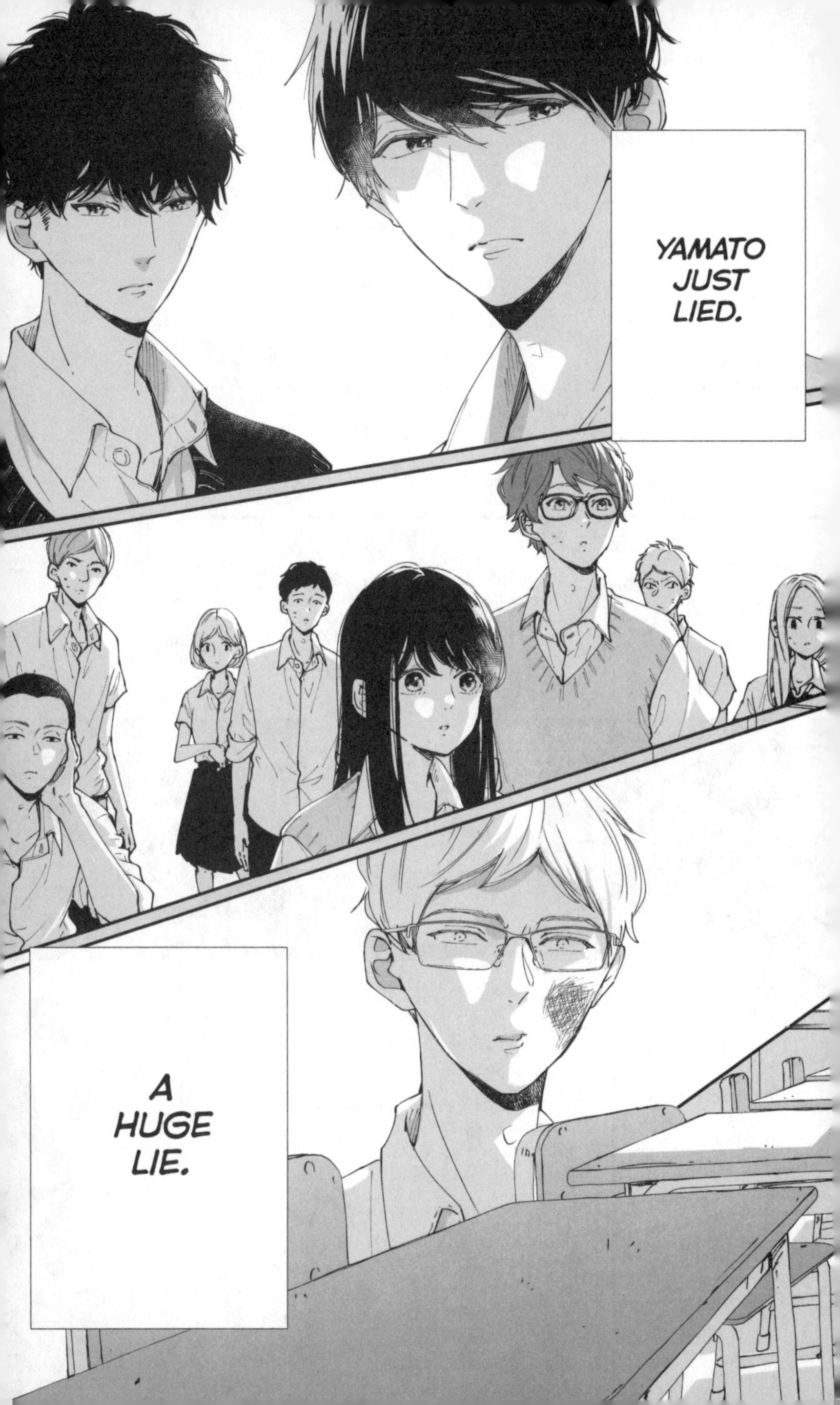
YAMATO JUST LIED.
A HUGE LIE.

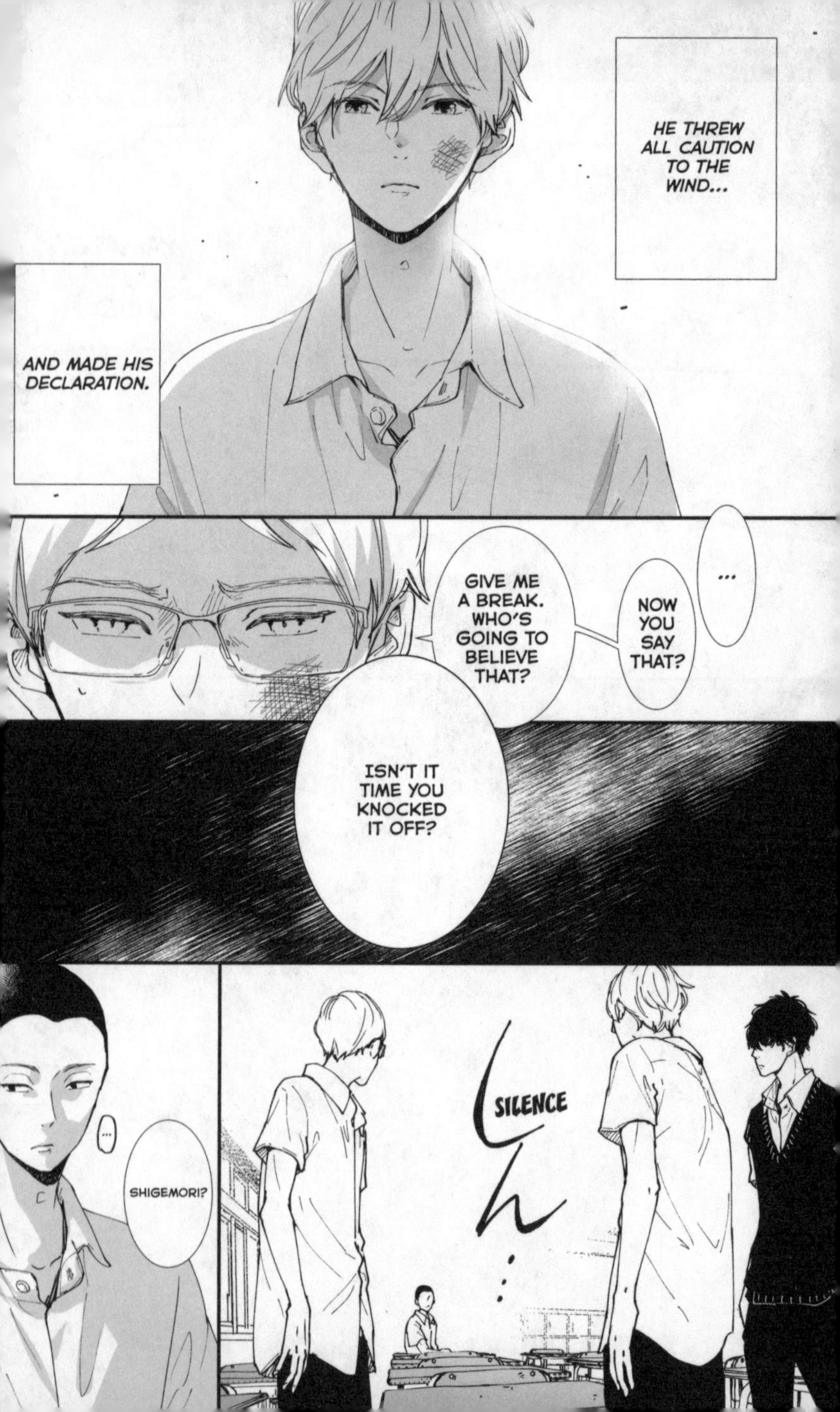
HE THREW ALL CAUTION TO THE WIND...
AND MADE HIS DECLARATION.
...
NOW YOU SAY THAT?
GIVE ME A BREAK. WHO'S GOING TO BELIEVE THAT?
ISN'T IT TIME YOU KNOCKED IT OFF?
SILENCE
SHIGEMORI?
...

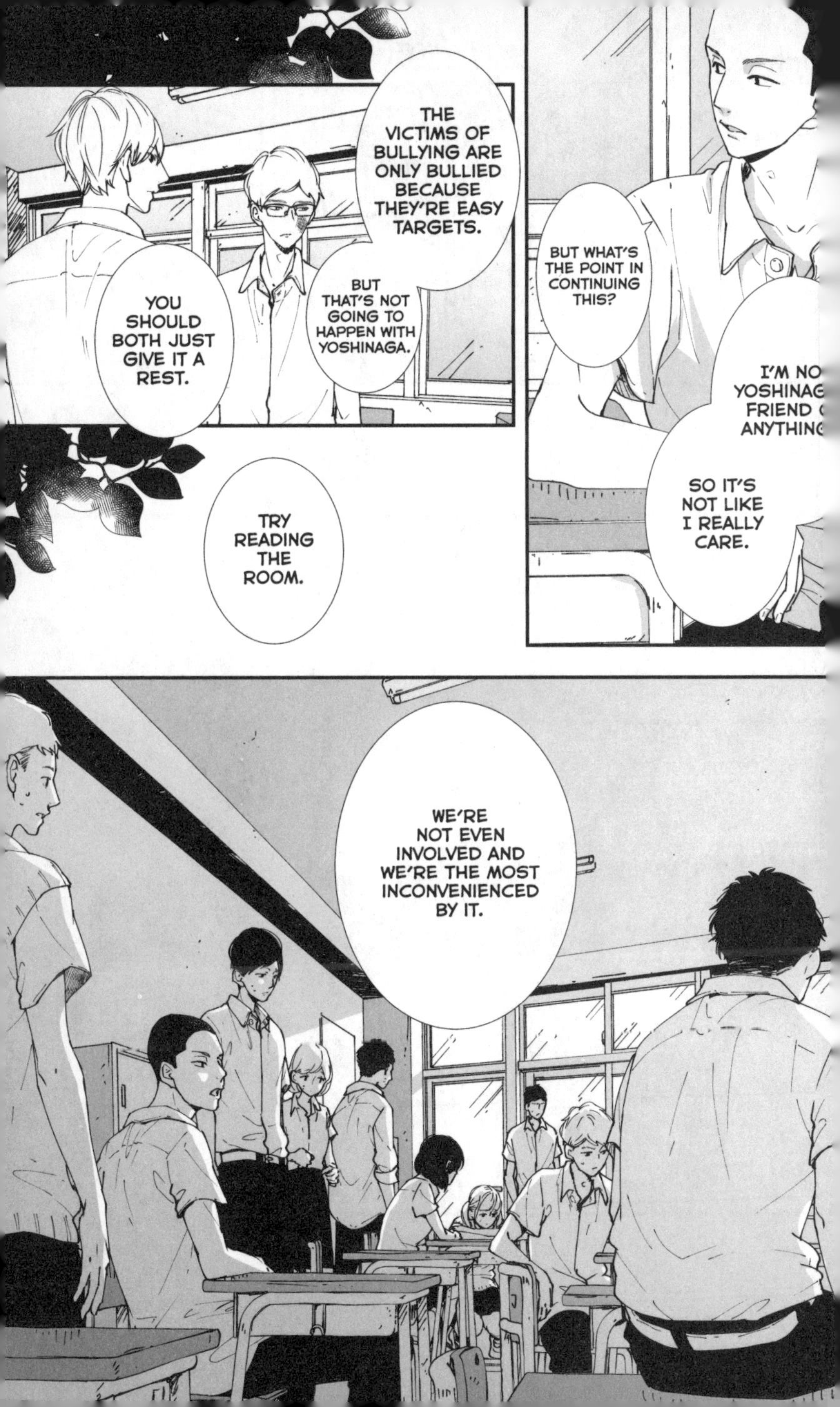
BUT WHAT'S THE POINT IN CONTINUING THIS?
I'M NO YOSHINAG FRIEND ANYTHING
SO IT'S NOT LIKE I REALLY CARE.
THE VICTIMS OF BULLYING ARE ONLY BULLIED BECAUSE THEY'RE EASY TARGETS.
BUT THAT'S NOT GOING TO HAPPEN WITH YOSHINAGA.
YOU SHOULD BOTH JUST GIVE IT A REST.
TRY READING THE ROOM.
WE'RE NOT EVEN INVOLVED AND WE'RE THE MOST INCONVENIENCED BY IT.

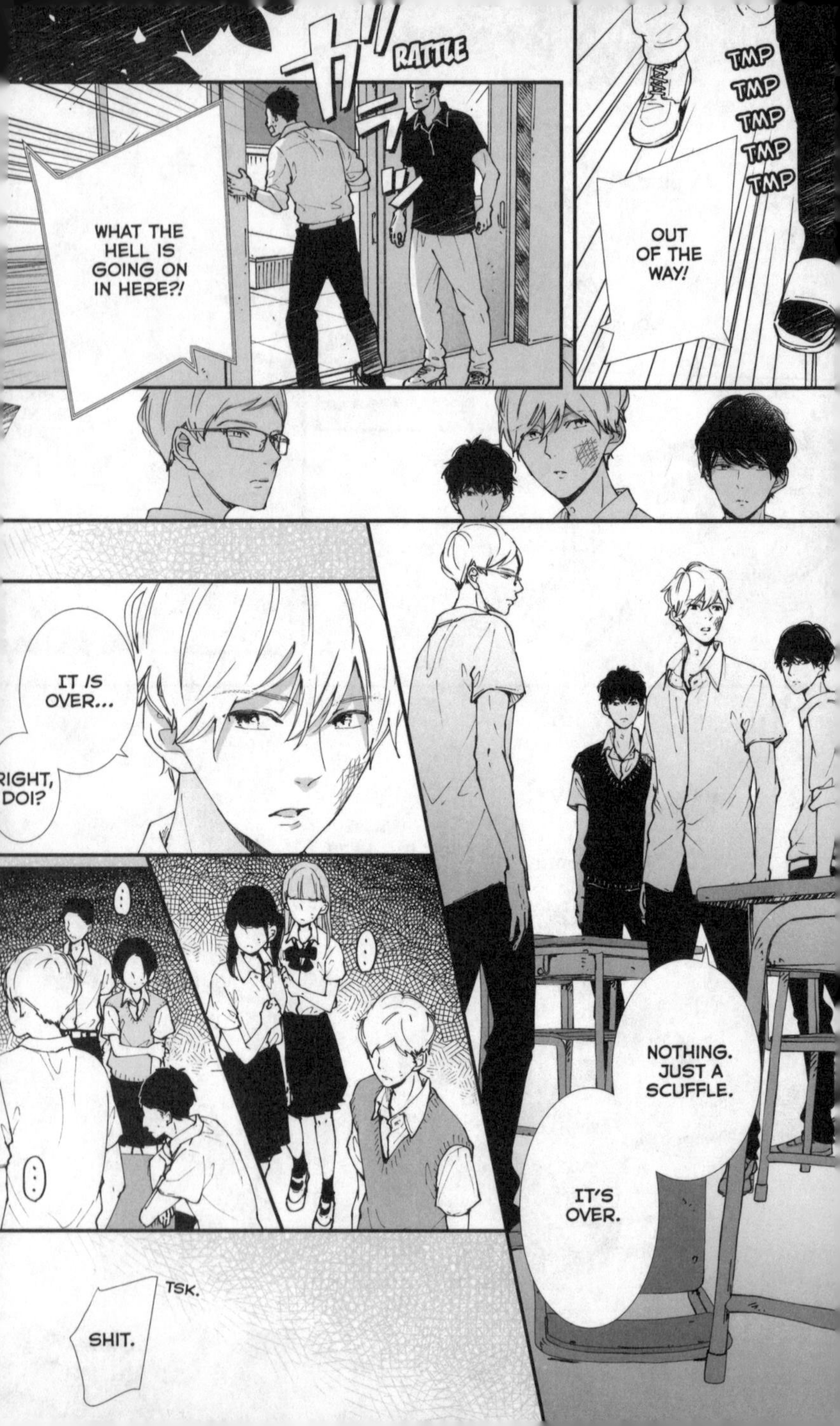
TMP TMP TMP TMP TMP
OUT OF THE WAY!
RATTLE
WHAT THE HELL IS GOING ON IN HERE?!
NOTHING. JUST A SCUFFLE.
IT'S OVER.
IT IS OVER...
RIGHT, DOI?
...
...
...
TSK.
SHIT.

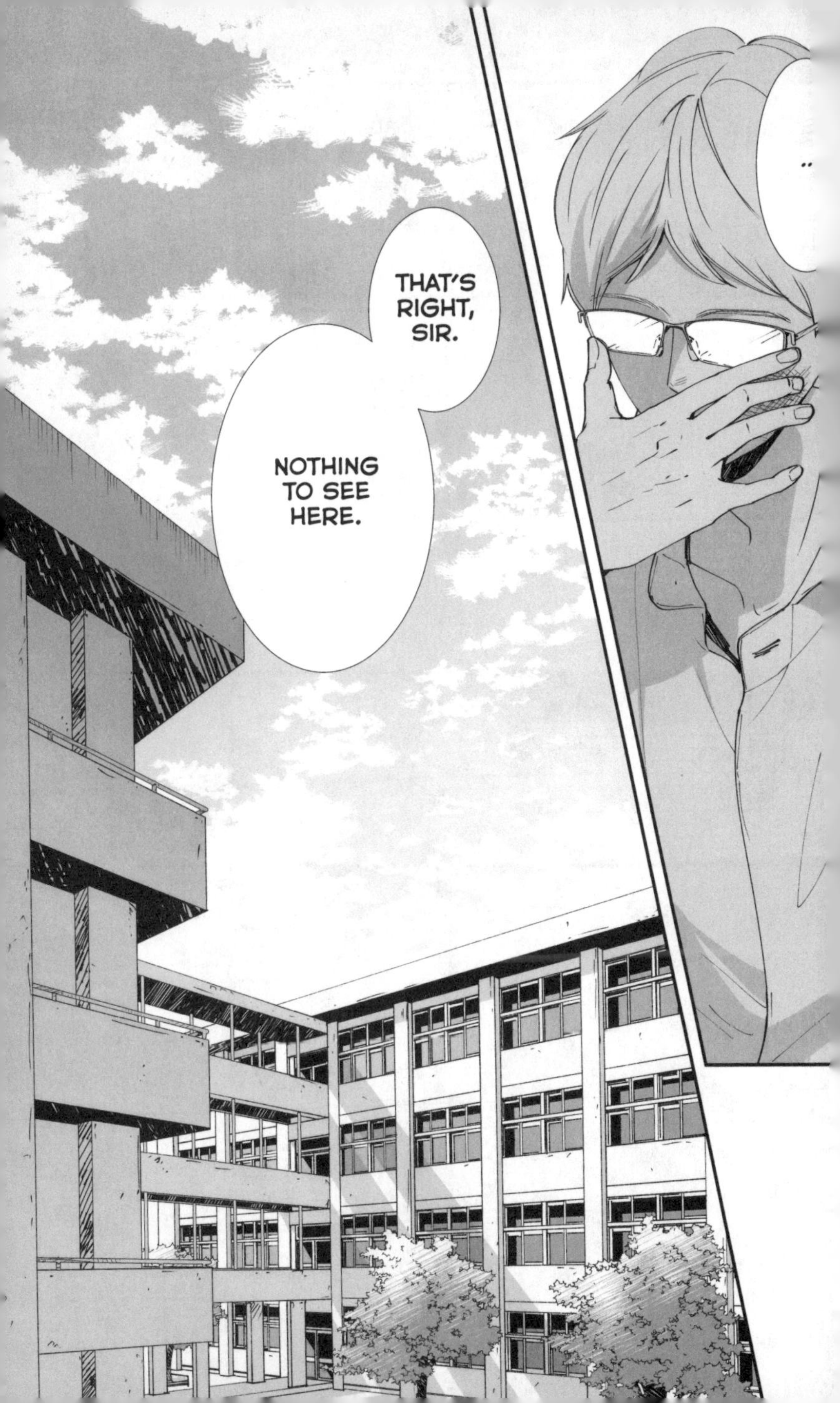
..
THAT'S RIGHT, SIR.
NOTHING TO SEE HERE.

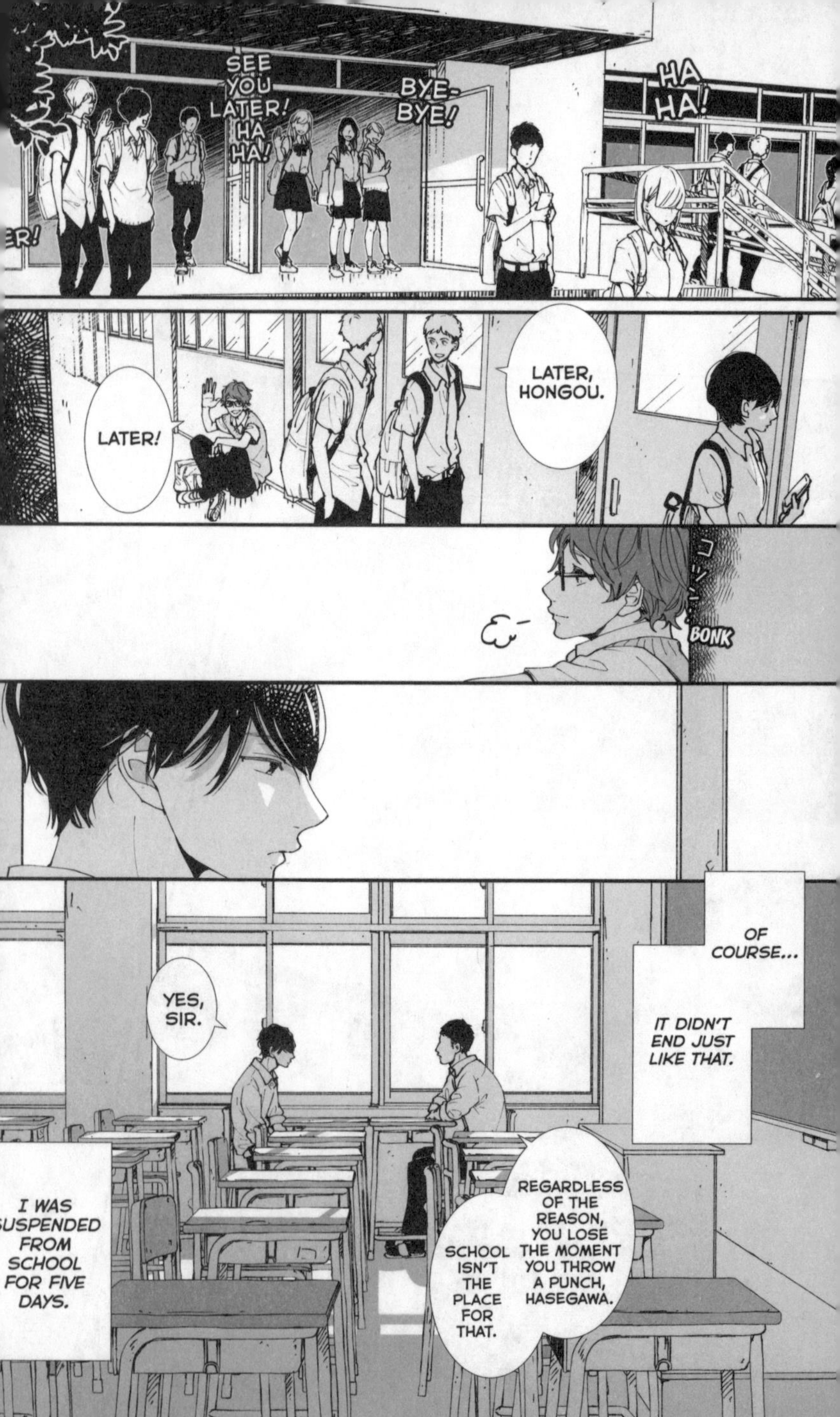
HA HA!
BYE-BYE!
SEE YOU LATER! HA HA!
ER!
LATER, HONGOU.
LATER!
BONK
OF COURSE...
IT DIDN'T END JUST LIKE THAT.
YES, SIR.
REGARDLESS OF THE REASON, YOU LOSE THE MOMENT YOU THROW A PUNCH, HASEGAWA.
SCHOOL ISN'T THE PLACE FOR THAT.
I WAS SUSPENDED FROM SCHOOL FOR FIVE DAYS.

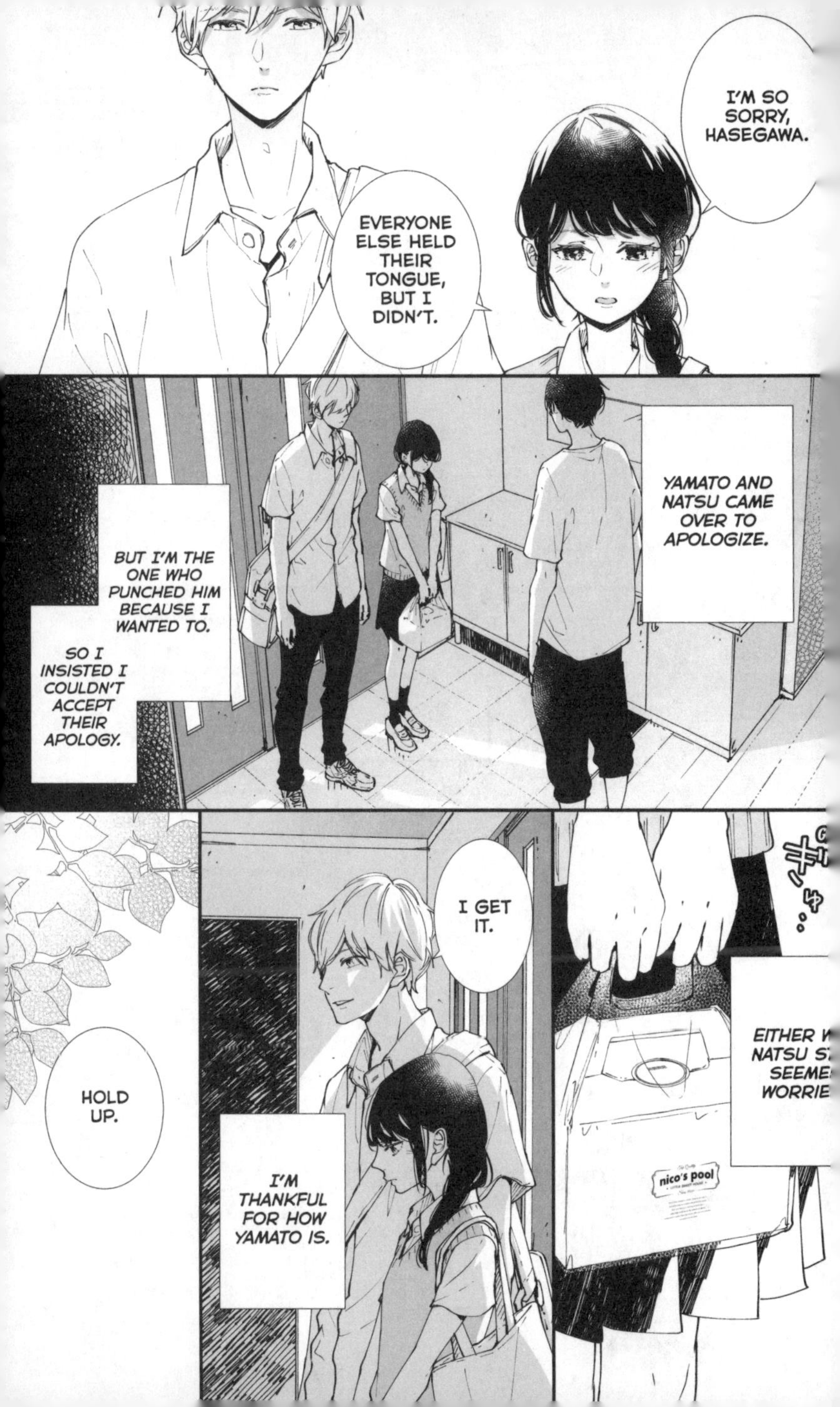
I'M SO SORRY, HASEGAWA.
EVERYONE ELSE HELD THEIR TONGUE, BUT I DIDN'T.
YAMATO AND NATSU CAME OVER TO APOLOGIZE.
BUT I'M THE ONE WHO PUNCHED HIM BECAUSE I WANTED TO.
SO I INSISTED I COULDN'T ACCEPT THEIR APOLOGY.
EITHER W NATSU S SEEME WORRIE
nico's pool
I GET IT.
I'M THANKFUL FOR HOW YAMATO IS.
HOLD UP.

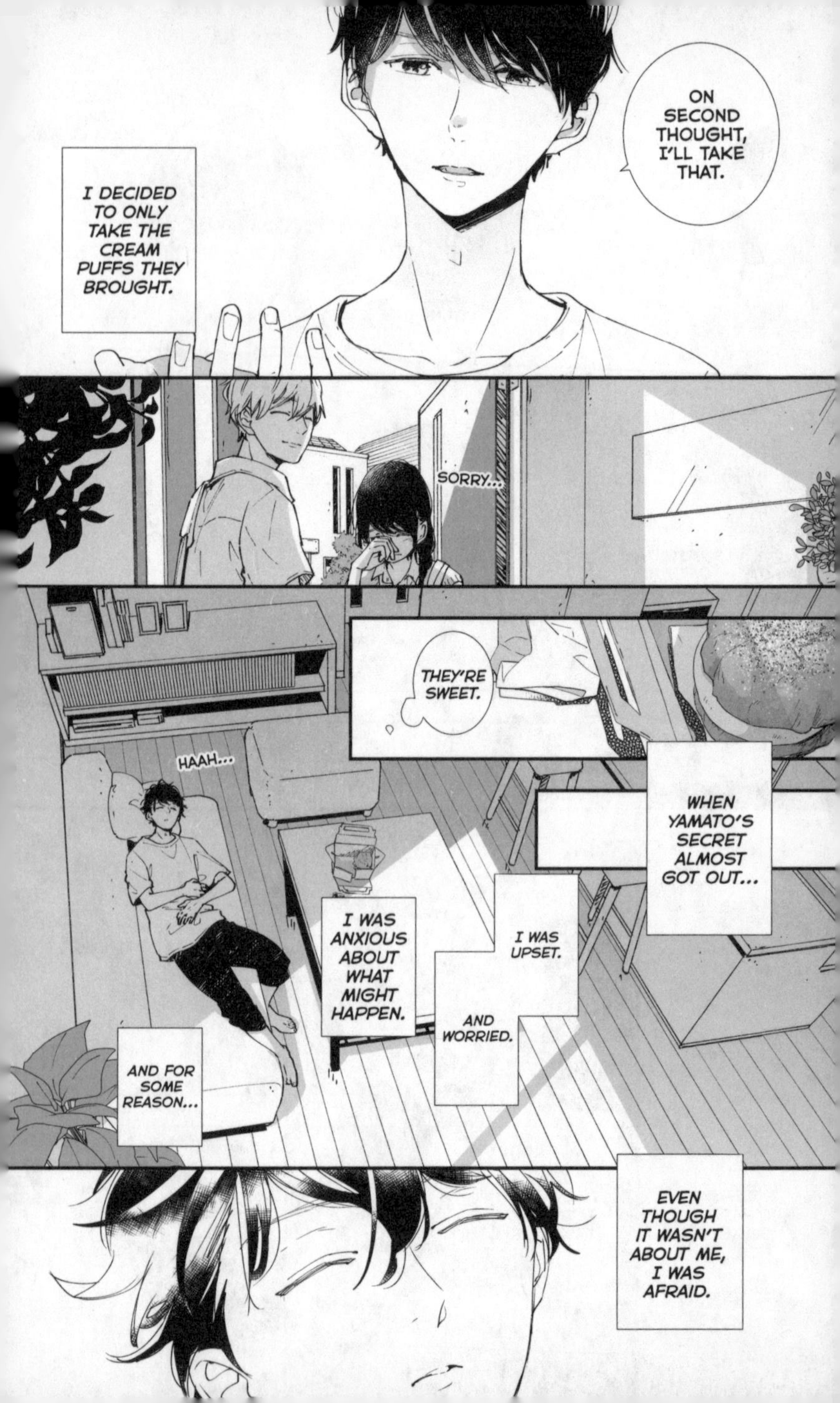
ON SECOND THOUGHT, I'LL TAKE THAT.
I DECIDED TO ONLY TAKE THE CREAM PUFFS THEY BROUGHT.
SORRY...
THEY'RE SWEET.
WHEN YAMATO'S SECRET ALMOST GOT OUT...
I WAS UPSET.
AND WORRIED.
I WAS ANXIOUS ABOUT WHAT MIGHT HAPPEN.
HAAH...
AND FOR SOME REASON...
EVEN THOUGH IT WASN'T ABOUT ME, I WAS AFRAID.

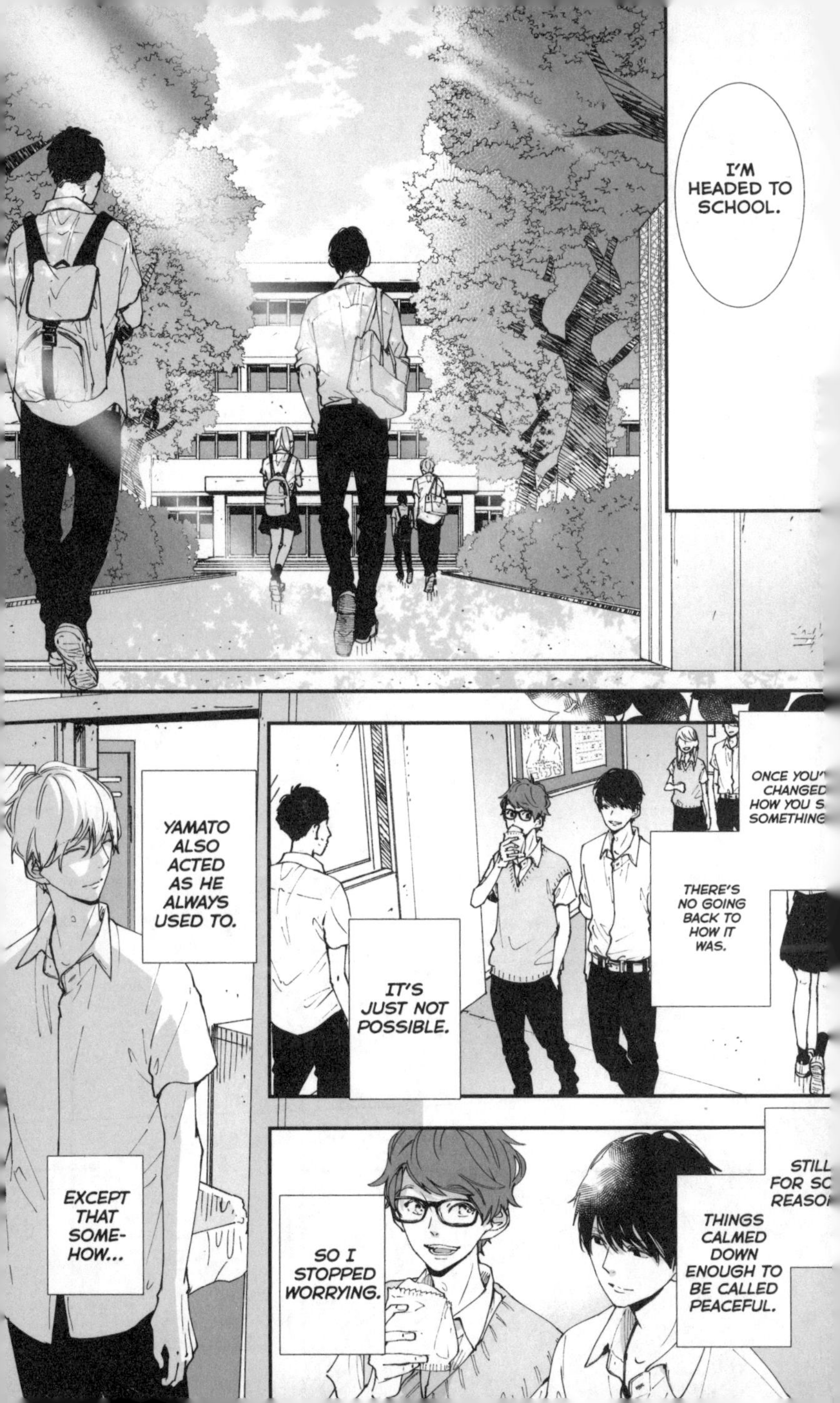
I'M HEADED TO SCHOOL.
ONCE YOU' CHANGED HOW YOU S SOMETHING
THERE'S NO GOING BACK TO HOW IT WAS.
IT'S JUST NOT POSSIBLE.
STILL FOR SO REASO
THINGS CALMED DOWN ENOUGH TO BE CALLED PEACEFUL.
SO I STOPPED WORRYING.
YAMATO ALSO ACTED AS HE ALWAYS USED TO.
EXCEPT THAT SOME-HOW...

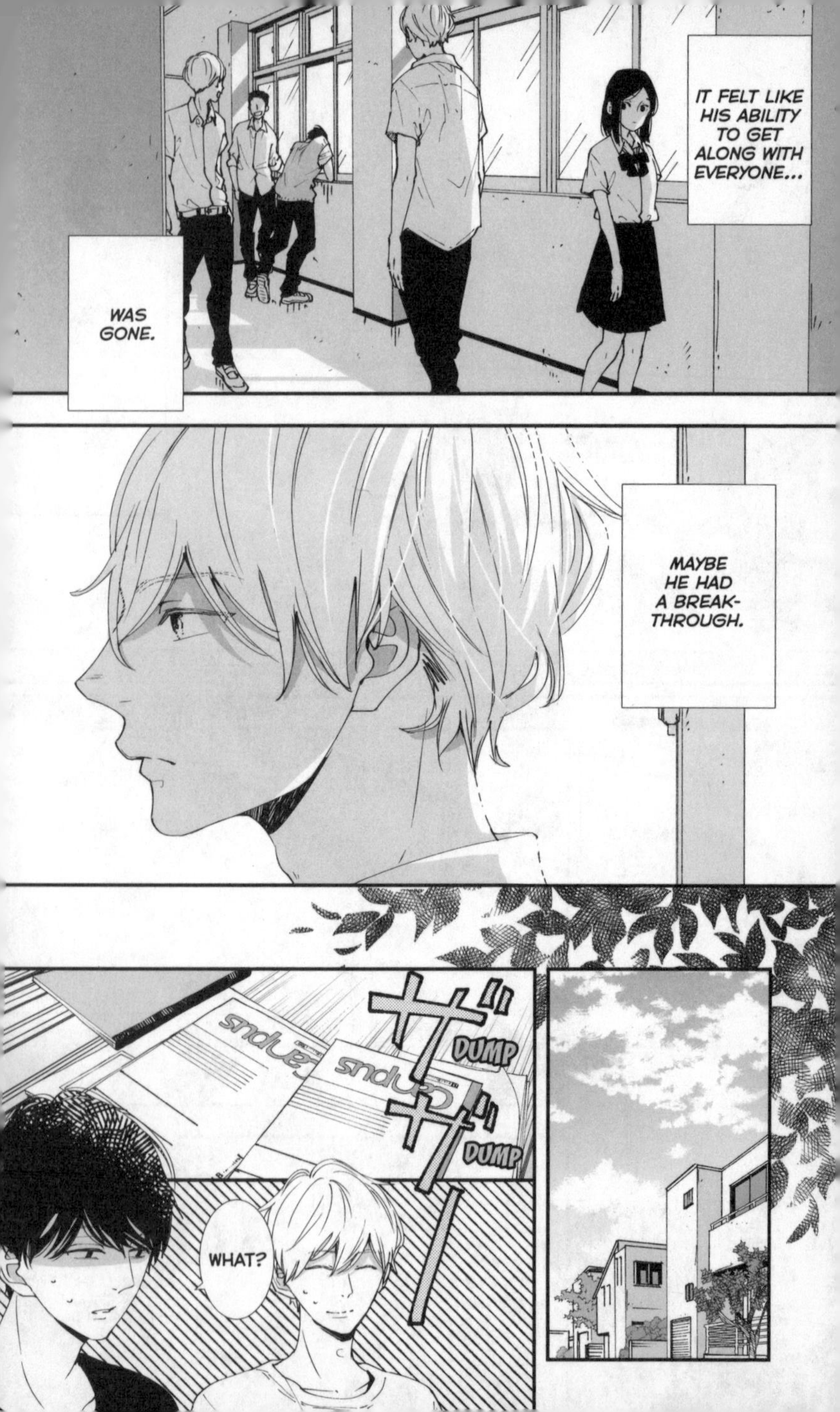
IT FELT LIKE HIS ABILITY TO GET ALONG WITH EVERYONE...
WAS GONE.
MAYBE HE HAD A BREAK-THROUGH.
DUMP
DUMP
WHAT?

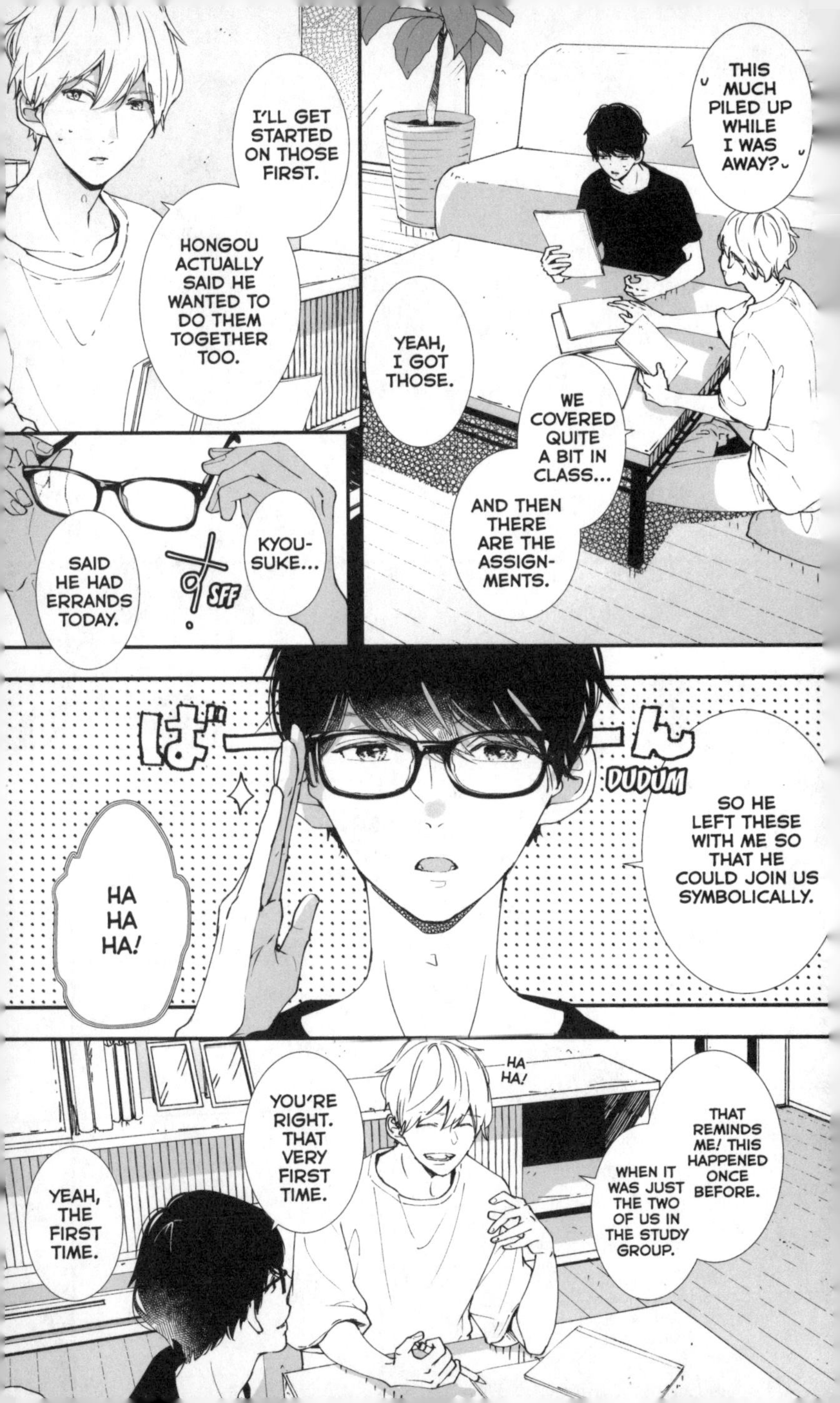
THIS MUCH PILED UP WHILE I WAS AWAY?
YEAH, I GOT THOSE.
WE COVERED QUITE A BIT IN CLASS...
AND THEN THERE ARE THE ASSIGNMENTS.
I'LL GET STARTED ON THOSE FIRST.
HONGOU ACTUALLY SAID HE WANTED TO DO THEM TOGETHER TOO.
KYOU-SUKE...
SFF
SAID HE HAD ERRANDS TODAY.
ばーーん
DUDUM
SO HE LEFT THESE WITH ME SO THAT HE COULD JOIN US SYMBOLICALLY.
HA HA HA!
HA HA!
THAT REMINDS ME! THIS HAPPENED ONCE BEFORE.
WHEN IT WAS JUST THE TWO OF US IN THE STUDY GROUP.
YOU'RE RIGHT. THAT VERY FIRST TIME.
YEAH, THE FIRST TIME.

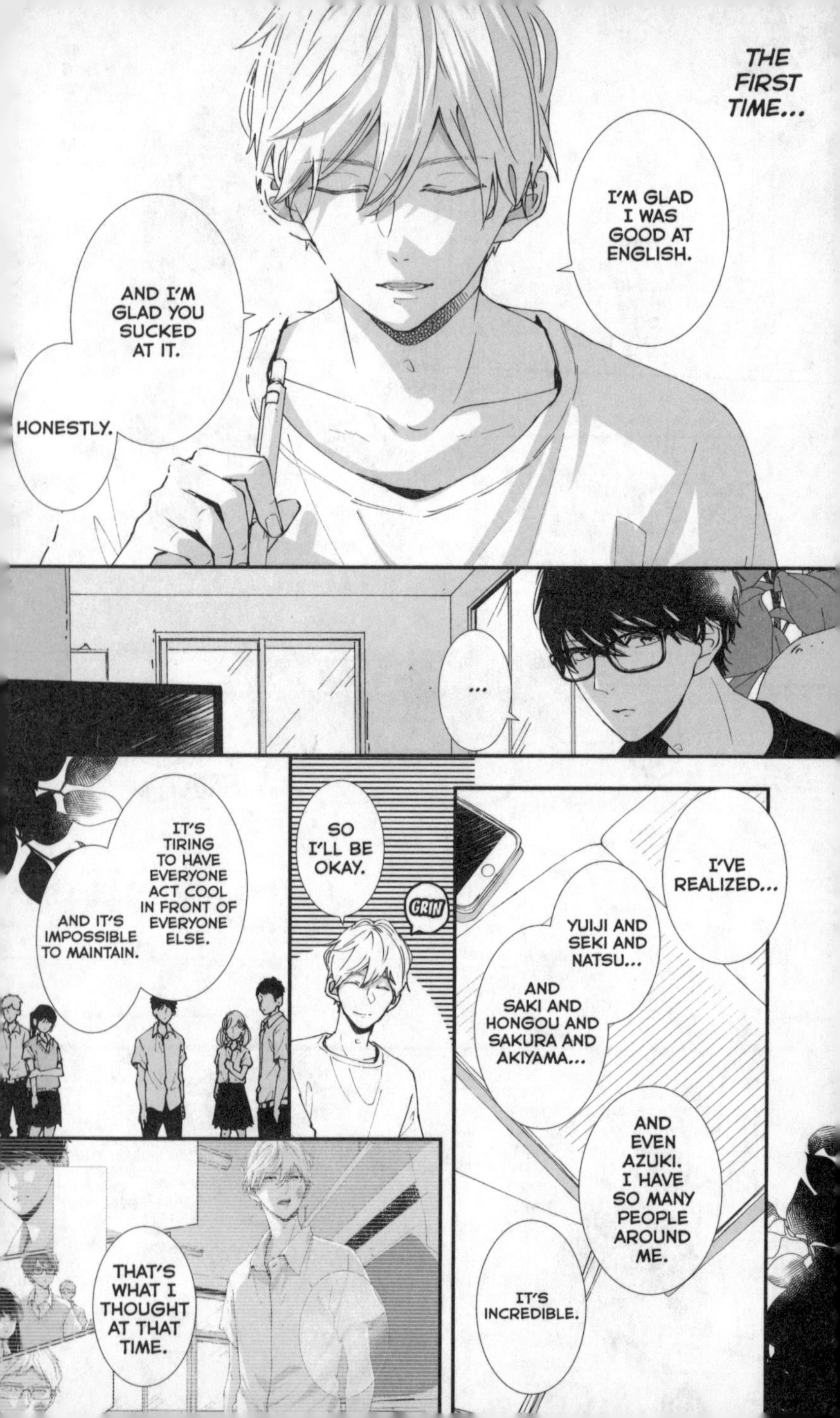
THE FIRST TIME...
I'M GLAD I WAS GOOD AT ENGLISH.
AND I'M GLAD YOU SUCKED AT IT.
HONESTLY.
...
I'VE REALIZED...
YUIJI AND SEKI AND NATSU...
AND SAKI AND HONGOU AND SAKURA AND AKIYAMA...
AND EVEN AZUKI. I HAVE SO MANY PEOPLE AROUND ME.
IT'S INCREDIBLE.
SO I'LL BE OKAY.
GRIN
IT'S TIRING TO HAVE EVERYONE ACT COOL IN FRONT OF EVERYONE ELSE.
AND IT'S IMPOSSIBLE TO MAINTAIN.
THAT'S WHAT I THOUGHT AT THAT TIME.

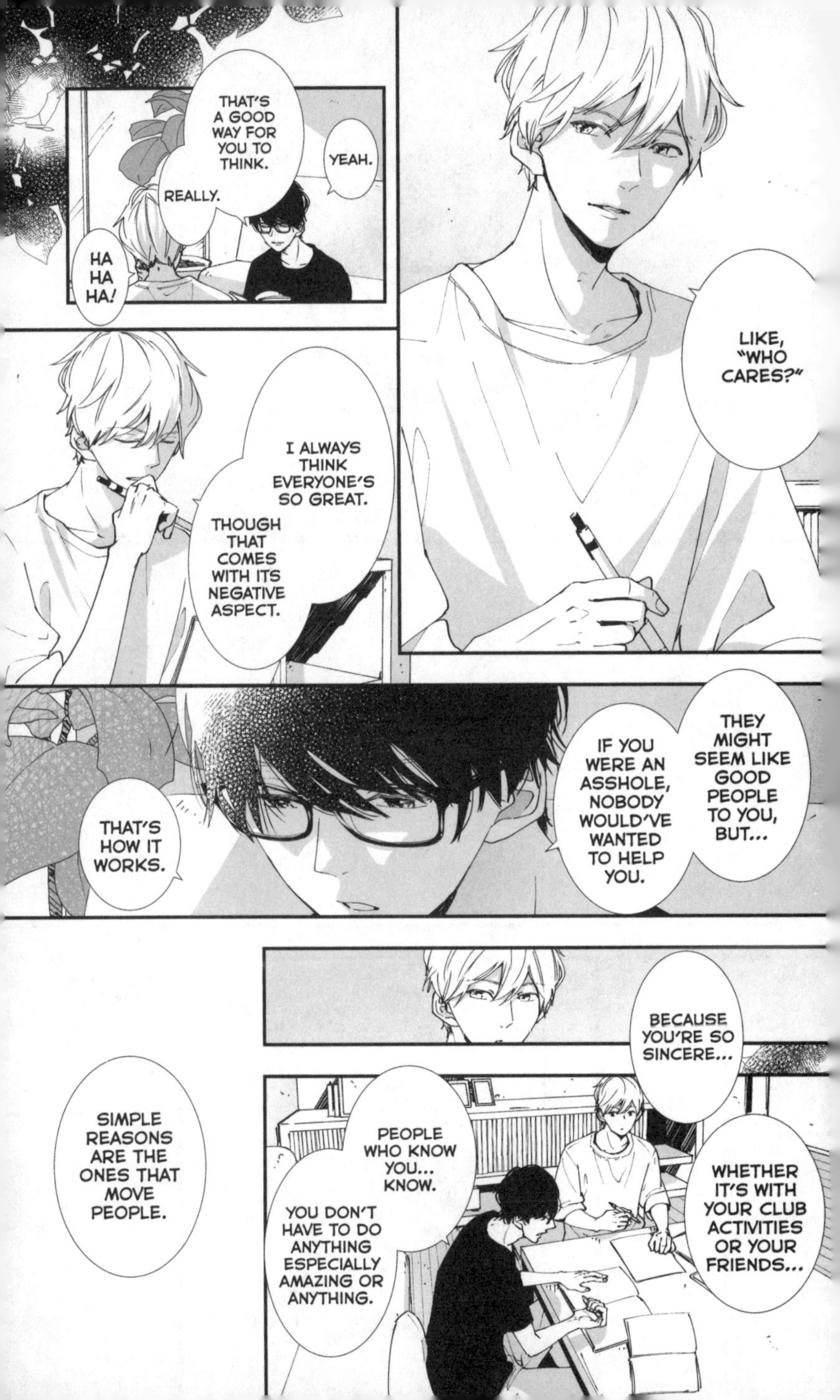
LIKE, "WHO CARES?"
THAT'S A GOOD WAY FOR YOU TO THINK.
YEAH.
REALLY.
HA HA HA!
I ALWAYS THINK EVERYONE'S SO GREAT.
THOUGH THAT COMES WITH ITS NEGATIVE ASPECT.
THEY MIGHT SEEM LIKE GOOD PEOPLE TO YOU, BUT...
IF YOU WERE AN ASSHOLE, NOBODY WOULD'VE WANTED TO HELP YOU.
THAT'S HOW IT WORKS.
BECAUSE YOU'RE SO SINCERE...
WHETHER IT'S WITH YOUR CLUB ACTIVITIES OR YOUR FRIENDS...
PEOPLE WHO KNOW YOU... KNOW.
YOU DON'T HAVE TO DO ANYTHING ESPECIALLY AMAZING OR ANYTHING.
SIMPLE REASONS ARE THE ONES THAT MOVE PEOPLE.

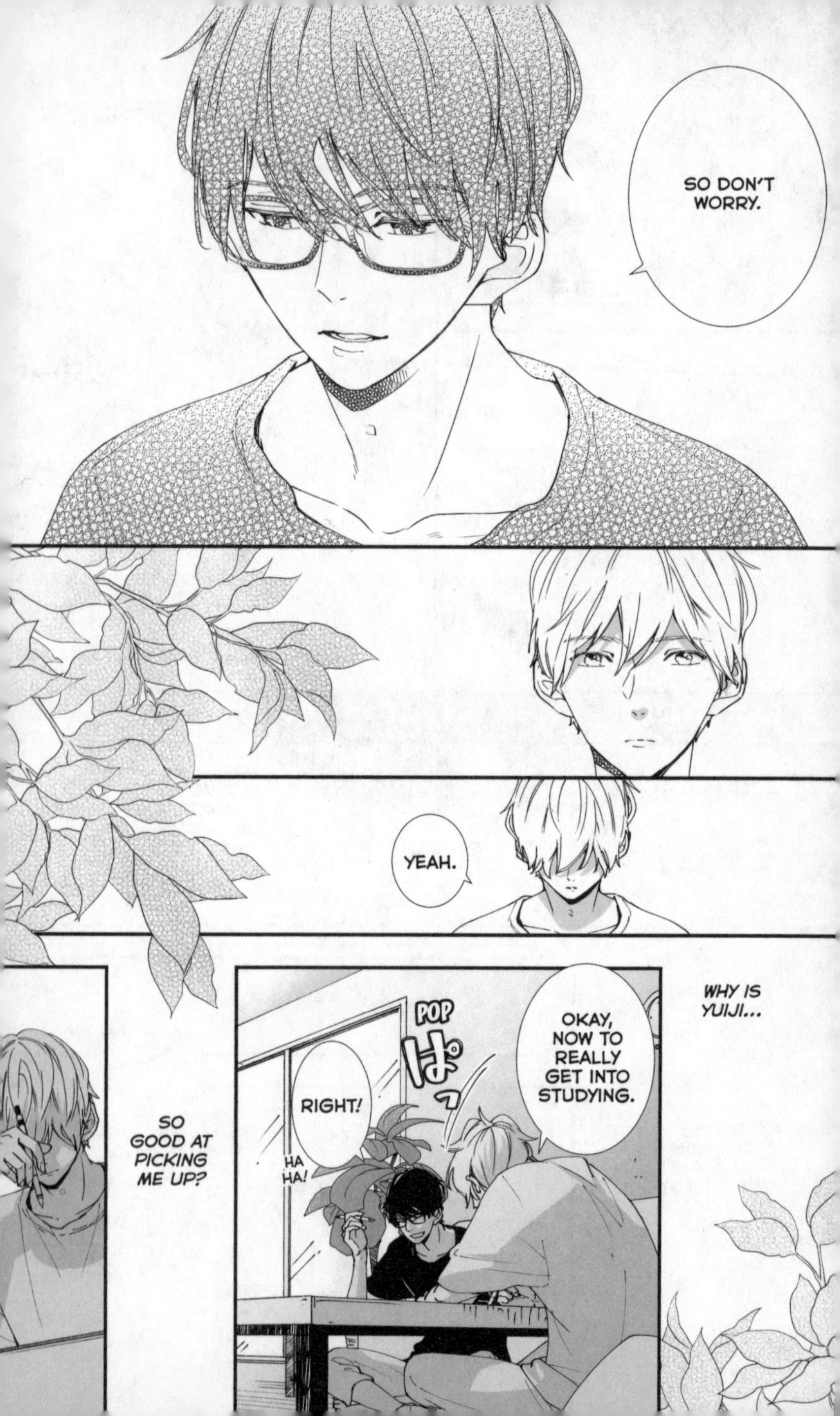
SO DON'T WORRY.
YEAH.
WHY IS YUIJI...
OKAY, NOW TO REALLY GET INTO STUDYING.
POP
ぱっ
RIGHT!
HA HA!
SO GOOD AT PICKING ME UP?

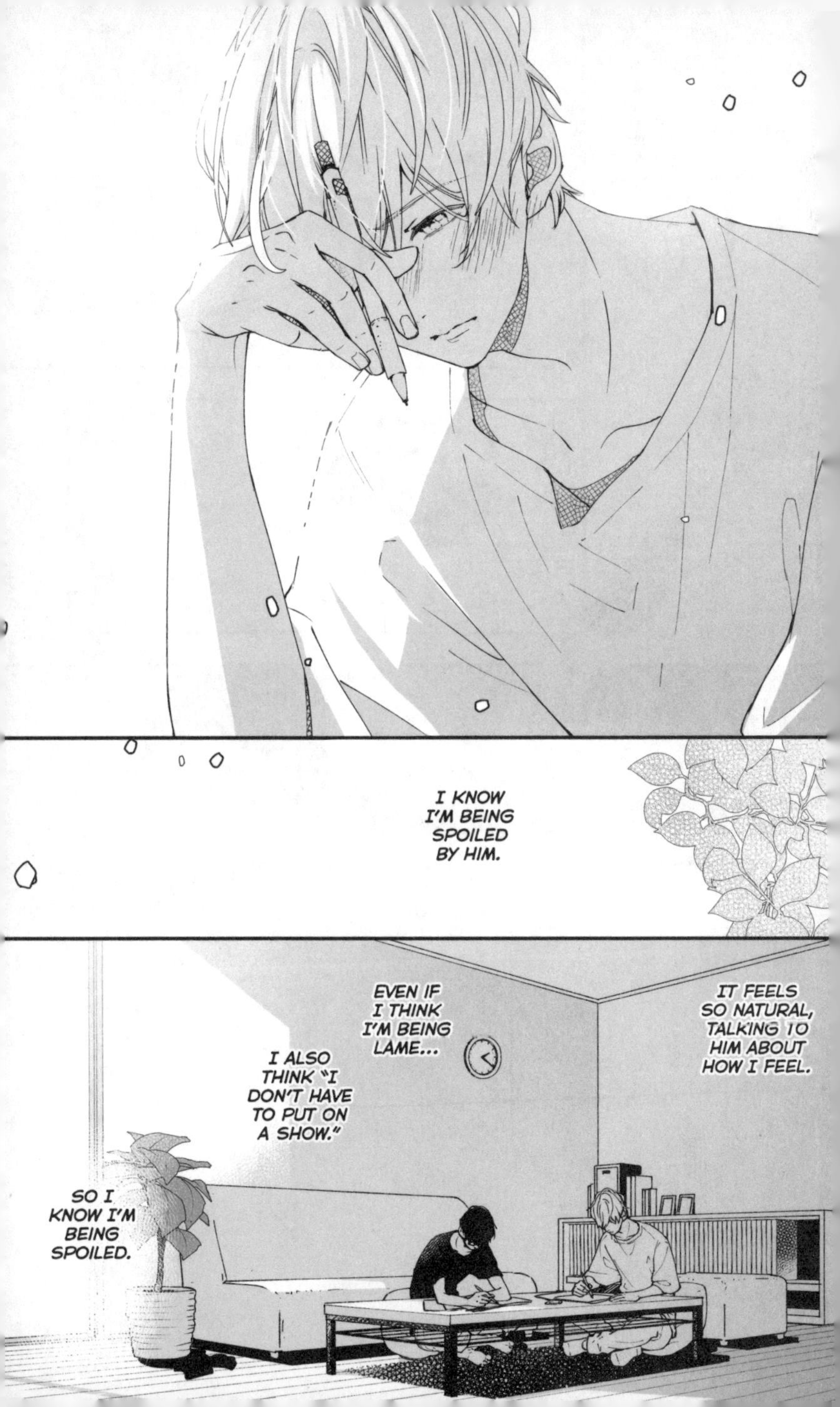
I KNOW I'M BEING SPOILED BY HIM.
IT FEELS SO NATURAL, TALKING TO HIM ABOUT HOW I FEEL.
EVEN IF I THINK I'M BEING LAME...
I ALSO THINK "I DON'T HAVE TO PUT ON A SHOW."
SO I KNOW I'M BEING SPOILED.

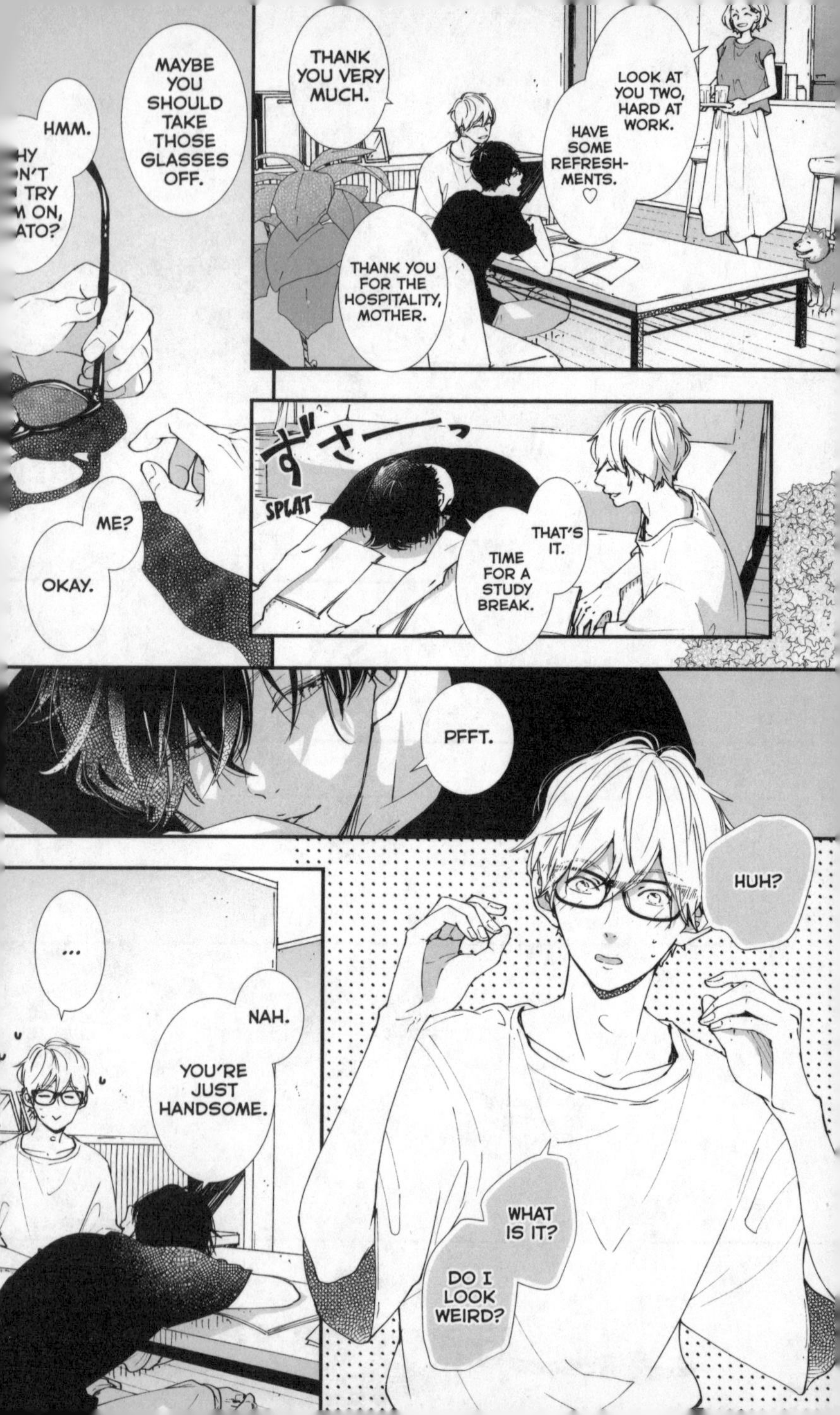
LOOK AT YOU TWO, HARD AT WORK.
HAVE SOME REFRESHMENTS. ♡
THANK YOU VERY MUCH.
THANK YOU FOR THE HOSPITALITY, MOTHER.
ずさーっ
SPLAT
THAT'S IT.
TIME FOR A STUDY BREAK.
MAYBE YOU SHOULD TAKE THOSE GLASSES OFF.
HMM.
ME?
OKAY.
PFFT.
HUH?
WHAT IS IT?
DO I LOOK WEIRD?
...
NAH.
YOU'RE JUST HANDSOME.

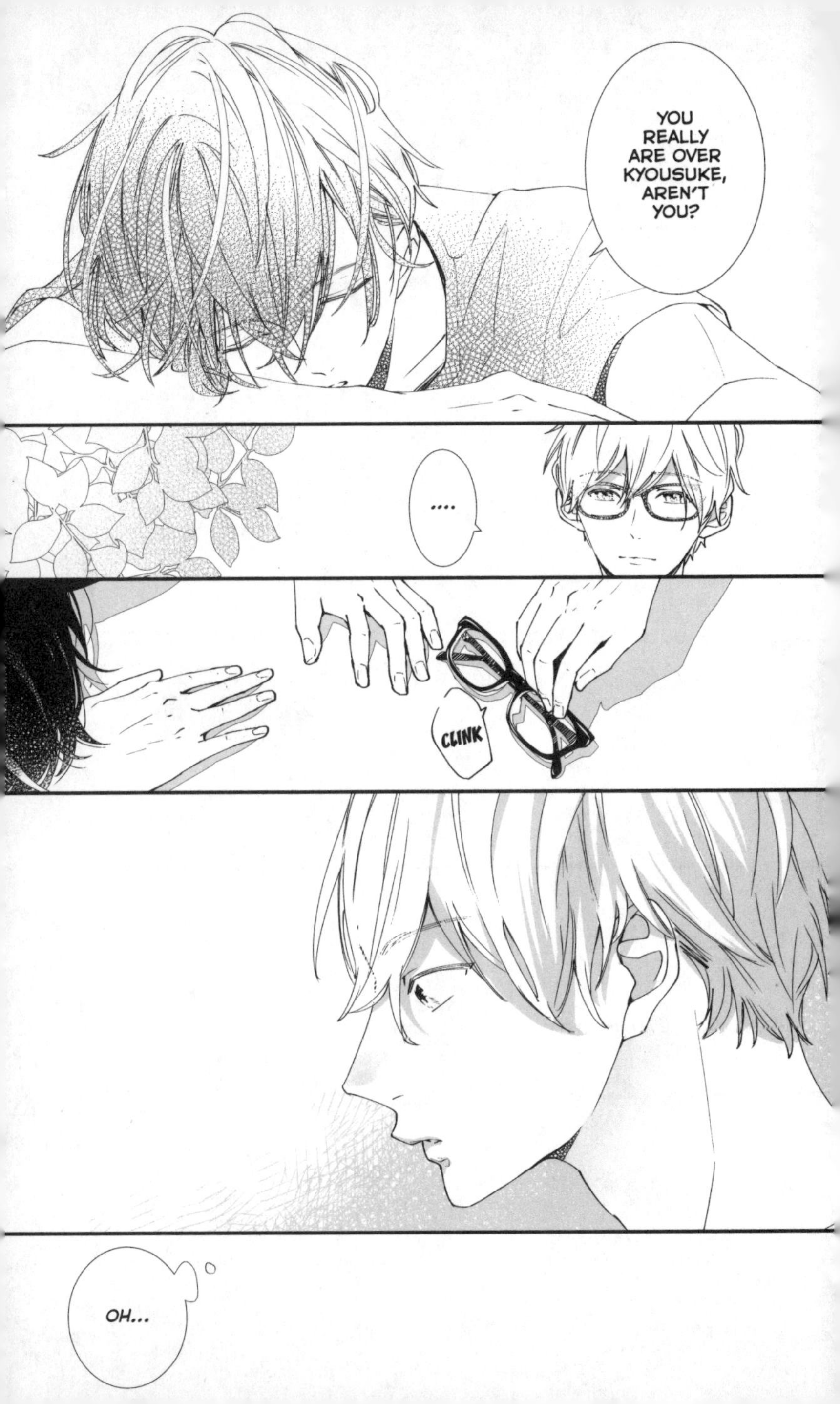
YOU REALLY ARE OVER KYOUSUKE, AREN'T YOU?
....
CLINK
OH...

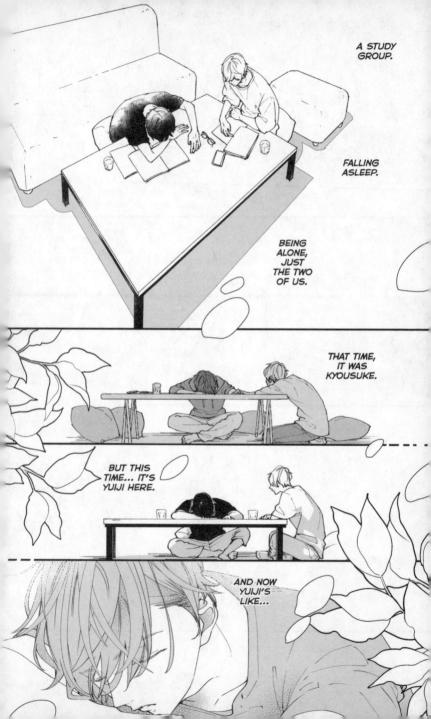

A STUDY GROUP.

FALLING ASLEEP.

BEING ALONE, JUST THE TWO OF US.

THAT TIME, IT WAS KYOUSUKE.

BUT THIS TIME... IT'S YUIJI HERE.

AND NOW YUIJI'S LIKE...

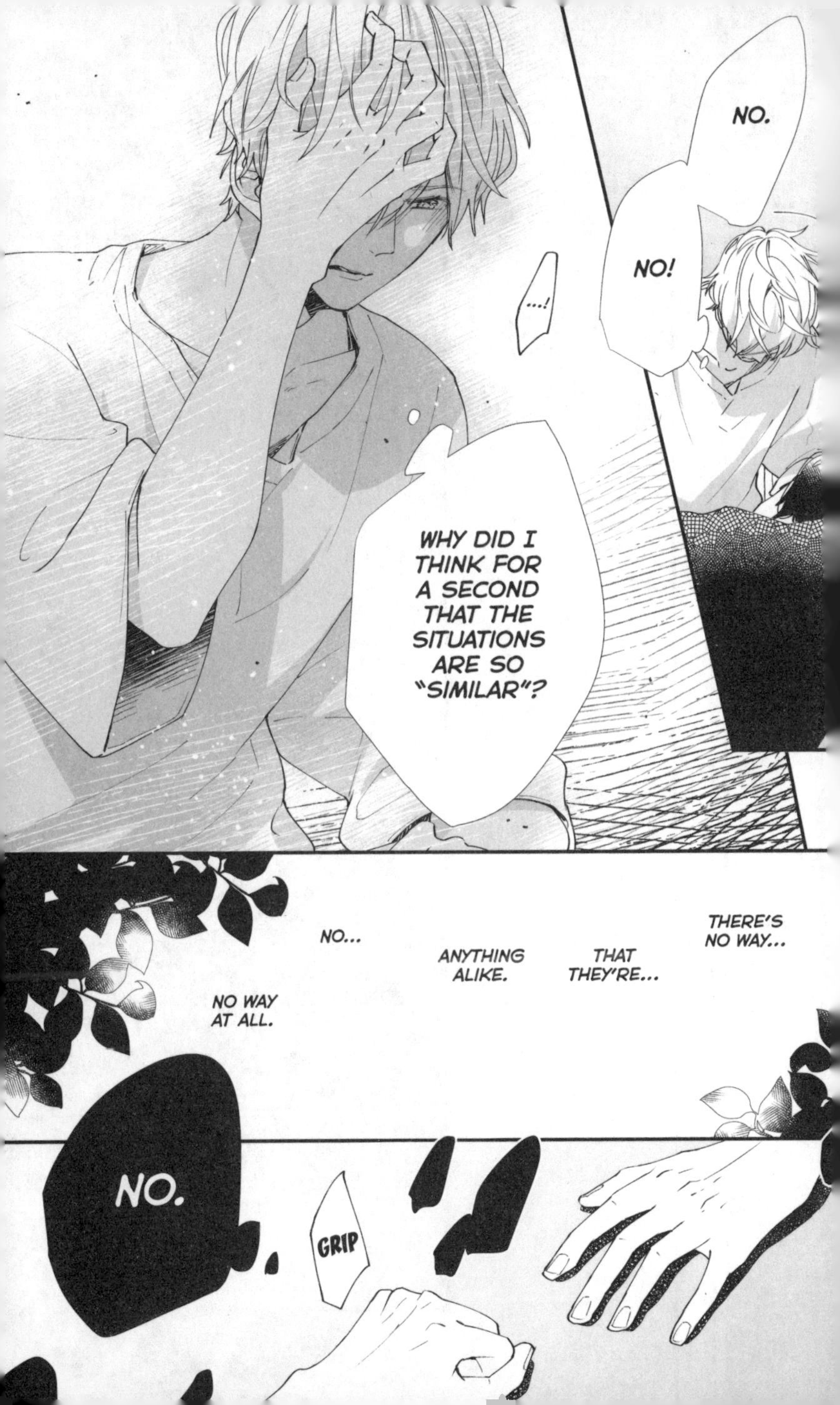
NO.
NO!
...!
WHY DID I THINK FOR A SECOND THAT THE SITUATIONS ARE SO "SIMILAR"?
THERE'S NO WAY...
THAT THEY'RE...
ANYTHING ALIKE.
NO...
NO WAY AT ALL.
GRIP
NO.

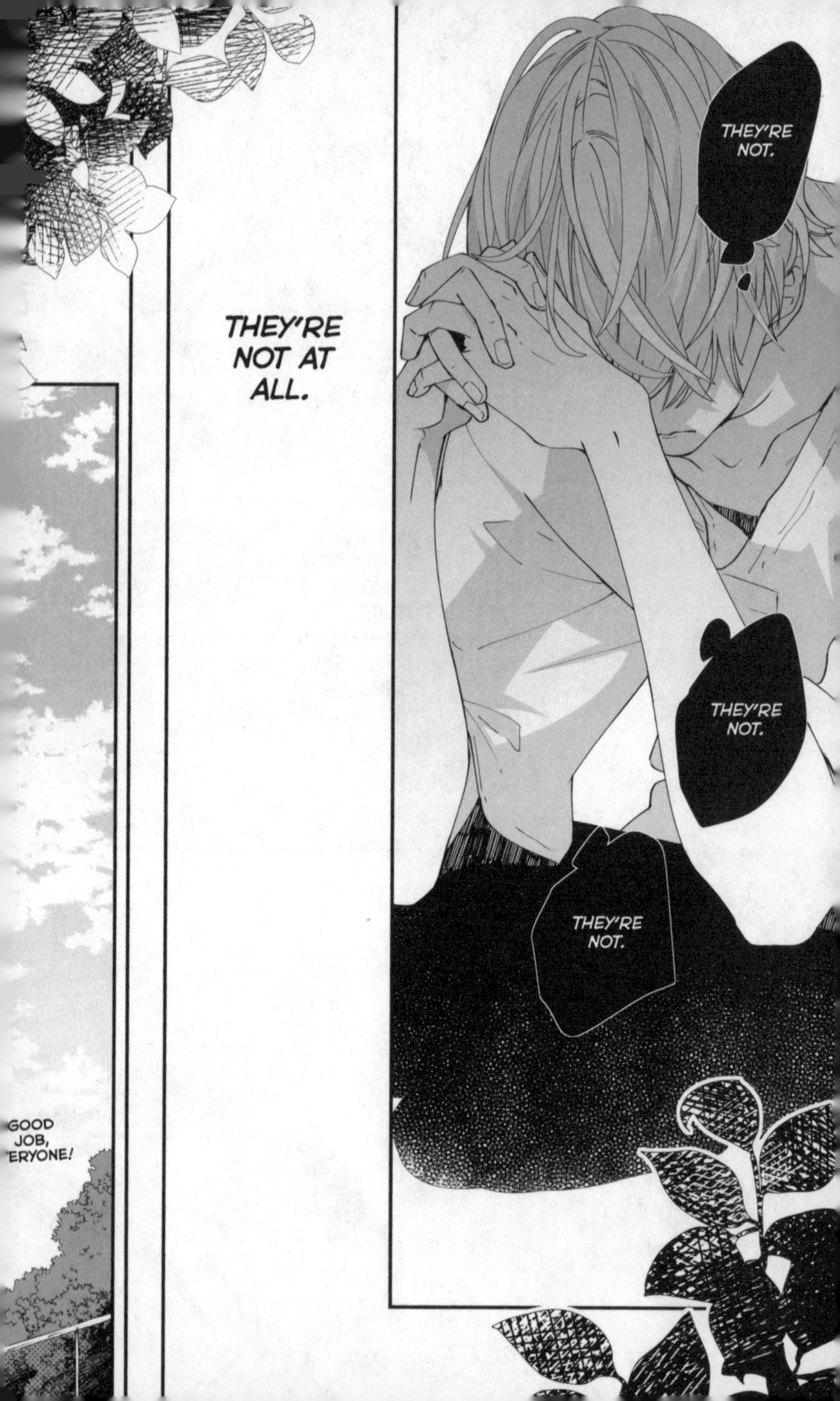
THEY'RE NOT.
THEY'RE NOT.
THEY'RE NOT.
THEY'RE NOT AT ALL.
GOOD JOB, ERYONE!

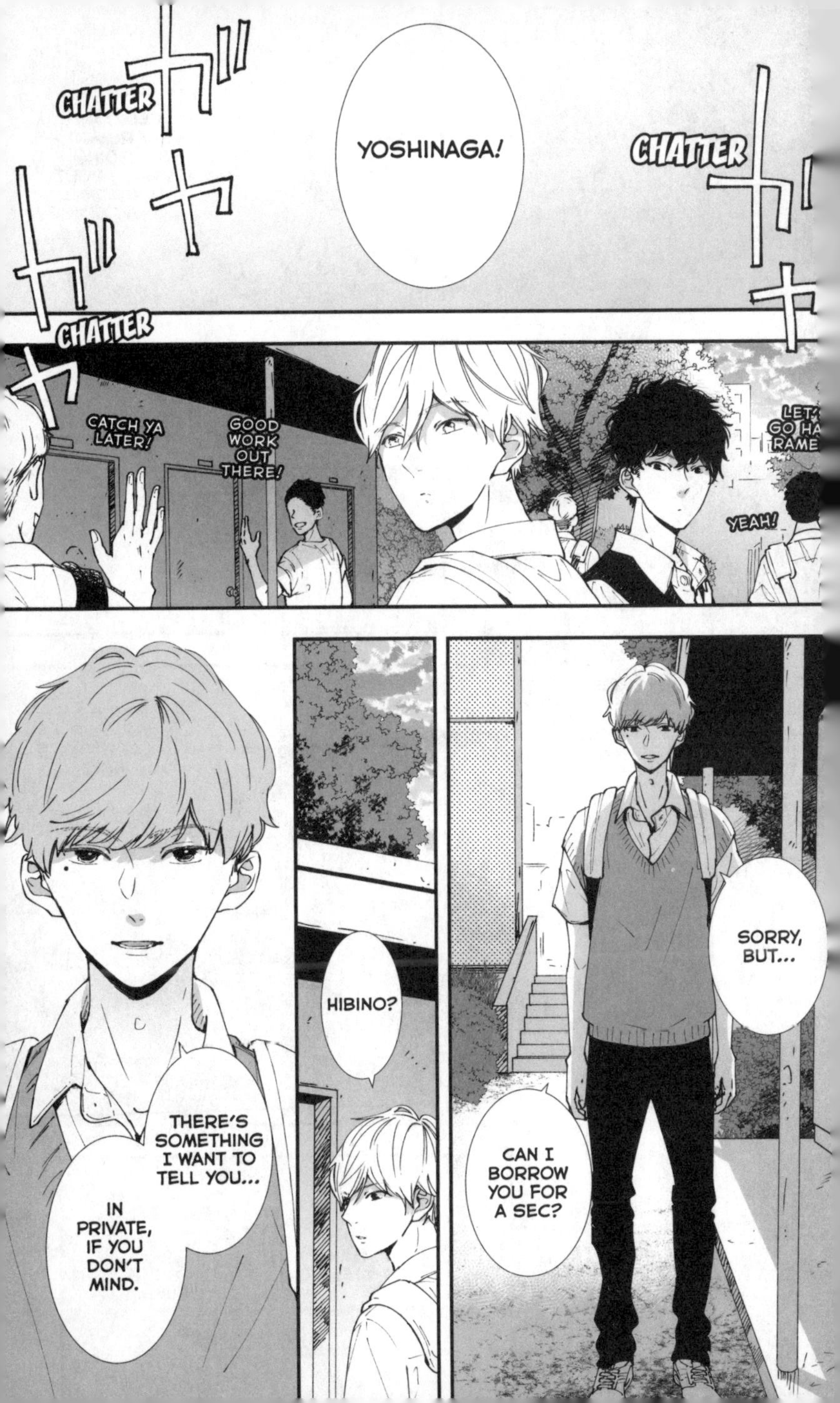
CHATTER
YOSHINAGA!
CHATTER
CHATTER
LET'S GO HA RAME
YEAH!
GOOD WORK OUT THERE!
CATCH YA LATER!
SORRY, BUT...
CAN I BORROW YOU FOR A SEC?
HIBINO?
THERE'S SOMETHING I WANT TO TELL YOU...
IN PRIVATE, IF YOU DON'T MIND.

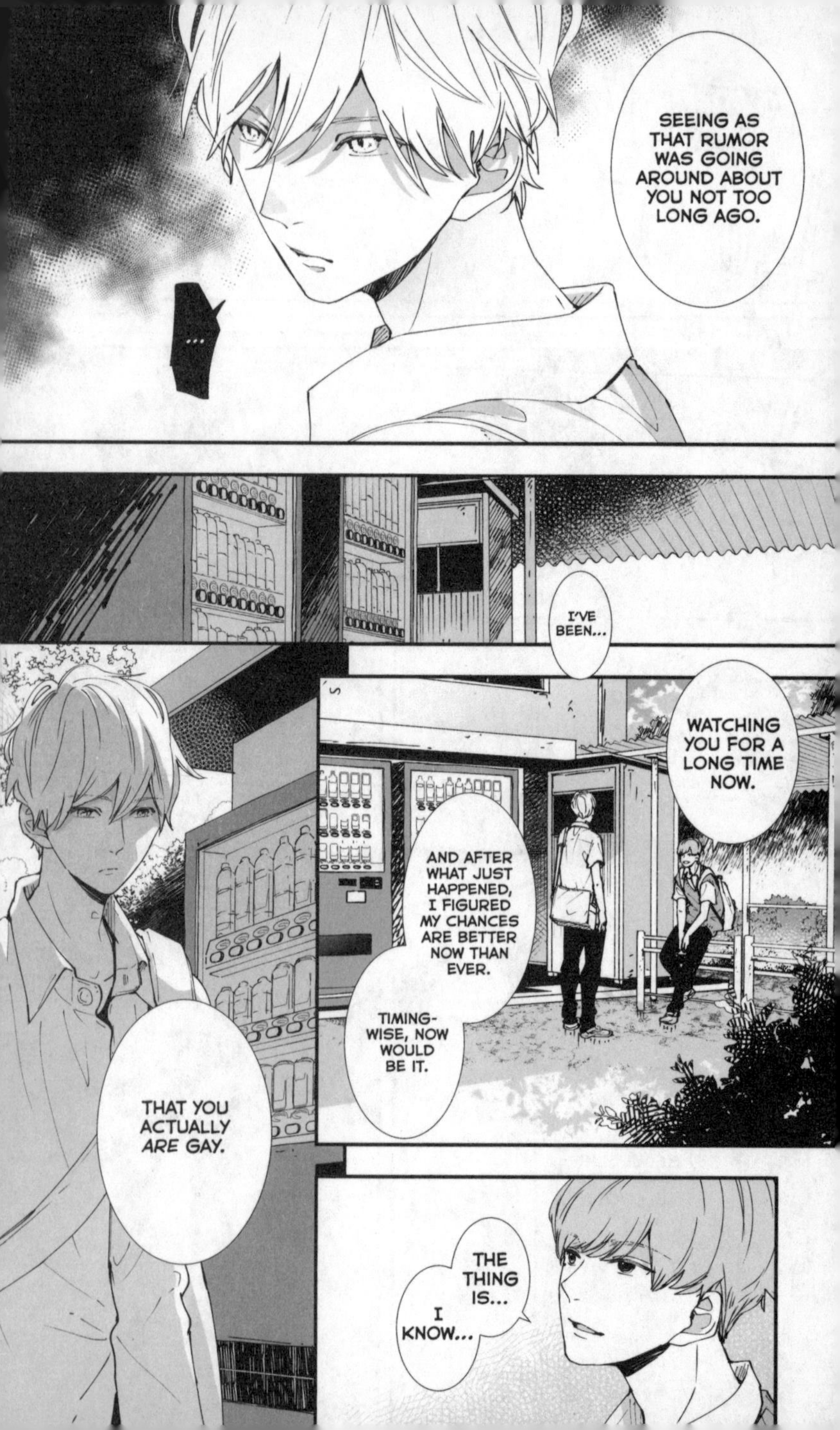
SEEING AS THAT RUMOR WAS GOING AROUND ABOUT YOU NOT TOO LONG AGO.
...
I'VE BEEN...
WATCHING YOU FOR A LONG TIME NOW.
AND AFTER WHAT JUST HAPPENED, I FIGURED MY CHANCES ARE BETTER NOW THAN EVER.
TIMING-WISE, NOW WOULD BE IT.
THE THING IS...
I KNOW...
THAT YOU ACTUALLY *ARE* GAY.

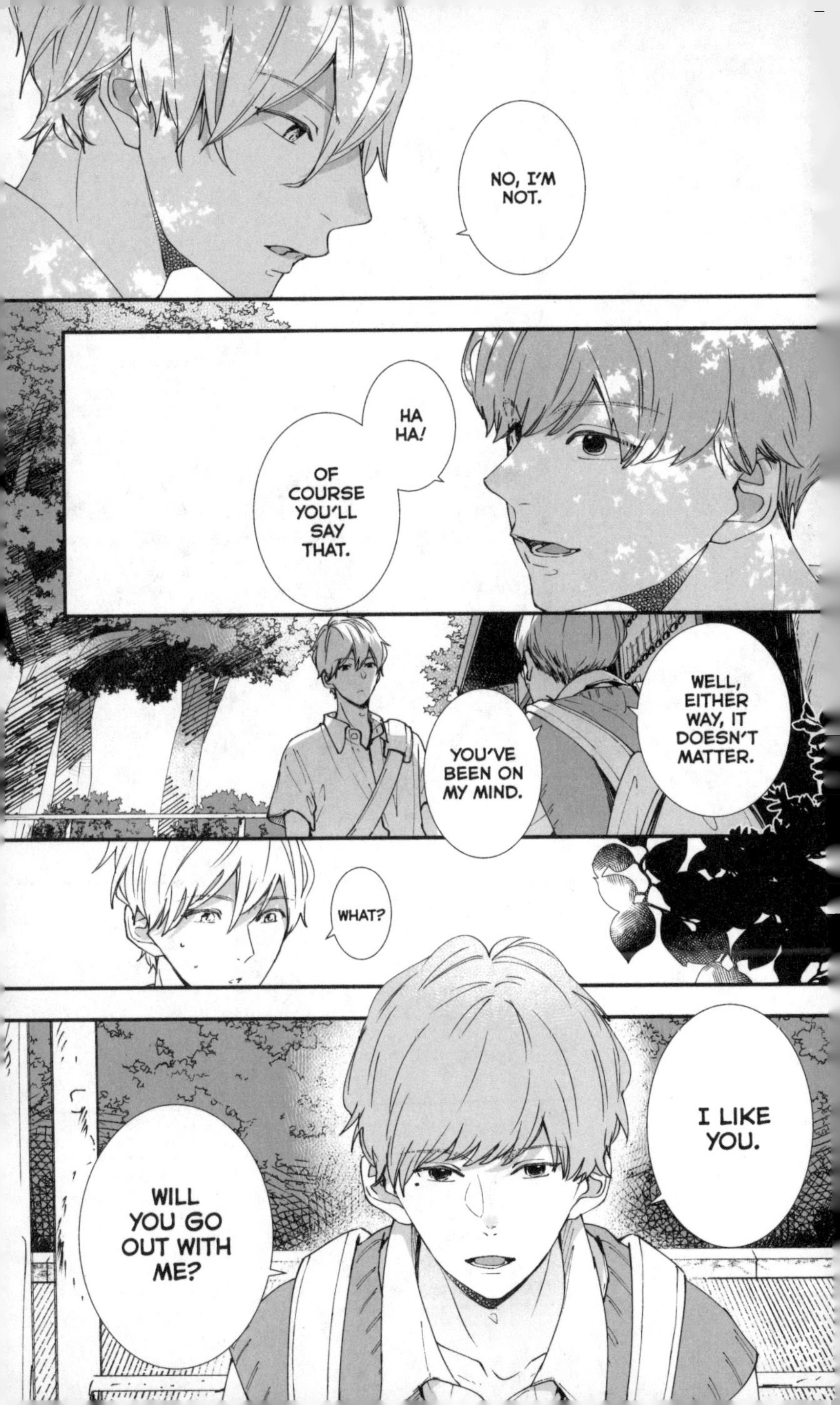
NO, I'M NOT.
HA HA!
OF COURSE YOU'LL SAY THAT.
WELL, EITHER WAY, IT DOESN'T MATTER.
YOU'VE BEEN ON MY MIND.
WHAT?
I LIKE YOU.
WILL YOU GO OUT WITH ME?

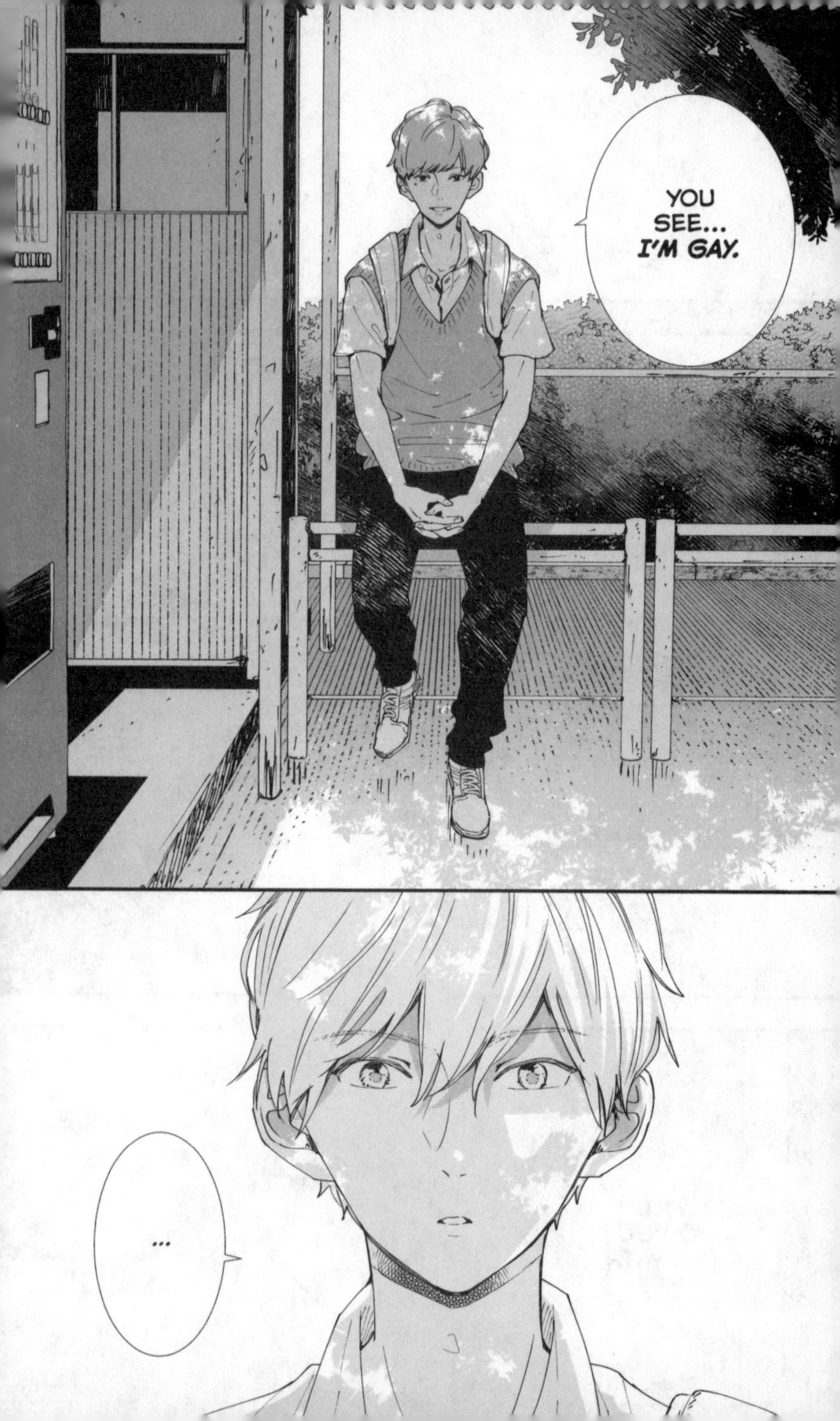
YOU SEE... I'M GAY.
...

KOIMONOGATARI

LOVE STORIES

VOLUME 2 • END

KOIMONOGATARI

LOVE STORIES

AFTERWORD

HELLO. THIS IS TOHRU TAGURA. VOLUME 2 HAS
FINALLY COME OUT! I'M SORRY IT TOOK OVER THREE
YEARS SINCE THE FIRST VOLUME. THERE WAS A
PERIOD WHERE MY HEALTH HAD DETERIORATED,
SO IT TOOK ME LONGER THAN I THOUGHT.

THIS STORY HAS A LARGE CAST, BUT ALL THE CHARACTERS
I HAD PLANNED HAVE NOW MADE THEIR DEBUT, AND
YAMATO'S DEVELOPMENT ARC WAS ABLE TO COME TO
AN END. NOW ALL THAT'S LEFT IS YUIJI'S ARC. ON THAT
NOTE, I'M SORRY FOR THE STORY NOT BEING MUCH
LIKE A BL EVEN AFTER TWO VOLUMES. THE NEXT VOLUME
WILL WRAP IT ALL UP. AND IT WILL BE A "LOVE STORY."
I HOPE YOU DECIDE TO STICK AROUND FOR IT.

I TOOK A PHOTO OF FUJISAWA STATION TO CREATE
THE BACKGROUND OF THE COVER FOR VOLUME 2. I'M
HAVING THE BOYS HOLDING DRINKS FROM (PSEUDO)
MCD'S, BUT THERE IS NO MCD'S NEAR THERE.

DEAR EDITOR,
I'M SORRY FOR CAUSING YOU SO MUCH TROUBLE
ALL THE TIME! AND ALSO THANK YOU SO MUCH.

THANK YOU, EVERYONE, FOR READING UP UNTIL THE END!

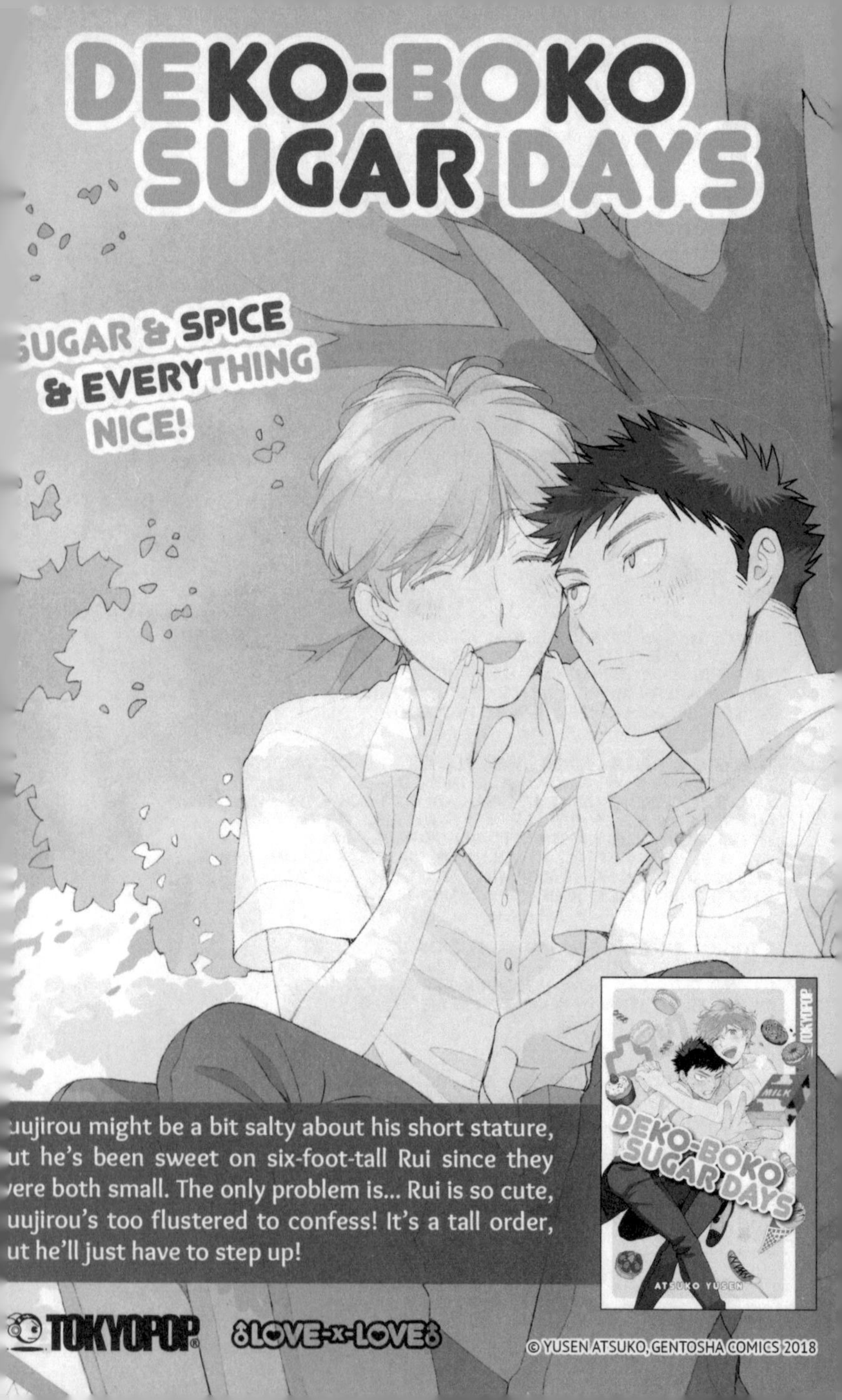
DEKO-BOKO SUGAR DAYS
SUGAR & SPICE & EVERYTHING NICE!
uujirou might be a bit salty about his short stature,
ut he's been sweet on six-foot-tall Rui since they
vere both small. The only problem is... Rui is so cute,
uujirou's too flustered to confess! It's a tall order,
ut he'll just have to step up!
MILK
DEKO-BOKO SUGAR DAYS
ATSUKO YUSEN
TOKYOPOP
TOKYOPOP
LOVE x LOVE
© YUSEN ATSUKO, GENTOSHA COMICS 2018

STAR COLLECTOR

By Anna B. & Sophie Schönhammer

A ROMANCE WRITTEN IN THE STARS!

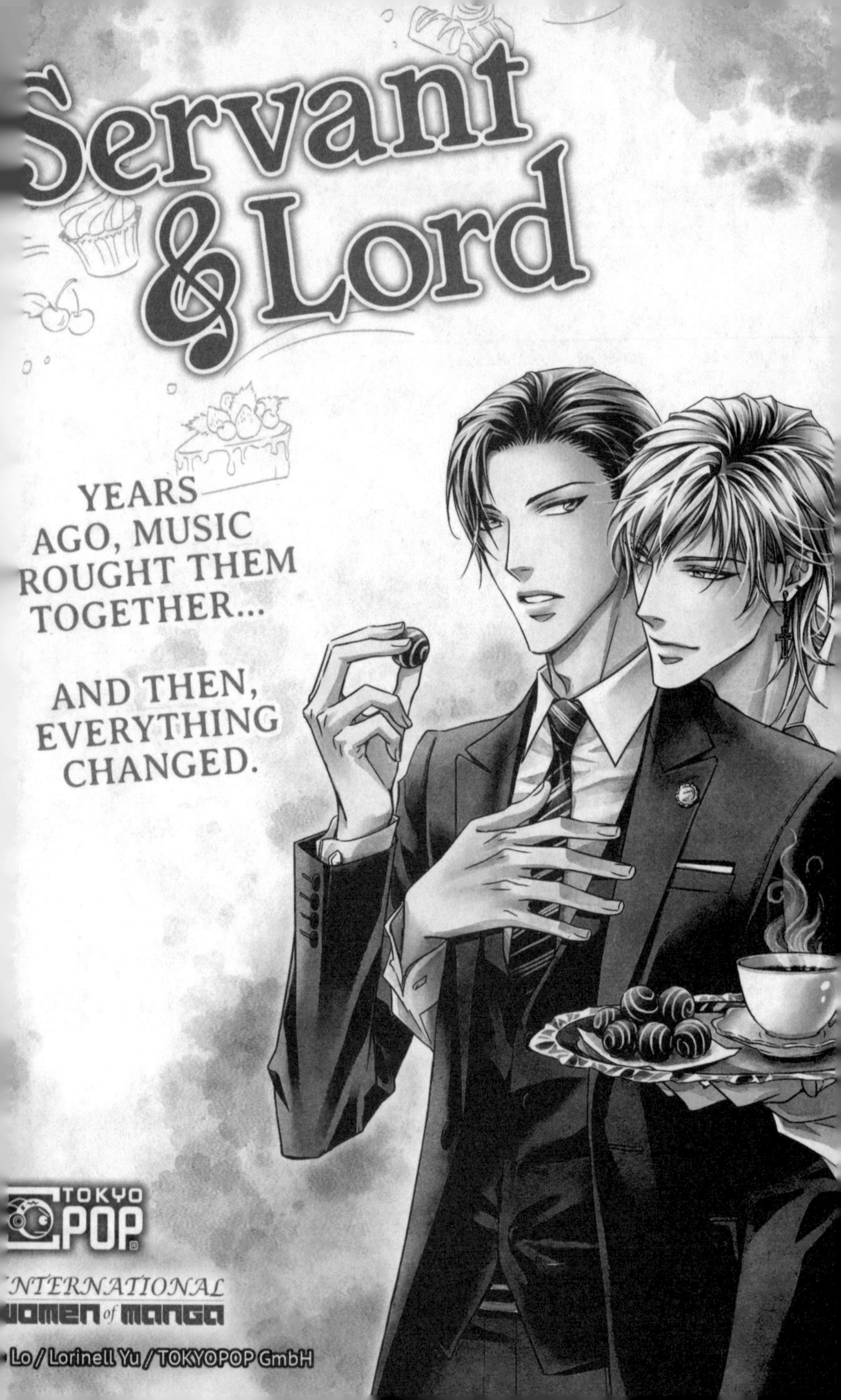

Servant & Lord
YEARS AGO, MUSIC ROUGHT THEM TOGETHER...
AND THEN, EVERYTHING CHANGED.
TOKYOPOP
NTERNATIONAL OMEN of MANGA
Lo / Lorinell Yu / TOKYOPOP GmbH

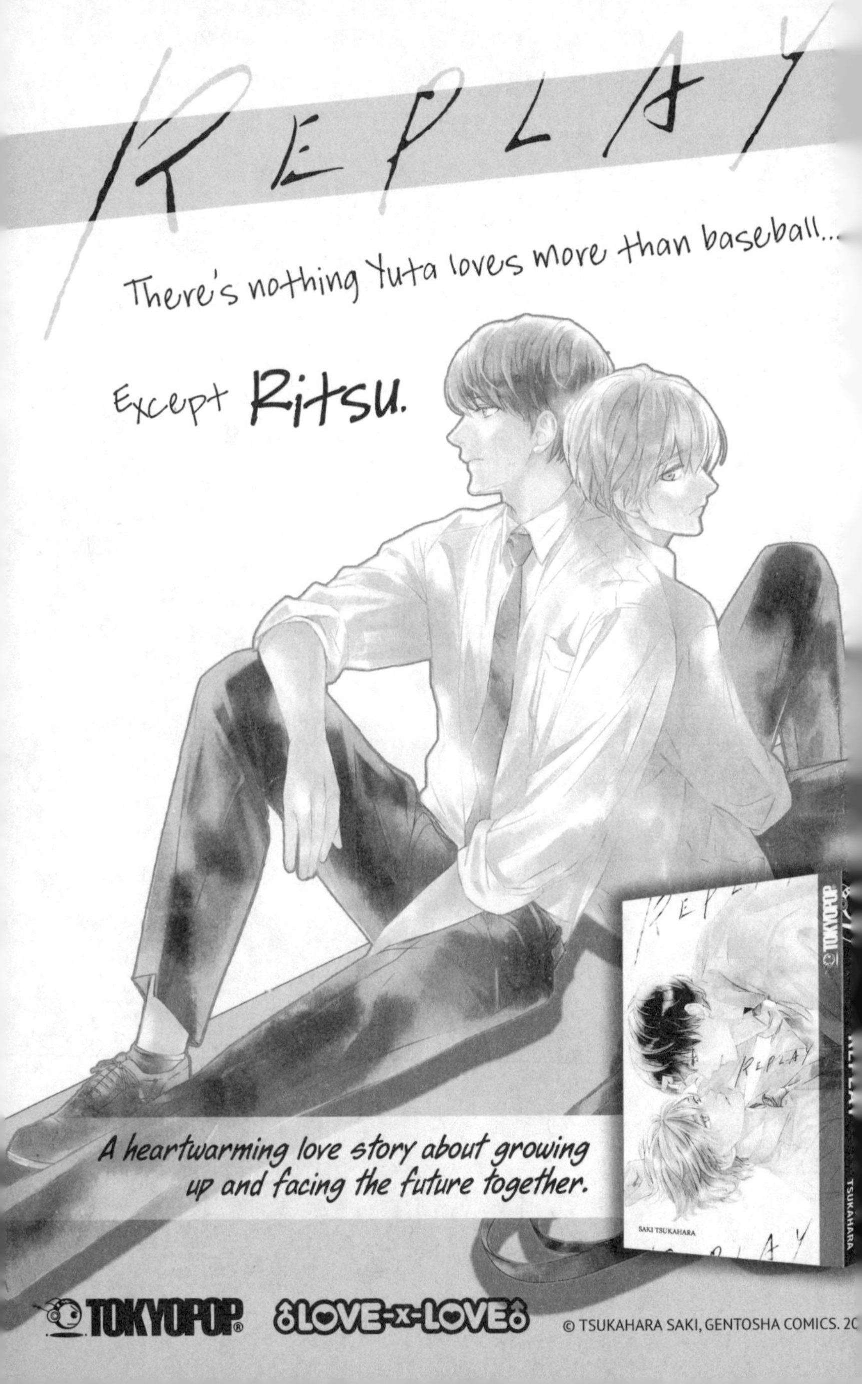
REPLAY
There's nothing Yuta loves more than baseball...
Except Ritsu.
A heartwarming love story about growing up and facing the future together.
SAKI TSUKAHARA
TOKYOPOP
LOVE x LOVE
© TSUKAHARA SAKI, GENTOSHA COMICS. 2C

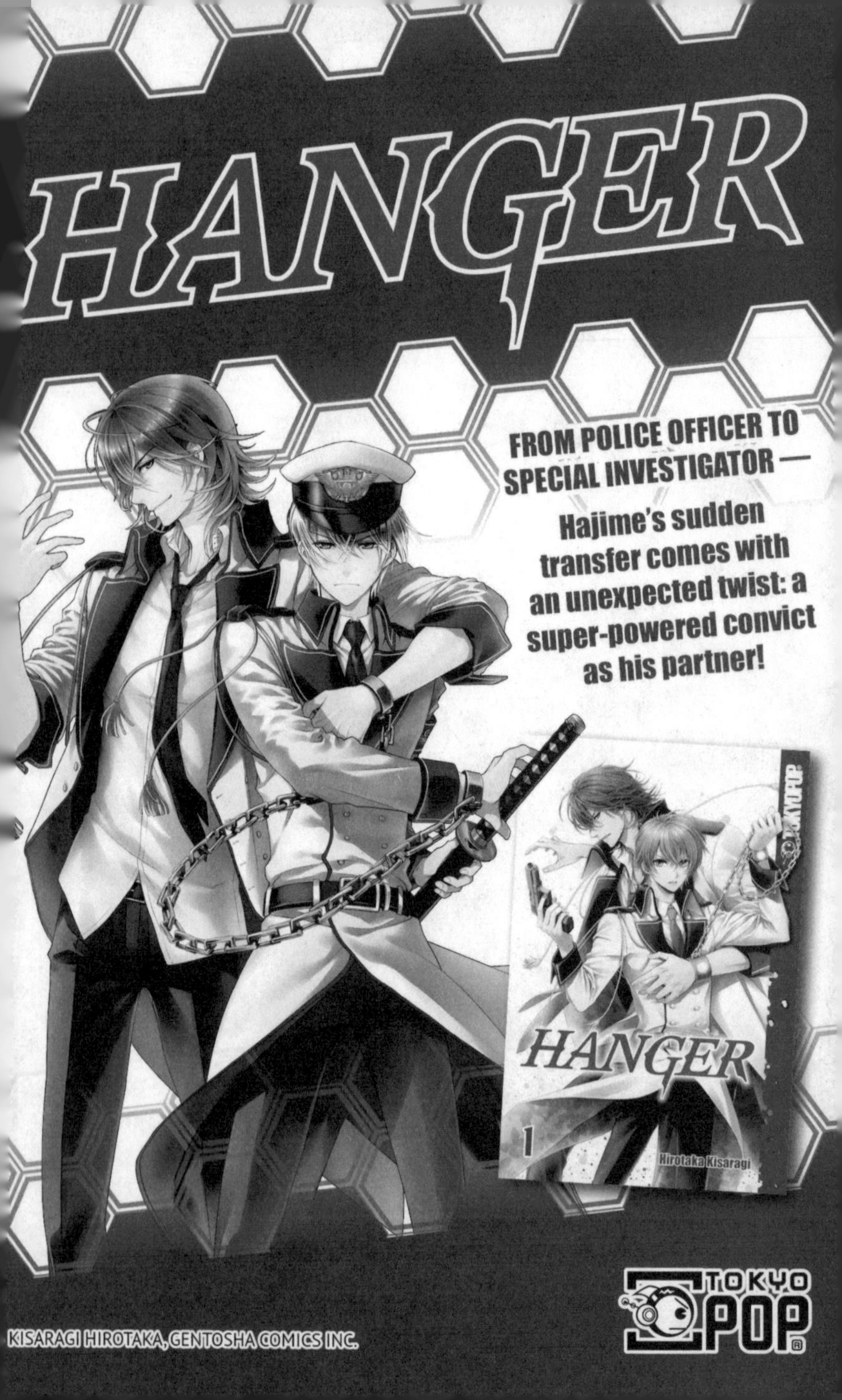
HANGER
FROM POLICE OFFICER TO SPECIAL INVESTIGATOR —
Hajime's sudden transfer comes with an unexpected twist: a super-powered convict as his partner!
TOKYOPOP
HANGER
1
Hirotaka Kisaragi
TOKYO POP
KISARAGI HIROTAKA, GENTOSHA COMICS INC.

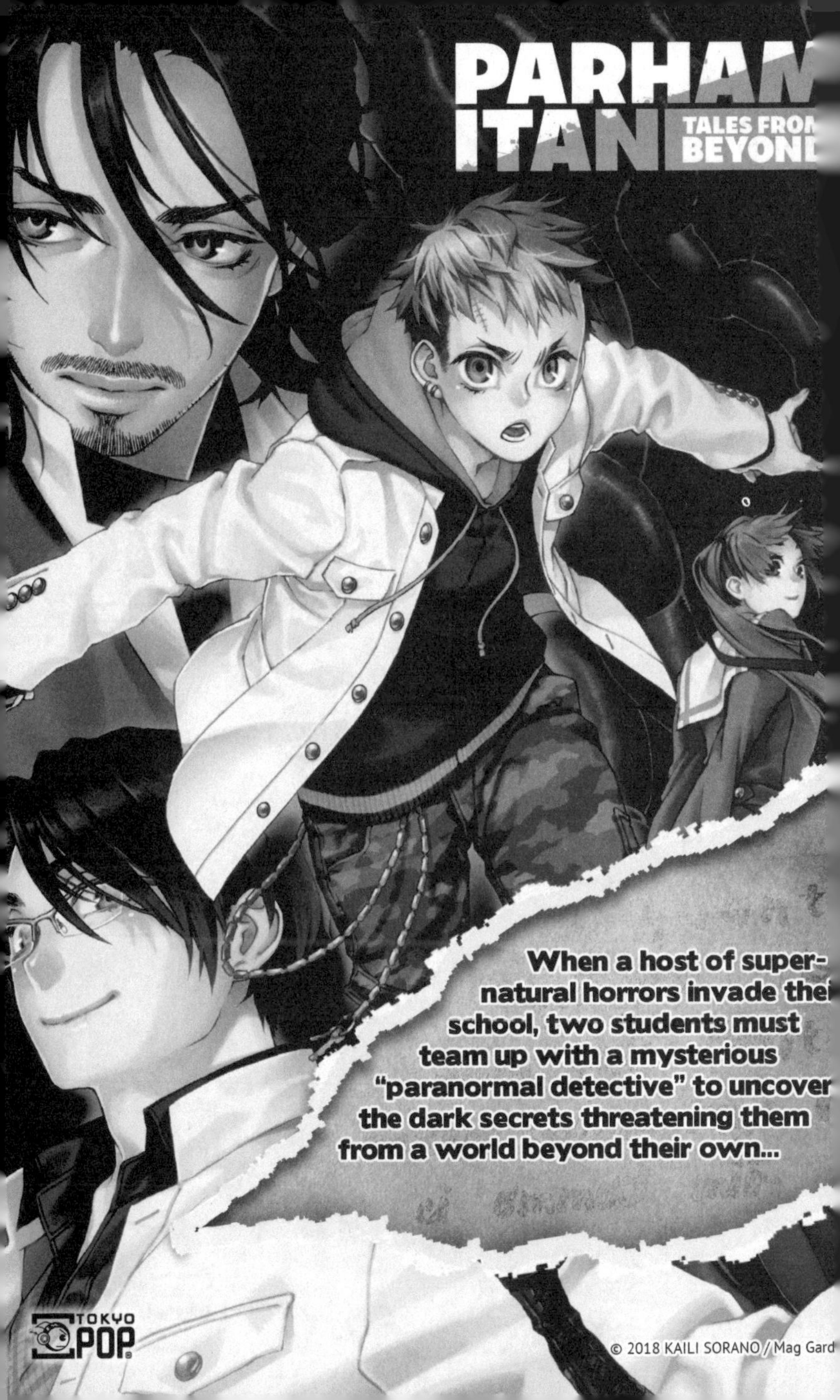

PARHAM
ITAN
TALES FROM
BEYOND
When a host of super-
natural horrors invade thei
school, two students must
team up with a mysterious
"paranormal detective" to uncover
the dark secrets threatening them
from a world beyond their own...
TOKYO POP
© 2018 KAILI SORANO / Mag Gard

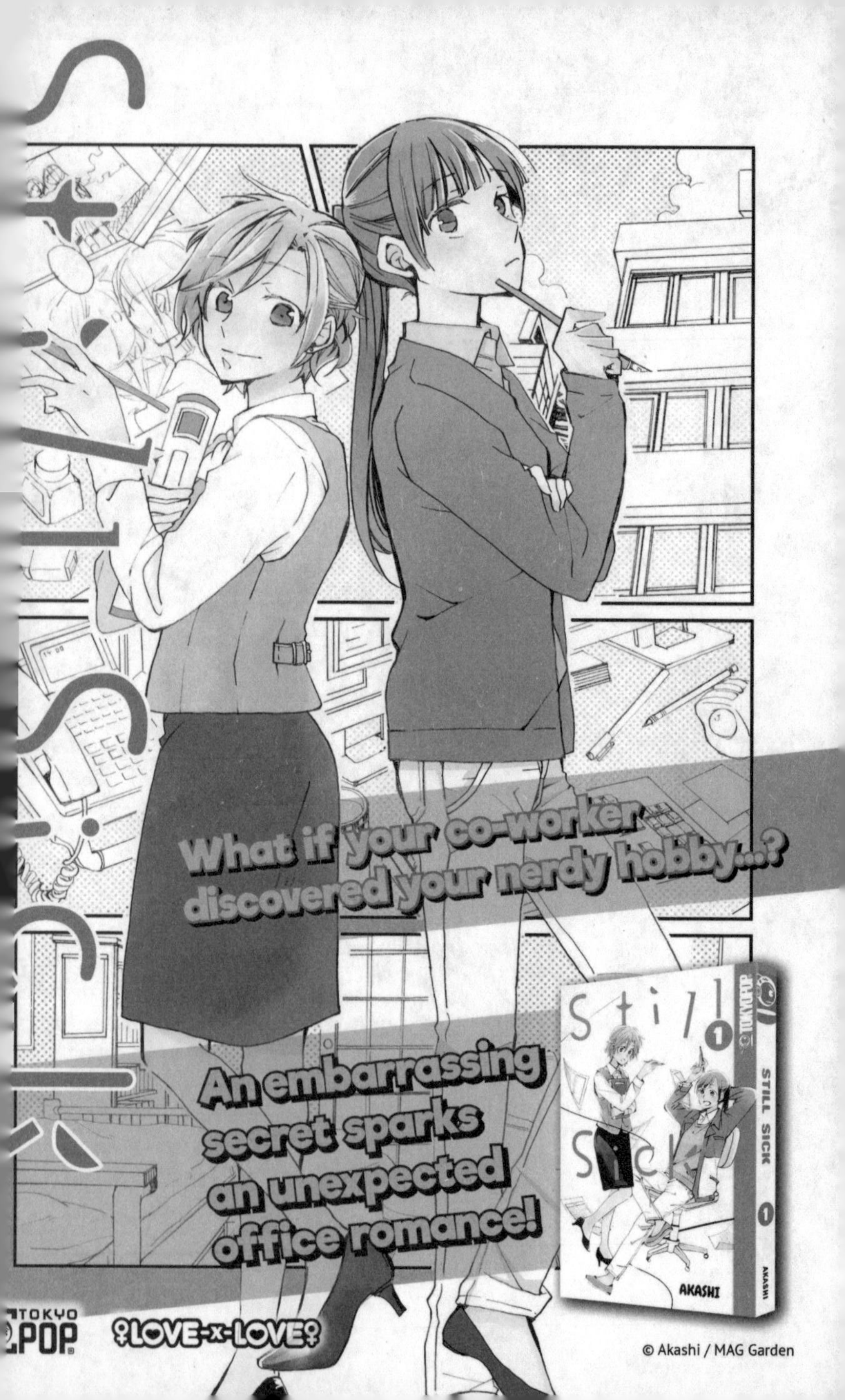

Still Sick
What if your co-worker discovered your nerdy hobby...?
An embarrassing secret sparks an unexpected office romance!
Still Sick
1
STILL SICK
AKASHI
TOKYOPOP
LOVE-x-LOVE
© Akashi / MAG Garden

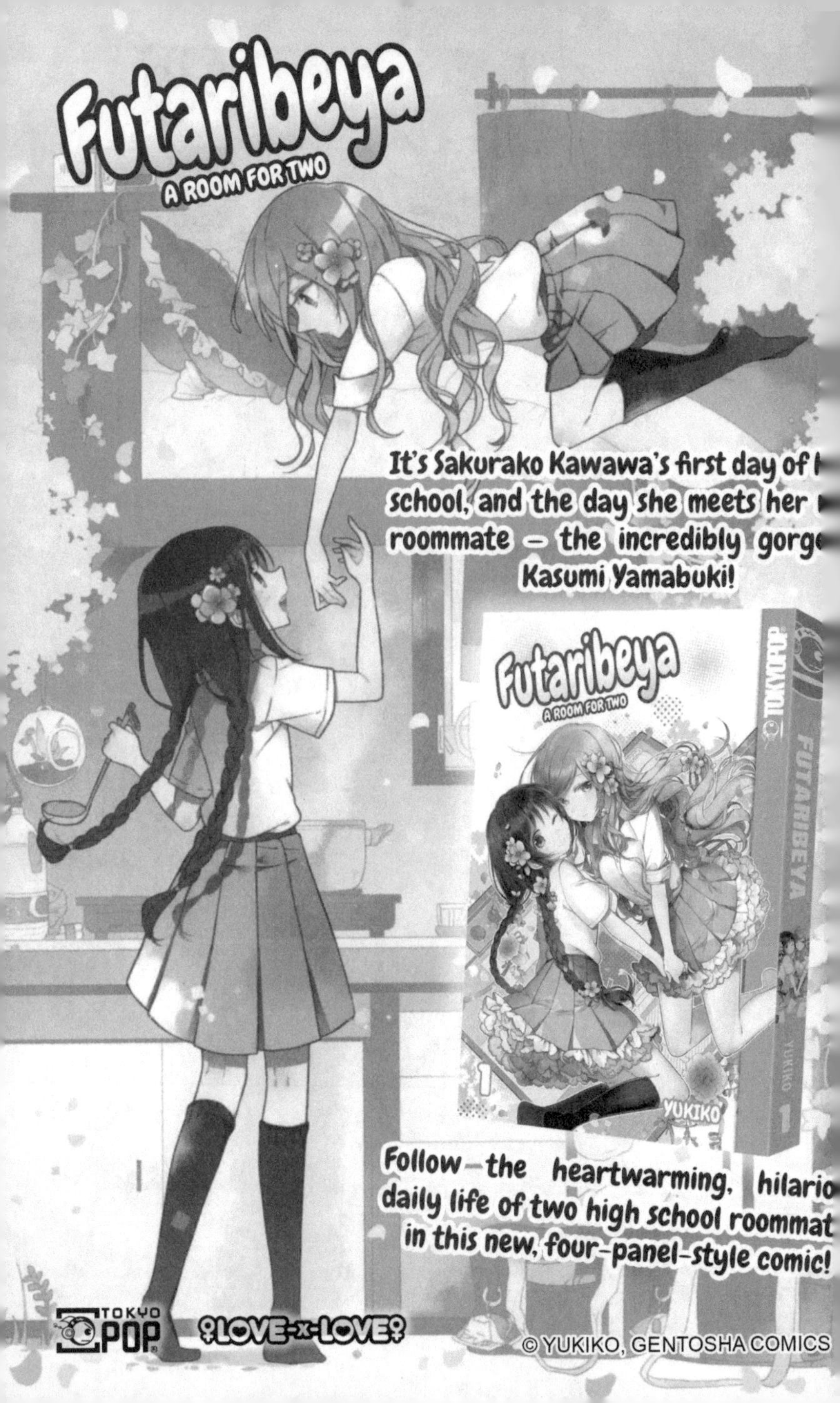
Futaribeya
A ROOM FOR TWO
It's Sakurako Kawawa's first day of
school, and the day she meets her
roommate – the incredibly gorg
Kasumi Yamabuki!
Futaribeya
A ROOM FOR TWO
TOKYOPOP
FUTARIBEYA
1
YUKIKO
YUKIKO
1
Follow the heartwarming, hilario
daily life of two high school roommat
in this new, four-panel-style comic!
TOKYO POP
LOVE x LOVE
© YUKIKO, GENTOSHA COMICS

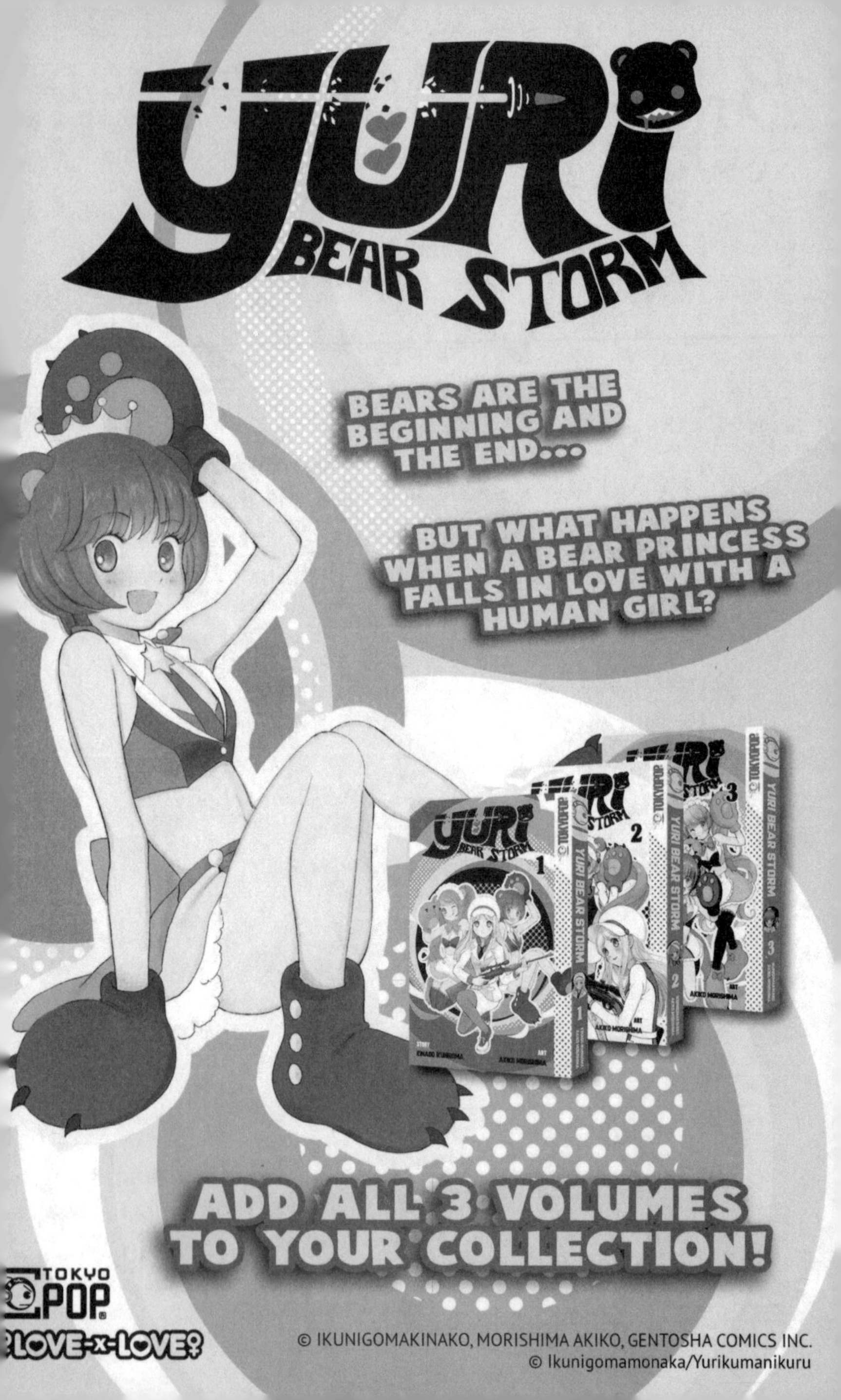
YURI BEAR STORM
BEARS ARE THE BEGINNING AND THE END...
BUT WHAT HAPPENS WHEN A BEAR PRINCESS FALLS IN LOVE WITH A HUMAN GIRL?
ADD ALL 3 VOLUMES TO YOUR COLLECTION!
TOKYOPOP
LOVE x LOVE
© IKUNIGOMAKINAKO, MORISHIMA AKIKO, GENTOSHA COMICS INC.
© Ikunigomamonaka/Yurikumanikuru

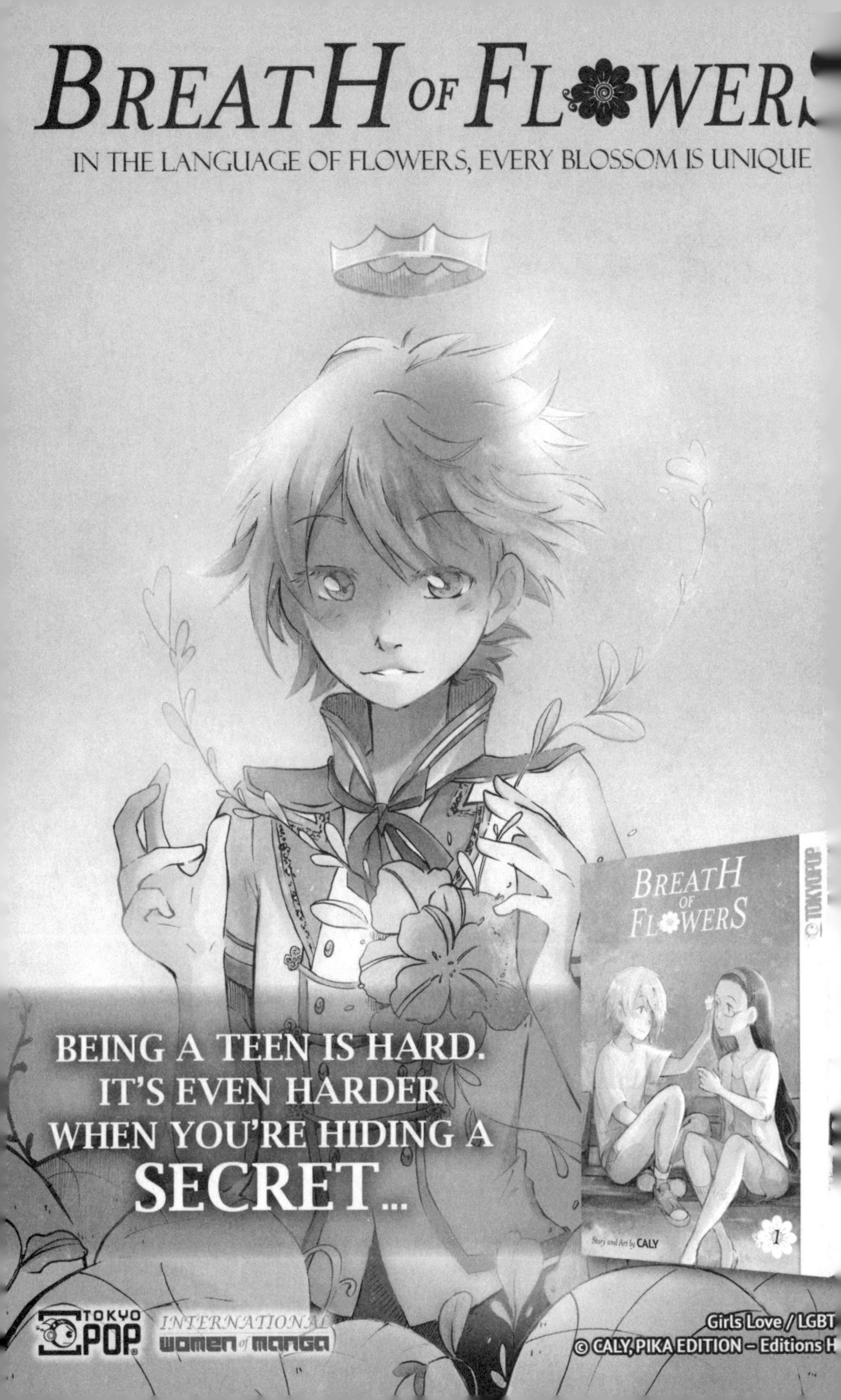
BREATH OF FLOWERS
IN THE LANGUAGE OF FLOWERS, EVERY BLOSSOM IS UNIQUE
BREATH OF FLOWERS
TOKYOPOP
Story and Art by CALY
1
BEING A TEEN IS HARD.
IT'S EVEN HARDER
WHEN YOU'RE HIDING A
SECRET...
TOKYO POP
INTERNATIONAL
women of manga
Girls Love / LGBT
© CALY, PIKA EDITION – Editions H

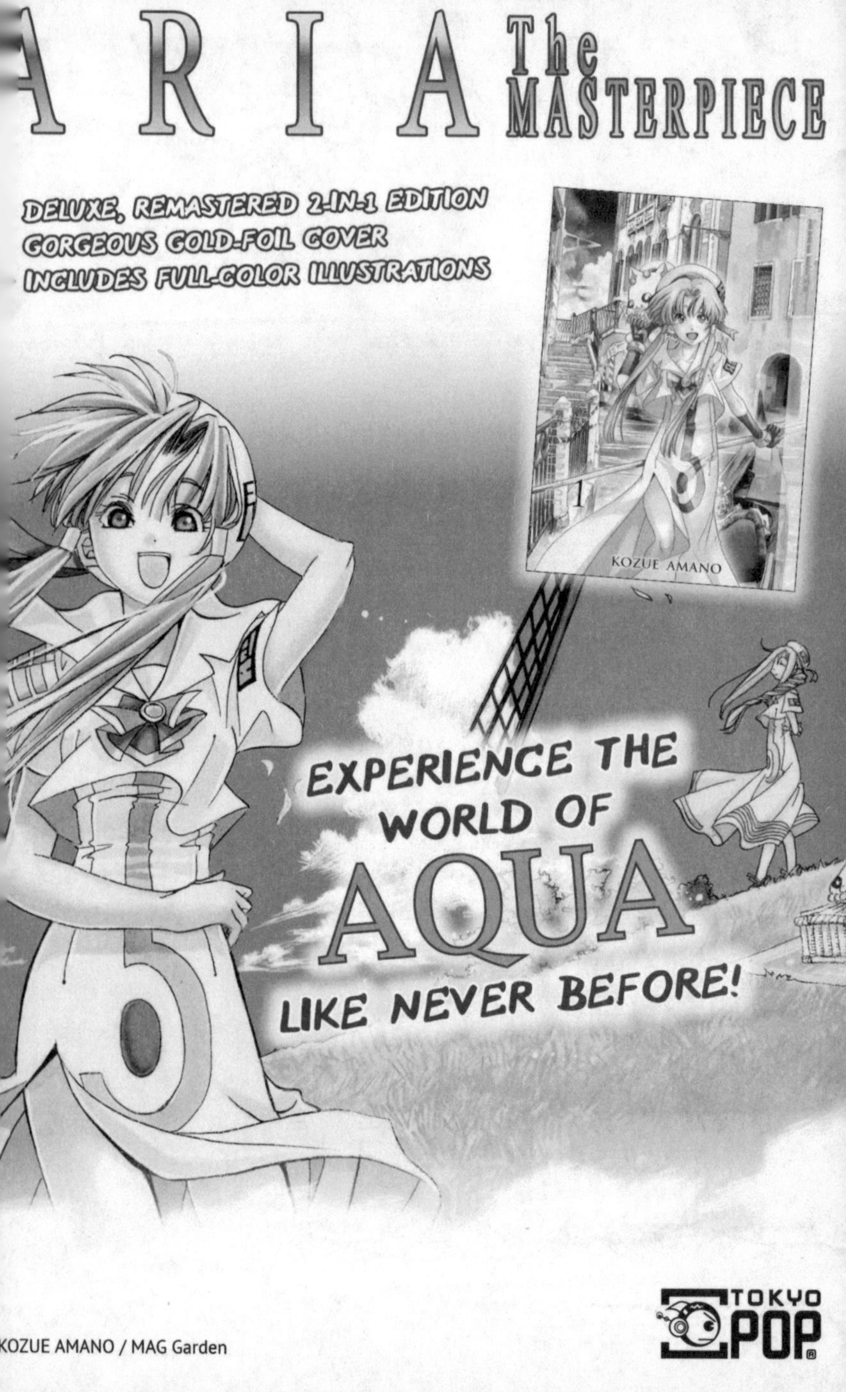
ARIA The MASTERPIECE
DELUXE, REMASTERED 2-IN-1 EDITION
GORGEOUS GOLD-FOIL COVER
INCLUDES FULL-COLOR ILLUSTRATIONS
1
KOZUE AMANO
EXPERIENCE THE WORLD OF AQUA LIKE NEVER BEFORE!
KOZUE AMANO / MAG Garden
TOKYOPOP

Long ago, an ancient hero sealed away the underworld. Now, with that sacred barrier broken, it's up to Rin and the mysterious demon Aghyr to restore balance to the Kingdom of Nohmur!

Koimonogatari: Love Stories, Volume 2
Manga by Tohru Tagura

Editor - Lena Atanassova
Marketing Associate - Kae Winters
Translator - Christine Dashiell
Cover Design - Soodam Lee
Retouching and Lettering - Vibrraant Publishing Studio
Editor-in-Chief & Publisher - Stu Levy

A  Manga

TOKYOPOP and 🐸 are trademarks or registered trademarks of TOKYOPOP Inc.

TOKYOPOP inc.
5200 W Century Blvd
Suite 705
Los Angeles, CA 90045 USA

E-mail: info@TOKYOPOP.com
Come visit us online at www.TOKYOPOP.com

🇫 www.facebook.com/TOKYOPOP
🐦 www.twitter.com/TOKYOPOP
📌 www.pinterest.com/TOKYOPOP
📷 www.instagram.com/TOKYOPOP

ISBN: 978-1-4278-6407-9
First TOKYOPOP Printing: August 2020
10 9 8 7 6 5 4 3 2 1
Printed in CANADA

STOP

THIS IS THE BACK OF THE BOOK!

How do you read manga-style? It's simple! Let's practice -- just start in the top right panel and follow the numbers below!

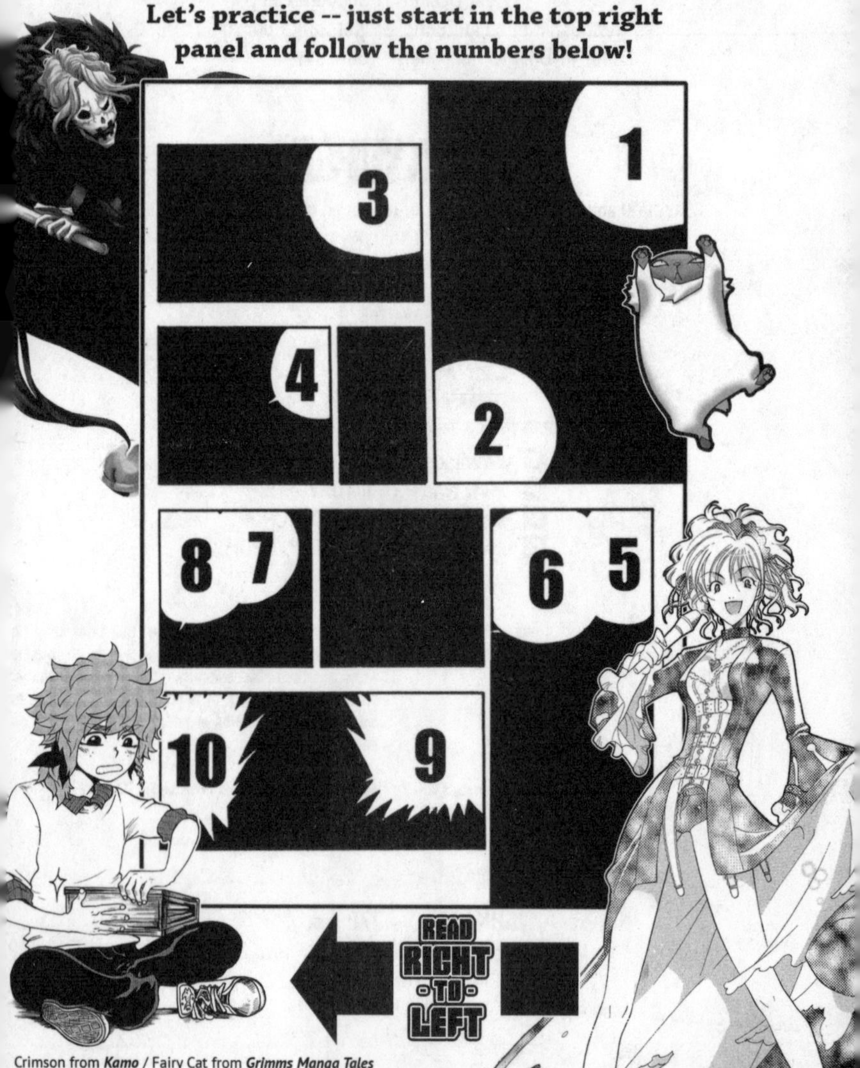
1
2
3
4
5
6
7
8
9
10
READ
RIGHT
-TO-
LEFT

Crimson from ***Kamo*** / Fairy Cat from ***Grimms Manga Tales***
Morrey from ***Goldfisch*** / Princess Ai from ***Princess Ai***